Praise for *A Consequential Life*

"During my four terms as Governor of North Carolina I sometimes thought we were having 'tough times.' After reading Bill Whichard's superb book on the life of N.C. Gov. David Swain–especially as President of the University of North Carolina in the Civil War–my time was a 'cakewalk.' But Swain didn't give up. Read about it!"

—JAMES B. HUNT, Governor, North Carolina (1977-1985 and 1993-2001)

"David Swain had a significant role in setting the direction of North Carolina during its formative years. Swain understood the role of government and education in creating a strong state. He had a vision for a better North Carolina that paved the way for who we are today. Justice Willis Whichard, in *A Consequential Life*, teaches all of us about David Swain, one of North Carolina's most important public servants. The book also brings to life North Carolina's early years and struggles through interesting stories and the words of Swain and his contemporaries. For me, as one of Swain's successors as president, it was particularly interesting to learn about his stewardship of the University of North Carolina as it was seeking to find its way to becoming one of our nation's top public universities. *A Consequential Life* is a wonderful addition to the history and understanding of our State and is a gift to all of us who love North Carolina."

—THOMAS W. ROSS, President Emeritus, University of North Carolina (2011-2016)

Praise for *A Consequential Life*

"Whether as a lawyer, state legislator, judge or university president, David Swain, as Willis Whichard reveals him, was a complex public servant who had a major influence over politics, the judiciary, slavery, UNC Chapel Hill, and other antebellum institutions in North Carolina. This is an engrossing and yet accessible biography that complicates our understanding of the former North Carolina governor."

—HILARY N. GREEN, James B. Duke Professor of Africana Studies, Davidson College

"The title to this new biography of David Lowry Swain—*A Consequential Life*—almost understates the importance and influence of one of North Carolina's early governmental leaders and long-serving President of the University of North Carolina. Swain's lengthy career in public service in a variety of positions and as perhaps the greatest advocate for the interests of Western North Carolina and his home in Buncombe County is set out in great detail. Of special interest is Swain's critical role in the N.C. Constitutional Convention of 1835 and the ensuing constitutional reforms favoring western interests. This is a timely story bringing to life an historic North Carolinian from an era of troubling social and moral dilemmas and allowing the reader to evaluate both the good and the bad of Swain's long career."

—ROBERT F. ORR, Associate Justice, Supreme Court of North Carolina (1995–2004)

A CONSEQUENTIAL LIFE

A Consequential Life

*David Lowry Swain,
Nineteenth-Century North Carolina,
and Their University*

Willis P. Whichard

Copyright © 2022 The University of North Carolina at Chapel Hill Library
All rights reserved

This work is licensed under a Creative Commons BY-NC-ND license.
To view a copy of the license, visit http://creativecommons.org/licenses.

Suggested citation: Whichard, Willis P. *A Consequential Life: David Lowry Swain, Nineteenth-Century North Carolina, and Their University*. Chapel Hill: The University of North Carolina at Chapel Hill Library.
DOI: https://doi.org/10.5149/9781469666198_Whichard

ISBN 978-1-4696-8403-1 (paperback)

LIBRARY OF CONGRESS CATALOGING-IN-PUBLICATION DATA
Names: Whichard, Willis P., author.
Title: A consequential life : David Lowry Swain, nineteenth-century North Carolina, and their university / Willis P. Whichard.
Other titles: Coates university leadership series.
Description: Chapel Hill : University Library, the University of North Carolina at Chapel Hill, [2022] | Series: Coates university leadership series | Includes bibliographical references and index.
Identifiers: LCCN 2021054803 | ISBN 9781469666181 (cloth) | ISBN 9781469666198 (ebook)
Subjects: LCSH: Swain, David L. (David Lowry), 1801-1868. | University of North Carolina (1793-1962)—History—-19th century. | Governors—North Carolina—Biography. | College presidents--North Carolina—Biography. |
LCGFT: Biographies.
Classification: LCC F258.S95 W47 2022 | DDC 975.6/03092 [B]—dc23/eng/20211206
LC record available at https://lccn.loc.gov/2021054803

Cover artwork:
TOP: David L. Swain, Portrait Collection
BOTTOM: University of North Carolina at Chapel Hill, Chromolithograph by E. Valois & Rau, circa 1861, University of North Carolina at Chapel Hill Image Collection.
All images are held by the North Carolina Collection, Wilson Special Collections Library, University of North Carolina at Chapel Hill.

COATES UNIVERSITY LEADERSHIP SERIES
Robert G. Anthony Jr., Series Editor
John A. Blythe, Series Assistant Editor

ADVISORY BOARD
Robert G. Anthony Jr., Chair
John A. Blythe
David E. Brown
Nicholas Graham
Michael Hill
Eric L. Johnson
Cecelia Moore
Regina W. Oliver
C. Edward Teague III
Jason E. Tomberlin

To the memory of Terry Sanford, a successor to Swain as governor of North Carolina, who joined Swain in implementing Archibald Murphey's vision of progress for the State, and William C. Friday, a successor to Swain as president of the University of North Carolina, who found Swain "a very interesting man" and thus strongly encouraged the author in this endeavor.

CONTENTS

Illustrations xiii

Foreword by Harry L. Watson xv

BEGINNINGS

Prologue 3

CHAPTER 1
Origins, Youth 7

CHAPTER 2
Law, Statecraft 25

GOVERNOR

CHAPTER 3
Vision 51

CHAPTER 4
Advancing the Vision 64

CHAPTER 5
Less Visionary Aspects 84

CHAPTER 6
Constitutional Reform 111

ACADEMIC LEADER

CHAPTER 7
The University of North Carolina 133

CHAPTER 8
Admitting, Parenting 137

CHAPTER 9
Student Misconduct 150

CHAPTER 10
Teacher 177

CHAPTER 11
Faculty 192

CHAPTER 12
Hedrick Affair 217

CHAPTER 13
Property 232

CHAPTER 14
Special Events, Distinguished Guests 252

CHAPTER 15
Public Policy 264

CHAPTER 16
Politics 284

HISTORIAN

CHAPTER 17
History Matters 301

CHAPTER 18
More Courting Clio 324

CHAPTER 19
Clio: Yet More 347

PERSONAL LIFE

CHAPTER 20
Family 371

CHAPTER 21
Other Personal Dimensions 392

CHAPTER 22
The "Peculiar Institution" 410

CIVIL WAR, RECONSTRUCTION

CHAPTER 23
Disunion, Disruption 429

CHAPTER 24
Reunion, Controversial Union 451

CHAPTER 25
Reconstruction 471

ENDINGS

CHAPTER 26
Decline and Fall 499

CHAPTER 27
Aftermath, Finale 523

Epilogue 531

Notes 565
Bibliography 689
Acknowledgments 715
Index 717

ILLUSTRATIONS

David Lowry Swain xxi
University of North Carolina president's residence 2
Swain's birthplace 9
John Louis Taylor 13
Eleanor White 23
Notice for Buncombe Turnpike Company 31
Internal Improvements Convention report 67
William Horn Battle, James Iredell, and Frederick Nash 87
First Presbyterian Church, Raleigh, NC 116
Campus view, pre-1847 132
UNC student report 178
Zebulon Baird Vance 189
Elisha Mitchell 201
Benjamin Hedrick 218
Thomas Day advertisement 237
James K. Polk, James Buchanan, and Andrew Johnson 254
John Motley Morehead 270
George Bancroft, Francis Lister Hawks, and John Hill Wheeler 342
Joseph Lane 367
Richard and Eleanor Swain 384
William Gaston 399
William A. Graham 401
Wilson Swain Caldwell and George Moses Horton's
The Poetical Works of George M. Horton 422
UNC campus, circa 1861 428

Smith D. Atkins and Eleanor Swain Atkins 469
Cornelia Phillips Spencer 480
Kemp Plummer Battle 512
William Woods Holden 521
Richard C. Swain as adult 535
Swain Hall 551

Note: Unless noted otherwise, illustrations are from the Portrait Collection and the University of North Carolina at Chapel Hill Image Collection of the North Carolina Collection, Wilson Special Collections Library, University of North Carolina at Chapel Hill.

FOREWORD

Willis P. Whichard concludes his sweeping examination of the life and work of David Lowry Swain (1801–1868), governor of North Carolina and president of the University of North Carolina, by calling him arguably "the most influential and consequential North Carolinian of the nineteenth century (p. 561)." Whichard makes a thorough case for this position, not only detailing Swain's contributions to the university, where he presided from 1835 to 1868, but also to state politics, public policy, economic development, and public education. Tracing Swain's achievements across these fields, Whichard places him in the vanguard of an long-honored cadre of antebellum North Carolina leaders, mostly from the reform-minded Whig Party, who included William R. Davie, father of the university, William J. Gaston, judge and congressman, Archibald DeBow Murphey, educational and transportation reformer, Joseph Caldwell, Swain's predecessor as university president, Willie P. Mangum and William Alexander Graham, both United States senators, John Motley Morehead, governor and railroad executive, and Calvin H. Wiley, superintendent of common schools. An older generation of historians would probably have included Thomas Ruffin, state chief justice, and Zebulon B. Vance, Civil War governor, in this list, but the shadow of proslavery rulings and Confederate leadership might make others pause today. Like Swain, these men were all widely recognized by contemporaries and by later historians for their wisdom, ability, and common devotion to the task of uplifting a state that was widely regarded as backward and stagnant. Whichard presents Swain as the underappreciated energizer of this reform-minded band, teaching and inspiring them and their sons, corresponding among them, organizing them politically, and concentrating their efforts for public purposes.

Briefly but tellingly, Whichard's impressive portrait does not omit the shadow that fell across the work of Swain and his colleagues. Like Ruffin and Vance, though less conspicuously, North Carolina's Whig reformers blinded themselves to the moral and economic failings of a society built on human bondage. Not only were the economy and society of the entire South founded on slavery, but even more, so were the personal careers and fortunes of its leaders. Swain himself was a buyer and seller of human property who exploited the enslaved in his household, on his farm, and in university operations while fervently attacking abolitionism. The law did not recognize the marriages of human chattel, but Whichard tells us that Swain even denied the comfort of nominal matrimony to couples he enslaved, to head off emotional ties that might complicate their sale.

Outside observers—most notably the traveler Frederick Law Olmsted and dissident yeoman Hinton Rowan Helper—freely blamed slavery for Southern backwardness, but found no audience in North Carolina's elite.[1] In their secret debating societies, Swain's own students warmly debated the economic consequences of slavery, but when Professor Benjamin Hedrick voiced the same criticisms in public, the faculty demanded his discharge, Swain agreed, and the trustees promptly obliged.[2] Antebellum North Carolina could tolerate some mildly antislavery opinions, but alone among the gentlemen Swain led and respected, only Judge William Gaston publicly condemned the peculiar institution as the obstacle that "keeps us back in the career of improvement..., stifles industry and represses enterprize..., [kills] economy and providence..., discourages skill, impairs our strength as a community, and poisons morals at the fountain head."[3] Swain and his corps of reformers heard and read Gaston's quiet warning in his 1832 address to UNC's Dialectic and Philanthropic Societies, but did not respond. In the broadest view, they tried instead to modernize a slave-based society without fundamentally changing it. Whichard points to this glaring weakness without dwelling on it, reasonably preferring that the facts speak for themselves, but his twenty-first century readers will probably struggle with the stark contradictions they bred among the reformers' visions, achievements, and shortcomings.

Beyond the costs of slavery, the North Carolina that Swain and his peers attempted to transform was cursed by an inaccessible coastline, impassable rivers, and a complex landscape of feverish swamps, washboard hills, and daunting mountains. While beguiling modern tourists and residents alike, this terrain impeded the movement of people, crops, and manufactured goods, and stifled the commercial prosperity that other states enjoyed after 1815. Instead of fixing this situation, many North Carolinians succumbed to a malady one labeled the "*Alabama Feaver*," and joined a stream of migrants seeking better opportunities in the Southwest.[4] The results at home were neglected fields, languishing towns, undisturbed forests, and stunted public services, including a complete lack of public schools, all summarized by North Carolina's humiliating nickname, "the Rip van Winkle state." As they saw it, the task confronting reform-minded North Carolinians was not simply the smooth operation of state government but a sweeping program of changes to "wake up Old Rip."

Credited by Whichard as the leader of this crusade, David Lowry Swain was born in mountainous Buncombe County in 1801, where his father was a respected farmer, hatter, and state legislator. Excelling in a private academy, the youth attended the state university briefly before leaving it for legal training in Raleigh. Returning home, he quickly followed his father into politics and served five terms in the General Assembly, where he worked diligently for local internal improvements (as transportation projects were then called), before becoming a Superior Court judge. In 1832, the General Assembly chose Swain to the first of his three annual terms as governor, where he guided the creation of North Carolina's Whig Party, formed to oppose President Andrew Jackson's Democrats and support public spending for economic development. When term limits ended Swain's governorship in 1835, trustees of the state university made him its third president, succeeding the deceased Joseph Caldwell. Swain would retain this position for the next thirty-three years.

Constitutional reform was the key to any other positive action by state government, and it loomed as the new governor's greatest task. North Carolina's 1776 constitution vested virtually all power in the General Assembly, composed of one senator and two representatives (known as "commoners") from each county, regardless of size, plus seven more commoners from each of the state's "borough towns." This plan gave control of the state to the eastern plantation belt, where counties were smaller, wealthier, and more numerous than in the western uplands, home to numerous small farmers with few or no slaves. Eastern planters were predictably unwilling to change this arrangement, particularly since westerners were calling loudly for state-funded canal and rail connections to coastal ports and distant markets, presumably to be financed largely by eastern taxpayers. Fearful of exposing slave property to tax-hiking nonslaveholders, easterners refused to relax their grip on the legislature or to spend any funds on western transportation. For "Old Rip" to wake up, in other words, westerners must first reapportion the legislature. Threats of extralegal measures, similar to those that precipitated the near-contemporary Dorr War in distant Rhode Island, grew louder.

As governor, Swain's powers were largely ceremonial, but he had pressed hard for constitutional reform and internal improvements as a legislator, and he continued to do so as governor. He became an active leader of internal improvements conventions and peppered the General Assembly with reports, statistics, and rhetoric calling for state action. The impasse finally collapsed when representatives from eastern market towns changed sides and voted with their western colleagues for constitutional reform, hopeful that one or more rail lines would open up the backcountry and revive their flagging trade. Swain chaired the ensuing constitutional convention and helped to engineer a compromise settlement that gave control of one legislative chamber to each rival section. When Congress soon distributed surplus federal revenue to the states, North Carolina was ready to benefit by investing its windfall in bank stock to expand available credit and corporate securities to capitalize two fledging railroads. Profits from these investments then supported a nascent public school system. Swain's advocacy had broken a developmental deadlock.

In his last official act as governor, Swain proclaimed approval of the constitutional amendments of 1835 before assuming his new post in Chapel Hill. Founded to supply the infant state with trained leaders, the University of North Carolina had opened in 1795 as the nation's first public university. When Governor Swain took its helm (no one called him "President"), the student body had not yet reached forty, and the numbers of faculty and buildings did not exceed a handful. Swain's greatest challenges were expanding the university's enrollment and physical plant, and he succeeded at both by 1860, with enrollment approaching five hundred (second place to Yale's nationwide) on a campus of comparable extent. As president, Swain also continued his role as champion of internal improvements and public education, and senior advisor to leading Whigs. Historians owe Swain deep gratitude for his favorite activity of collecting historical records and founding the University Historical Society to preserve them. Swain's most valued work, both to himself and his biographer, seems to have been his dedication to teaching. Though never praised for pure scholarship, Swain threw himself into teaching history, constitutional law, and moral philosophy, captivating generations of highly privileged young white men with tales of great statesmen, surely feeding their imitative ambitions and inscribing his own ideals of combined progress and conservatism on the state's political culture.

Like most Southern Whigs, Swain opposed sectional extremism, antislavery agitation, and the South's slide toward secessionism, but swung to the Confederacy when the attack on Fort Sumter led to Lincoln's call for troops. With a handful of students, Swain kept the university open throughout the war, but when General William T. Sherman's army approached at war's end, he worked with Governor Vance to arrange a peaceful transfer of power in Raleigh and the state government. Back in Chapel Hill, he formed an unlikely committee with law professor William Horn Battle and university janitor Wilson Swain Caldwell, legally Swain's own property until then, to negotiate the campus' surrender in exchange for the army's pledge to protect it. In the aftermath, Swain drew widespread criticism when his daughter married the Union commander in charge of Chapel Hill, and criticism increased as his health declined. Pressured by the trustees, he resigned his presidency in 1868 and died from a buggy accident soon afterward.

David Lowry Swain was widely admired in North Carolina, especially before his difficult final years, but he also attracted his share of critics. Perhaps the most trenchant was a subsequent UNC president, Kemp Plummer Battle, writing in his two-volume *History of the University of North Carolina*. Battle mocked Swain for his love of light conversation, puns, and genealogy, and dismissed his intellect, remarking that Swain "had a kind heart and genial manners. He was not an extensive reader. His range of learning was not wide, but accurate as far as it went." More seriously, Battle scored Swain for neglecting advanced scholarship, academic specialization, and educational rigor, as well as the university's endowment, library, and scientific equipment. Imbued with the ethic of the New South, Battle valued practical achievements over dead languages, politics, and constitutional theories, and regretted Swain's focus on statecraft and the classical curriculum, but finally blamed the state itself instead of its officer: "Undoubtedly he gave what the public demanded."[5] Whichard duly reports these and other criticisms of his subject but emphasizes positive achievements and leaves final judgment to his readers.

Nor does Whichard query the underlying mission of Swain and his fellow reformers. Did they face an impossible task? Could they have truly waked Old Rip with education and infrastructure? Or was the dead hand of slavery too heavy to remove with railroads and schoolhouses? Slavery made some Southerners rich; could it ever enrich the region? With funds tied up in mobile labor, would the South's footloose enslavers ever decide to stay put and invest in their own neighborhoods? Unpaid labor left a third of North Carolina's workers with virtually no income; could the remainder ever create enough demand for a self-sustaining process of growth and development? The United States' 1860 railroad map is thick with intertwining lines across the Northeast and Midwest while the South is barely scratched by export corridors for its favorite staples. Could state-funded construction ever make up the difference? And if not, how much can we admire those who attacked the South's problems without noticing their roots?

These questions are of course unanswerable, and perhaps beyond the historian's purview, but it's hard to forget that antebellum Southern leaders almost never raised them, despite the prodding of independent critics. Instead, men like Swain did the best they could without fundamentally challenging the world they inherited. Willis Whichard tells his story with a judge's sharp eye for detailed evidence and prodigious command of his sources. In his rich telling, Governor Swain emerges as a complex figure with varied interests and multiple contributions. Was he truly "the most influential and consequential North Carolinian" of his century? A final answer is elusive, but David Lowry Swain was clearly among the best and most accomplished that North Carolina's antebellum leaders could offer.

Harry L. Watson
Atlanta Distinguished Professor of Southern Culture Emeritus
Department of History
University of North Carolina at Chapel Hill

David Lowry Swain, 1801–1868

Beginnings

UNC president's residence, site of David Swain's funeral, undated but from Swain era.

Prologue
"A full attendance"

DAVID LOWRY SWAIN'S FUNERAL in late August 1868 was well attended. Held at his Chapel Hill residence at the early hour of 9:00 a.m., it attracted every class of the small university town's citizens, with "quite as many negroes as whites thronging the wide piazzas or standing in the yard under the shade of the oak trees.... A full attendance of the people of Chapel Hill followed the train around the house and to the garden," wrote a neighbor, "where they placed the remains of our beloved and venerated friend by the side of his daughter, to await the widow's final decision respecting them."[1]

Through most of Swain's life, this would have been expected. From earliest youth he had been a popular man of considerable power and influence. A true wunderkind, by age thirty-one he had served five one-year terms in the North Carolina House of Commons, prosecuted criminal-court dockets as solicitor for the Edenton District, and distinguished himself as a judge of the superior court. Shortly before his thirty-second birthday, the North Carolina General Assembly elected him the state's twenty-sixth governor, and he remains its youngest. In the context of his time, he was an activist executive, prodding the state to develop its infrastructure, thereby promoting economic development, which in turn would sustain universal public education. As his constitutionally limited time in the Executive Department was expiring, Joseph Caldwell, the state university's president, died. In a surprise action, the university trustees selected the thirty-four-year-old Swain to succeed him. He would occupy the position until shortly before his death almost thirty-three years later.

Neither Swain nor the trustees would have predicted so long a tenure, nor would they have foreseen his precipitate decline and fall toward the end. A normal, age-related diminution in powers, both physical and mental, bore partial responsibility. Significant hearing loss, in particular, eroded his considerable skills at negotiation and diplomacy.

Other forces, beyond his physical faculties and his capacity to control, were at work, however. Swain had been a late and tepid supporter of the southern position in the recently ended fratricidal conflict between the northern and southern states. Like other former southern Unionists, he had come to the Confederate position only when Abraham Lincoln called for seventy-five thousand troops to subject the southern states to what these men "perceived as corrupt, tyrannical oppression."[2] Once North Carolina, the state he had long served, joined the train of secession, he too entered its track. His earlier reticence was remembered, however, as well as his efforts to exempt his students from the Confederate draft. At least initially, his intelligence and his life experience precluded genuine, unmitigated enthusiasm for the cause.

In that context he suffered from the controversy engendered by his role in ending the Civil War in North Carolina. A public servant to the core, he suggested, and could hardly have declined, the request from his former student and his high school sweetheart's son, Governor Zebulon Vance, that he join another former North Carolina governor, William A. Graham, in negotiations with Union General William T. Sherman to remove the capital at Raleigh and the university at Chapel Hill from Sherman's war-ending path of destruction.[3] First walking, then riding by train in a southeasterly direction from the state capital, Swain and Graham accomplished that purpose admirably.

Swain's severely impaired hearing, however, probably precluded his knowing that shortly afterward he was taunted for it as a traitor who should be hanged.

In Governor Vance's absence while traveling westward to meet with the fleeing president of the Confederacy, Jefferson Davis, it was Swain who took the keys to the state capitol from a "Negro servant" and presented them to Sherman. Returning to his home at the seat of the state university, he would soon become the focus of more pervasive and persistent criticism. Federal troops, commanded by General Smith Dykins Atkins of Illinois, now occupied the small town, home of the first public university in the country to open its doors to students. When the commanding officer made a courtesy call on the university president, their mutual interest in the Revolutionary War surfaced.

Swain was the proud possessor of one of British General Charles Cornwallis's order books. Naturally, he wished to display it to his guest. The consequences of this friendly, seemingly innocent gesture could not have occurred to him, however, for when the book was produced by Swain's attractive twenty-two-year-old daughter Eleanor, better known as "Ella" or "Ellie," sparks flew instantly. The ensuing romance between the southern belle and the Union general spawned a scandal of epic proportions in the small town, but Cupid would not be denied. Only four months later the Swain parlor was the scene of their marriage. Many townspeople, even friends of the president and his family, refused to attend, some spitting and stomping on their invitations. On the wedding day, students tolled the university's South Building bell in protest.

Three difficult years later, injuries Swain sustained in a carriage accident immediately precipitated the funeral at his house. Arguably, however, they were not the more fundamental cause of his demise. He was, rather, as much a casualty of the Civil War, which left his university financially devastated and sparsely populated, as the soldiers who encountered more bloody deaths at Antietam and Gettysburg. He was slain, not by conventional weapons of war, but by the arrows of outrageous fortune, one slung carelessly from the bow of Cupid that inflicted wounds too severe for a man of his age and sensibility to survive. "The spirit of a man will sustain his infirmity, but a wounded spirit who can bear?" (Proverbs 18:14).

But this is the end of Swain's story, one that warrants narration from its beginning. That idea is neither recent nor original. Over a century and a quarter ago, Clement Dowd, biographer of Swain's student Zebulon Vance, said to Kemp P. Battle, the second of Swain's successors as president of the University of North Carolina:

> In looking through some old University Magazines and seeing so many valuable contributions to the long history of our state by that great and good man Gov. Swain, I wonder what has been done to perpetuate his memory.
>
> Has any body written or undertaken to write his life? If not, why not?
>
> Surely abundance of good material is not wanting and our state has had few if any more useful men—and certainly none more patriotic, his love for his native state being testified in deeds as well as words.
>
> If nothing has been done to rescue his memory from fast ensuing oblivion, it is late, but may not be too late for something to be done yet.[4]

Over half a century ago, historian Hugh T. Lefler listed among North Carolina leaders who merit more study and perhaps full-length biographies "David L. Swain, Governor and long-time President of the University of North Carolina."[5]

In his biography of his accomplished ancestor, the first duke of Marlborough, Winston Churchill wrote, "In a portrait or impression the human figure is best shown by its true relation to the objects and scenes against which it is thrown, and by which it is defined."[6] The objects and scenes against which David Lowry Swain was thrown, and that define him, include a state vast in geographical expanse while small but growing in population. In 1800, the year before Swain's birth, North Carolina had a population of 478,103; in 1870, two years after his death, 1,071,361.[7] The state was sufficiently lacking in basic infrastructure, economic development, and educational opportunity that it was popularly known as "the Rip Van Winkle state."[8] The historian Francis L. Hawks said of it, to Swain: "Poor, dear, old N. Carolina! God help you. With boundless resources, your own children are killing you. They are a century behind the rest of the states. God help you."[9]

Although Swain is known as the "commoner" who popularized the state's university and opened it to others like him,[10] it is nonetheless true that it then educated only white males, most of them sons of the planter, mercantile, and professional elite. The scene that defines him must also include human bondage as a common practice. The number of black people in North Carolina, most of them enslaved, increased from 140,000 in 1800, the year preceding Swain's birth, to 361,522 in 1860 near the end of his sixth decade. As a percentage of the total state population, blacks increased from 29.3 percent in 1800 to 35.5 percent on the eve of the Civil War.[11] Indeed, Swain can be properly portrayed only in a context that is Old South and at least largely old school.

CHAPTER I

Origins, Youth
"A dutiful and accomplished son"

Swain's paternal ancestors were of English descent,[1] though one relative believed the Swains originated in Denmark. "Conute Swayn King of Denmark made war with the Saxons of England," he wrote Swain, "and took possession of a part of the Island of Great Britton." "I have heard it remarked," he said, "that the name Swayn is frequent in Denmark."[2]

More immediately, Richard Swain came to New England from England in the mid-seventeenth century. He and a son were believed to be early purchasers of land on Nantucket Island in Massachusetts, and he to be a David Swain ancestor. William Swayne, a man of note in his day, was also thought to be a Swain progenitor. William had "imbibed Quaker sentiments" and emigrated to Nantucket to escape the persecution of his sect.[3]

More immediately still, David Swain's paternal grandfather, Samuel S. Swain, died an alcoholic, leaving in straitened circumstances a widow, Freelove Swain, seven sons, and two daughters. Except for George, David's father, the sons all died childless, and consequently, the Swain name is rare in Massachusetts and the North.[4]

Born in Roxbury, Massachusetts, on June 17, 1763, George Swain received brief schooling in Springfield before being apprenticed at age fourteen to a hatter. On September 1, 1785, he sailed with a friend and some stores for Charleston, South Carolina, but lost his possessions in a storm. From Charleston he went to Augusta, Georgia, where he stayed less than a year before settling in the county of Wilkes, later Oglethorpe, Georgia.

There he obtained prominence as a justice of the peace, member of the state legislature, and delegate to a state constitutional convention. Such success commonly breeds loyalty to place, but in the winter of 1795–1796, prompted by health concerns (probably malaria) and believing a mountain climate more suitable to his fragile constitution, George moved to Buncombe County in the mountains of North Carolina.

He never regretted the decision. "I then thought my system too much injured to obtain good health anywhere," he told David, "[b]ut ... through providential preservation I have not experienced a fever of any kind since I came to the country[,] and I would not now exchange our salubrious air [and] pure mountain water."[5]

The mountain ambience also brought George renewed prominence. At his shop near the current location of the Grove Park Inn, he continued to manufacture hats while engaging in a mix of other economic activities. On his small farm in the Beaver Dam section near Asheville, in addition to raising crops usual to the region, he planted fruit trees, some varieties imported from New England. His apple trees were the product of cuttings from Massachusetts, and they are still known in that region by the names he gave them.[6] In 1807 George became the deputy postmaster, later postmaster, in Asheville. He held the office for more than twenty years and is said never to have been absent on arrival of a mail and to have distributed every letter with his own hand.[7]

Finally, by the relaxed standards of his time, George was a physician, the second in Buncombe County. He was appropriately humble about the assumption of this status. Being called "doctor" in the county, and addressed as such by visiting medical men, thoroughly embarrassed him. Nevertheless, reports such as one of George's being away at the home of a man whose wife was ill were common.[8]

As in Georgia, George Swain participated in public life. When the town of Asheville was incorporated in 1797, he was one of five commissioners appointed to dispose of the town lots, make regulations, and impose taxes for the town government. When new commissioners were appointed in 1805, George did not then live in the town and was not reappointed. He was again appointed in 1807, however.[9]

North Carolina then had no common (public) schools, but George supported the limited extant means of education. In 1805 the North Carolina General Assembly established the Union Hill Academy as a seminary of learning. George and other trustees held title to the school's land. Later, when David attended there, the Asheville school was known as Newton Academy. George was one of five managers of a lottery created to benefit Newton and to promote the establishment of a female academy. When the lottery failed to raise sufficient funds to achieve these purposes, he and the other managers disbanded it and refunded the participants' money.[10]

On December 2, 1788, George Swain married Caroline Lane Lowry, widow of Captain David Lowry, who had been killed fighting in an Indian raid. She was

David Swain's Buncombe County birthplace.

two years older than George; family tradition held that she had employed him as a tutor to her four children by Captain Lowry.[11]

Caroline was from a prominent North Carolina family, said to have been connected with Governor Ralph Lane, who led an English colony to Roanoke Island in 1585. Born May 26, 1761, she was the daughter of Jesse and Winifred Lane of Wake County, North Carolina. She was a sister to Joel Lane, whose land became the site of the City of Raleigh, and Jesse Lane, father of General Joseph Lane, military general, governor of and U.S. senator from Oregon, and Democratic candidate for vice president on the John C. Breckenridge ticket in 1860.[12]

As to Caroline the historical record is scant. It is almost certainly safe to assume that, like most women of her time, she passed her days as a wife, mother, and homemaker. Her extant letters are scrutable but lack the grammatical correctness and precision of expression that would suggest a high level of education. Still, hers was probably beyond the then norm for women, particularly in the mountains of North Carolina.

The Swain-Lowry marriage produced five daughters and two sons. The first son was named for George. Caroline wanted the second named for her deceased first husband, and George consented. The boy, born January 4, 1801, in their log house in the Beaver Dam Valley, would be known as David Lowry Swain.[13]

Little evidence from David Swain's childhood survives. He is said to have been a good scholar at Newton Academy, doubtless aided by a lifelong strong, tenacious memory. Benjamin F. Perry, later governor of South Carolina, was among Swain's Newton Academy classmates. He described Swain at around age twenty as "about as awkward and gawky a young gentleman as I had ever met . . . six feet two inches in height, slender and ill-shaped, with a long pale face, thick lips, sharp nose and dull expression of the eyes." Beloved by the other boys, he was an accomplished Latin and Greek scholar who translated difficult sentences for the younger students. Amiable, well-tempered, "punctiliously honorable," and possessing no vices completed Perry's depiction.[14]

Swain's Newton Academy education was considered adequate preparation for entry into the junior class at the University of North Carolina.[15] Although he ultimately enrolled there, albeit briefly, he first explored other options. After half a day with the principal of an academy in South Carolina, he considered the students' classical recitations inferior to those of Newton Academy. Still, he was embarrassed by his ignorance in light of one student's performance on a geography exam.

Commencement exercises at Columbia College, later the University of South Carolina, exposed Swain to orations that "afford[ed] satisfactory information." There he enjoyed a dinner and a ball. Upon departure, however, he thought "the popular sentiment by no means favorable as to the merits of the college." After he chose Chapel Hill over Columbia, perhaps for this reason, his father encouraged "a well written complimentary letter excusing neglect and apologizing for a change of intention," thus suggesting that David initially favored attending Columbia.[16]

The Columbia-versus-Chapel Hill debate was less intense than that over college-versus-immediate law studies. George thought David might benefit from learning general principles of jurisprudence from North Carolina Supreme Court Chief Justice John Louis Taylor's lectures prior to entering college. Soon thereafter, when David visited Chapel Hill, George was curious to hear of his transactions there and to learn whether he had made the acquaintance of university president Joseph Caldwell.[17]

Chapel Hill prevailed over Columbia, but Swain's student tenure there was brief. One account says four days; others, four months.[18] A catalog of the university's Dialectic Society shows him as a "Transient Member." In his short stay he began to acquire friendships that would benefit him in later life, among them that of his roommate Leonidas Polk, the son of Colonel William Polk, one of Raleigh's leading citizens and a longtime university trustee.[19]

Swain's ephemeral UNC presence later formed the foundation of a university fiscal policy. In 1854 Elisha Mitchell, professor and university bursar, informed the Trustee Executive Committee that even brief enrollment merited denial of tuition refund. "The case of the present excellent President of the University is in point," he said. As a student Swain had recited to Mitchell once. His tuition was forfeited and had never been refunded. "When therefore the student joins college and *recites* though ever so small a number of times," Mitchell stated, "the money is retained."[20]

Given that Swain would devote almost half his life to the university, it is interesting that his early impressions of it disappointed him. Prosperity, David thought, had had a pernicious effect on the institution. The students were generally the sons of wealthy men; they were seeking pleasure and "any thing else but mental improvement." Dissipation, lewdness, and profanity prevailed, and few good scholars resulted. People there were skeptical as to whether a Buncombe County boy could be a scholar. The expenses, David feared, were too high, and the students too young. Finally, he found the instruction lacking. Few, if any, were acquainted with the classics. "The classical course I have read," he said, "is nearly twice as extensive as the one in vogue here." Moral philosophy and belles-lettres received little attention; history, none. David hoped he would yet be pleased but feared he would not.[21]

George had sound advice for any choice: cultivate a mind that common occurrences cannot affect and develop habits of endurance of hardship and difficulty that produce equanimity in any fate. Even he vacillated, however, about his son's course.

The family of publisher Joseph Gales joined Governor Gabriel Holmes and Chief Justice John Louis Taylor in recommending a plan for the immediate study of law, which David adopted. If the objective was to make David a sound lawyer, Judge Taylor thought time spent in Chapel Hill an "impolitic step." George thought the plan "judicious," gave it his blessing, and pledged his best efforts to support it. He agreed with Judge Taylor, he told David, that the knowledge of jurisprudence prior to entering the university would improve his "leisure moments" for reading legal authors and enable him "to form a better knowledge of those particular branches of science that will be most essentially necessary for one of your profession."

Joseph Gales affirmed the decision. David had properly placed himself under Judge Taylor's care for the present, he said, concluding, "I have no doubt he will derive much advantage from an attendance upon his Lectures, and a residence in this place for a few months previous to his pursuit of further scholastic studies."

Gales thought it probable that David would then choose "our University" over "one of the Northern Colleges," partly because he could remain in close communication with Judge Taylor.

Although seemingly content with this course, George nevertheless inquired of David as to Judge Taylor's opinion of his going to Chapel Hill. He also conveyed to David his brother George Jr.'s opinion that David should enter college; George Jr. offered to assist David, presumably financially, "rather . . . than you should miss the highest point of collegiate honor after a chase so long and ardent in pursuit of it." George Sr., despite having blessed David's decision to study law forthwith, wanted him to have every qualification his natural and acquired abilities could possibly afford, so came "to the determination of [his] entering college as soon as possible." A consultation with a judge strengthened this conclusion: George should give his son the best education "our University" could provide, and let him have the name of a graduate.

Soon, however, the father again expressed contentment with his promising son's decision to forego college for an immediate professional tutorial. It troubled him that many thought David "would not be considered emminat [sic] in a legal profession without a collegiate education." If the advantages were no more than David seemed to think, however, "the purchase [was] too high for these hard times." David thus should "do the best you possibly can in obtaining your profession and return to me with as little expense as you can reasonably."[22]

George's concerns about financing the studies lingered throughout David's time in Raleigh. The father complained about assisting numerous family members, thus explaining his difficulty in sending funds for David. Still, he would convey his shame over "keep[ing] the Judge so long out of his money" and apologize to David for not having sent it. He always wanted to know the state of David's finances. When David received money from George, it "was of course very acceptable" to him.

When David suffered a serious illness, he estimated his medical expenses, and George sent funds "either for the Judge or the Doctors as you think proper." David, conscious of the financial strain yet focused on his purpose there, avowed that he had never spent except when essential to his comfort or reputation, or refrained from it when either of these required it. When needed, he did not hesitate to request "a little cash as soon as convenient." It did embarrass him, however, to estimate his expenses and request them when his participation in the wedding of Chief Justice Taylor's daughter rendered needed outlays larger than anticipated.

As David neared the end of his Raleigh time, George was uneasy about his expenses and promised to send $25.00 weekly until all accounts were balanced.

John Louis Taylor, Chief Justice of North Carolina, 1819–1829, David Swain's law teacher.

He inquired whether David had sold his books and paid Judge Taylor. Calculating what he thought would be David's remaining costs, he sent most of the sum, requesting that David inform him as to what he would need "to wind up your accounts honorably with all your creditors."[23]

The funding sufficed. Earlier, despite a focus on his work so intense that he declined to speak even to the governor unless first spoken to, David had felt unprepared for the bar and thus had resisted the temptation to be tested. In due course, however, he found himself "engaged pretty closely in studies" as he prepared to stand for examination. A friend supposed him busily engaged as he anticipated "standing before the bar of that awful tribunal." Soon the friend congratulated him on his successful application and wished him professional success. David now told his father he would be returning home bringing about fifty volumes of books.[24]

Swain's Raleigh time was well spent. He revered Judge Taylor and apparently learned well from him. Another chief justice, more eminent still, crossed his path. Swain was on the grand jury when John Marshall convened the Circuit Court for the United States in Raleigh. Earlier he had described Marshall as about seventy years old with hair "white as wool" and a soft voice. "He speaks with the utmost simplicity," Swain wrote, "and even when addressing a jury, smiles, apparently as unconsciously as a child."

He was also introduced to Joseph J. Daniel—formerly a superior court judge, later a state supreme court judge—and "found him a much more familiar, plain, communicative man than too many who are clothed (legally) with his dignity." He highly admired William Gaston, Judge Taylor's brother-in-law, whom he considered as great a man as he had encountered; but in reporting Gaston's loss of a case, he noted that he "may sometimes be outwitted." Soon after his arrival in Raleigh he met Governor Gabriel Holmes and was "received with every degree of attention and familiarity." Later he attended "a small party" at Governor Holmes's residence and conversed with him.[25]

Witnessing courts in action supplemented Swain's book learning. He observed federal and state tribunals and considered the Wake County courts perhaps the ablest in the state. The legislative branch also captured his attention. He anticipated the introduction of a multitude of bills and reported action on some, including one for the formation of Davidson County. Arguing themes that would later occupy him as a legislator and governor, he expressed support for a turnpike from Asheville to the Tennessee line and doubted that the convention question—fair legislative representation for western counties—would be brought forward in that session. The formation of the new county, Davidson, would, he thought, appease western members temporarily. A nascent interest in politics, government, and all aspects of public life was clearly maturing in the youthful law student throughout this period.[26]

It was an interest his father encouraged. North Carolina was his native state, George told him, and it was hoped his future station. David thus should prepare himself in the state and, among other things, should consider becoming an orator. He should avoid narrow sectionalism in order to acquire the affectionate regard of every section of the state.

While David was away from Buncombe County readying himself, George was networking for him and promoting his future career, both legal and political. He reported a friendly disposition toward David from one Asheville lawyer and conveyed respects from another. He informed David on Asheville court happenings and local legislative candidates. David looked to George for election results and may have been disappointed when George deferred to D. M. Vance to send them. George sent David funds for clothes and a hat so David could "meet our Buncombe [legislative] members in a decent garb." He advised David not to be openly critical of the university lest he diminish his popularity with its supporters.[27]

George created opportunities for David to acquaint himself with leading state officials. He forwarded a plat with instructions that David give it to the secretary of state and request a grant as early as possible. He gave David messages to give to the governor. He conveyed the desire of Buncombe Senator Zeb Baird that David apply for one of the legislative clerkships in the ensuing session, and he encouraged Baird to let David compile items needed to amend laws of the Town of Asheville. George exhorted David to assist legislators with their work, to pay close attention to parliamentary order, rules, and debates, and to keep a detailed journal of same, "in case you should be called on hereafter to serve . . . in that capacity." David would never have the same chance before he was called on to act personally, George observed. David yielded to his father's prompting and essentially served as a secretary to the Buncombe legislative delegation in the 1822 session.

George once told David, "I am ready to make any sacrifice to give you an equal chance provided the blessing of heaven will second my efforts." Others joined him, one friend, for example, describing to David his campaign travels with Robert B. Vance, David's friend and the congressman representing Buncombe County.[28]

These efforts may have been superfluous, for there was nothing opaque about the young Swain's inclinations toward political life. At least from his departure for Raleigh, he was curious about political matters and laying the groundwork for a political career.

His youthful friendship with Robert B. Vance spawned a keen interest in Vance's political fortunes. He flattered himself with the hope that Vance would provide him "frequent and luminous strictures on the character and conduct of the great men of the mountains and . . . supply [him] with a regular narrative of the times." In early 1823 Vance opined to Swain that multiple candidacies in the mountain congressional election would result in the reelection of his opponent, the incumbent Felix Walker. David, though viewing the contest as close, had been more sanguine about his friend's prospects. He was ecstatic when Vance prevailed, and his Raleigh friends shared in his pleasure.[29]

Swain's contempt for Walker matched his respect for Vance. He did not know whether he would ever be "a candidate for populous favor," but he knew he would not "*creep* into any office." He preferred "but three decent men in the world who could say that Swain is a clever fellow than a whole host of Mr. W's friends if obliged to acquire and retain them as he has."[30]

Judge Henry Seawell was likewise a subject of Swain's scorn. Seawell's appointment as arbitrator under the Treaty of Ghent that ended the War of 1812 rendered "his vanity ... greatly grateful," Swain said, calling Seawell "one of the last of our prominent men whom North-Carolina would have delighted to honor." Swain had contempt, too, for the "obscure and ignorant" man who defeated Judge Paul Cameron for a State Senate seat from Orange County. He was pleased, though, when "more men of talent" were elected than he had expected.[31]

State issues were Swain's standard fare. Internal improvements in particular were a consummate interest. He learned too of proposed alterations in the state constitution more favorable to the West than expected. Internal improvements and regional empowerment through constitutional change would be absorbing concerns in his later time as legislator and governor.[32]

To consider the young Swain as concerned only about state and local matters, and thus provincial, would be inaccurate, however. He and his friends were, for example, keenly interested in the 1824 presidential election. More than a year preceding it, a friend wrote Swain that the contest was exciting more interest than ever was known on a similar occasion. Another soon said it was "in every mouth and I do not know when I have ever been more tired of a subject." He thought William Crawford would get a majority in a caucus, but one-on-one with John C. Calhoun or John Quincy Adams, either of them would prevail. He added, almost as an afterthought, "[Andrew] Jackson has some friends here."

By early spring 1824 the election "swallow[ed] up everything else," with Crawford and Jackson considered the leading competitors. Jackson, it was thought, could not be president: "There is too much innate virtue and intelligence in the great mass of the community for him to succeed." Although the Constitution might keep him in check, he would try its strength in a short time.

Swain appears to have been interested but discreet. He was at least thought to be a Crawford supporter and to have hinted at opposition to Jackson. This would accord with his later views on Jackson. It would also reflect a consuming concern for politics.

He once acknowledged to his sister that he recognized her complete disinterest in it, but said, "I have heard, read, thought and talked of nothing else this month past."[33]

While politics and public affairs were Swain's paramount interests, he had others. Robert Burns was his favorite poet, and he was thought to be "interested in every thing that concerns him." Lord Byron's dark poetry also engaged his attention. A correspondent identified only as "Eclletchete," apparently an Indian friend, wrote him of botany and botanists, with particular reference to André

Michaux. Swain's lifelong passion for history took root in this period. While a law student he traveled to eastern North Carolina and viewed "[t]he ruins of the palace built previous to the revolution for the English Gov. Martin, the house in which the state constitution was formed, and the former residence of Gen. Davie . . . with no ordinary interest."[34]

This excursion occurred as Swain recovered from a serious illness. A late summer and early fall 1822 epidemic afflicted more than a third of Raleigh's population. It was described as a bilious fever or marsh miasma, attributed to ponding water near the mill on Rocky Branch owned by the brother of Governor Gabriel Holmes's wife, Captain Theophilous Hunter Jr. Many years later scientists concluded the disease was probably malaria.[35]

In early August David reported that "Raleigh is at present sickly beyond all example." Governor Holmes and his family, Judge Taylor and his daughter, and many others were quite ill. David had experienced a severe cold and had feared the bilious fever but had taken Epsom salts and was entirely recovered. A few days later he considered himself "never more healthy than at present" and was confident he would be as healthy in Raleigh as in the mountains. A visitor reported to George that his son was in no danger; he was so correct in his habits, the visitor observed, that if anyone escaped the fever, he would.

Shortly thereafter, David's friend W. R. Gales advised George that his son was "slightly indisposed." A week later Gales had hoped David would be completely recovered but could only say he was well enough to converse with his usual volubility but still unable to write without difficulty. He thought David would be able to write home by the following week.

Gales had guessed correctly. A week later David told his father it had pleased a just providence to place him on the bed of affliction, where he had been confined for eighteen days with a bilious fever. He was sitting in a chair for the first time for the purpose of writing. Doctors had pronounced him convalescent, and his feelings indicated the same.

Meanwhile George had counseled removal from the city "to some quarter more healthy—or where a change of air might have a salutary effect." He advised David against resuming his studies too quickly and urged him to "carefully shun every fatigue and exposure." David took the advice seriously. As soon as he could travel, he went to the home of General Calvin Jones in Wake Forest to continue his recovery. He was again eating well and feeling much better. His reception had been cordial, and he was confident his residence there would be very pleasant.

After twenty-two days of change of scenery, air, diet, and exercise, David's health was improved, and his spirits had lifted. He recounted shocking mortality in Raleigh, however, "much greater than was at first generally apprehended." "Many poor persons, negroes and children have passed into the grave unpitied and unnoticed," he lamented.

He was shocked to learn that his recovery had been "wholly unexpected to my physicians and the family in which I board." He had been in delirium and thus had "felt little of the alarm" as his doctors found it almost impossible to make medicines operate upon him.

George Swain, deeply religious, was grateful to God and the friends God had provided to help David through this "perilous scene." He thought the medical bills reasonable in view of "the violence and protraction of [the] illness," and wanted to pay them as promptly as possible. He refused to let David postpone purchase of winter clothes due to the cost of his illness. "[W]isdom," he said, "directs us to shield the body from the cold."

George remained concerned that David was resuming his studies too soon; he should await "a compleat restoration of health." If David failed to report on his health, George reprimanded him. He communicated David's mother's desire to know the location of the destructive mill ponds "supposed by miasmata to have produced the late sickness in Raleigh."

David ultimately reported his health better than ever, or than anticipated, "after sufferings at the bare recollection of which I almost shudder." As late as June 1823, however, he reported two weeks of delicate health with symptoms of another attack of the fever. Almost a year later William Gaston hoped David's return to his native mountain air had produced a perfect recovery of his health and strength. Swain had been seriously, even dangerously ill, and the illness had bred lingering effects.[36]

One dimension of health, temperance, brought David unrelenting parental admonitions. George's experiences with an alcoholic father had rendered him hypercritical of consuming alcohol. David perhaps inadvertently aroused his father's concerns in this regard. While on a trip to South Carolina as he approached his twentieth birthday, he apprised George that his health had been good except for a brief period from the consequences "of drinking cider with too great a portion of ardent spirits." George apparently viewed this intendedly innocent confession as an alarm bell in the night.

"[C]onvivial entertainment at conversation parties" greatly concerned George. He lamented what "these seeming pleasures" had cost his father in pain, sorrow, property, and life. A lingering death, characterized by excruciating agonies, had been the result; the widowed wife and fatherless children, the ultimate victims.

The effects of alcohol consumption were debilitating, and David was encouraged to "drink the best cordial that God bestowed on man[,] Good Water."

"Don't think hard of my scolding you about conversation parties," George cautioned. He had no objection to sociability and wished David every improvement possible from good company. From mournful experience, however, he knew that alcoholic drink had "proved the baneful destructive enemy of genius of life, of health of reputation of every enjoyment that a rational and reasonable being ought to hold in the highest estimation." Although George had never followed his father in dissipation, he attributed his lifelong weak nerves to his father's drinking. Many, he informed his son, had killed themselves with intemperance.

In David's transient student days at Chapel Hill, George's temperance concerns generated a plan for action. He hoped, he told David, that the president and faculty would "zealously second you in putting my plan for the suppression of drunkenness into execution." There could be no more proper place "for giving a check to that enormous evil as our seminaries of learning." If he knew the president, Joseph Caldwell, he would write him, and he wondered whether David could "pave the way for the commencement of a correspondence of that kind?" His strongest opponents, he said, "became the warmest supporters of sobriety when brought to a right mind."

No evidence that David advanced his father's scheme survives. In his later life as president of the university, ardent spirits caused many problems with student discipline.

Likewise, there is no evidence of dissipation on David's part. Perhaps the father's admonitions took, but more likely the intense, ambitious son simply had no time to waste in a state of intoxication.[37]

Parental monitions extended beyond temperance to general piety. George Swain was a ruling elder in the Presbyterian Church and a man of deep and abiding faith. Caroline was an equally pious Methodist. It was perhaps on her account that Methodist Bishop Frances Asbury visited "Squire Swain's agreeable family" when he passed through the French Broad Valley in 1800 and later spent two days resting in their home. Humphrey Posey, a Baptist preacher of the mountain region, was also a family friend. Add the subsequent influence of David's teacher, the Reverend George Newton, a Presbyterian, and David later would say he was reared to love all good Christians.[38]

George's epistles are replete with inspirations toward a robust Christian commitment. Could he live his life over, he told David, his first step would be a study of the Bible. The twelfth chapter of Romans, in particular, should be memorized, for it contained every precept to guide clergy or laity. Christian fortitude, George said, was a better supporter of the mind than ignorance.

George would commend sermons to David, once praising one from the text: "Let us hear the conclusion of the whole matter . . . fear God and keep his commandments for this is the whole duty of man" (Ecclesiastes 12:13). A communication on faith from David afforded him much satisfaction, and David's joy on hearing a preacher made George wish he could hear him. "Acknowledge *him* in all thy ways and *he* shall direct thy paths," he admonished (Proverbs 3:6; emphasis in original). Long experience, George said, had taught him that all blessings stem from one doctrine: "Seek first the kingdom of heaven and its righteousness and all these things shall be added unto you" (Matthew 6:33).

Undoubtedly George was pleased when David reported hearing several preachers at the Presbyterian Church in Raleigh and his father's friend Luther Rice, a famed Baptist preacher and missionary, at the Baptist meeting house—"quite a mild and agreeable speaker," David concluded. He may have been less pleased when David recounted attending church with a friend because "some young ladies of our acquaintance" would be there. "[A]way we went like pious christians," David said, "but some how or other selected a pew much more convenient to the ladies than [to] the preacher." Soon, though, the "fools eyes' resting on the pretty faces of the girls" were fixed on the preacher, a Jew, and David had never listened to a sermon with more interest. Indeed, he went to hear the man three times in one day, and that not a Sunday.

Devoted faith, in George's view, produced appropriate conduct. He once expressed considerable gratitude that David was not implicated "in those pitiful love intrigues carried on by your intimate associates." The precise nature of the intrigues is unclear, but a "Miss Jane" had resorted to legal process. The "slightest shade," George told David, "has never attached itself to your character of that kind since you had a being."

Caroline, too, devoutly sought assurance that David's soul "was prepared for a blissful immortality," her only care being for his future welfare. Read the Bible, she urged, "and pray over it until you are charmed with it." "[D]avid, I wish you wood turn from the law to the gospell," she wrote, "in the gospell there is agrate treshure."

Siblings united with their parents in expression of righteous concerns for him. A sister thought how useful he might be if religion was added to his other endowments, but she "seriously fear[ed] lest his mind should be so crowded with the things of this world as to leave no room for the one thing needful." "I would rather know that he was an humble follower of the meek and lowly Jesus," she said, "than to see him promoted to the presidency of the united state."[39]

These concerns for him failed to make David a faithful correspondent with them. They filed their protests with their father. George Jr. had not received a letter and complained of neglect. A sister, Mary, wrote her father, "Tell brother D if he can not write to me I wish he would send a newspaper occasionally[.] I feel some anxiety to know what he has been doing in Raleigh this winter and whether he has got home yet."[40]

Friends shared their discontent. In light of Swain's slackness in responding to him, John L. Ellis thought their friendship must be secondary to many. He once noted his delay in responding to Swain, but reminded Swain of his own want of punctuality and gave him a reprimand. At times he had determined to put a final stop to their correspondence, he said, because he did not wish to intrude upon those who "manifest the least disinclination to reply with punctuality." He thought Swain "some-times unnecessarily busy" but hoped he was mistaken or that Swain would be less remiss. Like Ellis, J. R. Liles complained of not hearing from Swain. "I have not received a line from you since you left," he wrote, "owing as I charitably suppose to your many correspondents who perhaps have a juster claim."

For all his virtues, it appears that Swain was indeed an unreliable correspondent. His friend Robert B. Vance offered a reason: the ladies had entirely engrossed Swain's attention.[41] Vance was right, at least in part. Swain's communications in this period often related to women. Vance boasted to Swain that the most interesting and beautiful group of ladies imaginable had assembled around him. He begged Swain to write him "of these lovely fascinating beings who continue to be the directors of our destinies," and when away, requested that Swain give his respects to his female acquaintances.

One friend, inquiring as to the outlook for Swain, noted the absence of "prospects of a change of my dull life of celibacy." Another found in New Bern a greater display of female beauty than he had previously met but thinking of those who willingly put themselves in a state of slavery diverted him from matrimonial considerations.

The most cynical expression came from one frightened by an incident with a woman. "I inwardly cursed the sex which was the cause of it," he wrote Swain, "for a foolish babbling set of animals and of no use in this world but to make men." He planned to consult Swain to "see if we could not make men by steam or some other method by which we could do away with those useless beings called women."

Swain, too, could be caustic in appraising women. He accused one of a failing "common to the sex, too great a fondness for admiration." Still, he was concerned when his father failed to inform him of a marriage; he was not interested in the fate of all the mountain girls, he said, and his female company en route to Raleigh was so pleasant he was no longer haunted by them, but he did not want the common order changed without due notice.[42] Further, he found most of the young ladies he met "tolerably intelligent." To sustain a conversation with them on literary topics, he noted, a man must "have read the Waverly novels, the Spy, Peters letters, Lord Byrons works, Moores Melodies, & if in addition he can sing, play on the flute, violin, or clarinet, he may pass with great éclat."[43]

Although he was charged with being "the greatest gallant in the metropolis [Raleigh]," his accuser acknowledged that Swain had entangled himself with a particular damsel, probably beyond hope of extrication. Eleanor White, daughter of North Carolina Secretary of State William White and granddaughter of Governor Richard Caswell, had caught his eye, and she never lost it. Friends teased Swain good-naturedly. Despite his resolutions to the contrary, one observed, he "at length became a worshipper at the Shrine of Beauty in defiance of [his] boasted indifference to feelings of that nature." Cupid had found one spot sufficiently tender and unprotected "in which to plant a shaft to poison [his] peace." When Eleanor visited Buncombe County, another friend wrote sarcastically that it was "for *her health* Aye, Captain?"

Others were more supportive. One simply requested the truth as to whether Swain had fallen in love. His Indian friend Eclletchete enjoined him to get a wife and settle down so he could "make it my home at your house." A Raleigh acquaintance informed Swain that at Whitehall, Eleanor's family home, "they regard you in the light of a future son-in-law."[44]

Eleanor refused David's initial proposal, but he persevered, and they were married at the White residence in Raleigh on January 12, 1826. They initially planned a private ceremony, but upon arrival of some of Eleanor's relatives, opened it to a number of friends. Some were invited to tea at 8:00 p.m. to find upon arrival that the marriage had taken place at 7:00. A week after the wedding the couple left Raleigh for Buncombe County, traveling twenty miles before spending the night at a private residence. Swain soon received assurances from Eleanor's next-door neighbor that his bride could acquit herself of every duty and prove an agreeable and interesting companion on his journey through life. She had been bred in a good school by one who was herself an exemplary wife and widow, and would, he was confident, make one of the best of wives.[45]

Swain's time in Raleigh thus brought him a lifetime companion in Eleanor. It spawned other lasting friendships as well. A missive from one such friend is interesting in light of subsequent events; the friend, Lucius Polk, was en route to the

Eleanor White, who married David Swain on January 12, 1826. Courtesy of Suzy Barile.

wedding of one of his relatives, James K. Polk, later president of the United States. A remark in a Swain letter likewise acquires interest in light of his later career; he had visited with the family of the late Governor David Stone and had only one objection to its members: "They concern themselves too much with politics."[46]

Mixed emotions marked the end of Swain's tenure in Raleigh. He had left his mountain home "endeared by many tender associations," and he anticipated his return to it with much pleasure. Raleigh, however, had risen in his estimation, and he would leave it with sincere regret. He had acquired greater empathy with the afflicted while there.

The friendships were unexcelled in hospitality and disinterestedness. Indeed, he feared he was leaving more friends behind than he would find at home. As Swain neared the end of his life, a friend from his student days recalled that his sister had dreaded spending an evening with this "raw country youth, a son of her father's old friend," but noted "with what surprise and delight they afterwards spoke of [that] evening [which] sufficed to fix [Swain's] status in Raleigh."[47]

David left Raleigh with Judge Taylor's admonition to read law books, including *Coke on Littleton*, daily. The judge also gave him a list of books recommended for a small library. As his departure approached, David suggested that George request information from Judge Taylor as to his progress "or something of this kind." "I do not ask it because I believe he will report favorably," David assured his father, "but because I am inclined to believe he expects it."

George protested mildly. "I feel no small degree of reluctance," he said, "for my abilities were ever of an inferior grade and now my faculties are so greatly benumbed by age that I am not able to write common sense." He was ashamed of his relative ignorance, his tendency toward verbosity and redundancy, and his grammatical deficiencies. Nevertheless, he wrote, and he was amply rewarded with the response.

Long experience had taught him, Judge Taylor said, "not to pander to a father's expectations where they are unreasonable." This was not a problem with David. Among the youths he had instructed, he had "never met with a finer or more correct understanding than your sons." David was indefatigable in his studies and dissatisfied with superficiality. His foundational knowledge was well absorbed, and the groundwork would readily receive any superstructure that future experience or acquisition might add to it. His talents would assure him a high standing in the profession, and they were "combined with excellent qualities of the heart, . . . a high sense of honor and love of truth, and many virtues which must inevitably endear him to all who knew him intimately." These observations were not Taylor's alone; David's other acquaintances would agree. He was, in sum, "a dutiful and accomplished son" who would gild the evening of his father's old age.

Others affirmed Taylor's assessment. Calvin Jones, with whom David had stayed while ill, viewed him as having "the elevation of his native mountains and . . . in time [he] will be equally conspicuous and famed." A visitor to Asheville reported to George that David's "character stands very fair in Raleigh, particularly among the best and highest grade of people who know how to value men of stability and firmness."[48] Even discounting the rhetorical flourishes with which nineteenth-century men expressed themselves, a doting father could hardly have hoped or asked for more.

CHAPTER 2

Law, Statecraft
"Station[s] of some importance"

Lawyer

SWAIN'S TENURE UNDER CHIEF Justice Taylor's tutelage had prepared him for his chosen profession. In June 1823 he was licensed for practice in North Carolina's county courts, and in December 1824, in its superior courts. His hometown of Asheville, seat of Buncombe County, afforded a convenient locale for commencing a law practice. It was the first time a native of the county had returned there as a lawyer.[1]

Previous biographical snippets describe Swain's professional life as "very successful" and "lucrative."[2] Considered in light of his lifetime financial achievements, they are almost certainly accurate. Such cannot be surmised, however, from his contemporaneous correspondence. Laments of financial woes were the common currency of his letters from the court circuits.

Lack of business was not a problem. Securing ready compensation for it was. He had been busily engaged in arranging his papers and researching his cases, he once told Eleanor; his professional prospects were promising, but funds were so scarce that he obtained "almost nothing in ready change." Despite doing extensive business, he received no money; indeed, he said, there was none in the county.

On one occasion he "barely received money enough to pay my bills"; not only was he unable to collect $100.00 due him from an estate, but he also had to buy the deceased's land to preserve it for the family. Although he would have his share of a docket's cases, complaints such as "I found myself poorly paid after all for my long and loud speeches," or "I have never known so chaffy a court," were routine. Failure to secure sufficient fees to pay his bills in an eastern county made him disinclined to return there.[3]

Loneliness was his steady companion while traversing the circuits. Often these nomadic periods were prolonged. Once he had been away seven weeks; another time he wrote Eleanor in late August that he could not afford the pleasure of seeing her before Christmas.

Social life on the circuits afforded pleasant, offsetting amenities. In one week, Swain attended two parties, the first given by a client, the second by Governor James Iredell. He admitted to Eleanor that he had "seen many very pretty girls" at these soirees but redeemed himself by vowing that a brief embrace with her would give him more heartfelt pleasure than a month of such enjoyment.

Eleanor's deficiencies as a correspondent aggravated her husband's wayfaring solitude. In the seven-week absence, he had received three letters from her and was hopeful that the next mail would not disappoint him. She could not know how much he wished to see her and to avoid such long separations. Once he delayed writing because he had expected a letter from her but was disappointed. Anxious to know everything that interested her, particularly the state of her health, he was grieved when she "complain[ed] of melancholy." "I declare this long absence is insupportable, and becomes more intolerable every day," he would say.[4]

Swain's practice, like that of most lawyers of his day, was general in nature. It appears to have been predominantly civil, but at least occasionally he handled a criminal case. He once found it his duty to defend a criminal of a character, and in circumstances, he hoped never to hear of again. The defendant was a destitute, disfigured young woman, age twenty, on trial for infanticide, the killing of her first-born, illegitimate child. She protested her innocence, and Swain gave her demurrer some credence but thought convincing a jury of it would be exceedingly difficult. He must have been persuasive, for the woman was acquitted "without a scuffle." Swain was not modest about his role. "I acquitted the poor woman," he reported, "and have generally been pretty successful." He also found pleasure in securing an acquittal of a "negroe boy . . . charged with burglary" whom he did not believe was guilty; that he had to destroy the reputations of three girls who testified against his client was an unpleasant aspect of the defense that was, he said, "thrown upon me."[5]

On the civil side he reported numerous visitors who flattered themselves with the belief that they had important business. While somewhat deprecating their appraisals, he yielded to their importunities. Among them were two U.S. topographical engineers who were surveying the French Broad River to ascertain the practicability of uniting its headwaters with the Savannah River by means of a canal or railroad.[6]

Swain's legislative capacity factored in his acquisition of state legal work. Governor Hutchins G. Burton appointed him a commissioner, pursuant to legislative act, to implement a State contract with certain Cherokee Indians. Swain was to meet in Franklin, North Carolina, with Philip Brittain, another House member who was the other commissioner, to comply with the act.

Later, Governor James Iredell employed Swain to defend purchasers from the State against claims asserted by any Indian or persons claiming under such pursuant to a reservation under treaties of 1817 and 1819. Every such case was submitted to Swain's discretion, subject to guidance from the report made to the General Assembly in 1824 by commissioners appointed to investigate these Indian titles, and to the report of the committee of both legislative houses to which this report was referred. At his convenience Swain was to furnish the governor a list of the cases and the amount of his charges. Iredell also appointed Swain to attend the State Bank shareholders' meeting, vote for the State in the appointment of directors, and represent the interests of the State generally.

Governor John Owen, as president of the university trustees, employed Swain as attorney for the trustees in Buncombe, Haywood, and Macon counties. Swain was to collect sums due to the university, probably escheated funds primarily, in said counties; to sell and convey lands there to which the trustees held title; and to represent their interests generally.[7]

Swain is said to have had no superior in complex land disputes. One such case, described as "a complicated mass of litigation, involving more land than was ever sued for under one title in our State, except . . . the claim of Lord Granville's heirs," went to the U.S. Supreme Court. George Badger represented the State of North Carolina, which associated Massachusetts lawyer and senator Daniel Webster. It also associated a twenty-seven-year-old David Swain, to whose careful preparation, indomitable energy, patient research, and acumen Badger attributed the state's ultimate success. When elected governor while the case was pending, Swain returned one-half of his retainer to the state treasury.[8]

Estate work composed a portion of Swain's law practice. He served as coexecutor of the estate of his close friend Congressman Robert Vance, who was killed in a duel. He also served as administrator of his father's estate.[9]

Swain was known for his remarkably retentive mind. As a lawyer, it enabled him to cite cases from memory. It was said that in jury trials he could, without notes, repeat the testimony of all witnesses regardless of the length of the trial, a feat diminished only slightly by his admission that he could recall no instance in which a trial occupied more than a day.[10]

He maintained an Asheville-based legal career until his election as a superior court judge. His share of the business was then such that John Hall, son of the state supreme court judge of the same name, "removed to Buncombe to take charge of [it]." Over three years after he left the practice a former client, who claimed to have paid Swain "a liberal fee," was still seeking "some prominent character who will attend [in Swain's stead] in all the counties if need be."[11]

No legal practitioner altogether escapes criticism and conflicts. Swain was no exception. He, George Badger, and others contracted to represent the state in Indian land-claims cases for $500.00 each. They had to inform the governor, John Owen, that this was not intended to include suits in the federal courts. Still, the critics talked. "They are roasting the governor for the fees paid Badger, Swain & Seawell and me," wrote one lawyer, "but it cannot succeed." In another matter, the parties proposed Swain as a commissioner in a case in which he had had some previous, unspecified role. "The fact was disclosed," wrote later Chief Justice Thomas Ruffin, "but it shook not the confidence of either of the counsel."[12]

Swain was sensitive to reputational concerns. His papers contain a statement by Joshua Roberts, an Asheville attorney, regarding a conversation with Swain. Swain had told Roberts he was engaged "in a business of a delicate nature about which he might be much blamed at some future period." It related to land in Macon County that Swain had arranged to purchase for the state. Swain was distressed that he would have no one to vindicate his conduct, which he considered correct, except those interested in the transaction. He was prepping Roberts to be a "disinterested" witness if necessary.

So far as the records reveal, nothing improper occurred, and nothing came of the matter. These testimonials from leaders of the bar perhaps disarmed potential critics. But Swain had covered his tracks in case there was a future problem.[13]

Legislator

Professional standing was not the sole motivator of Swain's reputational concerns. His political future weighed at least equally in these calculations. He had barely alighted in Asheville as a lawyer when he bought one hundred acres of land to meet property qualifications and in 1824 returned to Raleigh as a twenty-three-year-old member of the House of Commons. His first election was not unanimous. A friend, feigning ignorance about the candidates, encountered a naysayer who said he would not vote for Swain. "He acknowledged that you were a pretty smart fellow and would hold a very high poll," the friend recounted, "but thought you a little roguishly inclined & not to be trusted because you were a lawyer."[14] It would be the first of his five one-year terms in the House and would launch a life of public service that held few remaining days in which he did not occupy some important public station.

Legislative careers tend to defy comprehensive analysis and description. The volume of discrete measures on which a solon must pass, combined with the collaborative nature of the process, render complete and accurate assessment of individual performance difficult, if not impossible. Brief mention of a Swain predecessor in the General Assembly, however, lends structure to his service and provides context for its evaluation.

Archibald DeBow Murphey represented Orange County in the North Carolina Senate from 1812 until 1818. When he served, North Carolina was so undeveloped, backward (educationally and otherwise), and indifferent to its condition that it was known as the Rip Van Winkle state. Murphey functioned as the leading rooster in Old Rip's barnyard, rousing the state to serious consideration of a system of public education, internal improvements, and constitutional reform. Governor William A. Graham, a Swain contemporary and fellow Murphey disciple, would say that it was Murphey who "inaugurated a new era in the public policy of this state" and left to posterity "the noblest monuments of philosophic statesmanship to be found in our public archives since the days of the Revolution."[15]

Although Murphey's county of Orange was centrally located, in the parlance of his time he was a westerner, and his followers tended to be as well, perhaps foremost among them three future "western" governors: David L. Swain (1832–1835), John M. Morehead (1841–1845), and William A. Graham (1845–1849). Swain was their early leader and a rallying point for Murphey's program. He is properly viewed as aligned with the progressive leaders of his section, a departure from "the laissez-faire concept of government so satisfactory to the conservative East," and as a catalyst for "an active progressive government striving to provide a solution to the problems which hindered the advancement of North Carolina."

Traditionally, legislative leadership had hailed from the East. Swain's far-western district thus made him something of an anomaly. Soon, however, he proved himself, to colleagues from all sections, a man of courage, a clear thinker, and a ready debater. "I will take deep pains to represent matters in their true light," he once said, "and convince my constituents if I can that I am neither to be bought [n]or bullied." Despite his youth, an ungraceful physical makeup, and a voice tone described as "hollow and high-keyed," he quickly entered the ranks of legislative leadership. His unattractive physical appearance bothered him little, if any. Henry Clay, perhaps the foremost lawmaker of the day, was also ugly, Swain once noted.[16]

Internal improvements were foremost in Swain's buy into the Murphey program; and although Swain represented a region with greater, even desperate transportation needs, his advocacy and efforts in this regard were devoid of provincialism. "[T]he prosperity and happiness of the state," he told his constituents, "depends greatly upon the success of our system of Internal Improvements, and . . .

sectional prejudices and narrow economy ought never to be suffered to influence our course." In the Buncombe Turnpike Company, his county's citizens had "participated in the public bounty." "[C]ommon justice requires at our hands the extension of like liberality to other sections of the State," he admonished.[17]

The Buncombe Turnpike was Swain's prime legislative accomplishment. Before he acquired solon status, a future constituent apprised him of local support for it. "I believe it [the projected turnpike] meets the ginneral (illegible) of a large majority of the cittizens of our County and is a very popler thing," he wrote, suggesting that "it is our Interest to alert their men (?) for the Intres of our Roads and Turnpick."[18]

Thus encouraged, the new Buncombe Commoner presented his first bill: to authorize the making of a turnpike road from the Saluda Gap in Buncombe to the Tennessee line. His membership on the Committee on Internal Improvements, whose duties he described as "arduous and important," aided him in securing early passage of the proposal.[19] Three Asheville men—Samuel Chunn, James Patton, and George Swain, the bill sponsor's father—were authorized to sell $50,000 of stock in the company. The collection of tolls further financed the project.[20]

A vested-interest holder attempted to block the turnpike. James Allen, who would represent Buncombe in the 1827 House of Commons, operated an older turnpike built across some precarious mountain heights. He protested the proposal for a new artery by the Buncombe Turnpike Company. When the company declined Allen's offer to contribute $5,000 toward building the new road along his right-of-way, he secured an injunction and sued to set aside the company's franchise. The North Carolina Supreme Court unanimously upheld a judgment against him. Allen brought further court actions, but despite his opposition, construction of the road proceeded. Allen and Swain became bitter enemies in the process.[21]

Ready perception of its value to the mountain region greeted the new road. Calvin Jones, with whom Swain had resided in Wake Forest while recovering from illness, wrote George Swain, "This road only is wanting to make Buncombe to a traveler the most interesting and agreeable portion of our country." In the context of the time, it would revolutionize commerce and development in western North Carolina. It opened the mountains to traffic from the Piedmont and to new levels of emigration, travel, and trade from Tennessee, Kentucky, and South Carolina.[22]

To the bill's sponsor it was "the first fruits of my political life." He observed the construction with obvious delight. "[T]he road ... is so different from what you once found it," he told his wife, "that one of the greatest pleasures I promise myself

> **Buncombe Turnpike Company.**
>
> NOTICE is hereby given, that in pursuance of an Act of the General Assembly of North-Carolina, passed at Raleigh, on the 30th day of December, 1824, Books are now open at Asheville, under the direction of the undersigned Commissioners, appointed by said Act, for the purpose of receiving Subscriptions to the amount of Twenty-Five Thousand Dollars, in Shares of Fifty Dollars each, (being the amount open to individual subscription, Five Thousand Dollars having been already subscribed by the State.)
>
> Notice is hereby further given, that the Books will be kept open at Asheville, as aforesaid, until the first day of March next, when the subscribers to the Stock of the Company will meet, and, if the sum of Twenty Thousand Dollars shall have been subscribed, the Company will be organized.
>
>   JAMES PATTON,
>   SAMUEL CHUNN, } *Commissioners.*
>   GEORGE SWAIN,
>
> Asheville, (N. C.) Jan. 1, 1825. [F 15 tu9]

Notice seeking subscriptions in Buncombe Turnpike Company, which David Swain called "the first fruits of my political life." From the *Charleston Courier*, March 29, 1825.

in future is to traverse it with you, and exhibit it in triumph. It is very certain that it will be greatly superior to any road of the same extent in the state."

While Swain's appraisal is self-interested, the turnpike's advantages were beyond cavil. As expressed by a writer to a Raleigh newspaper, "If any serious enquirer really wishes to know what may be done for $30,000.00 under proper restrictions, let him traverse the road ... it is one of the best ... in the southern [states] nor are there many better in the United States." Six years after passage of the legislation, the Board of Internal Improvements, of which Swain was a member, reported that during the first eight months after completion of the road the company had declared a dividend of 8 percent, and at the close of the following year a further dividend of 10 percent, upon the capital stock. The board's conclusion had to be gratifying to Swain. "No higher evidence of the prosperity, or the ability with which their affairs have been managed," the board said, "should be desired."[23]

Other Swain-sponsored measures, regional in nature, included a bill to improve the road from Old Fort in Burke County (now in McDowell) to Buncombe and a bill to keep open the French Broad River. As to the former, the Board of Internal Improvements later reported that the act had been "carried into effect" and "[t]he road ... is nearly completed and promises to be a very good one."[24]

Swain's votes on nonregional matters conformed to the philosophy he had expressed to his constituents. He consistently supported internal-improvements projects, without regard to sectional interests, and equally consistently opposed anti-improvements measures. Early in his first session he voted against a bill to repeal an 1819 enactment that created a fund for internal improvements and established a board for its management. A subsequent attempt to amend the act, apparently to weaken it, and in particular to reduce the salary of the state's civil engineer, drew Swain's negative vote. He then voted to allow per-diem expenses for the civil engineer while in the service of the board.[25] He favored the state's assenting to and enforcing acts of the Tennessee General Assembly relating to the Smoky Mountain Turnpike Company, and the state's subscription to the stock of said company.[26]

At the outset of the 1825 session Swain again attained membership on the House Committee on Internal Improvements. He again voted against the effort to repeal the 1819 act that had created a fund for internal improvements and a board to manage it. He appears to have favored autonomy for the board in that he voted to postpone indefinitely a bill that would have forced its hand in a matter involving the Roanoke Navigation Company. He was opposed to indefinite postponement of a bill to appropriate funds "for clearing out the flats below Wilmington."[27]

Conflict-of-interest issues regarding transportation projects are not solely a modern-day phenomenon. On one occasion a citizen, recognizing Swain as a leader on such matters, informed him that directors of the turnpike company were becoming contractors. He suggested statutory language to prohibit the president or a director of the Buncombe Turnpike Company from becoming a contractor for making or improving any part of a named road.[28]

Swain's support for internal improvements, combined with his legal ability, led Governor John Owen to select him, with George Badger, as attorney for the Board of Internal Improvements when it was sued because of an annulled contract.[29] Such support also led to membership on the board itself. His first nomination in the 1828 General Assembly failed, but in 1829 he was elected on the first ballot.[30]

Soon Swain was traveling with Governor Owen, the board's president, on an inspection tour of the Cape Fear River, examining efforts to improve its least navigable portions. He also became the draftsman for the board's annual report to the legislature, which provided him a forum from which to lament the lack of progress. It had been twelve years since the legislature had set aside a fund for internal-improvements purposes, he stated. Little had been done since except "to procure surveys, devise plans, and make estimates—all which have . . . been submitted to . . . the Legislature, and have produced but little practical effect." Absent a different course, the state should abolish the board and return the funds to the public treasury.

That, however, was not the preferred course. A policy "calculated to promote the prosperity and elevate the character of the state" would use the funds, and raise others, for internal improvements, which would lead to economic prosperity, which would then sustain public education. Internal improvements, one prong in the Murphey program, were Swain's hook into another prong, education. The conclusion that as a legislator Swain "offered no constructive leadership in the cause of education,"[31] while accurate in terms of concrete accomplishment, is incomplete and therefore misleading.

Swain shared Murphey's vision for universal public education, although then limited to white males. As a legislator he lamented that "[c]ommon schools are left dependent on individual patronage, and how often . . . are the bright buds of genius withered by the chilling frost of penury." The state constitution, he continued, "imposes upon us the establishment of common schools as an absolute duty." He confessed the state's abdication of this responsibility, saying: "But to subserve the purposes of general education, to place it in the power of the poor man as well as the rich, to hold his infant to his bosom . . . , confident [of opportunity and hope,] we have done almost nothing. Common schools are left dependent on individual patronage."[32]

Swain reprised this theme in the internal-improvements report, advancing economic development as a prerequisite to universal public education. "The best system ever devised for the general diffusion of education," he said, "is the general diffusion of wealth." The half million dollars the board was seeking could not educate the state's youth, but "judiciously used in the improvement of our physical condition," it could "enable them to educate themselves." Improving the condition of the country would "furnish the means of education, and lessen the temptation to crime."[33]

Able and articulate advocacy did not emanate in concrete accomplishment. As a legislator Swain's record on education is sparse. The 1825 session established the Literary Fund to prepare for state funding of a system of public education. Swain was almost certainly a supporter, but his vote cannot be determined. He was a member of the House Committee on Education in the 1828 and 1829 sessions, but the journals do not establish a significant role for him in that capacity. They reveal only minor actions such as his motion to refer the portion of the governor's message on education to the standing committee on that subject; his successful recommendation, for that committee, that the governor be directed to convey certain lands to Macon County and to establish Washington Academy; and his unfavorable report for the committee on a prayer from memorialists of Edenton Academy, in which the House concurred.[34]

Apart from adherence to Murphey's program for internal improvements and public education, Swain's legislative career is devoid of overarching themes. Several discrete matters merit brief mention, however. Swain was elected by a western constituency. It is therefore not surprising that he strove to advance western interests.

The foremost example is his support for forming new western counties. He steadfastly sought creation of a new county taken from Buncombe and Burke. His stated purpose was to accommodate a growing population and to relieve the citizens from long-distance travel to reach courthouses and attend militia musters. The more significant reason was to offset the dominant political influence of the East by providing enhanced legislative representation to the West. For obvious reasons, the eastern influence consistently scotched the proposal. Ever the optimist, Swain once informed his constituents that the measure was "gaining ground, and must ultimately succeed." In his lawmaking days, however, it did not.[35]

On matters in which western interests were less directly implicated, Swain's votes tended to accommodate Eastern interests. Racially related topics provide a prime example. Although westerners, including Swain and his family, owned slaves, legislation regarding, in the parlance of the time, "the Negro," was of greater concern to the Eastern slavocracy. Swain's initial foray into this arena, though, was prompted by his own constituents. Responding to a petition signed by his father, his brother-in-law William Coleman, and several Buncombe County citizens, he introduced a bill on the migration of free persons of color into Buncombe County, praying for a capitation tax of $50.00 or more on such. The tax was obviously designed to discourage their migration into the county and state. The Committee on Finance, to which it was referred, considered it inexpedient since its object could be obtained by a strict enforcement of the vagrancy laws.

In a subsequent session Swain voted for a bill to prevent free persons of color from migrating into the state and to provide for "the good government" of such persons already in residence. It contained "many salutary provisions," he reported to his constituents. He later failed to vote on a bill, which passed, to enforce more effectually payment of taxes by free Negroes and biracial persons.[36]

An inconsistency appears in one of Swain's actions on a racial matter. A bill was pending to allow the election of sheriffs in North Carolina counties by the qualified white voters thereof rather than the county courts. On two occasions there were motions to delete the word "white." On the first, Swain voted no; on the second, yes.[37] He was opposed to the bill, and the second vote could have been motivated by a desire to diminish the bill's chances of passage.

Throughout his legislative career Swain opposed these bills. His view prevailed in the 1824, 1825, and 1828 sessions. In 1829 he voted for a proposed amendment that would have imposed a term limit of three years and a waiting period of three years before the occupant could again seek the office of sheriff. The amendment failed, and Swain again voted against the bill, which, after several failed attempts, finally passed.[38] He also voted against a bill to place Quakers, Moravians, Dunkards, and "Menonists" on an equal footing with other freemen of the state.[39]

Bills to regulate "treating" at elections received Swain's support. "Treats," mainly food and drink, with spirits prominent, had been a feature of Andrew Jackson's campaign for president. That Swain was interested in national politics is evident from correspondence to him. But Swain was not a Jacksonian, and this feature of Jacksonian democracy apparently had no appeal for him; parental admonitions regarding spirits could also have influenced him. Because he represented a politically divided constituency, he largely steered clear of national races and issues in order to broaden his own base of support. For reasons not readily apparent, however, he was willing to assume any risks inherent in opposing this feature of the Jacksonian approach.[40]

As expected of a lawyer-legislator, Swain served on the House Judiciary Committee. In the 1827 session he was a member of a committee to conduct the balloting for a superior court judgeship when no candidate obtained a majority. He was on a similar committee in 1828 when Willie P. Mangum, whom Swain would later succeed, was selected to replace Thomas Ruffin on the superior court bench.

In miscellaneous actions on judiciary-related matters Swain opposed a bill to enlarge the jurisdiction of justices of the peace; made the motion when the House resolved to inquire into the unequal and insufficient administration of justice; voted to require clerks of court to keep offices at the courthouse; voted to require the state supreme court to sit in several places and against reducing the judges' salaries; served on a judicial-reform committee; and made the motion when the House resolved to inquire into the need for a new Revisal of the state's laws. On judiciary-related matters, it was often Swain who made the floor motions. When the skills of the legally trained were needed, his colleagues frequently summoned him.[41]

Internal House matters found Swain equally active. He was often the moving member on procedural matters.[42] He served on the Rules Committee, moved for adopting joint rules governing intercourse between the two Houses, and secured the printing of the Rules Committee report "in connection with the Constitution of the State and Bill of Rights and the Constitution of the United States," one copy to be provided to each member.[43] Sometimes he attempted to expedite the legislative process, moving, for example, to suspend for the remainder of a session the rule requiring public bills to be read on three different days (unsuccessfully), or to repeal a resolution requiring that all bills and resolutions involving expenditure of public funds be read three times on three separate days (successfully).[44] On his motion a public treasurer's report was sent to the Senate with a proposal to print one copy for each member, and on his motion the 1828 session commended House Speaker Thomas Settle, a future state supreme court judge, for the impartial and dignified manner in which he had discharged the duties of the chair.[45]

Given his retentive mind, it is not surprising that Swain became an authority on taxation and statistics regarding the condition of the state. He led the effort to require the comptroller of public accounts to develop, and attach to his annual report, a table of the amount of taxes paid by each county from the formation of the state government forward, with explanatory notes as deemed advisable. When the comptroller submitted the document, Swain proposed that two hundred copies be printed and deposited in the public library, with the next General Assembly to set the comptroller's compensation for this service.

He supported a bill, which failed, that would have provided statistical information about the resources of North Carolina. In the process of these endeavors, he acquired and retained knowledge that informed and enhanced his future service to the state.[46]

Swain also supported state assistance to John McRae of Fayetteville "to aid him in a publication of a Map of [the] State." His role in a measure, stimulated by Archibald D. Murphey, "to encourage the publication of a historical and scientific work on this State," is not clear. The bill passed the House, however, and in light of Swain's lifelong interest in preserving and perpetuating knowledge of the state's history, it probably received his enthusiastic endorsement.[47]

No matter how deeply committed to state-level issues, no legislator can altogether escape purely local concerns. Swain was no exception. He presented local bills for the better regulation of the Town of Asheville, to alter the boundary line between the first and second regiments of the Buncombe militia, to repeal an 1824 act regulating the mode of electing wardens of the poor and directing their duties so far as related to Buncombe County, and to incorporate the Vance Literary Society of Asheville.[48]

Constituent services, too, demanded his attention. He presented a petition from Polly Buckner of Buncombe County to be divorced from her husband, and one from Thomas Welch Sr. of Haywood County seeking redress for grievances arising from his purchase of Cherokee lands. On a broader scale, when apprehensive about the spread of smallpox in Buncombe County, Swain pledged to ascertain whether vaccine could be procured and, if so, to "send it by the present mail."[49]

Swain's legislative service led to his being considered for other positions. When former Governor John Branch left his U.S. Senate seat to be secretary of the navy in President Andrew Jackson's cabinet, legislators talked of uniting around Swain for the position. There was one insurmountable obstacle, however; he had not attained the constitutionally required age of thirty. "The 4th Jan. 1801 [Swain's date of birth] is a foreclosure," his brother-in-law wrote, adding, "If it will afford you any gratification I will now–say–your chance would have been a very good one." Thomas Ruffin wished Swain was "*old* enough and *rich* enough to go to the Senate."[50]

When Ruffin was considered for a vacancy on the state supreme court, there was interest in Swain for Ruffin's replacement as president of the State Bank, perhaps because of the knowledge and ability Swain had demonstrated in debating banking legislation.[51] Ruffin himself wanted an able man with industry, discretion, character, and balance; a man of business, likewise a lawyer and a good one. "I have no authority for saying the place would be conferred on *yourself*," he wrote Swain, but added, "I have thrown out in private the idea more than once." The leading stockholders and a decided majority would prefer Swain, Ruffin said, before any man in the state. He wanted to give Swain all the aid he could, and hoped to persuade him "upon public grounds, [and] on the influence of my own wishes as a citizen."

Ruffin was not appointed, and there thus was no vacancy at the bank. If there had been, however, there was considerable thinking that Swain would have filled it. "It was intended to have you made President of the Bank," Weston Gales told him.[52] Outwardly, Swain absorbed these lost potential opportunities with equanimity. The surviving records reveal neither disappointment nor despair.

Legislative life was not always pleasant. It made Swain angry at times. Once, for example, he wrote a bitter letter to a newspaper editor who had attributed his election to the House to his silence on the 1824 presidential contest. The editor had "attempted to subserve the *vile* purposes of *party* by prostitution of the truth," Swain carped.[53] At other times he was disappointed, both in the tone of legislative debate and in its results. When his bill to consolidate several banks into a State Bank failed, the defeat followed "an animated and too warm discussion," according to future chief justice Frederick Nash.[54]

Prolonged absences from Asheville forced him to send some of his practice to other lawyers. On a personal level, he was so busy in Raleigh that he could write only to his father, requesting that he share the letter because there was no time for others.[55] Over time this demanding and divided life took its toll. As early as his 1826 election, which he won by about one hundred votes, the campaign was "ardent" and "fiercely fought," and Swain was glad when the "hurly-burly" was over. He did not return to the House in 1827, and in 1828 his friends proclaimed him a candidate without his consent. Romulus Saunders, a former House speaker who would soon be the state's attorney general, had hoped Swain would offer, and he did. For a time, he had no opposition. If no opposition ticket ran, Swain noted, it would be a "first instance" for the county, and his election would be certain. "How it might result otherwise," he said, "I have no great anxiety to ascertain."

When opposition emerged, he did not deem it formidable. He had attended no public gathering and participated in no treat during the campaign, he said at one point, except for the annunciation of his name at court. Subsequently, though, the campaign began "to wax warm." In Swain's view the new candidates against him and Colonel John Clayton (each county then elected two House members) "had little to recommend them but the most untiring industry in electioneering." He was sanguine of success and flattered himself with expectations of the highest vote, but he was growing sufficiently weary of the process that he thought a loss would be "matter of little regret to me except at the moment of defeat." In all events he promised himself "with much confidence that I will not be so foolish again." To add to his electoral woes, his "pretty black mare" died from poison in August "and left [him] to wind up the electioneering campaign with a borrowed horse."

Swain was again successful; indeed, as he had predicted, he led the ticket, with 1,183 votes to Clayton's 1,041. Both Swain and Clayton had more than twice the votes of their nearest opponent. Historical perspective almost compels the conclusion, however, that with this election Swain was on a trajectory toward terminating his legislative service. "Today," he said as he reported the returns, "I have had to shake hands some 500 times, make speeches, tell anecdotes, talk law and politics untill my head is as empty as a tobacco box."

He would be "so foolish" once more. He was again elected and served in the 1829 session. By 1830, however, he had set a course against further electioneering. "I have given general notice that I am not to be considered a candidate for the General Assembly," he informed Eleanor, stating pensively: "What may be my ultimate course I can now determine with but little certainty and perhaps it is best so. I hope it will be calculated to promote my own happiness and that of those whose destinies ... [are] interwoven with mine."[56]

His standing in his district was excellent.[57] Absent extraordinary circumstances, he probably could have been reelected indefinitely. He was leaving public life, temporarily as it turned out, for personal, not political, reasons. But after five terms in which he was a quite active member of the House of Commons and in the life of the state generally, the man was ready for a change of pace.

Solicitor

There was one brief interlude in Swain's legislative service. Leonard Martin, a House of Commons member from Hertford County, died January 25, 1827. He had been in the House the previous day; less than twenty-four hours before his death, Swain had seen him and indicated that he had never seen him in finer health or more buoyant spirits. A capital city procession in remembrance of Martin extended for one-fourth of a mile and included all state officials and counselors.[58]

At that time a legislator could concurrently serve as the solicitor, or prosecuting attorney, of a judicial district. In addition to his legislative seat, Martin had held the legislatively filled office of solicitor for the first judicial circuit in the northeastern corner of the state. Notwithstanding Swain's residency near the other geographical extreme, he became a candidate, along with, initially, three others. After one withdrew, no candidate received a majority on the first ballot. Swain's name was then withdrawn.

But the race was not over. Names were added and subtracted, and the balloting remained inconclusive. Ultimately, three days after Swain's name had been withdrawn, it was again added, and he was duly elected. If he had been mistaken initially, he said, "subsequent occurrences have certainly gone far to wipe away such impressions." He had been placed in "circumstances as singular as they were gratifying."[59]

Swain's election was the product of the inability of the district's leadership to agree on a candidate. It also demonstrated, however, that his legislative service and general participation in affairs of state had endeared him, or at least made him acceptable, to a wide range of the state's leadership. A certificate from Governor Hutchins G. Burton invested him "with the office of Solicitor of the first judicial circuit of the State," noting his appointment by joint ballot of both houses of the General Assembly.[60]

The immediate aftermath found Swain reflective. "What may be my ultimate destination, time alone can determine," he said. He did not think anything less than absolute necessity could drive him from the mountains. He then revealed his probable underlying design: "it will increase my knowledge of the state and enlarge the boundaries of my intercourse with her citizens." In accepting the position, he had a longer-range political purpose in mind.[61]

While Swain was headed east for a spell, he was not forgetful of his western obligations and ties. He hoped his business there would not be "seriously deranged." He expected to procure Judge Willie P. Mangum's attention to a case in Rutherford County and to attend the trial of it there in the fall. His matters in Buncombe and Haywood counties he committed to other attorneys. He directed a circular letter to his Buncombe County constituents, noting that the legislature had seen fit to remove him from among them "to fill a station of some importance in another section of this State." He pledged never to forget the county that from infancy had given him "nothing but untiring confidence and kindness."[62]

Circuit travel in the east, like that in the west, left the new solicitor lonely.

Eleanor resided with her family in Raleigh during this period, but towns like Edenton, Hertford, and Plymouth, although closer to Raleigh than was Asheville, remained at a long distance given the modes and conditions of travel. Swain again missed her, and while he could never say with certainty when he would reach Raleigh, he would virtually command her not to be away at times when he had that prospect.

During absences he would share with her the nature of his life and cases. "I will have to prosecute three men for murder at Currituck which will most probably detain me the whole week," he once wrote. On another occasion he had little to do in Camden, so made a pleasant visit to "our seaports" in Norfolk. Still another had him setting out soon for Currituck County "where we have a long and tedious session in prospect as a white man and negroe have to be tried separately for murder."[63]

Swain found much about eastern North Carolina agreeable and appealing. The climate was healthy, the country pleasant. "[T]he farms, the machinery, and the prospects exceed any thing I have ever seen before," he wrote. At times he found "little good society," but he viewed a longtime jurist, John Robert Donnell of New Bern, with whom he visited, as "social and agreeable." Governor James Iredell and numerous old acquaintances greeted him in Windsor, which meant that he found himself "in the midst of very pleasant society." The governor, indeed, was to become the courier for Eleanor's letters to him.[64]

Swain's professional success in the East also exceeded his expectations. Solicitors then were allowed to practice privately on the civil side of the court dockets, and he thrived sufficiently that he gave serious thought to settling in the East. Early in his solicitorship he told Eleanor that, based on what he had experienced and could foresee, he would find little difficulty in obtaining a lucrative practice there. He had already secured "a commanding practice" in Washington and Tyrrell counties. A short time later, however, he thought he would "certainly never settle in this circuit" but might practice there for a brief time and reside in Raleigh (he was catering to Eleanor's well-known preference for a Raleigh residence).[65]

In the meantime, Swain's native population had not forgotten him. One constituent wrote from Asheville that he hoped Swain would "resign your solicitorship and reside here again." He soon would. In January 1828, he informed Eleanor that the present mail carried to the governor his resignation as solicitor of the Edenton circuit. His professional prospects and every other consideration except her predilection for Raleigh warranted the decision, he said. As to the latter, if he settled in the East, he would still be absent from her six months a year, "which ... would not be very pleasant." Governor Iredell had selected him as counsel for the state to defend the purchasers under (i.e., from) the state against the Indian reserves in Haywood County. He was obliged for the compliment and would be still more gratified if it should be backed by a liberal fee.[66]

The North Carolina mountains burrow deep within the souls of their native sons, and despite the acknowledged temptations of the East, it was probably inevitable that Swain's stay in the flatlands would be transient. His ephemeral presence there had undoubtedly accomplished his overt purpose, however: he had significantly increased his knowledge of the state and enlarged the boundaries of his intercourse with its citizens.[67]

For the remainder of his days, he would benefit personally from this experience; and numerous advantages, political and academic, would accrue to the State of North Carolina and its citizens.[68]

Judge

Swain's essay into private life proved short lived. In autumn 1830, a few months following his decision to foreswear another legislative candidacy, James Iredell declined reelection to the U.S. Senate. Although still not age-eligible, Swain again received a few votes for the position. Willie P. Mangum of Orange was chosen, and accordingly resigned as a superior court judge. Swain, Henry Seawell, and Patrick H. Winston were nominated for the vacant judgeship. Swain prevailed on the first legislative ballot. On January 12, 1831, Governor Montford Stokes issued

Swain's commission, his having for a second time been appointed to a high office by a joint ballot of both houses of the General Assembly.[69]

Seawell was unpopular but difficult to beat. This time, however, as stated by an Iredell County legislator, "we took up Old Warping Bars from Buncombe and warped him out." The nickname, derived from Swain's awkward and ungainly physical appearance, stuck until Swain became president of the University of North Carolina and the students renamed him "Old Bunk" for his Buncombe County background. That sobriquet would stay with him for life.[70]

Word of Swain's selection spread quickly. James Graham advised his brother, Swain's friend and future governor William A. Graham, of it. A Macon County correspondent thought it might make considerable changes in Swain's domestic arrangements; it would, in that he would never again reside in western North Carolina.[71]

One captious note was struck. A Salisbury newspaper noted Swain's election and his reputation as "a gentleman of promising talents and of considerable legal attainments . . . [who] with a few years' experience, will make a good Judge." Judge Seawell was, however, his superior in talent and legal acquirements, one who ranked with the ablest men of the profession. "If we wish our Judicature to assume character and dignity," the paper opined, "it is from the fathers of the profession, and not from the Juniors, that our Judges should be taken." "This remark is a general one," it continued, "and not intended to apply to Judge Swain," who, if he followed the right example, might yet "become an able and efficient Judge and leave no regrets with the Legislature for having appointed him."[72] The expressed intent aside, the commentary could hardly have been more pointed or critical of the Swain election, nor was it altogether baseless. Seawell was fifty-six years old, had been licensed in the legal profession for thirty-three years, and had extensive executive, legislative, and judicial experience.[73] Swain was not yet thirty, only seven years past Judge Taylor's legal tutelage, with no judicial experience and considerably less than Seawell's in the other branches.

The hardships of Swain's new post were not materially different from those of his old ones. Prolonged absence from home remained his prime complaint. He would be content in his station, he told Eleanor, "if it were not for these long periods of absence from my family." A basic task like getting his clothes cleaned could prove difficult. "I send my dirty clothes," he once wrote Eleanor, "which I wish washed by the time I get to Raleigh which will be about the close of the week after this." His shoes, too, were worn out and had to be replaced. At times the mails were "so badly arranged as almost to interdict communication," and he could be altogether "out of the range of mail communication."[74]

Road hazards were commonplace. Arteries were muddy, desolate, and unimproved from his time as solicitor. Swain traveled from Williamston to Plymouth and found that "[t]he intervening country presents a general aspect of desolation without beauty." On one occasion he sustained injuries from the overturn of his sulky. On another he missed lunch en route from Norfolk to the Currituck County courthouse.[75]

Health problems could arise at inconvenient times and places.[76] The work could be demanding. He had less leisure on the circuit than he had supposed, he told Eleanor, or than she herself seemed to suppose. He had at least a dozen unanswered letters on hand, all of which he cited "as an apology for not having written more frequently and at greater length." "My toils are incessant and confinement unremitted," he once reported. Fortunately, the labors of that week were "nearly closed," and only the Person County docket stood between him and a respite at the family hearth.[77]

As with Swain's previous positions, there were amenities.[78] Swain was a consummate social being, and in this respect the judicial life was pleasant. "I have met many old acquaintances in the various counties through which I have passed," he related early in his career, "and have been treated by them with great hospitality." Again: "[F]or a full week I have been eating and drinking most luxuriously with the lords of the law." He expected thenceforth to live more temperately, partly from choice and equally from necessity.[79]

Swain spent a week at the home of Supreme Court Judge John Hall in Warren County. "Mr. Seawell" offered him a ride when he was going from Raleigh to Granville County. His return to eastern counties he had served as solicitor brought renewed friendships and many engagements. From Windsor he recounted a visit to a couple in company with Governor Iredell. Indeed, the former governor was Swain's frequent companion. Diary entries show him dining with Iredell and others at Plymouth, traveling with him for the remainder of a circuit, spending an evening with him and others, receiving a visit from him when sick, and attending a party at his home.[80]

Other friends fell within the judge's social ambit. He renewed his acquaintance with William Gaston, a prominent older lawyer whom he greatly admired. While traveling from Tarboro to Williamston, Swain met with Joseph J. Daniel, a former superior court judge and later a state supreme court judge. He convened on one evening with his friends Miss Pettigrew and Dr. Warren. This visit evoked an expression of his regional bias. The "cherry cheeks" of Dr. Warren's children, Swain said, "would indicate the life-giving atmosphere of the mountains rather than the pestilential vapours of a cypress swamp." He attended church with one friend and walked over the farm of another. Calls such as those on attorney George Badger, Judge John Hall, and Governor Montford Stokes kept him busy when not in court.[81]

Religious services took some of that uncommitted time. Swain was not a church member during this period but worshipped regularly. Ecumenical in approach, he favored the Presbyterians (his father's denomination) and the Methodists (his mother's), but Episcopalians and Baptists would find him in their sanctuaries as well. It was common for him to note the biblical text and to evaluate the sermon; for example, "Mr. McDonnel preached a good sermon on Wednesday night from the text, 'I said I will take heed to my ways that I sin not with my tongue'" (Psalm 39:1). A funeral service by "Dr. McPheter" (probably William McPheeters, 1778–1842, founder of Raleigh's First Presbyterian Church) on the text "[t]his mortal shall put on immortality" (I Corinthians 15:53) also attained an appraisal of "very good" from Swain. An anniversary discourse on the Benevolence Society by a Baptist preacher, but in the Presbyterian church, drew his attention. Once he reported hearing three sermons in one day.[82]

At every opportunity Swain indulged his penchant for Clio, the Muse of History. In Caswell County he visited the grave of Bartlett Yancey, congressman and speaker of the North Carolina Senate, and exclaimed, "I could scarcely realize the idea that such a giant slumbered at my feet." The historic town of Edenton captivated him like no other. There he observed the records of an address by the 1760 provincial legislature praying for a redress of grievances from the king of Great Britain; one copy was addressed to Sir William Pitt. In recording diary entries on aspects of Edenton's history, he concluded that "[i]t is a beautiful spot and must have afforded a delightful prospect to the eyes of our ancestors."

Perquimans Court, too, found him examining "various old records," including court documents. He lamented the many ancient records, formerly deposited there, that had been pilfered by antiquarians or lost by carelessness and inattention. He later amused himself with the manuscript journals of Governor Arthur Dobbs's administration, commencing with 1754 "at which period Richard Caswell jr. [Eleanor's relative] was a member from Johnston."

Finally, Swain consorted with Joseph Seawell (Shocco) Jones of Warren County, who, in his view, had "taken more pains to obtain information with regard to the early history of the state than any individual with whom I have met." Jones informed him of many publications "in the library of Cambridge College upon this subject not to be found elsewhere." He had Herman Husband's pamphlet, which Swain read, as well as papers of Judge Archibald Murphey and Governors Johnston, Burke, Nash, and others. The most interesting of Jones's items that Swain mentioned, in view of the protracted controversy on the subject, then in its infancy, was "the proclamations of Gov. Martin of August 1775 . . . with regard to the Mecklenburg Declaration."[83]

History in the making, current politics, also caught Swain's attention. At the national level he noted an attempt to mate Jackson and Van Buren forces, President Jackson's veto of a bill to incorporate the Bank of the United States, John C. Calhoun's exposition on nullification and an article on it, and the adjournment of the federal Congress. At the state level he recorded the election of H. Seawell, N. G. Rand, and C. L. Hinton to represent Wake County in the forthcoming General Assembly. As a judge he was somewhat isolated from, but by no means disinterested in, the political life of the nation and state.[84]

Laconic Swain diary entries provide a limited insight into the work of his courts. His dockets contained a mix of criminal and civil cases. On the former side one entry reads: "Tried negroe Jordan for insurrection and rebellion. Verdict not guilty." One day brought twenty criminal convictions.

On another occasion Swain had completed the civil docket, except for questions of law reserved, by 2:00 p.m., after which he tried the "State [i.e., criminal] docket." Still another presented a session with twelve cases from Tyrrell County, twenty-four from Washington, and seventeen from Bertie. There were grand jury charges to be given and reserved points of law to be decided.[85]

To aid him in these tasks, Swain became a perpetual student. His readings included treatises by Blackstone, Kent, Chitty, and Gould, as well as the state's statutes and Supreme Court decisions. He once attempted to codify the state's statutory law.[86]

Surviving stories from Swain's bench time provide some sense of the man, his character and personality. Nathaniel Macon was a much older statesman when Swain entered the public life of his state and was late in life when a youthful Swain assumed the bench. Macon's testimony, it was believed, would determine a case before Swain to set aside a will. The opposing side would need to establish memory impairment to discredit his attestations. Swain consented to a request that he meet out of court with opposing counsel, his associate, and clients. In that session, counsel reported having met with Macon for four hours and said he had never before met "any man of his mould and breadth and bigness." He "could not make a dent in any testimony he might give" so convinced the local attorneys and the clients that the case was hopeless. It was dropped, and a $500.00 fee was returned to the clients. Modern-day ethical constraints would render the matter problematic in several respects, but Swain told the story years later as the most remarkable case he had encountered, and the most significant impression made by one man upon another.[87]

At the April Term 1832 of Rutherford County Superior Court, Swain was on the bench. Colonel James R. Dodge, Samuel Hillman, and Thomas Dewes Jr. were in the courtroom. While Dodge addressed the jury, Swain recalled a punning epitaph on a man named Dodge, wrote it out, and passed it around to the entertainment of the bar. When Dodge completed his argument, he found the following lying on his table:

> Epitaph of James R. Dodge, Esq.
> Attorney at Law
>
> Here lies a Dodge, who dodged all good
> And dodged a deal of evil,
> Who after dodging all he could
> He could not dodge the Devil.

Not to be outdone, Dodge quickly gathered his composure, scribbled as the others watched, and then read aloud:

> Here lies a Hillman and a Swain
> Whose lot let no man choose;
> They lived in sin and died in pain,
> And the Devil got his Dewes.[88]

Swain's physical appearance—tall, gaunt, awkward, loose-jointed, and knock-kneed—was the impetus for another story. When his sulky overturn resulted in a knee out of joint,[89] he was carried to a nearby house and a doctor was called. When the doctor began twisting and pulling Swain's leg to set it right, Swain interrupted to say, "Stop Dr. you have got hold of the wrong leg." The doctor replied, "Well Judge, you seem to need setting all over."[90]

Any attempt, from a twenty-first-century vantage point, to assess the work of a nineteenth-century trial judge would be futile. The North Carolina Reports contain twenty-three appeals to the Supreme Court from cases that Swain tried. He was affirmed in seventeen and reversed in six.[91] The statistic is meaningless, however. The most able trial judges are reversed on appeal, and weaker ones often avoid such by artfully dodging difficult cases or rulings.

From what we can know it is reasonable to assume that, notwithstanding relative youth and inexperience, Swain as a judge performed at least adequately and perhaps admirably. One account states that the only objection raised to his conduct on the bench was his leniency to criminals, that he was incapable of resisting an appeal for mercy or a tale of distress.[92] This is hardly a damning criticism for one whose religious precepts taught that the merciful are themselves blessed and shall obtain mercy (Matthew 5:7); indeed, the biblical verse is inscribed on the Swain grave marker in Raleigh's Oakwood Cemetery. If it was indeed a flaw or weakness, it was a consistent one; Swain would be the subject of similar complaints regarding his administration of student discipline as a university president.

By all appearances, the judicial role fit Swain well. He seems to have been happy in his work and, for the most part, with the lifestyle it allowed. He might well have chosen an extensive career in the judiciary, and having entered upon it at such a tender age, have had opportunities, state, federal, or both, for advancement. It was not to be, however. As with the Edenton District solicitorship, the North Carolina General Assembly would again find itself unable to attain a majority vote to fill a station of still greater importance, and it would again turn to the youthful statesman from the West as a felicitous compromise solution.

Governor

CHAPTER 3

Vision

"A sagacious and profound statesman"

THE NORTH CAROLINA CONSTITUTION of 1776 directed the State Senate and House of Commons, jointly, at their first meeting after each annual election, to elect a governor to serve one year. The person had to be at least thirty years old, to have been a resident of the state for at least five years, and to be the owner of a freehold in lands and tenements valued above 1,000 pounds. A provision that no one could hold the office longer than three of six successive years reflected a profound distrust of executive power, the product of the colony's and the country's experience with the British monarchy. The office possessed limited powers, often requiring for their exercise the concurrence of a seven-member council of state chosen by the legislature.[1]

When the General Assembly met following the 1832 election, the incumbent governor, Montford Stokes, had served two terms and was eligible for a third. He declined reelection, however, because President Andrew Jackson had appointed him chair of the Federal Indian Commission to supervise the settlement of southern Indians west of the Mississippi.[2] The absence of an incumbent was unexpected, and in its initial efforts to fill the vacancy the Assembly met stalemate.

A first ballot—with Richard Dobbs Spaight Jr. of Craven, Thomas G. Polk of Rowan, and John Branch of Halifax as contenders—failed to produce a majority for any candidate. Polk's withdrawal on the second ballot did not change the result. On the seventh ballot, Swain attained a majority and was declared elected. On December 6, 1832, Joseph J. Daniel, a superior court judge, administered the oath for Swain's first term.[3]

Swain's election was a surprise, for he had not been mentioned in the preelection speculation. Once nominated, though, he drew support from a coalition of Westerners (his natural base), national Republicans (Jeffersonians, not modern-day Republicans), and advocates of states' rights united only by their opposition to Spaight, a prominent Eastern Democrat who was the leading candidate. Swain's even temper, intellectual ability, well-regarded character, and moderation aided the coalescence around his candidacy. His silence on national political candidates and issues also facilitated his election, enabling him to draw support from Whigs and Democrats, Jacksonians and anti-Jacksonians. Popularity in both the East and the West was a substantial asset in the election and in his gubernatorial administration.[4]

Reaction was swift and mostly positive. A predecessor in the office, John Owen, took pleasure in Swain's election and assured him of his abiding esteem and friendship. A Charlotte couple against whom Swain had once entered a judgment congratulated him "on the important office you now fill," while hoping he would "relax occasionally from the affairs of state." A Fayetteville paper predicted that Swain's election would be popular with the people "for we believe there is no man of Judge Swain's age in the State, who stands higher in their estimation." It attributed his steady advancement in official positions "entirely to the force of his own genius and character" and thought his election as governor "as honorable to the Legislature as to him."[5]

The times in which Swain took office were, however, troubled: "Nullification was then rife, and not a few grave questions in politics were awaiting a decision." While also congratulatory, his politically knowledgeable correspondents focused on the "deep sense of crisis at hand which threatens the peace, the union, and the liberty of our common country." Former Governor John Branch warned of the impending danger. He feared "the horrors of civil war, and . . . the destruction of our state sovereignties by the establishment of a consolidated government comparatively irresponsible." He had, however, high respect for Swain as the chief magistrate of the state. One Swain friend, who had "but lately" taken his oath as a U.S. citizen as well as sworn allegiance to the State, was concerned that the oaths might soon become "at variance" with each other. This moment of peril, he thought, would demand the best exertions of Swain's talents to right "the impending calamity."[6]

James Graham, western North Carolina congressman and brother of William A. Graham, sounded a rare discordant note. Swain's election was no surprise, said Graham, for "popular preferment is the ruling passion of his soul." The new governor met an early rebuff from the legislative branch. Senator Henry Seawell of Wake proposed to pay Swain's full judicial salary for the court days he had missed while nursing injuries from a carriage accident; on first reading the Senate resolved "that the same shall not pass."[7]

Swain's 1833 election to a second term appears to have been routine. The

House and Senate journals contain no names in opposition; they merely state that Governor Swain, having received a majority of the votes, was elected. It was so ordinary that the reelected governor apparently chose not to give an inaugural address; unlike with his other elections, none has been found.

Swain's friendship with William A. Graham was in an early stage. Yet it must have pleased Swain that it was Graham, a first-term borough representative from Hillsboro, who, after reporting Swain's election, moved for a joint Senate-House committee to inform the governor and set a time for his oath. "Your body is liberal enough," noted a Graham correspondent, "to elect *Gaston* [New Bern attorney William Gaston, recently elected to the state supreme court], & *Swain*." On December 9, 1833, Charles L. Hinton, a Wake County justice of the peace, administered Swain's second oath as governor.[8]

Swain's third and last election was more problematic. It began simply enough, with the Senate routinely proposing to the House that they ballot for governor for the ensuing year "and nominating for that appointment his Excellency David Lowry Swain." The House readily agreed. Soon, however, the committee appointed to conduct the balloting reported that no candidate had received a majority of the votes. The bodies agreed to ballot again, and again no candidate received a majority. The Senate proposed that the Assembly "wait upon the sick members and receive their votes," but the House did not concur. On a third ballot, Swain prevailed by a slim majority. The margin obviously came from the swing of a sufficient number of the "scattered" votes to Swain.[9]

Why such difficulty, after an easy time only a year before? In the meantime, partisan politics had reared its head. Parties and partisanship were ill-defined in the North Carolina of Swain's entry into the governor's office. His posture as a nonpartisan advocate of internal improvements and constitutional reform was plausible and workable in his first two elections, allowing him to draw support not only from Whigs, the party toward which he was steadily trending, but also from Democrats, particularly Westerners who placed these objectives above partisan politics and also admired Swain. By 1834, however, Swain had an identity as the Whig candidate, and William D. Moseley of Lenoir, his opponent, as the Democrat.

Further, Swain had allowed his name to be floated as a possible replacement for U.S. Senator Bedford Brown, a Caswell County Democrat. Though young, Swain was hardly politically tone deaf. He perceived both the difficulties inherent in an attempt to oust Brown and the complications such an effort could present to his securing a third term as governor. Brown, he observed, could not be beaten "without a perfect union of all the elements of opposition and it will be barely possible ... with it." He was not disposed to take the risk "without positive assurances of the cordial support of all the *non contents* and even then if I do not decline I certainly will not seek."

Swain soon declared privately that he was not a Senate candidate and did not expect to be. Indeed, he was by no means certain that, "after the official expression of [his] opinions," he could retain the position he held. He was aware that his opponents, particularly in the East, were implacable and would misrepresent both his motives and "through me, the system I have been endeavoring to build up." He regretted not having disavowed a Senate candidacy earlier, and loathed "the events that are in prospect."[10]

Swain's reelection prospects thus were complicated by a confluence of stiffening party lines with his flirtation, in a partisan context, with a bid for federal office. Even some western legislators deserted him. Ultimately, however, he succeeded, enabling him to serve the constitutional maximum of three consecutive years in the executive office. His triumph was not greeted with universal applause. One disgruntled citizen, obviously affiliated with the opposition, found himself "unable to discover in the fact of Gov. Swain's having been already twice elevated to the highest office in the State, any reason why he should have reached that distinction a third time; especially when it is recollected that ... he has used all the means in his power, compatible with official dignity, to prostrate the men with whom I have acted, and to bring into disrepute the principles I have adopted." The carping notwithstanding, on December 10, 1834, Judge Henry Seawell of the superior court administered Swain's third and final gubernatorial oath before a joint session of the two houses of the General Assembly.[11]

In the year before Swain assumed the office, William Gaston aptly depicted the condition of the state Swain was to govern. "In truth there does seem to be a fatality ... attending poor No. Carolina," he said. The state's internal improvement plans had failed, and "profitless expenditure" had discredited future plans. The university was "tottering to its base." Discouraged citizens were emigrating or "sunk in apathy." The capitol had been destroyed by an 1831 fire, and divided opinion about moving it to Fayetteville was distracting. Later, with equal aptness, Gaston limned the constraints on a governor sufficiently audacious to attempt amelioration. The governor, he stated, had no political or lawmaking power. He could not appoint officers. Other than granting reprieves and pardons, "all that is required from him is, that he should be a gentleman in character and manners, and exercise a liberal hospitality."[12]

Perhaps in recognition of his limited powers, but more likely due to the surprise nature of his election and thus the sparse time to prepare, Swain's 1832 first inaugural message was brief, modest, and somewhat self-effacing. "I am," he declared, "duly sensible of the high responsibility which I have assumed." The times were "eventful," established governments abroad in turbulence, and domestic institutions designed "to ensure the greatest attainable degree of liberty and happiness" equally subject to "the mutability incident to all human things." "At such a crisis," he declared, "the office of chief magistrate acquires an importance increasing with the difficulties which surround us." While conceding that many could bring greater ability to the task, he asserted that "no one could serve ... with more fidelity and zeal."

Brief concern for an overbearing, overzealous national government followed, but Swain expected redress in the patriotism, wisdom, prudence, and forbearance, both of its officials and of the American people. The guiding Providence of half a century would, he believed, "yet sustain us ... as [a] free, a united and a happy people."[13]

Swain's annual messages to the legislature stand in sharp contradistinction to this rather unassuming inaugural. It was customary for the governor to make recommendations to the General Assembly in an annual message and other special communications. The standard governor's message of the time, however, was high on deference and low on conviction. "Colorless" is an apt description. Swain's messages deviated from this norm. While he too was respectful and considerate of the opinions of lawmakers, he had strongly held views on a wide range of public issues, which he stated forthrightly and unequivocally. Displaying both lawyer and historian personae, he marshaled evidence and brought an array of facts and figures to the support of his positions. The addresses extolled Murphey's vision for the State, offered a design for Swain and future governors in its implementation, and constituted a hallmark of his administration and legacy.[14]

The first of these exalted the superior status of the lawmaking body and acknowledged the executive's constitutionally mandated deference to it. Periodic assemblage of the representatives of the people, clothed with power and charged with the interests of their constituents, was, he said, the most striking characteristic of our republican system of government. The constitutional grant to them of the whole power of legislation was wise; he could not control their proceedings, and even the privilege of advising them derived from custom, not the constitution.

While previous assemblies had preserved constitutional rights and aspired to advance the state, little had been accomplished. Matters such as settlement of the state's Revolutionary War claims, and a more salutary policy regarding the Cherokee Indians than simply allowing other states to "fasten them upon our soil," could await another day. The appropriate focus of the moment was on "all that concerns the character and interest of the commonwealth."

Apathy had characterized the state's half century of legislative history. The operating expenses of the General Assembly, combined with those for internal improvements, exceeded the aggregate expenditures for the rest of state government. "That government cannot be wisely administered," he posited, "where those who direct the public treasure receive more for this service than the amount of their disbursements." He was urging upon the legislature "the propriety of entering upon a system of legislation required by the wants of your constituents, commensurate with their resources, and worthy of the confidence which they repose in your ability to administer their public affairs."

Unsurprisingly, internal improvements, the bedrock of the Murphey vision, received first mention among specifics. These included coastal inlet betterment, canals, highways, railroads, and swamp reclamation. A societal consensus dictated that "a more liberal system is essential to the future prosperity of the state." Individual exertion would not suffice; public treasury contributions were essential.

Admitting prior waste in such expenditures, it was, he asserted, much less than generally conjectured and an inevitable result of inexperience. Projects of interest to the whole community, he thought, were less likely to attract private enterprise and thus demanded the exclusive attention and patronage of government. As to local improvements, private companies should be incorporated in every section of the state where needed. Private investment would then evidence "the practicability and usefulness of any work."

Such improvements could lay the foundation of a school system "as extensive as our limits, and as enduring as our prosperity." The Literary Fund, established in 1825 to support public schools, he believed (correctly) still too small to justify entering upon a general system of education. In time the development of economic infrastructure would extend commercial facilities and stimulate agricultural exertion, thereby affording the blessings of universal education.

Banks would be "indispensable" to economic development. While ceding great deference to the opinions of those more conversant with the subject, he recommended the establishment of banks "at such places as the business of the country may require."

General revision of the state's statutory law he also found "deeply interesting to the community." Adoption of the common law of England, except as expressly modified,[15] had left "[t]he lives, the liberty and property of our citizens... subject to the enactments of a government, widely dissimilar from ours, which few have read, or had it in their power to read." Five centuries of legislation thus were "a sealed book to the great body of the community, and in some degree, even the profession whose interest and duty rendered the study of law the business of life." The upshot was to empower the judiciary, the interpretive branch, to encroach on other departments of government. Corrective legislative action, including repeal of obsolete statutes, was in order.

Among the laws wanting revision were those regulating land valuation for tax purposes. For years the state had engaged in deficit spending. The property tax, a major revenue source, depended on the integrity of the individual citizen in valuing his holdings. Correction of this defect could supply the deficiency in revenues. The entire system, including the taxes imposed by the county courts, demanded radical reformation, with the aim of uniformity.

In due time, he concluded, he would communicate further regarding matters of less interest but worthy of consideration. Conviction regarding the propriety of his proposals was devoid of any assertion of infallibility. His sole ambition was to unite with them "in the adoption of such measures as shall be best calculated to develop and improve our physical and intellectual resources; to promote the prosperity and advance the character of the State."[16]

The General Assembly parceled out Swain's proposals to the appropriate committees. Due to a lack of revenues, they stalled there for the moment, yet the governor had articulated a vision for the state's future. To one Swain correspondent the message embraced "[m]any topics of great and paramount importance"; if the legislature gave them their deserved consideration, the address would be long remembered, and the state permanently advantaged. To another, an émigré from the state whose interest was internal improvements, great blessings from such to future posterity induced him to hope Swain's message would be viewed in a favorable light, and efforts made "to bring to a successful issue the principles there laid down."[17]

Swain's 1834 legislative message acknowledged that the state had not attained the prosperity and happiness within its reach but expressed the conviction that it had improved the "science" of government and promoted civil and religious freedom at home and abroad. A brief bow to the separation of powers, as the guarantor of public liberty, followed.

Historical treatment of the General Assembly's right to call a constitutional convention preceded Swain's statement of reasons for recommending that one be called. The great object to be attained, he said, was a radical change in the basis of representation—removal of the Eastern-dominated disparity. Grounded in history rather than reason, the extant system had produced inequalities from which mischiefs and disorders had arisen and the best schemes for the welfare of the province been defeated. The minority ruled, and those paying comparatively little of the public expense controlled all the resources.

Not only natural disadvantages, Swain continued, but also various acts of federal legislation had hindered the state's progress. It had experienced privation in the adjustment of losses incurred by the Confederacy and by the states in the Revolutionary War. The fiscal system adopted upon the federal assumption of state debts was prejudicial to North Carolina, which had become a debtor state. The federal government was steadily extending its powers, augmenting its resources, and multiplying its expenditures, all to the detriment of the state.

Again, not surprisingly, when Swain turned from federal to state matters, internal improvements received top billing. Another year's experience had afforded conclusive proof that individual associations could not accomplish any plan commensurate with the state's necessities and resources. Emigration was depriving the state of many of its most intelligent and enterprising citizens and much of its wealth. In many respects the state could compare favorably with the most prosperous members of the Confederacy, yet obstructions to navigation of its rivers and the impossibility of the largest class of ships entering the ports connected with those rivers were great natural disadvantages. These difficulties could be obviated and conditions essential to a highly prosperous condition assured. The state had a wider sea coast than any other, and the best inlet and harbor south of the Chesapeake. "Under such circumstances," the governor postulated, "to permit public prosperity either to decline or remain stationary is as foreign from our duty as it is injurious to our interests and repugnant to our feelings. The period cannot be distant when other objects than the disbursements of sums smaller than the aggregate of legislative expenses shall be considered as falling within the legitimate range of your duties."

Sectionalism—"local divisions"—had thus far hindered progress. Swain hoped that they would not separate "without the adoption of such measures as shall make us a united people, as well in feeling as in interest."

Reprising other themes from his 1833 address, Swain again found the state's revenue system defective. Deficit spending continued to erode reserves. Fair evaluation of real property, and accurate identification of individuals subject to the poll tax, could avert an increase in the rate of taxation. Allowing landowners to assess the value of their freeholds ill-advisedly rewarded the less conscientious. Slave owners committed fraud with impunity in relating the age of their enslaved for poll-tax purposes. Correction of these evils could increase the revenue from these sources by one-fourth. Abolishing "the discrimination of ages" and imposing a tax on each enslaved person would be a simple, easy, and efficient remedy. Taxing pleasure carriages, other articles of luxury, and collateral inheritances could further enhance the state's treasury.

Legislation was needed to effect proper preparation of the Assembly's acts for publication. Members of the council of state should be required to reside in the immediate vicinity of the capitol, subject thereby to call without delay to advise the governor. The rights of the state's citizens to their enslaved, free from domestic aggression, demanded protection.

Finally, Swain reported his compliance with the legislators' directive that he appoint three commissioners to revise and digest the public laws of the state. His appointees—William H. Battle, Gavin Hogg, and James Iredell—had entered upon the immediate discharge of their duties. Illness of one had impeded their progress, but timely completion was still possible. A report, he promised, should be transmitted to them soon.

A nod to amicable collaboration between the branches terminated the address. "I have only to assure you," Swain said, "of my hearty cooperation in every measure which may be calculated to preserve the liberty and promote the prosperity and happiness of our constituents."[18] The address was, pronounced a Raleigh newspaper, "a finished state paper" authored by "a sagacious and profound statesman."[19]

Swain viewed his third inaugural, a year later, as a renewal of the solemn pledges of fidelity required by the state of its chief magistrate. Somewhat defensive in the wake of a contentious electoral contest, the re-elected governor expressed gratitude that he had neither believed nor desired that his administration would give universal satisfaction. Lessons learned early taught him that those who pleased most were not always the ablest or most faithful public servants. By rigid adherence to duty, he had sought the approbation of his own conscience, followed by favorable estimation of honest men. The first he had attained, and in the second had succeeded sufficiently to be sustained against "the high tide of party excitement."

Further reflections on federal-state relations had convinced him anew that eternal vigilance is the price of liberty, that widely shared power is always under diversion to the few, and that federal power and patronage are dangerous to public liberty. A frequent recurrence to fundamental liberties thus was indeed essential to the preservation of liberty.

Executive misrule had afflicted no state more than North Carolina; the grant of only "the attribute of mercy" (the pardoning power) to the Executive Department reflected this malignant history. Now, federal extractions of revenue had increased, while the state's had decreased. The state's legislators deserved thanks for their frugality, which could serve as an example for an economical administration of the affairs of the general government. "[T]he power and patronage of the General Government must be restricted to narrower limits," he admonished, "or liberty will but too soon exist only in name."

This critique of its extant administration notwithstanding, Swain yielded to no one in his admiration of the excellence of "our form of government." "To secure the purposes of its founders," he contended, "it is only necessary that it shall be administered with the wisdom and purity manifested in its formation." Implicitly covenanting so to administer the state's government, he took this, his third and last oath as governor, free of misgivings or mental reservations and determined to yield hearty and cheerful obedience to all its requirements.[20]

Swain's attack on the federal administration drew sympathetic journalistic commentary for its "sound political views" which, it was thought, should convince all leaders of that government's incursion upon their rights and the uneconomical nature of its current operations. The address's states-rights emphasis resulted in wide circulation in the papers of other states.[21]

Naturally, however, the observations also drew critical appraisal from newspapers holding other viewpoints. One, a frequent Swain critic, carped that the governor had "abandoned his equivocal position" to make "an insidious thrust" at President Andrew Jackson. Others thought partisan comment ill-suited for an inauguration, especially since the governor knew that a majority of the legislature, his principal audience, did not share his views. He was charged with waiting until he could no longer seek the post to clarify his position; in a new election, it was thought, Swain would be defeated. Critique of Swain's facts and figures followed, as the Jackson administration's friends defended it against the governor's charges.[22]

Whether or not to Swain's liking, he had now discarded his nonpartisan stance and with clarity marked himself as an anti-Jackson Whig. One supporter wrote approvingly of the "bold ground" Swain had taken and thought those who had unjustly considered him "two-sided and equivocal" must now admit "that he had fairly cleared *the fence*."[23]

Swain's final annual address to the General Assembly came shortly before his departure from the governor's office. It also came at, for him, an anxious moment, as he awaited the result of the election on proposed constitutional amendments to, inter alia, enhance the legislative representation of the West. Although major policy changes should await the outcome of that vote, the executive, he believed, should proceed to convey to them "the customary expression of opinion upon the most important topics which engage public attention."

The state, he reported, was experiencing relative prosperity: crops good, agricultural prices higher, citizens' pecuniary difficulties diminished. Comparative abundance had not stemmed the tide of emigration, however. The state continued to lose its most wealthy, enterprising, and intelligent citizens to the new states and territories of the West, not surprisingly in light of cheap land prices there.

This divestiture of human resources stemmed not from want of natural advantages, as to which the state was scarcely exceeded, but from lack of educational academies, especially for the poor; absence of internal improvements; and no fund worthy of the name for future development of the state's resources. While the state had underachieved, it had also been constantly retarded by applicable federal legislation—injustice in settlement of Revolutionary War claims, an oppressive revenue system, reduced real estate values due to low prices for government lands in the new states and territories.

The most quoted line from Swain's messages followed. In the state's first half century, he noted, state legislation amounted to little more than annual taxes of less than $100,000, of which half funded the legislature while the remainder paid governmental officers. "The establishment of schools for the instruction of youth, and the development and improvement of our internal resources by means beyond the reach of individual enterprise," he lamented, "will seem scarcely to have been regarded as proper objects of legislative concern."

A fair share of federal largess would help, particularly a "just proportion of the revenue accruing from the sales of public lands." Moreover, individual enterprise alone could not effect internal improvements commensurate with the state's necessities and resources. Private gain, rather than public need, would determine those investments. While private companies properly had an important role, public assistance was essential.

A jarring shift of focus then occurs. From a high-minded consideration of economic development, with its promise of universal public education and other benefits, Swain turned to a virulent attack on the fanaticism, in his view, of the abolitionists. The state had hardly been ignoring this perceived danger. The 1830 General Assembly had made publication of incendiary newspapers and pamphlets on the abolition of slavery a felony. A first offense was punishable by fine, whipping, and the pillory; a second, by death. The public safety, however, Swain asserted, required more to suppress "these wicked and mischievous publications, injurious alike to the best interest of the master and the slave." Cooperation of legislatures of the states "from which these missiles proceed" was now needed. The rationale: such an interference with our domestic concerns upon the part of citizens of a foreign state, either encouraged or permitted by the government, would at once justify a "resort to the modes ordinarily adopted for the adjustment of national differences." North Carolina thus had an indubitable right to request of other states adoption of measures "to suppress [these publications] totally and promptly." On this, he asserted, there was no diversity of interest and could be no difference of opinion. The entire South, he assumed, would unite with them in the adoption of measures "to ensure union of counsels and prompt and energetic action." The solons thus should consider adopting resolutions inviting the states with shared interests to cooperate in adoption of measures necessary to their common safety, and in calling upon the legislatures of all the states to enact such penal laws on the subject "as may be necessary to perpetuate the blessings contemplated in the formation of the Federal Constitution and the Union."

Clearly, this was Swain at his most radical, and equally clearly, he overstated. The very fact of the perceived threat addressed contradicts his assertion that there could be no difference of opinion on the subject. Such differences existed, even in the South, even in North Carolina. In light of his later reluctant-secessionist stance, one doubts that he was truly ready to go to war over slavery at this point; yet his reference to "resort to the modes ordinarily adopted for the adjustment of national differences" strongly suggests differently. National events shortly preceding Swain's time as governor may well have influenced this radical stance. David Walker, son of a free black North Carolina mother and an enslaved father, had given a speech in Boston in 1828 later published as an *Appeal to the Coloured Citizens of the World*. Walker condemned slavery and asserted the right of black people to citizenship based on their contributions to the building of the nation. His call for abolition suggested that violence was acceptable if necessary to achieve freedom. *The Liberator*, William Lloyd Garrison's journal committed to the immediate abolition of slavery, commenced publication in 1831. Later in the same year the violence Walker had found acceptable came, as Nat Turner led a slave uprising that exacerbated the slave society's fears that Walker and Garrison had generated.

North Carolina legislators shared these fears, and in this instance the General Assembly promptly acquiesced to Swain's request. This portion of his message was referred to a joint select committee, which soon reported resolutions seeking cooperation of other slaveholding states to prevent the circulation of any such publications within them. The resolutions deprecated any action of Congress toward liberating enslaved persons without the consent of their owners. The governor was to transmit a copy to North Carolina's senators and representatives in Congress and to the executives of other states, a task with which, one would surmise, Swain gladly complied. The enacted resolutions were ordered printed. A minority report, evidence of the fallacy in Swain's assertion that there could be no difference of opinion on the subject, was tabled but also ordered printed. North Carolina was not alone in this course; other "[s]outhern state legislatures asked northern states to prohibit the printing of abolitionist literature and suppress abolitionist societies." The "militancy of the southern defense of slavery" was regional in scope.[24]

Over a century and a quarter after this address, one of Swain's gubernatorial successors would tell the black leaders of his day that their enemy was not the white man but "a system bequeathed us by a cotton economy."[25] As governor, Swain was a vigorous defender of that economy, probably viewing its preservation and perpetuation as essential to achievement of his vision for the development of the state, economically and otherwise. His stance, even then more radical than political necessity required, would have been expected of any southern governor of his time.

Concluding with lesser matters, Swain touched upon the public treasurer's recommendations for improving the state's finances, the need for an exchange of court reports between the states, the propriety of revising the laws regarding the duties of the public printer, and the need to fill a superior court judgeship vacancy and to consider court reforms. He promised a report from the revisors of statutes at an early date, as well as one from the commissioners to superintend the building of the capitol.

Finally, cognizant of the constitutional limits on his tenure and the nearness of his departure from the office, he expressed deep gratitude for the public's confidence and kindness. He would "retire from the active and responsible duties of public life to comparative quiet and seclusion," but would continue to pray for "the preservation, in their purity, of our free institutions; and the advancement of our citizens in every thing calculated to promote their prosperity and happiness, and add lustre to the character of the State."[26]

CHAPTER 4

Advancing the Vision
"No children have as yet been educated at public expense"

O N JUNE 21, 1831, Judge Swain had witnessed the burning of the state capitol, more commonly referred to then as the "State House." On July 4, 1833, Governor Swain laid the cornerstone for the new one on the same site. Earlier, while commissioners for rebuilding the capitol considered several plans from noted New York architect Ithiel Town, William Gaston urged that his son-in-law, Robert Donaldson, a New York resident, inform Swain of his thoughts on the subject. "The Governor has a very high view of his taste and judgment," Gaston told his daughter, "and I am sure would take pleasure in furthering his views."

Absence of a capitol building during Swain's tenure raises the question of the then location of the governor's office. Based on modern archeological studies, it is believed to have been situated on the south side of the present capitol, immediately west of where the George Washington statue now stands; to have been thirty-six feet by twenty feet; and to have had a door on the east side and perhaps a second one on the north side leading to the State House.[1]

From this temporary seat of government Swain commenced his gubernatorial efforts to advance the Archibald Murphey vision of progress for North Carolina. To state that he implemented Murphey's vision would exaggerate. The limited resources of the state did not permit it. Indeed, the first prong of the vision was to enhance these resources to make feasible its educational dimensions. To conclude that Swain advocated and planned for implementation of the vision, however, does not overstate. He thereby advanced it, moving the state toward a time when public funds would support the education of its children.

A matter Swain had supported while a legislator, which would facilitate internal improvements development, came to fruition during his time as governor. In the 1825 session he had presented a petition from John MacRae of Fayetteville requesting financial aid in the publication of a map of North Carolina. As chair of the committee to which it was referred, Swain reported it favorably and introduced a bill granting a loan to MacRae for the purpose. The measure failed in 1825 but passed in 1826.

The map was published in 1832 to accolades that it was the largest, most detailed, and accurate map of the state to date. Early in his first administration as governor Swain informed MacRae that the General Assembly had authorized him to procure, at a price he deemed reasonable, a copy of the map for each state, territory, and district of the United States. Could MacRae deliver the number of maps required, and if so, when and at what price, Swain inquired. Whether MacRae received Swain's letter is unclear, for three-and-a-half months later he wrote Swain that the map was finished, and the twenty-four copies authorized by the legislature were now subject to Swain's order. It would aid their speedy transmission, Swain responded, if he received them in Philadelphia.[2] The governor undoubtedly derived considerable satisfaction from receiving and distributing this product of his endeavors as a member of the House of Commons.

Swain's first gubernatorial term brought two state-level internal improvements conventions. The first convened in Raleigh on July 4, 1833. Its journal commences with a statement addressed "To the Public," with Swain as the first signatory. It notes that simultaneously with the laying of the cornerstone for a new capitol on that date, many of the state's most intelligent and respectable citizens would gather to determine public sentiment regarding proposed internal improvements projects.

Former Governor James Iredell called the convention to order. On motion of John Owen, another of his predecessors as governor, Swain was unanimously elected president. Several resolutions followed. The first depicted the rationale for the gathering. The state's condition was "highly discouraging and mortifying": trade languishing, agriculture neglected, population departing, political strength withering, public and private wealth declining. Absent arrest of these evils, the state would sink into "ruin and contempt." Other resolutions suggested specific remedial internal improvements projects.

A committee appointed to consider these propositions concluded that it was then inexpedient to recommend specific works to the legislature or the people. Remediation demanded the active, zealous cooperation of the state's citizens. Provision of primary "marts" (markets) was the first grand object, and aid from the state treasury was appropriate.

A loan, on the faith of the state if necessary, would assist in the prosecution of the works; a tax on land, if necessary, would defray the loan. Counties and towns could subscribe to stock in any company incorporated for internal improvements. Once a private company raised three-fifths of the capital recommended to accomplish such, the state would subscribe to the remaining two-fifths.

Swain, as convention president, was to appoint a committee of twenty to publish an address on the subject to the state's people. He was also to appoint a committee of seven in each county to correspond together, distribute the address, and otherwise promote the convention's objects. A second convention should convene in November to deliberate further on the subject. William Gaston chaired the committee to compose the recommended address to the people. It reiterated the lamentable condition of the state, particularly its inability to fund numerous needed public projects and programs. Basically a plea for public support for internal improvements, it candidly acknowledged the purpose of the convention: "To awaken you [the citizens] to a sense of the vast importance and urgency of the subject." If successful at that, the committee concluded, specific plans could thereafter be more advantageously devised and arranged.[3]

As prescribed by the first, a second convention met in November 1833, with Swain again as president. It too deemed it temporarily inexpedient to designate specific projects for implementation. Instead, there should be a board of internal improvements, and an engineer or engineers to plan and conduct the works according to agreed-upon outlines. As to involvement of the state, the second convention was less modest than the first. The nature and magnitude of the task, it believed, were "entirely [beyond] the range of individual enterprise." Execution exclusively by the state, under the direction of its officers, was thus recommended. Internal improvements, simply put, were a proper function of state government. The General Assembly could command the resources of the government, but it could not force individuals to subscribe to stock companies.

Even the state, however, required credit to fund such projects. Five million dollars should suffice, it was thought, and it should be acquired by annual loans not exceeding $1,000,000. The state's "wasted fields, her deserted farms, her ruined towns, her departing sons, all reproach us with supine neglect," the convention concluded, and demanded the counseled course.[4]

More or less simultaneously, the Board of Internal Improvements, under cover letter from Swain, transmitted its report to the General Assembly. The document starkly revealed the state's financial handicap. The board had slightly more than $900.00 in the public treasury and slightly more than $32,000 due it on bonds for Cherokee lands and funds received or due from a judgment against the late John Haywood, hardly sufficient sums to finance extensive public works. Poverty notwithstanding, the board joined in the aspirations articulated by the conventions.

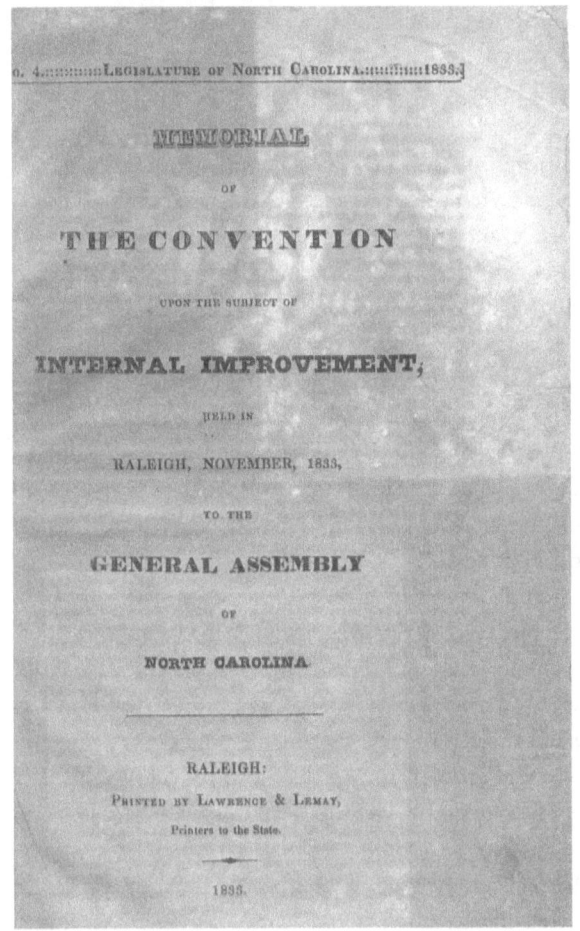

Title page, Report of November 1833 Internal Improvements Convention, of which Swain was president.

One suspects Swain's hand in the following statement: "The Board cherishes the hope that the period has arrived when the citizens of North Carolina are prepared to adopt a liberal system of legislation; and acting upon this expectation, they have determined to submit a plan of improvement which, if prosecuted with spirit, must, in their opinion, effect an important change in the character and condition of the State." The board agreed with the governor that the "great channels" of interest to the whole community were unlikely to be effected by individual enterprise and thus demanded "the exclusive attention and patronage of government." The most important objects were a good outlet to the ocean and a line of railroad "best calculated to attract to it the produce of the largest portion of our territory." Proposed investments of the Internal Improvements Fund and the

Literary Fund would produce an accumulation to pay the first million dollars of the sums borrowed for the purpose.

Caution was counseled. The General Assembly should not appropriate funds for any specific plans. Rather, competent engineers should survey the state, designate routes, make cost estimates, and provide the legislature with data on which to act. Projects whose goals and importance were not understood should be resisted. Such caution, prudence, and enlightenment of the public mind would, it was thought, render the program irresistible. One again suspects Swain's hand in the board's sanguine closing: "A scheme of this kind would, in the opinion of the Board, ensure the prosperity, and advance the character of the State."[5]

Little in Swain's plans was original with him. He was, as noted, taking up Archibald Murphey's vision for North Carolina from earlier in the century. Joseph Caldwell, longtime UNC president, had also championed internal improvements, especially railroads. At the national level Albert Gallatin and John C. Calhoun had advocated similar developments, and Swain drew on all of their ideas.[6]

He also received considerable advice—as well as affirmation, encouragement, and reinforcement—for his advocacy and efforts. A correspondent from New York offered detailed commentary on internal improvement proposals that would, he said, promote commerce. Gaston thought the proposals "too gigantic" for the state's resources and "too magnificant" for the public mind to absorb and support. Swain, however, was more confident. Perhaps, he thought, the citizenry could be induced to move on a "scale of enlarged liberality." While doubtful of success at the ensuing legislative session, he hoped another year would bring "something worthy of the state."[7]

In this response to Gaston, Swain enclosed an internal improvements plan from "a friend of ours" who insisted on anonymity, but in whose judgment he had great confidence. His scheme, Swain wrote, presented the subject "in a more imposing aspect than we have been accustomed to consider it." The anonymous friend was almost certainly James C. Johnston of Edenton, son of Samuel Johnston, one of Swain's predecessors as governor. Johnston had sent Swain three lengthy letters on the subject, congratulating and thanking him for awakening in the state "that spirit which so long has slept." While acknowledging the limited constitutional powers and duties of the governor's office, he touted its capacity to give impulse and direction to public opinion and action. The state was truly fortunate, he told Swain, to have a person of his distinguished talents and enlarged, enlightened, and liberal views at the head of its government. It would be more fortunate still if Swain could direct the now-aroused spirit of the state to some great object that would place his name "far above those of the *intriguing politicians* of the present day."

There were difficulties, Johnston conceded—sectional feelings, local prejudices, and selfish motives among them—but great minds could rise above obstacles. Raising the state to its just deserts would give Swain "a fame which will reach the latest posterity." It would bring "wealth activity and industry to [the state's] citizens, and immortality to yourself."

Johnston did more than puff Swain's ego, however. There was substance to his proposals. The state, he urged, needed a good outlet to the sea to provide a great market for its produce. He detailed placement of a canal between Norfolk and Beaufort for this purpose. The proposed canal would reclaim a large body of valuable land for cultivation, resulting in flourishing villages and a great highway of trade. Trade, tonnage, and revenues from such would increase. Inland navigation would be safer than that around Cape Hatteras.

Obtain cost estimates, he implored Swain, borrow the money, and tax land and slave owners sufficiently to pay the installments and interest. The Eastern slaveholding section would suffer more than the West, but while an Easterner, he was a North Carolinian first and desired improvements everywhere. A line of railroads from West to East would intersect water courses, improve navigation thereon, and create markets. Proper superintendence was essential, so boards should manage all arteries, with the governor as president of each. Such enhanced duties should bring an augmented gubernatorial salary.

Johnston objected to the state's partnering with individuals. The state's effort, he said, "should be on a large scale of general good—a line of canals on the seaboard and a rail road in the interior[.] [P]rivate companies with their own resources may make lateral rail roads and canals in to the main state line—whatever the state does should be with her own resources managed under her own direction by her own officers, accountable to her for their conduct and management." No improvements could be effected without taxation, which should be in proportion to ability to pay but would increase the property values of those who paid it."[8]

Joshua Forman of Rutherford, active in business and politics in New York before moving to North Carolina, advocated a board of commissioners to develop a general plan. The goal was not just passage of the first law, but a design that would sustain the project to completion. Forman volunteered to meet with Swain to discuss such matters at leisure and was grateful that Swain did not give up on them.[9]

Joseph Gales of the Raleigh publishing family, now living in the District of Columbia, was pleased with the "patriotic part" Swain had taken and trusted he would be able to carry his point. If so, he would rank among the state's greatest benefactors. James Mauney of Beaufort had noticed Swain's efforts with pleasure and hoped he would persevere with unshaken fortitude. He had no choice but to do so, in William Gaston's view; having intimately connected his public career with the cause, nothing would be more discouraging to its friends than for Swain to despair of it. Benjamin Wright had little concern in this regard. "The Gov. is bold in his plans," he told Gaston, "and I like this very much."[10] Correspondents weighed in from adjacent states on related plans, optimistic that Swain's exertions would end "the forty years slumber of old Rip."[11]

There were discordant notes, however. Joseph Seawell Jones advised Swain that he had differences with him on the subject. To have both a board of internal improvements and a board of engineers would, Jones thought, be too complicated. It would be more efficient to have a first-rate engineer backed by a board than to have a board of twenty engineers. Jones was always exploiting a patronage angle, however; he was anxious to bring an engineer friend to the state who would, he avowed, be of more service than anyone in the cause of internal improvements.[12]

James Wyche, state superintendent of public works, was another naysayer. In his view the legislature had given him duties without the means to perform them satisfactorily. With adequate means, he would perform them cheerfully, but experience cautioned against sanguineness in this regard. He thus asked Swain to appoint a successor but would serve on the board of internal improvements if not required to perform certain duties.

Swain regretted the inadequate legislative support but asked Wyche to remain in office. The cause, he told him, required constant attention, and it would be difficult to fill the position if Wyche resigned. Swain thus hoped Wyche would persevere until the General Assembly's attention could be directed to the office. Wyche apparently remained, but he continued to grouse. He questioned the value of Swain's proposed internal improvements tour. If Swain was firm in his positive view of it, he would not "much object," he said, "but at present I incline to the negative."[13]

A Western legislator thought Swain's views patriotic and praiseworthy but extravagant to the point of impracticality. He doubted that the convention could present any plan that the legislature would enact.[14] Undeterred, Swain pursued the cause locally when state-level conventions were not in session. William Gaston wanted him at the New Bern convention. "The knowledge that you will be at it will affect public opinion favorably," he wrote. A Wilmington resident offered lodging if Swain attended an internal improvements meeting there; and Edward B. Dudley, Wilmington resident and future governor, posed questions for determining Wilmington's course. He was confident of Swain's cooperation in all public endeavors for the good of North Carolina and of his cognizance of the urgency of their situation.[15]

Swain's presence at Pittsboro would guide its citizens in selecting measures to relieve its commercial ills. The topic had high rank among Swain's aspirations, the inviter noted, "if we may be permitted to draw any inference from the history of your past life." Finally, his appearance in Salisbury would aid the cause in the West and inform the East of the West's feelings "on this all engrossing subject." Thomas G. Polk, Rowan legislator, saw Swain's administration as "in a great degree ... identified with the success of the Internal Improvements of the State" and the people as determined to sustain him in this "great work." "[I]t is important therefore that you should be present," he wrote.[16]

Swain attended the internal improvements meetings in Pittsboro, Hillsboro, Kinston, Salisbury, and Wilmington. He received reports on those he could not attend.[17] Later, when Swain contemplated an Eastern swing as president of the Board of Internal Improvements, he feared "ill-natured suspicions" as a consequence. This, he knew, should not deter him from the discharge of duty, but he did not wish to go if his presence would not "effect anything for the cause of internal improvements." William Gaston provided perspective: "You can not escape from the suspicions and calumnies of political foes," Gaston said. He had no doubt Swain would do his duty, and he hoped he would "make my house your house" when in New Bern.[18]

Swain regularly submitted reports and other material on internal improvements to the General Assembly.[19] Too, he informed turnpike companies of duties the Assembly had imposed on them and urged compliance, not merely to avoid the penalty for neglect, but to ensure early transmission to the Board of Internal Improvements of the statement of their condition contemplated by the legislation.[20] He in turn received from citizens disparate reactions to legislative action or lack thereof. One thought the 1834 session might unite in legislating for the whole state and thus "immortalize itself" in internal improvements. Another, less optimistic, would have responded to legislative inaction by dividing the state's territory between Virginia and South Carolina. Absent a home market for the state's produce and money, he thought, the state "must come under complete vassalage to these States."[21]

Swain augmented his public leadership on internal improvements by promoting related private endeavors. He once received a letter from a Charleston resident who proposed to establish a steamboat line from Elizabeth City to New Bern. He became a reference for the prospective developer. He had known the man in his school days, he advised, and knew well his near relations and his character, both as an individual and as a merchant. Swain recommended him "as a gentleman of integrity, intelligence and enterprize entirely worthy of confidence and esteem."

He planned to write William Gaston also, and he sent a copy of his letter to the developer, who knew no one in New Bern, so he would know to whom to apply for advice and aid.[22]

Finally, Swain regularly sought information in this area of his responsibilities. The Literary Fund, of which he was president, owned swamp lands in the East. He wanted to know their extent in the region watered by the Albemarle and Pamlico Sounds, the manner and cost per acre to drain them, the effect of such drainage on the health of the adjacent county, whether it could be done within a reasonable period by individual effort unaided by public patronage, and if so, in what manner and upon what terms such lands should be transferred to individuals. He sought intelligence from the state treasurer regarding numerous statistical matters, including sums appropriated to internal improvements or debt thereon. He was advised that there was no standing appropriation of any state tax to objects of internal improvements; sums had at times been expended for specific improvements, and no debt was due on this account. Indeed, the state had no public debt.[23]

When Swain's time as governor ended, he had devoted considerable time and energy to championing internal improvements. "Having had some agency in exciting the 'whirlwind,'" he had said late in his first year, "I feel the responsibility it imposes upon me to aid in directing 'the storm.'" Largely due to financial constraints, his direction left no legacy equivalent to that of the Buncombe Turnpike in his legislative days. He had, however, awakened the state's citizens to their need and planted seeds for future governors and legislators to harvest.[24]

Much of Swain's travel as governor was on behalf of internal improvements and demonstrated the compelling need for them. No journey of significant extent was quick or easy. Swain's correspondence from this period, reminiscent of that from his legal career, memorializes some of the hardships of these expeditions. He once reported to Eleanor his arrival in Salisbury "without any serious accident, though the stage was swamped two hours at New Hope." In other respects, he said, the trip was pleasant enough. A follow-up letter, however, was more detailed and less upbeat. While he had arrived safe, it was only after "most fatiguing travel for two days." The roads were in "worse order" than he had found them in the past. He was still struggling with his itinerary, unsure whether to take the stage to Lincolnton or to procure a private conveyance to Statesville and take the Morganton line from there. Delay in his return travel, compelling an absence longer than expected, was a concern. He could not even get out of the Salisbury house because it was "so muddy," and he had seen no one except "professional gentlemen" who had called on him.[25]

On another occasion Asheville was his destination and his business largely personal, including both buying and selling land, and investigating for his mother-in-law proceedings regarding "her boy" (an enslaved person, apparently). He was in good health and pretty good humor but had "never sustained absence before with so little patience." The home fires beckoned him, and he would welcome their warmth "unperplexed by other engagements."[26]

Banks, which facilitated some internal improvements development, at times required gubernatorial attention. The 1832 legislature chartered a new state bank and tasked the governor with supervision of subscription to its capital stock and organization. Swain appointed commissioners to open the books for subscription to the stock, among them some familiar names in the period: his successor as governor, Richard D. Spaight, at New Bern, together with William Gaston, soon to be a state supreme court judge; the second of his successors as governor, Edward B. Dudley, at Wilmington; publisher Joseph Gales, developer William Boylan, and magistrate Charles L. Hinton at Raleigh; another future governor, William A. Graham, at Hillsboro, together with Frederick Nash, a future chief justice; and at Greensboro, John M. Morehead, also destined for the governor's chair.

Subscription sales met with difficulty. Edenton commissioners reported, for example, that "no stock in said Bank has been taken at this place." Others advised that the "charter is not considered to hold out sufficient inducements for capitalists to vest [sic] their funds in such an institution." Consequently, Swain appointed commissioners to open new books, but still to no avail. This did not disappoint, for Swain had disapproved of the bank's charter. Throughout his public career he had disfavored the legislature as the director of banking policy. Investors obviously concurred and voted against the bank by withholding their funds from it.

Swain also appointed commissioners to represent the state at meetings of shareholders of North Carolina's several banks. On one occasion he so designated William H. Haywood Jr., but advised that his attention probably could be focused solely on the Bank of New Bern. There would be an attempt, he thought, to assign "the effects of the Bank to Trustees and thus put a period to its corporate charter," in Swain's view "a palpable violation of the intended charter," which Haywood should resist by all means within his power.

An anomalous entry in Swain's gubernatorial letter books has William Hill, Swain's private secretary, and N. A. Stedman, state comptroller, appointing Swain himself to replace Gavin Hogg (resigned) to represent the stock of the state and vote its interests at a meeting of directors of the State Bank. By what authority they acted is not apparent. The defect, if such it was, was soon remedied, as Swain joined Hill and Stedman in designating William Boylan for the position "in the room of David L. Swain resigned." While governor, Swain did serve at one point as a commissioner from Raleigh to take subscriptions for increased capital the legislature had authorized in the Bank of Cape Fear.[27]

Although Swain's commitment to public education could scarcely have been more zealous, no action was readily available when the state treasurer sent him the chilling statement, "No children have as yet been educated at public expense." He thus had to say, as he neared the end of his time as governor, "The establishment of schools for the convenient instruction of youth, and the development and improvement of our internal resources by means beyond the reach of individual enterprise, will seem scarcely to have been regarded as proper objects of legislative concern." Murphey's first prong, the building of infrastructure to enable economic development, had not yet produced revenues adequate to support his second prong, universal public education.

Swain, however, correctly assessed the state's limited economic capacity. Near the end of his first term the Literary Fund, established to provide for public schools, had assets of slightly over $117,000. The fund had been "idle and unproductive" and had made no expenditures, Swain and the board reported, for obvious reasons: "It is apparent that no general good could be effected by an attempt to establish common and convenient schools in every county . . . with a fund amounting to little more than $100,000." Near the end of Swain's last term, the fund had made some expenditures, leaving remaining assets of just over $49,000. With the state's annual revenues at less than $100,000, half of which paid the legislature's expenses and the other half the salaries of state officers, the fund was hardly poised for significant growth.[28]

The emerging private sector in higher education in the state drew some attention from Swain. He corresponded with Samuel Wait, president of the newly established Wake Forest Institute, and once attended its examinations in the company of William Gaston.[29] Not surprisingly, however, since he served ex officio as its board president, the state university placed more demands on his time and energy. The University of North Carolina was not unknown to Swain when he became governor. He had had an ephemeral presence in Chapel Hill as a student. In 1831 he had been elected a trustee, so he had almost a year as such before assuming the governor's office.

In June 1831, Swain had been on the campus for the first meeting of the North Carolina Institute of Education. The institute's objective was to diffuse knowledge about education and improve the condition of the common schools (then private) and other literary institutions in the state. Swain returned for the institute's second meeting in June 1832 and was appointed, with Judge William Gaston and future chief justice Frederick Nash, to a committee to memorialize the legislature on the subject of popular education.[30]

As a trustee Swain had acquired responsibilities early. At his second meeting, his last before becoming governor, he was appointed to a committee to consider changing the period of commencement and adopting a uniform mode of conducting its exercises. By his next meeting his attendance was noted more prominently than previously: "His Excy. D. L. Swain ex off pres't." As ex-officio president while governor, he was faithful in attendance and an active participant in the board's deliberations and decisions,[31] among them a decision not to move the university from Chapel Hill to Raleigh.[32]

During Swain's time as president the board abolished its appointments and land and buildings committees, replacing them with an executive committee. The committee was to be appointed at every regular annual meeting, and the president was to be an ex-officio member. For the remainder of Swain's life, the board functioned largely through its executive committee.[33]

Among major executive-committee decisions with Swain as a member was that to sell Tennessee lands given to the university by Major Charles Gerrard, a Revolutionary War figure. The Land Committee had considered the subject in Swain's first year as governor. By his last year the executive committee viewed the university as "languishing for the want of ... funds." The Tennessee resources were far away, making it difficult to exercise supervision and control over them. It was thought that they should be converted into cash and invested in stock. Swain executed powers of attorney, signing them as governor and board president. He soon reported that the lands had been sold. To the present day, Gerrard Hall memorializes this benefactor's contributions.[34]

Swain also submitted to the General Assembly annual reports of the board's treasurer and information on other university accounting and financial matters. His most numerous reports advised of board vacancies occasioned by death or removal from the state of a trustee. The first advised of the death of Archibald Murphey.[35]

As board president Swain received his first experience with hiring university faculty. George Badger wrote him to nominate Walker Anderson, an 1819 graduate, for "Professor of Rhetoric and Belles Lettres." Anderson had indicated that he would accept. Anderson was employed and later served as chief justice of Florida.[36]

Nominations for honorary degrees came to Swain. One from John H. Wheeler, recommending the Reverend J. B. Perry of Philadelphia for doctor of divinity, was addressed to Swain as "president ex officio of the University of North Carolina."[37]

Abandoned property and property of intestate decedents without statutory heirs ("escheats") went to the university. These matters came to Swain as well. John M. Dick, Greensboro attorney and later superior court judge, once advised Swain of funds "to which I think the trustees of the university are entitled." He retained some doubt, however, so thought he should consult Swain as board president before instituting proceedings. After stating the facts, he solicited Swain's advice. Early attention to his request would enable him to present the matter, if appropriate, to the next session of Randolph superior court.[38]

Another suspected escheats situation demanded immediate investigation because those in possession of the decedent's human property—enslaved persons—would not hesitate to run them off and sell them. Informing Swain of this was, said the writer, "a duty which I owe to my alma mater."[39] Human subjects as escheated property could present complex issues. One situation found Swain dealing with a "boy now nearly or quite grown" who, the writer thought, "falls to the university for want of any next of kin to take." A father, apparently white, had attempted a testamentary manumission of the boy, but for reasons not clear, the attempt had failed. There was a question whether, no other request having been made, the mother, formerly enslaved but now free, could take him. Would Swain, the writer inquired, authorize him, as Swain's agent, to take the boy for the benefit of the trustees, or if he could not take him as his own, transfer him to the mother?[40]

As trustee president Swain was exposed to student disciplinary problems, good preparation for his later role as university president. In spring 1834 a circular letter to students urged them to politeness and good manners. Improper behavior, it said, was "becoming so common as to characterize almost every public meeting, not specially for sacred purpose." As "young gentlemen ... sons and representatives of some of the first families of this and other states," they should "cultivate civility and refinement of manners."[41]

As board president Swain also witnessed the better aspects of student performance. President Joseph Caldwell invited him and others from the community "to attend as Examiners at the annual examinations." Swain was to stay at the president's house. Caldwell hoped he would "feel that the interest of the state as of the university have no small claims to plead here on the services of its citizens." Swain served as an examiner in 1834 and 1835.[42]

Caldwell's death earlier in the year cast a pall over the 1835 commencement. When students prepared for the ball, they requested permission to place Swain's name on the advertisements and tickets as an attendant manager. This would, they believed, add dignity and stability to the conduct of the ball and render it more successful. Swain refused. He explained that on the evening preceding commencement Professor Anderson would deliver a funeral oration "commemorative of the virtues learning and talent of the late able and estimable President of the University." The following day the cornerstone of a monument to Caldwell's memory would probably be laid. The executive committee therefore thought the students would regard "festivity . . . as entirely inappropriate."[43]

Shortly after that commencement, the board recommended to the executive committee that it "open a correspondence with distinguished Literary men" for the purpose of securing a university president.[44] At its next meeting the board's president, Swain, would be named the president. The timing of Caldwell's death could not have been more propitious for enabling Governor Swain to become President Swain. But that is a later chapter in his story.[45]

"I am anxious before I go out of office to lay the foundation of a respectable library for the State, and more particularly for the Supreme Court," Swain said toward the end of his administration.[46] He succeeded in laying the foundations of the State Library and that of the state supreme court, and these, too, were among his contributions to the education of the state's citizens.

The 1831 fire that burned the State Capitol destroyed virtually all of the State Library collection. In January 1834, while the new capitol was under construction, Swain, as president of the Literary Fund, submitted to its board a resolution of the General Assembly requesting that the board "take the necessary measures for the purchase preservation and management of a public library for the state." Swain, as president of the fund, was to correspond with "gentlemen at the north" to procure catalogues of proper works for the State Library and to ascertain the terms upon which they could be procured.[47]

Gavin Hogg was in Philadelphia when Swain asked him to obtain the books for the state, but health concerns precluded his assistance. Swain then requested that Chief Justice Thomas Ruffin, also in Philadelphia, support the effort. Ruffin, however, would be there too briefly "to admit of his attending to the commission." Francis L. Hawks, a New York historian with North Carolina roots and ties, had offered to make such purchases. Swain, however, as he often did, turned to William Gaston. The court was greatly in need of a library, he told Gaston, and it "may be important to procure one before the termination of my administration." The sum expended was not to exceed $1,500, which, Swain promised, "shall be remitted the moment I am advised of a purchase."

His wait was brief. Within the month Gaston informed him that he had purchased books costing $1,361.75 for the supreme court library. "I think I have bought on very fair terms," Gaston represented, "and recommend the house as one fit to be employed on future occasions." James Donaldson, younger brother of Gaston's son-in-law Robert Donaldson, soon acknowledged receipt of Swain's check for $1,361.75, which he had delivered to the company. Swain could state in the Literary Fund report that a good law library, greatly needed by the supreme court, had been purchased under Gaston's direction.[48]

Swain's efforts to build the State Library collection were directed toward securing the books of Judge Archibald Murphey, who had died in 1832. Jonathan Worth, former House member and later governor, advised Swain that he and others had become Murphey's security so he could redeem the library, which he had pledged for a loan. Judge Ruffin, believing several of the volumes suitable for the State Library, had suggested that he write Swain. Worth was willing to sell them "very low." Some he thought "very rare and desirable for a State Library." He attached a list of the books. Swain responded that he had made a list of the portion adapted to the wants of the state. The Literary Fund was willing to pay a fair price for them once value was ascertained.

An exchange ensued between Swain and Doctor Victor M. Murphey, the judge's son. Murphey soon sent by stage as many of the books as could well go by that means; he would forward the remainder in a few days. Valuation was a problem. Notwithstanding that Judge Ruffin was a commissioner of the Literary Fund, Murphey would be satisfied with any value Ruffin and Swain determined. Shortly he forwarded as many of the remaining books as feasible. Could Swain send him the $60.00 needed for "my note in the Bank for which the books are bound?" Murphey asked. Again, he would be satisfied with any arrangements Swain made regarding valuation.

Swain's gubernatorial papers contain lists of the books purchased from the Murphey library and their valuation. They also contain an acknowledgement from Victor Murphey of receipt of a check for the books. These books were foundational to the reconstituted State Library, and Swain had a significant role in securing them.[49]

The 1832 General Assembly formed the state's first historical society. Swain was at least somewhat involved; shortly after he became governor, he informed Joseph Seawell Jones, Warren County historian, of the impending bill, and that he had proposed Jones as an incorporator. Swain and Jones were charter members. The society never became active, however. No one else took the essential initiative, and the duties of governance were temporarily consuming Swain's leadership skills. This task would have to await his time as UNC president.[50] Even as governor, however, when Clio called with clarity, Swain responded.

Learning and informing of the state's past was integral to his vision for education, not only of the people of North Carolina, but also of many beyond its bounds. The most notable example is the document he produced for John Hamilton, son of Alexander Hamilton, the first U.S. secretary of the treasury and a George Washington confidant. William Gaston brokered the arrangement, securing Swain's permission for Hamilton to contact him on "some points of historical interest."

Swain's consent notwithstanding, Hamilton troubled him reluctantly; having exhausted available resources in New York and Washington, however, he yielded to necessity. His objective was "to illustrate the early history of our Country in connection with the life of my Father." The New-York Historical Society had appointed him to secure copies of the legislative journals and laws of the several states, and Congress was seeking "all the materials that may be useful to some future Historian of our Country." The importance of the task, combined with an absence of alternatives, trumped his disinclination to impose on a sitting governor.

Hamilton's inquiries related to early sources of the state's revenues, federal-state matters in the state's early history, an Edenton court case, North Carolina's response to the Virginia and Kentucky resolutions of 1798, and its provision for its debts in 1790. Swain gave detailed responses, designed to be notes "from which historical narrative might be framed, and . . . too hastily written to answer any other purpose." He was, however, willing to vouch for the opinions expressed.

This modesty exaggerated. It is unlikely that the response was the product of comprehensive research and analysis. Governors then had little staff assistance; the document, or most of it, was probably Swain's work alone. This, however, renders it the more remarkable for its breadth and quality. Certainly Hamilton thought so. He thanked Swain for the attention to his requests. The replies were "fuller" than he had expected and would be of great use to him. Equal interest in other parts of the country, he said, would have prevented his "groping my way through the darkest period of our history." His general lament Swain certainly shared: that "we are a people of the present hour," not interested in the past.[51]

Among Swain's contemplated sources were the papers of William R. Davie, leading Revolutionary War figure. He contacted Allen Davie, the general's son, who responded that his father's papers were at his old residence in South Carolina. Regrettably, many had been lost or destroyed. Allen's son was there and would immediately forward any Hamilton letters found.

The governor admired Davie and had proposed to take charge of his manuscripts and permit their use "to advance the character of our native state, and the well-earned reputation of your father." He advised Allen that Matthew S. C. Clarke, clerk of the U.S. House of Representatives, and Colonel Peter Force of Washington were collecting materials for a documentary history of the United

States. Swain vouched for the character and industry of the editors and expressed confidence that their volumes "will be the most complete and authentic history ever published in any age or nation."

Allen Davie doubted the papers' utility in some respects but found them "curious . . . as showing how the fiscal affairs of our State were managed in those primitive times." The revenues, he said, had to support the governor, his family, and the legislature; the legislature applied the balance to the military service of the state. He had long thought North Carolina's services in the Revolution underappreciated, and those of Virginia and South Carolina overly so. When the papers were used, he told Swain, he wished to add explanations, "as I have had full and free conversations with my Father with a view to their publication."

Swain exulted in acquisition of the papers. He immediately advised Clarke, one of the editors of the proposed documentary history, of it. Davie had been, he told Clarke, "one of the most distinguished men of the interesting period in which he lived, and few individuals, certainly no one of the South, saw more constant, active, and arduous service in the War of the Revolution." Accordingly, no contemporary was better qualified to give a history of those times.[52]

Swain's historical collaboration with George Bancroft commenced during this time. Bancroft, arguably the foremost American historian of his time, had solicited Swain's assistance on North Carolina aspects of a projected history of the United States. For once Swain discarded his accustomed modesty. "I have perhaps devoted as much attention to the sources of history in this state," he boasted with justification, "as any individual who is not a professional historian."

Still, how to respond to Bancroft's inquiries "in any communication of ordinary length" perplexed him. The ensuing discourse was indeed lengthy. Swain noted that he had forwarded legislative acts and excerpts from his diary kept while on the Edenton Circuit. These needed explanation, however, and a broad-brush portrayal of the state's early history followed.

He had never satisfied himself as to the precise period when the first permanent settlement of the colony was effected, but he thought it was produced by the prosecution of Quakers in Virginia about 1660. He set forth the dates of several occurrences, noting that he had read Lawson's 1709 history and Brickell's published in 1737,[53] both written for the purpose of "puffing the country into notice and thus enabling the Lords Proprietors to sell their lands." He would send a manuscript of Governor Alexander Spotswood of Virginia regarding the affairs of North Carolina.

His library, he boasted, had the only complete series of revisals of the state's statutes. He would loan any of these Bancroft desired except the 1715 manuscript that was a public record. The first truly great man to preside over the state's affairs, in Swain's view, was Gabriel Johnston, who had many successes and few, if any, equals. One valuable resource, recently discovered, was in his possession: the original Proclamations Book of the Colonial Governors. George Pollock possessed Cullen Pollock's letter book and was "entirely disposed" to furnish copies of letters others desired. The public offices in Raleigh, too, contained many valuable papers "worthy of a more particular examination" than they had received. The most extensive and valuable collection, in Swain's view, was that of the late Judge Archibald Murphey, then in the possession of his son, Dr. Victor M. Murphey. Until shortly before his death in 1832, Judge Murphey had been writing a history of the state, "which however will never be completed."

At the end Swain resumed a modest posture, fearing the letter had grown to a point where Bancroft would find it "scarcely worth the labor of perusal." He offered it nevertheless as evidence of goodwill and of his "anxious desire for your perfect success in the great work in which you are engaged." The apologetic was risible; Swain had placed at Bancroft's disposal more valuable sources than he could digest in any reasonable time frame.[54]

When Swain mentioned the Murphey papers to Bancroft, he was in correspondence regarding them with the judge's son, Doctor Victor M. Murphey. Swain wanted the historical society to purchase them. Murphey said he would derive great satisfaction from presenting the papers to the society, but he needed reimbursement for losses sustained from the death of his father, who had died in debt. He proposed that the society purchase the materials at a price determined by any friend Swain considered competent to judge the value. Later Murphey missed a visit from Swain while substituting for an ill county clerk. He wrote Swain afterward, noting his plans to move to the West. Swain had told him of "Gentlemen" (primarily Bancroft, probably) engaged in preparing a national history, who would be pleased to secure his manuscripts. Murphey requested that Swain write to the one most likely to respond soonest to ascertain his interest. It would be "troublesome" to move West with the papers, and he again offered to dispose of them upon such terms as any competent judge would suggest. Swain could be the broker: "I will cheerfully abide by any contract *you* might deem advisable," Murphey wrote. It would work out, but not until after Swain left the governor's office.[55]

Swain heard often from Joseph Seawell Jones, the Warren County "historian and humbug." In March 1832, Jones had accompanied Swain as the latter attended court in Eastern North Carolina. Jones was at work on a Revolutionary history of North Carolina but evolved mainly as a defender of the existence and authenticity of the Mecklenburg Declaration of Independence, the Regulator movement, and William Hooper, a North Carolina signer of the Declaration of Independence.

Jones's earliest missive to Swain as governor inquired of Swain's attention to the Regulation. He had prepared, he said, "a copious and critical essay on that rebellion—defensive of its character." Partisans of Governor William Tryon, Jones lamented, had written most of the prior histories, and "the clamor of their [the Regulators] being all Tories during the war is not true." Boston-based Southerners who had seen his book objected to its severity, but it was, he insisted, true. Swain should prepare himself, however, for an *"uproarious production."* Jones feared condemnation "for some of my high tory principles which have crept into my history of our constitution."

Delays, sufficient to evoke fear Swain had forgotten him, Jones attributed to extreme busyness in investigating papers of the state and other federal departments. He had copied some documents relating to North Carolina history and made abstracts of others. President Andrew Jackson had assisted him with insights into the Colonial Office of London, which he was determined to visit, and had been kind in general, even allowing Jones to order papers in his name.

A mix of altruism and self-interest characterized Jones's communications. In the former category was his desire to get the historical society established "with proper solemnity" and his offer to assist Swain with the purchase of books for the State Library. He also, though, solicited the state's business for two enterprising Boston printers whom he had induced to establish a press in Raleigh. They would be ideal, he suggested, for the printing of state laws, supreme court reports, the Chapel Hill orations, and other state work. He assured Swain that they would not expect an exorbitant profit. Too, Swain could be most helpful with the sales of Jones's book. Jones asked him to speak of it as often as possible to promote its sales, and to apologize for any charge for it above $2.00. Finally in this regard, he was not above soliciting Swain's research assistance. Go to the secretary of state's office, Jones once begged Swain, look at the Council Journal of Governor Josiah Martin, and note for him the names of the councilors.[56]

Finally, there were miscellaneous historical matters. Swain took seriously his responsibility to secure historically correct information for the gravestones of state officials who had died and been buried in Raleigh.[57] Francis L. Hawks, another historian with whom Swain had a relationship, once forwarded, per Swain's request, a 1711 Christopher Gale letter. A Virginian, desiring information about Revolutionary War Brigadier General Francis Nash and not knowing to which government office to write, addressed his inquiry to Swain. In response to a citizen's inquiry as to "the various public offices filled by the late Gov. Caswell," Swain sketched the career of his wife's distinguished grandfather.[58]

Swain's influence in this area lingered long after he departed the governor's office. Four administrations later, a citizen informed Governor William A. Graham that he would visit the state archives seeking information on the early history of Tennessee. Graham's predecessor, Governor Swain, he said, had once assured him that he could examine the executive and legislative records of that period for that purpose.[59]

CHAPTER 5

Less Visionary Aspects
"Not in my power to do anything as it should be done"

WHILE SWAIN WAS ARTICULATING and advancing a vision for North Carolina's future, more routine tasks consumed his days. He did not yield to this fate uncomplainingly. "I have . . . so many letters to answer and so much preparation to make for the legislature," he once told William Gaston, "that it is not in my power to do anything as it should be done."[1]

Among the relatively trivial matters were housekeeping details left by his predecessor, Montford Stokes. It was customary upon the election of a new governor, Stokes informed Swain, that a sum be appropriated "for repairs of the Government Lot, purchasing furniture for the Governor's House, etc." After Stokes's first election, this had not been done, but $600.00 had been appropriated after his second. It was also standard for the departing governor "to state his account of purchases and expenditures, and to hand over to his successor . . . any surplus monies in his hands." Stokes had not fully expended his appropriation. Several needed repairs remained incomplete. He had given Swain's private secretary an account of payments made and would make a full settlement and payment of any balance. Upon inquiry regarding these sums from the House Finance Committee chair, Swain could only respond that Stokes had delivered accounts for expenditures of $228.00 and that he would transmit other vouchers when able.[2]

The state constitution empowered the governor, with the advice of the council of state, to make recess appointments to vacancies in constitutional offices, to expire at the end of the next session of the General Assembly. Swain made no appointments pursuant to this provision and never convened the council of state.[3] He made numerous appointments, however, some pursuant to other constitutional provisions, others to legislative enactment. Probably none impacted his life as much as those designating his gubernatorial staff. Shortly after taking his first oath, he appointed William R. Hill his private secretary. David Outlaw of Bertie also became a gubernatorial aide.[4]

Notaries public received their commissions from the governor. One request to Swain noted that the applicant practiced "Physic" and was frequently out of town, so would be pleased if Swain would appoint him a notary. The governor similarly appointed commissioners "to take the acknowledgements and proof of deeds and instruments under Seal."[5]

The ministerial duty of formalizing General Assembly appointments fell to Swain. He "appointed" district solicitors, a state solicitor general and an attorney general, judges of the superior and supreme courts, and a U.S. senator. In reality, however, he was giving ceremonial notification of action by the legislative branch. The missives consistently stated, "the General Assembly having elected him," or words to that effect. He also transmitted to the General Assembly letters of resignation from public officials.[6] Sheriffs in the districts certified congressional election returns to the governor, and the governor issued commissions to the congressmen.[7]

At times the governor appointed land surveyors. In Swain's first term he enlisted Asheville attorney Joshua Roberts to assist in securing an accurate survey of "the Hopewell Treaty line" and other property, the Hopewell Treaty being the first one executed between the U.S. government and the Cherokee Indians. Roberts soon related that Joseph Henry was agreeable to the task and requested that Swain forward maps or records with instructions. Later the General Assembly directed conveyance of the "common" adjoining the town of Franklin to the chair of the Macon County Court. The governor was to appoint a commissioner to determine the quantity of land "by actual survey," and Swain appointed Jacob Siler for this purpose.[8] When two commissioners for rebuilding the state capitol resigned, Swain appointed their successors.[9]

Although Swain did not appoint judges, he at times assigned them to hold courts. One correspondent wanted Judge James Martin for the Buncombe-Rutherford 1833 summer term. Another thought Judge Henry Seawell's lack of appropriate judicial temperament disqualified him. The duty could not be divided between two judges, still another advised; he had consulted William Gaston, and the duty ought to be assigned to one. Swain took the advice and designated Martin.[10]

When the Northampton County superior court clerk resigned, he requested Swain's view on whether he could turn the office over to his deputy. The act was silent, Swain replied, as to the privilege of resigning and to whom a resignation could be tendered. It seemed to him, however, that it should be submitted, not to him, but to the appointing power, the court.[11]

Acting pursuant to Swain's 1833 recommendation, the General Assembly authorized him to appoint three commissioners to revise the state's statutory law. He selected William Horn Battle, Gavin Hogg, and James Iredell. When Hogg became ill, Swain replaced him with Frederick Nash, later chief justice of the state supreme court. The revisal project continued over several years. Iredell once informed Swain of his lofty aspirations for the endeavor but confessed to finding the work impossible while he traveled his judicial circuit practicing law. "I have postponed that matter until my return," he advised.

Swain rendered periodic reports on the commissioners' progress. Their duties were arduous and important, he told the legislators, and there were few subjects in which the intelligent portion of the community felt so deep an interest. It was "a task to which the greatest learning, the purest patriotism and the clearest intellect is not more than equal." The assistance of a compensated clerk would expedite the endeavor, he advised on several occasions, apparently without result. The end product, the *Revised Statutes of 1837*, constitutes a significant aspect of Swain's legacy for state improvement.[12]

The August 13, 1833, death of Chief Justice Leonard Henderson created a vacancy on the North Carolina Supreme Court. Notwithstanding that his son was dying, the governor immediately addressed himself to what he perceived as a crisis to the judiciary. By all appearances Henderson had been a popular and respected chief justice. The court was a fledgling institution, however, having only functioned since 1819, and it was unpopular. Every General Assembly session brought efforts to abolish it. The surviving members at Henderson's death, Joseph J. Daniel and Thomas Ruffin, disliked each other intensely. Ruffin lacked respect for Daniel's learning and intellectual integrity. The bar thus feared that without an able and honorable replacement for Henderson, Ruffin could resign, and the court would die.

The election of William Gaston to the post was believed essential to the court's survival. One possible impediment was brushed aside. Gaston was a Roman Catholic, and the North Carolina Constitution barred from state office anyone who denied the truth of the Protestant religion. Gaston and others rationalized that insofar as the Protestant religion could be defined, it was the Apostles' Creed, which Catholics also believed; the fact that they held other beliefs that Protestants did not share could be disregarded.

There were further impediments, foremost among them the candidate's finances. Gaston had $8,000 in debts, and his selection would reduce his $6,000 to

William Horn Battle, James Iredell, and Frederick Nash (left to right), Swain's appointees as commissioners to revise the state's statutory law.

$7,000 annual income as a lawyer to a fixed salary of $2,500 a year. He requested assistance from Raleigh lawyer Thomas P. Devereux in negotiating a loan not to exceed $7,500. He thanked Judge Ruffin for his offer to be a surety, leaving that decision to Devereux. If arrangements could be made to satisfy his creditors and his family, ultimately Gaston was willing to "leave it to a few friends . . . to say what duty demands of me." He specified the friends: Swain, Devereux, and Raleigh lawyer George Badger. These three played the civic virtue card in their appeal to Gaston. Swain asserted that "if any other name is presented the Supreme Court dies with the lamented Ch. J." Only Gaston's election, Devereux claimed, could "restore confidence in the public mind" and save the court.

Later Devereux and Badger prepared a joint letter to Gaston while Swain attended a railroad meeting in Pittsboro. Duty required Gaston's consent, they maintained, averring anew that only he could save the court. They acknowledged that he should place family considerations first and that his "profits will be greatly reduced." These factors, however, should not be decisive. His ascension to the bench was the sole event that could preserve the court and make it "*worth* preserving." Upon Swain's return, he signed this missive, adding that Gaston's acceptance would "keep down all opposition, certainly all but one individual."

The one individual was Judge Henry Seawell, whom Swain considered "ignorant of his own qualifications and character." "The Court," he told Gaston, "would not survive his [Seawell's] election a fortnight." Seawell, Swain was advised, had yielded to importunities to "become a candidate *against the nomination of the Governor.*" Swain, however, did not make the nomination. With Gaston's encouragement, he announced that since the legislature would meet before the next court session, he would make no interim appointment. This proved wise, as the legislature soon overwhelmingly elected Gaston. Gaston served the court ably the remainder of his life, and his service is a legacy of Swain's leadership, which he exerted vigorously and unreservedly on behalf of Gaston's candidacy.[13]

Gaston once stated that granting reprieves and pardons was all that was really required of a North Carolina governor.[14] He understated, but considering Swain's workload in this area, especially if his other criminal justice tasks are considered, he might well have thought it largely accurate. The surviving record of Swain's administration at least seems to contain more material on this subject than any other.

Proclamations from the governor offering rewards for fugitives were common. One had been convicted of "Negro stealing"—theft of enslaved persons—and received a death sentence. He was believed to be beyond the limits of the state. Swain offered a $200.00 reward to anyone who captured and confined him to any jail in the state. He also ordered civil and military authorities to use their best exertions to apprehend him or cause his apprehension.[15]

Swain offered a $300.00 reward for capture of the alleged perpetrators of a gruesome murder. He thought they were in Alabama, "where they displayed the same turbulent disposition that . . . has marked their lives." His informant did not sign his name, however, because the accused had relatives living near him. He referred Swain to another area resident who confirmed that the individuals were those sought and offered to give Swain further information.[16]

Swain sometimes did seek further information before offering a reward. He wrote one claimant requesting a copy of the proceedings of the jury of inquest. At other times he explained the denial of rewards. One claimant had captured an accused murderer but, not having committed him to jail within the state, had not met the conditions of the reward offer. Another thought himself entitled to an entire award but said "sheer justice" required an allowance of $50.00 for expenses incurred. Swain believed he lacked authority to pay and referred the claimant to the legislature. Ultimately, he received the award plus expenses and thanked Swain.[17]

Extradition matters were equally common. Swain wrote governors of other states requesting the return of fugitives. Once he contacted the governor of South Carolina to request extradition of four enslaved persons. The governor responded that he had forwarded them to Swain's agent from the sheriff of the Marlborough District. Fugitive freedom seekers sometimes made their way as far as the northern states. Once Swain requested from the governor of New York the return of two enslaved persons who were the property of a Raleigh woman.[18]

Public officials and ordinary citizens petitioned Swain on extradition matters. Romulus Saunders, state attorney general, once reported a particularly shocking murder case and requested that Swain take steps to extradite the offender. The solicitor of the First Judicial District requested a demand for extradition of a man charged with murder who had fled to Virginia.

A citizen accused two individuals of horse stealing and alleged that they were fugitives in Georgia. Swain requested "a regularly authenticated copy" of the indictments and promised to make the demand upon receiving such. Still another informed Swain that his "mulatto man" had disappeared in the company of two white men "who it appears had decoyed him away." He had learned that the man was in jail in Petersburg, Virginia, and asked Swain to give it his immediate attention. The practice of "decoying off" enslaved persons with promises of freedom had become common, and "an example should be made of some such villain."[19]

Extraditions involved expenses. One correspondent informed Swain that in apprehending a fugitive he had been to trouble and expense and lost friendships. He hoped Swain would at least pay his expenses while detained in Alabama. He had also incurred fees to two lawyers while there. The governor should send him what he thought right.

Another, in transporting two fugitives from Virginia to North Carolina, had incurred expenses of $122.08. That might seem high, he noted, but he had considered the stage the safest transport and had never slept until they arrived at home. He hoped Swain would consider, in setting his fee, the length of time he was gone. Swain responded, thinking $200.00 a fair compensation. After deducting $2.00 due his private secretary, he transmitted $198.00. It was not over, though. The recipient acknowledged receipt of the $198.00 but submitted an additional item of expense.[20]

Petitions for pardons constituted the greater portion of Swain's criminal justice workload. It was a rule with him, he said, not to interfere with a sentence imposed in the judge's discretion "without a reference of the subject to the Judge and Solicitor by whom the law had been administered." Both sides, he believed, must be heard; respect for the judge and the attorney general made this course "imperative."[21]

Swain preferred escape of the guilty over suffering of the innocent. Mercy, however, was not necessarily a communal good. He quoted a maxim that mercy to the guilty is cruelty to the commonwealth. Once, in refusing to commute a death sentence, he said no case more clearly demonstrated the truth of the maxim. The example, he stated, "must be made." No prospect of mercy remained on earth, and the prisoner should direct his attention "to happiness beyond the grave." At times a "clear sense of duty" required that he "permit the law, severe as it may be, to have its course."[22]

Poignant pleas put Swain's philosophy to the test. One prisoner had been incarcerated on a forgery charge. His wife had died of a broken heart during his absence, leaving three children, the youngest only two months old, whom the prisoner had not seen. His constitution was delicate, and his health had diminished during his confinement. He "for the sake of my unoffending and suffering babes" besought Swain to "restore a lost and ruined father to his helpless Orphants." If done, his children would "reverence thy name."[23]

Another inmate had been convicted of assault with intent to commit rape on his own daughter, the conviction a product of members of his own family "among whom there existed a violent quarrel." Trial testimony was contradictory and weakened by other circumstances. The alleged offender's wife was having an affair, and many respectable persons believed the charge was made by the daughter at the mother's instance and lacked foundation. The inmate had been a kind husband and father and was in feeble health. The "encroaching weather" would "render his confinement dangerous." Swain remitted the remainder of the term on condition that the prisoner depart the state within ninety days and not return in less than three years.[24]

A former Swain legislative colleague had hoped an inheritance would enable him to discharge a fine. His mother, however, was more than thirty years younger than his deceased father. The father had willed all his property to her, and she was "likely to live a good while yet." "I have once been a little dissipated," the petitioner confessed in imploring Swain's assistance, "but such is not the case now."[25]

Several petitioners thought a death sentence for "Negro stealing" too severe, especially since the offender was under a similar charge in Georgia, where conviction brought only imprisonment. They urged Swain at least to defer the execution to see if the governor of Georgia might demand the prisoner. The criminal, a surgeon-dentist, had been a victim of intemperance, which had consumed his property and ruined his character. There had been much good about him, however, and he was now into religion.[26]

Pity for an enslaver as a basis for pardoning an enslaved person rings harsh in modern ears. Swain received such a plea, however. "Negro Martin" had been charged with assault with intent to commit rape. The testimony was too strong to justify the jury in acquitting, but the jurors thought clemency desirable because the imprisonment had subjected the master to heavy expenses and costs. The jurors thus pled that the master's losses "should in some degree be alleviated, if it may be done without injury to society."[27]

Pardon petitions could also present unusual offenses or offenders. Swain remitted time for two offenders who had maimed their victims, one by biting off an ear, the other by biting off a small portion of a nose.[28] A woman convicted of keeping a disorderly house was, a petitioner argued, being undeservedly punished. Her husband had died in service in the last war with Great Britain, leaving her destitute. She had offended as a means of livelihood, was old and declining, and the purposes of justice had been answered by the time served. Further, the county attorney was convinced that she had been twice convicted for the same offense.[29]

A free man of color had been convicted of trading with an enslaved person by purchasing a bushel of corn. He was imprisoned until the fine and costs were paid. His reputation was that of an honest and industrious man, and he was no doubt ignorant of the law. It was alleged to be common among farmers "to permit their slaves to make a little for themselves," and no doubt the offender was ignorant of the law and considered the act authorized. A wife and several children were suffering from his incarceration.[30]

At counsel's request, a physician examined a death row inmate who "with great composure and firmness" asserted that he was Christ. The doctor concluded that the prisoner's mind was so confused that "the action of the *Brain* had become permanent," beyond his control, and not feigned. The doctor had a good reputation. The petitioner hoped for a respite but begged at least for more time for the offender to prepare to meet his God.[31]

It could be the petitioner who was unusual. J. J. Daniel, one of the supreme court judges, once asked Swain to remit the remaining three weeks of a prisoner's sentence due to the presence of smallpox in the town, making his continued confinement there dangerous. Swain granted the petition.[32]

Swain was amenable to remission of corporal forms of punishment. He remitted the lashes portion of a sentence when the solicitor and respectable citizens represented the defendant as age eighty and thus unfit for corporal punishment. Youthful defendants received the same treatment. Two who had been sentenced to thirty lashes for petit larceny secured remission upon the representation that they were "infants and fit objects for the exercise of executive clemency." Horse thieves, forgers, and receivers of stolen goods received identical favor.[33]

Remission of prison sentences was not unknown. It occurred mainly in assault and battery cases, but at least once in a manslaughter case and once with a female offender convicted of keeping a disorderly house and retailing spiritous liquors. In most cases some portion of the confinement time had been served.[34] Swain was also known to remit fines or some portion thereof, especially if the offender was unable to pay or had paid sums in a related civil action.

On one occasion he declined to remit a fine when a state Senate bill to do so had failed to pass. He promised, however, to reverse his action if the prosecutor could furnish him with facts from which he could conclude that the fine was excessive.[35]

Some clemency requests to Swain were actively opposed. A prisoner convicted of "Negro stealing" was, said an opponent of clemency, a really bad actor, "a man of the most vindictive as well as unprincipled feelings."[36] Another, convicted of burglary and sentenced to death, was the subject of a negative petition from eighteen citizens. The offender, they stated, had badly beaten the female occupant, and left her for dead before robbing the house. He had a bad past, and a pardon would upset the community. They spoke the sentiments of three-fourths of the citizens, they claimed. This prisoner, another correspondent represented, had threatened to kill other people if he obtained release or to have his brother do it if he did not. Everyone feared him, and he should be hanged to prevent some good man from killing him "and then they will have to call on you for mercy."[37]

Two Granville County cases were especially troublesome for Swain. The first, that of Washington Taborn, a free Negro, had county residents ready to support a constitutional convention to make the governor elected by the people so they could "give vent to their hostile feelings [toward Swain] through the ballot box." Taborn had been convicted of burglary and sentenced to death. One citizen, considering him "deficient in understanding" and thus not a fit subject for capital punishment, asked Swain to pardon him and remove him from the United States. Others signed petitions on his behalf. A juror said that but for Taborn's bad character, he would not have been found guilty "owing to the insufficiency of the evidence." His bad character was well established, however; he had numerous "clergyable felonies," including one in which Swain had been the trial judge, and was considered a "bad man and lost to every feeling of moral sense."

Swain had inherited the problem. His predecessor, Montford Stokes, had promised a pardon if Taborn could emigrate to Haiti. The condition had not been met when Stokes left office, but Swain felt constrained by the pledge. His desire to show "proper respect for Governor Stokes," he said defensively, "ought to have prevented all excitement." The prisoner escaped twice, causing Swain to seek and obtain his extradition from Virginia, and provoking public outrage.

After some respites, Swain allowed the execution to proceed. Often, he said, "very sensible and honorable men ... are ... more under the influence of sympathy than judgment." While the law was severe, that was for the legislature. His sense of duty required rejection of clemency, with the hope that the offender would "find that mercy in Heaven, which the safety of the country seems to render it necessary to deny him now." In the end Swain was resolute, but his dalliances en route, while for understandable reasons of deference, produced detractors.[38]

The second offender, Robert Potter, was politically prominent, with service in the U.S. House of Representatives and the N.C. House of Commons. In the latter he and Swain had served together, and this made the matter sensitive for Swain. Potter's convictions were on two counts of mayhem. He had castrated two men, one an elderly minister, the other a youth, after accusing them of improper relations with his wife while he was in Raleigh. Potter, apparently unruffled by his confinement in the Hillsboro jail, was a candidate for the House of Commons. Citizens in Orange and Granville counties petitioned the governor and the General Assembly for his release. One Granville citizen conveyed the rumor that Swain had said he was determined not to pardon Potter, even if he were elected to the legislature; he requested a speedy reply and permission to share it with his fellow citizens. At one point Potter summoned Swain to court, in Frederick Nash's opinion "for effect—to give dignity and importance to his case in the eyes of the gaping multitude."

Swain again deferred to the legislature on the punishment. When Potter's prison term had been served and detention continued solely because of an unpaid $1,000 fine, which he claimed inability to pay, Swain remitted the fine. He ordered, however, that Potter plead the pardon in person at the next term of court. When Potter entreated that he would be murdered if he appeared at the courthouse, Swain relented. A citizen had affirmed that a Potter appearance would produce "certain destruction." Swain's yielding on the requirement would, the citizen represented, "in all probability save a fellow being from an untimely death." Swain yielded, but not without having experienced what he called "unhappy excitement."[39]

One death row inmate sought a pardon via a professed religious conversion. He had repented and "had found the Saviour precious to him." Swain's correspondent, while suspicious of the inmate's sincerity, had come to believe "that his heart was renewed." He had endeavored to impress upon him "the awful state" of a man who died with "a lie in his mouth" and had urged disclosure before he met "his final Judge." The prisoner, though, had declared his innocence of all but receiving and concealing the money involved. A Methodist minister was satisfied that his protestations of innocence were true. All Christians who had examined him agreed, the minister wrote. Swain was unmoved. He had examined the guilt question himself and regretted that duty required him to allow the law "severe as it may be, to have its course." Once all hope of pardon was gone, the prisoner confessed and exonerated the other suspect. It was now evident that he had lied to the Holy Ghost, his advocate told Swain, making his claim to faith "worse than an empty profession, it was as hypocritical as that of Judas."[40]

Except for a few pardons of innocence, almost always granted where such was established beyond cavil, recent North Carolina governors have been sparing with pardons. When assessed in this context, Swain can only be viewed as generous in this regard. True, he was cautious, requiring input from petitioners and prosecution alike. The foregoing amply demonstrates, however, that in fact he bestowed pardons liberally.

It is thus ironic that he is still remembered, and questioned, only for a matter in which he declined a pardon or commutation. Frances (Frankie) Silver, of Burke County, was convicted of the murder of her husband, Charles (Charlie) Silver, and executed. The victim actually just disappeared. Body parts thought to have been his were found in and about the fireplace of the rural mountain home he had shared with Frankie and their young child. While circumstantial, the evidence indicated that Frankie had killed him with an axe, dismembered his body, and burned the parts. The extreme brutality of the killing may have influenced Swain's decision. The facts that at one point Silver escaped from confinement, and at another made a confession, could also have been factors. But for injuries received in a sulky accident, which precluded his court attendance, Swain would have been the sentencing judge. His election as governor removed him from that possibility but left him with petitions for Silver's pardon that had been filed with Governor Montford Stokes. Others would be filed with Swain.

Over the course of Swain's consideration of the petitions, community sentiment shifted in Silver's favor. Neighbors were convinced that Charlie had been "a lazy trifling man" and that his treatment of Frankie had been "both unbecoming and cruel very often and at the time too when female delicacy would most forbid it." Frankie's lawyer believed the case one of manslaughter or justifiable homicide, not murder. Swain was implored to save the state from "the disgrace of seeing a woman executed under the gallows." Nine-tenths of the Burke County population, including "the better of the community," it was said, could "cheerfully sign a petition and ... rejoice at her pardon." They now believed Frankie had killed Charlie "in a fracas" and that "no good would result from the example of her execution."

"No one," Swain said, "can participate more deeply than I do in their sympathy for her melancholy fate." Sympathy notwithstanding, he let the execution proceed. Why, says modern-day writer Perry Deane Young, "is an enduring mystery." Equally mysterious, perhaps, is Swain's remission of the last four months of a ten-month sentence given to an accessory after the fact to the Silver murder.[41]

Less Visionary Aspects 95

The Silver case remains the subject of analysis and contention. Books, songs, and plays about it proliferate. As recently as 1994 a Burke County teacher, believing Frankie a victim of spousal abuse who killed in self-defense, joined her students in applying to Governor James B. Hunt Jr. for a pardon of forgiveness for her. Hunt reportedly never replied.[42]

Cherokee Indians and their lands presented episodic problems for Swain. He was new to the office when first advised that intruders from Georgia, South Carolina, and Tennessee were committing depredations on these lands: destroying soil, cutting timber, depriving both natives and white citizens of benefits from the gold mines. The area's citizens, his informer contended, deserved protection by the state. A suitable state-employed guard protected the Georgia and Tennessee mines; North Carolina's were of immense value and should have similar security.

The state constitution designated the governor captain-general and commander-in-chief of the militia. He could, with the General Assembly in recess and advice of the council of state, "embody [it] for the public safety." Swain, however, thought he lacked authority to mobilize the militia for this purpose, apparently considering the matter one for federal jurisdiction. He thus sought assistance from U.S. Secretary of War Lewis Cass, whom he hoped would bring the issue to President Andrew Jackson's attention. Swain informed Congressman Samuel Price Carson of his letter to Cass and requested his aid if necessary "to secure the prompt attention of the proper dept."

Swain also wrote several mountain residents, noting alleged trespasses and requesting information on changes in the area's Indian population caused by proceedings regarding them in the legislatures of Georgia and Alabama. Ever attentive to constituents, he told the citizen informer of his request to the general government which, no doubt, would be "properly afforded."

As Swain had expected, Cass replied posthaste. He could not definitively answer Swain's request for a detachment of U.S. troops to be stationed in the North Carolina part of the Cherokee Country to prevent intrusion upon Indian lands. Soon, however, he should be able to let him know the president's views.[43] This exchange launched communications between Swain and federal military officials.

General Alex Macomb soon wrote that he had ordered General Winfield Scott to send two companies of artillery from Charleston Harbour to the Valley Town in the Cherokee Country to remove intruders. Scott had instructions to receive Swain's directions on the subject "and will execute them according to your wishes." A letter from General Scott followed, enclosing his instructions to Captain George W. Gardiner, who was about to march to Tennessee. Swain was to give Gardiner instructions deemed proper.

Swain advised Gardiner that he had received Scott's letter, that he had information regarding trespasses upon the soil and gold mines of the North Carolina portion of the Cherokee lands, and that Gardiner was to adopt measures to prevent the continuance and repetition of such offenses. The intruders were violating treaties and acts of Congress and should be directed to remove immediately. In the event of noncompliance, force should be used.[44]

Meanwhile, other informers downplayed the situation to Swain. One had observed persons engaged in both farming and gold digging, but they had permits. He thought U.S. troops had "pretty well cleared the Nation of intruders last fall." If not prevented, however, whites would work the territory in the coming summer. Another informer believed there were perhaps fewer white persons in the North Carolina Cherokee Nation than for some years.[45]

These communications had satisfied him, Swain advised Gardiner, that earlier accounts regarding trespasses had been exaggerated. Gardiner was now on the site, he said, "for the purpose of executing the instructions of your Excellency," which Swain thought would have the salutary effect of deterring lawless individuals from "future aggressions of this character." The number of men needed, and the time they should remain, he left to Gardiner's discretion.

Gardiner perceived confusion as to the precise nature of his task. He did not have the treaties between the states and the Cherokees and thus could only advise his subordinates in general terms as to the proper course regarding intruders. Whether whites were authorized to occupy certain property, and whether native councils had power to permit whites to remain in the nation at their pleasure, were unanswered questions.

Mechanics, blacksmiths, millers, and others were "making a plea for their residence in the nation." The natives wanted a carpenter to stay "to build for them"; the carpenter needed a permit, however. There was little evidence of gold digging, and the gold diggers were the only white men who could be considered intruders. Gardiner thus thought a permanent guard unnecessary, detachments sent from time to time being sufficient for the service required.

This apparently satisfied Swain, who advised that he considered the object of the expedition accomplished. There were further reports of troop movements on the Cherokee lands, but nothing more. The military authorities would remain happy to receive any instructions "touching our duties in this quarter" and would continue to advise Swain of anything important.[46]

While dealing with trespasses on Cherokee lands, Swain was also attempting to establish their boundaries for purposes of a federal court suit. Romulus Saunders, North Carolina's attorney general, was doing research and advising the governor from Washington. In probing the line run in 1797 as provided by the Cherokee Treaty of 1791, Saunders had found nothing having a direct bearing on the question. A 1798 report by the secretary of war, in obedience to a resolution of Congress, shed some light on the issue.

Swain agreed that the document illuminated the article in the Treaty of Tellico defining the boundaries of the Cherokee Nation. For possible use at trial, he urged Saunders to secure a copy of the report and the letters upon which it was founded. He had earlier advised the surveyor, again for possible trial use, to keep "a full and regular journal of your proceedings." The interests of the state required a map of the Cherokee boundary lines, he advised in requesting one from the Agent of the Cherokee Nation, guaranteeing its careful preservation and return when the suit ended.[47]

Joshua Roberts, the surveyor, forwarded to Swain a letter from Andrew Pickens, former governor of South Carolina, showing that he possessed an original commission appointing commissioners, including his father, "to run and mark the Indian boundary lines agreeably to the Treaty of Holston." Pickens volunteered to send the commission provided it was returned following use. Viewing the document as important to the interests of the state, Swain was pleased. He hoped Pickens possessed other papers connected with the boundaries that would elucidate questions arising out of the treaty and the practice under it. Pickens forwarded the commission.

Swain also sought material relevant to the suit from the governors of Georgia and Tennessee. He received copies of communications on the subject from the Cherokee Removals and Acting Indian Agent. Secretary of War Cass failed to locate a map Swain thought had been in Cass's office as late as 1812, but he referred Swain to sources of possible enlightenment.[48]

Swain frequently communicated with the General Assembly on Indian matters, reporting particularly on the reasons for his actions, or lack thereof, related to the Cherokee lands suit. The General Assembly had directed sale of the lands acquired by treaty from the Cherokees as he thought proper. No course of action, he had found, was free from difficulty. The lands had been diminishing in value due to trespasses by squatters and others; this furnished strong inducement to dispose of them immediately. Counsel for the state was convinced, however, that any agreement at that time would only "create additional embarrassments." Among the plaintiffs in the suit were married women and infants whom no agreement could bind. Should decision be in their favor, claimants of full age would be entitled to the money and bonds received of the purchasers. The state thus could not satisfy both classes of claimants. It perhaps should sell within the year, Swain thought, but he did not consider himself so authorized absent repeal of a certain resolution.[49]

As to the greater issue of removal of Cherokees from the state, Swain was a supporter, or at least an endorser, of the desire for removal on the part of the state's citizens. Both Secretary of War Cass and Congressman Carson received his endorsement. The state was "interested in the removal," Swain told Cass. Although the legislature had made few representations to the general government, it was "not because such an event is not ardently desired by her citizens." It would not be long until the citizens largely got their wish.[50]

In this and other instances Swain declined to exercise his constitutional power to "embody the militia for the public safety." His position as its "captain-general and commander-in-chief" imposed responsibilities, however. Once at a Mecklenburg Declaration of Independence celebration, he reviewed two thousand militia under the command of General Thomas G. Polk.[51] The organization could be more efficient, he once told the General Assembly, if the burdens sustained mainly by the poor and middle classes were reduced by exempting militia men from service earlier in life. If a proper degree of military science were disseminated among the members, he thought, the organization could be more efficient.[52]

Swain had regular administrative duties related to the militia. Requests for blank commissions for officers were common. Inadmissible political beliefs could disqualify for such. A commission as captain of cavalry was once sought for a militiaman; it had previously been issued to another, Swain was informed, "but on account of his being a *Nullifier* the company have nullified him."[53]

Requests for arms were common. The General Assembly had authorized the governor to receive a part of the public arms for cavalry, wrote one applicant; how soon could such be procured for new companies being formed in Greene and Pitt counties? The governor's private secretary soon advised that the order for arms "now will be complied with." Another plea sought arms for cavalry sufficient to equip forty troopers; still another, to equip thirty-two dragoons exclusive of non-commissioned officers.[54]

There were inquiries as well as requests. One correspondent noted two brass field pieces loaned to the Wilmington artillery and ordered returned by the Ordnance Office in Washington, unless state authorities agreed to receive them as part of the arms of the state. At its own expense, paid mostly by one member, the artillery had them mounted. It would be a pity to give them up and would jeopardize the company "which is now with difficulty kept up." Swain was accommodating. He would accept the pieces as a portion of the quota of arms due the state under an 1808 act of Congress, and they could remain in their present location.[55]

Delinquency charges came to the governor, at times in lists,[56] at others as individual matters. They appear, at least mostly, to relate to failures to file required reports. The alleged malefactors generally viewed them with seriousness. One sent Swain a certificate showing deposit in the Warrenton Post Office; he trusted it would "be a satisfactory refutation of the neglect of duty with which I am charged." The statement and certificate, the governor replied, were entirely satisfactory.[57] Another had been away from home and had not received the pertinent forms; he had made them at the first opportunity and could not believe this could be considered a neglect of duty.[58]

Finally, Swain was the state's point person on militia-related questions from the federal government. The adjutant general assisted him in responding to one set from the Department of State: 65,599 men were required to serve three days each year, the general advised; there were two regiments of volunteers uniformed and armed at their own expense, and light infantry companies attached to the several regiments of regular militia. Another request from the Department of State sought the numerical strength of the militia at specified periods. Swain forwarded some requested information and promised more upon receipt.[59] Swain regularly received such communications from federal officials. It was customary for the U.S. secretary of state to send him documents from sessions of Congress, with sets for the executive, both legislative houses, and the university. When Swain discovered that records of a session were missing, ever the historian, he requested them.[60]

The mail ran north as well as south. Swain transmitted to the president and members of Congress reports, resolutions, and memorials adopted by the General Assembly. He requested and received from the secretary of state copies of reports and surveys. In contemplation of a revision of the state's assessment laws, he sought a copy of an 1815 assessment on which the federal government had collected a tax.[61]

The most common federal communications requested information about the state. There were requests for population figures on whites, enslaved persons, and free persons of color; the number of state courts and their post offices; missing portions of the state's statutes; information on the state's banks; books and documents relating to the Revolutionary services of North Carolina troops; and the governor's name and date of appointment.[62]

Pride in the country and its republican form of government was once at stake. U.S. Secretary of State Edward Livingston told Swain a controversy had arisen "of some interest to the reputation of our country, and which may affect that of representative government everywhere." The assertion had been made that U.S. citizens paid more taxes in proportion to population than did French subjects. From this came the facile conclusion that republican governments were more expensive than monarchical ones. Livingston was collecting "facts that may elucidate this question" and sought information on North Carolina's taxes, state and local, and its expenditures for education, internal improvements, and other governmental services. There was no appropriation; he appealed to the public spirit of the letter's recipient.[63]

Swain soon acknowledged Livingston's request and pledged to adopt the most effectual means to obtain the information. Information he had acquired for the Edenton District while a judge he forwarded immediately, together with general facts regarding the state's revenue; Livingston found this knowledge valuable and wished for a "corresponding spirit" elsewhere. Swain followed by seeking statistical data regarding the state from the treasurer, county court clerks, superior court judges, and North Carolina's congressional delegation.[64]

In dispatching the data he had gathered, Swain was modest, perhaps overly so. Securing information on which one could rely with confidence was, he said, impossible. Only fifty of the sixty-four county clerks had responded to his inquiries. The statements regarding taxes he thought sufficiently accurate for practical purposes; those on religion, "in a great degree conjectural."

Swain's modesty aside, the report presents an excellent, if somewhat incomplete, profile of the North Carolina he was governing. The state taxed real estate, polls (individuals), stallions, merchants, individuals exhibiting natural or artificial curiosities, "Negro traders," bank stock, billiard tables, and gates permitted by law across public roads. Counties taxed land and polls exclusively, and taxes varied from county to county. There was no tax for religious purposes, and it was impossible to ascertain the amount of voluntary religious contributions. The state had active Baptist, Methodist, Presbyterian, and Episcopalian congregations; there were four or five Roman Catholic chapels and a dozen Quaker meeting houses. More than sixty-five thousand militiamen devoted approximately three days per year to instruction in military tactics and provided their own arms and equipment. Two regiments of volunteers were armed and equipped at their own expense.

Swain followed Treasurer William Mhoon's lead on education, stating, "No children have yet been educated at the public expense." He proceeded, though, to discuss the Literary Fund and the taxes contributed to it. "When it shall become sufficiently large for this purpose," he concluded with anticipation and pride, "the annual income will be expended in the maintenance of free schools."

It must have disappointed him to admit that no state tax had been appropriated, and no debt incurred, for internal improvements. A fund for such had been established, however, with dividends from bank stock and proceeds from sales of Cherokee lands; and a board had been created to administer it. He noted that a large portion of the meager sums that had been devoted to this purpose had been "either wastefully or improvidently" spent.

Except for small loans from its own banks, all of which had been repaid, the state had incurred no debt since adoption of the U.S. Constitution. Its bridges had been constructed and kept in repair by the counties in which situated, with a few built by individuals and corporations. With a few exceptions—clergy and physicians, for example—all free males, and all male enslaved persons between ages sixteen and fifty, were "liable to work upon the public roads." Using the 1830 census, each white inhabitant's share of the state's total wealth was about $347.00. The state's one university and several seminaries of learning received passing mention, as did the political and other newspapers published in the state.

Swain's earlier information brought gratitude from the Department of State. If his level of cooperation were general, a spokesman wrote, the department would have little trouble presenting a work of general statistics on the country. The governor now tendered more extensive intelligence, with a willingness to examine any other points of inquiry that suggested themselves. The department appears to have been quite satisfied, however.[65]

Over Swain's administrations, and at his direction, State Attorney General Romulus Saunders was a frequent sojourner in Washington, D.C., researching and lobbying for resolution of the controversy over federal assumption of state debts in the post-Revolutionary War period. At Saunders's request, Swain sent relevant documents to Bedford Brown, one of the state's U.S. senators, and informed Brown that Saunders was the state's agent to solicit payment of its war-service claims. Saunders in turn advised Swain that, at Swain's request, he had examined correspondence between a former governor and the War Department relative to the origins of the state's claims for "militia advances made during the late war." He proposed to return for further examination. Over a year later, however, Saunders spoke of his inability to have accomplished anything further and indicated that it might take many months to examine the papers. He pledged to see the secretary of war on the subject.

Soon, though, Saunders advised Swain that the papers regarding "our militia claim" were not as well organized as could be wished; indeed, there was even confusion about their location. By the adjournment of Congress, he hoped to have them in shape for presentation to the secretary of war; and he remained sanguine about ultimate success, though it would require time and attention. Swain reassured him as to the propriety of his intended course.

Months later Saunders was ready to submit the matter to the secretary of war, but the secretary was absent. A resolution in time to present it to Congress, if necessary, remained possible. In the final year of Swain's administration, Saunders still could not give him a decision. He had spared no opportunity to press upon the secretary his keen desire for one, and he would not fail to advise Swain of it if it came.

Swain made periodic reports to the General Assembly, once enclosing a communication from Saunders on the prospects for adjusting the claims. The Senate appointed a committee that made a detailed report and requested that the governor take such measures as he thought necessary to resolve the claims. Shortly before Swain left office, a War Department correspondent informed him that the bearer of the letter would take charge of such books and documents regarding the Revolutionary War services of North Carolina troops, located in the offices of the federal secretary of state and comptroller, as Swain deemed it proper to loan to the department. This letter is the last item on the subject found in Swain's gubernatorial papers. He left office with the claims unresolved, but not for lack of effort.[66]

Swain also communicated with officials, particularly governors, of other states. He once sought from his gubernatorial colleagues information on the revenues and expenditures of their states and received some replies. The governor of Louisiana requested of him information on North Carolina's expenses, disbursements, and resources. Virginia's governor wanted North Carolina's legislative acts from a session back for his state's public library.[67]

Transmission of session laws from other states to Swain was common.[68] Specific topics could be the subject, among them anticipated damages from a pending tariff bill, an organization of the militias of the several states, the currency and removal of deposits of public money from the Bank of the United States, disposal of federally owned public lands, the call of some states for a convention to amend the U.S. Constitution, and a condemnation of federal appropriations for internal improvements in the several states.[69]

Swain often shared these communications with the General Assembly. Among those shared were resolutions adopted by the New York legislature regarding a more perfect organization of the militia of the United States, by the Pennsylvania legislature relative to the union of the states and the U.S. Constitution, and by the Georgia legislature, both calling for a convention to amend the U.S. Constitution and declaring the federal government's lack of capacity to carry on a system of internal improvements with the several states, or to appropriate money for such. The General Assembly, in turn, would authorize the governor to transmit the state's public laws to the Congress and the several states.[70]

Until his emergence as a national Whig by his third term as governor, Swain tended to be cagey and selective in expressing himself on, or involving himself with, national issues, and with good reason: he had a plate more than full with state problems without adding national ones.

Yet, in the American federal system he inevitably functioned, as state governor, in a national context. Willie P. Mangum, one of the state's U.S. senators, was accurate when he told Swain, "Your position before the people of North Carolina necessarily connects you to a great extent with all those questions."[71]

Swain had barely crossed the threshold of the executive office when "[a]n unexpected debate" occurred in the House of Commons "in which the doctrine of Nullification was incidentally discussed." In response to a request from the governor of South Carolina, Swain had transmitted to the General Assembly the South Carolina nullification ordinance and addresses. According to a contemporary account, "[c]onsiderable feeling was manifested, and much unnecessary warmth created." Ultimately the Assembly referred the papers to a joint select committee.[72]

Almost simultaneously John Hill Wheeler, a North Carolina historian then in the federal government, informed Swain: "Congress is doing nothing of importance, Nullification seems to be the order of the day. No one can tell in what it will end. The President [Jackson] is determined to sustain the laws."[73]

As he focused on his goals for Murphey's internal program, Swain had little appetite for this acrid external controversy. But he could not escape it. He soon was hearing from North Carolina citizens on both sides. In his first month as governor a large assemblage of Beaufort County citizens expressed their opinions on subjects "of high political concernment." A resolution replete with states-rights doctrine, including the alleged rights of states to judge the constitutionality of acts of Congress and declare them void, was adopted. Deference to the state, it held, was the only mode of authoritatively settling the issue. These sentiments, it was resolved, should be communicated to Governor Swain.[74]

Counter convictions came Swain's way from another coastal area community. John C. Ehringhaus, ancestor of a future North Carolina governor, transmitted a resolution adopted "at a Union meeting" in Elizabeth City that decried the nullification movement. The Constitution and Union were menaced, it said, by the South Carolina ordinance, which was revolutionary in character and subversive of the Constitution and "the dearest rights of our citizens."[75]

John Owen, a former governor, saw the specter of civil war "thicken[ing] around us." South Carolina's course, he said, was "worse than mad." Can that state reasonably hope for support from the Southern states? he asked Swain. South

Carolina would receive "but little countenance" from North Carolina, he trusted. It would, he opined, require all of General Jackson's popularity "to ride out the whirlwind and direct the storm."[76] An unidentified correspondent viewed South Carolina's course as "utterly destructive of the Union if persisted in." Swain, he hoped, would not be with the nullifiers. He took comfort in knowing Swain was a favorite of his friend Gaston, who could not be a nullifier.[77]

Swain appears to have been unresponsive to these missives, probably the wisest course at the time. Relief must have been his reaction when a South Carolina friend advised that the storm, a most trying time, was over. From Washington, D.C., Romulus Saunders, the state attorney general, also reassured the governor. Everything there was quiet, he said. This was only the lull before a much greater storm, but Swain and his contemporaries could not have so perceived.[78]

James W. Gwinn, a state legislator from Macon County, solicited Swain's views on the rechartering of the Bank of the United States. There was speculation on Swain's views, Gwinn posited, and it was "going to do [Swain] an injury" if it was not shown that he was "a thorough going Bank man," opposed to the president's course relative to the bank. "This course of politicks in the mountains," Gwinn represented, "won't go down." Macon men were Swain's friends and wanted to be his political supporters, but they needed to know his opinions, and Gwinn wished to "communicate them to my constituents before I start to Raleigh."

Gwinn, Swain responded, appeared to regard him as a candidate for the U.S. Senate, which he was not. He had no objection to communicating his opinions, however, when requested by a friend. Otherwise, "I think that it does not become me as the Governor of . . . North Carolina to occupy such a position and I do not speak or write to any one on the subject who does not first address me."

As to the bank question, Gwinn seemed to have understood his opinions correctly from their earlier conversations. They had not changed. Swain did not doubt the power to establish a national bank but was not anxious to see the present one rechartered, at least not without more modifications than he could reasonably explain. There were more important issues regarding national politics, and he might submit his opinions on them to the General Assembly.[79]

Friends kept Swain abreast of national political maneuvering and its impact in the state. Early in Swain's second term Senator Mangum conveyed the opinion that the ensuing six or eight months would probably settle the next presidency. Van Buren's friends would be exceedingly active, and "[a]ll the resources of that bad influence *around* and *under* and *over* the throne will be actively employed." Henry Clay or Justice John McLean would be the candidate of those opposed to Van Buren in the South. Clay, Mangum thought, had the best chance provided he did not "tread upon our principles." McLean's politics were unknown, and many would not support him until they knew them. Mangum favored kind treatment of President Jackson but the striking of a blow "at the kitchen [Cabinet] and the *policy* of the kitchen."[80]

Unlike Mangum, Swain's brother-in-law D. L. Barringer, a member of the U.S. House of Representatives, brooked no kindness for Jackson. Senator Bedford Brown, a strong Jackson/Van Buren ally, was a particular subject of Barringer's wrath. "[O]ur Brown," he said, "has he become very notoreus, for his puny efforts on behalf of Executive usurpation." Brown, Barringer thought, stood no chance of reelection. Barringer, rather than Brown, would lose his seat in the next election because of his virulent anti-Jackson stance. For the moment his nemesis Brown was on the prevailing side of the political divide.[81]

The state-level impact of the national political scene came to Swain through former Governor James Iredell. Van Buren Jacksonianism was fast declining in all the counties where he had been, Iredell indicated. The people were beginning to feel the scarcity of money arising from the general want of confidence. Merchants could not give them money for their produce because they could not get money for it in New York or Norfolk.[82]

Throughout Swain's tenure as governor partisan political lines in North Carolina were solidifying along this national divide. He had come to the office as a nonpartisan. It was impossible for him to leave it as such. Indeed, it was this that made his final election to the office so difficult and close, as aptly depicted by a very friendly, to the Whigs and Swain, Georgia newspaper. "We have the gratification of announcing the re-election, on yesterday, of DAVID L. SWAIN, as Governor of [North Carolina] . . . after a most violent effort to defeat him," it stated. The effort to defeat him was "a practical commentary" on the principles of Van Buren supporters. They were "driven by a blind enthusiasm" and "regardless of every thing but the advancement of party purposes."[83]

North Carolina's Democrats had become the party of the status quo, satisfied with the condition of the state, content with its Rip Van Winkle status. The Whigs were the party of change, viewing government as a liberating, perhaps motivating, force in the economy. With capital scarce, only government possessed the resources with which to build an infrastructure, mainly transportation facilities, that would open the state to economic opportunities. Despite Swain's nonpartisan instincts and inclinations, the Whig Party was the only philosophically comfortable home for the young mountain governor with his avidly pro-development agenda. Under his leadership the Whigs would become the dominant party of western North Carolina and would remain so until the 1850s.[84]

A national Whig leader was once Swain's choice to represent North Carolina in the U.S. Supreme Court. Supposedly, the state had acquired certain land titles under 1807 and 1809 treaties. The titles were disputed, however, and Swain considered the matter of sufficient import to employ legal counsel of topmost rank. George Badger—destined for President John Tyler's cabinet, the U.S. Senate, and an unconfirmed nomination to the U.S. Supreme Court—represented the state. Swain, however, directed Badger to employ Daniel Webster, Boston lawyer and Whig political figure, as well. Webster was in Ohio when Badger's letter reached Boston; consequently, he was several weeks in responding. Albeit belated, the reply was positive. North Carolina's retaining him in the controversy would give him great pleasure.[85]

For reasons unknown, Swain thought both local and national counsel was needed. The case had been transferred from the federal circuit court to the U.S. Supreme Court. Badger's attendance there was important, Swain instructed him, "uniting with Mr. Webster in the management of the cause." State pride and self-respect demanded local counsel. Swain and the state, Swain told Badger, were "unwilling to rely exclusively on foreign auxiliaries." Deeply affected by Swain's confidence, Badger swallowed his reservations about appearing in the nation's highest court. Swain had overruled these personal considerations, he said; he was bound to defer to Swain's judgment and adopt the course he had prescribed, placing whatever ability he possessed at the command of the state. It was Badger who then forwarded to Webster a $1,000.00 retainer draft.[86]

Swain explained his course to the General Assembly. The principles involved could seriously impact the rights of the state and were not free from difficulty. He thus had secured the services of eminent counsel in the highest tribunal in the Union and recommended that the General Assembly pay them. He had engaged Webster because he thought the magnitude of the causes justified and public opinion demanded it; Badger, because the trial had shown that "there was no other individual who to eminent ability united an accurate acquaintance with all the matters of law and fact involved in the controversy."[87]

Early in Swain's tenure as governor, a citizen posed legal questions for his response, stating, "I don't see why it is not salutary to put a governor in remembrance now and then, that he is a *Lawyer*." Swain's legal training and experience proved advantageous at times as ordinary citizens and lawyers, usually perceiving nowhere else to turn, dropped their problems at the governor's door. One citizen, for example, was attorney-in-fact for a neighbor with a claim to land in Georgia; he was authorized to sell the land and wished to know what Georgia law required to authenticate such a document.[88]

William Gaston asked Swain to check records in the secretary of state's office regarding a poor woman's entitlement to three tracts of land in Tennessee. He needed the information "as soon as practicable." A Stantonsburg lawyer needed to know whether two women of the state had been legitimated. They claimed heir status by virtue of legislative act, an assertion he thought false. Ignorant of the locale of private legislative acts, he addressed the governor on the subject. He would forward a fee when informed of the amount.[89]

An inherited legal problem vexed Swain through much of his administration. The 1831 fire that destroyed the State House severely mutilated a statue of George Washington by the renowned Italian sculptor Antonio Canova. Montford Stokes, Swain's predecessor as governor, had contracted with Robert Ball Hughes, a sculptor based in New York City, for restoration of the statue. Hughes was a procrastinator. A month before Swain assumed the executive chair, Governor Stokes sent Hughes a blistering letter of discontent.

Swain received the first of many communications on this subject within days of becoming governor, not from Hughes, but from another sculptor proposing to do the job.[90] Ignoring this alternative, Swain entered an extensive dialogue with Hughes, who soon defended his "injured reputation" and refuted "an unremitted attack on my character." The charges against him were groundless, he argued, and his conduct was honorable. He stood ready to complete his contract; his only object, in fact, was "a speedy and honorable completion of my agreement with his Excellency [*sic*] the Governor."[91]

Swain eventually acceded to Hughes's request to allow him to do the work in New York City. This brought no productivity, however. He then involved William Gaston, Gaston's New York son-in-law Robert Donaldson, and former North Carolina House Speaker Louis D. Henry in the effort. Still, nothing worked. Ultimately, with executive and legislative concurrence, the state terminated Hughes's contract.

Remediation of Hughes's failure to perform, which spanned the Stokes and Swain administrations, would be slow. In 1963, during the administration of Governor Terry Sanford, a commission contracted with Italian artist Romano Vio to re-carve the work using Canova's original model. In 1970, during the administration of Governor Robert W. Scott, the "duplicate original" arrived in Raleigh and was installed in the capitol rotunda locale designated for it well over a century earlier.[92]

Swain's interaction with the General Assembly in the Hughes matter was uncontentious. This appears characteristic. Swain annually transmitted to the General Assembly the proceedings of the president (himself) and directors of the

Literary Fund. From his other legislative communications, it is evident that this was of special interest to him.[93]

A Senate select committee once asked Swain to inquire whether there had been a "uniformity in the accounts produced by the printer" and related matters. Swain responded that he lacked authority to pass on these accounts, that payments were made upon the certificate of a governing board, not upon the governor's warrant. As a member of that board, however, he could state that the accounts of the printer had been compared with those of his predecessor to ensure uniformity, and he recalled no accounts having passed the board that were not reduced to some extent.[94]

When the 1834 winter session of the state supreme court was commencing, the comptroller of public accounts occupied the space the court had used as a courtroom since destruction of the State House. Swain advised the General Assembly that it alone had authority to provide other accommodations. A joint select committee was established to respond.[95]

The 1833 General Assembly authorized the governor to have stones placed at the graves of legislators interred in Raleigh. In late 1834, Swain informed the General Assembly that this had been done for four members, and he transmitted vouchers for same. He reported a sparsity of space for future burials and presented the question whether a public lot should be set aside for such future interment. He inquired, too, about including the heads of departments. The House proposed referral to the committee on finance, with which the Senate concurred. That committee recommended that Moore Square be appropriated for the burial of those public officials "who may die near the seat of Government"; the secretary of state was to have suitable markers placed, with the public treasurer to pay upon warrant of the governor.[96]

On one occasion the House requested information on whether grants had been issued under an act giving two named individuals mineral-development rights in the state's mountain region, and on what use they had made of those rights. Swain responded that Joseph Henry, a House member from Buncombe, had superintended a survey of the lands; that plats had been filed in the secretary of state's office, but grants had not been issued. He denied any skill in mineralogy and had not yet consulted a professor of this science. "The anticipation of the Commissioners seem [sic] not to be of the most flattering character," he concluded.[97]

Finally in this regard, it appears that the state seal wore out during Swain's governorship. The General Assembly authorized him to procure a new one. It almost simultaneously, however, rejected a measure to authorize the governor to procure and transmit acts of the General Assembly in certain cases.[98]

Then as now, both public ceremony and private entertainment invoked the governor's active participation. Fayetteville citizens invited Swain to join in their July 4, 1833 celebration. Their kindness on a former occasion, Swain responded, made "a renewal of these associations particularly desired." Raleigh, however, was celebrating the National Jubilee and considering subjects of interest to him and others. Delegates from throughout the state would be present, and he had pledged his attendance to "concentrate ... energies ... upon a system of Internal Improvements." He thus declined, with appropriate gratitude to the citizens of Fayetteville.[99]

Swain also would be laying the cornerstone of a new capitol building that day. Representing the building committee, Judge Henry Seawell presented him with documents and coins for deposit therein, to transmit to "distant posterity" a portion of their country's history. The day was chosen, Seawell said, because "[o]n this day more than half a century ago, the great master workmen, all of whom now sleep in death [Charles Carroll of Maryland, the last surviving signer of the Declaration of Independence, had died the previous November], laid the corner stone of our country's freedom."

Simple grandeur worthy of the state would characterize the structure, Swain responded, and posterity would hail it "as a proud specimen of the taste and public spirit of their fathers." He noted the day of national jubilee and the deposit of memorials to "the first effort of the people to achieve their independence;—the first legislative declaration of the rights of man." North Carolina was being "true to herself," he continued, "and her sons emulous of their ancestral glory."[100]

Later that year Thomas D. Singleton, congressman-elect from South Carolina, died while passing through Raleigh. A committee of citizens made suitable arrangements for Singleton's interment, and Governor Swain headed the dignitaries in the procession to the grave. In another funereal setting he served as a pallbearer for William Polk, one of Raleigh's leading citizens.[101]

When Joseph Gales retired as publisher of the *Raleigh Register*, Swain presided at a public dinner honoring him at Raleigh's Eagle Hotel. Nearly every respectable Raleigh citizen attended, as did a number of Gales's friends from a distance. Swain delivered the principal address at a memorial service in honor of Lafayette. In his last year in office, he was a speaker at a Mecklenburg Declaration of Independence celebration in Charlotte.[102]

Former Governor John Owen apparently anticipated the entertainment demands to which Swain would be subjected. Owen advised that he had obtained his wines and liquors from Wilmington, but he thought Swain could get them from Fayetteville on equally good terms. Owen also advised on where to obtain a carriage. Swain indeed entertained. During one legislative session he gave "a great *to do*" with about five hundred guests invited. On another occasion he requested Commoner William A. Graham's company for tea at 8:00 p.m. on New Year's Eve.[103]

He also received entertainment. Colonel Nathan Blount's house could be his when he was in Greenville. A court-going William Gaston would visit the executive office to invite the governor to dinner. An evening with Gaston's family delighted Swain even when Gaston was ill. The illness precluded Gaston's traveling to Beaufort with Swain, to the latter's benefit, Swain said, in that he received attention that otherwise would have gone to Gaston. Finally, Swain was among many dignitaries present at dinner parties for Chief Justice John Marshall during his circuit court sessions in Raleigh.[104]

Considering the myriad tasks that confronted Swain as governor, it is little wonder that he told Gaston he could not do anything as it should be done. Clearly, though, he considerably exceeded Gaston's minimalist expectations. Other than granting reprieves and pardons, Gaston had said, the governor only needed to be "a gentleman in character and manners and exercise a liberal hospitality."[105] Governor David Swain fulfilled that role, but he did much more. His was an activist administration, uncharacteristically so for his time. He dispatched the daily tasks of governance, which considerably exceeded the mere granting of reprieves and pardons, while simultaneously articulating and advancing a progressive vision for the state's future.

CHAPTER 6

Constitutional Reform
"We will ... pull down the pillars of the political temple"

Constitutional reform was an overarching issue in the Swain administration. The object long antedated Swain's governorship, indeed, predated his entire life. Rooted in the antidemocratic features of the 1776 North Carolina Constitution, it was an unfortunate and uncorrected dimension of the state's Revolutionary heritage, one that rendered sectional divisions and hostilities inevitable: this, too, when relinquishment of the state's "Rip Van Winkle" status was improbable absent unity of purpose and action.

The Declaration of Rights of the state's first constitution commenced with the revolutionary statement of political theory "[t]hat all political power is vested in, and derived from, the people only."[1] In reality, however, it was vested in only some of the people. Enslaved persons, women, and holders of less than a requisite amount of property were excluded. The 1830s agitation for reform came not from these omitted peoples, however, but from those subjected to regional or sectional discrimination. Truly popular government had never, in actuality, been even an ideal in the state.

The 1776 constitution made the counties and certain towns (Edenton, New Bern, Wilmington, Salisbury, Hillsboro, and Halifax, the relatively urban areas) the basis for representation in both houses of the General Assembly. Each county had one member in the Senate and two in the House of Commons. Each of the towns chosen for borough representation had one member of the House of Commons. Population (except for the borough representatives), geographical dimension, and wealth had no bearing.[2]

The county basis of representation placed controlling power in the East, the older, more settled section, with the larger number of counties. Property qualifications for officeholding narrowed the ruling elite still further, making eastern landowners the dominant class and giving them control of the state. The West came to have most of the state's white population, but the state government continued to be administered largely for the benefit of the East.

Naturally, the West grew increasingly embittered. Its vital economic interests, particularly the need for transportation facilities connecting it with the East, demanded a larger beneficence from, and involvement with, the state.

It was not an insignificant disparity. According to one analysis, probably at least essentially accurate, of the state's sixty-four counties, thirty-six were east of Raleigh. They contained only 41 percent of the state's voting population but sent 58 percent of the members of the General Assembly to Raleigh. Their voting population was only 8.7 percent of the state's total white-male population, but it chose most of the General Assembly and thus controlled the state government.[3]

Shortly before Swain took office, William Gaston aptly described the factionalized context in which he would govern. Gaston saw a quintuple division of the state. The largest party, but less than a majority, he denominated "the Eastern." It supported rebuilding the capitol at Raleigh but opposed a convention in any form. The next in magnitude, "the Western," wanted only "a reconstruction of our Constitution with respect to political power." It would keep the government at Raleigh or remove it to Fayetteville, whichever would promote the greater end of redistribution of political power. The third, "the Fayetteville," had removal of the capitol as its main object but was also willing to approve a general convention. The remaining two, described as "of about the same magnitude," were "the No. Western" and "the So. Western." The first wanted modification of the constitution and opposed removal, while the second sought removal but resisted constitutional change. Gaston's bottom line was, "The Eastern party with the slightest assistance from the others can do as they will."[4]

Earlier attempts at correction proved unavailing. An occasional new county created in the West was offset by additional counties in the East. The East was intransigent and had long maintained its stranglehold on the state's political life. A mountain correspondent's expression to Swain exemplified the resulting attitude of westerners. "[O]ne part of the state," he said, "Rules all the Rest with a Rod of Iron."[5]

This was hardly news to the youthful governor from the West. At least by the age of twenty, he appears to have been highly cognizant of it. Throughout his life he retained a letter from an Asheville candidate for the 1821 General Assembly that depicted the problem and the western viewpoint it generated. It clearly left an impression on the youth, for as a man and the governor of the state, he drew on it when addressing the 1834 General Assembly.

The convention question, wrote the office seeker, had "produced . . . excitement" and could no longer remain "at rest" in a republic the majority governed. When this was not the case, "perfect liberty and equality of rights [were] not enjoyed." One man in several eastern counties had as much influence in the legislature as eight in Rowan County. The minority thus ruled the majority in the western part of the state whenever its interest or caprice so inclined it. He thus favored a convention.[6]

The following year, while a law student and observer of the legislative process, Swain addressed the issue. Should the convention question "be again agitated," he hoped western members would "give convincing proof to the east that talent and acquirement are not... found on the seashore alone." As convening of the session neared, he anticipated "a warm struggle" on the question.

Soon the creation of Davidson County out of northeastern Rowan temporarily mollified the West. Swain was congratulatory toward "the conventionists in the West," whose proceedings had "done some good." The convention question would not, he predicted, be brought forward in that session. "The magnanimity of some of our eastern brethren in supporting the bill for the division of Rowan will appease the wrath of the western members for a season," he thought.[7]

The pacification was for a season only, however. When Swain became governor a decade later, the disparity remained, and the issue yet rankled. Given the new governor's long interest in the issue, it seems surprising that he did not attack it immediately. He was an astute politician, however, and it is a reasonable assumption that his sense of timing suggested awaiting a more propitious moment. Too, he had yet to encounter, as chief executive, the frustrations of stalled progress the imbalance produced.

Swain's first legislative session as governor in 1832 witnessed the customary rejection of a bill for constitutional reform. This defeat stimulated greater efforts on the part of the West.

Throughout 1833 Western newspapers and meetings demanded action, but there is no evidence of public participation by the western governor. His 1833 annual message to the General Assembly did not mention the issue.[8] This executive reticence did not escape criticism. A western newspaper complained of his "mysterious silence." He had not even hinted at the subject, leading to the conclusion that he had changed his opinion or had "*other good reasons* for his unexpected reserve."[9]

Swain was moving to mollify this western critique, however. On the same day the newspaper protested his inaction, he dispatched a special legislative message on constitutional reform. He informed the General Assembly of a referendum in which an overwhelming majority favored reform, though votes had been taken in only some of the counties. His opinions had been so frequently expressed and were so generally known that further comment was superfluous. In the referendum he had voted for a convention. He commended the subject to the legislators, reminding them of their power and responsibility to solve the problem. He hoped "a spirit of conciliation and compromise" would direct them.[10]

The 1833 General Assembly again rejected bills to submit amendments on the subject to a vote of the people. The West did, however, achieve passage of an act carving the new county of Yancey from portions of Buncombe and Burke, thereby diminishing the imbalance slightly. More important, some easterners now perceived that the disparity had to be redressed. One eastern opponent of reform commended the westerners' "industry and perseverance" and attributed to these virtues the creation of the new western county, noting Swain's early role.

Swain, he said, had brought the measure to each legislative session beginning in 1825; an eight-year struggle had accomplished the objective, and "a similar result will attend the other, and more important measure."[11] David Outlaw, a House member from the eastern county of Bertie, wrote Swain that he was "one of those both willing and anxious to settle the Convention question." Swain best knew "the views and feelings of the West." He should "state frankly what compromises . . . the West will be willing to accept." Outlaw pledged confidentiality if needed.[12]

Defeat of the internal improvements campaign augmented the demand for constitutional reform. *The Raleigh Register*, a moderate, Swain-friendly paper, used revolutionary rhetoric that Swain would later take up at convention time. Absent redress of the grievances, it posited, "the yeomanry of the West will take the remedy into their own hands." The agitation continued throughout 1834, culminating in Swain's addressing the problem in his annual message to the General Assembly that November.[13]

After recommending a convention as the preferred instrument of constitutional amendment, Swain stated the "great object to be attained"—"a radical change in the basis of representation." He noted that the statesmen of 1787 had considered substituting population or taxation, or a combination of the two, for "the arbitrary principle of county representation," which disregarded population, wealth, and territorial extent. Only Maryland and North Carolina had retained the British idea of equal county representation; other original states had discarded it, and none of the new ones had adopted it.

From the beginning it had been the source of constant contention between the populace and the sparsely settled counties. It subjected the majority to the rule of the minority. Those who paid a lesser portion of the taxes controlled "the entire resources of the country." Correct this, Swain exhorted, and "you will achieve a triumph of inestimable importance, and entitle yourselves to the lasting gratitude of posterity."[14] This address converted at least one of the governor's critics. The formerly captious western newspaper called it an "able state paper," which "excite[d] a hope that this 'vexed question' will now be amicably settled."[15]

The hope was attained, but not without difficulty. Legislative margins on an election to call a convention were thin: 66 to 62 in the House, and 31 to 30 in the Senate, where four eastern members courageously joined all those from the West in favor. The people's vote was, as expected, heavily positive in the West and equally heavily negative in the East. The outcome was positive, however: 27,550 for, 21,694 against, for a majority of 5,856.[16]

Swain took pleasure in directing the attention of the county sheriffs to the referendum. Perfect uniformity of action and universal promptitude would be necessary, he said, to effect the objects contemplated. The General Assembly had directed the governor to have four hundred copies of the acts calling a convention printed for transmission to each county; if any had miscarried, the governor or the *Raleigh Register* newspaper would immediately supply the omission.

Once the referendum carried, Swain ordered an election to be held on May 21, 1835, to select two delegates from each county to the convention to be held in Raleigh on June 1 (it actually began on June 4). Citizens were urged to take this responsibility seriously and not to elect demagogues.[17]

Fortunately for Swain, the legislation contained neither dual-officeholding nor residential limitations on delegate status. Either would have precluded his service. He held the state's highest office and would hardly have surrendered it for a brief, ad hoc assignment, however important. At least since his assumption of a judicial post in 1831, he and his family had resided in Wake, an eastern county, where his views on the convention issue would have been unfavored and his election as a delegate thus unlikely. Absence of residential restrictions, abiding popularity in his county of origin, and the favored status there of his position on the convention issue, combined to enable him to become a delegate from his native Buncombe.[18]

The convention thus convened in Raleigh on June 4, 1835, with Swain positioned to become the recognized leader of the western forces. Unlike most delegates, he could live at home. A three-block walk took him from his mother-in-law's home at the intersection of Blount and Morgan streets, where he and his family resided during his time as governor (the General Assembly was occupying the Governor's Palace while the new capitol was under construction), to the convention site at Raleigh's First Presbyterian Church.

Geographical convenience had a downside, however, in that Swain had to juggle convention service with gubernatorial duties and family responsibilities. The

Raleigh's First Presbyterian Church, building dedicated in 1818, site of Constitutional Convention of 1835.

conflicting summonses on his time and energy became acute when, during the latter days of the gathering, his infant son experienced a critical, ultimately fatal illness. He often missed votes and at least apparently was absent from sessions, not surprisingly considering the other demands on him.[19]

On opening day Weldon N. Edwards of Warren County nominated Swain as chairman pro tem. The motion passed unanimously, and Edwards escorted Swain to the chair. Following members' oath-taking, former governor John Branch nominated Nathaniel Macon, the state's longest-serving member of the U.S. Congress, now retired, to be president of the convention.

Upon unanimous passage Macon briefly addressed the gathering. His long absence from public life, he feared, had rendered him "rusty in the Rules of Proceedings"; he therefore invited correction from his friends.[20] The following day Swain stepped aside as Macon took the chair. Occasionally thereafter, but rarely,

Swain reassumed it. On one occasion he asked to be excused from presiding "as he felt somewhat indisposed."[21]

When the convention declined to employ the public printer as convention printer, Guilford delegate John M. Morehead, a future governor, suggested the need for an audit of the account for printing. Swain disavowed any intent to take part in this debate "except to state a single fact." The principal work of the printer, he said, would be to print and distribute forty or fifty thousand copies of the constitution, as amended, to the state's people. The expense would depend upon the style of printing and other matters. Because the convention could not remain in session until this was done, others than a committee of the convention must necessarily audit the account for this service.[22]

A motion that a committee be appointed to consider how to conduct business left blank the number of members. Swain moved to fill it with the number "13," one from each congressional district. The motion, with Swain's amendment, was adopted. A subsequent amendment changed the number to two from each congressional district, for a total of twenty- six. Swain was appointed to the committee and became its chair.[23]

The convention rebuffed a Swain effort to secure floor space for spectators. He would have so allotted "all the space on the floor east of the outer range of the pillars, together with the galleries." "Filling up the avenues with spectators in hot weather," came the response, "would much incommode the members in their business." It would add to the heat and risk diseases "generated by crowding people too closely together in hot weather." Swain's effort went for naught; spectators would have to be satisfied with gallery space.[24]

Another preliminary skirmish raised Swain's hackles. A delegate sought the number of votes in each county on "the Convention Question." Swain did not object to the information being procured; he believed it impracticable to obtain, however, and irrelevant. The suggestion that the convention had resulted from a "thin vote" offended him. With a single exception, he rebutted, "it was the largest general vote ever." In 1828, 51,776 had voted for presidential electors. The number of votes for and against the convention was 49,244. The convention was Swain's baby, and he was intolerant of any notion that a low turnout of the state's voters had spawned it.[25]

While geographical disparity in legislative representation was the foremost issue, there were others. As noted, the 1776 constitution had granted legislative members to several of the state's towns. Swain pled for retention of some form of borough representation. There should be a plan, he contended, "to secure representation to the large towns . . . and those which might spring up in any section of the State." This could be done without producing great inequality "by withdrawing from the estimate, in the apportionment to the counties, the population and revenue of these boroughs." The large towns, he posited, should not be deprived of their representation.

Hitherto, he continued, sectional differences had prevented legislative action for general improvement. He wished to secure the largest share of intelligence and liberality for the legislative councils. The illustrious borough representatives, living and dead, provided "little reason to disfranchise them." Their united vote had called the convention into existence, and their constituents had been the only supportive easterners. Such representatives and their constituents should not be "the first victims for sacrifice." Without borough representatives, the towns would not find their interests protected. The delegates had come to Raleigh to correct evil, not to destroy good. Their constituents had not sent them "to extinguish the lights which . . . had given the greatest lustre to our public councils."

An opponent of borough representation accused Swain of attempting "to array parties here." A recommendation, which Swain supported, that the House of Commons continue to have representatives from the towns of Edenton, Fayetteville, New Bern, and Wilmington (eliminating Halifax, Hillsborough, and Salisbury) was referred to the Committee of Twenty-Six, which gave it a favorable report. The convention, however, defeated it 73 to 50, with Swain voting with the minority. Borough representation thus met its demise over Swain's opposition.[26]

William Gaston had long represented New Bern in the General Assembly. He was among the borough members Swain had in mind who had given "the greatest lustre to our public councils." Likewise, Swain's regard and affection for Gaston almost certainly influenced his votes against religion-based disqualifications from officeholding.

Section thirty-two of the 1776 North Carolina Constitution provided that "[n]o person who shall deny the being of God, or the truth of the Protestant religion, or the divine authority of either the Old or New Testaments, or who shall hold religious principles incompatible with the freedom and safety of the State, shall be capable of holding any office, or place of trust or profit, in the civil department, within this state."[27] Gaston, a Roman Catholic, had served several legislative terms and was now a supreme court judge. He and his colleagues had rationalized his service on the theory that Catholics did not deny the "truth" as perceived by Protestants, to the extent such could be identified; rather, they adhered to additional beliefs to which Protestants did not subscribe. Even so, the provision produced discomfort, motivating Swain and others to seek its removal or alteration.

When James S. Smith of Orange said he "wished this section to be laid aside as Sleeping Thunder, to be called up only when necessary to defeat some deep laid scheme of ambition," Swain saw potential for arbitrary application. He thus expressed contempt for the concept. Waxing poetic, he "did not like to leave it in the hands of men in power, who might hereafter abuse it, by 'Dealing damnation round the land, On all they deem'd their foe.'"[28]

The published debates omit some Swain commentary on this issue, for they show members responding to remarks of his that are not in this record. Jesse Speight of Greene, for example, requested evidence to support Swain's assertion (not recorded) of a "warlike spirit on the part of Protestants," who were both at war with one another and in combination against Catholics. He countered, citing "the hostility of the Catholics to the Protestants." He might not object, however, to the substitution of "Christian" for "Protestant." No response from Swain appears.[29]

Swain voted for an amendment offered by Weldon N. Edwards of Warren "in effect, allowing freedom of worship and of speech, in all matters of Religion." The amendment failed 87–36. A series of other amendments, all of which would have diluted the religious-disqualification provision, failed by similarly overwhelming votes, with Swain consistently voting in the affirmative.

Swain now conceded that no amendment other than that to substitute "Christian" for "Protestant" was likely to be adopted; he thus encouraged the members to "forebear to offer any further amendment, and act at once on that." One member, however, desired a recorded vote on an amendment "to remove the disqualification for office . . . from all who do not deny the being of a God and an accountability to Him." The amendment failed 80–46, with Swain voting in the affirmative.

Further debate on the proposal followed, with Swain, so far as the record reveals, silent. The committee's recommendation ultimately passed by a vote of 74 to 51, with Swain again in the affirmative. The convention had spent several days on the question, only to reach the meager result of substituting "Christian" for "Protestant" in the religious-disqualification clause. Swain supported the change but would gladly have gone much further.[30]

Prior to the 1835 convention, free Negroes had been eligible to vote in North Carolina. By a vote of 66 to 61, the convention removed that right. It adopted a report "which abrogate[d], *in toto*, the right of free colored persons to vote." Little debate on the question is recorded, none by Swain. He voted in the negative, however. Later he supported an effort to revive the right by subjecting it to a property-ownership qualification, but that too failed.[31]

The convention dealt with several matters of basic governance: The governor would now be chosen for a two-year term, not by the General Assembly, but by citizens qualified to vote for members of the House of Commons, and simultaneously with General Assembly elections. Gubernatorial tenure would be limited to four years in any period of six. Swain neither debated nor voted on the proposition.[32]

The General Assembly, at its first post-1839 session, would appoint an attorney general to a four-year term. If it extended the terms of solicitors, it could extend the attorney general's to the same period. Swain called for the ayes and nayes on one vote on the subject, which passed 87 to 24 over his vote in the negative.[33]

Dual officeholding was prohibited. The holder of an office or place of trust in the federal or state government could not concurrently hold another under the authority of North Carolina or be eligible for service in its General Assembly. Officers in the militia and justices of the peace were excepted. Swain, almost certainly with his late father's career in mind, argued that the provision was overly broad in that it would exclude postmasters, even those with small operations. Burgess Gaither of Burke replied that no class of officers was more properly excluded, "for there was none more immediately under the control of the General Government." Joseph J. Daniel of Halifax joined Swain in a willingness to exclude postmasters, but theirs was a lonely position. The section passed with officers of the militia and justices of the peace the only exclusions.[34]

The convention rejected a William Gaston proposal to require that counties with more than two representatives in the House of Commons be divided into electoral districts "of contiguous territory, and of equal federal numbers." A tabling motion, "tantamount to a rejection," passed 77 to 41. Swain joined Gaston in voting "nay" on the tabling motion.[35]

By a vote of 84 to 40, the convention approved a provision that in the election of officers whose appointment the constitution conferred on the General Assembly, the vote shall be *viva voce* (spoken). Swain voted with the minority in the negative.[36]

Regarding annual or biennial legislative sessions, on Swain's motion the convention resolved itself into a committee of the whole. Swain was with the majority in an 85 to 35 vote for biennial sessions.[37]

Finally, debate on future amendments to the constitution spawned sectional conflict. With Swain in the chair, the body considered a report recommending submission to the people of proposed amendments upon the vote of a majority of the whole number of each house of the General Assembly. William B. Meares of Sampson, an eastern county, who had been in the minority on the committee, moved to substitute a three-fifths vote of each house for a mere majority.

Verbal skirmishing ensued, with eastern members basically supporting the more difficult course, and westerners the more lenient. Meares, while denying impetus from sectional feelings, readily acknowledged his opposition to adopting white population as the basis of representation, which "a large portion of the people of North Carolina" (westerners) favored. "To guard against this, was the object of his amendment."

This brought Swain to his feet. Where western interests were involved, he asserted, "Eastern gentlemen [had] a morbid sensibility." He had come to the convention with two objectives: to reform the inequality of representation and to expunge the religious disqualification from the officeholding provision. Against his better judgment and "to appease an idle jealousy," he had voted for the eastern proposition to make the capitation tax equal. The western delegation, to a man almost, had also voted for it, despite misgivings. There was, Swain thought, "much needless solicitude with regard to future amendments of the Constitution."

Charles Fisher of Rowan found Swain's "morbid sensibility" remark readily explainable. For decades the West had sought, and the East opposed, a convention. It was natural, then, that the West should want any easier mode, and the East a more difficult one, for calling future conventions. Such considerations, however, should not influence the present decision, and the causes that produced them should be banished forever. He was opposed to an easy mode of obtaining a convention.

The convention settled on a two-thirds vote of all members of each house to call a convention. A three-fifths vote of each house was required to propose a constitution alteration, subject to a six-months publication prior to a new election of members of the General Assembly, a two-thirds vote of the full membership of each house, submission to the qualified voters for the House of Commons, and approval by a majority thereof. Sectional tensions, however, constituted the real story of the debate; this issue simply brought them to the surface.[38]

Such tensions, indeed, were the raison d'être for the convention itself. Employing one of his many scriptural references, Swain posited that "the great business for which they had assembled was to heal the breach" (see Isaiah 58:12, calling for "repairer[s] of the breach").

Regional disparity in legislative representation was the foremost cause of the East-West breach, and Swain identified it as the "great business" the convention now addressed. The delegates had been sent there "for the express purpose of compromising this question of Representation."[39]

Inability of the West to secure eastern support for economically essential internal improvements, a cause Swain had long championed, was cited in support of a redress of the representational balance. North Carolinians, James Wellborn of Wilkes said, were ashamed to own their place of nativity, and if questioned about it, at least claimed to live "very near the Virginia line!" To assume that the West wanted power was a mistake; what it wanted, instead, was justice, "and it is on that principle that every decision should be made in this body." If the West had power, Wellborn concluded, "a system of Internal Improvements would be commenced, which would change the face of things, and put at once a check to the tide of emigration which is depopulating the State."[40]

Former Governor John Branch of Halifax made the eastern response to Swain and Wellborn. He was prepared to concede as much as possible. The situation of the East, however, was different from that of the West. It was called on to surrender power. Was it not then the duty of gentlemen seeking it to show their entitlement to it? Should not the chairman of the committee (Swain) assign the reasons that brought them to the conclusions developed in their report on proportional representation between Senate and House? They had met "as brethren, and should mutually concede as much as possible, manifesting a spirit of courtesy and kindness."[41]

In responding to Branch, Swain was defensive, impassioned, and in his most radical posture. If he knew his own heart, he stated, no gentleman had come to these deliberations "with less of party or sectional feeling, or more anxious to terminate forever the differences between the two sections of the State, than he." While confident that a correspondent feeling influenced the great body of the convention, he was nevertheless apprehensive as to the result.

Protection of life, liberty, and property was the purpose of government. The "*beau ideal*" of representative government, to Swain, "was perfect protection to *persons* in one branch, and to *property* in the other." He was willing to accept the compromise tendered by the legislature and sanctioned by the people if the duties of the convention should be justly and wisely performed. The interests of both East and West would be well served if this were done, "and thus terminate forever a bootless controversy, which convulsed the Colonial Assembly of 1746, and has been the bane of legislation ever since."

If injustice were done to any large portion of the community, Swain warned in conclusion, the struggles in which they were involved would continue. Indeed, he said, "[t]he general sense of injury will impel the people, as one man, to rend assunder the cords which bind the body politic, and stand forth here, in unshorn might and majesty." An observer portrays a still more radical and defiant Swain. "Let our Eastern brethren beware," he credits Swain with saying, "[i]f they do not grant our peaceful appeal for a change in the basis of representation, we will rise like the strong man in his unshorn might and pull down the pillars of the political temple."⁴²

While uncharacteristically revolutionary and extreme, that Swain said this admits of little doubt. It is confirmed by subsequent remarks from his friend and mentor William Gaston. Testifying to his "highest affection and respect" for Swain, and confident that "no menace was intended," Gaston stated that Swain "in earnest language had predicted that if a satisfactory arrangement were not now made, the People of the West would rise, like the strong man in his unshorn might, and pull down the entire political edifice." In doing so, Gaston reminded his audience, including his youthful protégé the governor from the West, that the strong man "buried *all* beneath one hideous ruin." Should the West violently overthrow the existing constitution, he concluded, "the mad triumph will be a triumph over order and law, over themselves and their friends and their country." The implication was unmistakable: like the strong man, his able and accomplished young friend the governor would emerge from such action "a martyr and a hero" but politically dead beneath the rubble.⁴³

Leaving this gentle but firm rebuke, Gaston conceded that the West had cause for complaint and that "on any principle of free government, the *present* distribution of political power can no longer be upheld." The adjustment sought was "moderate and reasonable," and "[n]o government on earth can be long insensible to the rooted dissatisfaction of a large number, and still less a majority of its citizens."⁴⁴

Other eastern delegates acceded to Gaston's approach, sacrificing narrow regional interests for the greater good of the state and ignoring their eastern President Macon's conviction that "all changes of Government were from better to worse." Each county would now have one representative, rather than two, in the House of Commons. The remaining number of the 120 members would be apportioned by population, giving the more populous West greater representation.

While not achieving full equity according to population, the improvement for the West was considerable. Earlier Swain had stated that he "was willing to accept the compromise... if the duties of [the] Convention should be justly and wisely performed." He apparently was satisfied that they had been, for he voted for the Report of the Convention containing the entire package of amendments, which was adopted 81 to 20. The twenty dissenters, including Macon, all represented eastern counties. The West was satisfied and wished to submit the proposal to the voters of the state sooner rather than later. Swain thus joined two other western delegates in active and successful opposition to an eastern delegate's motion to postpone the vote from November 1835 until March 1836.⁴⁵

Swain had been "anxious to terminate forever the differences between the two sections of the State."[46] This was an unrealistic aspiration. Under his leadership, however, the state had taken significant steps in that direction, and he and his western allies left the convention with a considerable sense of success and satisfaction.

Swain gained in stature from the convention, both with his peers and in historical perspective. Thomas I. Faison, a Sampson delegate, informed him later that there he "formed a favourable opinion of you which I have entertained ever since[,] believing you to have a noble and generous heart." The convention was the arena, writes one historian, in which Swain greatly extended his ascendancy in North Carolina; and with the single exception of Judge Gaston, he was the most powerful and useful member of the body.[47]

William Gaston credited Swain for the West's success and thought the effects of the convention "for weal or woe are probably to be felt for ages." Although dissatisfied with aspects of the convention's product, he advocated its ratification "not because the project is unexceptionable—but because it is decidedly better than any which can be obtained hereafter if this chance be lost."[48]

Swain soon sought a fair price for publication of ten thousand copies of the act to amend the constitution, and twenty-six thousand in octavo form, as ordered by the General Assembly. He issued a proclamation submitting the amendments to the people for a vote on the second Monday in November next. Polls were to be opened for three successive days to all citizens eligible to vote for members of the House of Commons. County sheriffs were to certify the results on the Monday following the election and to transmit them to the governor within twenty days thereafter.[49]

A Raleigh newspaper reported a perception of "great unanimity" in the western counties in favor of ratification. "If the West turn out in their strength," it speculated, "there is but little doubt they will carry the day."[50] Swain, however, did not relax. That eastern voters would oppose the amendments was certain, and there was legitimate fear of defections by westerners less than fully satisfied with the proposals. Swain thus traveled to his native county of Buncombe for a public address imploring a favorable vote.[51]

One unpleasant task remained for him. Some sheriffs failed to report the returns from their counties, forcing Swain to request their immediate attention to the matter. When complete returns were in, however, the amendments had prevailed by a vote of 26,771 for, 21,606 against, for a majority of 5,165. Only twenty-nine counties had a majority in favor, while thirty-nine reported a majority against. Every eastern county save one, Granville, voted to reject, while every western county supported ratification.[52]

On December 3, 1835, Governor Swain issued a proclamation declaring that the amendments had "become part of the Constitution of the State, and [would] be in full force and effect from and after the first day of January, eighteen-hundred and thirty-six." He then forwarded the secretary of state's certificate of the vote in the several counties to the General Assembly.[53]

When he issued the proclamation, one week remained of Swain's tenure in the governor's office. The inequitable treatment of his native West in the councils of the state had been a significant irritant throughout his public life. Securing substantial redress for it was probably the most important and enduring of his many public services and the highlight of his time as governor.

At times the mantle of administrative responsibility weighed heavily on Swain's shoulders. E. J. Hale, editor of the Fayetteville paper, once asked him, "Must I infer . . . that the cares of office bear so heavily on you as to render these days less happy than those in which I had the pleasure of seeing you more frequently than at present?" "If so," Hale continued reassuringly, "let it console you that you are laboring for the good of your native state, which can never forget the earnestness and grace with which you advocate her best interests."

William Gaston offered similarly cheering wisdom and advice at a difficult time for his young protégé. "To a man of sensibility, who is desirous to do his country service," said Gaston, "nothing can be more stinging than those caluminiest injurious suspicions which his base and profligate opponents put into circulation in order to remove him out of their way. But he who has engaged in his country's cause must make up his mind to endure, and if possible to despise those annoyances. It is certain that their evil is greatly exaggerated by allowing the imagination to dwell on them." There were few persons living for whom he entertained "a more affectionate respect," Gaston said.

Without question Governor Swain had opponents, even enemies. John Owen, a predecessor in the office, once warned him not to let "our sanguine friends throw us off our guard." "We have a wily foe to contend with," Owen persisted, "and some of them are quite as sanguine of success as we can be." Keep an eye on House Speaker Julius Alexander in particular, Owen advised; he would do all he could against Swain and was not to be trusted. Alexander, Owen concluded, was "a bad man and an ugly Christian."[54]

There were others, opponents and enemies. In the internal improvements debates, there was opposition to him in the Hillsboro and Roanoke River regions. Two newspapers, the *Western Carolinian* in Salisbury and the *Free Press* in Tarboro, frequently expressed opposition to him. By the time Swain left office, the legislature that had elected him governor three times was dominated by a majority opposed to him politically. His political opponents, indeed, controlled the state. Partisan politics had become so acute as to diminish, if not destroy, his former capacity for maintaining good personal relationships even with political opponents.[55]

Praise for Swain undoubtedly irked his detractors, and he received it. They would have found discomforting this commentary from a Wilmington paper: "So far as sincere respect and genuine good feeling toward him can gratify Governor Swain, he will not go away dissatisfied—these sentiments, we believe, are unanimously entertained in this quarter. We do not recollect of ever having felt a deeper love and veneration for the Republican manners of our countrymen, than we experienced during the Governor's visit. In him were found politeness without affectation, and dignity without vain pride; and on the part of the people, respect without awe, and friendship without flattery."[56]

This, from another paper, would also have induced their frowns: "Governor Swain is ardently and entirely devoted to his country in general, to his native State in particular; he is a zealous and competent advocate of constitutional law and liberty; an avowed enemy to usurpation and ignorant misrule, and the very opposite of a corrupt partisan, who would sell his country and deny his God for a smile from the man in power, or for the emoluments of office."[57] His enemies would not have cared for the tokens of esteem that came his way while governor, such as honorary membership in the Washington National Monument Society and the Franklin Literary Society of Randolph Macon College.[58]

Largely favorable judgments from the court of history would likewise have displeased them. Swain "present[ed] every quality that can dignify our nature," wrote one historian, admittedly his friend, shortly after his death. Later historians would echo the thought, however. He distinguished himself as one of the state's most progressive governors, said one. The editors of Governor William A. Graham's papers viewed him, as governor, as "a constructive figure of the first rank." A biographer credited him with starting a trend to make the governor the political leader in the state government.[59]

R. D. W. Connor, historian of North Carolina and first U.S. archivist, held a highly positive view of Swain and his gubernatorial administration. Connor viewed Archibald Murphey as the visionary but saw Swain as the pragmatist with the interpersonal skills essential to implementation of Murphey's vision of progress for the state: economic development largely through internal improvements, resulting in revenues sufficient to support universal public education. Swain's tact, personality, and forthrightness, Connor posits, led to abandonment of the old laissez faire policy, which the historian Thomas Carlyle called "anarchy plus a constable," and that had so long characterized North Carolina legislation. Swain thus is entitled, in Connor's view, to a high place among the progressive governors of North Carolina.[60]

Carolyn Daniel (later Wallace) reached similar conclusions. Swain was, in Daniel's view, one of the state's most outstanding governors and enlightened statesmen. He started the trend to make the governor a political leader, not a mere functionary performing legislatively prescribed, ministerial tasks, and he enhanced the vitality of the governor's office. The people of North Carolina, Daniel posited, "gave a clear verdict of approval to Swain when they elected governors who, like him, were active leaders, constructive statesmen, and staunch Whigs."[61]

On December 10, 1835, Richard Dobbs Spaight Jr. took his oath as governor, with Swain, now denominated "the late Governor," in attendance. Swain had defeated Spaight for the office in 1832, and it is unlikely that Spaight's election as his successor pleased him. It is almost certain, however, though admittedly speculative, that Swain was thoroughly courteous and cooperative in facilitating the transition. Anything less would have been inconsistent with his basic nature and habitual conduct.

Swain must also have had a grudging respect for the persistence and resilience that had brought Spaight to the position. His friend William Gaston reflected this when he informed his daughter that her "old friend Governor Spaight is at *length* elected Governor." "His is a remarkable instance indeed," said Gaston, "of what may be effected by perseverance."[62]

The fate of the governor's office under his successor's leadership probably was not Swain's foremost thought as he viewed Spaight's inaugural, however. There was his own future to consider. At the tender age of thirty-four, he was leaving the highest office the state government could offer, and he was constitutionally ineligible to hold it again in the next three years. Having previously served with distinction as a legislator and judge, he had already attained the rare status of a holder of elective office in all three branches of the state's government. Having abandoned his Asheville law practice when he became a judge in 1831, he could not have been anxious to rebuild it after a period of full-time public service.

A seat in the U.S. Senate, the next logical step for a state-level political figure, had been explored but abandoned. Swain had been considered for such as early as 1829, when he did not yet meet the constitutional age requirement of thirty. Again in 1830, when he would have met the age requirement by the time for taking the office, his name was mentioned, and he had some support.[63]

In 1834, the prospect of a Senate seat was more serious, yet ultimately failed, complicating Swain's bid for reelection as governor. Willie P. Mangum, then a

U.S. senator from North Carolina, had raised the possibility. In a flattering letter regarding national issues, Mangum told Swain the country was entitled to "the influence of your great popularity & weight of character in the pending struggle [the 1836 presidential election]." Swain, Mangum said, could do more than any man in North Carolina for the Whig cause, and "without seeming to mingle in the strife." If Swain's program of internal improvements found favor with the public, which Mangum doubted, Swain might "find it to the advantage of the public, as well as most conducive to your reputation and fame, to which no good man can be insensible, to remain in your present position." Absent such, however, Swain's friends would "most probably turn their eyes upon you to take your position in the Senate of the U. States." Mangum admitted a personal interest in having in the Senate "one who holds your principles in the main." The threat of Van Buren's election was an "emergency" in which, Mangum urged Swain, "the country has a right to the influence of your name and character."[64]

Mangum must have shared this view more widely, for he soon heard a contrary view from a Swain detractor. The writer expressed his closeness to, and support for, Bedford Brown, the incumbent, avowing that his support for Brown was all the stronger "when David L. Swain is to be the man who is to supplant him." Mangum, he knew, had "disapproved my course toward that *Judas* in the Hillsborough convention" (apparently the writer had supported Thomas Ruffin over Swain for chair of the Hillsborough Internal Improvements Convention). "When you come to act with him as it has been my fortune to do—and which I fear it will be yours ere long—you will then have realized all I have said of him, and to him," the writer concluded—hardly a ringing endorsement for a Swain Senate candidacy.[65]

Critics and skeptics notwithstanding, Swain continued to be viewed as the foremost alternative to Brown. Richmond M. Pearson was certain that Swain alone could take on Brown "with much certainty of success"; he had been taking pains to convince his friends of "this fact." David F. Caldwell believed Swain better qualified for the position than anyone else mentioned. James Graham told his brother, William A. Graham, he hoped Swain would be elected. "I see no reason why he should denounce Jackson or kiss the little toe of any would be President," wrote Graham, "Let him stand erect and bear stiffly up against party manoevers on one side or the other."[66]

William Gaston, as usual, was encouraging. Without any effort on Swain's part, he said, the public attention had been directed to him "as an individual who may be put in nomination for the appointment of Senator." Gaston counseled silence on Swain's part as "most consistent with self-respect." If satisfied the choice probably would fall on him, Swain should not "prohibit your friends from bringing you forward." "A hopeless contest," though, he said, "you ought not to engage in."

In Gaston's view Brown's reelection would be a surprise, and, he concluded, "I know of no person more likely to succeed than yourself." In a later missive sent closer to the election, Gaston acknowledged that Swain himself could best assess his chances of success. "[B]ut if there be a fair prospect," he closed, "and the sacrifice you are called on to make be not too great, I trust that you will permit your name to be used by your friends."[67]

Finally, the usual regional interests surfaced. "To the West," Thomas G. Polk of Rowan told Swain, "you are now looked upon as the individual who ought to be brought out against Mr. Senator Brown." Polk had met with "gentlemen" from several western counties regarding the course the West should pursue in the election. Macon and Haywood counties, he said, had elected representatives friendly to President Jackson but adverse to Van Buren. They would support Swain over Brown, it was thought. The same was true in Anson County except for one senator who had always been anti-Jackson. Some pledged to Swain against Brown were admittedly soft in their support and might defect if another candidate were presented.[68]

Ultimately Democrats concentrated their efforts on defeating Swain. One writer invoked support for Brown rather than "one who has been sitting on the fence and is just ready to take his stand with the stronger party, regardless of its principles." Swain was remaining silent, indeed not wishing to alienate his prior supporters on both sides of the emerging and rapidly coalescing political divide.

On November 20, 1834, the voting commenced. Henry Seawell nominated Swain, but at the urging of Swain's friends and almost certainly with his blessing, withdrew the nomination.[69] Thus, as Swain witnessed his gubernatorial successor's oathtaking ceremony, there was no U.S. Senate seat awaiting him in the foreseeable future (the subject would arise again). Absent such, five days earlier the still Whig-dominated University of North Carolina Board of Trustees had elected him to succeed the late Joseph Caldwell as president of the university.[70] As noted, Swain had barely paused as a student in Chapel Hill before departing to study law under Chief Justice John Louis Taylor. He had no degree, was not a prominent scholar, and a life in academic administration was uncharted territory. His mind thus almost certainly strayed from the solemn occasion of state before him to the more immediate and personal question of how he would fare in his next undertaking.

In his final address to the General Assembly as governor, Swain stated that when his term ended, he would "retire from the active and responsible duties of public life to comparative quiet and seclusion."[71] It is reasonable to doubt that he really wished for or expected that. If perchance he did, he was to be severely disappointed.

Academic Leader

Pre-1847 campus view, University of North Carolina.

CHAPTER 7

The University of North Carolina
"A pleasant, almost timeless rhythm"

CHAPEL HILL, DECEMBER 1835. A sleepy town in a sleepy state, though arguably at least, less so than before David Swain became governor. A town with one store, one practicing physician "whose saddle-bags contained all the physic of the neighborhood," no schools, no churches, no pastors, no lawyers.[1]

Home of the first public university in the United States to open its doors to students, which it had done in 1795 (Georgia had chartered a university earlier but opened it later). With fewer than one hundred students, still quite small, despite forty years of enrollment. While "public" as constitutionally and legislatively established, lacking financial support from state appropriations. Although in theory open to all white male citizens of the state, in reality largely limited to sons of the professional, mercantile, and planter classes: no women; no African Americans, most of whom were still in bondage; no Native Americans; and few from financially deprived families.

The president, newly arrived on December 11, was not a complete stranger to the quiet village. His earlier presence as a student at its university had been ephemeral. Almost four years as a university trustee had brought him back, however. He had strolled the small campus as a member of the trustees' visiting committee and had joined an overflow crowd at the 1833 commencement. As governor he had held still more exalted status as ex-officio president of that board.[2]

Swain had joined his fellow trustees in observing, and responding to, his predecessor's physical decline. Suffering from an incurable disease, in December 1833, President Joseph Caldwell had requested assistance. At his suggestion Elisha Mitchell, the professor of longest standing, had been made acting president—at first partially, later entirely—an arrangement that would continue until Swain's arrival.[3]

When the board expressed its sorrow following Caldwell's death on January 27, 1835, Swain made the motion. The deceased president, the board stated, deserved the lasting gratitude and reverence of his countrymen. Apparently satisfied with Mitchell's performance as acting president, the board postponed until its December meeting the election of a new president.[4]

The delay worked to Swain's advantage. Twenty-nine of the university's trustees had been present at the constitutional convention in Raleigh that June. They had sought worthy candidates for the university presidency by recommending that the board's executive committee "open correspondence with distinguished literary men and in other ways." This description of qualifications was hardly tailormade to fit a Swain candidacy. This, indeed, probably was in no one's contemplation, other than possibly his, at this juncture.[5]

Just when the thought entered Swain's mind is uncertain, but at some point it did. He is reported to have been in the governor's office one evening when Judge Frederick Nash dropped by. No political opportunity awaited him; the bar was crowded, and he had never been enamored with the practice of law; and at age thirty-four, with a family to support, necessity dictated that he work at something.

What would the judge think, then, of his being a candidate for the presidency of the university? Perceiving that Nash reacted with coolness, Swain asked him to consult with Judge Duncan Cameron, who loved the university; Swain would be governed by Cameron's opinion. Cameron's reported response was positive: "Well, I never thought of it, but Swain is the very man for the place; a man who has proven himself such a great manager of men would make a good manager of boys."[6]

Cameron made the motion for Swain when the trustees met to elect a president. Judge William Gaston seconded it. The minutes record that "the Board proceeded to ballot . . . when it was found that David L. Swain had received a majority of the whole number of votes and that he was duly elected."[7]

While Swain's selection was largely a surprise, speculation about it was not altogether lacking. One contemporary letter, apparently from a student to his father, stated: "As usual there is but little interesting news about Chapel Hill. . . . There was some talk of the trustees electing gov. Swain as President of the College. The students were surprised at the news. But I expect that it is yet very doubtful who will be the President."[8]

The selection, according to one newspaper, "excited equal curiosity and surprise." To some degree, party lines determined reaction. The trustee board, unlike the state legislature, remained in Whig control; and there was, and has continued to be, some thought that Swain's appointment was a reward for effective party service. Among those surprised and disappointed were professors who had thought themselves worthy and deserving of the position. One, William Hooper, was especially embittered and disgruntled; he said North Carolinians had elected Swain to every office within their power and were now sending him to the university to be educated.[9]

Compliments were equally forthcoming, however. One newspaper was "highly gratified" by the choice and rejoiced "because we believe it to be a judicious selection." Swain would, no doubt, devote "all the energies of his highly gifted mind to the advancement of the Institution." His ability, past performance, and devotion to the public welfare "afford[ed] a sufficient guarantee to the friends of the university that under his auspices, the Institution will prosper." William H. Battle soon told Swain it afforded him the greatest pleasure to see the institution flourish "because you preside over it." Battle's son, Kemp Plummer Battle, would later say that Swain was then at the height of his powers, mental and physical.[10]

The little town's residents were naturally curious about the new leader. Internet and multiple media sources did not yet exist to convey instant images of public figures. Informed members of this rather provincial nineteenth-century community certainly knew of Swain, but even they often did not know the man and had no mental image of his features.

There thus was some disappointment when the youthful, awkward looking, physically unattractive president arrived. Caldwell's was the accustomed presidential image, and in first-blush appearance, the new man was his antithesis. While pleasant and accessible, he lacked "the old school touch of quiet and dignified courtesy and grace—the old *prestige* and name which people had long revered and deferred to." He would grow to hold his own with anyone, to make himself felt "as a remarkable man, second to none in sagacity, prudence, and administrative ability." While never a scholar in the formal, classical sense, he knew much, would learn more, and knew how to use the knowledge he possessed. But this depicts the later President Swain, whom the villagers would always call "Governor Swain," not the thirty-four-year-old who first stepped into Caldwell's office as his successor on December 11, 1835.[11]

When Swain had been in the office a few months, one student thought him a misfit there. William Blount Rodman, later to serve on the North Carolina Supreme Court, wrote to his uncle that Swain was "far from possessing the information which I had supposed. . . . His previous bustling habits of life have unfitted him for this monotony of his present situation," he said. Social while others were studious, he lacked companions so was "melancholy and dissatisfied." When Swain had been there two years, Hamilton C. Jones of Rowan County told U.S.

Senator Willie P. Mangum he thought Swain was "sick of" his university role. His services were essential to the university's prosperity, however, so "we must hold him to it."[12]

Both Zeb Vance, probably Swain's most prominent pupil, and R. D. W. Connor, prominent North Carolina historian in his time, thought a Swain biographer would essentially have to end the monograph with the subject's arrival at the university president's office. From that point forward, in their view, few notable events occurred in Swain's life and career to attract the attention of the biographer. Swain's history simply became that of the university and little, if anything, more.[13]

Vance and Connor had a point. Academic years have a repetitive rhythm and routine. A novel set in an English boarding school captures this ambience admirably: "The years unfolded, season by season, term by term, with a pleasant, almost timeless rhythm."[14] As a consequence, standard chronological treatment of an academic personage, if achievable, is often redundant and thus dull.

Surviving records from Swain's time at the university do not readily lend themselves to strict chronological treatment. By taking a thematic or topical approach, however, rebuttal of the Vance-Connor thesis is achievable. Much of value and interest remains to be said about Swain's life and career. It is, in a sense, the university's history. Swain, however, was in many respects the focal point of the university's life, and it thus is his history too.

CHAPTER 8

Admitting, Parenting
"Friendly and paternal solicitude"

ADMISSION COMMENCES THE COLLEGE experience. The modern academic setting includes admission deans and offices. The process is elaborate, the requirements detailed and specific. In Swain's UNC time, by contrast, he was the portal of entry, and the process was casual and informal. Technically the faculty admitted students; in reality, though, it was the president. At one point the practice received official sanction: no applicant was to be examined until he had obtained a written certificate signed by the president. This president preferred older students; with an older than average senior class, in his view, the college went along well.[1] Admissions requests often came from prominent citizens. Early in Swain's tenure Robert Strange, then a U.S. senator from North Carolina, informed Swain that one of his sons would be accompanying another son "to see him settled at Chapel Hill should he have the good fortune to enter college." A young friend would also endeavor to enter. It was hoped that both would meet the approbation of Swain and the faculty.[2]

George Badger, prominent attorney and officeholder, commended an old friend to Swain's "kindness and attention" as he came to Chapel Hill "with a view of placing some of his sons under your charge for the completion of their education." Matthias Manly, a superior court, later state supreme court judge, introduced a prospective freshman "eminently fitted for literary pursuits." Swain would inform himself of the student's "acquirements," but Manly did not doubt their sufficiency. On another occasion Manly sought admission, without the customary charges, of a young townsman whose family fortunes had been "much reduced by ... the late Civil War."[3]

Willie P. Mangum, president pro tem of the U.S. Senate, sought Swain's advice, for Georgia legislator Joel Crawford, on educational opportunities in North

Carolina. Mangum had strongly advised Crawford to send his sons to the state. General D. L. Clinch had enrolled a son at Chapel Hill, one reason being his respect for "the character and Talents of the President." Aware that a Clinch son had attended the institution under Swain, Crawford desired a conversation with the general on the university's merits. "[W]rite how far Chappel *[sic]* Hill is likely to advance the end I have in view," Crawford said to the general in a letter Mangum forwarded to Swain.[4]

There is no evidence that partisan political affiliation influenced admissions decisions. Advocates for applicants might plead it nevertheless, hoping it advantageous. A Wilmington correspondent commended to Swain a young man whose father was "one of the most respectful and influential citizens of Onslow County," said the advocate, and "[i]f it may be lawful to say so, the main Pillar of the Whig cause in that benighted county."[5]

Sectional considerations entered the process. Historian Francis L. Hawks, a North Carolina native then living in New York, once introduced Swain to a friend, similarly situated, who was visiting Chapel Hill to enroll his son. It pleased Hawks that the father was sending the boy "*home* for his education." The youth was "Southron by birth," said Hawks, who was "more and more convinced that southern boys should be trained at the South."[6]

Ordinary people, too, sent admissions requests and recommendations. One introduced "a young man of ease worth and promise"; Swain would readily discover his talents and scholarship and hopefully secure him membership in one of the higher classes. Another, desirous of sending his son if the boy could gain admission, inquired about the requisite prior studies. Still another had seen his son's tutor move to the West and was "at a loss what to do" with the idle lad; unlike his father, the boy was "of fine disposition and studious habits."[7]

A former student might initiate the admissions process. One wrote, for example, to request a university catalogue for his cousin. A prospective student, desirous of knowing the rules and regulations and the required course, would himself write the president requesting "a circular."[8]

Candor about candidates' deficiencies, information unlikely in a modern admissions application, was characteristic. One mother acknowledged that her son was not entirely prepared to enter the university. He was deficient in arithmetic and had not read Latin and Greek to the extent required. Another thought her son "a little deficient" but "able to keep up with the classes." She was to blame if he was not ready, for she had kept him at home for a year "fearing his health of body and mind might be injured or destroyed by long confinement."[9]

Prominent advocates for those seeking admission were equally forthcoming.

One applicant, reported Senator Willie P. Mangum, had "wasted a great deal of his time" and had never studied until the last six to eight months. Charles Manly viewed his own son as so ill-prepared that he chose to delay his admission. The boy might "squeeze in," Manly thought. Manly's position as secretary-treasurer of the trustees, however, could lead to charges of "an odious precedent of favoritism"; therefore, he thought it "best to detain him."[10]

Concerns could be behavioral rather than academic. George W. Mordecai, Raleigh lawyer and businessman, had taken charge of a friend's (his and Swain's) son and was experiencing "great difficulty in determining what disposition to make of him." The youth was willing to go to Chapel Hill but "had discontinued his classical studies for some time." Further, Mordecai felt obligated to disclose that the prospect "had been dismissed from St. Mary's College, Baltimore" for a scuffle with a "servant girl" over a pitcher of water. Still, if Swain could accept the lad "and try to make something of him and prevent him from throwing himself away," Mordecai would experience great relief.[11]

Robert Donaldson, William Gaston's son-in-law, foresaw similar problems with his son. He sought from Swain a university catalogue containing entrance requirements, while noting a preference that Robbie "board & lodge where his Health & morals would be watched over more carefully than they could be in College Rooms."[12]

Swain could find admissions problems disconcerting, as when he was asked to have the Dialectic Society educate the son of Julius Alexander, whom the requester thought "incompetent for any kind of business." That Swain and the father had been bitter political enemies undoubtedly exacerbated an already difficult admissions dilemma.[13]

Difficulties could occur at the institutional rather than the individual level. Braxton Craven, head of the Normal College (later Trinity, still later Duke), once sent three young men to Swain. In every case he had recommended UNC to them rather than Randolph Macon or other institutions he might have been expected to favor. Craven was not nice about it, however. The university as a whole, he complained, "treats us ungently, and with but little of that courtesy due an honorable *inferior*." Students from his school were disadvantaged when seeking UNC admission; they did not get the same respect as those from institutions such as Wake Forest and Davidson. His lament notwithstanding, Craven hoped Swain would accept the students. Whatever the applicants said they had read, he assured Swain, "you may rely upon it they did it understandingly."[14]

Transfer inquiries and requests were common. Soon after his arrival in Chapel Hill Swain heard from a freshman at Randolph Macon College in Virginia who wished "to go to Chapel Hill as quick as I can." It was a matter of state pride: people there ran down "and calumniate[d]" UNC "because they consider[ed] it in *the way* . . . and . . . wish[ed] to keep several students who talk of going to Chapel Hill." No man was better qualified to advise and encourage him, he said, than Swain. [15]

Most transfer inquiries and information came from presidents and professors at other institutions. The president of the University of Nashville advised Swain of a student whose studies had been interrupted by ill health. He had been dismissed, without censure, at his own request, as had another who was of good moral character.[16] A professor at Randolph Macon College requested a copy of UNC's "laws, course of study and general regulations" for two young gentlemen who were considering matriculating there. Would they be admitted to the same class, he inquired? They were, he assured Swain, "of good morals, honourable deportment and creditable scholarship and prefer to graduate at your institution."[17] Harvard president Edward Everett certified to Swain that a freshman there had "by the advice of his friends left the Institution." His conduct had been becoming, his attention to duties exemplary, and his academic progress highly respectable.[18]

Transfer student reviews from Swain's peers were not always so positive, however. Basil Manly, a North Carolinian serving as president of the University of Alabama, once wrote Swain of a prospect who was "a noble fellow—misled lately by his passions, though not to a very culpable extent." He would still make an excellent student, entitled to the faculty's respect and confidence. Any others applying from that institution, however, "and not bearing an honorable testimonial," merited careful inquiry.[19]

Disruptions from the Civil War spawned transfer requests. A Minnesota correspondent introduced Swain to the son of a neighbor and friend who was a native North Carolinian. While a university student there, the youngster had been "[s]eized with ardor to maintain the rights of the Southern Confederacy." Impaired health had led to his honorable discharge. He now sought admission to the junior class at UNC. Want of patronage had compelled closure of the university previously attended; accordingly, the usual certificates from its president and professors were unavailable.[20]

Late in the war William A. Graham wrote Swain from the Confederate Senate to introduce three young gentlemen from Arkansas "who profess to connect themselves with the University of North Carolina as students." He did so at the request of that state's senator, R. W. Johnson. A contemporaneous letter from the boys' guardian notes their prior attendance at the Virginia Military Institute, "which has been broken up by the enemy." The guardian could find no better solution, he told Swain, "than to send them to the university you have made so conspicuous among the Institutions of the Earth."[21]

Such compliments, with their accompanying transfer requests, undoubtedly pleased Swain, not just for ego reasons, but because he focused on enrollment numbers. In Caldwell's time the number of students at the university had never exceeded 165. At Caldwell's death in 1835 the count was around one hundred. Swain commenced immediately to raise the numbers. By the end of his second year as president, William H. Battle congratulated him on the increase. It was, Battle thought, the dawn of a brighter day for his alma mater.[22] In Swain's early UNC years the enrollment was as follows: 1836, 89 students; 1837, 142 students; 1838, 164 students; 1839, 160 students; 1840, 171 students. "So steady and rapid an increase since GOV. SWAIN took charge of the Institution," said a Raleigh newspaper, "speaks well for his administration of the affairs of the College."[23]

Swain's letters reflect his pride in the growth over the years. The university was well and its prospects promising, he said in 1838. The freshman class, which included Francis P. Blair Jr. from a prominent Missouri journalism and political family, had sixty-five students. In 1840, the university was "very crowded." In 1848, Swain feared a reduction, but the next decade, instead, brought a trebling of the numbers. In 1851, with more than two hundred students, he could find little time to visit friends or for correspondence "except in relation to the college." In 1856, the number was 360, and in 1858, "upwards of 400."[24]

Enrollment reached its antebellum peak, in the 460 range, just before the outbreak of the Civil War. It then dropped precipitously, as the population group from which the university drew its clientele went off to war, many never to return. The fall of 1861 saw one hundred young men enrolled. The number grew to 115 in the spring of 1862. There were sixty-five in the fall of 1862, reduced to fifty-eight for the spring of 1863. By war's end there were only a dozen or so students, all, or at least almost all, with some disability that precluded military service.[25]

Once students arrived in Chapel Hill, an *in loco parentis* philosophy prevailed. The university stood in place of the parents; and in this regard, to a significant degree, Swain was the university. Parents were entrusting their sons to him. "I have been influenced to place [my son] at our own university principally because *you* preside over it," one father told Swain, "and having full confidence in your exertions to make as much of young men as possible." The son was aware, the father said, of the dangers college presented "absent the watchful care of a parent." The student would listen to and obey Swain's commands and advice. The father thus looked to Swain "for a rigid exercise of that controul and influence which *you* can so happily use in the government of young men."[26]

Charles Manly, who had problems with a son at the university, articulated the rationale for the philosophy. An incident with the senior class, he told Swain, "only confirms the good sense of the Law and universal experience that Boys are not able nor fit to govern themselves."[27] Governor John M. Morehead described the *in loco parentis* role in military terminology. He was sending Swain "three raw recruits," his son and two nephews, he once wrote, "out of whom . . . very good regulars may be made under the drilling of such a sergeant as yourself." In any matters of doubt as to honor or propriety, they were to consult Swain "on whom they may implicitly rely—that you will advise them to do nothing or pursue no course that you would not advise your own son." Indeed, Morehead implored, "[j]ust as you would desire young Buncombe [Swain's son Richard] to be treated by me, if under my care, so do you by the young Plebes."[28]

A presentation of a youth for admission requested that Swain "direct him how to proceed in establishing himself in college." Swain was also to inform the presenter, however, of "excesses of any kind." A father likewise submitted his son to Swain's "especial superintendence and guardianship, not only as it respects his literary interests but his general habits and conduct."[29] Other fathers made similar requests. Give his son "a parental supervision," begged one. "An occasional word of encouragement from yourself," said another, would stimulate his son "to proper exertions and . . . confer on me the greatest favor." Another would be pleased with information from Swain about his son, particularly whether he was complying with college regulations and being attentive to studies. The boy was capable, with application, of attaining a respectable standing in his class; he could, however, "be influenced by idle or vicious boys."[30]

One son, desirous of graduating with distinction and perceiving himself at a disadvantage with his professors, was too proud to approach them himself. He was not, however, above asking his father to request that Swain "speak to such Pro'f as I recite to and request of them that they will take such note of my recitations as that I may be raised to this distinction if I am worthy of it." The father, state attorney general when Swain was governor, complied.[31] In his *in loco parentis* role, Swain usually dealt with students' fathers. On one occasion, however, while traveling, he noted that the mother of a "truant student" had seemed very glad to see him.[32]

It was not just parents who invoked this role. The historian John H. Wheeler sent his "young Brother" to "join your Institution." The brother, who had been in the army during the Mexican War, had "a mind of a fair order." Wheeler requested Swain's "paternal care."[33] A correspondent with two brothers who had died fighting for the Confederacy was concerned for a brother-in-law. The young man had not chosen a college, but the writer, believing "[w]e must educate our boys and girls at home," was "decidedly opposed to his going North." "[S]hould he go to the institution of which you are the honored head," he continued, "may I not ask that you take such a fatherly interest in his well being as you may think best."[34]

Former Governor Thomas Bragg commended a nephew to Swain. Swain would, he hoped, aid the youth in procuring "board and quarters." The boy would deliver a letter from his father imploring Swain's care in more detail. Swain was to extend not only the ordinary care he bestowed on all pupils but also "to give him the benefit of that friendly and paternal solicitude which I assure you I should feel for a son of yours sent to me under like circumstances."[35]

Family ties were not essential; friendship sufficed. A Tarboro resident commended to Swain a young friend, a dropout who had consented to return to the university. He still needed advice, however, requiring the aid of a friend as well as that of a preceptor. An occasional kind and encouraging word from Swain was thus solicited.[36] Sometimes these solicitations addressed specific concerns. The contents of a university circular gave one father "great anxiety and distress of mind." He had learned that a favorite son was in danger of "becoming an habitual inebriate (that most disgusting of all vices)." Not only that, but it appeared that his example was likely to prove destructive to his associates. The father requested that Swain interview the student and report on whether he should remain in Chapel Hill.[37]

There were health concerns. One mother had withheld her son from school for a year for such reasons. She thought he could now keep up with his classes, but she and the father, she told Swain, were "anxious for him to be under your superintendence." Another parent desired Swain's attention to her son's eyes, his mind, and his general health. "Above all," she pleaded, "dissuade him from the use of that filthy, poisonous weed, Tobacco." Occasionally such concerns proved insurmountable. His son had been sick for a considerable time, one father informed Swain, "and would not be able to attend to his studies any more this session."[38]

Assistance in financial matters constituted a significant facet of Swain's *in loco parentis* role. Indeed, he was a smalltime banker to many students. A dismissed student once wrote him from an out-of-state university to acknowledge that he was "still fifteen dollars in your debt." When he visited home soon, he would refund the amount. A graduate wrote Swain on the "small loan" he had made to him. He hoped soon to remit the sum plus the price of his diploma. Circumstances had prevented another's "sending you the amount I borrowed of you when I left the Hill." He now enclosed it, with thanks for the favor and for Swain's many kindnesses. Swain sometimes elicited Judge William H. Battle's assistance in collecting small debts due him from students or former students.[39]

At times Swain was asked to advance a sum to a student with assurance it would be repaid. George Badger once sent his nephew to Chapel Hill with $10.00 and a request that Swain "advance anything for Thomas beyond what is sent" and let Badger know the amount. A father made new boarding arrangements for his son, with a request to Swain to advance any necessary sums, which he would refund.[40]

At other times Swain was asked simply to handle financial matters for students. One father furnished fewer funds than might be necessary because his son tended to be careless and extravagant. He wished to arrange with Swain, or someone he recommended, to take charge of the money and exercise control over the expenditures. As to the son, "[a]n occasional word of encouragement from yourself will stimulate him to proper exertions and will confer on me the greatest favor."[41] Governor John M. Morehead once sent Swain a check for $100.00 with a request that Swain cash it and give the funds to Morehead's nephew, a student at the university. While the Morehead-Swain friendship undoubtedly facilitated this transaction, Swain performed similar services for the famous and the unknown.[42]

Penurious parents and guardians also imposed on Swain. One father sent his last son to the university, commending him to Swain's "friendly notice." He wished to furnish funds sufficient "for comfort and respectability," but "not ... a dollar beyond." Swain should let him know if the amount sent was too much or too little. A guardian, whose ward had borrowed both money and items when leaving Chapel Hill, hoped it unnecessary "to make any apology to you as the head of the Institute and by character favorably known as a Gentleman." Swain was fully competent to determine the writer's legal obligation as the student's guardian, and he would "cheerfully ... submit to your decision as a Gentleman."[43] True penury produced requests for charitable accommodations. The student of an alcoholic father, whose use of ardent spirits had devastated his estate, found his "prospects very gloomy." He had always desired an education above all else. Perhaps Swain could do him some service or recommend him to some situation.[44]

Despite Swain's generally miserly regulation of the university's finances, in his first year as president, in an early forerunner to the modern-day "Carolina Covenant," a work-study program for students of limited means, he and the trustees notably advanced accessibility to higher education in the state. Prospective students who could not afford the tuition were no longer required to pay it. On July 9, 1836, the executive committee resolved "that any native of the State desirous of prosecuting his studies in the university who shall furnish satisfactory evidence of good talents, studious habits, and exemplary morals and who shall be unable to defray the expenses of tuition may at the direction of the Faculty be admitted to all the recitations of the classes free of any demand for tuition." These students could also secure a college room rent free unless all were necessary to accommodate paying students. A Raleigh newspaper captured the significance of the action. It hoped "that hereafter we shall never hear repeated the unfounded and senseless clamour, that it is a 'School for rich men's sons only.'"[45]

Student financial irresponsibility once became so extensive as to prompt legislative action. The General Assembly made students' contracts void unless entered with the written permission of the university president or a faculty member. If made more than two miles from Chapel Hill, the person with control or authority over the student had to consent. Swain sent a circular letter to his students' fathers and guardians advising of these provisions and requesting that they notify him of their concurrence. This would enable him to advise students and merchants that the fathers and guardians would pay no debt contracted by their sons and wards without their permission or that of a faculty member. It was a strong dose of *in loco parentis* policy, and one suspects that Swain requested and lobbied for the statute.[46]

Implementation of the policy took other forms as well. Early in his tenure Swain induced the faculty to take regular turns visiting students in their rooms at night. At faculty meetings he called for reports on these visits. Student attendance at off-campus political events required faculty permission. Two seniors were once allowed to attend the Whig Party convention in Raleigh because they had been appointed as delegates from their county. When Henry Clay made a Raleigh appearance in 1844, many students were anxious to attend. The faculty voted unanimously that "the President shall require a written request from his father from every student who may apply for permission to visit Raleigh on that occasion."[47] Even seemingly simple requests, such as for permission to attend a family wedding, went through Swain. A father wanted his son to attend his sister's wedding but not if the required week's absence would impair his class standing. If it would, the idea had to be abandoned, for the father's heart was set on his son taking honors.[48] The *in loco* role extended to some regulation of the village economy. The price of local boarding houses was not to exceed $10.00 per month. Students were prohibited from boarding at higher-priced establishments.[49]

Swain instituted the practice of regular quarterly reports to parents and guardians. Faculty members provided materials for these. A Swain note to Judge William H. Battle and his wife regarding their son, Wesley Lewis Battle, is representative. In the past ten weeks Wesley had missed prayers four times and recitations once. His class rank was very respectable in French, Latin, and Greek, and respectable in all other departments.[50] The president's communications to parents could be on health matters. He once wrote a parent, for example, "Basil was confined to his room by a bad cold on Monday and Tuesday, but is about again." Parents sent similar messages to Swain. One father was happy to say that his son was quite well, though not yet as strong as he could wish. He concluded on an optimistic note: "I hope he will be able to return next week."[51] Swain once advised the faculty that any member could feel free to communicate at any time with a parent or guardian concerning a son or ward at college. It was a prerequisite, however, that the communication first be submitted to the entire faculty for revisal.[52]

In his *in loco parentis* role, Swain apparently knew no limits. On one occasion a father committed his son to Swain's "parental care and instruction." "Advise him as a father," he said, "he will submit to your reproof and be grateful for your counsel." Later the father was grateful for Swain's "conversations with and advice to our unthinking boy." Swain had even proposed to take the boy into his own family. The father, however, thought he "had better return home."[53] At least for friends, Swain would extend this role beyond his campus. A father with a son at the University of Virginia once sought Swain's counsel for his boy. The concern was "respecting the effect that study may have on his eyes." He wanted the advantage of college for his offspring but not at the expense of his sight. He was writing, he believed, "to an old friend who would appreciate my motives."[54] Finally, Swain's *in loco parentis* role often extended beyond the student's time at the university. A graduating senior once complained to Swain at length about a distinction made between him and another senior. "I look to you Governor," he said, "to see that we are treated alike. . . . [M]y college life is over. Your decree is on this subject as final as death itself."[55]

Money matters often invoked Swain's postgraduation assistance. A father, upon learning that his son had left Chapel Hill owing a local woman between $36.00 and $40.00, sent Swain "Forty dollars in North Carolina money." He requested that Swain "hand it over to her" and send him a receipt. A former student, who left owing $12.00 in rent, sent the sum to Swain with which to pay the landlady, with thanks to Swain for the kindness and attention bestowed on him while in Chapel Hill. Another former student, pleading the dire pecuniary straits of his locale, apologized for his failure to remit money Swain had loaned him. More than two years later he still felt obligation to Swain for favors offered and conferred and had dedicated a book to Swain on that account.[56]

Swain's postgraduation influence was sought in securing positions. He had helped a student, while at UNC, become deputy marshal for Wilkes County. The superior court clerkship in Caldwell County was now open, and the former student sought Swain's recommendation "as soon as convenient." Swain was to mention it to other members of the faculty if he thought proper. His influence was sought by another who wanted "a warrant for an assistant surgeon's place in the Navy." One name was worth a host of signatures, and Swain's was the one he wanted.[57]

At times Swain's influence was solicited regarding a former student's business interests. The Raleigh agent for a fire insurance company, when asked on what terms he would insure a mill owned by a Mr. Wait, contacted Swain. Wait, he told Swain, "was a kind of protogee [sic] of yours and Dr. Mitchell's." If Swain was disposed to aid Wait in procuring insurance, he would "see and value his mill or certify to the character of any person who may value it."[58]

Testimonials from Swain were sought and valued. A former student seeking admission elsewhere would secure Swain's certification that he had been dismissed from UNC, without censure, at his own request.[59] A former faculty member had been no admirer of one of his students. He had become persuaded, however, that the man had changed for the better, now regretted "the stubborn foolishness of his college life," and "has capital traits of character." He thus "engage[d] [Swain's] kind offices in his behalf" as the man sought a school principalship.[60]

New Bern Academy once advertised for a teacher to head its classical department. An applicant was a UNC graduate and a former tutor there, before Swain's presidency. Still, Swain's opinion was "highly acceptable," and the trustees requested that he inform them regarding the applicant's qualifications.[61]

Calvin H. Wiley, North Carolina's first superintendent of common schools, regretted having neglected Swain since his 1840 graduation. When an applicant for "an office abroad," however, he requested Swain's assistance, stating, "North Carolina will never attain her proper position until she contains more than one Swain."[62]

Edward Mallett, UNC Class of 1849 and a Confederate soldier, had a difficulty with his colonel "on account of grave charges that I preferred against him." This diminished his utility "to the cause" and prompted him to seek assistance "in procuring a position in some other field of duty." Swain, Mallett told Kemp Battle, had expressed a great desire to assist him and had promised to use his influence with Governor Zeb Vance. Swain had also promised to confer with Battle, then private secretary to the governor. The effort apparently failed, for Mallett was killed in the March 1865 Battle of Bentonville. He left a dying wife and four small children penniless.[63]

When Swain gave a testimonial, it was eloquent. One for William L. Scott, for example, described him as a UNC graduate with the first distinction in scholarship; a distinction in deportment, more rarely attained; never absent from duty; "a young man of good mind, correct principles, exemplary habits, and ... believed to be unusually well qualified to undertake the government and instruction of young men desirous of being well prepared to enter college." Swain hoped this would place Scott "in the light you desire, whenever and wherever you may have occasion to use it."[64]

Former students often updated Swain on their postgraduate activities. Robert R. Bridgers, Class of 1841, informed him when he had employed a principal for the Tarboro Male Academy. He had made considerable additions to his library—two hundred or so books on law, the rest "select literary works"—and had been using both "to much greater advantage than at any time since I left college." Bridgers also had almost entirely renounced politics: "it is touch not, taste not, or I become intoxicated with them." The foundation for all his subsequent success, he acknowledged to his university's leader, had been laid at Chapel Hill.[65]

Another, who viewed Swain and his associates as "my old instructor[s]," had laid aside his "legal pretensions," having grown tired of the "slavish business." He had been licensed as a Methodist preacher and "commenced a school in our male Academy." He anticipated the time "when the good and clever" would view him as he viewed Swain and his faculty. Swain, he said, was faring well in his area: "I know of no one who has stronger, tho they be humble, friends than you have in that region."[66]

Still another noted that had he studied harder at college, he "could easily have obtained the first honor." Honor itself was not so significant, he said, "yet the efforts used to obtain [it] will be an immense advantage." Given another chance, he would "burn the midnight lamp." The course of instruction had been "well calculated to train the mind rightly," and he regretted his ingratitude for "the care and pleasure you took in instructing us."[67]

Serious illnesses and deaths of students probably affected Swain more profoundly than any others among the many difficulties that came his way. He once reported that he had never known so many cases of fever in the university. The last death there had occurred almost nine years earlier, but now one case was considered "almost hopeless." Another year produced among the students an extensive outbreak of the mumps.[68] Deaths were more traumatic still. University records from Swain's time report a student's passing "of a congestive chill after a sudden illness of two days only"; Swain's calling a faculty meeting to arrange the funeral of a senior "who died of a congestive chill"; Swain's conferring, assisted by other faculty members, with the father of a student who had died after a two-week illness; and Professor Wheat's announcing a freshman's death from pneumonia. A contemporary newspaper account reports a student death "of a congestive chill" following an illness of several days.[69]

One student death was particularly affecting for Swain. John Burton, son of Hutchins G. Burton, a Swain predecessor in the governor's office, died at the university "after a severe and painful illness." Swain had informed the parents of their son's illness, and the boy's mother had arrived in Chapel Hill before his demise. Judge Battle, in travel status, expressed surprise over not hearing from Swain during that period. Swain's intentions were good, Mrs. Battle responded, but she supposed "he was too uneasy in his mind about Mr. B[urton]."[70]

In their student days undoubtedly there were those who chafed under, even resented, Swain's paternal ministrations. For the most part, however, they grew to appreciate them and to love him. Eight years postgraduation, one former student told Swain he had been "instructed by my father in my early days to respect and obey you." These early feelings of respect and obedience "increased to love in after years from association and the many kindnesses received at your hands."[71]

CHAPTER 9

Student Misconduct
"Enough to ruin a saint[,] much more a mortal"

STUDENTS DID NOT ALWAYS accept quiescently the *in loco parentis* role that Swain and the faculty assumed. Unruly boys took their revenge in cursing, drunkenness, pranks, unauthorized absences, and occasional violence. The university experience, designed to educate, could also corrupt. In 1847, James Johnston Pettigrew told his father that "a sojourn of two years in this place [Chapel Hill] is enough to ruin a saint[,] much more a mortal." In student minds their misconduct was probably a legitimate form of rebellion, an assertion of independence from a domineering president and faculty. The consequence was that much of the time Swain functioned like a modern dean of students, dealing extensively with disciplinary matters. He rarely had the luxury of operating like a modern university president, focused on a far broader agenda and enjoying the luxury of delegating disciplinary matters largely, if not entirely, to others.[1]

Bylaws governing student conduct often proved ineffective. An exasperated Swain once penned a resolution proposing that a faculty committee be instructed to inquire "[t]hat whereas the students at the university are sinners, rude, irreverent and coyish, whether it be expedient to have the gospel preached to them and if so, whether any member of the faculty, or his family, can with propriety attend... such religious service?"[2]

Some student misconduct was organized and purposeful. A student organization called the Ugly Club, dedicated to resisting all forms of regimentation, was formed in 1838. It created nighttime disturbances, both on and off campus. Its instruments were horns, tin pans, and lusty lungs, indeed, "whatever ingenuity can devise to make noise, including... the college bell." On the first Saturday of that fall term a routine hazing party erupted into "a village-wide rampage with black-faced young men intimidating faculty and citizens, turning over privies and happily defying all attempts to restore order." During the club's many shenanigans,

Swain's white mule, old "Cuddie," might be found stabled in the upper stories of dormitories, including the halls of South Building.

Faculty minutes show "the precincts of the university and of the village having been seriously annoyed . . . by a set of individuals styling themselves the Ugly Club." When identifiable participants were arraigned, they expressed regret and promised not to participate in or countenance such activities again. One was placed on probation. Others, more culpable, were allowed to remain in school and to "recite with their class," with the faculty to determine at session end "the propriety of admitting them."

These sanctions had little effect, however. Only weeks later Ugly Club members, disguised to be unrecognizable, "spent the night in the most shameful excesses, offered the grossest insults to various citizens in the village, threatened violence to members of the faculty, and committed trespasses of a peculiarly low and disgusting character upon private property." "[T]his shameful riot," the faculty called the incident.

Two leaders of the "riot" were advised that only great propriety of conduct would entitle them to regular standing at the winter examination. One who failed to comply received a private admonition from Swain. He had exhausted the patience of the faculty, the president advised, and had received his last warning. Such admonitions notwithstanding, the club continued to rear its "Ugly" head. The 1839–1840 academic year saw the faculty take "measures to prevent . . . the riot and disorder . . . occasioned by . . . the Ugly Club." The summers of 1840 and 1842 brought faculty meetings to investigate disorders and deal with student cases arising from club proceedings. In 1840, the faculty heard student statements, and Swain and other faculty members admonished the students. They then deferred the matter, however. In 1842, the students involved averted dismissal by signing a pledge "not to participate in the disgraceful orgies of the 'Ugly Club.'"

A student diary entry provides a vivid account of a valiant Swain effort to repress the club and its activities. Notices proclaimed a meeting at the chapel at noon, "and that members of that ancient and venerable institution the Ugly Club were determined to sustain it." Swain, "excited by these notices," addressed the members at 10:00 that morning. He dwelt on the degradation of the club, the disgusting ceremonies, and the degradation of those who submitted to its inflictions of membership. Students should not submit to the club's impositions, he admonished, and he promised to hold safe those who knocked down anyone who attempted to "black" (disguise) him.

Swain's address inspired the freshmen to an anti-Ugly Club stance, said the diarist, in which they boasted of the achievements of valor they would perform if there was such a club. This, in turn, prompted a proclamation by the grand mogul of the Ugly Club in reply to Swain. Fearful punishments, he said, would be inflicted on all freshmen who resisted the club. The diarist concluded (wrongly), however, that there was no club and no such activity. Soon the trustees prohibited students from joining any secret club or association. The Dialectic and Philanthropic societies, established and respected literary clubs, concurred in the opinion that secret associations were injurious to the regularly instituted societies and to the university, and thus pledged hearty cooperation in any endeavor to suppress them.

In 1844, the faculty, supported by the trustees, required as a condition of resuming studies a student pledge not to "unite himself with an Ugly Club or any similar riotous proceeding." Students involved in Ugly Club incidents would be dismissed in a manner that would prohibit them from joining other academic institutions. Governor John M. Morehead, as president of the trustees, read those resolutions to the lower classes, and a long list of students signed pledges that they would not affiliate with the Ugly Club. For years students continued to sign an identical pledge. The club nevertheless continued to thrive until the Civil War.[3]

"Spirits" were the common fuel of student misconduct. Early in Swain's UNC tenure, the faculty resolved that henceforth the laws prohibiting introduction of spiritous liquors into student rooms would be strictly enforced. Students publicly intoxicated, or with liquor in their rooms, would be suspended or dismissed. The resolution, with accompanying admonitions from Swain, was read to students. Soon the university board of trustees gave its "entire approbation" to the promulgation and sought its "rigorous execution." The faculty was to dismiss "promptly and without respect to persons" any students found intoxicated or in whose rooms spirituous liquors were discovered.[4]

Attempts to enforce the policy were often unavailing. One incident prompted a circular letter from Swain to parents. Upperclassman had persuaded freshmen that "from the foundation of the Institution" their class had treated the upper classes. With a subscription of two dollars each from numerous freshmen, the upperclassman had purchased wine and ardent spirits from Hillsboro. On a Saturday night when students were not required to be in their rooms, there had been a "celebration of this Festival in the woods." Many students drank freely, a small number to intoxication. "The result," Swain informed parents, "was a series of disorders which were continued the greater part of the night." Parents would concur, Swain hoped, in the belief that suppression of such was "of vital importance to the Institution" and would cooperate in prevention efforts. Severe penalties would be imposed, of which parents should inform their sons "in decided terms."[5]

Two decades after the aforementioned faculty resolution, the problem persisted. Former Governor William A. Graham reported for a trustee committee that "riotous and disorderly behavior, the result for the most part of intoxication from spirituous liquors . . . has occasioned more scandal to the university than all other causes combined." To the committee's regret, active faculty endeavors to repress such conduct had "not been crowned with entire success." Prompt enforcement of pertinent regulations, without exception, was again the remedy of choice, its previous failings notwithstanding.[6]

No university occasion was off-limits to alcohol-fueled student misconduct. Even the president's recitation once drew a student "unduly excited by the influence of spirits." Another student was dismissed for having drunk too much wine before giving a speech and being intoxicated on the stage.[7]

Efforts to prevent introduction of intoxicants to the campus proved futile. The faculty once requested that local boarding house operators abstain from placing wine on their tables. More significantly, it became an indictable offense to maintain a tippling house within two miles of the university, or to sell within that distance wine, ardent spirits, or malt liquors, to be used by a student, without the consent of the faculty. Enforcement was a problem, however. Once Swain went to Raleigh to indict an offender for sending liquor to the students, only to find that the grand jury had been discharged the night before.[8]

Students found ingenious ways to circumvent the ordinance. Kemp Battle reports that a favorite scheme was to hide bottles of spirits in boots returned from the shoemakers, and that Swain himself once brought from Durham what he thought was a can of kerosene oil but was in fact corn whiskey. On another occasion a tutor caught a "Negro" on campus at night with a jug of spirits. He "arrested" the malefactor and ordered him to wait at Swain's gate while he hailed the president. When the tutor returned with Swain, however, the man and his liquor were gone.[9]

Advice about remedies came to Swain. In a missive intended "for your single self," a correspondent noted "that your boys are in the habit of drinking . . . to an excess which must sooner or later materially injure the college." His proposed remedy: bring one or two trustees to the Hill "and get the Societies to enter into mutual agreement to take the matter under *their* management and impose heavy penalties on those who may violate the regulations." Faculty or trustee lectures would be futile, the writer opined: "it must be done by consent of the students." His own sons promised not to touch spirits during the session, but Swain was to let him know if they reneged on the vow.[10]

At times the faculty determined that to give efficacy to the statutes criminalizing certain alcohol-related offenses, intoxicated students would be suspended. Such strict enforcement could produce harsh results. In one instance a student had fortified himself with wine "in order to give himself effect on stage." He imbibed more than intended, however, and it proved to be "more than he could bear." Despite the student's untarnished record for three-and-a-half years, the faculty believed it had no discretion but to impose a period of suspension.[11]

Swain was an active participant in enforcing alcohol policies. It was common for him to find spirits in student rooms, leading to suspension of the violators. On one occasion he discovered students assembled in a room during a recitation hour. The door was fastened, and when Swain entered, he perceived that wine or ardent spirits had been used. The students, who refused to admit that they had been drinking, were severely reprimanded. One student reported that the president was a frequent visitor in his room on Sunday evenings, when he would "drink water out of my tumbler instead of the dipper, to see if he could detect the smell of whiskey."[12]

Swain's home could be the scene of intoxication-related disciplinary matters. His kitchen witnessed a student, in company with "some [N]egroes" and in the state of intoxication, fire a pistol at "a [N]egro boy," inflicting wounds on the arm and hip. Elisha Mitchell once delivered a student to Swain's home "at a late hour in the darkness of the night." Mitchell had found a bottle labeled "Champagne" in the student's room. Swain determined that the bottle in fact contained champagne, and he dismissed the student with a private lecture. When the faculty determined that other students had been treated more harshly for the same offense, however, they dismissed him for the remainder of the session.[13]

Swain's enforcement endeavors extended beyond the campus to vendors of the spirits. The faculty would direct him to institute prosecutions for the sale of spirituous liquors and to investigate their sale in the village by designated peddlers. He at least believed his efforts worthwhile; he once told William Gaston's son-in-law, Robert Donaldson, that the law prohibiting the sale of spirits within two miles of the university, or to a student anywhere, had "produced a very decided improvement without as well as within the college precincts."[14]

At times other faculty members assumed the enforcement task. At one late-night faculty meeting, a note came to Swain with information that "a wagoner was then engaged . . . in selling spirituous liquors within a mile of the university." As the officer in charge of the college for the week, Professor Benjamin Hedrick was "directed to take one or two of the younger members of the Faculty with him, and repair to the spot" to detect the offender. Hedrick found several students there, one with a bottle of spirits in hand, all drinking but protesting that they were not intoxicated. The claims went for naught, as the faculty unanimously dismissed them.[15]

Mixed reactions came to Swain from parents of students dismissed for alcohol-related offenses. One father, whose son's use of spirits had produced "disorder" in his room, concurred in a three-week suspension, notwithstanding his son's theretofore "uniform correct conduct." Another father, though, prayed for immediate reinstatement of his penitent son. The trustees generally declined to intervene regarding such dismissals. In one instance though, Charles Manly, the board's secretary-treasurer, informed Swain that the dismissed student was from a good family, was popular, and had a strong case.[16]

Support for the policy could come from the highest of stations. President James Buchanan attended the university's 1859 commencement. "[I]f the evils of intemperance among students needed an additional denunciation," the faculty reported, "they ... received it by what was so well and so strongly said ... by the Chief Magistrate of the Union."[17]

Requests came to Swain for admission of students dismissed from other institutions for alcohol-related offenses. A South Carolina College correspondent commended a junior there who had been dismissed, with several others, for becoming intoxicated at "a Ladies Fair in this City [Columbia]." The student did not intend to reapply, and the authority of the law there having been vindicated, the recommender foresaw no weakening of the example for that institution's students by his admission elsewhere. The student was admitted to UNC and graduated a year and a half later. One suspects, however, that the admission gave Swain pause.[18]

Given the problems intemperance caused, Swain and the faculty gladly bestowed special privileges on promoters of temperance. When two students petitioned for leave "to attend the Grand Division of the Sons of Temperance ... as delegates from the University Division, and to be excused from making their lessons after returning," the request was unanimously granted. Student temperance promoters could be the subject of humorous ridicule, however. One morning a knot of students gathered about the campus well. When asked what they were doing, Zeb Vance replied: "Governor Swain was in hot pursuit of [a student]. Afraid of being caught with whiskey on him, [the student] threw his half-emptied tickler into the well. The temperance boys have been drinking the water ever since, hoping to get a taste of the spirits."[19] There was, Cornelia Phillips Spencer said of the university in those days, "a good deal of half hidden dissipation."[20] If she was right, the "half-hidden" variety supplemented much that was in the open. It, and the student misconduct it engendered, presented difficult and abiding problems for Swain and his faculty colleagues.

Illicit sexual activity presented similar, though less extensive, problems. It was Swain's lot to inform a student's father that his son stood accused of fathering an illegitimate child in the village. The faculty later directed prompt communication to the parent or guardian regarding any student known to have visited a house of ill fame. The faculty also appointed Elisha Mitchell to attend a trustee meeting for consideration of measures to prosecute persons maintaining such houses near the university. "[T]here are houses near the university in which lewdness and other devices are indulged," the trustees had been informed. The solicitor should, they implored, "give his warm and immediate attention to the subject." A year later the problem persisted, for Mitchell drew another assignment from the faculty: write the solicitor and urge him to prosecute "the lewd women who are known to be keeping bawdy houses near the village of Chapel Hill."[21]

Students boldly, at times violently, expressed contempt for the authority of Swain and the faculty. One nighttime disturbance left a student suspected of attempting to strike Swain with a chair. The faculty unanimously dismissed the student, and the trustees approved criminal proceedings against him to elicit the truth about the incident. When the trustees later considered a similar incident, they requested the presence of Swain and at least one other of the faculty members "on whom violence was ... committed."[22] On another occasion Swain confronted a drunken, boisterous student and found himself faced with the student's stick raised in defense. "[T]he governor ... lost both the buckles off his cloak in the engagement, the fellow whom he rushed upon having collared him."[23]

Faculty members had similar experiences. The Reverend John Thomas Wheat, professor of rhetoric and logic, once requested student aid in intervening between two students who were "desperately fighting." Instead, unknown individuals pulled him around and "menaced his personal safety." Another faculty member, while unarmed, was assaulted by a student, who was expelled for the assault, destruction of recitation-halls furniture, and insolence and general insubordination. The faculty instructed Swain to instigate both criminal and civil proceedings, to be published in newspapers, and Swain was to transfer copies to other colleges in his discretion. Swain complied, and a representative of South Carolina State College soon notified him that he had brought the case to the attention of that faculty.[24]

While such violent incidents occurred, nonviolent displays of disrespect were more common. Students brought before the faculty for disturbing Professor Manuel Fetter's recitation "were duly admonished by the President." When others disturbed Professor James Phillips's recitation by talking, the faculty requested that Swain address the class with threats of dismissal absent a change of deportment. An entire class (the junior) was the subject of the faculty's wrath, conveyed at its request by Swain, for "disgraceful behavior at Dr. Wheat's lecture."[25]

At times Swain sided with students in these matters. A faculty motion to dismiss a student for impertinence at Professor Henri Herrisse's recitation "was lost by the casting vote of the President." In place of dismissal, the faculty appointed Professor Phillips (which Phillips is not stated) to inform the student's mother of his conduct "and of his peculiar relations to the Faculty." Another student, accused of "stomping" in Professor Mitchell's class, reported to his father that he had consulted with Governor Swain, who "says that he knows nothing against me."[26]

More often, probably because of his larger role in the disciplinary process, Swain himself was the object of student insolence. Students disregarded his summonses, disobeyed his proscription against throwing bouquets on rostrums during senior speaking, and talked while he addressed them in chapel. One of two students, before the faculty for answering roll call with improper names, aggravated the charge by using "offensive language towards the President."[27] A disturbance at a hotel table invoked a summons to Swain from the proprietor. One of the student offenders kept his seat despite orders from Swain "to retire to college." He later "most humbly apologized," and by a small majority the faculty accepted the apology and allowed him to stay.[28]

Swain's early-rising habit presented problems for some students. Once Swain sent, at 6:00 a.m., for a student to report to him at 6:45. The student failed to appear, pleading as an excuse that he fell asleep. Another student offered as an excuse for disobeying a Swain order "that he was hungry."[29] Other instances of overt defiance included spitting on a recitation room floor just after Swain had admonished the class on that subject; refusing to meet the faculty at evening prayers despite repeated Swain instructions to do so; declining to retire from the well during study hours; and standing mute when Swain inquired about a pistol in a student's drawer.[30]

Faculty statements regarding such misconduct could be more generic, simply "defying the authority of the President" or "peremptorily disobeying the President." Students laughed when discipline was attempted, one faculty member claimed; and one faculty meeting on discipline degenerated, he said, into "what I call *circus*." "I have seen Gov. Swain on several occasions," he said further, "censure students for laughing when being reprimanded by the Faculty."[31]

Often the bad actors were related to the state's leading men, who were well known to Swain and he to them. Some of the men were Swain's close friends; all, or at least most, were well-recognized acquaintances with whom he had labored or collaborated in public service. There thus was an intensely human element, involving embarrassment as well as concern, to these disciplinary incidents.

Asa Biggs had served in the North Carolina General Assembly and the U.S. Senate. In the year in which he became a federal judge, the university dismissed his son William for insubordination in the chapel. William and other boys had scraped their feet and coughed, thereby drowning out Swain as he attempted to talk to them. They had also exploded torpedoes, small fireworks. Biggs conveyed to Swain his deep regret that his son "should so far have yielded to impulse," and he condemned such impropriety. Still, he was baffled as to why, out of the great number of guilty students, his son had been singled out for "dismission." The boy was a freshman, not yet sixteen years of age, and theretofore had conducted himself with propriety and been diligent in his studies. His elders among the students were equally culpable, if not more so.

Swain's response was both sensitive and defensive. He had read Biggs's letter "with disappointment and regret." His sentiments for Biggs were those "of kindness and respect"; he "hope[d] . . . they were reciprocated." Only very strong evidence, Swain said, would satisfy him that Biggs would do him "intentional injustice." A "disinterested person," however, would take a different view of the case than the son's statements had presented to Biggs. Swain had given notice "in the most empathetic manner" that the first person detected scraping his feet or exploding torpedoes would be sent home. "It was with deep and sincere regret, as well as surprise," Swain informed Biggs, "that I found your son had fallen under the rule." If Biggs desired an impartial opinion, he should contact Judge Battle, "a cool, dispassionate man, [who] has had much experience at the bar and upon the bench." Battle had been present, and a gross injustice would not escape his notice. Swain signed the letter "with renewed allowances of sincere respect and esteem, and earnest desire for your sons welfare." Biggs reciprocated the sentiments and assured Swain of his confidence in the faculty and strong feelings for the university. In a few weeks William returned to Chapel Hill and resumed his studies, but only after some awkward and difficult moments for Swain.[32]

Francis P. Blair hailed from a prominent Missouri journalism and political family. He would become a major general in the Union Army, a U.S. senator, and a vice presidential candidate. His student days at UNC, however, were troubled. Blair appears to have been an able student, for he attained distinction in math.

Early in his UNC career, though, he was "suspected of intemperance and other misdemeanors." The faculty voted to inform his father that he was "in imminent danger of forming habits of intemperance and irregularity." Blair had been absent from seventeen of sixty recitations since his arrival for the session. He was, said the faculty, "a young man of fine capacity [and] interesting manners, and capable, if the unfortunate propensities . . . can be controlled[,] of attaining to high respectability and usefulness." They had too little hope in such reformation, however, "to recommend his longer continuance in the institution."

Blair jumped to his own defense. If the faculty would countermand the letter to his father, he would pledge to abstain from spirituous liquors, faithfully comply with all his college duties, and abstain from the perpetration of disorders. The faculty must have had more confidence in him than previously indicated, for it granted his petition. The confidence proved misplaced. Only a few months passed before Blair's father, again advised to withdraw his son, petitioned the faculty to allow him to remain until commencement upon the son's promise to amend his conduct. Faculty indulgence was again extended. Ultimately Blair transferred to, and graduated from, Princeton.[33]

Former Governor John Branch's son William committed the now seemingly innocuous, but then prohibited, offense of taking a book into recitation class. Branch advised Swain that he was wrong in holding that William and other students had openly resisted a law or ordinance of the college "recognized and practiced by preceding administrations." Swain acknowledged that both he and Branch were anxious to avoid "unpleasant discussion on the subject" but said both would cherish getting the facts right. If he were in Raleigh, Swain said, he could show Branch he was wrong by reference to trustee records. Absent such presence, he trusted that a statement from the faculty would remove doubts about past construction and practice. "No one knows better than I do," Swain asserted, "how narrow is the isthmus which any man occupies who ventures to interpose between parent and child." The faculty had been anxious to induce William to abandon a position that left them no course but the one pursued, dismissal. It had failed, but it was hoped that at a future time both Branch and his son would approve.

As for William, he told Swain his father had concluded he might be admitted to Princeton upon Swain's certification that he was "free from censure" at UNC. He would now most assuredly comply with the ordinance, a course Swain had said would suffice to obtain "an honorable dismissal." Swain responded, not to William but to his father as, he said, the college laws required. William's statement that such a letter would allow him to join another U.S. college was "founded entirely in misapprehension." The faculty would give him every opportunity, consistent with the truth, to go elsewhere. It would be left to the authorities at other institutions, however, to receive or reject him.[34]

Governors' sons, indeed, seemed to have a proclivity for trouble. While Edward B. Dudley was governor, his son experienced an unspecified difficulty or indignity within the Di Society. Dudley thanked Swain for lecturing the boy "for his improper conduct." Swain would have his gratitude if he would check on the student "in such way as you think best." While inclined to support his son, Dudley considered the matter a proper one for faculty regulation.[35]

Almost certainly Swain's closest friend among his fellow governors was William A. Graham. The relationship involved not only personal and political ties, but also family ones: their spouses were cousins. The stress of Graham sons in university difficulties thus must have weighed especially heavily on Swain. At least Graham was understanding when his son Joseph was dismissed. He was "much obliged" for Swain's letter as to the causes. "I have for some time been apprehensive that without a change of his habits," Graham told his friend, "his college course would be of little profit." Joseph had permission to return to the university. Graham would nevertheless, at the end of the session, consider whether to transfer him to another institution or to business. The faculty later suspended another Graham son for two weeks for interfering with a faculty member while discharging his duty and offering him a gross insult. Swain, perhaps mindful of the prior problems with Joseph, dissented. Only a day later a less severe resolution evolved. Upon the student's "ample and satisfactory apology for his conduct," Professor Phillips requested, and the faculty unanimously granted, immediate reinstatement.[36]

The son-in-college experience was one of double jeopardy for former governor James Iredell. Not one son, but two, gave him trouble. The older, the third James in the Iredell line, was less than fully devoted to his studies. Twice his mother had written to urge "greater application" upon him, Governor Iredell once told Swain. James might be unable to pass his examinations, Iredell feared. If Swain agreed, he was to grant him permission to return home at once. Iredell would then "induce him by close application to his studies to endeavor to prepare himself for readmission to the college."[37]

The "T" in Samuel T. Iredell's name stood for "Tredwell," but it could have stood for "Trouble." Sam appears to have commenced his journey into delinquency with an unauthorized Sabbath-day trip to the country. He then discharged a pistol near a campus building during study hours and refused Swain's demand that he surrender the pistol. Combined with previous offenses, this led to dismissal. Soon, however, he "was restored upon a written pledge."

Sam was suspended once for having "given great trouble"; his parents were to be advised. At least two lists of students who failed to pay their tuition included his name. He was before the faculty for peremptorily disobeying the president; going to Raleigh and Hillsboro without permission; and being absent from prayers ten times, from church once. His father requested an excused absence for one unsanctioned trip home on the grounds that he was sick. The same letter, though, had to deny Sam's involvement "in the outrage on the President's domicil [sic]." He had "too much of the blood and the feelings of a gentleman to have engaged in any insult . . . to you and your family," Governor Iredell contended to Swain.

An attitude adjustment would have benefited Sam. Once, offered reconsideration of a sentence upon appropriate acknowledgments and promises, he expressed indifference about whether he stayed at the university. His father, he said, had always treated him as a gentleman, and always would. The father would believe him against any or all of the faculty. Not surprisingly, the faculty rejected his petition because it "regarded the tone of its language as inappropriate."[38] Somehow Sam survived his multitudinous disciplinary problems. He graduated with the Class of 1849.[39]

Like Iredell, Governor Charles Manly encountered difficulties with multiple students from his family. He once wrote Swain, "I am almost afraid to hear from my thoughtless idle son Basil," but requested "a line" on him from Swain. Three weeks later the faculty instructed their secretary to write Manly that it advised Basil's withdrawal for neglect of his duties. A Manly nephew was reprimanded for going to Pittsboro without approval. Swain was to communicate the facts to Manly, who was governor at the time.[40]

Finally, even the president of the university was not exempt from such family problems. In his senior year at the university Swain's son, Richard Caswell Swain, was reported to the faculty for talking at prayers.[41]

Absence of proper student decorum was sometimes attributed to excess leniency on Swain's part. Nancy Hilliard was hostess at Chapel Hill's Eagle Hotel. When any of her pets among the students got into trouble, she put on her bonnet, walked to see Swain, and begged for them, apparently with considerable effect. Swain may have been too parental in disciplinary cases, Cornelia Phillips Spencer would say, but he never regretted that "he has leaned too much on mercy's side." "He would condescend to an erring boy rather than give him up." As a parent himself, he was thinking of the parents' anguish when a ruined boy returned to them.[42]

Presumably the parents were grateful, and certainly the indulged students were. Samuel T. Iredell once thanked Swain profusely for saving him from "dismemberment... from the institution." Swain's "kind and benevolent interposition," Iredell said, "rescued me from that pain." He confessed to not having given Swain "that respect which was due." Swain, he said, "ask[ed] nothing but what is for our individual good and the prosperity of the institution." Almost a century after his death, Swain was praised for overruling the faculty in refusing to expel students, motivated by the belief that "the chief concern of the university was to make character and not to break people."[43]

At times Swain had companions in lenity. Longtime trustee Charles Manly once told Swain he had informed some young men that their case was without remedy, "that the law for dismission was peremptory," and that neither the faculty nor the trustees "could alter it." Manly was having sober second thoughts, however. The young men looked so imploringly that he felt sorry for them and wondered about moving for reconsideration.[44] At other times the trustees were less sympathetic with their president's seeming inability to resist tales of distress or appeals for mercy. His "suffer[ing] the Draconian code of the trustees to lie dormant, whilst he lectured, reproved and exhorted," eventually brought censure. Former Governor James Iredell read a trustee-committee resolution from the chapel rostrum at commencement, expressing the opinion that disciplinary laxity was injuring the institution. Swain was not quiescent about the accusation. He is said to have responded "with spirit, even with heat"; "with such emotion, not unmingled with indignation." The trustees apparently did not mention the subject again.[45]

They were once memorialized, however, by a dissident faculty member who complained of Swain's role in proceedings on a student's disorderly conduct. Henri Herrisse, instructor in French, had detailed for the faculty the classroom misconduct of a member of the junior class. Six faculty members voted to dismiss, with five in the negative. Swain joined the minority, producing a tie vote and causing the motion to fail. Swain then, in Herrisse's view, "little willing... to bear the responsibility of such an unjust measure," declared the motion out of order. Herrisse complained bitterly of the students showing him disrespect and the faculty not backing him. He lamented to the trustees a want of discipline and a general maladministration of the affairs and government of the college by Swain and the faculty.[46]

Swain informed Charles Manly, secretary to the board, that a committee chaired by Elisha Mitchell was preparing the faculty's response. Swain would reply "to such parts of Mr. Herrisse's Memorial, as relates [sic] especially to myself." He acknowledged that he had "sometimes been censured" for overindulgence to students. Such indulgence paled, however, when compared to that which he had granted to Herrisse. He had always regarded a faculty member as prima facie in the right in student disciplinary matters; he could not, however, "act upon the principle that the instructor never errs, and that the pupil is always wrong." No faculty member, he claimed, had had more issues with the young men than he had.

Herrisse was "much excited" by the perceived insults "heaped upon him" at the faculty meeting. He had, he said, intended to meet Swain "in the same kindly spirit" Swain had manifested toward him that evening. He had been prevented, however, by the assaults upon him by the other faculty members. He now said, with some ambiguity but in context quite possibly belligerently, that when things quieted down, "you will see me come out and give Governor Swain all that he asks and even more."

Rightly or wrongly, Swain viewed the statement, and Herrisse's general demeanor toward him, as hostile. Several faculty members took the same view and came to Swain's defense. Charles Phillips, for example, said, "This imputation of lax discipline is to say the least a very cheap criticism." Elisha Mitchell was more empathetic. Trumpeting his senior-faculty status and extensive experience in higher education, first at Yale, then at UNC, he proclaimed that the Herrisse "paper from beginning to end was an atrocious libel."

Herrisse now took his cause to the sitting governor, Thomas Bragg. Led on by Governor Swain, he informed Bragg, the two oldest members of the faculty had branded him "with the horrid epithet of infamous liar." Instead of a calm and dignified assessment or refutation of his arguments, the faculty "heaped upon me the most unjust and outrageous insults." In melodramatic fashion, Herrisse charged Governor Bragg with determining "whether I shall depart from this Institution with a mark of infamy which, whether innocent or guilty, must stick to me forever!"

Herrisse said to Swain, as he had to Bragg, that Swain's remarks "*did* create in my mind the impression of a threat on your part to raise a mob against me by reading my memorial to the classes." Swain's disavowal of such intention, however, had caused him to withdraw the statement. Still, the critique could hardly have been more explicit or damning. Discipline in the institution was lacking. "Impunity, repeated impunity," he stated emphatically, "removes all checks . . . and hardens the most timid of students." Students, he said, laughed when discipline was attempted.

He could not have been more candid in expressing his view of student disrespect for Swain. "Let the President himself venture to address all the classes in the Chapel," a "consecrated place," he said, and even useful, well-worded remarks from "the first officer of the Institution, a man of note, a man of age," would draw laughter and stomping "and almost drown his voice." Some delinquents, he said, appeared before the faculty for eleventh and twelfth times.

Swain, shaken by the allegations, encouraged a thorough trustee investigation. A board committee should visit the institution, patiently examine its records, and conduct "a searching inquiry into the . . . success with which instruction is communicated and discipline maintained." He acknowledged a rare insecurity about his survival in the university presidency, stating that if the allegations were true, he was "altogether uncertain of my station." Unanswered, they would negate his capacity "to exercise the influence over the Faculty, indispensable to the successful management of the affairs of the institution." An early decision on the issue was, in Swain's view, important.

Swain's concerns proved unwarranted. Whatever the faculty may have thought about his disciplinary standards and practices, it apparently thought less of the hotheaded Frenchman. The faculty resolved that discipline was as well maintained as it had known it to be. Individual members also came to Swain's defense. Professor Charles Phillips denied that there was any formal proposal or threat from anyone to read Herrisse's memorial to the students, "least of all from the President." Professor John T. Wheat opined, "in my humble judgment this impudent assault upon Pres. Swain's administration, by our allegorical accuser . . . is without a parallel." The trustees accepted the Swain-faculty version. Herrisse left the university at the end of the term, and the crisis passed. While it persisted, however, it was among the more unpleasant experiences of Swain's almost thirty-three years in the university presidency.[47]

The faculty must not have been too concerned about Swain's alleged leniency, for at times it entrusted disciplinary matters to his sole discretion. The president, it once declared, had "a plenary power to adjust the difficulty with" a certain student. Three students with discipline problems were "referred to the President for private admonitions." When a dismissed student petitioned for "an honorable dismission" that would enable him to enroll at Wake Forest College, the subject was referred to the president with "discretionary power." When several students in trouble were committed to different faculty members for disposition, a student named "Ruffin" was committed to Swain.[48]

At times the faculty gave Swain directives in these matters. He was to reprimand a senior "for misbehavior at Prayers," to advise a father to withdraw his son for neglect of studies and irregularity of conduct, to admonish students who had brought from Hillsboro "the liquors of the freshman treat" and to write their parents on the subject, and to "try the effect of a private interview" with a student whose father's whereabouts were uncertain. Two dismissed students were to "be received when they shall have made a proper written communication to the President."[49]

The faculty sometimes referred disciplinary matters to a committee, of which Swain was often a member. He, with Professors James Phillips and William Green, was once assigned to interview students regarding disorders in East Building. With Professors Elisha Mitchell and William Green, he was to question certain students regarding disturbances of a stated date. On one occasion Swain and Mitchell were to deal with certain student disciplinary and academic problems. Swain and Mitchell were also to interview three other students "in regard to the irregularities and improprieties of their conduct."[50]

Rumors of student misconduct sometimes exceeded the facts. A Raleigh newspaper once reported a fight between two UNC students that ended in the murder of one. One student, it was said, had struck the other with a leaded whip, then stabbed him. The stab wounds had proved fatal, and the murderer had escaped. Swain issued a circular contradicting "the grossly exaggerated statements of riot and disorder among the students." The university's friends, he said, could "felicitate themselves" upon the fact that in the school's sixty-four-year history, no death had occurred there by violence. Not only had no murder occurred, a "general character . . . for quiet and subordination" prevailed. University history, Swain stated, "will show that the subordination and general quiet prevailing during the last ten years is at least as great as that of any like period since its foundation." For appeal to the pious element, he noted that student interest in religion was on the upswing.

The circular proved reassuring. He was "profoundly pained," one university supporter wrote Swain, when he heard "of any disturbance at that seat of learning, which is likely to alienate our people from it." This circular, Swain could be "well assured," had "favorably impressed the public mind."[51]

While Swain could deny "riot and disorder" in this instance, such did occur, at least certain student misbehavior was so designated. The faculty used the gentler term "disorders" when students shattered a tutor's windows with stones and other missiles, endangered several faculty members, and took faculty members' horses on unauthorized rides. The sterner term "riotous conduct" described behavior toward a "Mr. Deems," presumably Charles F. Deems, adjunct professor of rhetoric and logic. Full disclosure by the students and a satisfactory apology to Deems might allow the malefactors "to join college and pursue their studies."[52]

In 1845, the trustees met "to consider of certain riotous proceedings in the College campus and buildings." They approved initiation of criminal proceedings by the faculty, and their president, Governor Graham, was to communicate the proceedings to the university president. Graham's ensuing letter to Swain stressed the importance of pursuing criminal punishments. Five years later similar occurrences brought similar language, "riot and disorder," and similar proceedings and sanctions. Certain students, "in direct violation of the college laws and shameful disregard of written pledges," had "committed wanton trespass upon the college property and indulged in excesses of other kinds." Those responsible were to pay for the repairs, but even so, the trustees approved criminal prosecution of the offenders. At the beginning of the next session President Swain was to read the 1845 trustee resolution to the students, together with Governor Graham's letter written in obedience thereto, and to announce the board's determination to enforce "the measures therein indicated as indispensable to maintenance of proper discipline."[53]

This failed to produce the desired effect. In the following year students were again before the faculty as Swain read their answers to questions about their participation "in the disturbances." Swain invited corrections; there were none. He then addressed them "in a most solemn manner" about their conduct before announcing "the sentence of dismission." The faculty departed for Professor James Phillips's house to write "the necessary letters" to their parents. The faculty's resolve failed, however, when one student acknowledged his connection with "the riot" and desired reinstatement. Swain read his petition, and the faculty unanimously granted it.[54]

While "riot" would overstate some forms of student misconduct, no term could exaggerate the appalling nature of one set of occurrences that affected Swain personally, deeply, and poignantly. A group of students "blacked" (disguised) themselves, went to "a Negro house," seized Suky Mayhs, "a common Negro prostitute," tore off her clothes, and painted her naked body. To conclude the night's "sport," they painted the gate to Swain's house. A few nights later they poured a quart of oil in the pulpit of the New Chapel and in Swain's piazza. They soon again painted Swain's gate. Horrific enough under the best of circumstances, these acts occurred while Swain's almost six-year-old son David lay ill, and then a corpse, at his residence. His daughter Anne was also there and dangerously ill.

The Philanthropic Society investigated whether its members were involved. It found no member implicated. If the truth was not elicited, however, representative members asked Swain "not to allocate the failure to any want of zeal, or sympathy in behalf of any injured and outraged parent, but to the difficulties which usually attach themselves to things of this nature." They detested the actions, as would "every high-minded honorable man." The enormity of the crime demanded punishment. When students refused to respond about their involvement, the faculty commenced "a general sweep," which proved unproductive. Apparently, the perpetrators were never identified.

The intensely personal nature of the outrages did not deter Swain from addressing them. He commenced with general remarks to the students on their duty to discourage such offenses. He then spoke "very feelingly to the death of his son and with deep sensibility of the general courtesy and sympathy exhibited by the students." The feelings produced, he said, could never be forgotten. His supposition that "such would universally be the case," however, had been disappointed. "I relied with confidence on the Honour of the students as my protection from all external care during that period of deep distress," he told his pupils, "[b]ut alas! I was mistaken." "[T]he privacy of the abode of my affliction was invaded," he continued, "even the sanctity of the dead was invaded by your ruthless inhumanity." "I will expose the whole affair," he pledged, "and its authors shall be brought to punishment." Swain begged the students not to force him into "such violent measures." He regretted the allusion to his "private wrongs." He would have preferred that "they should descend with me to the grave."

Swain frequently wiped tears, "and his whole frame seemed racked with the bitterness of emotions." The students experienced "intense excitement" and were anxious to discover the villain—"hard will be his fate," said one. The Phi Society report, while exculpating its members, expressed "abhorrence of the deed, and [an] earnest desire to discover its perpetrators if possible." The investigatory committee read its correspondence with Swain to the students, to which Swain replied, grateful for the result of the investigation and their sympathy. Like others, this incident passed, but it is unlikely that Swain ever altogether forgot it.[55]

Fights between students were common. One at Nancy Hilliard's tavern saw a student "well nigh beaten to a mummy." Swain and other faculty members separated the combatants and dispersed the crowd. Another brought dismissal to two brawling sophomores. When students requested clemency for one, Swain advised that the rules required the student to petition for himself, which he had not done. Upon a second petition, denied for the same reason, a large portion of the student's class protested by absenting themselves from prayers and recitations. That, too, violated a university regulation, and the students were warned to consider themselves dismissed upon a further occurrence. Swain sent a circular letter to parents explaining the resulting dismissals.[56]

Student possession of firearms was a problem. At the commencement of each session, Swain visited the college rooms to inquire whether the occupants had guns, pistols, or other deadly weapons. On one occasion a student, among "the stoutest fellows in college," replied while "shaking a very significantly brawny fist,

'None but this, sir?'" "The Governor," said the student's roommate, "was very much amused at the reply and laughed heartily." Swain was unaware, however, that the roommate "had a pistol in the draw [sic] and therefore said nothing."

A student publicly accused of an offense once approached his perceived accuser and "drew from his breast a pistol." Before he could cock it, however, he dropped it, and Swain ordered him removed from the hall. The perceived accuser then admitted to Swain that he had written the offending item. The confession put him in fear for his life, for he soon said, "At every step I am in danger of being attacked." "One attempt at my life is a sufficient excuse," he claimed, "for my going armed." It was a most unpleasant business, he said, to go to church with a lethal weapon in case a man should attack him.[57]

There were occasional destructive fires, likely student induced. In 1831, the university's first president, Joseph Caldwell, had constructed the first astronomical observatory connected with a university in America. It was on the highest summit of a hill north of the Raleigh Road, near the village graveyard. In 1838, early in Swain's administration, a fire destroyed the abandoned structure. Swain acknowledged the improbability of ferreting out the perpetrators by voluntary testimony, but he and the faculty had requested from the trustee executive committee advice on the desirability of resorting to the criminal law to discover the offenders. Kemp Battle viewed this episode as illustrative that Swain "could be abundantly firm when occasion justified." There is, though, no evidence that the offenders were discovered.[58]

In 1856, the belfry in front of South Building burned. A contemporary student account attributes the cause to boys "throwing balls of cotton saturated with spirits of turpentine." Swain thought "a judicial investigation" desirable and initially believed there would be little difficulty in ferreting out the culpable persons. That could not be done, however, without the intervention of the trustees. The trustee executive committee appointed a faculty committee of Swain, Elisha Mitchell, and William H. Battle to investigate the cause of, and the means taken to prevent or extinguish, the fire. The committee reported that there was no clue that would enable it to ascertain the facts. A longstanding rule was an impediment to the investigation; no student could be compelled to testify against his fellows or incriminate himself.

The faculty committee believed, nevertheless, that a grand jury inquiry could generate the facts. It thus submitted the matter to the trustee committee to decide whether a criminal prosecution should be instituted. The trustee committee requested that Swain request a judicial investigation and indictments of the guilty felons. This too proved unproductive, perhaps because two of the witnesses had left the state and the other "had quietly gone to sleep after ascertaining that the Belfry was on fire." Charles Manly ultimately advised Swain, apparently for the trustee committee, that "it would be as well to drop it for the present."[59]

Chapel was a favored venue for student misbehavior. Early in Swain's tenure several students had been "very remiss in their attendance on prayers," notwithstanding special warnings. Swain admonished them that even at examination time, absences would be recorded as usual, and the president would hear excuses. Without satisfactory explanations, the offending students would not be recommended for a degree.

New students had to be taught proper chapel decorum. Once the entire freshman class appeared before the faculty because a large number had created "disorder in Chapel." More commonly, individual students were the villains, often reported by the president. Their offenses included impropriety in the Prayer Hall on Sunday evening, answering improperly at prayers, irreverence at prayers, disorder at prayers, stomping in the chapel at evening prayers, sitting on benches forbidden to student use at prayers, failing to stand during prayers and at other appropriate times, and failure to remove hats when entering the chapel. Offenders would generally be "suitably admonished by the President," often with dire warnings of suspension or dismissal upon repetition of the conduct.[60]

Swain continued Caldwell's policy of attempting to confine students to the campus, and even on the campus, within a quadrangle of buildings and a restricted area of ground. At one point the trustees provided that permission to leave during sessions was to be granted sparingly; it increased the expense of education and was injurious to study and discipline. The faculty followed by not allowing students to absent themselves except upon written authorization from home. A student's petition for excused absence was to be sent to his parent or guardian.[61]

Even seemingly desirable off-campus activities drew close faculty scrutiny and occasional punishment. Early in Swain's tenure certain students' names appeared in newspapers "as a portion of the Whig dinner to be given in the Village." At a meeting Swain called, the faculty resolved that he should inform students who attended in the capacity of managers that they should consider themselves dismissed. A circular letter to parents and guardians on the subject was unanimously adopted. When Democratic presidential candidate Stephen A. Douglas spoke in Raleigh in 1860, numerous students requested permission to attend. The faculty resolved that only seniors with permission from home could go. When some students were charged with going without permission, the faculty determined that most in fact had it or "were ... of age." One student was dismissed but reinstated four days later.[62]

Swain encouraged faculty, but not students, to attend the State Fair. With Professors Fetter, Kimberly, and Wheat there, the faculty would be well represented, he once told Governor Manly, "at the great agricultural festival." He hoped the number of students would be smaller, however, "and that under the eyes of their instructors and governors, their deportment will be creditable to us." When students he charged with unsanctioned State Fair attendance "confessed the crime," they received a one-week suspension.[63]

Strenuous efforts to avoid it notwithstanding, students misbehaved in off-campus venues. An establishment called Moring's, eight miles from Chapel Hill, was once the scene of a disturbance involving UNC pupils. One, who had been intoxicated, was unanimously dismissed. Two others, not proven to have been in that state, were retained, but "the President was requested to make a statement to the parents ... of the part ... they had taken in this affair."[64]

Even vacation periods did not always exempt student behavior from university concern and discipline. When students found themselves in off-campus trouble, Swain appears to have seen that they received able legal representation. Governor Manly once wrote Swain that he had gotten Swain's "young friend Miller" off with a five dollar fine "to his grand joy and general surprise."[65]

As student enrollment increased, so too did trustee concern over "unallowed departures from the college by the students." Growth in the number of students, said the trustees, augmented the difficulties in enforcing discipline. This enhanced the importance of faculty exercise of greater diligence over student conduct, especially in preventing these "unallowed departures." The faculty was to employ all means to secure student discipline and to adopt new ordinances and rules if necessary.[66]

A great variety of other offenses commanded the attention of Swain and the faculty, among them ringing the bell and committing other violence to the Village Chapel; playing cards, aggravated by the fact that it occurred on a Sabbath evening; outrages upon the property of the college or of individuals; carrying three locusts into a recitation room; careening through the streets as revelers at 2:30 a.m. on a Sunday, with a senior class member who was consorting with "certain very improper company"; singing during examination hour in a passage of South Building; cruel treatment of new students by upper classmen; and combining to protest the faculty's refusal to readmit a student who had not, as the rules required, petitioned for his own re-admission. General disrespect for the faculty was an overarching concern; at one point the faculty resolved that "all allusions to the Faculty ... whether as individuals or collectively in the speeches delivered hereafter on the public stage be expressly prohibited."[67]

Student financial irresponsibility likewise commanded attention, so much so that Swain and the trustee executive committee sent circulars on it to parents, guardians, and the business community of the Chapel Hill area. Swain himself was a prime target of student financial misdeeds. Thus, the duty he recommended to others was, in his own case, to "be considered an imperative obligation." "[N]o one must be permitted to contract a debt in my name or on my account, here or elsewhere," he enjoined, "without exhibiting specific authority in writing[,] and such authority will rarely be given."

The trustees reminded area merchants that Swain had advised them of the 1855 statute prohibiting these unauthorized extensions of credit to students. Aggravated violations of the law had nevertheless occurred. The law, they admonished, was for the protection of parents and guardians, many of whom resided in distant states. They depended on "the honest State of North Carolina" to shield them "from impositions, and especially from all attempts to seduce [their sons and wards] into habits of imprudent and unlawful expenditure." All authorities of the institution thus would unite to enforce the law. The threats proved, like the idle wind, unmoving, and the efforts to prevent unsanctioned extensions of credit thus futile.[68]

Faculty disciplinary practices and procedures could be subjected to high-level legal opinion. Thomas Ruffin Jr., whose father was the sitting chief justice of the state supreme court, once went, not to his father, but to Judge William Gaston, a special friend of the university, for such a judgment. Swain, he alleged, had requested that he do so. The faculty, in cases of student disturbances, was polling an entire class and demanding "a yay or nay" from each member. Did not this, Ruffin inquired, violate the law, "which forbids a person bearing self evidence, and . . . should any one decline answering, is he by law, considered pleading non guilty[?]" A part of the junior class had declined to answer such a question, not only to screen the offender but also because it was "unjust to demand of us an answer, when there was no suspicion resting on . . . us." Given the choice of answering or being dismissed, however, "none was so bold and constant as to decline."

Gaston responded but declined to render an advisory opinion. Ruffin was honored by the response but disappointed that it lacked "an answer to my queries and my request." The faculty's right to make such laws was not at issue; rather, the question was their conformity with the law against self-incrimination, and whether, in refusing to answer, the student "would be considered by law as pleading non guilty." Ruffin reiterated that he was "urged by Gov. Swain to seek your opinion on these topics," but apparently to no avail.[69]

University trustees and administrators could resort to the law in disciplinary matters. Swain once told an alumnus that life at the university was "pretty much as in your day." The boys, he said, were about as troublesome as usual. They "would probably have been more so," though, he opined, had the trustees not had a dozen of them indicted at the last superior court.[70]

Mischievous misbehavior, rather than outright misconduct, aptly characterized two vexatious incidents during Swain's presidency. The senior class once invited Roman Catholic Archbishop John Hughes to preach the commencement baccalaureate sermon. Swain and the faculty feared that the reaction of orthodox Protestants would destroy the university's patronage. Hughes relieved their anxiety by declining the invitation. Four years later, it was renewed and accepted. There was criticism but no serious adverse consequences.[71]

The second incident occurred as the country and the university were in the throes of post-Civil War Reconstruction. It was tradition that the seniors selected the commencement ball managers and they in turn selected honorary managers. In 1866, the students selected as honorary managers "some most conspicuous Confederate leaders": General John C. Breckenridge, General William R. Cox, President Jefferson Davis, General Robert D. Johnson, General Robert E. Lee, and Governor Zebulon B. Vance. They did so without securing these leaders' consent. Further, it was a time when, with southern representatives excluded, the U.S. Congress had a two-thirds Republican majority and was considering its course with relation to the former Confederate states, including North Carolina. The university was an entity of the state, and the alarm and consternation thus were considerable.

The faculty promptly and unanimously directed Swain to inform the ball managers that their action was "grossly improper." Further, in the circumstances, it was "like[ly] to expose the Institution to undeserved suspicion." The trustee executive committee, with only Governor William W. Holden absent, unanimously approved the faculty's course.

If the influences proceeding from the university were "to be rather against than in favor of the government of the United States," said a Raleigh newspaper, "then we say let it sink at once." Swain, joined by trustee Bartholomew F. Moore, advised the paper that it could not have been "more surprised and mortified" than they were "at the indiscreet proceedings of the Ball Managers." The faculty had expressed similar views. As at President Caldwell's death, Swain said, "festive demonstrations" were improper. The commencement would now, thought Professor Charles Phillips, "be very notorious throughout our country." The 1866 commencement came and went, and the incident passed into history, but not without considerable distress to the university and particularly to its beleaguered president David L. Swain.[72]

The university's academic mission was not exempt from the students' misconduct and, more often, their laxity. On one occasion students "overtly and tacitly combined to absent themselves from recitation." Swain admonished the entire class "in becoming terms." Because of this one, in the future "a much slighter offense could draw down the penalty of dismission." Another occasion found Professor Fordyce Hubbard unable to gain access to his classroom. When ordered to repair to the chapel and recite the lesson, all but six of the students refused. The faculty requested that Swain meet with the students and give them such admonition as he deemed proper. A statement of the affair was to be sent to the parent or guardian of each delinquent.[73]

A group of Phi Society seniors once endeavored to dictate academic policy. The faculty initially refused to receive their anonymous communication to Swain. The message soon came back, however, with three signatures and these demands: (1) that a designated senior receive "first distinction," (2) that no Phi senior be refused his diploma, and (3) that a copy of the resolution be transmitted to the faculty in the name of the Phi seniors. If any Phi senior was denied his diploma, the document threatened, they would refuse theirs. Attempting to place a positive gloss on their audacious demands, they denied any spirit of opposition to the faculty, whom they respected as an enlightened body. They were merely compelled, they asserted, to support a fellow member "in his rights."

Summoned before the faculty, the students received a minilecture from Swain. The faculty had experienced extraordinary unanimity in the compilation of the report complained of, he told them. While not perfect, the faculty had approximated justice better than usual. It could not alter its decisions without losing its self-respect. More important, it could not yield to a remonstrance that "had the appearance at least of intimidation." The students could appeal to the trustees, but they would get no redress from the faculty. They should, Swain counseled, review their act and seriously reflect on the consequences to themselves and the institution.

Soon the faculty received a resolution from the entire Phi Society that thanked members of the senior class for their "noble stand . . . on behalf of an injured class mate." Their fellow members, they alleged, supported their cause and commended their motives. Still, they desired peace and concord, even at the expense of some concession. They thus had requested their brothers to "sacrifice their just proceedings to the decision of the Faculty." Should they see it proper to comply, they were to transmit a copy of these resolutions to the faculty. The complaining brothers acceded to the society's proposal and respectfully recalled the resolution. The complainants were then invited to a second interview with the faculty. Swain made brief remarks and concluded by stating that the matter would be laid before the trustees. Two of the three students then wrote letters of apology. There is no surviving evidence of such action by the third student or of trustee reaction.[74]

The senior class once acknowledged its failure to review several subjects and pleaded lack of time to do so. The faculty rejected its petition to be excused from examinations on that account. Such academic neglect could bring other consequences at commencement. One student, recommended for assistant marshal, had been "so unpunctual in the discharge of his college duties" that the faculty declined the appointment, thereby producing "some dissatisfaction in the college." The chief marshal, who had nominated the student, appeared before the trustees, to be advised by Chief Justice Ruffin, presiding in the governor's absence, to nominate another. The chief marshal considered the advice, but rejected it, and asked to be allowed to resign his position. The trustees acceded to the request.[75]

The disciplinary efforts of Swain and the faculty generally received parental and community support, though at times accompanied by agonizing commentary. News that his son had participated in the destruction of university blackboards was, to one father, "melancholy . . . destroying intelligence." He nevertheless requested from Swain "a full and frank account of my sons conduct." "If he has been thoughtless, negligent, or even mischievous," the grieving father told Swain, "my wounded feelings will find solace in the truth, and I can then cherish a hope, if I shall wish it, that he may be reinstated." The father enclosed a check to replace the blackboards and to repay Swain for the sum he had loaned the boy on which to travel home.[76]

It was with great distress that a father-in-law received Swain's letter informing of his son-in-law's recent improper conduct and consequent dismission. He understood the necessity of making an example of him, however, "to vindicate the character of the institution." The boy had shown deep contrition for his offense, and if he should return to college, his conduct would be exemplary.[77]

The passage of time brought perspective and changed attitudes to some who, as students, had been disciplinary subjects. One said he had believed Swain and the faculty had treated him "with a great want of respect." He had since realized that he was in error about Swain. No man had a greater appreciation for Swain, and he regretted having thought "for a moment that you were disposed to injure one who placed so high a value upon your services as I did." He hoped Swain would be "spared for a long time to your country and family."[78]

Occasionally there were later apologies. A former student wrote Swain from Petersburg, Virginia, during the Civil War to apologize for an incident when he was a student, "the little negro scrape I got into then." He had been arrested and a friend had advised him to see Swain, "as you were *ex officia* [*sic*], *in loco parentis* of all such boys as myself." A "servant" aroused a sleeping Swain, who sent for the boy to come to him. "It was certainly one of the severest trials I ever experienced," the youth said, as he inquired about "the case as it stands." He concluded with a fervent, touching prayer for Swain's longevity. His replacement would "be difficult to find." The student thus said, "May you live long to administer the affairs of that noble institution."[79]

Student misconduct could have later consequences. Swain might be asked about "the habits and character" of a student "when at College." He had thought them good, the inquirer would say, but had come to understand that the student had been dismissed for some impropriety and "was very dissipated and immoral while there."[80]

Swain's good report could be essential to a former student's admission to another institution. Through a supporter, one who apparently had not received an honorable "dismission" sought such from Swain. The young man wanted the good opinion of his numerous relatives, and the supporter thought he "perhaps... might be induced to act uprightly and study closely."[81] Another offered Swain "a short explanation of a few circumstances regarding my application for readmission into college." He confessed to having intercepted and altered, to his benefit, Swain's communication to his father. If he had to go elsewhere, he recognized the necessity of a certification of good behavior from Swain. "It would not be charitable," he acknowledged sheepishly, "to recommend an individual elsewhere when you refuse him admittance into your own precincts."[82]

Some student offenses now seem minor. Study hours appear to have been considered sacred. There were instances in which Swain admonished students for sitting out in the campus, or in front of East Building or in South Building, during these hours. Playing marbles during study hours drew his and the faculty's reproof, as did congregating in the campus during examinations. On one occasion "[a]fter some remarks from the President," students denied having thrown acorns, a denial of dubious credibility. A final seemingly minor matter acquires significance from the student's later role in the life of the university. "Mr. Todd [*sic*] R. Caldwell of the senior class was called up, & told that he must forth with remove his dog from the precincts of the university." Caldwell, who read law under Swain while at UNC, was later governor of North Carolina and thus ex-officio chair of the university's trustees.[83]

The foregoing could leave an impression that student conduct was consistently bad. On the contrary there were episodic intervals of "quiet." Swain once complimented the students on "preserving better order than he had previously seen during his Presidency." The following year he regarded senior-class deportment as superior to that of any class he had known.[84] Swain later expressed his pleasure with the deportment and apparent diligence of the young men. It was a period, he said, with "a little bell ringing late at night," but the general deportment was very good. He had not even written a "complaining letter" about a student.[85]

A few years later Swain wrote to Judge Battle, "We have never had a session of greater quiet than the present, or one characterized by greater sobriety and industry." The freshman class, in particular, deserved the credit. Later still, Lucy Battle reported to the judge that "[t]he Gov . . . was quite lively—told me . . . he has a goodly number of boys and all is as quiet as can be expected." The faculty resolved that discipline was as well maintained as they had known it to be. Swain noted that even the oldest senior professor "will admit that he has never known more general quiet sobriety than have advantaged the last 8 weeks."[86]

Such "quiet and sobriety" was not the norm, however. There were times when "the conduct of some students" rendered their president "so very much excited that he could not sleep." Apparently, he contemplated resigning on account of it. His daughter once reported him "*determined* to resign his situation here." The talk soon died down, however, even though "the boys ha[d] been doing very ugly." "All such disturbances you know excite the Gov. very much," Lucy Battle told her husband, "and it was probably under such excitement that he made the threat."[87]

In his history of the university, the Battles's son Kemp was apologetic for having perhaps "dwelt too much on the pranks and frolics of the students," which he attributed to "the defective system of discipline."[88] He should not have been, for a different approach would have failed to depict, fully and accurately, the university as it was in those days. Nor should a biographer of David L. Swain be defensive about treating at some length this aspect of his work as president of the university. After all, it consumed a considerable portion of the man's time and energy for the last half of his life.

CHAPTER 10

Teacher

*"Uncommonly interesting and inspiring ... always ready
to deepen an impression or illuminate a dark passage"*

A S HE HANDLED DISCIPLINARY matters, Swain was instructing. Most of his interactions with students were, to some degree, didactic in purpose. Throughout his UNC presidency, however, he was not just an administrator but also a classroom teacher. His teaching load did not differ dramatically from that of other faculty members. They were responsible for ten recitations per week; Swain, for seven. Recitation orders establish that he had a significant share of the tutelage assignments.[1] A professor had charge of each of the four classes; Swain had the seniors. Sometimes his absence caused postponement of senior speeches; at others, the recitations were distributed among faculty present "until the return of the President." He was considered the "Examiner" of the seniors.[2] Swain dignified the senior class. They were exempt from attending the most odious recitation, that before breakfast. He held as a maxim that "as is the Senior class so is the University." Its members received a one-month holiday before commencement. They were presumed to be improving their minds by reading and writing.

Faculty members with chapel duties could claim exemptions from Sunday recitations. Swain was among those upon whom this duty devolved when necessary. He would also substitute teach for other professors. In his final semester he reported "doing double duty" due to the absence of one faculty member and indisposition of another. For the first time in his life, he presided simultaneously over recitations from three classes: sophomore, junior, and senior.

Swain taught in the library. Its volumes were kept in the lecture room on the second story of South Building, and for many years it was called Governor Swain's recitation or lecture room. Only Swain and the librarian used it.[3] Swain took the

> UNIVERSITY OF NORTH CAROLINA.
> CHAPEL HILL, N. C., *___* 1867.
>
> Every Student is required to attend prayers thirteen times a week, and Divine worship on the forenoon of every Sabbath. The Freshmen and Sophomores have fifteen, the Juniors fifteen, and the Seniors eleven recitations a week. All absences, whether unavoidable or not, are recorded, and a very simple computation will show the proportion of duties performed or omitted.
>
> During the half session, which closed on Friday evening last, (a period of ten weeks,) Mr. *___* has been absent from Prayers ___ times, from recitations 5 times, and from attendance on Divine Worship, ___ times—of these absences, ___ from Prayers, ___ from Recitations and ___ from Divine worship were unavoidable.
>
> His relative grade of Scholarship in his class *is Respectable in Latin & Greek, Very Respectable in the Bible & French & Good in Mathematics.*
>
> *He received the Second Distinction in Mathematics in the General Report.*
>
> *His Deportment is Very Good.*
>
> Yours very Respectfully,
> DAVID L. SWAIN,
> President

UNC student report from Swain era.

classroom-instruction dimension of his duties seriously, so much so that he had students come to his house to obtain their "Reports."[4]

In Swain's view the chief function of the university was to prepare political leaders for the state. As one steeped in the art of politics, he was well suited to the task. He once told Charles Manly he wanted "instruction practical to the greatest possible extent." An ideal of public service permeated the life of the university under Swain's leadership.[5] Students were well aware of this objective. One recorded the president's expressing to a class that "the whole and sole object of study was to express our thoughts in the best language either in speaking or writing." Swain would cite examples of men whose character students "might study with profit ... whose schemes of life were well and wisely planned, and well and wisely executed." Unfavorable models received equal attention, among them a father who had been expelled from the university and whose two sons later incurred the same fate and "met most violent deaths."[6]

The subject matter of, and materials for, Swain's classes were well suited to this public-service orientation. He taught the seniors constitutional and international law, or, as he entitled it, national law, intellectual philosophy, and moral science. He taught by questions and answers, with close adherence to text. He required memorization, in order, of tables of contents or marginal topics, which classes often found burdensome. He lectured on topics such as the Magna Carta, the Petition and Bill of Rights, and the character of the great men of North Carolina and the United States. At one commencement he examined seniors on constitutional and international law in the presence of three trustees: the sitting governor, John Motley Morehead, and John D. Hawkins and Charles Manly, who also held public offices. A later audience was more sophisticated still: it included President James K. Polk; secretary of the navy John Y. Mason; Governor William A. Graham, ex-officio president of the trustees; former governors John Branch and John M. Morehead; and Judge William H. Battle.[7] A posthumous appraisal states that Swain "knew how to teach constitutional law and political economy as they were not elsewhere taught in America." In the context of a curriculum dominated by "the tiresome classics," his lectures on the rewards of a professional life were enticing, and the importance of public speaking came to be appreciated.[8]

A contemporary student diary offers insight into Swain's teaching manner and methods as well as his subject matter. An opening entry gives the subject matter as the Declaration of Rights prefixed to the North Carolina Constitution. As each section was recited, Swain would briefly state its purpose and the meaning of technical legal terms. The class reportedly was attentive as, in Governor Morehead's presence, Swain presented forcibly "from the President's chair" that in the United States power was vested in the people, not in "the King as the fountain of all power." Soon students were reciting to Swain from the federal Constitution, from which the diarist "derived much instruction." Impromptu classes, too, were interesting and informative. "The Governor sent for us about nine o'clock," the student once recorded, "and we went down to his house," where Swain addressed them "on the connection between the State and the General Government, the progress of liberty in Great Britain, and gave us some general remarks of an indefinite character."

Daylong sessions on political economy brought "pretty hard study" but no complaint. A student once bragged that he had "uniformly prepared the lessons well," motivated by Swain's inspirational teaching: "The peculiarly instructive manner of the Governor, his happy illustrations, and rich fund of anecdote, made the recitations more interesting and profitable than they would otherwise have been, and I hope that I have benefitted in no small degree by my study of this science."

Swain brought "real life" illustrations to his classroom. When banks were the subject in political economy, for example, "the practical operations of a Bank were explained . . . by taking up an exhibit furnished by the State Bank to the last Legislature." The course was inherently interesting to the student, but it derived "new attractions" from the fact that Swain, who had much information on all subjects, was "peculiarly at home here."[9]

On rare occasions Swain was "not as good as usual." The enthralled student attributed the decline to the subject matter, however, not the teacher. "The reason," he said, "was that the Chapter is very difficult, and subtle." Still, he was sufficiently enamored with the teacher and the class that he was "self-enraged" when "negligent forgetfulness" caused him to miss a session.

The governor's lectures were "obviously the result of long years of study and reflection." "The more acquainted I become with Governor Swain," he wrote, "the higher becomes my estimate of his abilities," continuing: "He shows so much information on every subject, and yet on all subjects offers such original views that I know not whether most to admire his knowledge or his mind. Each are extraordinary, and their possessor deserves even a higher reputation than he has."[10]

The diarist was persuaded that, with Swain's assistance, he could "lay the foundation for a superstructure of eminent legal attainments." Swain advised him on the study of law, even visiting him and his roommate in their room for that purpose. He examined them on their course of history and recommended that they "take up either Gibbon's Chapter on the Feudal System, or the Introduction to Robertson's Life of Charles V." Remarks followed on the character of the reading that should be given to works of law. Anecdotes from English, American, and North Carolina legal history amplified his points. Swain promised to pursue the subject further, and the budding legal scholar pledged to "make it a general rule to register here the substance of the Governor's conversations." He expected "to obtain in this way a very valuable fund of information" from "the most popular individual of the Faculty."[11]

Initially Swain held the title "President and Professor of National and Constitutional Law." When Judge Battle arrived in the 1840s as professor of law, the "Professor of National and Constitutional Law" portion of Swain's title was dropped. No reason appears in the university records. It may be that in those formative days of university-based legal education, the thinking was that there could be only one professor of law.[12]

Loss of title notwithstanding, Swain continued to teach the courses considered introductory to the study of law, concluding with one composed of lectures on the history of constitutional law.[13] Despite Battle's presence and the beginnings of a modern law school at Chapel Hill, students continued to "read law" under his tutelage. Before Battle's arrival Swain ordered, for himself and the university, books suitable only for legal instruction, among them Kent's *Commentaries*. He invited others, including some nonlawyers, to attend his examinations on Kent.[14]

Some who read law under Swain later held significant public offices. Tod R. Caldwell, one of Western North Carolina's best criminal lawyers, succeeded William W. Holden as governor of North Carolina upon Holden's impeachment, was elected to the position in 1872, and died in office. John Willis Ellis served in the General Assembly and as a superior court judge and was governor of North Carolina from 1859 to 1861. Samuel Field Phillips held several state offices and had a lengthy tenure as U.S. solicitor general. Nicholas W. Woodfin, prominent Asheville attorney, served in the General Assembly and the 1861–1862 state Constitutional Convention; he was a regular Swain correspondent and handled Swain's personal business in his native Western North Carolina.[15]

Swain's teaching repertoire included religious and moral instruction. He spent an hour on Sunday afternoons teaching the Bible to seniors. Student preparation at times went for naught, as the president consumed the hour lecturing on the advantages of reading the Old Testament "and the interest excited by a perusal of the volume, considered independently of its divine origin." He quoted distinguished men on the subject. To encourage scriptural learning postgraduation, Swain began the practice of giving each graduating student a Bible; the gifts bore his autograph. More broadly, Swain lectured on what to read and how. Even if his subject was "rather stale," wrote his admiring diarist, he was imparting much "useful—real practical" information and dispensing it so liberally that his audience took pleasure.

In the chapel at prayers, his subject, "addressed . . . at full length," was morality. All students, old and new, must be moral. "Moral Culture was far more important than the intellect: without the former[,] the latter was an actual detriment to society." Student days were the time for developing character. Uniformly, the university's distinguished graduates had been moral men. "A villain at eighteen is a villain at forty," hence the importance of character building in youth.[16]

One aspect of religious instruction, compulsory Sunday attendance at university chapel, proved a vexatious and divisive issue for Swain, the faculty, and the trustees. Student attendance at this service was a longstanding university requirement. Upon the 1848 completion of the Chapel Hill Episcopal Church building,

Professor William M. Green moved the faculty to allow student members of that denomination to attend Sunday worship in their church. Green's position ultimately prevailed but not without a contentious interim.[17] The faculty requested Swain to convey to the trustees that some members of the Episcopal Church wished their sons to be absent from public worship in the college chapel in order to attend their own church in the village. Swain was "to intimate to the Trustees that the Faculty are divided on the subject."[18]

In December 1848, there were numerous signatories to a petition to the trustees to allow students of age (majority, presumably, then twenty-one), and those underage upon the request of a parent or guardian, to select their own place of worship rather than being required to attend the college chapel. The petitioners believed it would be "in strict agreement with the liberal spirit of our constitution and laws, which favors no denomination, but guarantees liberty of worship to all." Simultaneously, Swain detailed for a correspondent his work on the "free to worship" question.[19]

The trustees bought into the proposal almost verbatim, ordaining that "hereafter students in the university who are of full age shall have the privilege of attending Divine Worship in any one of the Houses dedicated to that purpose in Chapel Hill:—And when they are not of full age they shall be permitted to attend at such places of public worship in Chapel Hill as their Parents or Guardians may in writing indicate." The faculty was to adopt regulations to ensure the attendance of each student at some place of public worship in Chapel Hill.[20]

Shortly afterward the trustees imposed a limitation. Students taking advantage of the policy had to select a church within two days of admission. Once made the selection was irrevocable until the term ended. There was one exception. They could opt to return to the chapel service; that, if done, could not be changed during the session. The duty of the faculty to adopt regulations assuring student attendance at some local place of worship was reiterated. In less than a month the trustees again altered the ordinance. Once made, the selection now would not be modified during the session.[21]

For approximately a decade the foregoing policy prevailed. The issue then, for reasons not clear, resurfaced. Parents petitioned Swain to permit their sons an alternative worship experience.[22] They were not the only ones concerned. The Diocese of the North Carolina Convention of the Episcopal Church petitioned Swain and the trustees protesting, on both religious and constitutional grounds, the requirement that students attend chapel worship rather than that of their own faith traditions. A citizen advised the trustees that allowing students to attend regular churches rather than chapel worship on Sunday mornings would be all right. They should disapprove of sectarian tenets being inculcated in the minds of the students, however: "[O]ur university is common ground for all to occupy," he said, "and every thing of a sectarian nature should be strictly avoided."[23]

Alexander Wilson, respected educator and a Presbyterian clergyman, offered Swain a thoughtful perspective. It was clear to him that the congregations had no cause to complain. Because there was considerable feeling on the subject, however, would it not be advisable to allow the congregations to have worship at 11:00 if they saw fit? Swain and his Presbyterian brethren of the faculty had "done everything that could be expected and desired ... to maintain the original plan of the college as far as religious worship is concerned." The time for a change had arrived, however. The village was now too large, said Wilson, to accommodate all the families, together with the students, if all denominations were to agree to close their house of worship when a service was held at the college chapel. Some denomination would necessarily open its place of worship; it would thereby gain an advantage over the others, creating dissatisfaction and jealousies. The university would experience no peace on the subject of churches until preaching at the chapel was dispensed with, and students were required to attend preaching every Sabbath forenoon at the church of their or their parents' preference.[24]

Initially the trustees tabled a resolution to give a student's parent or guardian the choice. Later, by a closely divided vote, they agreed to the change in principle and appointed a committee of Battle, Manly, and Winston to implement it. Swain voted for the principle. Later still, the board granted Swain dispensation to exempt students from chapel worship in designated cases. Exempt students were to attend worship conducted by the denomination to which they belonged or services indicated by the parent or guardian. The mandatory nature of such attendance, however, and its underlying philosophy, were clearly articulated. Worship and prayers were an important part of the intellectual and moral training of youth and of order in the community. They therefore were "embraced by the university establishment." All students, then, were to attend public worship on "the Lord's day." Further, without exception, unless temporarily excused by the president or permanently by the board of trustees, students were to attend "the Morning and Evening Prayers."[25]

The serious nature of Swain's subject matter, whether religious or secular, did not preclude his use of humor in conveying it to his students. Indeed, his admiring diarist appears mildly critical of him on this account. While a speaker preferable to Swain was rare in this student's experience, "[l]ike all others," he said, "he has his faults, and with much instruction is mingled much amusement."[26]

Another student journalist records a philosophy class in which the subject was double vision. Swain told an illustrative anecdote. Stanly, interested in a case in the supreme court, "resolved to have a little profit—and drink success to his case." When he reached his room, he invariably missed the keyhole with his key. Imploring him to relinquish the key, a comrade said, "I clearly perceive you don't see the hole." "The Devil I don't," Stanly responded, "I think I see two of them."[27]

The mass exodus from the university during the Civil War left the Class of 1865 with one graduate. The graduate later reported that the senior curriculum "was not at all relaxed" as a consequence. Swain would lead him to an open room, and the normal recitation would be held. At early morning prayers Swain would be standing in front of the chapel with underclassmen when the one senior arrived. He would "step out and with a sweeping oratorical gesture would say, 'See the best man in his class. Look at him. He is the very best man in his class.'" In the evening Dr. James Phillips would step in front of the senior "and with his fist doubled up and his thumb sticking out as if to prod me in the ribs would say, 'Eh! Eh! The worst man in his class,' and repeat the words with emphasis[,] only he pronounced worst as if it were spelled w-u-s-t with a very short sound of u." The student later said he came to understand that Swain and Phillips saw the calamity (Civil War) coming to the university to which they had given their best years and long affection. "[I]f under such circumstances they could find a little relaxation with such pleasantry when the situation was so perfectly fitted for it," he would say, "it was not for me to be annoyed by it."[28]

While Swain liked a good joke, one on him was not well received. A student, John H. Manly, often imitated Swain's peculiar voice. He could do so with exactitude, and he delighted in scaring his fellows as they engaged in their frolics. He never knowingly exercised this mimicry in Swain's presence, however. Manly once approached the post office window and said in Swain's voice, "Mr. McDade hand out my mail." McDade did so, and as Manly turned to leave, mail in hand, he found Swain behind him with a quizzical look on his face. With no reference to the prank, Swain simply said, "Mr. Manly I'll take my mail if you please."[29]

At a time when faculty members considered most students largely uninterested in their studies, UNC students generally liked Swain as a teacher and responded positively to his instruction. They took an irreverent view of him, calling him behind his back "Old Bunk" for his native county of Buncombe. His physical appearance too prompted impious comments. A bit "fuddled" by wine, a student once remarked that "Old Bunk" reminded him of chaos: he was "without form and void."[30]

Such irreverence notwithstanding, Swain's teaching clearly captivated many students. One once wrote of being "so much engaged upon Governor Swain and studies" that he had been unable to respond to a letter. Students preferred him to other professors. Once in Swain's absence his students spent three days under Dr. Mitchell's tutelage. He was heartily tired of it, a student noted, finding it "indeed... sometimes very dull."

A student, unable to write a composition for Swain, dealt with his writer's block by "giv[ing] up on the undertaking." Rather than disappointing Swain, however, he would "steal enough time from one of the other professors to perform this duty." Ultimately, he selected as his topic Francis Bacon's aphorism "[r]eading makes a full man, conversation a ready man, and writing an accurate man" (a close approximation of the actual quote). Swain seized the occasion to cite Governor Graham to the student as "a great man who had ballanced [sic] his education according to the maxim of Lord Bacon."[31]

Students honored Swain's teaching by acting on his suggestions. When he recommended Lord Brougham's discourse "on the Pleasures of Science," a student "got it from the Library and pursued it with delighted attention." "Certainly never was so much valuable and interesting information compressed into so small a space," he wrote afterward.[32] Students did not like to disappoint him. One took the affirmative in a composition on the question, "Can the Fine Arts ever flourish in this Country while it remains a Republic[?]" He could support his argument only weakly and was frustrated because it was "the worst composition I have ever showed to Governor Swain."[33]

Swain apparently commenced in a lower key but elevated the discourse as he proceeded. His "ardour, originally by no means small, increases with every lesson," said a student. The fund of anecdotes with which he illustrated his subjects, and his peculiar intonation of voice, attracted attention. "He has collected much information with regard to the State and its early history," wrote one journalist, "and may probably favor the public with a true and valuable work upon the subject." The historical work never materialized, but history indeed had a large place in his subject matter, and he was "fond of quoting Bacon's saying that Geography and Chronology are the two eyes of history."[34]

A student account of Swain's teaching style is elegant and descriptive: "Governor Swain when he Cases a subject with elastic wing his mind springs above its common level, he lays before you a view at first large grand and beautiful, he talks on and your vision is extended, he seems to scan the landscape and horizon. He talkes [sic] on new beauties before unseen rise up to view. We seem to be surrounded by a landscape of thought, and all dispersed over its uneven surface the bold features of mountains and hills of widespread forest and extended planes of fields."[35] Kemp P. Battle would say of Swain, posthumously: "As a teacher, while he could not be called erudite, he was uncommonly interesting and inspiring. He had a very extraordinary memory and was always ready to deepen an impression or illuminate a dark passage by illustrative facts and anecdotes, often humorous, drawn from his reading or his own large intercourse with men."[36]

Battle's last point is illustrated by a class in which Swain deviated from the standard lesson in rhetoric. He read, instead, from a lecture Judge William Gaston had given at the university and a sermon by Dr. William Hooper. The lesson apparently made an impression. The student who reported it wanted to take a copy of the sermon when he left college and would always keep Gaston's address. It was not just his "large intercourse with men" that formed and enhanced Swain's classroom instruction, however. He had, as one admirer wrote, "the happy facility ... of extracting instruction from every object around you."[37]

Swain departed from contemporary educational norms in another respect. Women could not then enter the university. There was one young woman, however, to whose education he contributed considerably. Cornelia Phillips Spencer, daughter of one UNC professor and sister of another, was an object of Swain's interest and attention, and she learned much from him. We would wish for more evidence of his support for higher education for women, but the surviving records have not revealed it.[38]

In the end students appreciated Swain's attention to and tutelage of them. While later reading law under Judge Richmond Pearson, future North Carolina governor John W. Ellis acknowledged to Swain "the attention which you paid to the instruction of the class; and the interest manifested by you, for our general improvement and advancement." Swain was, by Ellis's reckoning, "as willing to communicate as ... able to instruct." Swain's concern for those no longer "under [his] protection" was, Ellis believed, ongoing.[39]

James Johnston Pettigrew, who would become a Confederate hero in the Civil War, said of Swain: "[H]e makes a most excellent President, and fulfills his duty in the world's economy as well as any person of his abilities; so that you must prepare to shed tears, when he gives you a final shake and wishes you god-speed."[40] Another former student, while acknowledging that his scholarship had not been the best, said: "I did not fail to learn from you ... both in your recitation room and elsewhere.... I feel under lasting obligations to you for the interest which you communicated to the important studies and subjects which are attached to your department. I make these acknowledgements now because they were not manifested while I was there."[41]

Historian Stephen B. Weeks noted a tendency to underrate Swain and "to speak slightingly of his attainments in the field of letters." In Weeks's view, however, North Carolina had had no teacher who knew better how to use his attainments to best advantage, or a better gift for arousing the best in the minds of the young men around him. "[H]is scholarship in his own departments of instruction was never questioned in my day," said Weeks, and he was "second to no man in the State in dignity of character, influence or public estimation."[42]

Because of its distinctive origins and its lasting and significant effects, one Swain teacher-pupil relationship merits special mention. Zebulon Baird Vance was from Swain's native county of Buncombe. Swain and the Vance family were long and well acquainted. Indeed, Vance's mother had been Swain's friend and sweetheart in their days at Asheville's Newton Academy. Swain acknowledged this relationship when he read to the UNC faculty Vance's letter seeking admission to the university. His Buncombe County property was not very productive, Vance explained, so he needed a $300.00 loan to attend. He would take a general course of studies, while simultaneously studying law under Judge Battle and Samuel F. Phillips. The faculty granted the loan, which would finance Vance through one year at the university.[43]

A lovelorn Vance took a sleeping room on Swain's lot. He informed his amorous interest, later wife, Harriet Espy, that upon his arrival in Chapel Hill, he "met with a cordial and patronizing reception from Governor Swain." Due principally to the kindness of Swain, "whose good opinion I am so fortunate as to possess," Vance received kind treatment from all families in the village whom he visited.[44]

Vance would say that Swain used no lecture notes. Rather, he spoke from the vast store of learning he had accumulated out of reading history and law, when reduced circumstances deprived him of the desired college years. Swain, Vance said, would reach to a library shelf, pull off a book by a great poet, and hold a class captive. It was under Swain's richly endowed tutelage that Vance came to know intimately the framers of the U.S. Constitution.[45]

Stories of Vance's performances in Swain's classes survive. Swain once called upon students in his international law class to list the cases bearing upon the contraband of war. A student had written the cases on his boot, foot, and leg. Vance saw him reading the cases, jerked the leg onto his lap, read the names, and returned the limb to its normal position. When called upon, the other student could give only three or four of the cases. Swain thereupon said, smiling at his own pun, "Mr. Vance, advance to the front and cite the cases bearing upon this point." Vance gave every one of the thirty or forty cases "with the weary air of one who had been knowing the thing for ten years."

In lecturing on political economy, Swain related that the currency of the short-lived state of Franklin, once part of North Carolina, had consisted of coon skins.

"After awhile," Swain stated, "the traders got to sewing to possum skins the tails of coons." When Swain asked Vance what kind of currency he would call that, Vance, displaying the quick wit that would serve him well in politics, replied, "A retail currency." Vance's wit found further expression in his description of the incident from his student days mentioned briefly in chapter nine. A temperance lecturer had started a total abstinence society, which numerous students had joined. One day Vance was asked why a group of students had gathered round the campus well. Vance replied: "Why, they are members of [the] Temperance Society. [A student] got on a spree last night—Governor Swain was in hot pursuit of him. As he ran by the well he threw his tickler in and broke it on the rocks of the curbing. Those temperance boys have been drinking water since day-break to get a share of that half pint of whiskey."[46]

The relationship between Swain the teacher and Vance the pupil was a natural one, rooted in many commonalities. "You and I are the sons of old friends," Swain would tell Vance many years later, "natives of the same county, born under the shadows of the same mountain and nurtured under similar influences, physical, intellectual and moral." Their time together in Chapel Hill was the beginning of a long, cordial, and productive association.[47] After Vance's return to Asheville to practice law and pursue a political career, he made a point of spending time with Swain whenever the latter returned to Buncombe. "He was a most noble friend to me," Vance said during one of those visits, "and I feel desirous of showing him and his family all the humble attention in my power during his stay up here."[48] It was to Swain that Vance could always go for advice. They were on terms "of confidential intimacy," Vance later said, from his first entry into the university until Swain's death. After Swain's demise Vance, for the remainder of his life, revered his memory of Swain "with filial affection."[49]

Because of his versatility and extensive knowledge, John Ruskin was known at Oxford University as "the Professor of Things in General." At the University of North Carolina, the moniker could have applied to David Swain. A vast public appealed to him for information and advice on a broad array of subjects. His role as teacher, especially as law teacher, thus extended well beyond the UNC campus.

A fellow delegate to the 1835 Constitutional Convention considered moving his sister and her children to Chapel Hill. There were deterrents, however, concerns that "the wild young men would ruin the Boys," that there was no school for the girls, and that rent and expenses were high. Swain's advice thus was needed.[50]

Requests could be for geology reports or meteorological information, but more often the subjects were legal: the constitutionality of a tax imposed on a railroad company, "the constitutionality of the coal transportation," drafting a

Zebulon Baird Vance soon after his time as David Swain's student.

deed to reflect certain borders, "the proper manner of adjusting the difficulty" in a boundary dispute, or a reversionary-interest issue in a complex legal title. A former student and budding lawyer once promised that "any advice which you might choose to give with regard to the study will be thankfully received."[51]

Experienced lawyers too, even some among the best, sought Swain's legal advice. George Badger, later nominated for a U.S. Supreme Court seat, once sent Swain an extensive letter regarding various legal technicalities. Another correspondent accompanied a legal question with the earnest plea, "If you can answer the inquiry without trouble... I shall be greatly obliged."[52]

On a broader public level, Swain's opinion on constitutional questions was coveted. Was it constitutional for one person to hold the solicitor's position in two counties? asked Tod R. Caldwell, Swain's former pupil and later the state's governor. Caldwell held the position in Burke and had been elected to it in Caldwell. It was within the letter of the constitution, Caldwell thought, but he troubled over whether it was in "strict conformity" with its spirit. He could resign one if Swain thought he should not hold both.[53]

The anticipated appointment of U.S. Senator Asa Biggs to a federal judgeship would create a Senate vacancy. Was there precedent, Governor Thomas Bragg asked Swain, for filling the vacancy "by Executive authority"? If so, was the council of state "a part of the Executive in this state"? Absent precedent, Bragg ultimately asked, "what think you of the matter?"[54] Another governor, Jonathan Worth, had the benefit of "repeated letters" from Swain on Reconstruction matters. He later desired that Swain and Judge Ruffin "attend" him in Washington on such matters. Their inability to do so resulted in no inconvenience, Worth said, "save the want of their Counsel," which he clearly considered valuable.[55]

Speaking invitations afforded Swain with teaching opportunities. These were common and often flattering, as illustrated by one for "an address on the anniversary of the Institution." "The importance of the subject, your familiar acquaintance with the history of the university, together with the interest you exhibit in its reputation and prosperity," a student committee said, "pre-eminently qualify you for the discharge of this duty."[56] When the Dialectic Society invited Swain to give the literary societies' annual commencement oration, Swain deflected the proposal with the suggestion that they secure an outside speaker. A repeat invitation a few years later anticipated a similar response. To "add dignity and importance" to the occasion, the invitation stated, "the discharge of this duty should be in trusted only to an individual of known ability and high standing in society." Swain's preference for "some person of distinction from a distance" was recognized, but that had been attempted without success.[57]

Upon the death in 1846 of Helen Caldwell, President Joseph Caldwell's widow, Swain spoke at the service. The occasion, he noted, perhaps providentially coincided with the fiftieth anniversary of Caldwell's assumption of the university presidency.[58] For the later dedication of the Caldwell monument on the UNC campus, Charles Manly was the scheduled speaker. Manly, however, in Swain's words, was "felled by disease." The duty then went, in Swain's view, to Paul C. Cameron, as president of the Alumni Association. Cameron, however, was resistant. He suggested to Swain other possible speakers yet thought Swain himself "*ever ready*" for such an assignment. Visitors to Chapel Hill would be pleased, he flattered Swain, "to hear a Eulogy from one who has so well sustained the position of successor to Dr. [Caldwell] as yourself." A mandatory injunction followed: "And as I am 'in authority,' I shall require you to be ready!" Cameron soon relented and recognized a duty to perform the task if Swain thought it "worthy of the occasion and myself."[59]

"[A] flattering compliment" came from a Swain presentation to a legislative committee on the state of the university. Members were "so struck by his eloquence that they requested him to address the whole Legislature." The Commons Hall was "to be given up to him on [a] Monday night." It was hoped that he could "convince somebody of something."[60] Chapel Hill's July 4 celebration, and a "model" reply to the best annual student English composition, provide other examples of Swain oratory.[61]

Requests for written material from Swain, also standard fare, likewise provided occasions for teaching. Some were university related: one for a history of the university to be published in the *American Quarterly Registry*; another for a listing, for publication, of all UNC graduates to 1841. The data Charles Manly, secretary to the trustees, could supply for this purpose were incomplete. He could identify the honorary degrees for 1840 but could locate neither the "Report of the examinations nor the list of Honorary Degrees for 1839."[62] Other requests were more generic. The *American National Review* wished him to write for it "on some national topic." A northern publisher desired his opinion on the new edition of its *Geography and Atlas*. An article from him, it was believed, would be helpful to a new monthly literary magazine on common-schools education.[63] A committee preparing to establish a university in Greensboro solicited his opinion.

In fulfilling his multifaceted role as president of the University of North Carolina, David Swain was, ever and above all else, a teacher.

CHAPTER 11

Faculty

*"Probably as strong a faculty as was
to be found in the Old South"*

THERE WAS ANOTHER CONSTITUENT group, faculty, with whom Swain dealt on a regular basis. By modern reckoning it was quite small, fewer than a dozen plus some "tutors." Public perceptions of their role and lifestyle would fully resonate with some current ones, however. William H. Battle once conveyed to Swain sentiments that would be familiar today.

The world at large, Battle said, thinks that "the President [,] professors [,] and tutors of the university are among the favored few who receive ample pay for comparatively easy work." "I know the contrary," Battle continued, "and am glad that others have had the opportunity to be enlightened upon the subject, as well as myself."[1]

From the outset of his presidency Swain acquired, enhanced, and embraced power and influence with the small faculty. He instituted a policy of holding regular weekly faculty meetings and recording them. They were often held at his home, at times quite early in the day. Faculty meetings were cancelled when he was absent. That a little wine was served afterward perhaps aided his acquisition of authority. Soon the trustee executive committee ruled that during regular sessions, no professor or tutor was to absent himself without prior leave from the president; by 1845, no faculty member was to be appointed without his consent. While he was garnering personal weight of command, Swain was also gathering around him "probably as strong a faculty as was to be found in the Old South."[2]

Swain usually consulted the faculty before acting. Faculty meetings would be called "to consider divers confidential communications laid before it by the President." He could be annoyed, however, when they differed with him. "By adroit management he generally carried his point, without causing dissatisfaction. He had decided attitudes in regard to his prerogatives." When other professors investigated and interviewed faculty prospects, they reported their impressions to Swain. Hires were then often made on his motion or nomination; he executed faculty directives to notify new members of their appointments. It was Swain who then, in consultation with faculty and trustees, handled their housing arrangements in Chapel Hill.[3]

Swain was the steady liaison between the faculty and the trustees, particularly its executive committee. The trustees transmitted reports and memorials on faculty salaries to Swain; he, in turn, was to consult with the faculty on salaries and duties and to report back to the board as soon as practicable. When the faculty desired adoption for UNC of provisions in the laws of other state universities, it resolved that Swain should bring the matter to the trustees' attention. When it wanted the Department of Modern Languages to remain unaltered, it requested Swain to inform the trustees; if the trustees nevertheless chose to add a professor, Swain was to advise of its preference for the position. When the trustees delegated faculty questions to the executive committee, the faculty bought into Swain's proposal of a faculty committee to work with the trustee committee to resolve them.[4]

While ultimate faculty-hiring authority rested with the trustees, Swain could, with reasonable confidence, rely on the executive committee to conclude that the opinion and recommendations of the president, backed by the faculty, would "be sustained by the unanimous voice of the board of trustees." He was sufficiently secure in his position that, with the concurrence of Judge Battle and Governor Graham, he would hire an instructor with "preeminent" qualifications, knowing it was subject to the executive committee's sanction. When uncertain of Swain's support for a faculty applicant, that committee would defer to "the expediency of waiting to hear from [him]."[5]

While mostly bold in his dealings with the trustees, Swain could be deferential. Once when he differed with Professor Mitchell on an issue of university policy relating to faculty, he did not mince words in conveying his views to the executive committee. He acknowledged, however, that if the committee held the contrary opinion, his view of his duties must "fall within a narrower circle."[6]

As with students, Swain was the portal of entry for faculty applicants. Many contacted Swain themselves. One, who understood that a faculty member was about to resign, offered himself for the vacancy. He had been educated in France and Germany, he informed Swain, and had resided in Italy for some years. Others offered themselves for a chair either in history or in rhetoric and logic. When the departures of Professors Herrisse and Hedrick were impending, there were immediate volunteers for their positions.[7]

Curriculum enhancement might be suggested to create a faculty position.

The addition of architecture, "or such of its branches as would be useful to the students," was once recommended by one who apparently saw himself as the instructor. A practical knowledge "of Architecture Building and Surveying together with land scape gardening," it was thought, could be an appropriate branch of instruction.[8]

A UNC position was not always the objective. One UNC graduate sought Swain's knowledge as to any institution where he might teach. He was studying law under Judge Richmond Pearson, but if Swain could in good conscience recommend him for a teaching position, he requested that he do so.[9]

Advocates for faculty aspirants, too, implored Swain on their behalf. When Andrew D. Hepburn was elected to the university's chair in rhetoric and logic, he had numerous supporters. One, the Reverend Joseph R. Wilson of Augusta, Georgia, father of future President Woodrow Wilson, told Swain he knew few gentlemen who would better grace the chair than Hepburn.[10]

Personal friendships could complicate the faculty hiring process. Two in particular proved troublesome for Swain. Francis L. Hawks was a native North Carolinian, a clergyman, and a historian with whom Swain roamed the fields of Clio extensively. Hawks applied for a professorship as early as 1847. A laconic entry in the executive committee records states that the secretary was to inform him that no vacancies existed, and the committee did not then deem it expedient to create new positions.

As Swain and Hawks labored together in the vineyards of history, the question resurfaced. The timing was not propitious, however, and compensation was an issue. He should fill the chair "with a resident professor," Hawks, then living in New York, advised Swain, "and let me come in as I can, as a volunteer." Swain maintained hope, nevertheless, advising Hawks that he had been anxiously awaiting the development of his plan. The board, he thought, would soon fill the chair in rhetoric and logic but would defer decision on a professor of history.

Hawks responded that "[t]he present unhappy state of affairs between the North and South" rendered impossible a statement of his plans. His current geographical location notwithstanding, he was a Southerner and would "sink or swim with the South." If the salary was adequate, he would accept a chair at the university. He would even serve in two professorships if there were two salaries. He could not lecture gratuitously, however. Swain soon advised that he and the board, despairing of securing Hawks's services, had filled the professorship. Despite extensive consideration by all parties, the friendship between the two principals, and expressions of interest and support for Hawks from others, the discussions came to naught.[11]

John Hill Wheeler, a co-laborer with Swain and Hawks in historical endeavors, was aware of the negotiations between Hawks and the university. Like Hawks, Wheeler was a North Carolinian but was then living elsewhere, in Washington, D.C., where he had held several governmental posts. Also, like Hawks, he was interested in a faculty position at his native state's university. Finally, and again like Hawks, he and Swain were friends, in this case, according to Wheeler, "of more than 30 years standing."

Wheeler appears to have been more active than Hawks in pushing for a UNC position and enlisting others to do so on his behalf. As the historical labors between Wheeler and Swain were at their height, Wheeler told Swain, "My ideas are still the same should any vacancy occur at Chapel Hill." He soon learned that Professor W. M. Shipp had resigned to be president of Wofford College, and he conveyed to Swain his desire, held for five years, "to return to my native state." He had a master's degree in history from UNC and knew Spanish from having served as U.S. minister to Nicaragua. He wished to know the salary and prerequisites and stood ready to provide testimonials.[12]

Swain soon heard from Wheeler's supporters. Wheeler had studied well, said one, had a facility for imparting knowledge, and possessed proficiency in French and Spanish that would be useful. Thomas Bragg, whose time as governor of North Carolina had just ended, forwarded papers Wheeler had placed with him for delivery to Swain. Swain's cousin, Joseph Lane of Oregon, soon to be the vice-presidential candidate on the 1860 John Breckenridge ticket, apparently weighed in for Wheeler. Swain told his distinguished relative that Wheeler had no friend more disposed to promote his best interests than he, but that the conflicting claims to consideration presented difficulties as perplexing "as that which seeks for solution at the Charleston convention" (where the national Democratic Party would split, paving the way for Abraham Lincoln's election). Even former President James Buchanan had expressed the gratification he would feel if the university employed Wheeler, Swain was informed.[13]

Historian George Bancroft, responding to Wheeler's importuning, told Swain that "a comfortable and respectable b[e]rth" for Wheeler would be most "agreeable" to him. Other than Swain himself, Bancroft opined, Wheeler had probably given as much attention to the history of North Carolina as any man in the state. Soon, though, Swain had to advise Bancroft that while their opinions on Wheeler coincided, and he would be gratified if he could provide for him, "[a]t present it is not in my power." Few applicants, he said, could present the necessary attainments in general literature, as well as in local history. Religious denominational concerns had surfaced, but an Episcopalian-dominated board would hire no one "unless they can command the services of one, whose reputation will leave no room to doubt that superiority of qualification, and not religious preferences, . . . impel the selection." Thus, as with Hawks, Swain's long negotiations with a friend over a faculty position were to no avail."[14]

One instance of employing a Swain friend did materialize, with felicitous and lasting benefits for Swain and the university. Formal, university-based legal education was not then the norm. Prospective lawyers read law under an established lawyer or judge until they considered themselves prepared for the required examination. One such student gave Swain a vivid description of the distress he experienced in this process. "I have not made any considerable progress in law," he said. A "long apprenticeship" made law itself less "enticing." But, he told Swain, "I must not falter." Greater honor would follow if he surmounted the difficulties.[15]

Swain, however, had a vision for formal legal education at the state's public university. He had not been in Chapel Hill long when Judge William Horn Battle and former Governor James Iredell started a private school in Raleigh to prepare aspirants for the bar exam, then administered by the state supreme court. Swain had his eye on it, for he told a friend that "Battle and Iredell are doing well with a law school." Soon he was suggesting to Battle that he move himself and the school to Chapel Hill. Battle apparently had dropped hints of his interest, for Swain noted "[a] rumor" that Battle had "entertained some thoughts of a removal to this place." Swain then articulated a forward-looking perspective on university-based legal education. The university, he said, offered one in Battle's situation "some strong inducements to such a course." Three years earlier Swain himself had undertaken to give "instructions in legal science" to two or three undergraduates. Had he declined, the students were going either to the University of Virginia or to William and Mary, in both of which "the study might be prosecuted in connexion with their scholastic pursuits."

The endeavor had grown beyond what Swain had expected or desired, and he was fully prepared to transfer it to Battle, or to divide it with him, whichever Battle preferred. A permanent school would secure support in Chapel Hill better than elsewhere in North Carolina, Swain thought, and he was anxious to engage Battle on the subject. "My plan would be to make the law school an integral part of the university," Swain stated with clear vision, "and to confer degrees as at Harvard." Judge Joseph Story of the U.S. Supreme Court was a law professor at Harvard, so why, Swain asked his friend, "should not Judge Battle become so here"?[16]

Battle delayed a response in order to process the matter with friends. He admitted that for some time he had thought a removal to the university would be advantageous to him and his family, both financially and "to have my sons more immediately under parental supervision during their progress through college." Subsequent reflection had strengthened this impression, and Swain's generous offer had produced "a decided conviction" that he should "make the necessary arrangements to locate myself near you."

The change could not be immediate. Except for "some eight or ten negroes," the whole of Battle's property was invested in a cotton factory and in houses and lots in Raleigh. He could not move without disposing of this property; but once that was accomplished, unless the legislature located him "in this judicial circuit," he would "take up my abode for, at least, several years on your hill of science." To take all the law students off Swain's hands was unthinkable, apparently because of Battle's ongoing judicial service, but Battle was "willing to join with [Swain] in the establishment of a law school at [Chapel Hill]." "[A] school of that character," Battle presciently told his friend, "would be more likely to secure a liberal and permanent support at the University than at any other place in the state."[17]

Within the year, the trustees adopted the following ordinance, one of lasting significance to the state, the university, and generations of law students: "that the Executive Committee be ... authorized at their discretion to establish a Law Professorship and to prescribe such rules and regulations as to the duties and emoluments of such professorship, and also as to the class of students who may attend instruction therein as [they] may think proper." The timing produced awkward moments for Battle. He was "in treaty" for the sale of his house and lot in Raleigh but had not heard whether Swain had succeeded in renting a house and lot for him in his village.[18]

The matter was soon resolved, and Battle notified his wife Lucy that he would "endeavor to get a view of the house in which we are to live, so as to be able to satisfy your inquiries in relation to it." The executive committee soon approved an application for Battle to purchase a small piece of university land adjacent to his house. It deferred to Swain to report on whether the price would be detrimental to the interests of the university, how much land Battle wanted, and the price.[19]

All the while Swain, Battle, and the trustees were collaborating on the future of legal education at the university. Swain once informed Charles Manly, secretary to the board, that he and Battle had consulted on the law professorship resolution and were preparing a plan. He advised Battle of Governor Graham's objection "to so much of the regulation of the Law Department as relates to the admission of regular students." Battle was not surprised. Some trustees, he said, had urged against permitting students "on regular standing" to engage in the study of law during their college course. Battle would acquiesce in any arrangement Swain might make. His personal interest should not impede any plan the executive committee wished to establish or be considered in doing anything that might retard the university.[20]

Ultimately, this significant entry appears in the executive committee minutes: "President Swain attended the meeting of the Committee and presented a programme embracing a Law Professorship with the Hon. Wm. H. Battle at its head which with some modifications was approved." The committee also resolved to confer the honorary degree of master of arts upon Battle.[21]

Soon, as Battle traveled his judicial circuits, his wife informed him of students arriving in Chapel Hill to study law under him. The judge inquired of Swain about advertising for the Law Department. Was it too late to do it for the ensuing session? If not, it would be a favor to him if Swain would prepare the advertisement and have it published at Battle's expense. Swain soon was telling Battle that he had never had "so correct and promising a class of law students as the present."[22]

A history of legal education in the United States shows a law school at Chapel Hill from 1843–1845 under the proprietorship of Battle and Swain, with the UNC Law School commencing in 1845.[23] From Battle's arrival in Chapel Hill in 1843 until the formal establishment of the university law school in 1845, Swain and Battle were all but Siamese twins in the legal education endeavor. A sharp demarcation between Swain's 1843–1845 and post-1845 roles would, however, be inaccurate. Swain remained involved and was the link between an oft circuit-riding Judge Battle and his program and students. He also developed an easy intimacy with Battle and the Battle family and frequently assisted Lucy and the family in the judge's absence.

At such times Lucy would share with Swain correspondence about the law school and respond to the writer with Swain's thoughts on when he could get licensed. Swain, in turn, would convey to Battle, through Lucy, news of the death of one of Battle's former students—with great regret, said Lucy, because Swain viewed the decedent as "a very smart young man." When a circuit-riding Battle was to miss commencement, Lucy was to tell Swain that, if present, Battle would recommend a certain student for the degree he desired. He hoped Swain would arrange it in his absence. When Swain attended Hillsboro court, he complained to his jurist companion that "[t]he bar is by no means equal to what it was when I held the court in 1831."

Swain offered Lucy both money and shopping advice. On one occasion he bought eleven barrels of corn for the Battles. When Lucy lacked funds with which to pay a debt, Swain paid it for her. He was a warmhearted man and a sincere friend, she told her husband, who had been "so kind." She complained when Swain failed to visit her but soon noted that he had "turned over a new leaf" and had visited her often since. While Swain and Battle handled Battle's prolonged absences well, Swain preferred Battle's presence in Chapel Hill. He "always inquires very particularly about you," Lucy once told her absent husband, "and I have no doubt but he will be as much pleased when you return as any one except myself."[24]

Swain had been at the university fifteen years before the General Assembly established the Town of Chapel Hill. Until then he was at least in essence the town government, and not much changed with the formal creation of a municipality. Cornelia Phillips Spencer accurately states: "Gov. Swain always declared that Chapel Hill was co-existent with the university, and they must sink or swim together. He was always as much interested in the growth and prosperity of the one as the other." The Battle family's situation is illustrative; they would seek Swain's approval even about minor matters regarding their town property.[25]

The coming of the Battles to Chapel Hill would have long-term implications for Swain and the university. It marked not only the commencement of a law school at the university but also the beginning of a long and significant relationship between the university and the Battles' son, Kemp Plummer Battle. In September 1850 an obviously pleased Lucy told her husband, "Kemp is a bona-fide tutor of Mathematics and since he has told the Gov. [Swain] that he will accept, is much happier." A simultaneous laconic entry in the university's faculty minutes confirmed the occurrence: "Mr. Kemp P. Battle having concluded to accept the appointment of Tutor in the Mathematical Department, appeared and took his seat."[26] Battle would be a longtime, valuable servant of the university, its president from 1876–1891, the author of its history, and a professor of history until his death in 1919.

Another significant Swain-era faculty hire, one that Swain considerably influenced, also involved the son of a prominent faculty member. Charles Phillips was the son of Professor James Phillips. When Ralph H. Graves resigned as tutor of mathematics in 1844, Swain advised the executive committee that Charles, then "a member of the Theological Seminary at Princeton," would "be universally accepted by the Faculty." Professor James Phillips noted to a friend that "the Gov. has selected Charles" as Graves's successor, which Professor Phillips found disconcerting.

Charles's longevity in the position was not assured, however. Swain later reported that Charles had received an offer from Davidson College, which would be more lucrative, thus creating "some *danger* on [the] prospect of his accepting." The fear was justified. In light of it, Swain grew assertive, writing to trustee Bartholomew F. Moore that Charles would remain at UNC. Charles had "been busy screwing [his] courage to the sticking point," apparently toward accepting the

Davidson offer, but this proved too much for him. Swain's missive to Moore had given "the lever its last and most effective turn." Phillips's obligations to Swain were "too numerous and too serious to allow me to thwart his wishes where his feelings seem to be so much engaged."

Apart from the personal considerations, Phillips told a friend that his choice would have been different. Instead, he thanked Swain for "the reception of another and the most distinguished mark of your favor" and wished him "an ample reward for your prolonged self- denying services for the public and for your friends." Phillips would serve the university into the post-Swain era and would be with Swain at his bedside when Swain died.[27]

With the employment of William H. Battle and Charles Phillips, the university entered a period of faculty stability. This stability ended in the summer of 1857 with the sudden, tragic demise of Elisha Mitchell, longtime beloved and respected professor of chemistry, mineralogy, and geology. Mitchell died from a fall while exploring the North Carolina mountains to acquire new scientific information. Swain learned of Mitchell's fate from his former student Zeb Vance, who wrote to convey "a most melancholy and unfortunate piece of information." "Our dear old friend Dr. Mitchell," Vance continued, "is no more." Mitchell was lost among the mountains, Vance said, and the utmost searches had proved unavailing. Vance had traced the professor's path to the extent possible, but the general opinion was that he had met with an accident and perished. "That he is still alive there is hardly a possibility much less a probability." Swain should, however, await the next mail before notifying the family, "by which time," promised Vance, "I will write again and give further news, if by that time the body of our dear friend should be found."[28]

The small, close-knit academic village received the news with profound trauma. Charles Manly was "greatly shocked at [the] intelligence." Swain was to "lose not a mail in telling me all you hear." While particularly sad for the Mitchell family, Manly's sorrow extended to "all the College Authorities, [and] the whole State at his loss." Manly had wept, while finding some comfort in the knowledge that Mitchell "died in the harness a martyr to the cause of science and truth." No one felt the loss more keenly than Swain, who had lost his "right arm, through thick and thin." "His afflicted widow and children feel his loss, more sensibly," said Swain, "but perhaps not more deeply than I do." An in-the-moment realist, however, Swain observed that the past was beyond control, and "energetic and discreet measures are demanded for the future." The most unpleasant task would be to settle with Mitchell's administrator complicated accounts of the institution, which Mitchell had also served as bursar.

Professor Elisha Mitchell.

Until the executive committee could meet, Swain admitted that he would "assume Dictatorial powers." "I . . . need . . . offer no apology for the apparent boldness and precipitancy of my action which may not be found in the necessities of the times and of my position," he told Governor Manly. Still, prompt action from the executive committee was "not merely desirable but important." The executive committee forthwith granted Swain "carte blanche" authority to fill the two positions (professor and bursar). With faculty concurrence, Swain was to distribute Mitchell's duties among those faculty members willing to undertake them. If necessary, he could appoint more tutors. Mrs. Mitchell was to receive Mitchell's salary for another half year, and she and the family were to continue in university housing for the same period.[29]

Mitchell had taught Swain during the latter's brief time as a student, and Swain clearly revered his old professor, so much so that his desire to see Mitchell properly honored trumped his usual adherence to historical and scientific accuracy. This, indeed, significantly preceded Mitchell's untimely death in 1857. In the summer of 1835, Mitchell had made his first attempt to determine, by barometrical measurement, the highest peak of the Black Mountain. His account was published and was the first authoritative pronouncement that the summit of the Black Mountains in North Carolina was higher than that of the White Mountains in New Hampshire and the highest in the United States east of the Mississippi River. The modest and unassuming Mitchell was never adamant about the claim and certainly never suggested that the peak be named for him.

Swain lacked such reticence. In 1839, at Swain's instance, Roswell C. Smith's *Geography and Atlas* called the peak "Mount Mitchell" and stated unequivocally that it had "been ascertained to be the highest point of land in the United States, east of the Rocky Mountains." Swain again gave it the Mitchell name in an 1840 issue of *The Raleigh Register*, stating, "We are gratified to see the reputation of the Senior Professor in our university established upon so durable, firm and elevated a basis."

Mitchell was initially buried in Asheville, but the following year his body was reinterred on the top of Mount Mitchell. Swain took the occasion to defend the claim that Mitchell was the first to visit the peak and to deny a similar claim by longtime Western North Carolina Congressman Thomas L. Clingman, whose name had been given to the mountain on a map published by William D. Cooke in 1847. Swain accused Cooke of making no effort to obtain the best private materials on the controversy. Swain, half owner of the land on which the ceremony took place, offered to donate "the top of the mountain to the trustees of the university on condition it shall be called Mt. Mitchell." Two days after the reinterment Swain repeated his oration at the Asheville courthouse "to a large auditory."

The controversy "was never defined to general satisfaction." A leading historian of Buncombe County accuses Swain, not of deliberate falsehood, but of zeal in excess of his judgment. He did not know the correct calculation of the altitude, says the historian, and in a "partisan spirit," based his position on an incorrect calculation, scarcely satisfactory to the measurer himself.

Swain persisted, however. Shortly after Mitchell's death he resolved to collect the various documents relating to his death and burial and to publish them in a booklet that he hoped would be read beyond the state. As part of that compilation, he prepared an expanded version of his remarks in Asheville two days after the reinterment ceremonies. After consultation with Zeb Vance and former Governor Graham, he deemphasized details of the Clingman-Mitchell controversy, attempting to avoid accusations that might "afford Mr. Clingman opportunity for another triumph, or indeed to enable him to make a decent defense." Instead, he focused on the names that had successively been given to the peak and made the case that the Mitchell name had always been associated with it until Cooke had attached Mitchell's name to a lesser peak in 1857. "To remove an ancient landmark," Swain concluded, "is both a private and public wrong": "a double wrong... as inconsiderate as it is unjust."

Swain prevailed, but one historian has accurately noted that the historical foundation for his case was shaky at best. It was not the finest hour for a man devoted to historical preservation and accuracy. It demonstrated vividly, however, his deep loyalty to a friend and a desire to promote the friend's memory and the reputation of the university that the friend had served so ably for forty years.[30]

In the wake of Mitchell's death, Charles Manly had both concerns about and confidence in Swain. He had seen Swain in tight places before, however, and knew he generally responded well. Among other tasks, Swain was assisting with closing out Mitchell's affairs. The professor had accumulated a library approaching 1,900 books "containing works on every branch of science." Many, including Swain and the trustees, thought it would be a pity to have so valuable a collection scattered over the state. Ultimately a trustee committee, with Judge Battle as chair, authorized a purchase of the library for $3,500. It was placed in the university's library room under the care of Professor Fordyce M. Hubbard, who was to catalogue the books and make a full report. The university was also authorized to purchase Mitchell's "articles of chemical and philosophical apparatus" upon "such terms as may appear reasonable." Because it was believed that Swain would be in Buncombe when a trustee subcommittee met, Battle, rather than Swain, served on it. All, though, desired the benefit of Swain's views and information.[31]

Foremost among Swain's many tasks upon Mitchell's death was hiring his faculty replacement. The process took time. Some three months after Mitchell's death a Raleigh newspaper reported that the trustees would make no permanent appointment of a successor until their annual meeting in December. This was thought proper in that so few North Carolina native sons were qualified for the position. Applicants were to present their claims, without delay, to Governor Thomas Bragg, president of the trustees, or to Swain, president of the university.[32]

Early in the endeavor, attention focused on Professor William J. Martin, a graduate of the University of Virginia then on the faculty at Washington College in Pennsylvania. Swain received numerous recommendations for, and testimonials to, Martin and his credentials.[33] Two in particular made a strong impression. Both came from Professor William H. McGuffey of the University of Virginia, well-known educator and author of a popular children's reader. In McGuffey's opinion Martin was greatly superior to another candidate "in both talents and attainments."[34]

Swain sought more specific information from McGuffey and conveyed his views on qualities desired in the candidate. He should "have a well established character as a Christian," Swain said, continuing: "Other things being equal I would prefer a product of the University of Virginia and a member of the Baptist Church.... All the leading denominations are properly represented in our Faculty except the Baptists; and we have no one who has undergone the peculiar system of training and instruction which characterizes your university."[35] The statement would cause trouble for Swain. It was construed as saying the reputation and influence of the University of Virginia were so great, and it had such a strong hold on the admiration and affection of the UNC faculty, that the UNC president had expressed himself as, all other things being equal, preferring a graduate of that institution. The UNC trustees, it was said further, had endorsed that opinion by electing Martin to the chair.

Swain defended his position, but in reality mostly repeated it, with some elaboration. It had been his objective, he said, to find among UNC graduates an able young man and "an accomplished Christian gentleman" with a capacity for instruction. It was no discredit to UNC, however, that none of its graduates had been considered. Because the university was a state institution, he had always thought all parties in the state, political and religious, should be represented in its governance. No member of the faculty was a Baptist; accordingly, other things being equal, he would prefer a member of that denomination. If no UNC graduate met the qualifications, again other things being equal, he "would prefer a Southern to a Northern man" (Francis Hawks had urged this position upon him). He was not aware, however, that he had "ever been suspected of great partiality for either Va. or S.C. or want of proper respect for any other state."

Finally, as his present faculty had been educated "on the old plan," other things being equal he would prefer someone prepared in the system at the University of Virginia. In no forum had he expressed any other opinion, he concluded emphatically.[36] Swain was not alone in being defensive. Governor Graham characterized a newspaper article on the subject as "puerile." One newspaper protested "against being styled, even inferentially, an 'accuser' of Gov. Swain."

The entire affair was a tempest in a teapot. The university had a position to fill, and it filled it with a man perceived to be the best available. Professor Martin proved a longtime hire and appears to have produced general satisfaction. From the University of Virginia, Professor McGuffey conveyed his gratification and urged Martin to join the UNC faculty without delay. Battle, who heard "the *great news*" through Swain, was glad Martin had made so favorable an impression but wondered how "the boys" liked him as a professor. The students respected him "very highly," Lucy Battle happily reported, while noting that "he is said to be very strict in the recitation room." Swain mentioned the "singular coincidence" that Martin had "commenced his duties just forty years after the arrival and entering upon duty by his predecessor [Mitchell]."[37]

Controversy over the Martin appointment passed, but denominational concerns in faculty hiring, which had predated the Martin matter, persisted. The concerns, indeed, predated Swain's presidency. In 1818, President Joseph Caldwell had been subjected to the criticism that the university was a Presbyterian institution.[38] Swain encountered the denominational problem early in his presidency. Following the University of Virginia model, the trustees determined, upon petition of the societies, to establish a university chaplaincy. A chaplain was to be appointed annually, taken alternatively from the state's four leading denominations: Baptist, Episcopalian, Methodist, and Presbyterian. It was Swain's duty, if practicable, to obtain the concurrence of the several denominations.

His initial attempt at this failed. Swain informed the Right Reverend Thomas A. Morris, bishop of the Methodist Episcopal Church, that the faculty had determined to offer the position to a minister of his church. Swain had a candidate in mind: the Reverend Edward Wadsworth, husband of a sister of Mrs. Swain's. Both university and family purposes thus would be served by getting Wadsworth to Chapel Hill. At one point Wadsworth was committed elsewhere and would have had to decline, but he could now accept if the bishop's approval could be obtained. Swain, noting that the Methodists were the most numerous denomination in the village, assured the bishop that he had authority to guarantee "a competent provision for his support."

The bishop, however, refused. The village was too small, he informed its leader, thus presenting "an insufficient prospect of successful labor" to make it a regular station to be supplied annually. To supply it once every four years "would not probably justify the deduction of time and labor to be made from our regular work as itinerant ministers." Further, when his denomination's next turn came, it might not have a minister whom Swain's board would approve. The bishop wished Swain and the university well, but good wishes could not camouflage the fact that his response constituted a rebuff to both.

The rebuff did not sit well with Swain. He confessed to "more indignation ... than I choose to express." Only with some difficulty had he constrained himself "from returning a response to the Bishop that would make a durable impression upon his memory." A viable opportunity to escape the accusation that the university was under the influence of two denominations only, Presbyterian and Episcopalian, with the incidental advantage of making his wife's sister a resident of Chapel Hill, had evaporated, much to Swain's chagrin.

All the university's "church duties," Swain now said, fell on Dr. Mitchell, an ordained Presbyterian clergyman. Given his other responsibilities, he could not be expected to bear this extra burden much longer. There could be no doubt, in Swain's thinking, "that the regular maintenance of public worship is not merely necessary to the prosperity but indispensable to the existence of the institution." The only question was whether it should be sustained "by a chaplaincy of the character proposed or by a regular member of the Faculty." Because the Baptists had their own institutions, Swain suspected an application to them would meet a similar reception as the one to the Methodists.

Swain's proposed solution, which the faculty essentially adopted with trustee concurrence, was to employ the Reverend William Mercer Green, UNC Class of 1818 and rector of Saint Matthews Episcopal Church in Hillsboro, as professor of rhetoric and logic. To enable him also to fill the chaplaincy position, Green would have no governance, and reduced recitation, duties. With two Presbyterian clergymen on the faculty, Mitchell and Phillips, Swain thought the relative influence of the two denominations could be preserved. Green would be expected to attend morning prayers throughout the year and to preach in the college chapel once every Sunday, with occasional relief from Mitchell or Phillips. Mitchell and Phillips would cover evening prayers. When Mitchell volunteered to relieve Green of one-half of his Sunday morning preaching duties, Green took on additional teaching and coaching commitments. The crisis thus passed temporarily but not before rendering an ecumenical-minded Swain angry and disappointed over this failure to achieve enhanced denominational balance for the university.[39]

In 1849 Professor Green left to become bishop of the Protestant Episcopal Church of Mississippi. A trustee informed Swain that the Methodist Church had had only one instructor in the university and but meager representation on the board of trustees. "This should not be so," he said: "The institution being the property of the state, the various denominations of Christians have a right to demand an influence in the management proportional to their numbers." It thus would be well for Green's successor to be a Methodist.[40] Mitchell's death in 1857 brought similar demands that a Baptist fill his position. A Baptist minister told Swain the denomination's members believed the trustees were "desirous to do justice to them as a denomination." There had long been no Baptist on the UNC faculty, and it was not to be supposed that the trustees would appoint anyone other than a Baptist.

As noted, to a point Swain agreed. He informed the minister that, other things being equal, he was disposed "to give the preference to a member of that denomination." The preference for a Baptist could not be indulged, however, "in favor of any one whom I may suppose to be inferior to a competitor, in more important qualifications." To another minister he acknowledged the desire of faculty and trustees to see all the leading denominations of Christians in the state "interested and represented in the government of the Institution." This sentiment was "fervent if not universal."[41]

There was still no Baptist when a further vacancy occurred in 1859. John Hill Wheeler was interested but acknowledged to Swain his lack of awareness "of all the difficulties arising from denominational preferences and perhaps sectarian or sectional preferences." Wheeler took a rather ingenious approach to the problem. Testimonials about him from clergymen, "worthy and prominent ministers of the Baptist denomination," were being forwarded to Swain. He supposed these letters from "leading members of the Baptist Church" would remove any impediment to his appointment from "denominational jealousies." Charles Manly, meanwhile, cautioned Swain that "there are considerations of much higher import than such as are merely denominational."[42]

While thus engaged with Baptist advocates, Swain found himself and the university under attack from the editor of a Methodist publication. Governor Manly and Judge Battle advised Swain "to take no notice of him whatever." No man ever yet had a fair fight with an editor, they cautioned, and it was a game he could not win. This Methodist organ sought to promote antagonism between the church and the university so "this sect" would withdraw its patronage, and children and wards, from the university in favor of Trinity College. No matter what Swain said, they counseled, the editor "has the type and will have the last say."

The editor, however, got personal beyond Swain's capacity silently to bear it. Swain acknowledged his Methodist roots proudly and at length. More than eight decades earlier his mother had been a member of the first Methodist church near the Wake County Courthouse. Of her eight deceased children, six had been Methodists, two Presbyterians. His childhood home had been a haven for itinerant Methodist preachers as early as the beginning of the century.

Swain's wife was of Methodist parentage and predilections, and they had been married by a Methodist minister. Many of his friends had been, and many now were, Methodists. "It will require strong evidence, I suspect," he asserted, "to convince any one of them of unfairness on my part to the Church to which they belong. My whole course of life private and public negatives the presumption."

The allegations that Swain's Methodist antecedents justified claiming him as a Methodist, and that he had united with the Presbyterians when they "were restless under the preponderance of the Episcopalians" on the UNC faculty, Swain said, "are fancy sketches." The subsequent averment that Swain's policy had been "to secure a balance of power between the Presbyterian and Episcopal churches, thus securing the support of both; and to admit only so much Methodism into the Faculty as would bring in Methodist patronage, is alike unfounded and uncharitable." During his first seventeen years in the UNC presidency, there had been three efforts—two successful, one not—to secure Methodists as members of the faculty. Presbyterian numbers on the faculty had, in fact, diminished.

The editor briefly tipped his hat to Swain and the university. The university was "an ornament of State," and the "personal worth and public services of Gov. Swain [were] among the treasures to be preserved in its future history." The attitude of the university toward the churches, however, he continued, "very properly comes within the limits assigned to religious journals." He then posed the "plain question": "Are the Methodists of North Carolina thus [i.e., properly] represented?"

Methodists considerably outnumbered other denominations in the state, the editor continued. Yet there was only one Methodist among the fifty-five university trustees and none on the executive committee. On the faculty for several years one Methodist, Charles F. Deems, had served in a subordinate professorship. Upon Deems's departure Professor A. M. Shipp, also a Methodist, had been appointed professor of history. Swain would not deny these facts, said the editor, but he had cited none of them in his letter. The evidence, he again said, showed that Swain's policy was to secure a balance of power between Presbyterians and Episcopalians to acquire the support of both "and to admit only so much Methodism ... as would bring in Methodist patronage." "We say *his* policy," he said, for "he is captain of the ship."

Swain's plea regarding the chaplaincy situation was reminiscent of the name of his native county: "Buncombe." All that could be claimed for Swain's letter was that he had failed in his efforts to secure a more equitable representation for Methodist and Baptist churches. Concluding, the editor claimed "for Methodism a representation in the Board and the Faculty equal to what is possessed by other churches."[43]

Manly and Battle had been right. There was no way Swain could get the last say in this war of words. Even after Swain's demise, the issue lingered. The Reverend Solomon Pool, a Methodist and Swain's successor as UNC president, was said to have been a product of Swain's "chatholicity [sic]" in hiring, employed because of Pool's "ecclesiastical relations." Swain, it was said, was "always on the lookout to coordinate the various denominations of Christians" and had secured Pool's election as a faculty member for no other reason than that he was a Methodist. His juggling of these concerns brought Swain posthumous criticism even from one of his closest friends and staunchest supporters. He was known, said Cornelia Phillips Spencer, "to sanction the election of an inferior man because the applicant was a member of some church which in his opinion ought to be represented in the faculty in order to attract students from that denomination."[44]

The university's academic curriculum changed little during Swain's tenure. Modifications were episodically contemplated, however, and sometimes implemented, usually with Swain, faculty, and trustee collaboration. The faculty once considered the addition of a course in experimental philosophy. Swain requested that the trustees take no action until further word from him. The issue had been resolved, he soon informed them, "to the entire satisfaction of all parties." A course of lectures in experimental philosophy was underway. Hopefully, Swain said, it would be a credit to the professor and the institution. At that juncture his own recitations had frustrated his desire to attend the lectures.[45]

Should seniors be permitted to study French rather than Greek or Latin? Swain once posed to the faculty. It resolved the issue in the negative but allowed two lessons a week in Latin to replace one in Latin and one in Greek.[46] Another time the trustees instructed their executive committee and Swain to provide at the university instruction in civil engineering, agricultural chemistry, and the application of science to the mechanic arts. One or more professorships could be established, with salaries not exceeding $2,800 in the aggregate.[47]

The subject of agricultural instruction arose frequently. One of the most expert agriculturalists in New York, "an accomplished gentleman and a gifted man," wished to spend a summer in the South and to defray expenses by lecturing at the university and other places. "What say you?" inquired a Swain correspondent.[48] A reply has not been found, but similar questions would recur. Indeed, Charles Manly was once willing to allow the professorship in history to "die out and go in for Agriculture on the *larger scale*." Francis Hawks wished to know how an agricultural college would do in North Carolina "as a branch of the university." From New York, Robert Donaldson urged the idea upon Swain as a means to educate farmers' sons for their profession.[49] Toward the end of Swain's administration the faculty met "to consider sundry papers that the president laid before them concerning the Agricultural School." While very much in the air at the time, the idea would not fully materialize until some years after Swain's demise and then on a new campus in the state capital.[50]

Upon Judge Thomas Ruffin's motion, the trustees once directed Swain and the faculty to reexamine the course of studies and consider whether "it be not too extended for the Term now allotted to the Four classes." Ruffin also advised Swain that he perceived great advantage in the continuance of geological and mineralogical studies in the state.[51]

On another occasion Swain proposed, and the faculty agreed, that seniors should be permitted to make certain substitutions in their curriculum. As the state developed and expanded its system of common schools, Swain took an interest in the university's role in teacher preparation. Initially unprepared to respond to a trustee inquiry on college honors, Swain, upon checking the institution's records, could advise that from its beginning the practice had been to distinguish about a third of each class. In small classes, he informed, individual honors were ordinarily assigned, while in large ones as a rule they were given to two or more students together.[52]

Swain was blessedly free from the problems of big-time college athletics. There were, however, occasional issues regarding athletic instruction or activity. A Major Roberts sought employment as an instructor of athletics, including fencing and boxing. William Graham, the sitting governor, informed Swain of executive committee approval "provided that it be done in hours of leisure among the students, and shall in no manner interfere with the studies or policy of the College." Faculty supervision was required, and the instruction would be suspended if it "conflict[ed] with the proper business and order of the Institution." Graham later advised Swain that the committee's former communication should "not be understood as implying anything in favor of Mr. Roberts." Further, if he was, as Swain had been informed, a London prizefighter, "he is no fit instructor for the young gentlemen of the University." The faculty should "exercise a sound discretion . . . keeping in view the intimations already given by the Committee." When the faculty exercised that discretion, it declined to grant Roberts the instructional opportunity.[53]

The deaths of prominent friends of the university also brought collaboration efforts between and among its president, faculty, and trustees. William Gaston, perhaps North Carolina's foremost lawyer and jurist and a trustee since 1802, died suddenly on January 23, 1844. Since Swain's time as a young law student under the tutelage of Chief Justice Taylor, Gaston's brother-in-law, Gaston had been a mentor and friend to him. His passing was thus a poignant moment for Swain. Upon learning of it, Swain called a faculty meeting. Not yet a member of the faculty, Judge Battle sat with it by invitation. Swain read a letter from Charles Manly to his son, a student at the university, detailing the circumstances of Gaston's death. He made remarks regarding Gaston's abilities and high moral character, "alluding . . . to the valuable services which Judge Gaston had rendered this university."

He then appointed a committee to prepare appropriate resolutions, with Battle and Professors William M. Green and Charles F. Deems as members.

The faculty soon passed several resolutions honoring Gaston's memory. Professors Green and Deems were appointed to solicit the executive committee's cooperation in applying to the Gaston family to have his remains deposited at Chapel Hill. This would, it was thought, "add a charm to the locality of the community" and keep before the students "such ever present remembrances of the great as may incite them to a vigorous prosecution of their studies and an assiduous cultivation of their hearts." Such language was characteristic of Swain, and one suspects his authorship. The effort failed, however. Gaston was temporarily buried in Raleigh and ultimately moved to Cedar Grove Cemetery in New Bern to be interred near his parents.[54]

Swain was the faculty's link to other colleges and universities. He conveyed to his faculty invitations to their celebratory occasions. He was, in effect, the university's ambassador to them, attempting both to learn from them and to sell them on the merits of the University of North Carolina. In 1842, Swain left the UNC campus for several weeks "to visit some of the Northern Colleges on business connected with the interests of the university." Acquaintances at one institution introduced him to faculty at others. One at Yale, for example, presented him to a Dartmouth professor as "a very superior and excellent man" who was "anxious to understand our institutions." His visit to Yale was later remembered with much pleasure and the hope that he would repeat it.[55]

At Harvard Swain missed the "public dinner and exercises" of the Phi Beta Kappa Society, an event, it was thought, that "would have been a pleasant occupation" to him. He apparently made a favorable impression there, nevertheless. A few months later the governor of Massachusetts wrote an article "paying a high compliment to the Old North State—to the Professors of the university and the students." Later still a Cambridge scholar, "as a small token of high respect," sent Swain a copy of a dictionary he had published. Swain spoke well of the volume, perhaps thereby inducing the author again to send a copy when a new and revised edition was published. Swain had hopes of visiting Cambridge again but noted that the four hundred boys under his jurisdiction consumed his time and attention.[56]

Intra-faculty harmony pleased Swain. On one occasion he reported that the freshmen in the Math Department had been given over to Mr. K. P. Battle "who has acquitted himself well in his new vocation." Battle had assumed his duties at a time characterized by more harmony in the faculty than previously known. "There is at present no great point about which we differ," Swain related.[57] Such accord did not always prevail, however. On one occasion Professor Charles Deems accused Professor Solomon Pool of spreading falsehoods about him. He could not trace them to anyone else, he told the university's president, whom he authorized to "show or give this to Prof. Pool."[58]

More serious allegations had Professor Wheat sexually harassing a female member of Professor Hubbard's family, "kissing and hugging . . . and patting her neck! rather too extensively." To Swain it was said to be "a scandelous [sic] state of things to exist between two brother clergymen and professors." Moreover, it was a "common topic" in Raleigh. Swain intended to call a faculty meeting to "put it down." To make matters worse, Wheat, rather than being embarrassed and apologetic, in Oliver Twist fashion asked "for more," namely, that his professorship be placed on an equal footing with others and that "window blinds [be added] to his house!" There were rumors, supported by "pretty strong hints" from Swain himself, that the university's leader was sufficiently dispirited by the accusations that he intended to resign. He did not, and this crisis too passed, but not without considerable agony for a man with both his sense of propriety and his abiding concern for his university's reputation.[59]

Charges against faculty members came from outside the university as well as within. One accuser informed Swain that Professor Fetter was slandering him. Swain should "make him work and not listen to any of his tales." The writer planned a trip to North Carolina to sue Fetter for $5,000: "it will stop his gab for a while," he thought. Faculty, students, and villagers would be his witnesses.[60] Another accuser could not identify a specific perpetrator but claimed to Swain that he had been a victim of a "loose, slip=shod [sic], cold-blooded proceeding." He had received, under Governor Bragg's frank, the testimonials that had been transmitted to Governor Manly (which suggests that he was a disappointed faculty-position seeker). He sought return of the letters U.S. Chief Justice Roger B. Taney "and my other dear and honored friends" had written. While he acquitted Swain of any intention to wound his feelings and was apologetic about "the necessity of addressing this distastful [sic] communication" to him, his complaint had to be discomforting to Swain.[61]

Like students, faculty members could be "ruined by . . . fondness for ardent spirits." Early in Swain's presidency the university employed Charles Marey to teach French. Swain once found "an uproarious row" in Marey's recitation room. He discovered the instructor too intoxicated to teach and subjected to merciless mocking by his class. Swain relieved him and took charge of the class, to be met with this challenge from Marey: "If you give this order as President of the University, I obey. But if you give it as David L. Swain I demand satisfaction!" Swain assured him that the action was official, and the instructor left Chapel Hill, soon to die in a brawl in Charleston.[62]

Temporary absences by faculty members, even for good purposes, produced controversy and extra work for Swain. Chemistry Professor John Kimberly once received leave to spend a year in a laboratory at the University of Berlin. The request was controversial, however. Charles Manly advised Swain that the furlough request, "unaccompanied by any note or Comment from the Prest., and without any expression of opinion by the Faculty, will, *in my opinion*, meet with little or no favor." Manly, Governor Bragg, and Judge Saunders regarded the plea as "notice to quit." Most of the trustees disagreed. The leave was granted, and, apparently, beneficial. As he contemplated resumption of his duties at Chapel Hill, Kimberly advised Swain that he had "kept steadily in view the objects for which I came." The trustees, he thought, would not regret the indulgence shown him.

There was a downside for Swain, however. Kimberly had seen the benefits of enhanced resources, and he wished Swain to call to the trustees' attention "the want of the university for a proper chemical Laboratory for the department of Practical Chemistry." Present arrangements were inconvenient for both teacher and student: "additional fixtures . . . are absolutely indispensable in a well-conducted laboratory." It was disagreeable for him to say it and would be for Swain to hear it, but Kimberly was no longer disposed to make personal sacrifices for these needs. It was time to impose fees on students for laboratory supplies and to give them "timely notice of the existence of such a tax."[63]

Faculty compensation issues presented administrative duties for Swain. Professor James Phillips once approached him seeking a $100.00 advance on his end-of-session pay. Phillips's son Charles, a student at Princeton Theological Seminary, needed "some money *now*," and Phillips could not provide it without assistance. "I do not like to trouble others," Phillips told his president apologetically, "and would myself suffer inconvenience rather than do so."[64]

More commonly, faculty pay was the issue. Once, for example, some professors and tutors memorialized the trustees "praying an increase in their salaries." The board recommended an increase in some but resolved that the president, himself a trustee, was the proper conduit for such requests. Swain was to consult with the faculty, present a scheme of salaries to be paid and duties to be performed, and report to the board at the earliest practical period. The faculty advised Swain of a preference among the plans for increases but stated that it would accept whatever additional compensation the board thought proper to bestow.[65]

Salary was an issue, probably the foremost one, in faculty hiring and retention. When Swain attempted to employ his friend Francis L. Hawks as professor of history, Hawks declined because of the low salary. The Reverend Charles F. Deems, who had once been on the faculty, likewise rejected a subsequent offer, notwithstanding that it was "one of the most handsome compliments which could be paid any gentleman." He was grateful for the warm welcome from the faculty, but because he could not take the position without sacrifice on the part of his family, he declined the honor.[66]

Efforts to retain extant faculty by financial incentives sometimes failed. Professors John Wheat and A. M. Shipp departed despite successful petitions for salary increases and the granting of other benefits. Wheat's letter of resignation was "very kind ... towards all the authorities of the institution," Swain said, "but places us all in a very awkward position nevertheless." Simultaneously, there were "unparalleled exertions," in Swain's words, to lure Professor Phillips away (Charles, probably, though unclear). "The number and impertinency of solicitors is amazing," Swain lamented, and he would be surprised if they failed. "What shall be done in this emergency?" he plaintively inquired.[67]

Sudden, unexpected deaths of faculty members also created emergency situations. In 1867, the Reverend James Phillips, longtime math professor, fell from his seat on the rostrum in the college chapel and died almost instantly. In paying tribute to him, a deeply grieved Swain said few men had filled a professorship for "so many years" with equal "ability ... and usefulness." Phillips's pupils everywhere would always speak of him "with feelings of respect and affection approaching filial reverence."[68]

Earlier in Phillips's teaching career, he had lacked this venerable status, indeed, was quite unpopular with the students. Phillips had mandated that textbooks not be carried into the recitation rooms, a rule some students openly defied. Charles Manly, secretary to the trustees, notified Swain that he had received an anonymous letter postmarked "Chapel Hill" and signed "A number of students." The letter contained various charges against Phillips and urged that he be "put on trial." He was, the students alleged, haughty, tyrannical, partial, and inattentive to his duties. He had shown them no experiments in philosophy; apparatus procured for that purpose, the students stated, had "never been touched by him." The letter was anonymous due to "the dread of being visited with still harsher treatment by him." If, upon inquiry, the charges were "not made good," the students agreed to "stand convicted as Slanderers and Libellers."

Manly inquired of Swain whether to call a meeting of the executive committee to submit the letter to it. This apparently did not occur. Instead, the faculty dealt with the matter internally. When twelve students again broke the rule, they were called before the faculty. Nine surrendered and promised compliance, but three, including a son of former Governor John Branch, were dismissed. By the time of Phillips's demise, however, this incident was long in the past, and his passing was genuinely mourned by trustees, students, and faculty alike.[69]

As noted, probably Swain's greatest difficulty with faculty was over matters related to disciplining delinquent students. He once drafted a statement to the faculty detailing a major difference of opinion in this regard. It was written "[i]n no unkind spirit," he assured them, "but from a solemn sense of duty," which bound him to protest certain proceedings regarding the freshman class. Had the faculty confirmed the sentence of "dismission" to the ringleader of the misconduct, and imposed a penalty of two-weeks suspension on the other members of the section, he would have been gratified. He would, however, have preferred the "dismission" of all to their suspension with the condition the faculty had annexed. The proceedings, he said, from beginning to end, were without his knowledge and not in conformity with his judgment.[70]

John DeBerniere Hooper, UNC Class of 1831 and a professor in the Latin and French Department, resigned in 1848, apparently over student-discipline issues. He had harsh words for Swain. In Swain's comments to the faculty regarding his withdrawal, Hooper said, he had "reflected the right of control." Indeed, Hooper had understood him to "make a threat to which I could not yield without a sacrifice of self-respect." Their different views on the authority vested in Swain's office "would not probably have produced any unpleasant collision but for a mutual misunderstanding entirely accidental." An "unpleasant collision" there was, though, and Hooper was "acting on principle." He regretted, however, that he had "sometimes expressed myself in a manner less courteous than you had a right to expect." Swain was quite sensitive, and no doubt Hooper's words stung him intensely.[71]

The Henri Herrisse affair, discussed earlier, was almost certainly Swain's most distressing problem with a faculty member over such matters. The relationship between Swain and Herrisse had commenced with considerable promise. A "Young Frenchman" had opened correspondence with him, Swain told Charles Manly, "with a view of obtaining a place here, as an instructor in the French language." Swain received a glowing testimonial to his merits, and Professor A. M. Shipp thought him "in every respect a worthy young man." After two years as a UNC instructor, Herrisse reported Swain and others as saying he had "given more satisfaction than any of my predecessors."[72]

The deterioration in this initially cordial relationship commenced with Herrisse's complaints about the want of discipline and maladministration of the affairs and government of the college by Swain and the faculty, detailed above. It did not end there, however. Matters would decline to a point where a frustrated

Swain would say that Herrisse aspired to "discharge" every "executive function" of the university. He had "earnestly kindly and perseveringly endeavored to restrain and correct these idiosyncrasies," Swain avowed, and "make him what he ought to be [,] a very useful acceptable and respectable instructor."[73]

Probably the most unforgivable of Herrisse's many sins was his self-appointment as a one-man faculty recruitment committee. He had the audacity, without notice to Swain or the faculty, to correspond directly with two men whom he encouraged to apply for tutorial vacancies. Further, he freely admitted to a difference of views with Swain on the enforcement of discipline in the college, and while regretting their difference, thought it only "natural that I should desire the election of a gentleman whose notions in such matters are in accordance with mine." He also admitted to opposing a faculty prospect because, if elected, he would vote with and sustain the views of the president.[74]

It was not a pretty scene. Herrisse would accuse Swain of leading an effort to have him branded an "infamous liar" and charge that Swain was going to raise a mob against him. Charles Manly would call Herrisse "that malicious little foreigner" and "the French Revolutionist." The executive committee would resolve that Herrisse had acted "through a want of information . . . of the usages of the institution, and the necessity of harmony in the action of the Faculty," thereby justly subjecting himself to the faculty's complaints.[75]

Ultimately the faculty sided with Swain by resolving that campus discipline was as well maintained as they had known it to be. Herrisse resigned, absolving all others by stating that he had had no prompters or advisors other than "my conscience and my duty." This crisis, too, thus passed, but not before getting as ugly as any ever did in this usually quiet, compatible academic village in this period of its history.[76]

CHAPTER 12

Hedrick Affair
"Not warranted by our usages"

HERRISSE HELD ONE OF his colleagues, Benjamin Sherwood Hedrick, professor of agricultural chemistry, in particularly high esteem. Sadly, Hedrick, like Herrisse, would see his UNC career prematurely terminated, and with only one dissenting faculty vote, Herrisse's.

Unlike the Frenchman Herrisse, Hedrick was a native North Carolinian, the firstborn in a Davidson County slaveholding family. He had graduated from the university in 1851 with highest honors. A circular letter from Swain in Hedrick's sophomore year showed him with no absences from prayers, recitations, or divine worship, and said, "His scholarship is very good."[1]

As Hedrick's graduation approached, Swain functioned as a placement officer for him. Swain wrote his close friend William A. Graham, then secretary of the navy, recommending Hedrick "for the clerkship within your gift." Testimonials from Professors Mitchell and Phillips vouched for Hedrick's qualifications. Swain concurred in the confident opinion they expressed of Hedrick as a scholar and a man. Swain's support for Hedrick was not altogether disinterested. He had conveyed to the faculty and to Hedrick, his "anxiety to see him devote his life to scientific pursuits." He had done so "with a view, in due time, to a situation as an instructor here."[2]

Hedrick seemed to Graham "a very suitable person for the appointment." Graham thus transmitted to him a commission making him "Clerk to the Superintendent of the American Nautical Almanac." Swain conveyed his gratitude. When Hedrick was one year into the position, Graham informed Swain of a letter from Hedrick's supervisor on "his exemplary character, . . . progressive improvement in science, and usefulness in the public service." He had approved the supervisor's recommendation to promote Hedrick and double his salary.[3] The Almanac Office was in Cambridge, Massachusetts, where Hedrick made his home for the next

Professor Benjamin Hedrick.

two-and-a-half years. In the fall of 1851, he entered the Lawrence Scientific School at Harvard University, from which he earned a doctoral degree three years later. It pleased Graham that Hedrick considered "the course of studies at Harvard . . . less extensive than that at Chapel Hill, at least in the department of Mathematics."[4]

Swain did not sit for long on his desire to bring Hedrick back to Chapel Hill. If the trustees were to establish a scientific school at the university, Swain soon inquired of Hedrick, could he present his name for a professorship? He needed a prompt answer. Hedrick was willing if the trustees offered compensation Swain thought he should accept. From the outset, it had been his intention to return to Carolina at the first "fair opportunity."[5]

The executive committee appointed Hedrick professor of agricultural chemistry. It simultaneously appointed Charles Phillips, son of Professor James Phillips, as professor of civil engineering. Swain was to submit, as early as practicable, "a plan in detail for the organization of this [Scientific] School," to be operative in January 1854. Swain informed Hedrick of the action, imploring that "you must notify me of your acceptance forthwith."[6]

Hedrick's acceptance did not come "forthwith." There was a complication. Davidson College, too, was interested in his services. A correspondence ensued between the two newly appointed professors in which Phillips was negative about Hedrick's coming to Chapel Hill. Phillips doubted that of the sixty-odd UNC trustees, six could intelligently discuss the new school. He feared that it would not be what "its projectors" anticipated and "that there will be humbug." Phillips's father, he told Hedrick, said Hedrick should go to Davidson "Gov. Swain to the contrary notwithstanding." He wanted Hedrick to make the decision best for himself and his fellow men, and he understood that he was "in a delicate and doubtful position."[7]

Hedrick soon chose to return to his alma mater. He informed Swain that he accepted the appointment and would devote all his time "to . . . better qualifying myself." "The pursuit of Chemistry in its various branches," he assured the UNC president, "is that above all others which my inclinations lead me to prefer."[8]

A promising start characterized Hedrick's new relationship with his alma mater. Charles Phillips found their employment "most unexpected . . . so complimentary." Swain, he informed Hedrick, was willing to crowd his senior teaching into one session to give them an opportunity to instruct the seniors in engineering and agricultural chemistry. Swain expected them to think over the teaching loads, acquisitions, and other matters for the new scientific school, and to help him "consult intelligently" with the executive committee regarding them. Swain had "disapproved" three of his seniors, indicating, Phillips thought, his "intent on raising the standard of scholarship here." He would have no "heartier cooperator" than Phillips, who doubted that Hedrick would be "backward in this good work."[9]

Swain was indeed supportive of the young professor. Through Phillips he assured Hedrick he need not fear "a protest on your bills" to the amount of $500.00. He assisted him in the purchase of equipment for his courses. Swain was also securing from Hedrick "information and assistance in the practical application of science to the arts." He sought advice on improving the university's diplomas. On a more mundane level, he entrusted Hedrick with $100.00 with which Hedrick shopped for him in New York. Hedrick's purchases for Swain included a stove, a washstand, and chairs.[10]

Unfortunately for Hedrick, however, his political views deviated sharply from those of most white North Carolinians, including the political establishment. On the foremost issue of the time, slavery, there was then little tolerance for dissent. North Carolina was an active participant in the southern slavocracy. The Free Soil Party, which would evolve into the Republican Party, opposed the expansion of slavery into the territories. In the 1856 presidential election, the first following Hedrick's appointment to the UNC faculty, Hedrick opined, in response to a question from a student, that the best candidate was the Free Soil Party's John C. Fremont. If there was a Free Soil ticket on the North Carolina ballot, he would vote for it, he said. This, to most North Carolinians, particularly to those whose opinions mattered most, was unpardonable heresy.[11]

In 1856, First Amendment free-speech jurisprudence was yet to evolve; academic freedom was at best a nascent, and by no means a fully developed, concept, though the UNC faculty had resolved in 1838 that it "disclaim[ed] all right to restrain or control the expression of political opinion, where the language is not in violation of the Principle of philology or good taste." Regardless of the side or the issue, it was Swain's policy to keep the university out of politics. Five years earlier, for example, when a student group wished to form a "Southern Rights Association," he had informed its members that it was contrary to the laws of the institution to establish a society of any description without the consent of the trustee executive committee. The university was patronized by all denominations and all parties, and nothing should be done that might disturb the harmonious relationship between the institution and its friends and supporters.[12]

William W. Holden's *North Carolina Standard* newspaper fanned the flames of the controversy. In September 1856, it published a letter from "An Alumnus" captioned "Fremont in the South." The letter quoted from a prior piece with that caption, which stated that any Fremont men among them should "be silenced or required to leave." Was "an open and avowed supporter of Fremont" who "supporte[d] the black Republican ticket," he asked, "a fit or safe instructor for our young men?" If the writer's information was correct, clearly the answer was "no," and the instructor should be dismissed: "we call upon the proper authorities to take action for the sake of the prosperity of our Alma Mater and the good of the State," he concluded.[13]

Hedrick's fate was probably already sealed. If not, however, he proceeded to assure it by responding. The letter, he said, constituted "an uncalled for attack on my politics." But he then affirmed his support for Fremont and gave reasons. The first was "because I like the man." The second, still more fatal to his cause, was "because Fremont is on the right side of the great question which now disturbs the public peace." Opposition to slavery, Hedrick said, was "neither a Northern nor a sectional *ism*." Instead, it originated with the great Southern statesmen of the American Revolution, who were certain the enslaved would be free. Because he held "doctrines once advocated by Washington and Jefferson," he said, "I think I should be met by argument and not by denunciation." Hedrick further opined that the subject belonged exclusively to the trustees, thereby denying the state's broader public a stake in matters affecting its university.[14]

Hedrick's efforts to defend himself did not end with the *Standard*. The trustees would be the ultimate arbiters, and he addressed them via letters to Governor Thomas Bragg, ex-officio president, and former Governor Charles Manly, the board's longtime secretary. He had acted as quickly as he could, he said, to deny reports that he had advocated "abolition doctrines." He had thought the matter forgotten until the first *Standard* editorial had appeared, and even then supposed it would go no further until the article signed "An Alumnus" was published. When Hedrick realized the *Standard* "was bent on agitation," he concluded that the better and more honest course was "to come out openly and avow my sentiments—that would at least prevent misrepresentation, and . . . gave the reasons for my opinions" so the world could judge their soundness. Above all, he denied any attempt to make converts among the students.[15]

Writing to Manly, Hedrick pleaded for a full and fair hearing. No one, he claimed, exceeded him in acknowledgement of "the justness and propriety of the usage which prohibits members of the faculty from agitating topics relating to party politics." There were instances, however, when he thought the usage could be disregarded. He had always endeavored to be a faithful, law-abiding member of the community. "But all at once," he continued, "I am assailed as an outlaw, a traitor, as a person fit to be driven from the state by mob violence." He resented this "as a tyran[n]ical interference with the rights of private opinion." In perhaps the most unrealistic of his contentions in the North Carolina of 1856, he stated, "What I have said about voting for Fremont amounts to almost nothing."

Continuing in a contextually fanciful vein, Hedrick contended that his statements on slavery were neither fanatical, incendiary, nor inflammatory. He again denied having ever held abolitionist views. To be driven out now, after having just taken root, seemed hard. This "trouble about politics," he thought, would "soon pass over." If not, and his usefulness was lost or greatly impaired, he would not ask to be retained longer.[16]

As Hedrick articulated his defense, the *Standard* continued its drumbeat against him. A letter from "A Trustee of the University" conveyed astonishment and regret that a professor at the university "should so undervalue the reputation and interest of that institution as to advertise himself the advocate of the sentiments he avows." His conduct would sink the institution "unless the trustees forthwith expel that traitor to all Southern interests from the seat he unworthily fills."[17]

To another writer to the *Standard*, Hedrick's communication had created "surprise and disgust wherever read—surprise that any Southern teacher should be a Fremonter, and disgust that said teacher should adopt the twaddle of Northern agitators and fanatics as his apology." A similar issue, the writer asserted, had never presented itself in the Founders' lifetimes.[18]

Hedrick's defense in the *Standard* prompted Swain to call a meeting of the UNC faculty and direct its attention to the letter. He vocalized the longstanding university policy: "In an institution sustained like this by all denominations and parties, nothing should be permitted to be done, calculated to disturb the harmonious intercourse of those who support and those who direct and govern it." Even Hedrick, Swain told the faculty, had testified, as student and professor, that he "knew of no institution, North or South, from which partizan politics and sectarian religion are so carefully excluded." The policy was both necessary to internal harmony and due to persons of different tenets and opinions who "have a right to respectful consideration."

The faculty referred Swain's communication to a committee composed of Professors Mitchell, Phillips (probably James, though not specified), and Hubbard. The committee reported that Hedrick's conduct was "not warranted by our usages," nor were his "political opinions ... entertained by any other [faculty] member." Although the members had only "feelings of respect and kindness" for Hedrick, they regretted "the indiscretion into which he seems ... to have fallen." After brief discussion the faculty, by 12 to 1, adopted the resolutions. Herrisse was the lone dissenter, based "simply on the ground that the Faculty is neither charged with Black Republicanism, nor like [*sic*] to be suspected of it."[19]

Ever sensitive to public opinion, Swain wanted to place the faculty's action before the public without delay. He told Charles Manly he would have had a copy sent to *Standard* editor Holden at once but for a belief that it would be more respectful to submit it to the trustee executive committee first. If that committee could not be convened immediately, however, and if Manly thought well of it, he might send the faculty proceedings to the *Standard* editor forthwith. He had addressed the student body on the subject and thought things would "go quietly." "I perceive no symptoms of excitement at present," he said.[20]

As to Hedrick, Swain credited him with "the courage of a lion and the obstinacy of a mule." Swain was "not certain that he does not covet the crown of martyrdom." With that thought in mind, the better, more pragmatic course might be "to bring the resolution of the Faculty to bear upon him at the present, and postpone the exercise of Supreme authority until the election is over, and the Board in session[.]" If martyrdom were awarded immediately, and Fremont won the election, Swain posited, "you make his fortune." "Sparing him at the present will give the free soilers no strength at the South," he continued, "while the charge of persecution for expressions sake will add to the tempest of excitement which is sweeping over the North." Displaying some sensitivity to First Amendment and academic freedom concerns, he concluded, "In the mutation of parties, no one knows when, and what issues may arise, and freedom of speech in religious and political matters must be restrained, if restrained at all, very skillfully."[21]

To delay the ultimate vote, Swain suggested a trustee committee investigation. He left no question about the ultimate outcome, however. "A professor," he said, "must be removed not extraordinarily or capriciously, for mere difference of opinion in religion or politics, which the Committee may deem sufficient, but for *misbehavior*[,] inability, or neglect of duty." Hedrick could very properly be arraigned for misbehavior "in departing from our established usages." This, and this alone, should be the "count in the impeachment."[22]

As to the *Standard*, Swain need not have been concerned. Its next issue published the faculty proceedings, with laudatory commentary. It was natural, it said, that Hedrick's conduct "should excite anxiety in the minds of the President and Faculty." By promptly repudiating "his conduct and ... dangerous and unconstitutional political opinions," they had guarded themselves against "the remotest suspicion of sympathizing with him in his views." Swain's communication to the faculty, the commentary continued, had stated only the truth of history in relation to the university, partisan politics, and sectarian religion. The institution had habitually avoided both, "and herein has it found one of the main elements of its prosperity and constantly increasing usefulness." The only remaining task was "to cut off, *if it should be necessary*, the offending member." The loss of his usefulness as a professor at the university was obvious.[23]

As to the trustees, Swain's suggestion of delayed action was unrealistic. Charles Manly advised him that Hedrick's political essay had given "great pain" to the trustees and friends of the university. The executive committee had met the day the essay was published. A resolution had requested Hedrick's resignation and, in case of refusal, recommended dismissal. It had been withdrawn, however, and the committee had unanimously agreed to request that Swain use his influence to persuade Hedrick to resign.

The intimation that the trustees wished him to resign should be sufficient, Manly opined. The intensity of the committee's thoughts and feelings about the matter, if Hedrick did not resign, was vividly expressed in what followed: "[B]ut if he wishes to be dismissed, that he may fly to Yankeedom ... and find refuge in the bos[o]m of Black Republicans with the blood of martyrdom streaming from his skirts, then he will not resign but will wait to be kicked out. I hope therefore that you will put on your Diplomatic cap and manage this thing right."[24]

A few days later Manly notified Swain that if Hedrick did not resign, the board would "take him up next winter and cut his head 'clean off' but so as not to suffer the blood of martyrdom for opinions' sake to decorate and adorn his garments." There were reports, Manly stated, that students intended to tar and feather Hedrick.[25]

Any Swain efforts to delay were unavailing. Five days after passage of the faculty resolutions the executive committee met. The prompt action of the faculty received the committee's "cordial approbation." Hedrick, the committee resolved, "has greatly, if not entirely destroyed his power to be of further benefit to the university."

When Hedrick resisted resignation, the committee dismissed him for "misbehavior," specifically the publication of his defense. Manly advised Swain, "As to Hedrick, he is beheaded." There had been letters from trustees, a public meeting, and the southern press, he stated, "all demanding his instant removal." Students had declared that "the danger of a college riot" was imminent; if the executive committee passed over the matter, "violence and bloodshed would ensue." The committee had determined to take responsibility. Swain was to notify Hedrick of the decision. The full board later approved the removal and elected John Kimberly to the vacant professorship.[26]

The *Standard* reported the news "with much gratification." "[T]he viper turned upon his *Alma Mater*," it concluded, "and upon the state of his nativity with envenomed fangs."[27]

Hedrick could not look even to his own family for "consolation and support." An uncle wrote to thank Hedrick for his condolences upon the uncle's loss of a legislative election. Nothing else in this correspondence was kind. The uncle had learned with extreme regret that his nephew had turned "public polition [*sic*]." For faculty to be "partizans," regardless of the side, inevitably created difficulty, strife, and embarrassment. With great pain, the uncle had learned that Hedrick had "taken public ground for Fremont." As an individual he had this right. However, he said: "You are a member of the Faculty of a Southern State Institution, patronized almost entirely by the South. And if there is any possible good to accrue to you personally or to your country, by your rendering yourself obnoxious to the Trustees and Pupils of the Institution, I cannot see it." He predicted, accurately: "You will soon become obnoxious to the whole Southern students; your intercourse with them will be unpleasant; the Trustees will look upon you with a suspicious eye; and your situation at the Hill will soon become precarious. All this, too, without you or any body else being benefited by your turning *politician*."[28]

A friend, while sorry the "excitement" had proven a "serious inconvenience," profoundly differed with Hedrick on the issue. "You seem to view [slavery] only in its social and pecuniary bearings," said the friend, "while to our view, as a great movement of divine providence it appears in its most imposing aspect." Many enslaved persons, he observed, had been Christianized by coming to this country.[29] Manly had accurately forecast Northern reaction, however. Francis L. Hawks informed Judge Battle from New York that "as I expected, here he is of course a martyr."[30]

Hedrick initially appeared to understand the grounds for his dismissal. He told one correspondent: "[T]he outside pressure is so strong that for fear of injuring the university, they may dismiss me. They will not however put my dismissal on the ground of holding impious opinions, but for violating the 'usages' of the Faculty by publishing my political opinions." So great was the agitation, he acknowledged, that even his best friends thought his continued faculty presence "would injure the interests of the university."[31]

Yet he soon quarreled with a *Wilmington Commercial* article stating that the trustees had established a standing rule that neither professors nor scholars should engage in political conflicts, and that it was under this rule that he was dismissed for his perseverance in wrongdoing after being duly admonished that he was violating a law of the institution. Any such rule was a pure fabrication, he said, attributing to Swain a statement that it was made from "whole cloth." That he had persevered in violating a rule of the institution, after admonition, was utterly false. The trustees had never been able to give a reason for his dismissal except that "[*Standard* editor] Holden and the Mobocracy" required it and they must be obeyed. While it was true that faculty members had refrained from any prominent part in politics, they had always expressed their party preferences as freely as others.

The *Commercial* published the communication, but dismissively. It considered it "reliable—certainly quite as much so as any statement made by Mr. H can be." By using the term "Holden and the Mobocracy," the paper said, "he offers an insult to the great and powerful and patriotic party with which we have the honor to act." It went on to mock Hedrick's elegant style.

Hedrick fired back that it was a misapprehension to view his communication as an attack on the Democratic Party. It was intended for no party but "for Holden and those who embrace his mob-law doctrines." After getting him dismissed from the university, Holden had begun to assail his private character. It was hard, Hedrick admitted, after being despoiled of his living and treated as one with no rights, to be subjected still to a tirade of abuse for having characterized as false what, upon examination, could so easily be shown to be so.[32]

Following the executive committee's vote, Hedrick debated whether to appeal to the full board. Initially he concluded that "it would be folly." Soon, however, his wife Ellen encouraged an appeal if it would "get you right before the good people of the State"; and Hedrick, writing now from exile in Cambridge, Massachusetts, said he expected to do it. He did not consider a return to Carolina safe at that point, however, for fear that "Holden might take advantage of my presence to get up a mob." Holden might even "get up a negro or two to help him out."[33]

Soon Hedrick expected no relief from the trustees. "They will probably let the Executive Board disgrace themselves and the state and make no resistance," he predicted accurately. Ellen, too, had been getting advice that "it would not be worthwhile." "[N]ow the stream is against you," she said. When a response from Swain offered "no encouragement at all," Hedrick was convinced of the futility. "[I]f the trustees are determined that Holden shall rule them," he stated, "they may have him for King."[34]

Ellen now saw all hope of their remaining in their "dear Carolina" growing "dimmer and dimmer." She even thought Hedrick would be in danger if he returned to the state that winter. Word from Eastern North Carolina was that there every man was against Fremont and all parties had been prepared to take up arms had he been elected. To the West, people in Alamance and Randolph called Fremont "the n----- "; and with one exception, a man who "thinks about slavery pretty much as we do," all the men thought it was right that Hedrick had been "sent off." She was pleased that he had given up the appeal, for she did not believe the board would sustain him.[35]

Hedrick promised he would not set foot in North Carolina again until he was "well armed." He would avoid difficulty to the extent possible but would be able to defend himself. Still, until his successor was appointed, he did not give up altogether on restoration to his UNC chair. He then said, "The mobocracy have so far relented that I am not in violence now, and they are so shamed of their conduct towards me, as to try to trump up some legal pretext for my dismissal—but so far without success."[36]

Hedrick's appeal decision and any thought of his resuming residence in North Carolina were complicated by what Ellen described as the "negro mess" or "negro fuss." As Hedrick traveled, a fugitive in the North, she informed him from Chapel Hill, "We have had some excitement here regarding the negroes rising." The report was that "there was quite a crowd of negroes here Saturday night come to hear who was president." If it was Fremont, they said they were free to kill white people and to have half the land. "I suppose the negroes did have some such notion," she said, "from what I have heard."

The movement was not confined to Chapel Hill, she soon added. In Wilmington the police guard had been doubled because of the threat. "I believe almost if Fremont had been elected under existing circumstance," she concluded, "we should have had something of a general massacre in the South."37 Hedrick was sorry to hear that people in Chapel Hill were "so stirred about the negroes." He blamed "[m]en like Holden . . . for all of it." He acknowledged, though, regarding his already dim prospect for an appeal, "this mess about the negroes will make it still worse."38 Hedrick himself made a convenient scapegoat. "Miss Iene [sic] tells me they are laying this negro mess to you," Ellen apprised him. Some had said there would be "murderous times" if he returned but that they would take his part "if any man laid hands on [him]."39

Hedrick's father had concern for his son's safety. Ellen should tell him, "not to come to [North Carolina] shortly as there is mutch [sic] talk of insurrection. . . . I have always advised him to come back but those disturbances among the darkies has made the fuss much greater against him." Ellen did not quarrel with the advice but did see a downside: she did not want to leave with those unacquainted with him believing him "an ally of the abolitionist." "Old Holden," she concluded, "ought to be sued for slander."40 After a few weeks Ellen advised, "The negro mania has subsided here." Hedrick hoped "the good people of the old North State are done with the negro question . . . and . . . will go to discussing something more profitable." It was wishful thinking; only the immediate crisis had passed.41

During this crisis Swain visited Ellen. He wished to see the *Standard*, curious as to whether it "said any thing about this excitement among the darkies." It did not. He then inquired about Hedrick. Ellen informed him that he had been invited to lecture in Washington, to which Swain did not reply.42 A few days later Ellen returned the visit. She sought information about her husband's possible appeal, wanting in particular the board's resolutions. "I want to see the Governor," she said in anticipation of the visit, "but he talks so little to me that it only provokes me, I can't get a thing out of him any way." Swain inquired as to the latest news about Hedrick, his general wellbeing and what he was doing. When Ellen asked about the board resolutions, Swain pleaded that he had been very busy; later, however, he sent them, noting that he had found and transcribed them for her. She remained somewhat critical of him, nevertheless. "I think that his thoughts are hard to find out," she opined to her beleaguered husband.43

By contrast, if Hedrick himself was similarly critical, with one exception noted *infra*, his comments have not been found. He thanked, not Swain, but Manly, for the uniform kindness he had always showed him. "You helped cut off my head," he said, "but I know you made the blow fall as lightly as you could." Manly responded by suggesting that Swain's wise counsel could have saved Hedrick from his misfortune at the hands of the executive committee. "His experience and knowledge of men," Manly continued, "would have told you that in times like these, on the eve of a heated political election for Pres't of U.S. such a step would be downright suicide."[44]

Manly's comment appears to have had an impact, for both Hedrick and his wife now regularly looked to Swain for counsel and information. Ellen soon requested a visit from him. She "didn't know whether it was quite right" but wanted his opinion on a note from her husband and a *Standard* editorial about him "full of continued multiple lies." Swain assured her Hedrick "could show they were falsehoods." He offered to "be of any service."[45] Hedrick asked Ellen to tell Swain of his invitation to lecture to the Republicans in Washington "and see what he says." He planned to write him soon about some things, he informed her. The letter to Swain that followed was a long one, largely seeking Swain's advice about an appeal. If he received any encouragement from Swain and others, he would "do my best to beat Holden yet."[46]

Swain's response was cordial but not encouraging. He thought only the trustees, not the executive committee alone, could make the decision, though "[i]t would be very easy to make a judicial question of it." There would be no impropriety in Hedrick's memorializing the board on the subject, and the way he proposed to do it was proper. He thought, however, that the board would uphold the executive committee's decision. "So far as the expression of public sentiment reaches me," he added, "it sanctions the course of the Committee." "I need not say," Swain closed, "that I regret most sincerely the occurrance [*sic*] and the course and that it would afford me the most sincere pleasure to be placed in the . . . situation in which we stood at the beginning of the session."[47]

In his next letter to Ellen, Hedrick made his one comment that could be viewed as critical of Swain. "The 'old Whigs,'" he said, "may be very good men, but they will not set themselves against the disunionists." "They are silent when they should speak," he continued, "If they do not be careful they will wish to speak when it is too late." While Swain had been removed from overt partisan political activity for more than two decades, he was an "old Whig." The remark thus fit him, as it did Hedrick's first employer, Governor Graham. The criticism, if it was such, in no way diminished Hedrick's affection for Swain, however. In the same letter he requested that his wife "[t]ell Gov. Swain that if he wishes to invest in new lands now is the time."[48]

The Hedricks's interest and confidence in, as well as affection for, Swain persisted. Ellen kept her fugitive husband abreast of Swain's activities. She would look to Swain, she said, for information that might be helpful to them. Did Swain have any intention of going North during summer vacation, she inquired of her husband? Hedrick, in turn, informed her when he learned from a northern publisher that one of his agents had visited Chapel Hill and "thinks the Gov. very learned in Historic lore."[49]

Swain likewise displayed steadfast affection for Hedrick and enduring confidence in his learning and ability. He joined other UNC faculty members in a letter of recommendation for him, noting his graduation with "first distinction" and his return to the chair of agricultural chemistry. They had no hesitation in saying he was entitled to the highest consideration for his ability and attainments in math and analytical chemistry.

In addition to this testimonial Hedrick asked of Swain an individual one. Trustees at Columbia, where he sought employment, wished to know whether candidates could teach and maintain discipline. He would be greatly obliged for Swain's individual recommendation, "particularly ... on the points mentioned."[50]

Both Hedricks continued to react to, and endure consequences from, the affair. Her husband had, Ellen thought, been "most shamefully treated." All they could charge him with, she said, was favoring Fremont. More than his article in defense, she believed, it was the editorials "that raised so much noise in the country." She "hated so much to leave old Carolina for ever," she acknowledged, but if the state refused them, it would "be the worse for it." The thought of her husband "travelling about in the cold just for the meanness of a few men here" angered her.[51] There were adverse financial consequences. A friend declined to loan Hedrick money, essentially pleading that he, too, was broke. Another, though, loaned him $50.00, with explicit instructions that "it was not to be returned until you could do it with perfect convenience to yourself."[52]

Publications now refused to provide an outlet for his views. One regretted discontinuance of their relationship "owing to the state of public feeling in regards to the step you have taken on the subject of politics." Continuance, it said, "would be disastrous to the interests" of the publication. Another would decline "to publish any thing further on the subject, either your defence or anything else." "It is not," the publisher informed Hedrick, "a subject for discussion in a Southern paper."[53]

Hedrick had maintained friendly relations with Charles Manly, but even Manly was curt with him. Writing from New York City, Hedrick requested of Manly a copy of Swain's letter to the executive committee about his matter. He desired it so that "he should stand correct on the record when the history of that disgraceful affair is written." In a time before open records laws, Manly denied the request. He regarded correspondence and communications between the university president and the board of trustees or its executive committee as "strictly confidential" and did not "feel at liberty to give copies without the express direction of all parties concerned."[54]

Contrastingly, as he traversed the North while fleeing from North Carolina, Hedrick found considerable sympathy. A Cincinnati resident informed two professors of Hedrick's desire to instruct in the North. "[O]f his expulsion from his professorship at Chapel Hill . . . for holding and expressing the sentiments of Washington, Madison and Jefferson on slavery," he wrote, "you may have heard." Another said of Hedrick that he "had to leave that college [UNC] for the awful crime of loving Liberty more than Slavery." The writer trusted "that Northern freemen will do what they can to aid this accomplished scholar and, what is better, *independent* man."[55]

Some of Hedrick's northern contacts were well known. Horace Greeley, publisher and leading abolitionist, was among his advocates. Writing educator Horace Mann on Hedrick's behalf, Greeley said, "The bearer is Prof. Hedrick late of N.C. University whence he was ejected for declaring for Fremont and Free Territory." Greeley had asked Hedrick to call upon Mann, "for I think you would like to see him."

In Cincinnati, Hedrick conversed with Ohio Governor Salmon P. Chase, later Lincoln's secretary of the treasury and chief justice of the U.S. Supreme Court. Chase, Hedrick reported to Ellen, was "rather vexed at the idea that I should leave Carolina—said I was wanted there." Urging Hedrick to "keep my stand," Chase predicted a bright future for him. Hedrick further reported that his "Defense" letter had "received the highest praise from the highest literary men." Ellen need not send him more copies, he said, because he believed "everybody here has read it."[56]

With the election over, Hedrick advised Ellen in December 1856, the "political excitement" in the North had dissipated. "Every thing about the election seems to be forgotten," he recited, "and all parties are disposed to give old Buck [President-elect James Buchanan] a fair trial [,] and it is generally thought that from recent assurances he will make a good president—and favor making Kansas a free state."[57]

As for Hedrick, he was "tired of living the life of a fugitive." In mid-January 1857, he returned to Chapel Hill where he remained until mid-April "without molestation." He settled his affairs, sold what little property he had, and left, noting that whether he would return remained "for the future to decide."[58] He would neither reside nor work in his native state again. Living in the North, he held teaching positions and government jobs.[59] Some relationships in his native state and region continued, including a cordial and useful one with Governor Swain, who, as we shall see, solicited his occasional assistance.

Reverberations from his unpleasant departure continued on the campus he left behind, however. Years later, shortly before Swain's tenure at UNC ended, A. D. Hepburn, professor of rhetoric, prohibited a student speech as violating the standing rule of the trustees "which forbid[s] all political discussions." It was his role, he noted to Swain, to determine "the fitness of an address to be delivered to any of our celebrations." He had always obeyed the law of the trustees "prohibiting young gentlemen from discussing political topics in any of our com[mencement] exercises or senior speeches," he carefully assured the university's president, almost certainly cognizant of the sad fate of the last UNC faculty member to defy the rule.[60]

CHAPTER 13

Property

*"We are ... improving the campus,
making important additions"*

EVEN BEFORE SWAIN'S FINAL term as governor had ended in December 1835, the trustees delegated a university property matter to him. He was to negotiate with Professor William Hooper on purchasing, for the trustees, Hooper's dwelling house or that of his stepfather, the late UNC President Joseph Caldwell. Swain was to report to the executive committee the terms on which either could be bought. If neither could be, Swain was to rent for the ensuing year at board expense.

Swain later reported that he had purchased Hooper's residence for $2,500 plus interest from date. A prompt decision on some questions about it, he indicated, "would greatly promote my convenience." It was the first of many university property matters the trustees would direct Swain to handle, and the broad discretion granted him then was characteristic throughout his presidency.[1]

The faculty soon directed that Swain, with two professors of his choosing, constitute a committee to superintend improvements on the college buildings. The trustees requested from him a report on the condition, property, and relative standing of the institution, which they planned to publish. The General Assembly then sought a report on all property received by the university from all sources since its inception in 1789, together with the number and condition of the university buildings, whether any addition to them was required, and the amount of property and funds the university then possessed. The trustees designated Swain and former Governor James Iredell as a committee to prepare the report. Swain soon presented it, and it is reasonable to assume that it was largely his work product.[2]

Growth of the university, and consequently of the small village that contained it, required housing for the village's inhabitants. The university owned the land surrounding it, and Swain became an integral agent in its allocation to purchasers. The trustees delegated to him, usually acting with another professor or two or another trustee, authority to sell the lots and to set the price. Although ultimately the trustees ratified the transactions, they basically "rubber stamped" the decisions he and those working with him made.[3]

Judge Battle was Swain's most frequent companion in these endeavors. University records show Swain and Battle, as agents of the trustees, agreeing to sell a local resident a lot adjoining the resident's own and certifying that another had contracted to buy a tract of land from the trustees. Later the executive committee delegated to them a determination of the advisability of sale of a portion of a vacant lot on Main Street, and if so, the cash value. Battle was still traveling as a judge, and Swain had to advise Charles Manly that a decision must await Battle's "return . . . from Rocky Mount, which is daily expected." A few days later Manly noted receipt of their report.[4]

The trustees authorized Swain and Battle to select a lot, not exceeding two acres, for buildings for the female academy at Chapel Hill. When Professor Fordyce Hubbard encountered difficulty in procuring a suitable residence, they empowered Swain and Battle to take action they deemed proper. When a resident wished to buy a small, university owned lot convenient to his workshop, Battle reported for the twosome: the lot was so positioned as to serve no purpose for the university, he and Swain had determined, and they thought it "well and fairly sold at the price of $75."[5]

Eventually the land sales committee contained a second former governor. The trustees now referred all applications for the purchase of lots in the village to former Governors Swain and Morehead, along with Judge Battle. Swain began to submit reports to the executive committee from the three of them.[6]

Some lots were sold for church purposes. In 1847, Swain reported to the sitting governor, William A. Graham, that four men representing the Baptist Church had applied for two acres for a church lot. He was delighted. "As the Episcopalians Methodists and Presbyterians are to have churches," he told the governor, "I heard with some surprise and great pleasure that the Baptists had raised a subscription of $2,000 for the same purpose." Later the trustees authorized lots sold to the Methodist Church. Later still, the trustees authorized the sale of a lot to Professor James Phillips for a Presbyterian Church.[7]

Housing for students, too, was a concern. Swain once told Battle, "there is scarcely a vacant bed, or a vacant seat at a dining table in the village." There were then 287 students in the university, and more were expected. Another occasion found him reporting to Governor Manly, "There are now 324 students in actual attendance and the pressure upon the dormitories is not greater than upon the boarding houses." Swain's interest in student housing surpassed mere adequacy; it encompassed quality as well. As a trustee, he once moved for a committee to examine student rooms and report on their order and cleanliness.[8]

From the outset of Swain's presidency broader building concerns occupied him. In his first summer he vented his dissatisfaction. "By the superintendent charged with the improvement of the premises," he told trustee William A. Graham, "little, very little is apparently to be effected." Whether the superintendent's delinquency was responsible he could not say, but the appropriate trustee committee should make that judgment. An entire plan of improvement was yet to be settled upon, and the committee's delay provided the superintendent a plausible excuse for tardiness. Graham thus must come to Chapel Hill for "a particular examination of the localities, and susceptibilities of the place, upon the spot."

Campus buildings were a particular source of Swain's frustration. "The college buildings ought to be *insured*," he next told Graham, "and then the sooner they are burned *down* the better." A strange but interesting comment, suggesting that the university would do well just to start over in this respect.[9]

Upon Swain's arrival in late 1835, the extant campus buildings were Old East (1793), Person Hall (1797), South Building (1814), and Old West (1822). Construction of Gerrard Hall had commenced in 1822 but since 1827 had lagged due to lack of funding. Swain charged the superintendent of buildings with its completion, and it was finished in 1837 in time to accommodate the second of Swain's thirty-three commencements as president. Buildings planned and constructed during his tenure were Smith Hall (later Playmakers Theater) in 1851, and New East and New West in 1859.[10]

Early in Swain's time at the university the trustees authorized him, as their agent, to purchase Joseph Caldwell's residence for $2,500. The premises were set apart as a future residence of the college president. Swain was to remove buildings and make repairs as he deemed proper for accommodation of a family at board expense. Other university residences were to pass into the occupancy of senior faculty as they became available. The trustees appropriated a sum for repairs to the college buildings, to be expended under the direction of the faculty and drawn from the treasury by warrant of the president.[11]

In Swain's first year, Elisha Mitchell proposed an arrangement of the campus buildings and grounds. Swain thought the proposal "merit[ed] at least respectful consideration," but any sequel is unclear. It is clear, however, that almost from the beginning Swain sought economies in campus-building maintenance. Instead of employing independent contractors as carpenters for "little jobs," he proposed employment of a man with a fixed compensation who would also keep the college servants at work. Kendall Waitt was employed at a $500.00 annual salary. After several months the plan was abandoned, and the university returned to the old method of individual job hires. The temporary arrangement was regarded as an experiment, with little of either gain or loss to the trustees.[12]

Swain soon waxed effusive in describing improvements to the campus. Both instruction and discipline were better, he said, and "[w]e are besides improving the campus, making important additions to the apparatus." They were "about to change the dull aspect of the exterior of the college edifices" by covering them with a new preparation, at least believed to be more aesthetically appealing.[13]

Among the improvements were enhanced quarters for the campus's two literary societies. In Swain's third year the Dialectic and Philanthropic societies memorialized the trustees relating to the erection of a building or buildings for their better accommodation and for the greater security and preservation of their libraries. The trustees referred the memorials to a committee composed of Swain, William A. Graham, and Andrew Joyner. Shortly Swain reported for the committee recommending, as soon as funding allowed, erecting two fireproof halls of the same dimensions and external plans, for the accommodation of the two societies. The university was to pay at least two-thirds of the cost. The trustees concurred.[14]

There was then no activity for several years. In 1843, the trustees instructed Swain to correspond with Robert Donaldson of New York, Judge Gaston's son-in-law, regarding procuring plans for the halls. The university soon employed Alexander Jackson (A. J.) Davis, a New York architect whom Donaldson recommended, and the following year plans and specifications for enlarging the East and West buildings for this purpose were approved. The Phi formally thanked Swain for his interest in the project and the assistance he had given it. Its members desired that Swain use his discretion about the supply of bricks "and other necessary means." They would be "perfectly satisfied with any arrangements he may make."[15]

Swain now requested information on how much of the funding the societies could contribute. The Di indicated that he could rely with confidence on $1,000 being paid upon request; if it could make collections during the summer, it could expect a much larger sum. The Phi had $500.00 on hand and thought it could count on $500.00 more at commencement of the next session. There were many subscriptions by former Phi members, but they were so old that it was uncertain how much could be counted upon. The members, however, were zealous in the undertaking and would use every effort to procure the necessary funds.[16]

The trustees now recommended that the bids or proposals on the plans and designs of Davis be rejected and that Swain and Judge Battle be appointed a committee "to let the work and make contracts," and supervise the project. A few days later Governor Morehead, as trustee president, laid before the board a contract, executed by Swain and Battle on its behalf, "for the erection of Society Halls and the execution of the work on the [Old] East and West Buildings as therein set forth." The board authorized Swain to sign it, which he did.[17]

Among Swain's suggestions was that a cabinetmaker, rather than a carpenter, be employed to construct the shelves and alcoves in the halls' libraries. Rejecting lower bids, he employed for that purpose Thomas Day of Milton, North Carolina, a gifted cabinetmaker and a free Negro who had come to the United States from the West Indies. The handsome shelves executed by Day, and the beautifully sculptured marble mantels, were the most conspicuous features of the libraries. Swain reported to the trustees his payment to Day of $246.83 for the work, which Day acknowledged.[18]

Upon completion the trustees directed that the presidents of the two societies draw lots to determine which would have the eastern, and which the western, building. The edifices were to be known as the East and West buildings and to be regarded as the halls of the societies, each to bear the name of the society to which it might be allotted. When the lots were cast before Swain, William A. Graham, and Charles Manly, the East building was assigned to the Phi and the West to the Di.[19]

In 1849, the executive committee considered a communication from students requesting "the erection of a Ball room." The committee thought it desirable to erect a building to be used by the trustees and the Alumni Association as a dining hall, a ball room at commencement, and for other board directed purposes. It was to be single story, brick, and "within the college campus and form a part of the Public Buildings." Swain and Battle were to procure a plan with cost estimate, to designate a site for its location, and to report to the board as soon as practicable.

In consultation with Swain, Battle, and the trustees, architect A. J. Davis submitted preliminary drawings that autumn. Further conferences, including some over a five-day period Davis spent consulting with Swain and Battle in Chapel Hill, led to revised drawings. The result, Davis told Swain, was "to improve the plan," making it "creditable to any University" in "classical taste, . . . general character, and proportions, what-ever defects there may be in the details, or execution." Ultimately, the plans contained "the classic design of a Greek temple." On Swain's motion the trustees named the structure Smith Hall "in honor of the late Governor Benjamin Smith[,] a munificent donor of land to the university." Although intended for multiple purposes, particularly a library, apparently the new edifice was used largely as a ball room.[20]

> **THOMAS DAY,**
> **CABINET-MAKER,**
> RETURNS his thanks to his friends and the public for the patronage he has received, and wishes to inform them that he intends continuing his business at his old stand, and is well prepared to manufacture all kinds of
> **Mahogany, Walnut, and Stained Furniture.**
> He has on hand a small stock of Mahogany Furniture, made of the best St. Domingo mahogany, in the newest fashion, and executed in the most faithful manner;—and also some Walnut and Stained Furniture, and high and low post Bedsteads, turned according to the latest paterns; all which he will sell at reduced prices and on the most accommodating terms.
> Feb. 22.   62—6w

Advertisement by Thomas Day, Free Negro Cabinet Maker, whom Swain employed for work on society halls. From the *Hillsborough Recorder*, May 4, 1825.

As student population grew in the 1850s, perception of a need for additional buildings also grew. In the summer of 1855, Governor Thomas Bragg and most members of the trustee executive committee, accompanied by U.S. Senator George Badger, visited the campus to make arrangements for a new building or buildings. They determined to await the opinion of a competent architect. Based on a communication from Swain, Battle thought the trustees would "probably decide upon a large and imposing edifice to correspond in location, size etc. with the South building." Swain, Battle said, thought "the committee were pleased with the condition of affairs on the Hill," and Swain was "evidently much pleased with their visit."

The following year the trustees appointed a committee of three—Battle, Graham, and Swain—to consider additional buildings. They could employ an architect to furnish plans and specifications. Later trustee action authorized them to "devise a scheme of college extension and improvement on the scale not to exceed thirty thousand dollars." Ultimately the trustees authorized the committee to move without delay on the necessary contracts and the erection of two college buildings. The maximum price was increased to $40,000.

Notwithstanding considerable experience with A. J. Davis and his many architectural contributions to the campus, the committee employed a competitor, William Percival, as the architect. Percival's Richmond firm opened a branch office in

Raleigh from which to supervise erection of the New East and New West buildings. The buildings were completed and ready for occupancy in September 1861. The cost, which included erection of a cupola and belfry on South Building, was $54,798.62, thus exceeding the limit imposed by the trustees by almost $15,000.[21]

Robert Donaldson—North Carolina native, UNC Class of 1818, and son-in-law of UNC trustee William Gaston—brokered the more durable and productive relationship between the university and New York architect A. J. Davis. In 1842, Swain visited Donaldson at his New York estate, Blithewood, and was impressed by his achievements. The following year the trustees authorized him to seek Donaldson's services as an advisor. Donaldson would cheerfully cooperate in improving the college grounds per the trustee resolution; indeed, he would consider it a filial duty to his alma mater. Donaldson immediately advised Swain that he had consulted with Davis about the society halls. He was thoroughly acquainted with Davis's business and represented that Davis would give designs for exterior and interior arrangements, libraries, busts, and works of art. It was his recommendation that Davis visit Chapel Hill to confer with the young men of the societies.[22]

Swain, having visited with several trustees, perceived himself authorized to invite Davis to visit the university "with a view to the execution of working drawings [and] specifications on the terms indicated" in Donaldson's letter. He went into salesman mode, touting, to Donaldson but obviously intended for Davis, his small academic village as "the most moral and best governed" in the state. He then waited "in constant expectation of hearing from [Donaldson regarding the] Society Halls and College grounds."[23]

The response was positive. Donaldson had found Davis ready to visit Swain. Davis had requested a draft for $100.00 for that purpose. He would make any pencil drawings desired, and more elaborate drawings and specifications if required. Davis was, Donaldson told Swain, the most skilled draftsman he knew, and he certainly could help to improve the college buildings and grounds.[24]

Swain forwarded to Donaldson the $100.00 Davis had requested. Donaldson informed Swain that he had given Davis some of his ideas "of the best mode of executing the improvements at the university," including specifics. The executive committee soon approved Davis's plans for enlarging the college buildings and for the society halls. He was now engaged in completing the drawings, and the trustees would pay $2,800 toward the work in such installments as Swain might direct.[25]

With the relationship now established, Swain and Davis began direct communications with each other. Davis had consulted a "stucco man" regarding the college buildings, he now informed Swain. The executive committee had adopted his plans and "seemed disposed to carry through the proposed alterations in the South Building, such as *adding a Dome* and *fitting up the attic*."[26]

While Swain had direct communications with Davis, he sometimes used the sitting governor, who chaired the trustees, as an intermediary. He once requested, for example, that Governor Morehead convey certain propositions to Davis and request that Davis transmit "the minute specifications." Swain would then be positioned to make a satisfactory arrangement with one of the contractors.[27]

As noted, given the long and strong relationship of Swain and the university with Davis, it is surprising that they employed William Percival as the architect for the construction of New East and New West. In one of Swain's early communications about the project, however, he speaks of it not being done "without Mr. Percival." He desired that Governor Graham and Judge Battle, the other members of the building committee, "have an interview with him, ascertain his views, and when he will be ready to report plans, etc." It was a favorable time to secure competent and responsible contractors on good terms, and Swain was "anxious to have our work offered to bidders at the earliest day practicable."[28]

Swain's involvement in the university's buildings, their construction, maintenance, and occasional enhancement, was extensive. On construction projects he functioned as a combination of owner-foreman, penning descriptions of tasks to be performed, dimensions, lists of measurements, and other details. The trustees placed funds in his hands to disburse for repair work on college buildings and approved his reports on their use. They paid for additions and improvements upon his certification of acceptable completion. They once authorized him to ascertain the cost of repairing the tin roof of South Building and covering the Old Chapel (Person Hall) with tin and to enter contracts for these projects. He proceeded to negotiate their terms with a Wilmington firm.[29]

The president essentially took bids on university construction projects. He once informed a contractor of plans to advertise for proposals for buildings. The contractor first indicated that he was willing to perform the work "upon as good terms as any responsible Builder." He later expressed concern, however, that he was at a loss about how to compose an estimate "unless the proposed improvements were more specified or I had some explanation from you." He would call on Swain and hoped "you will soon have the whole matter drew up specifically and it will take me but a short time to make out my proposal."[30]

Swain also served as the paymaster on these undertakings. "Received payment from D. L. Swain" was a common refrain. A "free Negro carpenter and cabinet-maker" once asked Swain to send his payment to a third party "as he has done some other business . . . for me."[31]

Friends advised Swain on these matters. Upon learning of a contemplated increase in university buildings, Francis L. Hawks said, "Do not *close up* the quadrangle but put your new edifices at the sides. This will give an imposing front and show all the buildings."[32] Swain felt free to call upon friends for assistance with these projects. He once sought to hire the Battles' "servant" Harry "to put some paling about the Stewards Hall." Lucy Battle informed him that Harry could not be spared until he had moved some buildings for Judge Battle. She hoped, though, that he would be ready as soon as Swain was.[33]

Faculty housing, too, occupied Swain. Professor F. M. Hubbard once requested that Swain present to the trustees a change in the terms under which he held his house. Professor John T. Wheat's family petitioned Swain for addition of "*Blinds* or shutters" to their home. They acknowledged the burden they were imposing: "You will greatly oblige us by adding this to your other cares at this time." The trustees granted their request.

The trustees appointed Swain and Battle a committee to deal with Professor John Kimberly regarding repairs on, and occupancy of, his house. On one occasion Swain wrote the trustee executive committee regarding improvements to the houses of the professors generally. The committee resolved to make repairs, improvements, and additions. It designated Swain and Professor William M. Green a committee to cause the contemplated improvements to be made on the best terms and to supervise their faithful execution.[34]

Swain's own residence got his attention. Early in his tenure he sought permission to build, from brick formerly used in the erection of an observatory, a kitchen on his lot. The executive committee ordered that it be built "after the plan proposed by the Faculty's building committee." Later, pursuant to agreement of the caretaker, the wings of Steward's Hall were given to Swain to be used in erecting a servant's house. At about the same time the trustee treasurer was authorized to repay Swain for expenses incurred in rebuilding the stables and other repairs on his lot.[35]

In 1850, the trustees noted that the Caldwell House had been purchased as the president's residence and should be occupied by him. Swain was "authorized and requested to take possession." The house Swain then occupied was to be used by the professor of rhetoric and logic. The trustees authorized repairs to both "and fences to be properly replaced." Swain applied for insurance on the house, paid the premium, and directed issuance in the name of the trustees. The trustees then authorized affixation of the corporate seal to a note from the board to the Mutual Insurance Company for the policy.[36]

A few years later the trustees authorized their building committee—Battle,

Graham, and Swain—to contract for repairs and alterations on the house. They recognized the importance of Eleanor Swain's concurrence. If she would not write him about the repairs, Charles Manly told Swain, he would be forced to "adopt some other plan to get the thing up, for the repairs must be made just as she says."[37]

Swain's concern for the campus and its appearance extended beyond buildings to grounds. Early in his administration he proposed, and the trustees approved, enclosing or walling in the college campus, thinning the grove, and planting ornamental and shade trees near the buildings. Four years later he professed to have "a great deal to say" regarding improving the groves and grounds. He hoped the enclosures could be completed that fall. He would then be anxious to plant many trees of various kinds and to arrange the walls, grass, and plants. He invited dissent but indicated that he might "petition for a re-hearing" if it came.[38]

Swain planted shrubbery and trees, great elms that enhanced the beauty of the campus. Faculty yards were also adorned with trees, some of which prospered more than others. Lucy Battle once informed her itinerant husband that their firs looked "pretty well[,] much better than the Governors." Swain, she said, thought they would all die. If so, however, his brother had "promised to send some in the Fall with the roots so managed that he thinks [they] will live."[39]

Elisha Mitchell was Swain's close companion in the construction of the stone walls that bounded the campus. The bountiful supply of large attractive stones around Chapel Hill made the task feasible. Mitchell, functioning as superintendent of buildings and grounds and drawing on his earlier experience in New England, laid them out, did some of the work himself, and was paid extra for it. A trustee minute entry shows him receiving $500.00 "for the stone walls erected by him around the campus and college grounds."[40]

Enslaved persons, including some of Mitchell's, performed some of this work. A receipt in the university records shows Swain paying Willis Duncan $8.00 for thirteen-days' work "in building stone walls, underpinning." Duncan signed with an "x," thus displaying illiteracy, which would have been consistent with an enslaved status.[41] While Mitchell gets the lion's share of the credit for the stone walls, they were part of Swain's program to beautify the campus, and Swain was both involved in and supportive of the endeavor. Indeed, Mitchell himself once said that, at least at one time, between them Swain bore the heavier burden.[42]

Swain also extended himself in efforts to obtain and retain a gardener for the campus grounds. He corresponded briefly with Albert B. Dod of Princeton, who informed him of two persons "who might be safely recommended to the post." They were not willing to leave their present positions but perhaps could make a trustworthy recommendation. Dod also suggested application to a New Yorker with several of his fellow Scotchmen in his employ "who are in general our best gardeners." Nothing came of this, however.[43]

A. J. Davis, university architect, had just the man in mind and thought he would be content to work for a time for a moderate remuneration. "His connection with your university would be a stepping stone to his deserts," Davis told Swain, "and would probably lead to some practice in your state."[44] The identity of this candidate is unclear, but over a year later Davis commended Patrick Cavanagh to Swain. Davis considered him "a patient industrious man, and one who would serve you as gardener so far as his capacity might enable him, most faithfully." Cavanagh's present employer held him in high esteem, however, and wished to keep him.[45]

This esteem must have been sufficiently great that the present employer managed to retain his services. Davis soon identified another prospect. He had arranged for P. G. McLaughlin to go to Chapel Hill as the landscape gardener. McLaughlin would require an advance of $30.00 "to defray his expenses on the road." Davis would advance the sum, which Swain could repay when convenient. Davis would provide McLaughlin with a rough sketch of the university grounds "merely as a hint, or first thought." This plan too soon failed. McLaughlin advised Swain that when he learned his board would consume half his salary, he had to decline. The heat of a North Carolina summer, to which as a northerner he was unacclimated, was a further deterrent. While uneasy that Swain might be viewing him as irresponsible, he told the president, whom he addressed at "Chapel Hill University," that he could not get a competent man for $400.00 a year.[46]

The executive committee instructed Swain to open a dialogue with Robert Donaldson of New York, with the object of obtaining the services of one skilled in laying out "pleasure grounds, landscape gardening, etc.," at prices that could be had and services that could be attained. Donaldson had ideas "[w]ith respect to the college grounds" and thought it would not be difficult "to procure such a Gardener" as Swain wished. He soon advised Swain that he had "called at Thorburne's seed store and described the kind of Gardener you require and they will be on the lookout for one." He had also written his brother James "and requested him to engage a suitable Gardener for you and to communicate with you on the subject."

Donaldson proceeded to recommend an agricultural society at Chapel Hill as a preliminary movement to the "Botanical Garden & Model Farm." The society could try experiments under the direction of the gardener. One particularly well-placed UNC graduate could assist: Donaldson's 1818 classmate at UNC, James K. Polk, then president, would "no doubt send from the Patent Office in Washington the rare and valuable seeds which are annually distributed there."[47]

James Donaldson now advised Swain of his involvement but candidly told him it would be difficult to find a suitable person "willing to go so far South without a larger compensation than $500 per annum." When a gardener arrived, James expressed his pleasure and hoped Swain was favorably impressed. He continued to be disappointed when one abandoned Chapel Hill and inquisitive about how new ones were working out.[48]

Over the course of Swain's presidency, the university employed several gardeners, probably foremost among them John Loader and Thomas Paxton. The trustees were consistently supportive, renewing the appropriations for a gardener and for the improvement of the campus and college grounds year after year. At one point they authorized the bursar to employ "a competent white man to superintend the campus and the enclosed grounds, to preserve and cultivate the shrubbery and plants; to keep up the fences and prevent trespass by stock and all nuisances; [and such other work as the bursar might direct.]"[49]

Mitchell thought giving "grace and beauty to the approaches to the buildings and to the walks around them" might influence the young men for good and "impress strangers favorably."[50] Whatever the effect or lack thereof on student behavior, Swain's efforts to improve the grounds are a significant part of his legacy. With the aid of his architects, gardeners, and others, he transformed the small campus from its primeval forest state into a grand grove, with macadamized walks, shrubbery, trees, flowers, stone walls, and other enhancements that have stood the test of time. Some, probably mostly untraceable, grace the university's grounds even today.[51]

While Swain gets credit for enhancements to the campus grounds, he receives criticism for failing to build the university library's holdings. A year into Swain's presidency the university librarian reported on the state of the library. For years, he stated, gentlemen had made valuable donations of books to the library; but now, for many years, "this spirit of individual munificence has entirely ceased." Recently there had been no appropriations for it. "[T]he Library," he stated, "has increased but little since the additions made to it by the purchases of Dr. Caldwell in Europe." He had put the library "in as good a condition as the room in which it is located is susceptible of." No department, however, was sufficiently supplied with the necessary books; that of modern languages was "particularly deficient." The university library then contained approximately 1,900 books.[52]

An account a year later reflected no change. The library, the next report stated, continued to be housed in the junior recitation room, but Swain and the librarian contemplated a room for it in the South Building attic. It speaks volumes that a single recitation room could contain the entire university library.[53]

Swain could have taken these reports as a clarion call to action but did not. Battle reports that Swain occasionally took joint charge of the library with the librarian but gives no indication of what he did with it on such occasions. The trustees made appropriations for it, at least sometimes at Swain's instigation. They once, for example, on his motion resolved to appropriate $1,000 a year for five years to increase the library under his direction. Swain was accused, however, of failing to spend even that for the purpose intended, preferring to apply the funds to an increase in the university's endowment. Several years later Bartholomew F. Moore, chair of a select committee of the trustees, reportedly said that "not a volume has been purchased by the Trustees during the last quarter of a century. No stranger is ever invited to examine our present collection."[54]

Louis Round Wilson, later longtime UNC librarian, has offered several explanations for this omission. It could be attributed, he suggests, to the excellence of the Dialectic and Philanthropic societies' libraries for student use, the extensive private collections of the individual professors, the methods of teaching during this period, and the fact that Swain kept many of the historical materials for his own use in his home or in the library, located at that time in South Building near his office. Wilson further posits that the failure may be attributed in part to Swain's devotion to other university interests that he promoted assiduously, including training young men for public service and accumulating historical materials relating to the university and the state.[55]

The assertion that there was *no* enhancement of the collections in Swain's time, however, exaggerates. Professor James Phillips kept Swain informed regarding books he purchased. Whether they were for himself or the university, however, is indeterminate. Swain himself placed orders with booksellers in New York, including one for Kent's *Commentaries on American Law* and the works of classical writers such as Horace, Livy, and Virgil. Again, however, it is impossible to say whether they were for his personal collection or the university library's.[56]

A London firm once offered Swain services in executing orders for foreign books. In at least one instance Swain placed with a publisher an extensive order for books for the university. In another he sent Benjamin Hedrick, then at Cambridge, Massachusetts, a list of books in which he was interested. Hedrick went to New York looking at books but made very few purchases; he planned to buy some when he returned. Late in the Civil War, the university purchased the library of a deceased person "at the price of $970 in Confederate money."[57]

Most of the library books acquired during Swain's time came as gifts from interested publishers, friends, and alumni, and most of the time these were directed to Swain. Harper and Brothers in New York once sent Swain several volumes of a series of classical works it was publishing; it wanted to furnish "accurate and uniform editions of the classical authors read in colleges and schools." The gift was not altogether disinterested, however. The firm had received letters of approval and encouragement from presidents and professors at prominent colleges and would, it indicated to Swain, "be very happy to have the privilege of including one from your pen."[58]

Another northern firm sent Swain a copy of *Delafield's Antiquities* "as an evidence that our obligations to you are not forgotten." A Boston correspondent sent a set of scientific reports "as far as the same have been completed," adding a few other pamphlets and books he thought might be of interest. One from Wilmington advised Swain of "1 square paper package under yr. mark per Sen. Henry Clay from New York."[59]

Apparently in response to a suggestion that the "State Papers" the U.S. Congress published would be a desirable addition to the university library, Swain made inquiry, was advised that the university was entitled to them, and was promised that they would be forwarded with the next congressional documents. The inquiry also produced a list of other works that the Department of State had furnished to colleges. If UNC had not received them, they would be sent upon Swain's request to the secretary of state. Later George Badger offered to send an astronomical volume from the U.S. Naval Observatory if desired.

A representative of the U.S. Department of the Interior, in response to Swain's request, sent to the governor of North Carolina two sets of documents of the Thirty-sixth and Thirty-seventh Congresses. He regretted that it was not in his power "to furnish you a set of the [U.S.] Statutes at Large."[60] These latter documents came following a post-Civil War Swain request to former UNC professor Benjamin Hedrick, now in Washington.

Until 1860, Swain informed him, congressional acts had entitled the university to a copy of all documents published under the authority of Congress. The secretary of the interior had annually transmitted to the university a box containing these items. They were now greatly needed, Swain implored Hedrick, "and I trust we will be still regarded as entitled to them." He would be greatly obliged if Hedrick would present the subject to the secretary of the interior.

Later Swain noted to Hedrick his success in obtaining some documents and the secretary's regret that he could not furnish the Statutes at Large. He was now anxious to obtain all subsequent publications that could be forwarded by express in like manner. The governor of North Carolina would pay the freight. Swain had also been promised all the Smithsonian collection of publications since 1860 but had not received them. He sought Hedrick's assistance in securing them. Over a year later Swain was still seeking Hedrick's aid in securing these publications. He had received none of the public documents since those of the Thirty-sixth and Thirty-seventh Congresses. Subsequent documents could be sent by express marked to the governor for the university. The result of these solicitations is not apparent, but Swain's effort to secure all such documents that he could for the university is clear.[61]

Swain once exhibited to the faculty anti-Masonic publications from a benefactor in Boston. The faculty unanimously voted to receive them.[62] Following the death of longtime congressman and senator Willie P. Mangum, Swain rejected, as duplication, an offer of his books. There was scarcely a volume in Mangum's library, he said, that was "not to be found in our collection." "Our library of public documents is fuller than the State Library is at present," he said, "or likely to be in the future." The reason: "Members of the General Assembly so frequently forget to return the volumes they are privileged to withdraw, that few series are found to be complete."[63]

Potential library additions were lost in other ways. Early in the Civil War a Charleston friend ordered books imported from London, intending to present them to the university. The books were captured by the squadron blockading Charleston, however, and carried to Philadelphia as a prize or contraband of war. The friend was trying to recover them, but there is no evidence that he succeeded. He had intended that Swain know nothing of them "until they were presented at Chapel Hill." "The horrid war that is carrying death and mourning into so many of our families," he said, "now makes that impossible."[64]

At an 1855 UNC faculty meeting Professor Mitchell moved that if funds permitted, the faculty recommend that the trustees appropriate $500.00 to $1,000 for books needed immediately. The rationale: "more than 30 years having elapsed since there has been any considerable expenditure for the increase of the Library." "Considerable" is the operative word here. There had been some expenditures for the library, and the president had made determined efforts, with some success, to secure for it every possible government publication available without cost.[65]

Swain is rightly credited with providing a beautiful setting for the library's collections. While Smith Hall was under construction, he reported that the new library was advancing rapidly and "promises to be our handsomest edifice." He was again working with New York architect A. J. Davis in the production of "a structure of impeccable proportions, the perfect portico with classic Corinthian pillars showing a delightful variation from the Hellenic norm in the capitals of wheat and cornplants, with foliage of grace and beauty, symbolic of the native American landscape."[66] Credit is also due to Swain for the physical enhancement of the societies' libraries. He encountered frustrations in that process. There were, he once informed Governor Manly, "some differences of opinion between the contractors and myself in relation to the interior finish of the libraries." These made "a reference to Mr. Davis indispensable."⁶⁷

Swain appears, however, to have insisted on high-quality work on these libraries and to have gotten his way. It was here, as noted, that he successfully lobbied his trustees to be allowed to pay free Negro Thomas Day one-third more than another bidder requested for the shelving. He did so well aware of the likelihood of criticism if this became known and thus cautioned Day to maintain silence about the figure. "I have concluded," he informed Day, "to accept your bid for shelving the libraries, though it is higher by more than $100 than the sum proposed by a very respectable person in this place." He would rely for justification on the impressive way he expected Day to execute the work, but he admonished him, "[f]or the present you must not mention to anyone the amount you are to receive."⁶⁸

No doubt Swain took comfort in the belief that Governors Graham and Morehead agreed with him that a cabinetmaker, rather than a carpenter, should be employed. At one point he expressed to Graham his concern that he had not yet succeeded in getting a contract for the shelving. Soon, though, he had Day, who initially assigned some preludes to the task to Swain. "I must beg the favor of you," Day said, "to measure the length of your Books the Debth [sic] of the shelves accurately and send me."

Day resisted Swain's overture to take rent-free lodging in Chapel Hill. By remaining at his residence in Milton, he could "select better timber ... and prepare it much better." He would "bring it in waggons and put it up much sooner and better and cheaper to myself than to come ... [to] that neighborhood." You may fully rely on the strictest attention being paid to the whole matter," he assured Swain, "and I have no doubt you will be satisfied when the work is done." Day was grateful for Swain's kindness in employing him.⁶⁹

Other friends also assisted. James Donaldson advised Swain from New York that he had ordered four mantelpieces for the library rooms. They would probably be shipped to Wilmington in the ensuing week.⁷⁰

Instructional materials unrelated to the libraries brought both inquiries and information to Swain. Early in his administration a correspondent wrote, not to Swain, but to publisher Weston Gales, noting that UNC, or some institution in the state, had written to a source in London on "the acquisition of a Cabinet of minerals fitted for public instruction." The writer knew exactly what was wanted and the place to obtain it. It consisted principally of crystals. Absent encouragement about keeping it in the United States, the cabinet was going to Europe. Had he known Swain personally, the writer would have considered the matter of sufficient importance to take it to him directly, "knowing his devotion to everything that tends to diffuse useful knowledge."[71] A Swain response has not been found. Swain knew Gales well, however, and it is almost certain that Gales would have brought the matter to his attention.

A physician's death brought an offer of a "complete anatomical preparatory apparatus." Any "blockhead" could "stick up his shingle" as a doctor of medicine and "practice by experiments upon human life," lamented the writer, an 1824 graduate and a trustee. The university thus should have a medical department, and the deceased physician would have been "highly gratified" to have his apparatus devoted to that purpose. It also, the writer opined to Swain, "would be a great acquisition to our university."[72]

An 1859 exhibition in the State Capitol displayed scientific and agricultural materials from the university. "The cabinet at Raleigh," Swain boasted to Governor John W. Ellis, "will serve to gratify public curiosity in many instances, and will occasionally attract the attention of sojourners and travellers."[73]

Simultaneously with this exhibit Governor Ellis, state geologist Ebenezer Emmons, and Swain joined to secure for the university "specimens illustrative of the geology of the State." It would not be as full as the state collection, the geologist informed Swain, but such collections were significant, "especially when deposited with an Institution so important as the University of Chapel Hill." The geologist needed to know the size of the room and space Swain could devote to the collection "and about the size of specimens you wish." He also hoped to furnish UNC with "a series of opinions illustrating the geology of New York."

Governor Ellis committed to the project. He had seen Emmons and was willing to contribute to the collection of specimens at the university as far as he was able at no cost to the university except perhaps for the freight. Swain thanked Ellis for the geologist's services in disseminating geological, mineralogical, and agricultural knowledge, and pledged the cooperation of the university's Scientific School faculty.[74]

On July 20, 1791, before the university even opened to students, its trustees arranged for appointment of an attorney in each district of the state to mind the interests of the university and account for collections on its behalf. From its beginning the university received property that escheated to the state, property to which there was no other legal claimant. The primary function of the attorneys in each district was to identify and collect these assets. These were coveted positions. A Fayetteville attorney, an 1842 graduate, once informed Swain of his belief that the university had no attorney in his county. He would like the appointment, he said, for he thought something could be done there for the university "by an active and careful friend of her interest."⁷⁵

As a trustee Swain was a member of a committee that prepared ordinances and regulations the executive committee adopted "in relation to Escheats and derelict property." As president, he reported to the General Assembly on such property. He took this responsibility seriously, sometimes conferring with other trustees, such as Governor Graham, on the subject.⁷⁶ The escheats apparently were not highly productive of university income. Governor Manly once reported to Swain that his books showed a yield from this source of only $13,238.92 from 1840 to 1855. Faced with proposals to divert the funds to the common schools, Manly doubted it worthwhile to contend against the effort. Supporters of the change, he told Swain, "laugh in your face and say 'Oh the university is rich and don't need this little mite—we want to give it to the little barefooted white headed children at home.'" One senator in particular, Manly said, when told "he had treated us badly," laughed it off.⁷⁷

Earlier, however, Swain had served on a trustee committee to examine ordinances on the subject and to report on whether the university should surrender the right to escheated property to the state. He made an elaborate report to the board against the idea, in which the board concurred. He then fought tenaciously, in the General Assembly and the courts, against efforts to divert the funds elsewhere. There were brief intervals in which the university lost them, but with those rare exceptions, his efforts succeeded.

In 1857, the House of Commons passed an escheats-confiscation bill overwhelmingly. A motion to reconsider failed by 90 to 11. "It is too pretty a topic for a Demagogue to relinquish," Manly told Swain. Governor Thomas Bragg also informed Swain of the massive House majority against the university and of his fear that the bill would pass the Senate. "Nothing but an immediate and strong effort will arrest it if that can," he advised Swain: "I can see no impropriety in your coming down. The impression I find prevails that the Institution is rich and does not need the proceeds of escheats. No one can so well explain this as yourself."

Swain went to work. Manly soon informed him that he believed the confiscation bill was dead. "[T]he stalwart and timely blows which you have laid upon [it] ... have put it past surgery," he said. Manly's information was that if called for a direct vote, the bill would be killed. The following day he told Swain, "The Gen. Assembly died out last night ... and with it the confiscation bill."⁷⁸

The university's lawyers in the counties often contacted Swain to inform or inquire regarding property perceived to have escheated to the university. One, who thought gold mines in his district might be university property, asked whether the property would be subject to the debts of the company from which it had escheated. "This subject may not directly belong to your station," he acknowledged, "but if not I hope you will see to it for me."[79]

Thomas L. Clingman, prominent Western North Carolina political figure, posed questions regarding a tract of land he thought had escheated to the university. "[W]hat could we get a release from the university for" he inquired of Swain? He had discussed the issue only with Nicholas W. Woodfin, who handled Swain's personal legal matters in Western North Carolina, and to avoid embroilment with the claimants he hoped Swain would discuss it with as few persons as possible.[80]

Unresolved legal issues could present escheats-entitlement questions. Bartholomew F. Moore, attorney and UNC trustee, had the transcript of a case where a man had died more than half a century earlier. There was an allegation that he had left three brothers, whose last-known residences were in Georgia. It was not known whether they were deceased or had left children, and he wanted Swain to inquire as to heirs. If the man had left heirs and there were now descendants, he told Swain, neither the university nor the Literary Fund had any interest.[81]

More complicated still was "a question of some interest and some novelty" on which a lawyer wanted Swain's advice. A British soldier had deserted during the Revolutionary War and joined the American Army. He was never naturalized and had left no children but did leave a widow, a native of the state. The soldier had purchased an estate in Iredell County, now worth a few hundred dollars, which had been unoccupied since the widow's death in 1824. Recently a trespasser had possessed it and continued to hold it. Was it desirable to bring a suit for the university the lawyer asked its president?[82]

Information about escheat matters came to Swain from Charles Manly, longtime secretary-treasurer of the trustees. "It is not unlikely," Manly once informed him, "that we are interested in the Maxwell Chambers estate to the tune of $150,000."[83]

The trustees authorized Swain to resolve a sensitive matter involving escheated property. David Allison of Philadelphia, one of many land speculators following the American Revolution, died owning North Carolina mountain land and without heirs. A Haywood County resident claimed the land in opposition to the university. N. W. Woodfin, university attorney in the area, entered a compromise with the claimant that the trustees later repudiated. It had never been communicated to them, they said, and it was the product of false representations by the claimant. Following their repudiation of Woodfin's settlement the trustees empowered Swain to compromise the matter. Swain was to go to Asheville forthwith and would be allowed his expenses and necessary disbursements. He returned with a proposed compromise under which the trustees would relinquish all interest in exchange for $3,450. The trustees accepted the compromise and requested that Swain prepare the quitclaim deed.[84]

There is some evidence that Swain received legal fees for this task, notwithstanding that it was university business. Charles Manly told Swain that when he sent the deed "it will be a fit occasion to present your bill for Compensation and Expenses . . . on your Buncombe negotiations." When Manly sent Swain the executed deed for delivery, he also sent a check for $125.00, which appears to have been for a legal fee.[85]

Land and money were not the only subjects of escheats. Human property too came to the university. Early in Swain's time there, Matthias Manly, former commoner and later supreme court judge, notified his brother Charles of such a situation. He believed "a negro girl and two or three children" had "escheated to the university." An "old Negro man" had been emancipated a few years before "after which he purchased this girl who is his daughter." The man had died "without having any heir of inheritable blood or making any provisions for his daughter and grandchildren." A note on the letter cover states: "Answered and 'instructed' to take possession and sell *for cost*." A contemporaneous executive-committee minute entry notes that the administrator of an escheated estate was ordered to sell the "Negroes" and convert the estate into cash as soon as possible.[86] A later missive from Charles Manly to Swain states "the negroes in our Columbus case have been sold for $2210."[87]

As in all areas of human endeavor, this one was subject to mistakes. A letter from the British Consulate in Charleston addressed Swain "with respect to a negro girl . . . who is in danger of being sold, as a slave, with her child, at Newbern N.C. under an advertisement . . . which a correspondent states to me emanates from an agent of the N.C. College." The escheator for Craven County, an 1824 graduate, had erred. There was no doubt that the "girl" was "a free British subject, brought at an earlier age from Jamaica to the U. States." The consulate hoped Swain would instruct his agent to withhold further proceedings "[p]ending the requisite negotiation on the subject."[88]

CHAPTER 14

Special Events, Distinguished Guests
"Do not fail to attend our commencement"

SWAIN GAVE SERIOUS AND sustained attention to the university's annual commencements. At his first in 1836 he set the tone for those to come. Despite recent misfortune, a young William A. Graham, recently elected a trustee, had to come. Swain's "invitation" was mandatory: Graham "must attend." The Swains were "new house keepers" but could "manage to keep a room, and a bed sufficiently large for the repose of your family, and you *will* be expected to occupy it."

Loss of a scheduled speaker failed to dampen the celebratory occasion. A protracted session of Congress once detained the Honorable Henry L. Pinckney of South Carolina, the literary societies' chosen orator. He forwarded an address, however, for a suitable person to read. The task fell to the new president, and he reportedly performed it "in a most emphatic and impressive manner." It was a notable beginning. "We . . . deem it but sheer justice to the new President, Gov. Swain," said a Raleigh newspaper, "to say that he discharged his duty to the entire satisfaction of all, and gave promise of making an able and popular President."[1]

Swain's second commencement brought enhanced praise from the same source. The institution had been extremely fortunate in Swain's succession of the venerable Caldwell, the paper stated. Initially, some friends of the university had considered his selection "*an experiment full of hazard*": "[T]hey doubted whether he possessed that maturity of character and austerity of demeanor which seemed to be demanded for the station, or could at once lay aside the seductive charms of political life and popular fame." The test of experience had dispelled the doubts, however. "[T]he acknowledged ability, dignity and energy with which he has administered his office," it concluded, "has fully justified the expectations of those sagacious gentlemen who were foremost in pressing the office upon him."[2]

Swain's fourth commencement in 1839 drew all living former governors of the state save one. Montfort Stokes had left the state, President Andrew Jackson having appointed him chair of the Federal Indian Commission to supervise the settlement of southern Indians west of the Mississippi River. Those present were John Branch, James Iredell, John Owen, David L. Swain, and Richard Dobbs Spaight Jr. Swain took advantage of the occasion to tout the improving condition of the university. His earnest wish was that it would continue to flourish and "to send forth from its walls a race of men to bless and adorn our highly favored country."[3]

Future Swain-era commencements also drew several governors. In 1854, there were seven, six from North Carolina and one, A. V. Brown, from Tennessee. Brown delivered the address for the literary societies. In 1863, Zeb Vance, the sitting North Carolina governor, attended, together with former governors Graham, Manly, Morehead, and Swain.[4]

A committee of visitation from the trustees attended and participated in the commencements. Swain, as a trustee, served on the visiting committees, even though as president he was hardly a visitor. Among the visitors' duties was attendance at the pre-commencement examinations of all classes. Judge Battle viewed the practice as having the good effect of stimulating the students toward more diligent preparation.[5]

Trustees, undoubtedly with Swain's prompting, took these duties seriously and were apologetic when they could not fulfill them. William Gaston and William A. Graham regretted it when court commitments compelled their absence. A son's serious illness once precluded Chief Justice Thomas Ruffin's attendance. Despite the unexpected nature of the invitation, Governor Morehead would give the annual address if Swain could not get someone else. "I say *we must have a speech*," he told his fellow former governor.[6]

Swain continually used the imperative in his commencement invitations. "Do not fail to attend our commencement," he once wrote to Calvin H. Wiley, state superintendent of common schools. He could be equally imperious in securing assistance with commencement-related matters. The fact that Judge Battle was busy holding court in Wilmington, for example, was no impediment to a gentle reminder from Swain: Battle must not forget his promise to inquire into the expediency and practicality of securing a supply of a certain item for commencement.[7]

The event was a command performance for faculty, the best of excuses for absences notwithstanding. Soon after Swain arrived on the campus, a young professor determined to leave before commencement to visit a young lady whom he was shortly to marry. When censured by Swain, he appealed to the faculty, which sustained his position. Swain went to the trustees, however, and prevailed. It became trustee policy that no faculty member should leave Chapel Hill until the

Presidents James K. Polk, James Buchanan, and Andrew Johnson, who attended UNC commencements in 1847, 1859, and 1867, respectively. Images of Polk and Buchanan courtesy of Prints and Photographs Division, Library of Congress. Image of Johnson from Portraits Collection, North Carolina Collection Photographic Archive.

Monday after commencement. Swain knew the state's people and their penchant for rituals of this nature. He thus used the occasions to promote the university, and he had no tolerance for treating them with less than the utmost seriousness.

Inadequate salaries notwithstanding, faculty members often contributed to the dispensing of hospitalities for the event. They also contributed to the purchase of Bibles for the graduating seniors. As the highest-paid faculty member, Swain's donation was sometimes the largest of these sums.[8]

While all Swain-era commencements were special, those of 1847, 1859, and 1867 were especially so. At each the sitting president of the United States was in attendance. To the first of these, the campus was a familiar place. James Knox Polk was, and remains, the only graduate of the university to occupy the office. A member of the Class of 1818, Polk graduated with first honors in mathematics and the classics. There was a degree of novelty in his 1847 visit nevertheless, for he had not returned to the village in the ensuing twenty-nine years.[9] His election had brought congratulations to Swain as president of Polk's alma mater, who could, said a Washington official shortly after the event, "justly be proud of the President elect." The university expressed its pride in the newly elected president by awarding him an honorary doctor of laws degree the following year.[10]

Polk's visit spurred considerable primping of the campus buildings. It was the first time in the university's history that the sitting president was to appear. Swain informed the sitting governor, William A. Graham, that Professor William

Green, chair of the committee on arrangements, would be dispatched to Raleigh to confer with him and the executive committee on the subject. In anticipation of the visit improvements had been made to the East and West buildings, and the contractors were anxious to have them approved.

Professor Green would confer with Graham on other improvements that should be undertaken immediately if they were to be executed in time for commencement: enlarging Gerrard Hall, painting houses occupied by faculty members, rewashing old portions of East and West, and repainting window sills and lintels.[11] At one point Swain informed Battle, absent riding the judicial circuits, that the appearance of the college buildings had improved considerably since his departure. One suspects that a rather spiffy academic village greeted the country's chief magistrate, then in the third year of his presidency. Indeed, President Polk noted that the buildings had "been greatly enlarged and improved since my day at the college."[12]

Anticipation of Polk's 1847 sojourn produced one sour note of partisan politics. Lucy Battle was sorry he was coming. If it were Henry Clay, Polk's Whig opponent, she told her husband, "I should think of it with pleasure." "[O]nly think how deceitful the Whigs will almost be compelled to be," she observed.[13] Even Lucy, however, was captivated by the prospect of a presidential visit. Professor William M. Green, Polk's UNC classmate, had heard from the president, she informed Judge Battle, and "he says he will certainly be here at com. if it is *possible*." When she had visitors, the one topic was the president's visit at commencement. Governor Swain, she said, was about to send the traveling judge some information on the subject. Swain was "much occupied," and she rarely saw him. According to the students, Swain thought of little else; some even said he was "crazy upon the subject of the Presidents visit."[14]

William A. Graham, sitting governor and thus trustee president, soon notified Swain that the executive committee was aware of the impending visit. Graham proposed that Professor Green, attended by a committee of not more than twelve members of the senior class appointed by the literary societies in equal numbers, receive the president at Gaston, the north terminus of the Raleigh and Gaston Railroad, and accompany him to Chapel Hill via Raleigh. If rooms were provided for the president in the college buildings, Governor Graham directed, "have a general superintendance of his quarters and accommodations." A ball was not recommended; rather, "an illumination on the evening of com. [should] be substituted."

The executive committee soon took official action. The faculty was to make arrangements for the reception and accommodation of the president and his suite "as they deem proper and expedient." The board treasurer was authorized to pay all necessary expenses.¹⁵ At length Swain could inform Judge Battle that the presence of the president and the secretary of the navy was considered certain. Their attendance would draw a large crowd, "and we will have enough to do, in the mean time, to make suitable arrangements for their reception and accommodation."¹⁶

Now came a communication, official yet intensely personal, from the president of the University of North Carolina to the president of the United States. He had heard of President Polk's contemplated excursion with great pleasure, Swain avowed. He regarded it as "so decided a manifestation of grateful remembrance and filial affection on the part of the most eminent of [UNC's] sons with feelings of kindness as well as pride." More than "mere eminence of station" generated his pride. Although the two had never met, Swain had observed Polk's "whole course of life" and had done so "with a particularity that you would scarcely have anticipated." He had been the college roommate and later "the familiar friend and associate" of Polk's brother Marshall, an 1825 UNC graduate with first distinction. "Under such circumstances," Swain claimed, "I feel that I have almost a right to consider myself an acquaintance and friend, and at all counts venture to hope that in the course of a few weeks there will exist no reasonable doubt on either hand." The president would want his stay in Chapel Hill to be quiet. In the bustle of commencement week, that could be difficult. His best bet could be, Swain posited, "to take shelter under my roof." Until informed of Polk's pleasure, he would reserve "a small chamber for the accommodation of Mrs. Polk and yourself."¹⁷

Polk's visit materialized essentially as planned. He and his suite arrived from Raleigh around 5:00 p.m. on May 31, 1847. He chose to stay at Nancy Hilliard's Eagle Hotel rather than at the Swain residence. Hilliard had erected an addition to the hotel for the express purpose of entertaining and accommodating the president and his party. A metal plate over the entrance greeted him with the following inscription:

ERECTED TO RECEIVE
PRES. POLK
ON THE OCCASION OF HIS
VISIT TO HIS ALMA MATER

A procession of faculty, students, and citizens received Polk there. He was conducted into the hotel by Professor Green and the committee of students who had met him in Raleigh. From there he went to Gerrard Hall, where a large assemblage awaited him. Swain then addressed him, in Polk's words "tendering to me a cordial welcome on my return to the classic shades of the University." There are conflicting accounts of Swain's remarks. James Johnston Pettigrew, who had attained first distinction in the 1847 graduating class, wrote a friend that "Swain was considerably frightened, and made a rambling speech about the comparative merits of Tennessee and North Carolina." By contrast, a Raleigh newspaper viewed the address as "distinguished throughout by eminent courtesy of sentiment and chasteness of diction." Battle's history reflects the latter version.[18]

Later in his stay Polk dined with Swain. A nostalgic pilgrimage took him to the room he had occupied as a student in the southwest corner of the third floor of South Building. He remained through the conclusion of the commencement exercises and received high marks for "his total absence of ostentation, his sincere and unassuming courtesy."

On his return trip to Washington the president reportedly arrived in Raleigh "in excellent spirits." He thus must have considered the outing a success. He wrote in his diary that it was "an exceedingly agreeable one," adding: "My reception at the University and the attentions paid me on the route going and returning, was all that I could have desired it to be. My visit was wholly unconnected with politics, and all parties greeted and welcomed me in the most cordial manner."[19]

Shortly before Polk's term as president ended, Swain wrote to Mrs. Polk, recollecting "the brief but very pleasant intercourse which Mrs. Swain and myself enjoyed with you and the President 18 months ago." Both he and Mrs. Swain would be pleased, he said, "to hear either from you or the President." Unfortunately, the window for that opportunity would soon close. Five months later the university faculty appointed a committee "to consider and report what notice should be taken of the death of the late President of the United States, James K. Polk, who was an alumnus of this Institution." At a meeting of the Alumni Association during the following commencement, upon Swain's motion a committee was appointed to prepare a suitable memorial of President Polk to be filed in the archives.[20]

There were rumors that President James Buchanan would attend the 1858 commencement. "Have you heard that the President of the U. States has threatened to come to our next commencement?" Lucy Battle asked her husband. "Now that," she continued," is a big piece of news." The president did not come, however. The Dialectic Society had invited him, but he found it impossible to comply. "[S]hould Providence preserve my life and my health," he promised, however, "[i]t is my purpose . . . to be present at your next commencement."[21]

True to his word, in 1859 the president came. In early May Governor John W. Ellis, having been advised that Buchanan intended the visit, extended the formal invitation. Shortly before, the trustees had appointed a committee to extend an invitation and to make suitable accommodations for the president and his party. Taking advantage of the circumstances, the commencement ball managers petitioned the trustees for $150.00 in addition to the appropriation already made for that purpose. The presence of the president and members of his cabinet would increase their expenses, they claimed, and "it is necessary that our preparation should be better than heretofore." Noting "the peculiar circumstances," the trustees allowed the request.[22]

President Buchanan now "cordially and gratefully" accepted Governor Ellis's invitation. He had long desired to visit "the old North State," he told Ellis, "and become better acquainted with a people for whom I have ever entertained the highest respect and esteem." That the occasion was literary, not political, he said, made it "just such [a] one as I should myself have selected."[23]

Ellis soon informed Swain that the president would reach Chapel Hill at 1:00 p.m. on the Wednesday of commencement week. The governor would proceed at once with the president to Swain's house. The military was anxious to participate. He would order them to attend if desired; otherwise, they would be discharged at Raleigh. The influx of visitors would be so great, Swain responded, that the military companies meeting the president at Raleigh could not be invited. Nor was changing the order of the university exercises to accommodate the president's schedule, as Ellis had suggested, achievable. There was no time for a reception. The president should, upon arrival, proceed directly to the Chapel.

Charles Manly talked to Governor Ellis and advised Swain that there would be no military display. Ellis, aided by consultants, soon fixed upon the president's schedule. They had unanimously concluded that the party could not arrive in Chapel Hill early. Buchanan would get too little sleep if they departed early in the morning. He had "made a special request ... that he should be subjected to as little fatigue as possible," Ellis advised Swain, which, he said, "is most natural considering his age." The president would stop to greet people at every station along the way and would be almost constantly engaged while at the Hill.[24]

President Buchanan now communicated directly with President Swain. Though grateful for the kind invitation from Swain and his spouse to lodge at their home, he was "under the direction of the Committee, and their will must be my law." He would be gratified, however, "if they would enable me to become your guest."[25]

The primitive nature of mid-nineteenth-century travel rendered Buchanan's southward journey long and difficult: horse and carriage to Baltimore, boat to Norfolk, train to Raleigh, and stagecoach to Chapel Hill. He was nevertheless said to have been "perfectly delighted with his trip." He greeted citizens along the way. A military display, said to have been the first ever witnessed in North

Carolina, greeted the president in Raleigh, where he held a levee in a parlor at the Yarborough House.

The following morning, with a discharge of artillery, the presidential party departed for Durham's Station, from which carriages transported them to Chapel Hill. At the boundary of the village on the Durham Road they were greeted by a large gathering of faculty, students, trustees, citizens, and visitors. An escort to the home of President Swain followed.[26] Upon their arrival Swain noted the presidential visit twelve years earlier, when James K. Polk "returned to the scenes and companions of his boyhood." Buchanan's sojourn was "the more complimentary because the associations were less intimate than his." Buchanan's visit "as Chief Magistrate," said Swain, "is a compliment of which we may well feel proud." The university's welcome was not merely in his official character, however, "but as Mr. Buchanan, and a citizen of Pennsylvania."

A prototypical Swain historical exegesis followed, in which, as one commentator expressed it, "[t]he Governor let fly at him the battle of Alamance." Swain concluded by extending to the president "for myself and citizens, a unanimous and heart-felt welcome." In response Buchanan thanked Swain and the attending citizenry for their kindness. "I have always had a partiality for this good Old North State," he said, commending its "eminently prudent, wise, and conservative sons" who had "always stood by the Constitution and laws." Its young men should "devote themselves to the preservation of the principles of the Constitution, for without these blessings our liberties are gone."

Cognizant of the precarious state of the Union over which he presided, Buchanan left the young men with this admonition: "Let this Constitution be torn into atoms, let the Union separate, let thirty Republics rise up against each other, and it would be the most fatal day for the liberties of the human race that ever dawned upon any land." The human race, as well as the people of the United States, coveted the preservation of the Union, Buchanan concluded, and he hoped to "be gathered to my fathers before I should witness its dissolution." The "kind and cordial reception" of the university community no doubt would prove "one of the most interesting periods of my life."[27]

The crowd then requested a speech by Secretary Jacob Thompson, who, "in reminiscent mood," spoke of his appreciation for the late President Caldwell. Swain, Buchanan, and Thompson then proceeded to Swain's residence, where the latter two were guests ("the Committee" apparently permitted Buchanan to lodge there). At 2:30 p.m. Swain's front yard was the scene of a large dinner for the distinguished guests, faculty, trustees, and other prominent visitors.

At the commencement ceremony the following day, the audience rose and cheered when Presidents Buchanan and Swain entered the hall. Buchanan received an honorary doctor of laws degree as had President James K. Polk earlier. Five governors of North Carolina were in attendance: the incumbent, John W. Ellis, and former governors Thomas Bragg, William A. Graham, John M. Morehead, and David L. Swain. Following the ceremony Buchanan and Thompson held a reception under the Davie Poplar.[28]

By all appearances Buchanan enjoyed the occasion immensely. Certainly, Swain did. One account stated: "Gov. Swain was perfectly happy. His face, not a very expressive one, was the picture of stolid delight. He reminded me of a man surfeited at a feast. Were he translated to Heaven now, he would be unhappy–he would find it *flat*, I am sure."[29]

At the 1866 commencement, the university awarded the honorary degree doctor of laws to President Andrew Johnson. Johnson thanked Swain for the faculty's "complimentary action," the motives that prompted it, and the "friendly expression" that accompanied it. Like President Polk before him, he then attended the university's commencement the following year.[30]

This time Swain's invitation to the president had a dual purpose. The monument to the president's father was to be dedicated in Raleigh, and the university's commencement was to occur later in the same week. The trustees and faculty of the university, in "hearty concurrence," desired Johnson's presence on both occasions.[31] As he anxiously awaited Johnson's response, Swain noted that if it was positive there would "no doubt be an overflowing attendance." If the president accepted the invitation to the monument dedication, he expected to meet him in Raleigh on Monday preceding the university's commencement on Thursday. The governor had promised to give him the earliest notice practicable of the president's intentions.[32]

Governor Jonathan Worth soon informed Judge Battle that the president had accepted the invitation to both events. Swain then received confirmation from President Johnson. "I have today accepted the invitation to be present at Raleigh on the 4th," he informed the elated UNC president, "and also the request of the University of North Carolina to attend the commencement at Chapel Hill on the 6th June." A personal note added that he hoped to have the pleasure of seeing Swain.[33]

Swain received regrets from two of the state's most prominent citizens. Former Chief Justice Thomas Ruffin was "infinitely obliged" for Swain's offer to be the guest of his family "with the President and the Governor." He was, however, "so prostrated and feeble that I cannot attempt it." He wanted to attend, both as a matter of *State Pride*[,] of which we have too little," and as a display of respect for the president's official position and personal merits. Ruffin wished the president success "in pacifying the country and upholding the conservative provisions of our National Constitution, which he and I agree is still our Constitution and ought to be observed." "But alas!," he concluded, "[e]ighty years have done their office on me—body and also mind—and I can do but little good at best, and for the present, at least, none at all."

Swain had also extended a special invitation to former Governor William A. Graham. Because of the recent death of the Swains' daughter Anna, about which Mrs. Swain "seem[ed] . . . inconsolable," she desired to see only intimate friends. There were places for Graham and his family, however, and she would be very glad to have them. Circuit court duties made it unlikely that Governor Graham could be present. If he could, he would comply with Governor Worth's request that he accompany the president from Raleigh to Chapel Hill; however, "if Ch. J. Chase or Judge Brooks shall proceed with the business of the court[,] few members of the bar can be absent."[34]

The visit generated poignant memories for the president. In response to Swain's welcoming remarks, he told of walking along the street in front of Swain's house as a young man en route from his native Raleigh to his adult residence in Tennessee. Footsore and hungry, he had no idea where he would acquire supper or a bed for the night. He was informed that a "kindly and hospitable" man named James Craig lived nearby. Craig gave him food and lodging, as well as provisions for his further travels. His next visit to Chapel Hill was as president of a republic of forty million people.

Two cabinet officials, Secretary of State William H. Seward and Postmaster General Alexander W. Randall, accompanied President Johnson. General Daniel E. Sickles, military governor of the state under Reconstruction, was also present. They occupied the platform, together with President Swain, Governor Worth, Judge Battle, the Reverend Doctor F. M. Hubbard (chaplain of the day), and the senior orators.

The societies met to initiate honorary members. President Johnson joined the Dialectic Society and gave an informal talk. A small minority, to convey their hostility to the Reconstruction Acts, denied membership to General Sickles. Secretary Seward, Postmaster General Randall, and Colonel J. W. Bomford, a subordinate officer of General Sickles, joined the Philanthropic Society. One sour note crept in. Seward was critical of the dwellings in Chapel Hill. Kemp Battle's history, in turn, is critical of Seward's critique. Seward, Battle said, should have remembered that these were ancient buildings "and such are seldom improved, particularly under so economical a President as Governor Swain." Battle also noted that six years had passed since the beginning of the Civil War, "and not only the buildings had deteriorated but the loss of the University endowment prevented their repair."[35]

James Craig's cool drink for a tired, thirsty young man was not the last one for Johnson in his native state's academic village. One account notes that he "wanted a more bracing drink now," and since his host, President Swain, was a teetotaler, an equally thirsty student came to the rescue. He had a bottle of rye in his room in South Building, the student told Johnson, and the student could find sugar and ice.[36]

Diplomas in Latin were awarded at these and other university commencements. The signatories were Swain, the faculty, and trustees.[37] From time to time master of arts degrees were awarded to persons with at least two years in one of the learned professions. Swain administered the issuance of these. To Swain, notifying the recipients of this degree was a "pleasant duty." Absorbing the complaints of disgruntled nonrecipients was not so pleasant, however. James H. Viser, an 1840 graduate, once conveyed his perplexity over Swain's silence about his request for the degree. By the rules and usages of the university, as Viser understood them, a graduate "who has pursued any one of the liberal professions for two years is entitled to the degree as a matter of course."[38]

Swain also had a key role in awarding honorary degrees. While the faculty and trustees approved them, the recommendations, at least usually, came from Swain. Typical faculty minute entries have Swain notifying the faculty of his intention to nominate certain honorary degree recipients.[39]

The 1845 commencement brought honorary doctor of laws degrees to President James K. Polk, U.S. Attorney General John Y. Mason, and U.S. Senator Willie P. Mangum. To Polk, the honor was "most unexpected, and . . . highly appreciated." Swain had informed the president that unless specifically desired by the recipient, no diploma is issued for this degree. Polk desired one, however, if not "inconvenient."[40]

Between the Polk and Buchanan visits, Swain recommended for honorary degrees, among others, A. O. P. Nicholson, an 1827 UNC graduate who served as chief justice of the Tennessee Supreme Court and a U.S. Senator from that state; John Randolph Clay, a career diplomat then serving as U.S. minister to Peru; and Aaron V. Brown, an 1814 graduate who served in Congress, as governor of Tennessee, and as a postmaster general. Swain clearly used these degrees to promote the university and to build or enhance friendships both for it and for himself. In thanking Swain for his degree, Brown at least implicitly acknowledged this, stating, "You were right in supposing you could command me in any matter touching yourself or the interests of the university over which you preside."⁴¹

The Buchanan commencement in 1859 witnessed, in addition to Buchanan's, the awarding of honorary degrees to Judge Mitchell D. King of Charleston, South Carolina, and J. H. Otey, an 1820 UNC graduate and the first Protestant Episcopal bishop of Tennessee. In thanking Swain for the "unexpected [and] distinguished" honor, King noted his enhanced gratitude because the university's official communication included "a friendly letter from yourself."⁴²

Commencements were not the only occasions for distinguished guests. Edward Everett, Massachusetts statesman and orator, soon to attain enhanced fame as the second most significant speaker at the Gettysburg Battlefield dedication, once brought to the campus his oration on the life and character of George Washington. He came upon the invitation by the faculty, initiated by the students. His sojourn, Everett said, was "extremely agreeable [with] nothing to regret but its shortness."⁴³

A visit by General Joseph Lane of Oregon must have pleased Swain immensely. The two were first cousins, born in the same house in Buncombe County. When he journeyed to Chapel Hill, Lane was in the U.S. Senate. The *University Magazine* noted that he "was the guest while here of his cousin our worthy President, which we suppose was his principal purpose in honoring us with his presence." Both Lane and Everett were soon to be vice presidential candidates, Lane on the 1860 John C. Breckinridge ticket, Everett on the John Bell ticket.⁴⁴

CHAPTER 15

Public Policy
"In close touch with public life"

EARLY NINETEENTH-CENTURY NORTH CAROLINA evolved from a state without strong political parties to one in which two major parties, the Whigs and the Democrats, dominated its political life. Swain, as noted, also evolved during this time from a nonpartisan into an active Whig.

His transition from the governor's office to the university presidency changed things. Cornelia Phillips Spencer states that he now "[kept] himself aloof from state politics." Swain felt the relative isolation keenly. He once told a relative, in late March, "I have not been more than half a mile from my door since Christmas, see very little company here except the Faculty and the young men and probably possess little more information with relation to events, especially political[,] . . . in this State, than you do." Earlier the relative had said to him, "A man who knew you less intimately than I do would envy your happy state of indifference on political matters."

The implication is clear. The relative knew better, and he was right. Swain was anything but indifferent to political matters, and he was scarcely a political eunuch. On the sidelines to a relative degree, yes; oblivious to, dispassionate about, and detached from such matters, not at all.

J. G. DeRoulhac Hamilton notes that Swain "was kept in close touch with public life by those who sought his advice." Kemp Battle's history states similarly: "His curiosity for the news was insatiable. Every person arriving on 'the Hill' was called on at once by the President and catechized as to what had happened of interest or importance within his knowledge." Abundant evidence in the historical record supports these conclusions. Indeed, the expectations were sufficiently clear that T. L. Clingman, prominent Western North Carolina politician, once concluded a letter to Swain by apologizing for "not attempting to give you [a] birds eye view of things here [Washington]."[1]

Swain's new status did not end old political rivalries. One in particular reached white-heat stage in Swain's first year at UNC. When Swain was elected governor, Richard Dobbs Spaight Jr. was among the defeated aspirants. When Swain, by then a Whig, left the office, Spaight, a Democrat, succeeded him. Whatever the degree of rivalry and disdain between them, however, neither could have foreseen the sizzling exchange soon to occur between them.

In late August 1836, Swain sent Spaight a letter, on its face thoroughly innocuous, indeed, informative and helpful. Swain reminded Spaight of a gubernatorial duty to appoint commissioners for a railroad. It was important, Swain stated, "that these appointments should be made forthwith." The North Carolina delegates to the railroad's convention had authorized Swain to prepare an address. Swain enclosed the journal of the convention, which listed the delegates, all "respectable gentlemen" interested in the enterprise and thus suited for appointment as commissioners.

Spaight's response was terse and acerbic. "I do not receive any letter unless respectfully addressed to me," Spaight wrote, "especially one addressed as yours is—I have only at present to call for an explanation." If the entire address had been in the same handwriting, Spaight continued, his course would have been a very plain one.

Apart from the returned envelope and Spaight's reference to the disparate handwriting, Swain would have been clueless about the rationale for this venomous outburst. On the envelope, between Spaight's name and his city of residence, this interlineation appeared: "Puppet of van buren." The interlineation was clearly in a different handwriting from that in Swain's letter and on the rest of the envelope.

Spaight's letter acknowledged this. For some reason, however, this obvious fact failed to assuage his anger. Upon reading Spaight's response, it was Swain's turn to be angry. In formal and less-than-amiable fashion, a note on the inside page of Spaight's letter states that Swain "declines receiving the communication." He was willing to withdraw the original, substitute a copy, and "disavow the offensive epithets on the face of the letter." There is no evidence that this note went to Spaight. Swain's response that was sent, however, with Charles Manly as courier, was no less formal, touchy, and carping. "It is impossible for any individual of ordinary intelligence," Swain wrote, to see his letter "without perceiving... that the offensive epithet... is an interpolation," in another hand, and "inserted after the direction of my letter was complete." If the envelope was not sufficiently clear to convince "even... your Excellency" that the interlineation was in a different hand, he said, the letter itself should have evoked a perception of "the utter improbability" that "while attempting to accomplish an object of great public importance," he would simultaneously "by a paltry act of this nature, defeat the object he was endeavoring to attain."

Spaight's attempted rejoinder apparently was sufficiently acerbic that Manly returned it to him, refusing to deliver it to Swain. Manly reported to Swain, "it was xceedingly [*sic*] offensive and if read must have changed the position of the parties." He had taken it from William Dallas Haywood, Spaight's courier, with a reservation that he "could only receive it provided it was of such a particular tenor and such as I conceived I *could properly* receive and transmit to Gov. Swain." To Manly's obvious disappointment, the letter, in his view, did not meet these criteria.

Clearly Manly was concerned for this new president of the university he had served long and well. Swain's future movements in the matter, Manly admonished, should "be taken with the greatest caution." Discreet counselors were important. An immediate and frank discussion with Judge Cameron, in particular, was highly recommended. "I am sure you appreciate with me," Manly said, "his ability and fidelity."

The next Spaight letter to reach Swain continued the nasty tone. Spaight presumed Manly had informed Swain that his communication was not satisfactory. He had completed another note, but William Dallas Haywood had declined to carry it to Swain. He thus would "have to postpone making a communication until an opportunity is afforded through a friend."

At this point there is a hiatus of several weeks in the preserved correspondence. Weldon Edwards then wrote Swain "[a]s the friend of Gov. Spaight" to return Swain's original letter to him and to request his attention to "the offensive epistles." He noted that he would wait on Swain at 4:00 p.m. that day (Christmas Eve, 1836) "and make exchanges of copies of the correspondence referred to in their interview this morning."

In response Swain detailed anew his defense. "A very slight examination of the address will satisfy you," he told Edwards, "that the offensive epithet . . . has no resemblance to my hand writing—and I trust you know me too well to suppose me capable of either committing or countenancing so palpable a violation of common decency and common sense." He then set forth the letter's chain of custody while en route to Spaight and speculated that "[t]he offensive interpolation . . . is probably the act of some individual in Raleigh who had casually observed the letter at the bar of the hotel—and been weak and wicked enough to do the deed."

The discovered correspondence ceases with this letter. Swain and Spaight lived many years yet. Obviously, some resolution was reached. For weeks, though, there was every indication that North Carolina's sitting governor and his immediate predecessor were marching steadily toward a duel, over something Swain almost certainly did not do and that was, in any event, hardly worth the risk of death.[2]

The public arena brought Swain other unpleasantness. Soon after the Spaight imbroglio, he was surprised when a member of the General Assembly spoke of him to other members in less than "a spirit of kindness." Another unamicable accusation had Swain on several occasions refusing to speak to, or notice, the accuser. He would pass Swain in the streets of Raleigh and bow to him, the man claimed, only to be ignored. The two men came to "a better understanding" but only after exchanges that detailed a rancorous interpersonal history.[3]

Another incident, perceived as political, which Swain vigorously denied, anguished him perhaps unduly. It was common for him to spend summer vacations in Asheville. The town was his native habitat; he had practiced law there before public duties prompted him to move eastward; he had family and friends there; perhaps most important, he retained property and business interests there and westward. Counting the summer of 1844, he had spent seven of his nine university summer vacations there.

Swain declined an invitation to speak there on July 4, 1844. He informed the local committee "that no address need be expected from me." In mid-June he had departed Asheville for Macon County, where he had business interests, and did not return until the eve of the Fourth. He then found that with numerous citizens expected for the celebration, local and beyond, "of the various gentlemen invited from abroad" only he was present. Given these circumstances, he consented to importuning that he speak.

William W. Holden's *North Carolina Standard* attacked Swain harshly for this "stump speech." "Can it be possible?" it asked captiously. Had Swain "so entirely forgotten his . . . high position and . . . duties . . . as to have come down into the arms of partizan warfare?" If so, he deserved censure. If the state had a Whig university, parents needed to know, so they could choose to send their sons elsewhere. The paper was no enemy of the university, it proclaimed, but such a charge would not deter it from speaking out freely "in relation to the conduct of President Swain."

Another paper, the *Signal*, had called Swain's action an unprecedented "outrage upon propriety." The *Standard* agreed. Prior complaints of political bias at the university had been denied, said the *Signal*, but it was now certain "that the sons of Democrats must receive instruction from one who descends from the stump of whiggery to teach them, or else they must be driven from their own state to find instruction elsewhere." This was not a trifling offense but an intolerable outrage, worse even than "the desecration of the Fourth of July to purposes of a party celebration, under party banners." The Whig Party was in a lamentable condition, said the *Standard*, when it had to "call[] down Gov. Swain from his seat in the University and tell[] him to talk to Buncombe."

The *Standard* published Swain's response. Since becoming president of the university, he said, he had received numerous invitations to attend political meetings, including this one "from the citizens of my native county." Of these, he had replied to none. Under the circumstances it was natural that he should be pressed to speak, and "it might not have been considered kind or courteous, or even just in me to reject."

His address had begun by stating that "the discussion of party politics was inappropriate to the day"; even if it were otherwise, in his "present position" it was inappropriate. Since his last political speech nine years earlier, before assuming the university presidency, he had attended no political meeting and had heard no political address. On this occasion he had not planned "to allude to any controverted topic." His "extempore" comments had dealt with the structure of government and the importance of enlightened public opinion. "I was gratified at the close," Swain said, "by repeated assurances that [the remarks] were favorably received by all parties."

Over half of the living graduates of the university, Swain claimed in closing, "received their diplomas at my hands." If any from that time knew or believed they had been indoctrinated politically by university officers, he invited them to "avow it openly and tender the evidence on which the allegation rests."

The *Raleigh Register and North-Carolina Gazette* published Swain's letter and rose to his defense. The assaults on him were "most gratuitous," it proclaimed. Nothing proved the talk "a political one." On the contrary, published accounts raised a strong inference that Swain "did not allude at all to party topics." Had the speech been political, however, the *Register* continued, it would have been no ground for censure: "[A] man's being at the head of a Literary Institution certainly does not stop him from the expression of his political opinions among his old friends and neighbors." Knowing Swain's "proverbial caution and discretion," however, the paper was confident that an improper word had not escaped his lips "unless ... it be considered rank heresy to advocate the diffusion of learning in any shape." "These attempts to excite vulgar prejudices against Literary Institutions," it concluded, "are among the worst signs of the times."

The *Standard*, by contrast, while it published Swain's letter, found it "not satisfactory to us." The Whigs had met at Asheville for two consecutive days under the portraits of Henry Clay and "other large characters." Swain had been on his feet more than once in those two days of "Whiggery." The paper was a friend of the university, it asserted, but jealous of the institution's reputation and that of its officers. The public, the paper concluded, would no doubt render an impartial and just decision.[4] Like others during Swain's tenure, this controversy passed, and the university moved on. For a time, though, it was a source of considerable discomfort for the institution's highly sensitive president.

Fortunately, negative episodes were aberrations, not the norm. Apart from these rare instances, Swain was busily engaged in positive, constructive activity. Indeed, it was appropriate that almost everyone continued to call him "Governor Swain" rather than "President Swain," for in a real sense he was governor for life. The university presidency became a felicitous base from which he continued to promote the Archibald Murphy program of progress for the state, the predominant task of his gubernatorial labors.

Swain received occasional recognition of the continuing impact of those endeavors. An 1830 UNC graduate once thought Swain's "warmth in favor of Rail Road has abated of late years" (he was mistaken). "The western part of the state, however," he said, "is about to realize the fruit from the seed sown by you and your collaborators twelve or fifteen years since."[5]

The former governor remained a leading source of information about the state's progress with internal improvements generally. A nephew once anxiously awaited Swain's answer on the fate of internal improvements bills, "and particularly that which provides for the making of a turn pike road to the Georgia line." He had contemplated moving from Western North Carolina, but if the mountain counties were going to be improved, he would prefer to stay there with his friends.[6]

In his time as UNC president, railroads were the focus of Swain's internal improvements efforts. Early in his tenure, for example, he addressed a Fayetteville July 4 celebration on the Fayetteville and Yadkin Railroad. The talk apparently had an effect. Governor Edward B. Dudley soon told Swain that "[t]he good citizens of Fayetteville have again been roused to the importance of the Rail Road to the Yadkin and a better disposition has been indicated to take hold of the work." Dudley had summoned the Board of Internal Improvements to meet in Fayetteville "to afford an opportunity to render all the assistance in our power." Swain's presence "would be very acceptable" because it would enable the board "better ... to dispose of the matter satisfactorily."[7]

Such letters were common; his presence at railroad meetings was avidly sought. Governor Morehead once told him, as a Greensboro railroad convention approached, "[y]ou will be indispensable at our convention." The waters were troubled, Morehead said, and Swain's presence was needed in time "to do the *strong work*."[8]

Governor John Motley Morehead, who urged Swain's attendance at railroad conventions.

Swain was a delegate from Orange to an 1849 "Rail Road Convention" in Salisbury. Two years later he informed Calvin H. Wiley, soon to be the state's first superintendent of common schools, that he would probably attend the upcoming North Carolina Railroad Company stockholders meeting in Greensboro. The following year he reported himself in Raleigh to attend the same meeting.[9]

Correspondents kept Swain informed on, and solicited his assistance regarding, railroad matters. "The great railroad is now before our Legislature," a South Carolinian once wrote. John C. Calhoun had proposed a route that, in the writer's view, would prove impractical. He urged Swain to have the North Carolina legislature await South Carolina's action, and he hoped North Carolina would not attempt to control the western part of the route. "Your concurrence in that bill," the writer closed, "we feel to be of the utmost importance."[10]

Christopher Memminger, another South Carolinian, later secretary of the treasury for the Confederacy, also corresponded with Swain on "the prospects for our Rail Road." In due course, Memminger said, it would stretch up to Swain's mountains and push into Buncombe. Would some agitation on the subject be good, he inquired? Memminger later reported that his railroad meeting "went off as well as could be expected." He included details regarding the planned road and its financing. Memminger had just completed construction of a summer residence at Flat Rock, near Asheville, and Swain was always welcome to visit him there.[11]

The arrival of the railroad in Raleigh brought enthusiastic accounts to Swain. Cars with passengers now ran "to the Institute [Wake Forest]," said one, but they would reach Raleigh within two weeks. People generally were "in high spirits of the coming of the Rail Road to town." If Swain wanted to see "a crazy population," said another, "just come to this city": "We are all in a bustle. Men women and children white folks n----- and all." A "great celebration on the Completion of the Rail road" was in preparation.[12]

Swain heard from people with dreamy plans for railroads. One feared Swain would pronounce him "visionary" when he heard "the Magnitude of the scheme." He gave him information on what he "so much wanted" in the western portion of Swain's state. The states might have to look to "the General Government" for aid, he said, "as it would be one of that class of Improvements coming within the views of some of the most *strict constructionists*." A railroad extending across North Carolina and Tennessee was his vision, he told Swain, and he hoped "that a gentleman of your distinguished standing and fine opportunities will give these matters some consideration and influence."[13]

Difficulties with the railroads also came to Swain's attention. A correspondent who had thought it "a favorable time to make some moves about the western rail road" indicated a change of position due to a change of economic circumstances. "[A]ny attempt now at a subscription," he said, "will be premature" because "considerate men will not under the existing state of the country incur new responsibilities." A "most melancholy account" of everything relating to the railroad would require "the utmost exertions of all [its] friends . . . to prevent the project falling through." No one, said the writer, had it more in his power to save it than Swain. The death of its president, it was feared, was "an irreparable loss" to one railroad company. A temporary president would be elected, but some of the directors thought Swain "might be prevailed on to accept the appointment."[14]

Swain was not just a passive recipient of such information. He was expected to provide it himself. Governor Dudley once expressed pleasure that Swain "had entirely placed matters and things in their true position to his satisfaction and . . . [that of] our friends and the friends of internal improvements." If in Swain's "perigrinations to the West" he learned "anything cheering for the Fayetteville Road," Dudley wanted to know it. With proper exertions, he believed, the road "may be made." If it could be completed to the Tennessee border, and thence by that state to Nashville, it would contribute to a splendid route from New Orleans to

Boston. Failure, by contrast, would thrust the state "into another Rip Van Winkle nap." To Dudley the enterprise was a legacy item, "the most important event of my life." He thus keenly desired Swain's presence at a shareholders meeting in Flat Rock or at a later meeting of the road's agents.[15] As indicated by Dudley's interest in extending the railroad across Tennessee, Swain's efforts had interstate interests and dimensions.

At times Swain was the communicator, rather than the recipient, of railroad items. He once, for example, informed Governor Graham regarding organization of the road through Davidson County. Several men, Swain thought, could "without inconvenience" subscribe to the stock in varying dollar sums. Another was thinking about a subscription in which Swain would join.[16]

Swain once published in leading newspapers an account of a trip from Goldsboro to Charlotte by stagecoach, detailing the time and expense involved. He then related similar data from his trip by rail in South Carolina and Georgia. The stage ride suffered in the comparison in efficiency and expense. Swain concluded: "You travel along the route of the proposed Rail Road at a fifth of the speed, and at four times the expense, in approaching the capital of your own State, that is required to take a Georgian or South Carolinian to his capital or to any of the great markets of those states." With unmistakable clarity, he was trumpeting the case for the railroad.[17]

Governor Morehead had made Swain the chair of a North Carolina delegation to the Memphis Convention held in July 1849 to promote a transcontinental railroad. It was Morehead's request that Swain travel over the Georgia railroads, thus leading to these persuasive advocacy pieces.[18] These, however, were but a small piece of Swain's efforts for this cause. He also wanted to "extend any encouragement" he could to "the Central Rail Road," Swain told Charles Manly in the spring of 1849; he therefore was considering attendance at the Internal Improvements Convention in Salisbury in June. He indeed attended and gave one of several "able ... and effective speeches" that "above all ... were instructive." Swain's "abounded in valuable statistical information." It was hoped that he would publish it.[19]

The issue had become "a life and death case with our country," opined a Salisbury newspaper, quoting Swain to the same effect. Swain's was an impassioned appeal, "full of stirring eloquence and withering satire." The building of the road "was no longer a question of mere dollars and cents," Swain had said, "it was a question of *life* and *death*." Surrounding states, more advanced in internal improvements, were fully developing their infrastructure. If North Carolina failed to do so, it "would be driven out of the great marts of the world."[20]

As his remarks drew attention to the subject, Swain received other speaking invitations. Cadwallader Jones, convinced that Swain's aid would "be of the greatest consequence to the success of our efforts," invited him for addresses in Hillsboro and Chapel Hill. Governors Graham and Morehead received similar invitations. Their addresses, it was said, "collected facts and statistical information connected with this subject" and "submitted them to the consideration of the people" in a "faithful and lucid manner." Few who heard them, it was thought, could fail to be convinced of the necessity of the railroad.[21]

Charles L. Hinton, state treasurer, requested a Swain visit to Raleigh to "attend a meeting on the subject of the railroad." All there were anxious to hear him on the topic. "I think you may do much good by an address," Hinton said. When he later perceived "luke warm indifference with regard to the road," Hinton desired a letter from Swain "intended to arouse them." The "whole matter," Hinton said, "rests with Morehead, Graham, and yourself." He got his wish, for he soon wrote Swain again to report: "Among our people there has been a much better feeling on the subject of the Rail Road during the week. Your last letter has done good."

Hinton joined Morehead's supplication ("come COME!!") that Swain attend the railroad convention in Greensboro. "The very efficient aid you could render is of vast importance at this particular time," he said. While he doubted the profitability of the enterprise to investors, the importance of the work to the public had not been overrated. Indeed, Hinton said, "the character and prosperity of the state depends [sic] upon it."[22]

Years later, Swain pled the case for internal improvements in his native Asheville. It was a nostalgic visit. Twenty-two years had elapsed since he had resided there, and nine since his last visit. Passage of the years had taken a toll: "his locks had been touched by the frosts of time; he knew that he was growing old from his years if not from his feelings." Had he remained there and continued the practice of his profession, he would now be the patriarch of the Buncombe bar. Instead, those once his pupils were now the bar leaders, and he was entitled to the appellation of "old Fogy."

Sentimentality warmed Swain to the task: resumption of his evangelical efforts on behalf of internal improvements. The Central Rail Road would be extended from East to West, he predicted, and it would be done by North Carolina capital and men. He opposed importing labor for the purpose. North Carolina "had the bone, the muscle, and the sinew in our own borders"; if the state could not construct its roads with what nature had bestowed, he did not favor building them. The address, said a local newspaper, "abounded in noble and generous sentiments, and reflected the true spirit of a devoted North Carolinian. . . . At the conclusion, the thanks of the meeting were tendered to the speaker for his 'very eloquent, interesting and instructive address.'"[23]

As noted, in Swain's view internal improvements were not merely an end in themselves; they were also the means to economic resources sufficient to achieve and sustain universal public education. As a youthful member of the General Assembly, he had said: "Improve the condition of the country—advance the general prosperity—increase individual wealth—and you furnish the means of education, and lessen the temptation to crime." The "best school fund," he had said, was individual wealth, "and the most certain security against vice, universal education."[24]

When Swain left the governor's office, the state had no public (then known as "common") schools. As citizen, legislator, and governor, he had been their advocate. The governor served ex officio as president of the Literary Fund, and in that capacity, Swain had worked to build resources toward the day when the state could afford common schools. In his years as UNC president, that vision never left him, and he had the opportunity to implement it.

Swain thus was a natural choice when the Literary Board, directed by the General Assembly, concluded that the time for secondary public education had arrived. In 1838, the board resolved that Swain be requested to suggest a plan "best suited to the wants and resources of the state." Governor Dudley, as board chair, transmitted the resolution to Swain. "The Board," Dudley told him, "have great hopes that you will take this subject under consideration and afford them the benefit which many circumstances have so fully placed in your power to do, and in which they are in great need."[25]

Swain asked Charles Manly to inform the board that he had received the communication "requesting my attention to the subject of common schools." The governor should transmit to Swain certain laws, reports, and other documents. Once done, Swain told Manly, "I will communicate my views to the Board with pleasure." In less than three months Governor Dudley acknowledged receipt of Swain's report. "The Board," the governor "pretty confidently" predicted, "will adopt it with great pleasure." Governor Dudley advised Charles Manly, Swain's courier to the board, that he had read Swain's report and was grateful to him.[26]

The nineteenth-century common school program has been attributed "largely [to] the work of President Swain of the university." He was, however, following in the footsteps of his predecessor, Joseph Caldwell, in acknowledging both the obligation and the value of relating the university closely to education generally and to other public interests of the state.[27] Swain would continue this practice throughout his tenure as university president. In an 1859 speech to the Educational Association of North Carolina, regrettably not preserved, the minutes show that he addressed the preferred method of imparting instruction, showing by various illustrations the applicability of his method to the teaching of common-school branches. He discussed the use of physical punishment in schools and the advantages and disadvantages of "mixed schools" (referring to gender, not race).[28]

Swain's efforts were not universally applauded. A university orator once requested his permission to speak on the want of state pride and to connect his subject with "a neglected *University* (so called) and the present impracticable scheme for common schools." The orator felt sure "that perseverance in this miserable common school *law* will terminate in the bankruptcy of the [Literary] Fund." The state should "begin at the top," he said, by fostering colleges, and should "convert our university so called into a university in fact." The only practical policy for the state was "to *establish—promote—*and uphold the *higher seminaries of learning*." A Swain response has not been found, but his unfavorable reaction is not difficult to imagine.[29]

Swain took pride in the quality of the teachers the university prepared for the state's common schools and other educational institutions. He carefully guarded the university's premier role in this endeavor. Braxton Craven, president of the Normal College (later Trinity College, still later Duke University), once sought Swain's support for giving his school that task. The need for teacher training institutions was obvious, Craven said. "Such institutions," he continued, "should be separate from the university and yet of a high collegiate order." Could Normal College be made a state institution, Craven asked, "standing in relation to teaching and general education, that C. Hill oc[c]upies in relation to polite literature and statesmanship?" Or could North Carolina establish a Normal College "for the thorough education and training of teachers?" The money could perhaps come from the Literary Fund, and once started, "the College could easily sustain itself."

Craven had drafted a bill for the purpose but preferred "submitting the whole to you for revisions." Better yet, he preferred letting the bill "go into the Legislature under your auspices." It would then "do better than under any other man's in the state." Such competition with the university for both students and funding probably held little appeal for Swain. A modern biographical sketch of Craven concludes that "[l]ittle actually came of [his] experiment in teacher training."[30]

Calvin H. Wiley, Swain's former student (UNC 1840), would become the state's first superintendent of common schools. His book, *The North-Carolina Reader*, a collection of essays, historical sketches, and statistical information, was designed for use in these schools. Wiley tendered the book to his old professor for review and critique and received a lukewarm response. The book was equal to his anticipations, Swain said, "and yet greatly inferior to what I know you can make it in a second edition." Swain would forebear criticism but would "take pleasure when we meet in commending its merits, and calling attention to its defects, that you may be both encouraged and admonished to amend it."

Swain encouraged Wiley, nevertheless. When in Raleigh, he had heard frequent commendations of *The Reader*, and he had no doubt of the sale of the first edition. Further, consideration would be given to "the propriety of accepting the *Reader* as a text book in all the Common Schools in the State." Further still, Swain contributed financially to a fund to pay the cost of publication. And he provided a statement for public use. Its introduction into the common schools, Swain said for public consumption, would "not merely tend to awaken a more lively and general interest in the history of the State, but excite patriotic emotions in the youthful bosum [sic], which cannot be without effect upon the character of our future rulers."[31]

Wiley's was not the only common-schools text of interest to Swain. In 1857, the Southern Commercial Convention resolved that Swain, with other educational and religious leaders, "be requested . . . to take this matter (of Southern school books) under their auspices and select and prepare such a series of books, in every department of study from the earliest primer to the highest grade of literature and science, as shall seem to them best qualified to elevate and purify the education of the South." The group was to convene in Columbia, South Carolina three weeks later. Swain's leadership in this area thus extended at least to the regional level.[32]

Nor was *The Reader* Wiley's only publication of concern to Swain. When Swain assumed the UNC presidency, *American Annals of Education* was believed to be the only publication in the country devoted to systems of public education in the United States and Europe and measures for their improvement. Swain had been urged to secure it for the State Library. At least one publication was needed, a correspondent urged, to watch over "our schools and School Books."

Swain's action, if any, on this request is unknown. When Wiley proposed a *Common School Journal*, however, Swain was supportive. Such a "well considered" publication was no doubt needed, he told Wiley, and he granted permission to use his name "in commending your scheme as worthy of success." Wiley apparently had inquired regarding university advertising in the publication. Swain could "promise nothing." The trustees alone had the power to advertise. They had never done so, said Swain, but they could "perhaps be induced to change their determination so far as your journal is concerned." While he wished to see publication of the journals of the provincial conventions and congresses, as Wiley proposed, Swain was too busy to help. He did, however, become a subscriber to Wiley's *Journal*.[33]

Swain was both a recipient and a donor of materials and information relating to common schools. The superintendent of schools in Florida once sent him a copy of Florida's legislative act to establish a "common school system and to provide a school fund." He wanted Swain's views on North Carolina's "plan of education, pointing out its defects, and suggesting improvements." He sent Swain the materials and inquiries "knowing that you take an interest in any thing that tends to elevate the condition of man."[34]

A Connecticut writer thanked Swain for sending a document relating to common schools. He yet desired "more complete and satisfactory information reflecting the past and present condition of the educational institutions of N. Carolina." In particular, he wanted Swain's "views as to the defects, excellences or improvements" of North Carolina's educational system. This information would "contribute to the more thorough knowledge, than the public now possesses of the state of education in the United States," and there was no one else in North Carolina to whom the writer could apply.[35]

In the post-Civil War period philanthropist George Peabody established a fund to assist with universal public education, especially in the South. Swain's input on using the funds in North Carolina was solicited. The aid, he was told, was to be "strictly to common or elementary schools." "Where there are no public schools this seems to be the best method," his correspondent said, "It enables us to reach directly the class of children we wish to." Anything in this regard from Swain would be "valuable on account of your rare opportunities of observation, your intimate knowledge of the subject," the writer told Swain shortly before Swain's death.[36]

Finally, the post–Civil War period brought renewed and reenergized vigor to Swain's advocacy for public education. The state's circumstances had changed dramatically. "The slaves are gone," said Swain, "a great deal of property has been destroyed; we can safely say that the State emerged from the war worth just half she was when she went into it." Now, more than ever, he urged, "This state needs education." Why? "Its people are impoverished." If the educated men of North Carolina properly used their talents, there would soon be no illiterate people in the state. "Let each one that is educated be a Missionary here at home," he concluded, "and this State will grow and prosper and become densely populated like the countries in Europe."[37]

Internal improvements, public education, and a confluence of the two for the betterment of the state and its people were Swain's foremost extracurricular interests in the arena of public policy. Many of the state's other concerns attracted his attention and involvement, however. Some were, like internal improvements and public education, carryover items from his time as governor. In his first gubernatorial term Swain had recommended, and the General Assembly had authorized, the appointment of commissioners to revise the state's statutory laws. Swain had appointed three of the state's most able lawyers—William Horn Battle, Gavin Hogg, and James Iredell—for the task. When Hogg became ill, Swain replaced him with Frederick Nash, later chief justice of the state supreme court.[38]

In preparing the work the commissioners relied heavily on Swain's advice, much of it given after he left the governor's office. At one point Battle informed him that his views on the second volume were being implemented; the commissioners had included nearly all, if not all, the articles Swain had thought proper to insert. They then asked Swain to prepare the preface. He was, Battle and Iredell believed, "[t]he only person that can do full justice to it." They were waiting to hear from Swain on the preface before concluding in what form to present the article he had sent on the state's judicial history. The index needed Swain's undivided attention as well. The printing of both volumes would be completed early in the next month, Battle soon informed Swain.[39] The *Revisal* was a lifetime source of pride to Swain, but pride he deflected in favor of the commissioners. Any compliment, he said, should be to the judgment and tact exhibited in the selection of Hogg and Iredell "to give character to the enterprise and Battle to do the work."[40]

Cherokee Indians and their lands presented episodic problems for Swain throughout his administration as governor. Later, at the time of the Cherokee removal (the "Trail of Tears," late 1830s), Governor Dudley advised Swain that, as expected, General Winfield Scott had called on North Carolina "for a full regiment for the Cherokee service[,] and orders had been issued to supply the same." Swain had recommended, and Dudley had approved, "the selection [probably to command] of Lieutenant Colenel Bynum agreeably to his rank." Dudley sought Swain's advice as to the best officers from the counties of Buncombe, Burke, Rutherford, Wilkes, and Yancey.

Macon County was on the removal route, and a Macon correspondent soon informed Swain that the area was "somewhat alive with war like preparations and rumours of war." He had been told, however, that the Indians were not likely to resist or conceal themselves. The government, he said, was incurring considerable expense daily "in the Indian service." By his visit to Asheville that summer (1838), Swain could report that "[t]he Indians have all left the country."[41]

Construction of a new state capitol building was incomplete when Swain left the governor's office. He stayed in touch with both the progress and the problems until completion.⁴² Swain's concern as governor for the total development of the state did not wane when he left the office. Almost half a decade later he noted that Raleigh continued to improve rapidly, and Chapel Hill was by no means what it had been a few years earlier. No region of the state, however, had kept pace with improvements in the trans-Allegany section. Real estate values there, Swain noted, had appreciated by 25 percent during his residency in the East.⁴³

Swain's successors in the Executive Office, particularly those with whom he shared strong friendships, stayed in touch with him. John Motley Morehead once raised with Swain the question of whether the legislature placed excessive confidence in the governor. "Our Legislature," he told his friend, "seems to have unbounded confidence in the financial talent and integrity of their Executive—no matter who he may happen to be." There might be some evils in the system, Morehead suggested, "not before seen."⁴⁴

When Governor Charles Manly contemplated recommending constitutional amendments to the General Assembly, he solicited Swain's counsel. There was public interest in "radical and important changes." They related to extending the suffrage and election by the people of judges, justices of the peace, and heads of the state departments. Manly had few confidants, social or political, he said, and he would "rely on our long and well established friendship for advice." Swain's suggestions on any other topic would be listened to with pleasure.⁴⁵

During the Civil War, North Carolina elected Swain's student, Zebulon B. Vance, to the governor's office. Swain quickly assumed direction of the planning for Vance's inauguration. He acknowledged to Charles Manly, who apparently had formal charge of the event as he had with similar ones, that he was "poaching on your manor." No one knew better than Manly, Swain said, what ought to be done or how to do it, and no one could do it better. Given the difficult times, however, the occasion had significance beyond the norm, and Swain would not be deterred by customary protocol or niceties.

The judges of the supreme court, Swain directed, should be invited. One, Judge Battle, planned to attend; should the chief justice be absent, Battle would administer the oath "to our pupil," who had read law with him. Presence of the surviving former governors was a must. Governor John Branch was Swain's only surviving predecessor. Then, said Swain, came Morehead, Graham, Manly, Reid, Bragg, and Winslow. They represented all parties and sections, "and their presence will be received as a decided indication that the state is a unit." Governor Henry T. Clark, Swain continued, had called his attention to the record of Governor Caswell's inauguration in Revolutionary times and had seemed favorably impressed by it.

The implicit suggestion was that it perhaps should be imitated in some respects. Finally, Swain enclosed a letter to the governor-elect, with a request that Manly read it ("if you can," he inscribed parenthetically, thereby acknowledging the poor quality of his handwriting). If Manly knew Vance's whereabouts, he was to add the address and, presumably, post the letter.[46]

The legislative branch still had Swain's attention as well. He once was advised of preparations for a forthcoming meeting of the General Assembly when "quite a brawling session of it" was anticipated. Later Judge Battle informed Swain that Samuel F. Phillips would give him all the legislative news. Phillips followed with an interesting account of a debate over whether Warren Winslow, who had succeeded David Reid as governor when Reid resigned to take a U.S. Senate seat, could also continue to serve as speaker of the state senate. By a single vote the Senate had allowed Winslow to retain both positions. Phillips had conveyed Swain's position on the issue, in which Judge Battle concurred, to several persons, including Winslow. Phillips did not indicate what Swain's position was, but clearly his opinion still mattered.[47]

When Dorothea Dix urged the General Assembly to erect a state hospital for the insane, Swain accompanied her. She is said to have leaned on his arm as she entered the House of Commons. Swain then collaborated with New York architect A. J. Davis on construction of the facility. Swain continued to send to Dix materials about her project and other matters. She once told him, "I become anxious sometimes for the completion of the Hospital at Raleigh—and much desire to visit North Carolina."[48]

Swain also had concerns about state asylums for the deaf and blind. He expressed surprise when the university trustees residing in Raleigh preferred that city as the locale for "*female* mutes." He knew both places well, Swain said, and the women would be safer in Chapel Hill. Government efforts on behalf of the blind, he thought, should be organized on a regional basis. He doubted the propriety of North Carolina doing anything "unless the cooperation of S.C. and Georgia can be obtained."[49]

Governor Graham soon advised Swain that the Literary Board had employed an agent to endeavor to ascertain the number of blind persons in the state "who are proper subjects for education... and what are the dispositions of their respective counties to raise contributions for their aid." Graham, the sitting governor, planned to defer establishment of a school for the blind until he had this information. It would be several months before he determined between "a school here, and sending our pupils abroad."[50]

At times Swain held offices in organizations. In 1850, a group "interested in the

Industrial pursuits of the People of North Carolina" met in Raleigh. A particular object was to consider "the propriety of following the example of other states by holding State Fairs." The participants decided to establish a society to be known as "The North Carolina Industrial Association." At each annual meeting of the association a fair was to be held "for the exhibition of articles of production, i[n]genuity and skill in the Agricultural, Manufacturing, Mining and Mechanical Departments of Industry." Swain was elected a vice president.[51]

State boards also benefitted from Swain's service. The 1857 General Assembly established a "Sinking Fund," composed of all funds derived from the state stock in the various railroads and plank roads, turnpike and navigation companies, whether from dividends or the sale of stocks. The act appointed the fund's commissioners: Thomas Ruffin Sr., Weldon N. Edwards, and Swain. When health problems precluded Judge Ruffin's attendance at commissioner meetings, Ruffin deemed Swain's presence "the more important." Swain performed those duties for many years.[52]

Like all public figures Swain endured occasional discomfort with the press's treatment of him.[53] From time to time he also found it necessary to deny rumors or accusations. When the North Carolina Constitution of 1868 was under consideration, a section on education was attributed to him. It was an "absurd suggestion," Swain said. He had met with the education committee and recapitulated statements previously made "in relation to the past history, present condition and the measures indispensable to the continued existence and prosperity of the university." He denied making any reference to the common schools, however, or to education in general. He had spoken only to "the particular sections which related to the university."[54]

On some matters of state, Swain had a less glamorous role as courier, or broker, between interested parties. Elisha Mitchell once paid for a survey of roads from Raleigh west to the Georgia state line. He had written a piece for the Fayetteville paper, apparently related to the survey, which Swain and Governor Graham were to modify. When Swain delivered the item to Graham, he was to return to Mitchell the map of the state's geological formations Mitchell had left in Graham's office. Mitchell's endeavors became a source of controversy, bringing a request for Swain to serve as broker. "I must ask you," Asheville attorney Nicholas Woodfin wrote Swain, "to suggest to Professor Mitchell not to express any preference in his report to the Legislature for one of the proposed rout[e]s for the turnpike over the other." Mitchell could only prejudice the question, Woodfin said; the location had to be left to future surveys or the proposal could not possibly pass.[55]

While state affairs were foremost on Swain's public-policy agenda, national matters received his attention. He and national officials from North Carolina, in particular, were sources of information for one another. In William A. Graham's years in Washington, Graham wrote Swain frequently. He inquired of North Carolina's early monetary policy, a subject, Graham said, "which I know you investigated thoroughly during your Legislative and Executive careers." He asked because in 1837, John C. Calhoun had "referred to our paper money as an illustration of the success of Government paper, which he then considered as the best of all currencies."[56]

The 1793 settlement of the debts of the United States and the states was, Graham thought, another subject of Swain's expertise. North Carolina, Graham believed, had never admitted to the justice of the federal government's half-million dollar claim against it. The matter was settled "under your administration," said Graham, so Swain would have knowledge of the particulars. Public affairs in the nation's capital, Graham said, were then "in an uncertain condition," as an attempt was underway to compromise the bank bill.[57] Graham promised to send Swain a copy of the census if he could procure one. He had previously been unable to do so, even for himself. There was nothing new in political circles, he said, beyond what Swain read in the papers. Further, Graham said, "there seems to be no prospect of a reunion between the Whigs and the President [Tyler]."[58]

A more serious form of alienation was the subject of a later Graham-to-Swain missive. "The elements of discord have not entirely subsided either at the North or South," a worried Graham, now U.S. secretary of the navy, reported. It was then thought, however, almost a decade before South Carolina's secession, that it would not happen.[59]

John H. Wheeler also communicated with Swain from his national government posts. He informed Swain when he became President Franklin Pierce's "official secretary." Later in the Pierce administration Wheeler was the U.S. minister to Nicaragua. He informed Swain of his life there and advised that he greatly welcomed "[n]ews from a loved and distant Land." Swain was, Wheeler said gratefully, "so punctual and so satisfactory a correspondent."[60]

Declining public service opportunities was not in Swain's nature. He recognized his limitations, however, and declined tasks beyond his capacity. In the Buchanan administration he was invited to test the correctness of an assay at the U.S. mint in Philadelphia. If he thought he possessed the requisite scientific knowledge, Swain responded, he would do it, notwithstanding the pressing nature of his other duties. He readily acknowledged, however, that he did not. He was grateful to Buchanan for "tendering a distinction which under ordinary circumstances would have been most cheerfully accepted." North Carolina Congressman L. O. B. Branch had recommended Swain to the president. His declination, Swain assured Branch, "has no tendency to impair the grateful sense . . . of your kindness in suggesting and the President in tendering the appointment."[61]

Correspondents kept Swain informed during the 1840s war with Mexico.[62] On a visit to Shelbyville, Tennessee, he responded positively to a "call . . . for my appearance" at a festival honoring returning troops.[63]

CHAPTER 16

Politics

*"To promote with zeal whatever tends to enlarge
the resources and character of the State"*

WITHOUT A COMMITMENT TO political action, policy concerns generally prove fruitless. Swain's perception of the common good knew no severance of the two. His regard for the people making and implementing public policy, and the task of placing them in positions to do so, was ceaseless. This conclusion derives more from communications to Swain than those from him. It is a safe assumption, however, that he received and reviewed these missives willingly, indeed eagerly. With the 1840 presidential election pending, Swain said, "I am some times surprized to see with how little concern I can contemplate all their proceedings."[1] Almost without exception, the surviving evidence compels the conclusion that he was kidding himself, or perhaps engaged in wishful thinking.

As the nation approached the 1840 presidential election, Raleigh attorney and politician George Badger said to Swain, "I hope we shall beat those Van Buren democrats badly." Swain's brother-in-law, Daniel L. Barringer, viewed his state of Tennessee as Whig and going for Clay. In the spring of 1840, Swain himself regarded the Virginia election results as fatal to the incumbent president, Martin Van Buren. "Nothing but the natural death of Gen. Harrison [William Henry Harrison, the Whig candidate]," Swain said, "can preserve his (Mr. V. B.'s) existence beyond the 4th March." The "public mind," Swain later said, was "more generally tranquil" than he had known it to be. The lethargy of the Whigs concerned him, however. There was little energy among the party leaders, "and their [the Whigs'] continuous domination is in more jeopardy from this than any other cause."[2]

A Swain relative hoped he would not blame the Van Buren administration for the pressure in the money markets. The fault lay with the banks, he said, not with

Van Buren. Such kind words for the incumbent were rare. Swain soon declared George Badger "the most active and zealous politician in the State, and the great propagandist of the Log Cabin and Hard Cider candidate [Harrison]." Harrison would, Swain thought, "prove a more acceptable candidate in N.C. than Mr. Clay would have been." He had never known the Raleigh-area Whig Party to be more sanguine, "too much so," he said with concern.[3]

The sitting governor, Edward B. Dudley, continued the chorus of criticism. He noted how "obtuse and reckless those Van Buren leaders may be to every feeling and principle but such as they suppose will promote their peculiar interest." Dudley "hope[d] the most for the Whig cause" but feared the worst. A Wilkes County resident furthered the adverse assessment, referring to the Van Buren presidency as "this wicked administration of the general government." Almost all in Wilkes County were "united in opposition to this wicked and corrupt government." "I am now more composed than ever," he told Swain, "in my principles of Whiggery." It is not difficult to surmise where Swain's sentiments rested in the 1840 presidential election.[4]

That election brought a Harrison victory, a result favorable to Swain and his fellow Whigs. Harrison's was a short-lived presidency, however. George Badger, who remained a Whig champion, was not alarmed. No doubt Swain and his other friends had felt "[d]oubts and fears" as a result of Harrison's sudden and premature demise, Badger said, but he thought the country was safe with the new president, John Tyler.[5]

Badger's sanguinity soon proved misplaced. William A. Graham, now in the U.S. Senate, informed Swain of "pretty spicey attacks on Tyler." The "great body of our friends," Graham reported, "have no confidence in him." In his entertainments Tyler was embracing both parties in roughly equal numbers. He was refusing to remove officers from the prior Democratic administration; and when there were vacancies, he nominated "personal favorites," sometimes "persons removed by Harrison."[6]

William H. Haywood Jr., soon to be in the U.S. Senate, thought it "an unfortunate circumstance that Mr. Tyler's differences with his Cabinet and party should have precipitated the next Presidential Election upon us out of time." North Carolina, he told Swain, "always suffers and never profits by this contest." The state lacked statesmen, and its "publick men" thought little of its welfare and advancement at any time, and even less "in a period of national excitement." Haywood only hoped the state could "keep our position without *receding* until the next great Presidential battle is fought."[7]

Willie P. Mangum of North Carolina, then president pro tempore of the U.S.

Senate, was upbeat about Henry Clay's 1844 chances. All indications were favorable, he told Swain; indeed, no one seemed to doubt Clay's success. Mangum was prophetic, however. "In that confidence I fear," he said, "the greatest danger lies." When James K. Polk was elected, Mangum did not gloat over his accurate prophecy. "What think you of our American Democracy now?" he asked Swain. Mangum had despaired of seeing a really great man in the presidency, but when Clay came forward, his hopes revived. Now he was mortified at the pitiful gullibility of the people.[8] In partisan terms Clay's loss was Swain's also. He perhaps took some consolation in the fact that his university had produced its first (and to date, only) president, James K. Polk, UNC Class of 1818.

As the 1848 election approached, Clay retained significant support. Battle, holding court in Asheville, told Swain that in the mountains "Mr. Clay is *very decidedly* the first choice." Battle had "not heard a single Whig express a contrary opinion."[9] The Whig Party was not monolithic on this election, however. Daniel L. Barringer advised Swain from Tennessee that all there seemed "to be going for Rough & Ready [Zachary Taylor]." Swain let Battle know that George Badger was "an ardent Taylor man" and not pleased with Clay's "recent course." The renomination of Clay, Badger had said, "would be the signal for the dissolution, not the dismemberment, of the Whig party."[10]

"Rough & Ready" made it to the White House but did not survive the term. As the 1852 presidential election approached, Swain's close friend, William A. Graham, was serving as secretary of the navy in the successor Millard Fillmore administration. From Washington Graham reported to Swain: "The City is full of delegates to the democratic convention, and the welkin rings with the agitation of the Presidential question. But all is yet uncertainty as to the candidate of either party."[11] Soon the uncertainty would lift, and Graham was on the national Whig ticket as General Winfield Scott's vice presidential candidate. This contest held more than ordinary interest for Swain. He soon advised Graham that, in his opinion, the Scott-Graham ticket was stronger than the Whig gubernatorial candidate, and it "must succeed!" Swain conveyed reports from Battle that Battle had "advices from Buncombe" assuring him the tide was turning and all would be well.[12]

Swain received other opinions from the mountains. His nephew thought Fillmore and Graham would have made a stronger ticket there than Scott and Graham. He would support Scott for want of an alternative but did not admire him "as a civil or political man." "In my judgement," the nephew concluded, "[Scott] is unfited [sic] for the presidency." Asheville lawyer Nicholas Woodfin thought if certain conditions were fulfilled, the Whigs could carry that part of the state "about as strongly for Scott as for Taylor in . . . 48." He later reported organizational efforts there for the Scott-Graham ticket. The conditions must have been met, for Woodfin now said, "I think we will give them about the Whig vote in this section."[13]

As the election approached Graham informed Swain of "quite a demonstration" at Salisbury. "The Whig feeling," he said, "seemed to be aroused." Mass meetings were being held, and Graham hoped the excitement would become general. Some friends, though, were "lukewarm . . . in respect to Genl. Scott."[14] At election time both Swain and Graham were deficient on news. "We have no definite advices here," Swain told Graham, "[on] the result of the elections." The indications seemed to be that the Whigs had carried the state. Graham had news only from Orange and Alamance, which, he said, "is good enough, but might have been better."[15] When the overall results came, they were not good for the Whig ticket. Swain would not again have as personal a stake in a presidential election. His long collaboration with William A. Graham would continue, however, to the benefit of North Carolina and its citizens.

United States senators were then elected by the legislature. Perhaps for this reason these elections appear to have had a lesser place in Swain's reckoning. When William H. Haywood Jr. resigned his U.S. Senate seat in 1846, a Swain correspondent noted Haywood's address to "his friends in North Carolina." It was, he said, "a long labored article that will answer every purpose but satisfy the mind of the expediency of his course." George Badger was elected to replace Haywood, and two years later Swain thought Badger could not be reelected. It was a rare instance in which his judgment on a matter of this nature proved wrong.[16]

Four years later Nicholas Woodfin saw both Democrats and Whigs as lacking in organization. He told Swain he thought the Whigs had "as much prospect of electing a Senator as they [Democrats] have." Woodfin was right. North Carolina sent two Whigs, George E. Badger and Willie P. Mangum, to the Senate that year. As to Badger, Swain had told Graham that he was "exceedingly sanguine about the results" of that election. The outcome established that he had had good reason to be.[17]

United States House elections likewise do not figure prominently in Swain's surviving correspondence. Early in Swain's UNC tenure William H. Battle had little hope for election of a Whig candidate in his congressional district but was "very anxious" that William A. Graham should succeed in Swain's. Graham did not.[18] A few years later Graham's older brother, John Graham of Rutherford, was defeated for a House seat by Thomas L. Clingman of Buncombe. Probably because it was the district of Swain's nativity, his relatives and friends there kept him posted on the contest. If certain maneuvers succeeded, one speculated, it would be a very close election; if not, Clingman would win by a large majority. Graham's interference with the post office (probably referring to the appointment of a postmaster) would injure him, reported another, and Clingman "must be elected by a considerable majority."[19]

Nicholas Woodfin had no doubt that Clingman would be elected—in Buncombe, with a majority of more than two to one. Graham would carry his home county of Rutherford by about one hundred votes, said another, but Clingman's majority would be not less than one thousand.[20] Clingman indeed won and remained in Washington until the Civil War. There were occasional objections to his conduct in the office. A Swain nephew protested Clingman's "violence as a partizan." Nicholas Woodfin once viewed him as deceiving the voters "by pretending to be for the Union and Whig policy." As for election results, though, Clingman led a charmed life.[21]

One U.S. House election in particular pleased Swain. When Clingman was appointed to the U.S. Senate in 1858, Zebulon Vance, Swain's former student, was elected to Clingman's House seat. Lucy Battle told her husband that Swain "was gratified at the result of the elections." The teacher is almost always pleased when the student does well.[22]

Swain's interest in and concern for North Carolina politics and government did not die until he did. As the 1842 election approached, there was dissatisfaction with the Whig governor, John Motley Morehead. William H. Haywood Jr. opined to Swain that the state was in great danger of losing the little ground it had gained in the past twenty years. Morehead, Haywood thought, was "not the man for the times." Swain, however, believed Morehead would have "an easy triumph" over Louis D. Henry and that the Whigs would probably control the General Assembly. He was less certain of the latter than he was of Morehead's likely success.[23]

Swain's confidence in Morehead's chances may have been buoyed by the fact that Swain had convinced General Balis M. Edney, later U.S. minister to Guatemala, not to run. Edney, like Haywood, according to Swain, "had become dissatisfied with Gov. Morehead and was intent upon a race." Following "a most earnest appeal" from Swain, Edney withdrew from the contest. When Edney later planned a race for Congress that would "inevitably cause the defeat of the Whigs," Swain doubted that a "second interference of a like nature would be received with equal kindness." He thus passed the task to Senator Willie P. Mangum, whose "diplomacy would probably prove more successful."[24]

Swain thought the Whig gubernatorial baton would pass from Morehead to Charles Manly. It went, instead, to William A. Graham, with Manly later succeeding Graham. As Graham approached reelection time, Nicholas Woodfin raised with Swain the specter of a Graham withdrawal. The West should then put in a claim, Woodfin said, and if Swain would "lend us the use of your name," the Whigs could control both the governor's office and the legislature. The latter was, he said, "otherwise quite doubtful." "Will you think of it before declining," Woodfin pleaded.[25] Swain declined, but Whig prospects did not suffer. Battle soon reported to Swain from the West that no one there had doubts about Graham being reelected by a large majority. Battle later asked his wife to tell Swain "that the Whig spirit is getting up in the mountains." It would, Battle hoped, "show itself pretty strong for Graham at the ensuing election." It did, as Graham defeated the Democratic candidate, James Biddle Shepard.[26]

Political differences reside in the best of families. A nephew once expected Swain to "scold me for what I have done." He was a Democratic candidate for the legislature. "They would not let me off," the nephew pleaded. He had no reluctance about the Democratic cause, however. "[I]f possible," he told his Whig uncle, we will "drive whiggery from its mountain fortresses for ever." "Modest language for so young a man, you may say," he said, but then attempted to explain his position. With ultimate audacity, he asked his uncle, a Whig, to send him a suit of clothes, quoting literary references on the need for a lawyer to be well dressed.[27] Later another nephew, also a Democrat, defeated Nicholas Woodfin for a State Senate seat from Buncombe. Woodfin had been Swain's student and was his lawyer and close friend. Judge Battle's favorable reports on Woodfin's prospects proved overly sanguine. When Lucy Battle read to Swain her husband's letter about the elections, she reported Swain as "very sorry" to hear of Woodfin's defeat. "[I]n truth," she said, "I do not believe that he is at all pleased at his nephew's success any way." One strongly suspects Swain was not pleased with either of these nephews.[28]

Judicial politics acquired Swain's interest less often but could be of considerable concern. Following Judge Gaston's sudden death in 1844, John H. Wheeler speculated to Swain that Judge Frederick Nash would be Gaston's replacement. Wheeler guessed correctly.[29] Not surprisingly, William H. Battle's subsequent supreme court candidacy involved and concerned Swain more than did others. Judge Joseph J. Daniel died in February 1848. Battle and Judge Richmond M. Pearson were the leading candidates to succeed him. Early in the effort Battle, holding court in the West, opined to Swain that "on this side of the mountains it is in my favor." Battle was no Pollyanna, however; he was aware that "public opinion is a very uncertain matter."[30] Swain soon informed Battle that Pearson had presided over a nearby court session "very acceptably to the law, with one or two exceptions, and to the community generally." It was evident that Pearson was in campaign mode. "I never knew him apparently more solicitous to please," said Swain, "or more successful in the effort." Perhaps as part of his effort to please, Pearson had suspended a judgment on Swain's recommendation.

Swain's support for Battle did not preclude a cordial conversation between him and Pearson, in which Pearson opined that the contest was "confined" to himself and Battle.[31] The cordiality of this conversation may have led to false rumors that Swain was supporting Pearson. Battle heard the rumors and considered them "circulated designedly with a view to influence the course of Gov. Graham." Pearson supposedly had told one of his students "that he had no doubt . . . that he should receive the appointment for that you [Swain] had declared for him." Battle assured Swain that he had not done him the injustice to suppose this was true. He also reported that the West generally shared Pearson's view "that the appointment . . . will be conferred upon him or myself." "[T]he scale," Battle thought, "[is] inclined in my favour." He acknowledged his surprise, however, in learning that several members of the bar at Davidson Court had united to recommend Pearson.[32]

A Swain nephew soon wrote him to lament Battle's defeat. Before he mailed the letter, however, he added a postscript noting a newspaper account of Battle's selection. William A. Graham was the governor who made the temporary appointment; it thus is likely that Swain influenced it, though this cannot be documented. In the end, however, Pearson's prediction of geographical determinism proved correct. Whig legislators came to Raleigh determined to elect Pearson from the West for the permanent commission. After numerous inconclusive ballots, Battle withdrew, and Pearson was elected. The legislature immediately returned Battle to the superior court, and in 1852 to the supreme court, where he served until his 1868 defeat in the state's first popular judicial elections.[33]

When Nicholas Woodfin proposed Asheville attorney Joshua Roberts for a judgeship, he and others sought a character reference from Swain. If Swain had other friends seeking the position, however, his declining would be understood. He should not give the recommendation, Woodfin said, "unless your sense of propriety should dictate that course."[34]

Upon the death of U.S. District Court Judge Henry Potter, Swain, pursuant to a request, recommended New Bern attorney John H. Bryan for the vacancy. He had known Bryan twenty-seven years and considered him "one of the most accurate lawyers in the State . . . of unquestionable integrity, and . . . of exemplary moral deportment, "a qualification," Swain said, "which I fear does not always occasion the full degree of consideration to which it is entitled." Swain's recommendation did not prevail. Asa Biggs received the appointment.[35]

Charles Manly sought Swain's assistance about Manly's brother's reelection to the state supreme court. It was "a matter of almost life and death to him and his family," Manly told his friend, "and very dear to me." "Now can't you give us a lift in this emergency?" Manly pleaded. Swain was modest but cooperative. He did not know whether he could exercise any influence, he said, but he would try. Swain pledged to go to Raleigh and to talk to some important Whigs.[36]

Judge Thomas Ruffin's plans were always of interest to Swain. He speculated on Ruffin's "early resignation" some two years before it occurred in 1852. When Ruffin was again elected to the supreme court in 1858, Swain received the news "with no little surprise." With others he questioned whether Ruffin would accept. Swain thought he would if a fourth judge was added to the court. After meeting with Ruffin, he said Ruffin would accept unconditionally. He also assured Ruffin of Judge Battle's gratitude for his acceptance. Later, in thanking Battle for his expression of regard and confidence, Ruffin noted that Swain "had given me premonition."[37]

Aspirants to other state-level positions sought or received Swain's endorsement. He recommended Samuel Field Phillips for secretary of the North Carolina Rail Road Company. Phillips would have doubted his own qualifications, he said, "had not Gov. Swain given me his unsolicited advice to make the application."[38] Prominent Rutherfordton lawyer John Gray Bynum had been suggested for district solicitor. Unfamiliar with the manner of conducting elections by the legislature, he sought Swain's opinion as to his prospects. "I know of no one," he said, "by whose advice I would be more willingly governed." Nor did he know of anyone who could be of more service to him in the endeavor.[39]

Shortly after his 1851 UNC graduation, Bartholomew Fuller took an interest in the state comptroller's position. Swain offered to be useful to him "in any way at your entrance upon the struggles of life." He was uncertain as to Fuller's chances and whether it would be "a desirable situation for you for any considerable length of time." If it would introduce Fuller to the public, however, and if Fuller desired it, his success would afford his old teacher much pleasure. Swain said he had known the holders of the office over the past thirty years. "[I]n comparison with any of them," he reassured his pupil, "your claims are entitled to favorable consideration."[40]

Graduation from the university was not prerequisite to a Swain commendation. Robert B. Peebles completed only the sophomore year, though he did so with first distinction. Swain recommended Peebles highly when he sought a position in the military. He was, said Swain, "a young man of good physical and mental constitution, studious habits and correct moral deportments." To these qualities he added "the activity and energy requisite in military life." Swain was "loath to part with him, as a member of the university," but saw him as "qualified for usefulness elsewhere, and worthy of the lieutenancy to which he aspires." His confidence proved well placed. Peebles never graduated from the university but served as assistant adjutant general, a member of the General Assembly, a trustee of the university, and a judge of the superior court.[41]

Swain was the preferred intermediary when a correspondent desired a letter from Governor Dudley to the American minister at either London or Paris. The letter would, said the requesting party, "give weight to my investigations respecting better modes of working over of Gold and silver than are pursued in this State at this time." Swain, it was hoped, would communicate with Dudley on the subject. He asked "the more unhesitatingly," the writer said, "because I know no person who feels more sensibly than you a disposition to promote with zeal whatever tends to enlarge the resources and character of the State."[42]

Swain's influence on federal appointments was frequently sought. One solicitor wanted "a berth" for his brother-in-law in the Zachary Taylor administration. If Swain could have some of his friends recommend him, it would add a favor "to the countless number I have already received." Another wanted assistance with retaining a friend as the navy agent at Pensacola, Florida. President Polk had appointed the agent, and with the advent of the Taylor administration, he was "threatened with 'removal' on account of his politics." His Whig friends, no less than his Democratic ones, were anxious to prevent this.[43]

While Graham was in the U.S. Senate, he and Swain collaborated to secure for Professor James Phillips an appointment as a visitor to the U.S. Military Academy at West Point. Swain later communicated often with Graham's colleague, U.S. Senator Willie P. Mangum, regarding an appointment for a "Mr. Lucas," possibly Joseph Bibb Lucas, UNC student 1845–1849. Mangum informed Swain that "the Senators have no patronage in this respect." Swain's "strong statements," however, might "give ground to hope for success."[44]

Those seeking local positions filled by federal appointment also sought Swain's assistance. He helped one applicant secure a deputy marshal post in Wilkes County, only to have him seek further assistance when he wished to be superior court clerk. If an agent was to be appointed in Macon County to receive Cherokee Bonds, a friend of Swain's nephew there wanted the position. When a candidate had been recommended for postmaster, apparently in Chapel Hill, and "nothing ha[d] been heard from the Department," Swain sought assistance from his former student and faculty colleague Benjamin S. Hedrick. The candidate,

Swain said, was both well qualified and ready to accept. He requested that Hedrick "call at the Department immediately and urge the appointment forthwith."[45]

One change in a postmaster position was personal. In Asheville, Swain's nephew had been removed from the position and another appointed. The appointment, the dethroned nephew told his influential uncle, "produced a greater excitement among the people than any thing that has taken place here." Upon the election of James K. Polk three years later, Nicholas Woodfin advised Swain of a discussion about filling the Asheville postmaster position. All the Whigs and many Democrats, Woodfin reported, insisted that Swain's nephew should be reinstated. Senator William H. Haywood Jr. soon informed Swain, however, that while the incumbent had been removed, someone other than his nephew had been nominated as his successor.[46]

In addition to assisting with appointments and jobs, Swain brokered efforts to obtain government services or aid. He wrote North Carolina Governor David S. Reid to open doors for a cousin of John Y. Mason, UNC Class of 1816 and secretary of the navy in the Polk administration. He wrote Senator Willie P. Mangum seeking assistance for the holder of two Treasury notes, the right halves of which had been lost. He later sent Mangum an affidavit which, he said, provided "the only deficient link" in the testimony required for payment of the claim. He knew no "purer man" than the applicant, Swain represented to Mangum, saying "my agency in this business has been prompted by no motive but regard for [him]."[47]

One public assistance matter occupied Swain over a period of time. A Chapel Hill resident had previously lived with her guardian in Florida. While there, Indians had attacked the guardian's premises and the ward had suffered "great privations, narrowly escaped loss of life, and sustained the loss of all her property." A bill to compensate for her losses had been introduced in the U.S. House of Representatives "but was not reached in the Senate." Swain asked U.S. Senator David Reid to inquire into her case and advise about what should be done "to secure the redress to which she seems to have a very strong claim." She was "altogether dependent upon her exertions and the sympathies of more fortunate friends." Should her case go to the Court of Claims, Swain asked Reid, or to the Congress? Reid could not find that the claim had been presented to the Senate. He lacked sufficient information to determine the justice of it. If just, Reid said, "it will afford me pleasure to do any thing I can to get it allowed." The Congress was the proper place, he said, for the application.

Swain later forwarded to Reid the applicant's "Petition for redress." Apparently, it too was insufficient, for Reid soon wrote the applicant seeking further information. Once the necessary papers were in hand, Reid promised to "try to have justice done you." The applicant should "[s]how this letter to Gov. Swain, who will no doubt aid you in making up the case for the action of Congress." The outcome of the claim is not clear, but Swain's persistent efforts to assist a needy person are.[48]

Congressman Thomas L. Clingman once told Swain he believed him less interested in political matters than formerly. John H. Wheeler, from one of his Washington posts, likewise viewed Swain as "so much removed from politics that . . . nothing would interest you." Both were wrong. A Swain missive to Kemp Plummer Battle more accurately reflects his lifetime mindset. He designed to visit Raleigh, Swain informed Battle, where they could "have a full conference in relation to great matters of state." "[G]reat matters of State," and the filling of posts from which they could effectively be addressed, never ceased to engage him.[49]

Nor did Swain's UNC position eliminate his potential for some of these positions. He had not been at UNC long before there was serious talk of him for governor, railroad president, U.S. senator, and judge. Edward Dudley, the second of Swain's successors in the governor's office, wanted Swain to be president of the Fayetteville and Western Railroad. Dudley had sons at the university; on their account, he told Swain, he would "wish to keep you where you are." "[B]ut really my dear sir," he added, "I should prefer to see you in the field [for the railroad presidency] to any man in the State." It would pay him a salary of $2,500, said Dudley, "which appointment merits your acceptance." If Swain was going to quit the university (there were rumors to that effect), Dudley said, "how can you do better than refreshing the pocket a little." Swain's appointment "would give entire satisfaction to all parties," said another, who hoped he would accept the appointment if tendered.[50]

The Western Carolinian reported Swain's resignation as president of the university, his appointment by the Board of Internal Improvements as head of the Fayetteville and Western Railroad, and the appointment of Judge John D. Toomer as his successor at UNC. Thinking Swain would be leaving the university, the father of a student wished to resolve a matter regarding his son's indebtedness. Charles Manly was sufficiently concerned about the possibility that he offered to move that the executive committee increase Swain's salary to $2,500, in "the hope that you might be induced upon mature reflection to continue at the head of the Institution." The extant salary, $2,000, would be sufficient for a Swain successor, Manly said, but Swain had been tried and had proven himself "*worth the money.*" "Please give me a wink or a nod upon this subject soon," Manly implored Swain, "which I will regard as *strictly confidential.*"[51] The newspaper soon changed course. It now knew the reports "that Governor Swain had been placed at the head of this enterprize ... to be premature." For the university trustees, the immediate crisis passed. The concern that they might lose their president had been well founded, however. Swain later told Eleanor that he "should have obtained the Presidency of the Rail Road with great ease if I had desired it."[52]

The trustees' relief was short-lived. The following year, 1840, Swain was "talked of" as a U.S. Senate candidate, even listed among "probable candidates." A recent UNC graduate feared that "the Legislature of No Ca will next winter deprive the University of its President." T. L. Clingman noted that those from the far West were generally inclined to support him but added that without Swain's help "we shall not be able to get along." Nicholas Woodfin informed Swain of "a large Log Cabin and—Cider dinner" to which "all those who are spoken of for the Senate" would be invited. All hoped Swain could find it convenient to attend. Woodfin later advised that the jealousies among those engaged in public strife could enhance Swain's chances as a compromise candidate.[53] Again the potential loss of the university's president failed to materialize. The relieved father of a prospective student told Swain: "I had been informed that on the Whigs gaining the ascendency you would go into the Senate, and I had intended my son for Yale. But finding you remain I wish my son to be with you."[54]

A further threat remained, however. There was a vacant judgeship, and State Treasurer Charles L. Hinton told Governor Edward Dudley that if it were offered to Swain, he would accept it. Swain should let him know if he had gone too far, Hinton told him. If he had any influence with the council of state, Hinton said, he would oppose the nomination, "for really I don't know how your present situation would be supplied." But Swain should write him immediately. Swain's tepid, equivocal response was anything but a Sherman-like disavowal. He did not think the situation would arise that required an answer, he said. There were two other possibilities, William H. Battle being one, who could obtain the office with his "hearty concurrence." No circumstances could induce him to come into conflict with either one.

Clearly, though, he was seriously considering himself for the university position to which he later recruited Battle. By being on the bench "and connected with the university simply as Law Professor," he told Hinton, "I could advance the interests of the institution more effectively than by remaining in the Presidency." He could, he thought, give the senior class the same amount of instruction as previously "in Political Economy, Metaphysics and Constitutional Law." The remainder of the scheme was detailed and well conceptualized: "My official station, and returning at stated intervals fresh from the people would give me additional influence over the young men. My intercourse with parents and guardians on the circuits would enable me to remove groundless prejudices, to conciliate public favour and to command patronage. The reduction of my salary would enable the Trustees to add another member of the Faculty. If I were certain that the executive committee would concur in these views, and a seat on the Bench were tendered me, I would not decline it. As it is I do not feel myself at liberty to enter the arena."[55] That this equivocal response would have produced an offer of the judgeship is unlikely, and there is no evidence that it did. Two conclusions can be reached with confidence, however. The seeds of what would become the University of North Carolina School of Law were then germinating in Swain's fertile mind; and in these early days of his lengthy tenure in the UNC presidency, he was not altogether averse to leaving it.

Prospects of his doing so would recur. The 1840 election of Whig presidential candidate William Henry Harrison brought press accounts suggesting Swain as secretary of the navy. A year later rumors that Governor John M. Morehead would decline a second term produced the proposition that Swain had done more for the Whig cause than anyone else and would be the best candidate the party could run. Unless Swain felt "located for life," his brother-in-law later told him, he should go to the U.S. Senate if he could.[56] In 1848, T. L. Clingman advised Swain that his name had "been mentioned in connection with political affairs for this year." If the eastern candidates for governor should quarrel among themselves, causing the Whig convention to turn to a western candidate, Clingman hoped Swain would not refuse it.[57]

The more serious 1848 prospect, however, was a U.S. Senate seat. With the House of Commons evenly divided between the parties, and Whig incumbent George Badger just short of a majority on repeated ballots, Swain received several votes, some even coming from Democratic members. When Badger ultimately received the needed votes, two House members stayed with Swain. The possibility produced rumors that if elected to the Senate, Swain would move back to Buncombe. If he had any thoughts of doing that, a nephew wrote, he hoped Swain would buy his house.[58] The thought of Swain in the U.S. Senate never died altogether, and he was mentioned as a possibility for the state supreme court when Chief Justice Thomas Ruffin resigned in 1852.[59]

Occasionally other academic opportunities beckoned. Mississippi had not yet chosen a president for its university, a correspondent advised Swain in 1847. How would he "like a removal to the far west," the writer asked. It was probable that the Mississippi university board would be glad to secure his services. No Swain response has been found.[60] In 1856, Austin College in Texas was hiring a president. If Swain became a candidate, he was advised, he would be elected unanimously.

The starting salary could only be $1,500. If the college prospered, however, as it would under him, the president's salary would be increased. Denominational loyalty was invoked as a recruiting device. Swain was a Presbyterian; Austin was a chartered Presbyterian College. It would be a pleasant thought for Swain, said the college's advocate, to know that he was aiding the cause of both education and Presbyterianism.

A few weeks later the college's board elected Swain to the presidency. It did not have the appearance of a promotion, the advocate conceded, but he thought it suited Swain to come to Texas, which was destined to be "the Empire State of the great south west." Apparently, Swain had not discouraged the effort. He had told the Texas trustees, the correspondent reported, that Swain had given him encouragement that he would accept "*only* so far, that you said that you had serious thoughts of coming to Texas, and you intimated that the Law Department would fall in with your taste." The school had "no distinct Law School," said the writer, "but we thought as President you might . . . find it convenient to have a Law Chap, and this would be a great thing for our College." The $1,500 cap on the president's salary, the writer had told the trustees, was not thought to be of great importance to Swain "as you desired to 'Colenize' [*sic*] your blacks in Texas." There were then, he represented, "two very fine plantations offered for sale."[61]

No other identified source suggests a Swain interest in resettling his "blacks" on a Texas plantation. Clearly the Austin College proposal was serious, but it was one that Swain ultimately rejected. He would remain at the head of the University of North Carolina until a little over a month before his death in August 1868. It was a felicitous choice, for it is doubtful that he could have found a better base for his multifarious activities. In particular the university presidency provided a foundation for his considerable contributions to the preservation and dissemination of history.

Historian

CHAPTER 17

History Matters
"Laudable labors of rescuing the past from oblivion"

As a law student David Swain had viewed eastern North Carolina historic sites "with no ordinary interest" and had described his visits to them with considerable glee. During spare moments as a jurist, he had gathered and commented on musty old court records. As governor his leadership in matters of history had been uncommon and exemplary, particularly in commencing extensive collection of documents significant to the state's past. As UNC president, Swain's penchant for Clio became passion, obsessive in nature and lifelong in duration.[1]

Swain was modest about this proclivity for the past. While he acknowledged "some fondness for antiquarian research," he disavowed aspiration "to the higher and more arduous office of Historian." Others might consider him well qualified to write the history of North Carolina; he did not.[2] Assessed by modern perceptions of the term, Swain was right; he was not a historian. His institutional education in history was sparse, if not nonexistent; he had made only the most fleeting appearance on a college campus as a student. It is unlikely that a longer stay would have produced more extensive preparation. In the 1820s, American colleges and universities were only beginning to teach American history, and graduate programs in history were nonexistent. Although well-grounded in extensive and careful research, Swain's historical writings were light on, if not lacking in, citation of sources.

A divinity school professor once said to the author, "If you have thought about God, you are a theologian." Applying a similarly less-exacting standard to the history profession, Swain was a historian, indeed a very good one. Pervasive thought on the subject was characteristic of him. He read and studied it constantly and devoted much of his life to collecting and preserving its sources. First billing went to his state's history, but his interests ranged far into the field.[3]

Swain was, Cornelia Phillips Spencer said, "a storehouse of facts and anecdotes, and genealogical and traditional lore, such as no other man's memory in the state could compass," and he "knew more about most things than any other man in the state." A northern correspondent similarly viewed Swain's memory as "a kind of Cyclopedia for the living great men of our country."[4] While sojourning in the American North, Kemp Plummer Battle once wrote his father of visiting a library containing "the best collection of American books in the world [and] some fine manuscripts at the sight of which Gov. Swain's eyes would sparkle with delight." "[T]o [Swain] more than any other man," a later writer would say, with considerable supporting evidence, "North Carolina is indebted for the preservation of her history and the defense of her fame."[5]

The 1832 General Assembly had formed a historical society. Swain, an incorporator and a charter member, had been involved in selecting other incorporators. This society never became active, however.[6] In 1841, the State Literary and Historical Society was organized in Raleigh, with Swain as a member of the executive committee. It at least made an abortive attempt at activity. William H. Haywood Jr. volunteered to confer with Swain "on the subject of Historical Society." L. S. Ives, an Episcopal bishop, was scheduled to address the society but cancelled because of illness; in his apology to Swain, he promised a makeup address "at any future time." Ultimately this society, like its predecessor, failed to materialize in any significant way.[7]

Lack of formal organizational structure did not impede Swain's historic preservation efforts during this period. Recognizing that Swain had long been engaged in "preserving curiosities in the literary and epistolary line," Duncan Cameron sent him a "letter from the late Judge Haywood." William Gaston promised Swain his addresses at Chapel Hill and Princeton. Richard Washington directed Swain to potential sources for the papers of Governor Richard Caswell, Eleanor Swain's grandfather.[8]

Soon a new organization provided structural support for Swain's theretofore rather solitary endeavors. The Historical Society of the University of North Carolina held its first meeting at the university's 1844 commencement. Swain was the progenitor and, as president of the university, the ex-officio society president. Although it was often said that he was the society,[9] every university faculty member served on the executive committee. Thus, in theory at least, the academic community as a whole was engaged. Over time faculty interest faded, except from those on whom Swain specifically called.

Prior to the society's organizational meeting, Swain had apprised the public of its purpose: to endeavor to excite such interest in the public mind about the history of the state as to induce the legislature to obtain from England "the most interesting documents" relating to the royal government "together with such papers as may be found to reflect light on the obscure history of the Proprietary Government of Carolina." A second purpose: "to collect, arrange and preserve at the University *as early as may be possible* one or more copies of every book, pamphlet and newspaper published in this State since the first introduction of the Press among us in 1749; all books published without the State, in our own or foreign countries, on the History of Carolina, and, especially, all the records, documents and papers to be found within the State that may tend to elucidate the history of the American Revolution." Swain acknowledged that "many valuable papers connected with this most interesting period have been irrecoverably lost." Enough remained, however, "to satisfy the most skeptical that Mr. Jefferson's statement that 'there was no doubtfulness in North Carolina; that no State was more fixed or forward,' is sustained by clear and indubitable testimony."

The society solicited communications "from gentlemen every where who have it in their power to contribute in the slightest degree to the undertaking." Many families, Swain posited, would have collections of letters written during the Revolution and shortly thereafter; arrangement and presentation of these under the auspices of the society could honor "the memory of the writers and actors of these eventful and illustrious days."[10]

In the society's second year it again solicited historical materials for its collection. A document, written by Swain and signed by several others, appealed to the people of the state to assist "in collecting and preserving court records, educational records, newspapers and magazines and other historical material." Every North Carolina county, it was thought, would have books or papers of great importance to history. In particular, Mecklenburg, Cabarrus, and Rowan might contain evidence about the Mecklenburg Declaration of Independence. Principals of various academies in the state were implored to participate. Finally, the society sought new members and cooperation in organizing branch associations throughout the state.[11]

In June 1845, the society issued its first annual report. It reiterated its document-collecting purpose. Expressing surprise that for seven decades of the state's history no institution with similar purpose had existed, it lamented the irrecoverable loss of many manuscripts as a consequence. To prevent the progress of that evil, it stated, "is a principal object of this Society." An adequate history of the American Revolutionary War was yet to be written, and the society perceived a duty to render accessible to historians "*all* the facts which may be connected with the war in North Carolina." All intelligent citizens of the state should unite in this cause.[12]

The report, and Swain's distribution of it, drew thanks and praise. For too long the history of the state had gone unwritten, a newspaper opined, and too much ignorance about it abounded. The society's object—"to repair this injustice, to remove this evil, to insure the hearty cooperation of every North Carolinian whose soul is not dead within him"—was a worthy one.[13] The report noted books, newspapers, and manuscripts the society had collected in its first year.

Even in its first months, Swain had reveled in its success. "I am succeeding quite as well as I at any time ventured to anticipate," he wrote a friend, "in collecting materials for history, and arranging a cabinet for the Historical Society of the University." The recently obtained papers of General John Steele of Salisbury, a member of the First Congress under the Constitution, contained much valuable information regarding "that most interesting portion of our history." Swain had letters "from the elder Adams, Jefferson, Madison, Hamilton, Wolcott, Gallitin [sic] & others of other states, besides a voluminous correspondence with Davie, Macon, A. Henderson and many other leading men of our own State." A source had provided an "interesting relic—the original order-book of Lord Cornwallis" from his 1781 expedition through the state, an item that would figure prominently in Swain's future.[14]

The society was well received. One invitee accepted membership with pleasure, heartily approving "of the laudable object your society has in view." He would stand ready to make whatever contributions the society might require of him.[15] Further, the desired materials came. Swain learned that he would receive the "orderly" book of General Waddell's detachment of forces sent against the Regulators in 1771. The small volume relating to the "Regulator" soon arrived. It would explain itself immediately, the sender assured Swain, to one as conversant as he with the history of North Carolina. Helen Caldwell, widow of Swain's predecessor as UNC president, sent Swain letters constituting "a mixture of public and private affairs." "[T]he Govr can select such as may be useful to him and send the rest back," she said.[16]

Some materials came with a cost. A receipt shows Swain paying the Historical Society of Pennsylvania a small sum for provision of some English records. Some attempts at securing materials failed. Once Swain sought certain records "as an act of courtesy to the Historical Society of the University and did not succeed"; on reflection, he was satisfied that the records belonged to the state.[17]

Swain had help with his collection efforts. A scholar working with William R. Davie's papers "ventured to suggest to [Davie's son] the propriety and the desirableness of having them permanently deposited with the Historical Society." It "would have great force, and make it more likely" if Swain would do the same.[18]

Other historical societies also assisted. Swain petitioned the Historical Society of New York, Swain's term for what was likely the New-York Historical Society, for aid in securing "the long missing papers" of Hugh Williamson, a North Carolina delegate to the Federal Constitutional Convention. He urged "an early and safe transmission to me," pledging to "cheerfully remit any expenses for freight." Ultimately the Williamson papers were not found there, but Swain was establishing interstate relationships in his historical endeavors.[19]

Similarly, the South Carolina Historical Society granted North Carolina's society the right to examine and copy any of its papers relating to North Carolina. Swain would be "welcomed to every facility offered for the prosecution of the noble object to which you are devoted." One South Carolina correspondent appended a personal note to Swain, saying, "I believe you are the embodiment of the North Carolina Historical Society."[20]

The society, acting through Swain, sometimes loaned its collections. One borrower was apologetic for not having sooner acknowledged the papers Swain had sent him; they had, however, been more than three months in transit. Another, researching in the "very barren field" of Indian history in North Carolina, was grateful for Swain's offer of any materials in the archives of the Historical Society.[21]

Carping about the society was rare but occurred. Early in its existence a correspondent advised Swain that he was weary of generalities at the society's meetings. He offered a remedy. If Swain could get him papers relating to Governor Burke or General Steele, "or whom you please that is worthy," he would "make an offering to the Society not unsuited to its anniversary." A later correspondent pleaded for greater society activity. More scholarly lectures, it was thought, would do much to awaken the desire to continue its publication of valuable papers. Swain, Francis L. Hawks, and William A. Graham had broken ground and led the way "in this most interesting and important work," but were there not others who could contribute?[22]

The society offered its first honorary membership to former president John Quincy Adams. The invitation noted that North Carolina's first constitution "owed much of its excellence to [the] able suggestions and criticisms" of Adams's father, and that "many of its most important details were the suggestions of the extraordinary ability, the large reading and great experience of the Elder Adams." In his ready acceptance Adams acknowledged "the early part taken by my father" in the separation of the American colonies from the British Crown, "far in advance of most of his countrymen." Honorary membership in an organization with the society's purpose would be "among the most precious honours" of his life.[23]

Thus, the university's historical society provided Swain a mechanism, a formal structure, through which to conduct his endeavors for history. He soon had another, as the state of North Carolina, almost certainly with Swain's prodding, awakened to the importance of preserving the records of its past. The 1844–1845 General Assembly authorized the governor to collect the necessary papers to complete a series of letter books. He was to collect either the original papers or copies of the proceedings of the several town, county, and district committees organized to carry into effect the Articles of American Association and the proceedings of the various committees and councils of safety convened under the authority of the provincial legislature. Without such papers, Harvard historian Jared Sparks told Swain, no writer could do justice to the history of any state.[24]

The 1846–1847 General Assembly authorized the governor to collect, arrange, and publish a new edition of a pamphlet containing numerous historical documents, including the Mecklenburg Declaration of Independence. Finally, the 1848–1849 legislature empowered the governor to procure, from the public offices in London, documents deemed worthy of preservation in the state archives; it approved an expenditure of $1,000 for copying these records.[25]

Charles Manly became governor of North Carolina in January 1849. Like Swain, Manly was a Whig. He was also a longtime university trustee and the trustee board's secretary-treasurer. Through these political and university ties, Manly and Swain had developed a close friendship. Thus, it was hardly surprising when Manly appointed Swain as the state's historical agent to execute the purposes of the 1848–1849 resolution. Arguable cronyism notwithstanding, Swain's credentials for the position were beyond cavil.[26]

Swain was said to be "very much pleased at the idea of going to England," the only question being, in May of 1849 or of 1850? He soon resolved in favor of the latter and informed Governor Manly that he would not be ready for the trip until he could ascertain more precisely what information could be obtained in North Carolina about his mission. He had written historian George Bancroft, American ambassador to the Court of Saint James, for more definite information regarding papers on file in the public offices in London. Unless a message from Bancroft altered his view, he would postpone his visit to London until May 1850.[27]

While no personal visit to England was in the offing, Swain received communications on securing historical documents from there. A Liverpool correspondent, aware of Swain's wish for a history of his state, had asked the secretary of state for colonial affairs "what privileges could be granted to a person from the United States, who would wish to consult the original 'grants,' and other documents . . . in that office that relate to North Carolina." The papers, he was informed, were in the State Department. Another, en route to Muscat as U.S. consul, offered to stop in London and copy state papers relating to North Carolina "at a moderate charge."[28]

Meanwhile Swain's in-state efforts drew positive responses. Fayetteville merchant John Huske advised that it would afford him "great pleasure to promote the object you have in view on this matter." He knew little, however, of the life of his father, an early state and local official and merchant; he thus was forwarding Swain's inquiry to an aunt, who knew more than anyone else.

The death of Duncan Cameron—prominent North Carolina planter, judge, politician, and banker—brought an expression of trust in Swain as the state's historian. "I shall cheerfully furnish *you* with any paper that may come into my hands of any interest," wrote Cameron's son, "for I am sure that in your hands all that a son would live or die for would be safe." Unfortunately, however, the son had handled but few of his father's old papers and knew that his father had given away many.

Frederick Nash, chief justice of the supreme court of North Carolina, thought it beyond his power to assist Swain in preparing a biographical sketch of his father, Governor Abner Nash. He was five-years old when his father died, he said, and could only recall having seen him once other than in his coffin. Still, Nash provided Swain with valuable information. According to his mother, Nash said, anxieties and labors during the struggles of the Revolution, especially while he was governor, broke his father's health. He died en route to Philadelphia "to take his seat as a member from this State," having gone into the Revolutionary War a wealthy man and emerged from it with nothing.[29]

In these endeavors Swain learned that Harvard University possessed a large folio entitled "Governor Tryon's North Carolina Papers." The initial discoverer, not identified, had requested a copy for the UNC Library but had met objection on the ground that it was unique, and its value would be greatly depreciated by a duplicate. He was told to send a formal request, but he planned, should that fail, to write Governor Swain and suggest that he apply for it.[30]

That attempt indeed failed, and Swain commenced corresponding with two historians, George Bancroft and Jared Sparks, that produced the copy. Bancroft wrote Swain from New York that he would let him know what he heard from Cambridge regarding "permission to make a copy of Governor Tryon's letter book." He soon advised that a copy would cost about $100.00 and that a letter from Swain to the Reverend James Walker, president of Harvard, "would, I believe, produce the result you desire."[31]

Sparks then indicated that while original manuscripts could not be taken from the Harvard Library, copies were freely granted. The college, he told Swain, had acquired the manuscript from a Mr. Stevens in London, who had found it there in the hands of a bookseller. It had, Sparks affirmed, "all the appearance of having been the original record." Was it not probable, Sparks asked Swain, that some of the papers relating to the proprietary government of North Carolina were among the South Carolina papers in the British offices? Or possibly in manuscripts in the British Museum or in the possession of descendants of the Proprietors? If Swain indeed wanted the complete collection of these early documents, Sparks opined, it was "necessary that some competent person should go to England, and make a thorough research, particularly in the public offices."

Sparks engaged a copyist. An interim report advised Swain that the transcription was incomplete. After another month Sparks informed Swain that the work was finished, and the volume was in the hands of the binders. He would forward it as Swain might direct. Swain apparently failed to respond, for when Sparks soon indicated that the volume was bound, in his possession, and made "a good appearance," he reiterated, "I shall be happy to forward it in any manner you may direct."[32]

Swain soon had the volume, had read it through, and had found it as interesting and valuable as anticipated. The copyist had performed his task with remarkable neatness and accuracy. It was "very remarkable," Swain told Governor Graham, that such a volume should have been in the Harvard Library for years and escaped the attention of both Bancroft and Sparks. Swain was, he informed Graham, willing to continue the work of the agency if the legislature would enable him to "effect the design without submitting to an unreasonable sacrifice." Traveling expenses "and clerk hire" would satisfy him.[33]

Ultimately Swain deposited the Tryon volume in the Executive Office in Raleigh. He apparently ignored a news item that erroneously referred to it as a copy of "Tyson's North Carolina Papers." The item, while wrong in that respect, properly praised Swain's work as the state's historical agent, stating, "A correct history of his native state has been almost a passion with Mr. Swain for many years, and his qualifications for the task allotted him are of the first order."[34]

State history includes a composite of local histories, and Swain eagerly solicited these, both through the society and in his role as the state's historical agent. Former students were among those he importuned. One responded that he was sure the records of Anson County contained entries on Tory-Whig conflicts "and perhaps other facts of moment to the historical researcher." Since leaving the university, the graduate professed, he had intended to research the state's Revolutionary history. Swain's letter had reawakened this desire, and "hidden memorials of our Revolution" were calling him to county court records and other papers in a part of the state noted for constant warfare between Loyalists and Whigs. He would take pleasure in sending Swain such facts as he could collect. It was regrettable, however, that the society had not been formed sooner, for much was now lost and many with knowledge had died.[35]

An Edenton correspondent told Swain he had secured from the clerk of superior court there "several very old records" from which Swain would derive important information about the early history of that area. The clerk was willing for Swain to examine them as long as he wished. Certain "collectors books" Swain could keep "as the property of the Historical Society" unless an act pending in Congress required otherwise. "I have also learned lately," said the correspondent, "that the papers so ruthlessly destroyed by the former clerk here, belonged chiefly to the collectors office, and amounted to several barrels full."[36]

A Wilmington writer, professing himself "nothing of an antiquarian," nevertheless forwarded an undescribed letter which, he said, "may at some time be useful to the historian of North Carolina." There could be no better disposition than to place it in Swain's possession, and Swain could use it as he pleased. A local political figure in Elizabeth City likewise conveyed disappointment. He had searched the archives there and had found nothing predating 1730, "and that very unimportant." He hoped Swain's collections in Europe would amply remunerate his "devotion to this subject," and that upon his return he would occupy his leisure "in embodying your treasures in such a readable form, that our people may learn something of their former history."

Two correspondents brought Revolutionary War information, one of the Battle of Trent Bridge in Jones County, the other a more general history of the war in Western North Carolina. John Gray Bynum, author of the latter, was a prominent lawyer in Rutherfordton. His legal prominence notwithstanding, he was flattered that Swain wished him to write the history of Kings Mountain. A contemplated move to Wilmington would afford him more leisure for the task, which he would finish as soon as possible. Meanwhile he would try to furnish the *University Magazine* with articles "on incidents which cannot well be introduced in the history of the battle."

Allen J. Davie, William R. Davie's son, had long wanted some "capable person to publish recollections of the state of North Carolina." Swain's geographical location and position in society rendered him the best person to do it, "and the whole state," Davie said, "will have the most perfect confidence in the ability with which it will be executed." Davie had suggestions for appropriate harvesters of local histories. William Gaston could afford much information about his part of the state. Settlement of the Cape Fear and its local history was the province of the Moore family; Hugh Waddell could assist, "as his relation the late Mr. [Judge] A[lfred] Moore would have been if living the best authority in these matters."

From his father's papers and recollections, William A. Graham "could afford . . . much information as well as personal anecdote." Governor Iredell and James C. Johnston could cover the Edenton District. As to the Halifax area, Davie's father's papers could assist "so far as they concern the Revolution." North Carolina had not received due credit, Davie opined, "because we had *no writing man*." Swain thus should "seriously think on this subject"; "in my opinion," Davie concluded, "you could make it a work important and acceptible [sic] to your Native State."[37]

Swain hardly needed this prodding, yet it undoubtedly spurred his efforts. A further nudge came when the 1854–1855 General Assembly again authorized the governor to procure from London documentary evidence of the state's colonial and Revolutionary history, to appoint an agent for that purpose, and to pay the agent's necessary expenses from the public treasury. The governor, now Thomas Bragg, again tendered the agency to Swain, who "consented to render any services in my power to enable [the governor] to effect the wise and patriotic designs of the General Assembly."

He had already accomplished one of the Assembly's expressed purposes, Swain informed the governor, namely securing a copy of Governor Tryon's letter book. But he was not "unmindful of the more arduous task . . . the duty of endeavoring to ascertain . . . materials which. . . illustrate our annals throughout the two centuries which have elapsed since the earliest settlement." He was familiarizing himself with the materials to ascertain the necessity of a visit to the mother country. Once his collections from domestic sources were as complete as he could hope for, he would arrange and examine them and "be prepared to communicate my views upon all the subjects embraced by the Resolutions."[38]

Swain pursued these domestic sources via a form letter, apparently sent to one or more persons in each of the state's counties. He informed them of the General Assembly's action and stated his purpose to secure "every species of documentary evidence essential to the true and full development of our history, which has been preserved in our own, in our sister states, and in the mother country." He desired "all the information within your reach which may serve to illustrate the history of the state, or your own county."

Among the favored items were accounts of Indian tribes, their wars among themselves, and their contests with white people; records of associations and accounts of other proceedings to resist the Stamp Act; records of associations organized under the Articles of American Association adopted in 1774, and of

Revolutionary Committees of Safety; journals of Provincial and Revolutionary Assemblies; court records; parish and church registers; records of births, deaths, and marriages; ancient newspapers, pamphlets, and books; and accounts of early settlements and battles. To guard against pertinent omission, there was a catch-all clause: "in fine, every thing which, in your estimation, may possess historical value."

In addition to aiding in such collections Swain requested that recipients "prepare, or secure the services of a competent person, to prepare a sketch of the history of your county." Take John H. Wheeler's *Sketches of North Carolina*, Swain suggested, and rewrite the histories of their counties, "correcting errors, supplying omissions, and enlarging or retrenching as you may deem best calculated to present your views of the past and the present, fully and fairly, to the consideration of the historian." "[A]s little delay as practicable" was implored. To some recipients Swain addressed more targeted inquiries. He had no doubt that the public records of Orange County contained "a good deal of valuable historical information," he noted for William A. Graham. "Whom can you induce to search them for me?" he inquired.[39]

Reflecting respect for Swain and interest in his project, numerous responses followed, foremost among them some from legislators whose resolution had spawned the endeavor.

Though fearing inadequacy for the task, Commoner E. A. Thompson told Swain that nothing could afford him greater pleasure "than to be able to afford you any assistance or information from my county [Wayne] relative to your laudable undertaking." Senator Ralph Gorrell of Guilford had long desired a good history of the state by one of its own sons, so would most cheerfully comply with Swain's request. Because court records were burned by the British at the Battle of Guilford Courthouse in 1781, pre-Revolution materials were scarce in his county. Earlier deaths, taking much information to the graves, would also limit his service; but he solemnly pledged, "my best efforts will be used to carry out your design."[40]

Federal officials, too, gave or promised cooperation. Edwin G. Reade of Person wrote from the U.S. House of Representatives to suggest men in his district for the task. Robert Paine of Chowan, the first district representative, did the same. Court and church records in Edenton, he said, "will afford some information of use to you." Asa Biggs of Martin, then in the U.S. Senate, would, upon returning home, make inquiries "and try to assist you as far as we can."[41]

Citizens throughout the state were equally forthcoming. An Edenton resident considered it "the plain duty of all on whom you call for aid to contribute what they can to the good work." In response to Swain's circular, Dr. Edward Warren had agreed "to act as Historiographer of this county" and no doubt would discharge the duties well.[42] Matthias Manly, soon to be on the state supreme court, promised to cooperate and to communicate historical facts of interest. Such facts were few, however, and he was not sanguine that he would stumble across anything that would serve Swain's purposes. Another respondent enclosed what he had collected in Pitt County and promised to assist in Orange when he returned from the spring court circuit.

The circuit courts proved a fertile source of local historiographers. A Swain request at his last circuit had prompted one lawyer to secure such for fourteen counties.[43] Two gentlemen, Swain was told, had agreed to perform the duty in Martin County. The informant would "endeavor to render all the assistance in my power to accomplish the very desirable object contemplated in your proposed plan." William B. Rodman, formerly a Swain student and later a state supreme court justice, had been intending to give his grandfather's papers a careful examination; if he did, and found anything of interest, he would gladly communicate it to Swain.[44]

From Hillsboro came old superior court records, writs of attachment and the like done according to the old English practice, "all directed against the celebrated Herman Husband—the ring leader of the Regulators." County court records from Richlands dated back to 1734; the sender lived on Samuel Johnston's father's farm, where nothing remained to mark the spot except broken bricks and earthenware. An eastern North Carolina writer was preparing to expound on several of the state's rivers and would share information regarding them with Swain; he was, he said, Swain's "grateful pupil," who hoped to aid his teacher in his "researches as regards the history of North Carolina."[45]

Responses to Swain's circular were not uniformly encouraging. One from Moore County pledged to place all available information in the hands of Clement Dowd. Dowd, in turn, offered "[a]ny servises [sic] I may be able to render you, Governor," but recommended that Swain "devolve the duties of Historiographer of the county on some one more competent."

The writer of a "little work" on the history of Salisbury found it difficult to obtain its history under the royal government; indeed, he said, there was but little up to 1800. Stanly County was so new it was thought to have no history. The circular recipient there had honored Swain's request to rewrite Wheeler's sketch of the county but could offer no more.

An examiner of Lincoln County records also lacked confidence he had discovered anything of material assistance. There were court records, including one in which William R. Davie produced a license and was admitted to the bar; he sent these "such as they are" and would be pleased "if such *scraps* of information will be of any service to you." Union County too, it was feared, could furnish little of historical interest. There was the Waxhaw settlement; a battle between Whigs and Tories during the Revolution, with Cornwallis's headquarters nearby; and Davie's leadership of the Whigs. Drifting into historical controversy, the writer related Union County's claim to be the birthplace of Andrew Jackson, noting supporting details from oral tradition.[46]

Notwithstanding this focus on local histories, Swain's broader vision persisted. Renewed status as the state's historical agent revived his interest in securing materials from the mother country, to which the latest General Assembly resolution had authorized a visit. The obscure portion of North Carolina history, Swain told Harvard historian Jared Sparks, was that from the earliest settlement to the close of the proprietary government in 1729. Bancroft's researches exceeded those of his predecessors, Swain said, but his collection of materials was "very meager."

Ever frugal, however, Swain was averse to costing the state travel expense without a reasonable prospect of effecting "the wise and liberal purposes of the General Assembly." Thus, this question to Sparks: Was it important that an agent go to London, or could the researches be made, and the relevant copies secured, by correspondence with public offices and private persons? Sparks dodged the travel abroad question but was glad to find Swain making good progress. He hoped Swain would persevere "till all the materials relating to N. Carolina are obtained from the British offices."[47]

Swain's historical agency efforts extended to other states as well as the mother country. A Georgia correspondent examined that state's colonial documents folio from the State Paper Office in London but reported to Swain that he "found nothing that could aid you." Swain, he stated, already possessed anything there relating to North Carolina.[48] A Mississippian proposed to bring manuscripts to Chapel Hill for Swain's inspection. A North Carolina history, he said, should be the work of one of her own sons. "Your reputation as a civilian and scholar," he encouraged Swain, "is as well known here as in North Carolina, and we take a deep interest in the efforts you are making to recover her lost records and fading traditions."[49]

In South Carolina, Swain importuned James Johnston Pettigrew for assistance. This former student could direct Swain's letter to the president of the Historical Society of South Carolina. Pettigrew himself knew the history of both his native and adopted states, North Carolina and South Carolina, respectively; if he had the leisure, he, better than any other person, could perform research for Swain in the Charleston Library and the historical society archives. Particularly desired were copies of any relevant documents from England.[50]

Tennessee Episcopal Bishop James H. Otey, UNC Class of 1820, dispatched to Swain an engraving of Charlotte, King George III's queen. He trusted that it would reach Swain safely and requested such confirmation. Another writer reported an inquiry from a Swain student "regarding the state of Frankland [sic] organized in early times on the borders of N. Carolina now comprised within the state of Tennessee."[51]

Amidst a bevy of historical facts, Swain implored "the aid of the Historical Society and public authorities of Virginia." He sought names of the first colonists there, the place of the first settlement in Albemarle, and all information the society's collectors and the state's public officers could supply regarding the state's historical figures. If such information rendered it proper, he contemplated a visit to Richmond. Bancroft had mentioned important facts in public records there that had escaped the notice of preceding historians; some had eluded even his "keen research," Swain thought. "The laudable investigation of your annals, which is now happily committed to your direction," a Virginian wrote Swain, "will lead ... to the elucidation of many questions of common interest to our two states."[52]

One out-of-state correspondent invited Swain, rather than returning notes he had forwarded, to "remit me what you think them worth to the Historical Agency of North Carolina." Swain considered himself possessed of such authority. Reciting legislative leave "to procure documentary information in relation to our history," he assured one provider of materials that he would "examine them carefully and pay for them whatever sum they may be in my judgment worth, in the light in which I am permitted to examine them."[53]

Swain's avowed determination "to secure every document attainable at home, or abroad, that I may consider essential to the illustration of our history, with as little delay and expense as practicable" was extravagantly ambitious. Still, public confidence in his capacity to accomplish it was abundant. "The State is fortunate," said one newspaper, "in procuring the services of a gentleman so eminently qualified for the duty to be performed." "A correct history of his native state has been almost a passion with Mr. Swain for many years," said another, "and his qualifications for the task allotted him are of the first order."[54]

Others thought similarly of the need for a history of the state and of Swain's qualifications to produce it. One newspaper that considered his research efforts "unwearied and sagacious" looked with confidence to him for "a lucid and full history of North Carolina." Later a Charleston correspondent similarly urged Swain not to waste time in getting this done.[55]

As a student at the university, William Rodman, inspired by "conversing with Gov. Swain," devoted his spare time to history. As Swain approached his grave,

Rodman still could say, "Unless I mistake you are the man for this work—or rather the chief of the men by whom it is to be done."[56] The idea of "a correct and thorough" state history, said a Salisbury newspaper "must not be suffered to pass from the public mind." "[F]rom his long habits of research, and the vast fund of information at his command," Swain was the man to do it. No surer means existed to "embalm . . . his own virtues and excellencies" in the people's memories, "and there could be no 'better monument' to his services to the State." He should commence at once, it prophetically advised near the last year of his life, "seeing he has no time to lose."[57]

William Lee Davidson, donor of the land for Davidson College, said much the same, again in Swain's latter days. All eyes were turned to Swain, said Davidson, "to give No[rth] Car[olina] that enviable position in the *written history* of America to which she is so justly entitled."[58] This cajoling came too late. A file in Swain's papers marked "Notes on N.C. History" contains a draft that could have been intended as a nascent history of North Carolina. The author died before achieving anything approaching completion. He had, however, as H. G. Jones has noted, "blazed the trail of others who, through the use of his materials and encouraged by his unfulfilled plans, were to do better what he might have done poorly."[59]

From the outset of his tenure at Chapel Hill, Swain concerned himself with the history of the university. Soon after Swain's arrival and evidently at his suggestion, Hinton James penned recollections of his time as the university's first student in the 1790s. "Please give my most respectfull respects to Governor Swain," James directed, "and assure him that I sincerely regret that I cannot say more on this subject, that it would give me great pleasure at all times to add to his convenience in any way I possibly could."[60]

An early Swain-era entry in the university faculty minutes is telling: "The propriety of writing a history of the university was brought before the faculty by the President." Swain then sent documents to a northern education publication from which the recipient hoped to compile "a brief notice of the History of the college." Obviously spurred by Swain, a historian inquired of him, "When must I write the history of the university? When receive the materials?" Understanding that Swain was anxious to collect all possible information on the institution's early history, the nephew of a former professor sent him a file of his uncle's letters.[61]

To Swain's disappointment, some of the university's early history was lost forever. He once sought a report on the sale of lots in the village in 1793, the year the university commenced. The report, trustee secretary Charles Manly informed him, had been destroyed in the 1831 State House fire. So too had nearly all university papers prior to 1810.[62]

Given available materials, Swain facilitated their use for university history purposes. A William R. Davie memorialist sought such relevant papers as Swain possessed, "especially information touching Gov. Davie[']s labors in founding and fostering the University of North Carolina." Swain obviously obtained what he could, for he soon received assurances that a correspondent had given to a relative, for the memorialist's purposes, "[e]very letter about the house from the late Genl. Davie, which referred most remotely to the university." Diligent search would continue, and Swain's capable hands would receive any further finds.[63]

In 1854, the General Assembly invited Swain to lecture on the history, present condition, and prospects of the university. Warren Winslow and S. P. Hill, speakers of the Senate and House respectively, introduced him to his Commons Hall audience. University trustees requested a copy of "the eloquent and interesting address" and ordered one thousand copies printed and distributed among trustees, alumni, and students. The subject, one "interesting to every friend of Education," was "ably discussed by the distinguished speaker," opined a Raleigh newspaper: "no man could have done it fuller justice." "The university mainly owes its present success to his efficient supervision," it concluded.[64]

A handwritten note on a circular invited Swain to submit, for *An Encyclopedia of American Literature*, a brief narrative history of the university, "with both historical and personal entries of its foundation, Presidents and Professors so far as they involve anything of a special literary or general interest." A northern educator-editor similarly sought Swain's account of "the history and services" of his institution and invited his cooperation in building an educational periodical "of a truly American and comprehensive character."[65]

In January 1859, the trustees requested of Swain "a History of the Institution from its Foundation" for presentation at the board's next annual meeting. With a breakdown of the national consensus looming, it was a difficult time for Swain and the university, and there is no evidence that he performed the task. Not long after his death, however, Cornelia Phillips Spencer described a very valuable book of Governor Swain's "containing the history of the university—as collected by himself—newspaper articles etc. etc." "These new owners," she told Swain's widow, referring to the leadership of the university during Reconstruction, "are exceedingly anxious to get hold of all such things." With Eleanor Swain's authorization, Spencer would retrieve it from a Mrs. Saunders—not further identified, but apparently the wife of Colonel William L. Saunders, historian and UNC trustee—and send it to her. Spencer soon reported having sent for the book. "If it is the one I think," she told Eleanor, "it is very valuable." There the trail ends. The present research has not disclosed the volume. It would appear, however, that

Swain had at least gathered materials toward compliance with the trustees' request for a university history.⁶⁶

Swain occasionally gave public lectures on historical topics. University officials and students were his principal audience, but Chapel Hill residents were invited and attended. At the 1866 commencement, for example, as orator before the literary societies, he gave a series of historical parallels between North Carolina and the world at large, and then with Great Britain and other countries.⁶⁷ University duties constrained him, time-wise and geographically, yet outside speaking invitations proved difficult, if not impossible, to resist. His initial response to one of these stated, unequivocally, "[m]y time will be so unremittingly and laboriously employed...that I cannot hope to find leisure for the composition of a historical lecture." Hedging followed, however. Resistance to the proposition was admittedly difficult. He therefore would pledge "if you can do no better, to attend... and participate...whether I have opportunity to reduce my thoughts to writing or not." Ultimately his resolve proved infirm. "I will be with you," he stated, "if not hindered by causes which I cannot control[,] and...I will do all in my power to accomplish your purposes."⁶⁸

A Wilmington Literary Association invitation produced from Swain an introspective and expansive response. For some years, he replied, he had worked to supply historians with necessary materials for composition of the state's history, particularly about its first settlements. He had desired time in Wilmington, "with the hope of being able to learn the first elements of our history." Thus, he cheerfully accepted, saying, "I have interesting and valuable collections of which it will afford me pleasure to speak at the earliest favorable opportunity, and especially in relation to your town." These collections contained an important manuscript, received from a Wilmington citizen, relating to the city's history. He could exhibit it to the association and make appropriate acknowledgments.

A newspaper account of the lecture has Swain correcting "erroneous impressions" concerning leading events of the Revolutionary War in the Cape Fear area. Citizen refusals to yield to exorbitant demands of Crown officers were, he said, an "incident highly honorable to the people of this section." "Governor Swain," said the article, "produced a large number of letters brown and discolored by age, from men of the Revolutionary era, and read a few of these for the edification of the audience." The lecture was well received. The association president soon forwarded to Swain a resolution of thanks for his "able and instructive lecture." He requested a copy for publication.⁶⁹

A subsequent lecture series in the state capital saw Swain as the opening speaker. His subject: "Geographical and Physical History of North Carolina." A "large and intelligent auditory" attended, and uniformly laudatory press coverage followed. The "able and interesting" lecture, said one paper, "was characteristic of the learned president of the university, and showed a depth of research which, probably, no other man in North Carolina is possessed of." The lecture, it said further, held "an immense fund of historic lore" and was "particularly well versed in the history of the state, which is proud to own him as her son." That many said they could have listened several hours longer was "a just and deserved compliment to the erudite and accommodating lecturer."[70]

Two well-known Swain lectures were published together. The first was at the dedication of Raleigh's Tucker Hall. Swain there posited that few topics in ante-Revolutionary times exited more interest than location of the state's seat of government. He proceeded with a heavily factual account, showing detailed research, on initial steps and the ultimate 1788 siting of the capital "within ten miles of the plantation where on Isaac Hunter now resides in the County of Wake." His depiction of the later burning of the capitol building is poignant and highly descriptive: "It was my lot on the 21st of June, 1831, to stand a helpless spectator, when that noble edifice adorned with the statue of the father of his country was a sheet of blinding, hissing flame, and to hear amidst the almost breathless silence of the stupefied multitude around it, the piteous exclamation of a child, 'poor State House, poor statue, I so sorry.' There were thousands of adults present as sorrowful and powerless as that child."

Swain's personal involvement did not end there, however. He continued: "It was my lot as Chief Magistrate on the fourth day of July, 1833, to lay the corner stone of the present capitol, supposed on its completion to be the most magnificent structure of the kind in the Union." Finally, he told of later taking the keys to the capitol from a "Negro servant" and surrendering the structure to Sherman as the Civil War ended, receiving from Sherman assurance that the capitol and the city would be protected, and the rights of private property duly regarded. Subsequent highlights include histories of Raleigh businesses and personalities, the North Carolina Supreme Court, and the state's legal system.

To consider Swain an early feminist historian would exaggerate, but the address then contains this interesting, arguably prescient, observation: "Rarely since the completion of the Pentateuch has full historic justice been meted out to woman." After relating women's history in biblical accounts, he asks, accusingly—"Why are not similar pictures presented in modern times?"—and briefly paints some such pictures, concluding with the contributions of Dorothea Dix. Sectional concerns conclude the address: "Let us hope that when we meet here on the 4th July 1868, Southern voices will again have been heard in the halls of Congress, and that millions of Southern hearts, as in former days, will be prepared to respond 'Liberty and Union, now and forever, ONE, and inseparable.'"[71]

The second address dedicated a Raleigh monument to Jacob Johnson, father of Andrew Johnson, the sitting president. President Johnson returned to the city of his birth for the ceremony. A history of Raleigh and the capitol commenced the discourse. Swain took the liberty of elucidating the contributions of his maternal relation, Joel Lane, who conveyed to the state, for its capital city, one thousand acres contiguous to his residence at Wake Court House. A reference to William White, North Carolina secretary of state from 1798–1811 and Swain's father-in-law, also entered the discussion. Details about various public officials, and a history of local journalism, followed.

"It was in the midst of such society," Swain then said, "that JACOB JOHNSON lived and moved and had his being." The shift was incomplete, however, as Swain continued to depict the city and its inhabitants since Johnson's time, weaving some of Johnson's history and contributions into the mix. A more blameless history, Swain said, he had not encountered. Johnson's claim to fame was his rescue of two men from drowning, leaving effects that ultimately took his own life. "He had many friends in every walk of life," Swain asserted, "and no enemies."

Topics of dubious relevance followed: a history of the fathers of the three North Carolina-born presidents, for example, and material on Leonidas Polk, Episcopal bishop, Confederate officer, and Swain's college roommate. Time did not permit speaking of Jacob's son, but Swain deemed a plea for sectional unity an appropriate close. "The time has arrived when patriotism, not less than Christianity, requires the forgiveness of all that we can forget. Let the crossed swords on the monument, surmounted by the stripes and stars, form an appropriate 'Memorial Association' for the Confederate and Union dead, and no strife be witnessed above their graves, but patriotic and generous emulation to do most to promote harmony and restore 'the more perfect Union' designed by the Constitution of our common country!"[72]

Some of these lectures were published in the *North Carolina University Magazine*, together with Swain's articles and other historical material, much of which he facilitated and encouraged. First published in March 1844, the journal ceased publication in December 1844. It then had only two hundred subscribers. A second series, commenced in February 1852, claimed 525 subscribers. By 1853, the magazine was said to be "rising rapidly and certainly to the dignity of a first class Southern Literary Magazine."

In 1861, as the country descended into the Civil War, the magazine encountered serious financial problems. Student editors were "in danger of sustaining inconvenient loss," Swain said in an appeal for public support. To new subscribers he promised "the ten numbers of the current and the ten engravings of the last volume." The solicited response, he hoped, would "not merely indemnify the editors for their outlay, but enable the publisher to continue the magazine another year." Swain's expectation was overly sanguine. The appeal failed, and the journal again ceased publication. It did not resume until 1878, a decade after Swain's death.[73]

Cornelia Phillips Spencer saw "Governor Swain's hand in almost every number" of the magazine. "There was a time in his life," she wrote, "when every other interest seemed subordinated in his mind to that of elucidating our State Revolutionary History." Spencer described a wedding party at which Swain stood with his head bent forward and his eyes fixed in vacancy. "Look at him," she quoted his wife as saying, "he's thinking about the American Revolution this minute." "And," said Spencer, "I dare say he was."[74]

From the magazine's initial publication this Swain obsession dominates its pages. The first issue contains an article entitled "Revolutionary History—North Carolina." The author is not identified, but Swain is the leading suspect. If he did not write it, he almost certainly solicited it. Comments on the North Carolina founders followed. The edition laments the failure of the earlier historical society in Raleigh but praises the new one at the university for obtaining "several manuscripts of importance, consisting of journals and letters written during the Revolutionary War." While bemoaning the loss of much valuable material, it notes private papers yet extant that "would throw light upon the Provincial and Revolutionary history of North Carolina." The magazine provided Swain a further opportunity to tout the University Historical Society's purpose: to excite interest in the public mind regarding the state's history for the purpose of inducing the legislature to secure from England documents relating to "the Regal Government," together with papers that would elucidate the obscure history of the proprietary government of Carolina and that of the American Revolution.[75]

Swain boosted the society's reputation, and perhaps its membership, by the magazine's publication of Bishop Ives' "Introductory Lecture" at the Society's meeting. The Swain imprint is evidenced in a segment entitled "Stray Leaves of History," for example, and in an anonymous article signed only "XY," but likely his.[76] Nothing changed when the magazine resumed publication in 1853 after a seven-year hiatus. History material remained predominant. "Life and Character of . . ." articles were common. Swain himself wrote several articles, among them "British Invasion of North Carolina in 1776," "War of the Regulation," "Life and Letters of Cornelius Harnett," and "Life and Letters of Whitmell Hill." The articles are extensive; they display considerable research and knowledge, but generally cite few, if any, sources.

The magazine was a vehicle for Swain's solicitation of materials for the society: books, newspapers, and manuscripts. It also published letters from Swain to historians elsewhere that vividly demonstrate his wide-ranging aspirations for his historical endeavors. Publication of his 1856 letter to Governor Thomas Bragg detailed for a wider audience his role as state historical agent.[77]

One magazine item shows Swain soliciting historical information when motivated by charitable concerns. The historical subject was the "revolutionary services" of General John Ashe. Pure history was not the purpose, however, but rather to aid the general's destitute daughter who "demanded relief." Official duties and a family situation prohibited Swain from undertaking the war-pension claims task. His request for assistance, though, was made with "much zeal and kindness," and to the recipient it was a "pleasing task," one in which he could "engage with ardor," to subserve "the [ben]evolent purpose of Gov. Swain."[78]

Another item shows sensitivity on Swain's part rather remarkable for his time, especially when considered in light of his support as governor for removal of the western North Carolina Indian population. In a "Historical Sketch of the Indian War of 1776," he presented, prophetically, this moral issue: "Yet that question will arise—'Had we a right to force the poor occupants from their possessions and appropriate them to ourselves?' Human nature may be ever too cowardly to interpose an objection to the titles acquired by our fathers; but the time will come, when retributive justice will plead the Indian's course with more than an angel's eloquence, and with greater success than is ever witnessed in earthly tribunals."[79]

Swain obtained considerable affirmation from the magazine. Requests to receive it pleased him. A possessor of volumes one and three offered any price within reason for volume two. The public, he said, credited Swain for "[t]he articles of a historical nature," which gave the magazine great value. The opinion was not solely his; rather, it was "general among my acquaintances here."[80]

Matters from Swain's past found their way into its pages. An issue carried his exchange while governor with Alexander Hamilton's son John, covering matters of North Carolina history and demography. Everything "emanating from the pen of the Governor" contained much useful information, wrote a newspaper, as it postponed publication of his magazine article on the "War of the Regulation."[81]

Material tendered for publication was forthcoming. A reader offered "the original proceedings of the meeting for founding and locating the university," matter, he intimated, "which would make a good article for the Magazine." Another insisted on Swain's reading of an item, requesting prepublication suggestions "to make it appear as well as possible." He would gladly have resigned his subject altogether to Swain, who would have been "so much more able to do it justice."[82]

Editors of the magazine recognized and acknowledged their indebtedness to Swain. When publishing one of his articles, they predicted its reading by "every Carolinian who wishes to be informed concerning the revolutionary era." Mindful of the limitations Swain's academic duties imposed on him, they craved "some historian who devote [sic] his time and talents more sedulously to the important task of rescuing some of the events and some of the names of . . . revolutionary heroes and statesmen from the temporary oblivion that enshrouds them." To satisfy, partially, their debt to Swain, the editors named a prize for him. It was awarded to the student, editors excluded, who contributed the best article during a collegiate year. The recipient had a choice, a medal, or money for "the purchase of valuable books."[83]

One magazine matter proved difficult, even embarrassing, for Swain. He advised William A. Graham that he had prepared Graham's father's Revolutionary War manuscript for magazine publication. The manuscripts were in no fit state for publication, Graham soon responded. If Swain desired to publish them, Graham insisted, "they must be recast, with some attention to grammatical propriety." His father had not written them with publication in mind, Graham told his friend.

Swain responded that he seemed to favor the father's style more than Graham did. "It will compare favorably with the most accurate portions of the two volumes of Moultrie," Swain stated, referring to the Revolutionary War general from Charleston. Still, "the numerous and glaring typographical blunders" in the October issue portion concerned him. Swain blamed the printer but found them "wholly without excuse." Careful "to guard against fire and other accidents," Swain was anxious to place the whole in print. The manuscript apparently had been lost; and had it not been recovered, Swain opined, "some of the most interesting facts in our history would have forever eluded research."

In a few weeks Swain informed Graham that the manuscripts had been copied and corrected "for the press." The need now was a competent editor, one familiar with the names of the persons and places to which they related. Graham had sent corrections for the article, he replied, and would "cheerfully examine and correct the remaining papers of the series," but needed the originals to do so. Problems persisted, however. Graham's next missive complained that "the typography is so wretchedly mean and insignificant that . . . it will bring discredit on anything appearing in it." There were other serious production problems. He had returned the paper to the printer "calling these things to his notice," but lacked confidence that he could improve it.

Swain was apologetic. "I am very sorry to hear that [the printer] is not taking more pains with the forthcoming number of the Mag," he told his friend, "I hoped that the intimations which I made to him upon the subject while in Raleigh would have produced some effect." He remained excited about the publication, however. In the February, March, and April numbers, he said, the manuscript would "occupy the space ordinarily appropriated to history." Upon receipt of the April issue, Graham thanked Swain, but still groused. "The printed article wants much correction to make it readable," he said, "and I think there may be some mistake of names." He now feared that they were "wearying the readers."[84]

CHAPTER 18

More Courting Clio
"An ardent delver in the rich mines of American history"

Considered in the context of the long, durable Swain-Graham partnership on matters of history, the discomfiture over the magazine article was a trivial flap. Swain had barely completed the transition from governor's office to university campus when he broached with Graham a subject first raised in Swain's time as governor: securing the Archibald D. Murphey papers. They were in Graham's care, Swain understood: Was Graham authorized to sell them, and if so, at what price? The Revolutionary War, a predominant topic in the Swain-Graham dialogue, entered this early missive. George Bancroft, Swain reported, had sent Swain his early chapters on the history of the Carolinas. Graham could perhaps offer Bancroft useful suggestions. Swain also sought Graham's aid regarding a catalogue of the university's graduates who had received "literary distinctions."[1]

The partnership flourished during Graham's 1845–1849 tenure in the governor's office. The old aspiration of securing the Murphey papers resurfaced during his first year there. Graham had hoped to see the papers on a visit to Hillsboro; the possessor, however, had been "absent on his canvas for the clerkship." When Swain later obtained "a portion, possibly all," of the collection, he was disappointed. It proved neither as extensive nor as valuable as he had hoped.

A diminution of expectations notwithstanding, Swain avidly detailed the collection contents. Murphey, he had discovered, had been "the last depository of the long lost papers of Gov. [Abner] Nash." These had been "put up in separate bundles, with labels in Judge Murphey's hand writing." There was a considerable bundle obtained from Governor Samuel Johnston and Judge James Iredell. A "little tract" by Maurice Moore, father of U.S. Supreme Court Justice Alfred Moore, denied the right of the mother country to tax the American colonies. There was a letter in relation to the Mecklenburg Declaration of Independence, about which Swain found "no paper reflecting new light on the subject."[2]

Swain forwarded to Graham a memorandum in Governor Richard Caswell's handwriting which, Swain surmised, "show[ed] very clearly where his papers ought to be." Where they actually were, he suspected, was "by no means so certain." Graham's review convinced him that it was written at the close of Caswell's second administration. He could perhaps find "the whole budget" from that time, he thought, "unless they [sic] were destroyed in the [1831] burning of the capitol." A "P.S." informed Swain that the secretary of state had brought Graham several bundles of Caswell's letters, labeled as stated in the memo, embracing the years 1777–1778.[3]

Governor Thomas Burke's papers were among those the General Assembly had asked Graham to collect. Swain could advise that they were in his possession and "in good order." Graham had the right, Swain thought, to consider them public property and to take them when he wished. Graham thus could advise Burke's daughter that Swain's "researches upon this subject have been quite extensive"; the papers, he said, would "sustain the character of the author for ability, patriotism, and scholarship." As to Swain, Graham would be glad to have his aid in editing the letter books, especially those of Burke.

Soon Graham advised Swain that he had found in Caswell's writings a series of letters from Burke as a state delegate to the Continental Congress, reporting the progress of events and transmitting reports of the congressional debates. They were more elaborate than anything else Graham had seen from Burke's pen and evinced "a right-mindedness, high spirit, and patriotism, surpassed by no member of that body." They also displayed considerable political wisdom and knowledge of the philosophy of government. Burke's letters would be copied in Caswell's correspondence. Graham would, he promised Swain, examine the files of 1782 for further Burke messages as well as for "the resolution of request to John Adams for his views on the form of Government."[4]

The men's history topic exchanges demonstrate the wide range of their interests. Swain once gave Graham a detailed history of paper currency and the monetary system. The treatise is dense for the average reader, but it displays Swain functioning at a high level of scholarship. Graham was curious about the location of "the old sword of State." Swain developed a list of presidents and their college degrees, earned and honorary; he omitted only William Henry Harrison who, he told Graham, "is not known to have been thus distinguished." Graham was, Swain thought, the proper person to examine a manuscript on the history of the

Presbyterian Church in North Carolina.⁵ Swain aptly captured the enthusiasm they shared for all matters historical when he said to Graham, "Everything throws light upon everything."⁶

Post-Graham's governorship, the Swain-Graham history collaboration continued unabated. When *University Magazine* editors wanted a sketch of Archibald Murphey, Swain advised that Graham was the only person for the task; he also recommended publication of a Graham address to the Historical Society of New York, his term for what was likely the New-York Historical Society. When Graham desired the *Journal of the Board of War* (Revolutionary, presumably), within a week Swain had obtained it for him, with accompanying correspondence. Could Swain give him an account of an expedition against the Tories in Cape Fear in 1781, Graham once asked, complaining of "the want of convenient references in my isolated situation here [Hillsboro]."⁷

Judge Duncan Cameron's death prompted Graham to suggest a Cameron biography with Swain as author. In response Swain essentially acknowledged his penmanship of Cameron's obituary but said nothing more. The death of another North Carolinian, prominent attorney and officeholder George E. Badger, found Graham preparing the memorial, with Swain's assistance.⁸

This more contemporary history was secondary, however, to that of the Revolutionary War period and the North Carolina leaders of that era. Swain would tell Graham that he possessed Governor Caswell's Letter Books, and they were subject to Graham's order. He had also found Governor Burke's Letter Books. Swain and Graham were contributing to a forthcoming book, Swain a chapter on the British invasion of 1776, Graham one on the British invasion "of 1780, '81."⁹

A manuscript of the "closing scenes of the Revolution" was the subject of a Graham request to Swain. Previously, he had sent Swain "the copy of revolutionary narrative ... commencing with the retreat of the British from Charlotte, and ending with Morgan's safe retreat across the Yadkin." If Graham desired, Swain would send him a long letter from General William Lenoir "containing his reminiscences of the Battle of Kings Mountain."¹⁰

When Graham was asked to introduce a volume of his father's papers, he turned to Swain for suggestions. When Swain desired information on extortion indictments against Edmund Fanning brought in 1768 and tried in Orange Superior Court, he turned to Graham for research assistance. In commenting on a Graham speech, Swain critiqued him on a matter of English history: "Your reference to the 'merrie monarch'—Charles the second, instead of the *moody* James the second, as occupying the throne during the perpetuation of the judicial butcheries of Jefferies," he told his friend, "is erroneous."¹¹

In one Swain-to-Graham missive, Swain mused philosophically on history. Written early in the Civil War, it details the North Carolina system of taxation at the commencement of the Revolutionary War and immediately following. It was history for admonition, not merely information or entertainment. "Our fathers," Swain wrote, "learned many things in the school of experience during the revolution of '76, by which they profited *for a time*, and from which we ought to profit now." "No error was committed then," he continued, "that we have not committed within the last nine months [i.e., since the outbreak of the Civil War], or do not promise to commit very soon." His conclusion: "History is philosophy teaching by example, but her teachings, if they cost less, are rarely heeded in time."[12]

Shared historical interests spawned a similar bond between Swain and Wilmington's Griffith J. McRee. Family lore had steered McRee toward broader historical concerns. He had, McRee informed Swain, been amusing himself with an old ledger containing letters from his great-grandfather, a large merchant at the commencement of the Revolutionary War. "I know that you take a deep interest in the early history of the State," he told Swain, "and take the liberty of sending you some extracts from the letters." They might, McRee thought, shed some light on the early history of the state and the spirit of its people. Swain examined the letters with keen interest. They sustained Wilmington's reputation for early and ardent patriotism, he responded, and evidenced intellectual vigor and disinterested dedication to the principles of the Revolution. Swain would be interested in similar papers that came into McRee's possession. If "odd numbers" of the *Cape Fear Mercury* from the revolutionary period could be found, this too would be a "most interesting circumstance."[13]

Later McRee forwarded a commission to a great-grandfather who had participated in General Braddock's sufferings and defeat. Swain's letter of thanks lamented his inability to determine whether North Carolina had supplied troops for Braddock's army; a contemplated visit to Raleigh, however, might reveal records in the public offices that would "reflect light upon the subject." He was, Swain informed McRee, "succeeding quite as well as I at any time ventured to anticipate in collecting materials for history, and organizing a cabinet for the Historical Society of the university."

Among the acquisitions of which Swain boasted were the papers of the late General John Steele of Salisbury, whose 1789–1815 correspondence afforded "much valuable information in relation to that most interesting portion of our history." From the national level there were "letters from the elder Adams, Jefferson, Madison, Hamilton, Wolcott, Gallatin and others of other states, besides a voluminous correspondence with Davie, Macon . . . and many other leading men of our new state." "[A] very interesting collection of papers" had come from the daughter of Governor Burke.

Another source had provided a "most interesting relic," Lord Cornwallis's original Order Book showing daily marches and campsites on his 1781 expedition through the state, an item Swain longed to exhibit to McRee. McRee's region, Swain thought, contained similar Revolutionary period items Swain desired for the Historical Society, among them letters to the late General Lillington from Generals Washington, Greene, and others.[14]

A small volume relating to the "Regulator," in the handwriting of Governor John Owen's father-in-law, came to Swain courtesy of McRee. There were also "some old files" of North Carolina newspapers, one dating to 1788. From them Swain was to secure desired information "relative to the Cape Fear," and then to return them. With the returned files Swain included letters from Governor Burke's papers, some of which McRee would, Swain believed, read "with great interest." If obtained, an Order Book Swain desired was to be sent with these letters, when returned, "enveloped carefully together [and] sent to me by Mr. J. Iredell, Jr. [actually, the third] when he returns to college."

Swain informed McRee that the current governor, John Motley Morehead, had recently recommended completing the series of Letter Books in the Executive Department, from 1782 to the present, by procuring and placing on record the correspondence of the Revolutionary period. Governor Graham, Swain thought, would be well qualified to select and arrange the papers that should be recorded, which were "really public property."[15]

When McRee wrote a brief history of Wilmington, Swain read the manuscript carefully and, per McRee's request, secured a second reader, who suggested publication in the *University Magazine*. Publication would, Swain presumed, "communicate needed and most interesting information to the citizens of Wilmington and probably have the effect of calling forth similar histories of our other principal cities." Initial publication in the *Wilmington Chronicle*, Swain thought, might induce contributions of additional information for a revised and enlarged edition. If McRee concurred, Swain would return the manuscript for that purpose. McRee had no objection to *Chronicle* publication.[16]

Swain's communications to McRee demonstrate his passion for historical accuracy and detail. When McRee indicated that letters in his possession confirmed "the Mecklenburg Proceedings" and the Edenton Tea Party, and contained brief histories of all the Tories, Swain sought "more definite information." The Iredell and Johnston papers, he thought, might contain certain material information "which has not fallen within the range of my researches." He wanted the precise date and locale of the settlement in the County of Albemarle and the first permanent settlement upon the Cape Fear. The former he hoped to determine from public records in Richmond; could McRee aid him with the latter? McRee, in turn, acknowledging Swain as the state's expert on the subject, peppered him with questions on the Revolutionary period.[17]

Swain was the more didactic member in this dialogue. He once commended McRee for receiving criticism kindly. Swain deemed this "evidence not merely of amiable feeling, but good sense." That encomium preceded a rather severe critique of a McRee treatise on the Revolutionary War Battle of Moore's Creek.[18]

In 1857–1858, McRee edited and published two volumes of the papers of James Iredell, his wife's grandfather, a George Washington appointee to the original U.S. Supreme Court.[19] Family glorification was a byproduct, however, not McRee's principal purpose. Tensions between the North and the South were escalating toward civil war. McRee's goal was to convince citizens of both regions that North Carolina and the South, like the New England states and the North, had produced great men of the Revolutionary period. Among other things, he told Swain, he would show that Iredell was the first U.S. expositor of judicial review, that he "anticipat[ed] the remarks of Marshall in Marbury vs. Madison."[20]

Swain was a regular McRee correspondent, sounding board, and adviser. Indeed, he furnished McRee with some of the original Iredell papers. They were probably a product of his University Historical Society collection efforts. Early in the endeavor Swain informed McRee that he had delayed a reply to McRee's last letter, hoping "to find a safe opportunity for the transmission of the Iredell and Johnston papers." "They will fill a small trunk," Swain informed him.[21]

Transmittal of the letters consumed more than a year. McRee ultimately requested that they be sent "by Express." They would be carefully processed and returned. If he did not publish what he wrote, Swain's historical society would get the manuscript. Several weeks later McRee altered his instructions. Send the Iredell-Johnston correspondence to Charles E. Johnson of Raleigh (husband of another Iredell granddaughter), he instructed, confident that Johnson would take care of it and see that it was transmitted to him carefully. The collection was larger than he had supposed, McRee acknowledged. When added to "the very full material at Raleigh," it would furnish "matter for two good sized volumes—too much for the pages of the *University Magazine*." Still, he would "solicit [Swain's] attention."

McRee now had a greater appreciation of his subject, so much so that he proposed "as far as practicable to let the correspondence tell the tale." Iredell's addresses to grand juries had so impressed him that he would design their publication "in illustration of his talent." An Iredell speech shed light on his dissenting opinion in *Chisholm v. Georgia*, McRee said, which "sets him forth as the first authoritative expounder of the doctrine of States Rights (Sovereignty of the States)[,] ... the sole hope of the South for the future."

Swain responded, sending via Johnson a small trunk containing the papers, with confidence that McRee would properly care for them. McRee acknowledged receipt, complaining of Iredell's handwriting, but reinforced in his exalted opinion of his subject. The letters, he opined to Swain, "indicate a degree of cultivation far beyond my conceptions."

McRee proposed to publish the greater part of them, and thereby to "contribute most to the honor of North Carolina."[22] These sentiments pleased Swain. He delighted in McRee's concurrence "that the collection was the finest specimen of revolutionary literature that had fallen under [his] observation."

Swain was "much gratified" by "the zeal and success" in McRee's entry upon his labors. While "such enterprises" had not been well received in North Carolina, in this case Swain "venture[d] to anticipate auspicious results." Readers from beyond North Carolina would be drawn to the work by "[t]he extent and character of the materials..., the interesting period of state history which they seem to illustrate," and the newly revealed biographical subjects. Volunteering "to have a pass at" McRee's manuscript, Swain also offered to aid in his research. He needed to ascertain the nature and extent of the materials available "upon the Cape Fear," and he projected a visit "with a view to examine your collections, and those of your Hist[orical] Soc[iety]." McRee pledged to communicate to Swain everything in his possession.[23]

McRee soon availed himself of Swain's offer, tendering numerous questions about the history of the Revolutionary period. He was apologetic when he did so again. "You must pardon the trouble I give you," McRee stated. He could not afford to visit Raleigh and trusted Swain's knowledge to relieve him of that need. He expected to "go North next week" to publish his first volume.[24]

Swain was responsive, on one occasion referring McRee to John Hill Wheeler's *Historical Sketches of North Carolina* for information on Iredell's tenure as North Carolina attorney general. McRee detailed publication decisions for Swain, who was pleased that Appleton in New York would be the publisher. This would "present the book to the public in a dress worthy of the subject."[25]

Early in 1857, McRee still could not say when his first volume would appear; indeed, the second would be ready for the press before the first was issued. Swain regretted that subscriptions were lagging; perhaps, he suggested, McRee should use Francis Lister Hawks's agents. He thought it unlikely that the General Assembly would "do a great deal of good." By March the work was completed but sales potential was such that McRee would absorb losses.

He would withhold publication of volume two until he felt "able to encounter additional loss." At the first opportunity Swain's papers would be returned.[26]

Swain at long last found himself examining McRee's first volume. McRee had, Swain said, produced "a very valuable and interesting work and a most important contribution to our historical literature." "[A] spice of candid but not unkind criticism" tempered the praise. Analysis of the partisan divide of Iredell's time followed, implicitly suggesting an omission on McRee's part. McRee was also wrong, in Swain's estimation, about the date on which Abner Nash had succeeded Richard Caswell as governor. Swain appraised Iredell, however, as "not merely able and learned but a gentleman of singular pur[i]ty." He promised to "look with ... anxiety and expectation for your second volume."[27]

Perhaps mindful of his critique of volume one, Swain desired to see volume two before it went to press. But for his imminent departure for Raleigh, which precluded "time to look them up," he would have sent McRee letters from Judge Howard to Judge Iredell purportedly in the Richard Henderson papers. It was too late, however. The second volume was in the press, McRee advised: "480 pages have been printed." Otherwise, he would gladly have availed himself of Swain's counsel. While he would have preferred Swain's prepublication examination, he did not "think that there are any statements in the volume about which you and I are likely to disagree." Apparently there had been intimations, perhaps by Swain, of involvement by James Johnston, Samuel Johnston's son. McRee denied this. He alone was responsible and should be blamed for the work's faults and credited for its merit.[28]

Swain solicited, and McRee pledged, cooperation in securing historical materials. He once told McRee he hoped "to secure your cooperation to as great an extent as your convenience may admit." Both before and after this request, McRee indeed cooperated. He once sent Swain a small pamphlet for the historical society "because I wish it submitted to your inspection." "If I can at any period influence the destination of the [Iredell] papers," he promised Swain, "I will do so for your Historical Society." "When I have completed my work," he continued, "I think ... you will have everything of interest." More generally, McRee promised that "[a]s far as I can I will aid in your collection of historical materials." Certainly, if anything "novel" came to him, he would place it at Swain's disposal.[29]

Francis Lister Hawks was another of Swain's colleagues in his North Carolina history endeavors. A native of New Bern and an 1815 UNC graduate, Hawks had studied law under William Gaston in New Bern and at the Tapping Reeve Law

School in Litchfield, Connecticut. In 1826 he left the legal profession to study for the ministry. For the remainder of his life, he served churches and seminaries, mostly in the North. He never forgot his native state, however, and devoted considerable attention to its history and the preservation of it.[30]

At least as early as 1848 Swain knew Hawks was working on a history of the state. Their collaboration on it appears to have originated in a disagreement. In 1852, Hawks forwarded to Governor Graham a paper he had delivered to the New-York Historical Society. The address had been provoked by historian George Bancroft's disparagement of North Carolina, "especially with reference to the Mecklenburg proceedings." Bancroft, Hawks said, had "made free use to me of Gov'r Swain as his authority." "Now I know the grounds of the Gov.'s opinion," Hawks continued, "and I further *know* he is mistaken, as I will show hereafter, if I live." He would soon write to Swain, he promised Graham, "and ere long go to see him on this very subject." If Mecklenburg made no declaration other than that of "May 30, 1775 [*sic*, "31" is the correct date]," Hawks said, she made no declaration of independence at all, "for *that* is not one."

Hawks soon asked Swain to meet him in Raleigh for an interview and to bring an old map of the state he had once shown him. A lengthy collaboration between the two men on North Carolina and its history had commenced, one in which Hawks came to consider Swain essential to his endeavors. Hawks soon volunteered to lecture at the university, apparently in an attempt to integrate Swain more thoroughly into his efforts. Swain's "approbation and countenance" was, Hawks said, "indispensable," and he wanted Swain's views. "I must devise some plan of being in North Carolina and near *you*," Hawks wrote in seeming desperation, "if I am ever to finish the history of the State. If I cannot be near you and the materials I shall abandon the undertaking."[31]

When Swain was again designated the state historical agent, Hawks rejoiced. The North Carolina story would not be complete, he said, without the documents in the Colonial Office in London. Descendants of the Lords Proprietors also should possess "much of value." Only an agent familiar with the state's known history, however, could "do us much good." It was beneficial, then, "that the work is committed, to your hands." Together, Hawks thought, they could "make a true history of N. Carolina."[32] A *Raleigh Register* statement that Swain was writing, or about to write, the history of the state upset Hawks. He had thought the work would be a joint effort and that "the world should know it." If Swain was on a solitary endeavor, Hawks needed to know, as it would materially alter his plans and purpose.[33]

A Swain response has not been found. Hawks, apparently satisfied there was no competing endeavor, continued to ply Swain with information about his. He had a large volume of documents, primarily regarding the Episcopal Church in North Carolina and other Christian denominations. He would add copies of these "to the stores of the Historical Society of the University." Ultimately, he wanted the society to own his library of books on America, which was considered one of the most valuable libraries of American history in the United States. He could not afford to give it away, however, and thought $5,000 a low estimate of its value.

The *Weekly Raleigh Register* of April 29, 1857, announced publication of the first volume of Hawks's *History of North Carolina*. Hawks thanked Swain for his "kind letter about the first volume." Swain told Governor Graham he was very impressed with it. It gave "more evidence of painstaking research," he said, "than any of his friends generally ventured to anticipate. I know of [no] introduction to the history of a single State, so prepossessing and imposing." Another reviewer was less favorable; he wished Swain or George Badger "had undertaken the office performed by Dr. Hawks" because Hawks had made "glaring misrepresentations."[34]

Hawks was at work on the second volume. He would come to Chapel Hill to examine materials and would favor Swain with a fragment of the manuscript. Hawks hoped his "minute research" would be more apparent in the second volume than in the first. His desire was "to get at the truth," but, he said to Swain, "I cannot tell you how much I rely on *you*." The work would be their "joint production, and I mean the world shall know it to be so."[35] As he neared completion, he told Swain the volume would soon be "ready for your revision." He resolved against sending it chapter by chapter: better to have "the whole field ... before you at once," he said. It contained a great deal that would be "perfectly new to our countrymen in general," and three-fourths of it was "founded on unprinted documents." Following Swain's promised aid and revision, it would be "a very full and authentic, and in some particulars, novel history of North Carolina under the proprietary government, as far as that history is now known."[36]

Hawks now suffered a sinking spell. He was, he told Swain, very tired. "I must find a less laborious field of labour or die," he lamented. He was collecting materials for a third volume. It was, however, "utterly *impossible* to write it properly out of North Carolina," and finances were a consideration. He wished the state would pay him for the work, but he would not have his "countrymen think me selfish, interested or mercenary."

Against his inclination and wishes, Hawks soon considered writing no more. It would be better to leave the remainder untold than to tell it defectively. Unless he could spend at least half his time in Carolina, he preferred to abandon the project. His native state, he thought, had little interest in his labors for it. With

Swain's help, however, he might tell the story rightly. So, what about a position for him at the University of North Carolina "in subordination to you as president," he asked?[37]

Swain refused to countenance Hawks's negativity. Hawks was mistaken, he assured him, if he thought a general desire for completion of his history was lacking. No one else would curry greater favor for a similar undertaking. The state was "sluggish," as Hawks well knew, and could not be expected "except in great emergencies [to] be incited to prompt action." Hawks needed state patronage to enable him "to spend a considerable portion of your time among us," and Swain would exert every reasonable effort "to further your designs." Swain had conferred with Professor Charles Phillips; if a plan could be devised to compensate Hawks sufficiently "without involving the trustees in difficulties with the other Professors," it would have Phillips's "full concurrence." Swain had to inform Hawks, however, that Governor Graham thought his propositions for a state documentary history, and an edition of the statutes at large, were more than the legislature would sanction. He did not share with Hawks Graham's conclusion that the public was "a little impatient of delay in the Doctor's work."[38]

E. J. Hale, Fayetteville publisher, sent Swain copies of Hawks's volume two. Hale, however, found sales disappointing. The loss on the first volume was around $600.00, and on the second, $1,400 to 1,500. Hale viewed with some hope Swain's suggestions "about the Common School Libraries" as sources of sales but doubted that they could apply to the legislature for financial assistance. Hawks, Hale feared, would be disappointed and cease his labors. He was "appalled at the labor before him, and fearful that he will not live to accomplish it." But, Hale thought, signs of appreciation would bring him to the work "with new zeal."[39]

Swain was more optimistic. He viewed the governor, Thomas Bragg, and his own friends in the General Assembly as "disposed to do all that I desire" in relation to the Swain-Hawks historical endeavors. The matter had been referred to an able joint select committee from each House, he informed Hawks. Governor Morehead, then in the House of Commons, was the chair; and Swain had no doubt about a favorable report. But for the extraordinary caution regarding appropriations that characterized the General Assembly, Swain would be sanguine of success in both houses.

Hale had the more realistic perspective. Morehead soon informed Swain that he too had thought there would be no difficulty "about passing the resolution relating to Hawks History." The bill, however, had been laid on the table "as quietly as if the thing had all been previously arranged." Thus "Democracy [i.e., the Democrats] is determined that the poor children of the State shall not learn the early History of the State while they are in the ascendant," Morehead complained.[40]

The Swain-Hawks memorial was an ambitious one, going well beyond financial assistance for Hawks's completed work. They had for some years, the two informed the assemblymen, been collecting and preserving all historic facts connected with the early settlement and progress of North Carolina "from the commencement of her political existence up to the present time." They had accumulated a large mass of written documents but had seen, with deep regret, that "many of our earlier archives have been injured by time, that portions of them are already illegible." Without prompt action, these soon would be lost.

They proposed publication by the state of a chronological series of the state's archives, which would form the "Documentary History of North Carolina." Materials would consist of all appropriate public records, all documents of public interest belonging to private families in the state, and documents in the public offices of England. Copies of a large body of the materials were already in this country in the possession of historian George Bancroft, former American minister to the Court of Saint James. Bancroft had offered the use of the materials on the sole condition that the state would print them as part of its documentary history. He also had offered to help obtain from the public offices in England copies of any documents omitted from his collection.

Publication and the appropriations could be spread over a period of years. The volumes would belong to the state, and any profits would go to the state. Several other states had done this, but none in the South. It would be nice if North Carolina could be the first in the South. The documentary history work would require editors with "a tolerably extensive knowledge of the history of the state in all its periods." If the General Assembly deemed the memorialists competent, they would do it gratuitously. They would also edit the statutes "on the conditions already named."[41]

Governor John W. Ellis soon communicated to the memorialists a legislative resolution requesting that they "edit and publish" two volumes of the "Documentary History of North Carolina or of the Statutes at Large" within the next two years. The edition would consist of not more than one thousand copies of each volume. There should be an understanding before the work was commenced; in particular, the cost of copying Bancroft's manuscripts should "be distinctly ascertained before any expense is incurred." To "keep as much of our money at home as we can," the book should be printed in North Carolina. Swain could perhaps select a young man from the university's senior class to undertake the work.

In a joint communication Swain and Hawks advised the governor that they were ready to begin and to proceed "until the whole is accomplished." They proposed to commence with the years 1748–1783, "a stirring period in our annals, most likely to be acceptable to our countrymen, many of whom are the direct descendants of the men whose doings they will read." They would then "present *finally* in chronological order every Document worth preserving in our history from *the first settlement of the State*." Brief historical annotations would be needed "for elucidating documents."

The governor found the plan "in all respects a proper one." He would rely on Swain's "well known business talents" for proper economy in relation to the work.[42] The governor was more than an approving bystander. He had found "a number of revolutionary papers" in the capitol and had transferred them to his office for preservation. He intended to have an index made and desired to know whether Swain, Hawks, or anyone had examined them and what suggestions they had regarding them.[43]

Hawks was eager to proceed once Swain was satisfied the state would comply with their conditions, including that they would publish "*all*, and not leave the work incomplete." His standards were high. He depended on Swain "to see that we can do something really valuable and creditable to the State and to ourselves"; neither of them "should be found doing a miserable piece of imperfect, fragmentary patch work."[44]

Shortly, however, the difficulty of doing a complete work became evident. Swain had charged Hawks with ascertaining the number of volumes Bancroft's manuscripts would probably make. "Can documents regarding our revolutionary struggle be condensed into two compact volumes?" he asked. Hardly, was the essence of Hawks's reply. Hawks had visited Bancroft, and they had concluded that Bancroft's manuscripts would "fill 8 vos. of 500 pages each." Further, they were "chronologically arranged and bound in many volumes." There was no reference to the geographical region to which the documents referred; this "would have to be culled out of numerous bound volumes." Bancroft thus "would have to destroy his volumes if he let us have his Carolina papers." They could not buy all his volumes even if he were willing to sell them. Despite the difficulties Bancroft would probably allow copying done at Hawks's study and "under my eye." He could employ a copyist at any moment if Swain thought it best.[45]

Limited further byplay occurred between these two protagonists. Hawks promised Swain a list of Bancroft's papers as soon as possible. When weeks passed and the list was not forthcoming, Swain inquired about it; he wondered too about Hawks's professed intention regarding commencement. Hawks responded that he had reviewed the documentary matter covering 1748–1783 and had a list ready for Swain. The material could comprise three to three-and-a-half volumes of five hundred pages each. Swain, for his part, was ready to "sit down to . . . the examination of your permanent index of the Bancroft MSS."[46]

The truth, however, is that the project was on a downward trajectory, largely on Hawks's account. The first indication was Hawks's confession of fear that "before we see the end, of which Harper's ferry was an overt demonstration of the beginning, the State will have need to husband her money for other purposes, than that of preserving her past history." The impending Civil War was depressing him. "It almost kills me," he continued, "to think she may be obliged to use it in making a bloody chapter in her future history."

Swain would soon express disappointment that Hawks had not visited him. If Swain had the promised index, he could determine the gaps in Bancroft's collections and ascertain other sources for them. He had purchased Governor Martin's manuscripts for the state but had found them neither as extensive nor as valuable as he had hoped. He would retain them, however, for Hawks's examination upon his expected visit. E. J. Hale, Hawks's publisher, informed Swain that he too received no response to his letters to Hawks. Hale thought Hawks "deeply mortified" by the failure of his *History*, and that it thus was doubtful whether he would write any more. Was Swain aware, Hale asked, that Hawks had lost a son-in-law two months earlier? When Swain complained to Hawks about his unresponsiveness, Hawks pleaded in mitigation the distraction of the horror of the Civil War.[47]

The correspondence conveys an impression that Hawks was both distracted and depressed from a confluence of personal and societal circumstances. The upshot was that the projected endeavor with Swain languished, and their documentary history never materialized. It was, as noted, an ambitious undertaking that perhaps would have faltered in any event; but without question, the Civil War was a considerable and compelling distraction to both men. The surviving records reveal no suggestion of a post-war attempt at revival of the project, and neither man lived sufficiently long after the war's end to have completed it. Hawks died in 1866, and Swain in 1868.

While it lasted, however, the collaboration was meaningful and important to both men, and Hawks's published work benefitted from Swain's input. Samuel Ashe's *Biographical History* calls Hawks's history of the state "invaluable" and accurately states that it "bears [Swain's] imprimatur."[48] Hawks himself was effusive and protracted in his assessment of Swain's contribution to his work, saying:

> To North Carolinians the author hardly need say that President Swain has rendered to him every assistance in his power; and such has been his de-

votion to the subject for years, that everyone knows such assistance could not but be valuable indeed.... When the author undertook his task, it was with the agreement between President Swain and himself, adopted at his own request, that his labors should undergo their joint critical supervision, in manuscript before being sent to the press. He has therefore now to announce to the reader that the book in his hands has undergone such revision, and if there be in it that which is erroneous in point of fact, it is because the authorities have misled the revisors. They believe the story to be true.[49]

John Hill Wheeler was another historian of North Carolina with whom Swain worked episodically. Born in Murfreesboro, North Carolina, Wheeler, like Swain, read law under Chief Justice John Louis Taylor. He received a master's degree from UNC in 1828 and held various state and federal offices and diplomatic posts. In 1844, Wheeler began efforts to obtain original documents relating to North Carolina history. In addition to Swain, he corresponded with historians George Bancroft and Peter Force. His *Historical Sketches of North Carolina*, published in 1851, was dedicated to the three of them. The dedication said of Swain that his "native worth, ... services and ... talents, are alike [the state's] pride and ornament." Wheeler's book was the first such publication to use a substantial body of original source materials from home and abroad and is regarded as having perpetuated more errors than any nineteenth-century history of the state. It is said that Swain once attempted to count the book's errors and put it down upon reaching the figure of one thousand.[50]

An early Wheeler-to-Swain missive enclosed copies of "the Colonial Indexes," one for Swain and three for the university. Wheeler had followed Swain's suggestion by preparing "short explanatory notes to show when the documents were ordered, by whom, and where from." The documents contained discrepancies, but he considered it his duty to publish them "*verbatim* and *literatim*." Wheeler was now "heavily employed" in preparing his "Sketches of the Bench and Bar of our State." Once he had "something worth seeing," he would visit Swain, from whom he hoped to have "much aid."[51]

Wheeler lamented his inability to acquire "the early dates of the members of the Legislature" due to the 1831 fire that destroyed the capitol and its library. Later, though, he thanked Swain for furnishing him the list from 1776 forward from papers in Swain's possession. He was writing about North Carolina's counties and wanted Swain's assistance regarding his native Buncombe. When he thought Swain would not go to England to procure the Colonial Documents, Wheeler offered his services for this purpose.[52]

Swain collaborated with Wheeler and Calvin H. Wiley, the first state superintendent of common schools, on their joint historical endeavors. He loaned them materials, requesting that they be "*carefully perused and returned to me.*" Tell Colonel Wheeler, Swain commanded Wiley, "that I placed Jacob Henry's speech in the hands of his nephew forthwith[,] who promised to send a copy by the present mail." Henry, the first Jewish member of the North Carolina House of Commons, had represented Carteret County in the 1808 and 1809 sessions. Wheeler was to secure unruled paper for Swain's use in printing circulars. Swain was, he assured Wiley, "at present entirely at your service."[53]

A perceived slight to, or plagiarism of, Wheeler's work prompted a quick retort from Swain. Historian Benson J. Lossing, with whom Swain had a correspondent relationship, published a sketch of Governor Richard Caswell, apparently drawn from Wheeler's *Sketches*, but omitted to acknowledge such. Wheeler, Professor James Phillips and Governor Graham informed Swain, had complained of the omission. The reason is not altogether clear, but Swain apparently perceived himself implicated in Wheeler's complaint and addressed the matter head-on. Lossing had applied to him for the piece, Swain acknowledged. Because Eleanor Swain was Caswell's granddaughter, however, he preferred that it come from someone else. Professor Fordyce Hubbard had then volunteered for the task. Among other sources Hubbard had drawn on material about Caswell in Swain's Governor's Letter Book, a source based on "careful research, into many unpublished papers." Swain thus indirectly was a source and apparently had been for Wheeler as well but was not responsible for Hubbard's failure to cite Wheeler.

Lossing's sketch of Caswell, Wheeler acknowledged, "gave me cause of complaint." Both he and Lossing, however, "acquitted [Swain] of all complaint." He had derived his material facts on Caswell from a William Gaston article in the *Raleigh Register*. It appears that Swain had called the article to Wheeler's attention, for Wheeler acknowledged Swain's liberality and kindness at the time. In any event he was happy to learn Swain had done what he could "to give credit to the proper source" and that it was Lossing's oversight that had deprived his work of proper mention.[54]

When Wheeler desired to contribute "a rare and valuable collection of books" on North Carolina history, he sought Swain's advice about the most appropriate recipient. Benson Lossing, Wheeler said, thought some of them very valuable. A copy of John Lawson's early history, in perfect condition, was not included, however. Wheeler would take Swain's advice about the proper repository and was glad to know their friendship was as vivid as ever.[55]

Wheeler also offered to procure the *Annals of Congress* for Swain's Historical

Society. Through his Washington connections, he could secure a complete set free of charge. When Swain expressed appreciation for the value of the annals, Wheeler was pleased. At his request U.S. Senator Thomas Clingman had designated a set for the Historical Society.⁵⁶

Early in the Civil War Wheeler remained focused on a manuscript regarding David Fanning, a Revolutionary period figure. Both Governor Morehead and George Bancroft had read it and found it interesting and authentic. At length Wheeler sent four copies to Swain, who would agree, he thought, that it was "a treasure trove to the annals of North Carolina history." It would, Wheeler hoped, stimulate Swain to make similar offerings to the "Historical Documents relating to the Old North State." From Governor Burke's papers Swain "might make a very interesting document."⁵⁷ If Swain replied, the response has not been found. Again, national events and their effects on his university rendered this a relatively unproductive time in Swain's life as a historian.

Wheeler, by contrast, stood ready to improve his *History*. His inspiration came from materials collected in England (a visit made at Swain's suggestion), his Fanning endeavor, and notes made from *University Magazine* material. In Wheeler's mind Swain remained critical to his endeavors. He would send his new materials to Swain "by the first safe hand," he said, and would be happy to submit his work to Swain before submitting it to "the Press." In a book published long after Swain's death, Wheeler graciously acknowledged that Swain had materially aided his efforts for history.⁵⁸

A Swain relationship with George Bancroft—prominent national historian, government official, and diplomat—has been noted. Early in his UNC tenure, Swain informed Governor Graham of "a protracted correspondence between Mr. Bancroft and myself on the subject of Am[erican] History." Upon formation of the University Historical Society, Swain sent Bancroft a copy of the introductory address. He also sent indexes to the Colonial Documents relating to North Carolina and proceedings of the Wilmington Committee to carry into effect the Articles of American Association.

"You do me but justice when you suppose that the most pressing demands upon my time will not lessen my fondness for historical inquiries," Bancroft, then secretary of the navy in Polk's cabinet, responded in his letter of thanks, "nor shall I fail to continue to collect valuable materials, in which you have already rendered me valuable assistance." Swain had asked of Bancroft names and addresses of secretaries of the historical societies in the United States. It was a request Bancroft could not fulfill; should he acquire the list from friends, however, he would send it.⁵⁹

While the U.S. ambassador to the Court of Saint James, Bancroft assured Swain that he had "spared no pains" in searching the British State Papers Office. The object was "a copy of the Resolves of the Committee of Mecklenburg," and he had met with "entire success." A history of their provenance followed. Bancroft enclosed for Swain a letter from Georgia Governor James Wright to the secretary of state dated June 20, 1775, containing the following statement: "By the enclosed Paper your Lordship will see the extraordinary Resolves of the people in Charlotte Town in Mecklenburg County; and I should not be surprised if the same should be done everywhere else." Bancroft was securing copies of letters relating to the Regulators, whom he considered "on many accounts important." He was always glad to hear from Swain and to be of service to him or his state.[60]

Both "for its intrinsic merit and as proof of your continuing friendship," Bancroft prized highly "the revolutionary incidents by Mr. Carruthers" Swain had sent him. He wished Swain to give his new volume "a searching critical perusal" and advise of any errors. Subsequently he informed Swain, probably in response to Swain's critique, that he intended to revise his chapter on early Carolina history to give it more definiteness. Swain had again sent him pamphlets, for which he was grateful.[61]

Questions regarding English history as North Carolina history background were among those Swain posed to Bancroft. Bancroft once pledged to communicate anything he might have on the Earl of Shaftesbury. Later he forwarded to Swain an extract of a letter received from the earl, who wished he could have discovered among his family papers "any documents relating to the states of N. and S. Carolina" but feared there were none. Bancroft also knew nothing of the family of James Henry Craig, he advised Swain. If Craig was a baronet, however, his name and a family account would be found in a volume of the English ancestry. Simultaneously Swain continued to send North Carolina history materials to Bancroft. Bancroft acknowledged receipt and would "read with great pleasure and instruction" the biographical sketch of North Carolina's first attorney general, Waightstill Avery, Swain had sent.[62]

When the *University Magazine*'s lead article was on the Revolutionary War Battle of Moore's Creek Bridge, Swain sent it to Bancroft. Other issues of the magazine came courtesy of Swain, together with a continuing flow of pamphlets. This became expected behavior on Swain's part. A Fayetteville correspondent once sent Swain two copies of a *Fayetteville Observer* article on the Battle of Moore's Creek Bridge. Swain, if he thought proper, was to forward one to Bancroft.[63]

Bancroft in turn sent Swain excerpts from the *Journals of Pennsylvania* "proving that Herman Husbands [*sic*] was a member of the Legislature, 1777–1778."

George Bancroft, Francis Lister Hawks, and John Hill Wheeler (left to right), prominent historians with whom Swain worked. Courtesy of Prints and Photographs Division, Library of Congress.

When Bancroft planned a trip to eastern North Carolina, he requested of Swain letters of introduction to New Bern, Beaufort, and Lafayette (Fayetteville). If Hawks was still with Swain, Swain was to bid him to send such letters as well.[64]

Swain's dealings with national historian Benson J. Lossing have also been noted. When Lossing's *Pictorial Field Book of the Revolution* was in the course of publication, he requested of Swain a brief sketch of the public life of Governor Richard Caswell. Lossing knew of Swain's interest in matters historical, had learned that he had married Caswell's granddaughter, and thought he would be "fully informed on the subject of [Caswell's] public career." Swain promptly forwarded the desired item, apparently, from Wheeler's just-published *Sketches*, together with an autograph letter, "a fair specimin [sic] of the style of [Caswell's] epistolary correspondence." He would be happy to be of further assistance.

A grateful Lossing promised return of the letter and, accepting Swain's offer, requested further favors. Could Swain find autographs of some or all who signed the Mecklenburg Resolutions "drawn up by Dr. Brevard"? The names might be attached to letters or documents in Swain's possession "or where you might readily lay your hands upon them." As a stranger he was asking a great deal, but Swain's "interest in historical matters" made Lossing feel that he "would gladly reciprocate."

Swain responded promptly. The only such autograph he had seen was that of Waightstill Avery. All signers were respected gentlemen and pure patriots, and a few were good scholars. Securing their autograph signatures was doubtful, however. If anyone could make such a collection, it was John H. Wheeler; Swain would ask Wheeler to write to Lossing. George Bancroft and William A. Graham were other potential sources. Graham, then secretary of the navy, was the grandson of John Davidson, one of the Mecklenburg signers, and the son of General Joseph Graham, "whose certificate is part of the State pamphlet in relation to the Mecklenburg Declaration." Not only could Graham supply "the autograph portrait" of his father, but there was "no North Carolinian more accurately acquainted with the history of the state, than he." Lossing should visit historic sites in the Charlotte area, including the birthplaces of Presidents Polk and Jackson. "Are you aware that Genl. Jacksons birth place is really in this State and not in S.C.?" Swain inquired.

He would welcome the Avery signature, Lossing responded. When he wrote Secretary Graham, he would use Swain's name. He hoped to secure more signatures through Swain's kindness in sending his letter to General Wheeler. The history of the Revolutionary struggle in the Carolinas had been neglected in the general histories notwithstanding, particularly in the Old North State, "patriotism as deep and abiding and as early and efficiently manifested as in Boston, the boasted 'Cradle of Liberty.'"[65]

Kindred spirits had found one another. Lossing soon took Swain's advice and contacted Secretary Graham; Swain wrote to Graham on Lossing's behalf. Swain continued to press on Lossing the North Carolina position on Andrew Jackson's birthplace. In a didactic mood, Swain assigned a reading list on the subject, adding that "after these are read and digested I will be glad if opportunity offers of at least half an hour conversation."[66]

Eventually Swain secured for Lossing the promised signatures of Waightstill Avery and John Davidson. Those of Colonel William Polk, his father Colonel Thomas Polk, and Governor Thomas Burke were added bonuses. Burke's, in particular, Swain forwarded with pride. "There is no one of our revolutionary heroes to whose memory so little justice, and so much gross injustice has been done as to him," Swain opined.

Swain also favored Lossing, as he had others, with the First Report of the University Historical Society and an invitation to lodge with him when visiting Chapel Hill to examine the university's collections. At that time Swain would undertake to extract himself from his official duties "to relate as much of N.C. history as you will be willing to hear." Further, he enclosed an endorsement of Lossing's *Pictorial Field Book of the Revolution* that Lossing could use as he wished. Although he had detected occasional errors, Swain found it the most interesting and accurate published history of the Revolution, "a really magnificent work which reflects very high credit on the author."[67]

Swain's critique of Lossing's work illustrates the care with which he approached the historian's task. With one exception, he was satisfied with the narrative. The exception was that Lossing spoke of Ezekiel Polk as a Mecklenburg delegate in 1775. Swain was by no means certain Polk was not a delegate. His name did not appear in the delegate list, however, and absent proof that he was, better to avoid any offense that would be given by the statement. Swain's influence prevailed. Lossing made the suggested correction, gratified that his work met Swain's approval. Swain's blessing, together with Bancroft's, satisfied him that he had "fairly stated facts." He thus could "not care a fig for censorious criticism."[68]

Lossing acquired an autograph letter of Henry Clay and promised it to Swain by the first safe conveyance. Swain thought Lossing, and perhaps Bancroft, would be interested in a *University Magazine* article entitled "Closing Scenes of the Revolution in North Carolina." Lossing was correct, Swain said, that the William Blount who was a Constitutional Convention delegate from North Carolina was the William Blount who was later governor of Tennessee and "expelled from the U.S. Senate in 1799." He continued greatly to like Lossing's book and hoped his vacation would permit a continuous evening of reading.[69]

When Lossing came South, Graham reported to Swain that he did it "in such haste, that he did not obtain full information on Historical subjects." "[T]here was too little care in getting his materials, authentic and reliable," said Graham, "and too much facility in adopting the ... objectionable facts of other writers who had preceded him." Perhaps for that reason Lossing soon admitted to Swain that he had made "a careless blunder."[70]

The South was an object of Lossing's concern when he published a history of the United States for schools and families. Southern people, he told Swain, had been taught by fanatics to be suspicious of all books published in the North, especially schoolbooks. The cause was a compulsion on the part of many writers "to say some impertinent word about slavery when the pen gets below 'Mason's and Dixon's Line.'" He, by contrast, tried to state facts and leave inferences to the reader. With this apologia, Lossing sought Swain's careful reading and his opinion of the book's merits. If Swain could confidently commend it, Lossing would be grateful, "for your voice in such a matter would be [powerful] below the Potomac and the Roanoke." Another impending enterprise of his would also benefit from any publicity Swain might choose to give it.

Swain received the volume, but pressing business allowed only a casual perusal. A more deliberate examination would follow during his western vacation in December. He had seen enough, however, to conclude that the teacher who executed Lossing's plan intelligently "will find his pupils acquiring systematic and accurate knowledge of the history of our country." It was the most comprehensive and accurate text Swain had reviewed, especially regarding the Revolution and the formation of the government. Southern readers would find events in their region accurately portrayed "to a degree very unusual in ordinary works of this kind."[71]

Sectional tensions were too intense for Lossing's book to escape them, however. When Lossing gratefully acknowledged Swain's commendation, and the notice of it Swain had placed in the *Southern Weekly Post*, he decried the work's reception in the North. An abolitionist newspaper in New York—edited by Henry Ward Beecher, Harriett Beecher Stowe, and others—had treated the book in general terms of commendation, only then to say it was "proslavery in its tendency." It warned parents and teachers against "such partisan publications." This was, to Lossing, "disgusting." The historian, he said to Swain, "has no business to impertinently thrust his own opinion forward. He should state historical *facts* according to the record and have the reader to form his own opinions." If the Union was destroyed, Lossing predicted, "it will be the work of *fanatics* of the North and the South."[72]

In a poignant note Lossing enclosed for Swain "a little volume from my pen" written as his wife was dying from uterine cancer. He, with Lyman Draper, was at work on the life of Daniel Boone. He and Draper had ascertained that Swain had, or was about to have, "the long- missing manuscripts of Colonel [Richard] Henderson of *Transylvania* notoriety." Could Swain procure a loan "of such papers as have a bearing upon Kentucky history, and especially what might illustrate any matter in the life of Boone?" If necessary, he would cheerfully pay to have them copied; it was important to have the substance of them for his Boone work.

Swain forwarded the paper, together with a copy of the *University Magazine* "containing Rev[olutionary] matter." He also sought for Lossing's work the aid of a Henderson grandson. The grandson referred the matter to the legal representative of his grandfather's executor, but he could find no papers. He would continue to seek them, and if merited, send them to Swain. "Your name," he told Swain, "would be guaranty sufficient that the book forthcoming will be *History* & its actors have full justice done them."[73]

Lossing was grateful when Swain's *University Magazine* took "very kind notice of my little volume of American biography." A point of censure in the review evoked his bitter protest, however. The reviewer had criticized Lossing's inclusion of "two colored women," Katy Ferguson (born enslaved, became a child welfare worker and school founder) and Phillis Wheatley (enslaved as a child, became a poet and first African American to publish a book). "Why not? if they are worthy," Lossing asked. He pitied "the man" who could not appreciate Ferguson's contributions and virtue; for a woman of Saxon blood with her accomplishments, the reviewer "would have been jubilant in her praises." Such destruction of "the sanctity of a human soul" grieved him deeply. The writer was unjust toward him, he said, "and cruel toward the memory of an eminently good woman." The reviewer, identified only as "C," had similarly considered Wheatley "beneath notice." Washington, however, had not, Lossing argued, as evidenced by a long and complimentary letter he wrote to her.

Swain's response, while refuting Lossing's charge of racism, nevertheless rings harsh in modern ears. He now revealed the reviewer's identity: Lossing's "acquaintance Miss Phillips, now Mrs. Cornelia A. Spencer of Clinton, Ala." She had penned it at Swain's request. Because she knew he would not approve, however, she had deviated from her usual practice of a pre-publication perusal by Swain. Spencer's objection, Swain said, lay in misogyny, not in the racism Lossing had perceived. "[H]er criticism was produced not by the circumstance that [Ferguson and Wheatley] were *women* of *colour*, but simply that they were women"—very good women indeed, in Spencer's view, but not possessing intellects that placed them "among the celebreties of the country."[74]

Swain and Lossing did not meet in person until the winter of 1865–1866. For many years previous, however, they had enjoyed and benefitted from what Lossing would call "a pleasant correspondence." In his last surviving letter to Swain, Lossing told him their correspondence had been pleasant and profitable to him, and he would ever remember the pleasant acquaintance.[75]

After Swain's death Lossing developed a magazine designed to be "a treasury of American historical, biographical and other matters of value that might otherwise be lost." Swain would have been interested in it, Lossing thought, "for he was alive to all such matters." Swain was, said Lossing, "an ardent delver in the rich mines of American history. No man ever worked those of his native State so industriously, patriotically and wisely as he; and when he was summoned to a higher sphere of life, he was about to arrange his collected treasures in proper form for use."[76]

CHAPTER 19

Clio: Yet More
"A passion for the antique"

AS NOTED, LYMAN DRAPER, historical collector and writer, was Lossing's companion in a work on Daniel Boone. Like Lossing, Draper looked to Swain as a resource. He sought, for example, a copy of any portrait of Colonel Richard Henderson in Swain's possession. He said, acknowledging Swain's expertise, "You will, I presume, be likely to know, whether any such portrait exists." Loss of the Henderson papers, once in Joseph Seawell Jones's possession, would, Draper feared, render his narrative devoid of interest.[1]

Earlier, when preparing a book on *Lives of the Pioneers,* Draper had searched for a history of the Franklin republic in East Tennessee, 1784–1788. On the recommendation of Congressman Thomas L. Clingman, he had turned to Swain, who was from the area "and had taken interest in such matters." "[C]ommunicate what light you possess," he urged Swain, and send any information regarding major figures that the published accounts omitted. Draper would be grateful for whatever material Swain could furnish him.[2]

Five years later, while Draper was grateful for Swain's earlier assistance, Jones remained the subject of his angst. The early settlement of Kentucky was Draper's current interest, and the Henderson papers "would be of great service." Leonard Henderson, late North Carolina chief justice, had confided the papers to Jones, who had noted them in his *Revolutionary Defence of North Carolina.* Draper's several letters to Jones had elicited a sole response, disclaiming possession of the papers. He had left them with a friend from whom he had become alienated, said Jones, and would cheerfully grant their benefit to Draper if he recovered them. If Swain could assist, he would be grateful and would gladly serve Swain in any possible way.[3]

In Draper's last known communication to Swain, he requested a copy of UNC Professor Fordyce Hubbard's paper on William R. Davie. The long interval in their correspondence had been, Draper said, "a painful one to every lover of his country." (The Civil War had intervened.) He had not ceased his historical labors; while he had published nothing, he hoped to publish again soon. Reconstruction politics then entered the conversation. "I, as a Northern Conservative," wrote Draper, "hope and pray that you Southern people may not come under negro dominion."[4]

For several years after Swain's death, Draper continued to draw on his historical collections. Eleanor Swain, Judge Battle, Governor Graham, and Cornelia Phillips Spencer were the facilitators. Graham once had a needed item, having "borrowed it from Gov. Swain in his lifetime." Draper also sought to complete his set of the *North Carolina University Magazine*, which, he stated, "contains valuable matter on the Revolutionary history of the two Carolinas—contributed largely by the late Gov. Swain."[5]

Among the topics of Swain's interaction with prominent historians was the much-disputed Mecklenburg Declaration of Independence, a subject on which "[t]he literature ... is voluminous enough to form a small library by itself."[6] Indeed, a new book on the subject was published as this chapter was in process.[7] To enlarge that small library, or attempt a resolution of the abiding debate, is beyond the scope of this endeavor. It must suffice to note that in his time Swain was an active participant in the controversy; that his was an evolving position over his lifetime; that he commenced as a believer, or at least a promoter, of the declaration's reality; and that he died a serious skeptic, perhaps even a confirmed nonbeliever.

The April 30, 1819, issue of the *Raleigh Register and North-Carolina Gazette* first printed the declaration, allegedly adopted by a convention of citizens in Charlotte on May 20, 1775. According to this account, the delegates declared that "a free and independent people ... are and of right ought to be a sovereign and self-governing association under the control of no other power than that of our God and the General Government of Congress." Captain James Jack dispatched the resolutions to the North Carolina delegates at the Continental Congress in Philadelphia; they commended the Mecklenburg citizens, but concluded that action toward independence was premature. The original record of the meeting was reportedly destroyed in a fire at the home of delegate John McKnitt Alexander in 1800.

An exchange between two leading patriots of the American Revolution fueled the disputation about the declaration's existence. On June 19, 1819, John Adams sent Thomas Jefferson a republication of the *Raleigh Register* article contained in the *Essex Register*, a Massachusetts paper. How could the declaration have been concealed from him so long, Adams asked? Had it been communicated to him at the time, "it would have been printed in every Whig News-paper upon this Continent." Over a year before Jefferson's 1776 declaration, Adams would have made "the Hall of Congress Echo and re-echo" with it and commented on it right up to July 4, 1776.

Jefferson, in response, was the quintessential skeptic. "[Y]ou seem to think it genuine," he told Adams, "I believe it spurious." The article appeals, he said, to a burnt original book of a deceased person; to a joint letter from several deceased North Carolina leaders; and to a letter to Hugh Williamson, "whose memory, now probably dead, did not recollect, in the history he has written of N. Carolina, this Gigantic step of it's county of Mecklenburg." Jefferson would be a nonbeliever, he vowed, "until positive and solemn proof of its authenticity shall be produced."

While the matter remained "an incomprehensible mystery" to Adams, he gave the declaration far more credence than did Jefferson. "Though Mr. Jefferson believes these Resolutions to be fabrications," Adams said, "yet it is impossible not to believe from the similarity of expressions in his Declaration of Independence that he had heard those words repeated in conversation though he had not seen the resolutions in form."[8]

In 1831, the state of North Carolina published an official response. The preface is thought to have been written by Swain at the request of Governor Montford Stokes. Although it is unsigned, it is very Swain-like, and he almost certainly was its author. If so, his initial commentary on the controversy unequivocally takes the prodeclaration side. Jefferson's reply to Adams, states the preface, imposed on the General Assembly the task of proving Jefferson mistaken. Without question, it says, the author of the Declaration of Independence was a man of ability, purity, and patriotism. His letter to Adams, however, "was written in haste, upon a very superficial and imperfect view of the subject."

William R. Davie's copy of the declaration, Swain (presumably) said, was now in the Executive Office of the State. There was other supporting evidence. Colonel William Polk, a man of ultimate credibility, still lived, and had heard his father proclaim the declaration to the assembled multitude. General Joseph Graham, father of William A. Graham, had been present in his youth, and his affirming letter would "be read with pleasure and perfect confidence throughout the wide range of his acquaintance." There was Captain Jack's certificate, which was made a part of the report, stating that the sentiments were publicly expressed from the courthouse door in Charlotte and read aloud in open court in Salisbury when Jack was en route to Philadelphia. Swain then reached a sweeping conclusion: "It is not hazarding too much to say, that there is no one event of the Rev[olution] which has been or can be more fully or clearly authenticated."⁹ Swain, it should be remembered, had then lived only thirty years and harbored youthful political ambitions. To have denied the Rip Van Winkle state's foremost claim to fame would have been immensely unpopular and perhaps politically suicidal.

Soon afterward, as a still youthful governor, Swain remained unequivocal in his support for the declaration. "[T]he *facts*" connected with the declaration, Swain said, were "correctly stated in a recent duo-decimo by J. S. Jones, entitled 'a vindication of the Revolutionary History of North Carolina, from the aspersions of Mr. Jefferson.'" Jones's treatise adamantly defended the declaration's existence and attributed Jefferson's denial of it to pride of authorship and jealousy. He perhaps drew on one of his correspondents, who called Jefferson "a greedy monopolizer of applause." The Mecklenburg delegates could never be forgiven, Jones posited, for preceding Jefferson's illustrious declaration by fully a year. With Adams's letter, in Jones's view, "[t]he altar and the god ... sunk together." By crediting Jones with correctly stating the "facts" regarding the declaration, Swain had again staked a prodeclaration position. [10]

On the declaration's sixtieth anniversary, May 20, 1835, Swain, in his last year as governor, attended the Mecklenburg celebration.[11] It is difficult to conceive of a governor present for such an occasion standing altogether silent. Assuming that he spoke, it is equally difficult to imagine words other than a ringing endorsement of the alleged patriotic stance under celebration. Again, at this time Swain still saw himself as a future U.S. senator or the holder of another high office, and a contrary position would have been immensely unpopular.

Four years later, in 1839, Swain, now president of the university, declined a Mecklenburg invitation to a public dinner "to celebrate the day becoming its patriotic recollections." He also spurned a similar invitation from citizens of Cabarrus County. The rejections in no way represented a lack of enthusiasm for the occasions, however. To the Cabarrus committee he wrote, "I admire the spirit with which the memory of the illustrious events of that day is cherished by your citizens; and no circumstance of mere ordinary inconvenience would prevent my uniting with you in the high festival."[12]

Five more years passed, and for the 1844 celebration Mecklenburg citizens sought a suitable speaker. "[T]he selection has fallen upon yourself," Swain was advised. The reason: "considerations growing out of the Connection of your life with the best improvements in the social condition of the State," and "[t]he zeal you have ever manifested in bringing to light the memorials of her revolutionary history and the station you now occupy and adorn at the head of our university." Unlike prior observances, this one had a purpose beyond celebration: to promote the Mecklenburg Monument Association, the goal of which was "to erect a monument in memory of the Mecklenburg Declaration."

Swain did not attend, but the event, "a joyous affair," had consequences for him. He was unanimously elected president of the Monument Association. In light of their zeal for the honor of the state and confidence in Swain's ability to advance their objective, his electors brooked no doubt of his acceptance. "Much ardour was manifested by the friends of the Monument," and $500.00 for it had already been raised.

The electors had correctly assessed Swain's sense of duty. He immediately embarked on the task, suggesting the upcoming July 4 as "a suitable occasion to brighten the remembrance of what was done on '20th of May, 1775.'" Solicitations should be made to the clergy and other learned professions. The cause, however, was "the cause of all freemen," and thus Swain urged it upon all alike. Other states had erected "proud and enduring memorials" to less significant events. If North Carolina persisted in its failure to erect this one, Swain said, it should have the "epithet of 'degenerate.'" [13]

Yet Swain clearly harbored residual doubts, for he was also searching for proof of the declaration's existence or other enlightening information regarding it. Among other efforts he deputized two Charlestonians as research assistants. One, while pessimistic about "finding any thing here that will interest or profit you," nevertheless pledged that "[a]ll our Libraries here shall be carefully ransacked for the class of documents which you wish to consult." Swain, he said, should let nothing discourage him. Thousands of North Carolinians, particularly descendants of the declaration's signers, awaited the results of his promising labors. The second Charlestonian advised Swain, with regret, that he had "failed in meeting with the original or entire publication of the Mecklenburg declaration of Independence." He had examined old papers in the Charleston Library and other sources. Inquiries to informed friends had proven unproductive.

A dissatisfied Swain requested further exploration but with the same result. He had again examined the old newspapers, said his correspondent, "but am sorry to say that I can find nothing editorial, explanatory, or commenting on the Mecklenburg revolutionary proceedings."[14] An 1845 circular letter from the Historical Society, almost certainly Swain's product, thus could only say, "It is yet to be ascertained whether the records of Mecklenburg, Cabarrus and Rowan [he could have added other places] do not contain important evidence with regard to the Mecklenburg Declaration of Independence."[15]

In an 1853 lecture to the Historical Society Swain again alluded to the declaration issue. He recited a history commencing with the 1819 *Raleigh Register* publication, which "first directed public attention to the Mecklenburg Declaration," and mentioned the Adams-Jefferson correspondence. He then made the following somewhat concessive statement: "The living positive witnesses who avouched the fact of the declaration, were numerous and respectable; but in the absence of written contemporaneous evidence, had there been no subsequent developments, the issue, out of North Carolina, would probably have been decided against us."

Perhaps to suggest that such written, contemporaneous evidence in fact existed, Swain then cited an August 8, 1775 proclamation by Governor Josiah Martin. Martin, it said, had seen an "infamous publication" in the *Cape Fear Mercury* "importing [sic] to be resolves" of Mecklenburg people "most traitorously declaring the entire dissolution of the laws, government and constitution of this country, and setting up a system of rule and regulation, repugnant to the laws and subversive of his Majesty's government, etc." Harvard historian Jared Sparks had then found in the State Paper Office in London an original letter from Governor Martin to Lord Dartmouth dated June 30, 1775. The letter referred to resolves of a committee of Mecklenburg which "surpass all the horrid and treasonable publications that the inflammatory spirits of the continent have yet produced." A copy of the letter, Martin said, had been sent by express to the Congress meeting in Philadelphia. Swain continued with a detailed revolutionary history but did not return to the declaration question and carefully avoided stating a firm opinion on it. The concession regarding out-of-state opinion showed some retreat from his adamant "pro" position of 1831, however. A Philadelphia reader of the address "trust[ed] that some day the newspaper, containing the Mecklenburg Declaration of Independence will turn up, wrapped round a bundle of continental money."[16]

This did not occur and still has not. But Swain and his co-laborers in Clio's vineyard were continually searching for the document and pertinent information regarding it. John H. Wheeler, for example, was "anxious to know whether there is any Declaration of Independence of the 20th May 75 on file in [Raleigh]." He was inclined to think not but believed Swain would know and would inform him. Later he feared it "cannot be found, nor even a copy."[17]

An exchange with Francis L. Hawks contains perhaps the clearest articulation of Swain's evolving skepticism. "I imagine few of [North Carolina's] sons have looked more into her history than you and I have," Hawks told Swain. For that reason, Hawks was always sorry to differ with Swain "on a question connected with the history of our dear old State." Clearly, though, they differed regarding the existence of the "Meck Dec," the subject of a Hawks lecture he was forwarding to Swain. Hawks knew Swain's views, he claimed, and had seen the grounds of Swain's conclusions.

Hawks found in George Bancroft a scapegoat for Swain's, in Hawks's opinion, misguided views. Bancroft, in Hawks's view, "was disposed to disparage [North Carolina] and do her wrong." Worse still, he invoked Swain as authority for his opinions; he "meant to shelter himself behind you," Hawks told Swain, "to make a Carolinian seem to disparage Carolina." Hawks clearly had little regard for Bancroft and feared he would take advantage of Swain unless Swain was on guard. "[Y]ou may find yourself in his volumes in a mode not quite agreeable to your feelings," Hawks cautioned his friend.

Swain read Hawks's lecture and expressed pleasure that he had expressed his views. Anticipating a promised visit from Hawks, Swain pledged to place before him all the evidence he had collected on the subject. A revealing sentence followed. "In the meantime," Swain said, "I will not conceal the conviction I feel that the authenticity of the paper... of the 20th remains to be established." Swain clearly wanted the account to be true. "I... will be almost as much gratified as yourself if you shall succeed in maintaining the affirmative," he told Hawks. But the evidence then at his command, as a careful historian, did not get him there.[18]

More than four years later Hawks was the speaker for the Mecklenburg celebration. An invitation to Swain to accompany him stated confidently, "I think I can *now* make the fact of the declaration of May 20 clearer than ever." The University Historical Society had invited Hawks to give an address during commencement week. He could accept, but it would require his giving the historical portion of what he had written "for the celebration of Charlotte." He had "new testimony" that would, he thought, "conclusively show a meeting held on the 19th and 20th and a declaration made substantially and indeed literally as we have seen it."[19] There is no evidence that Swain, the society's founder, accompanied Hawks to Charlotte, or that either man succeeded in moving the other to his point of view.

Bancroft's perceived villainy is not apparent from his correspondence with Swain that shortly followed Swain's with Hawks. Their relationship appears, rather, to be one of two honest seekers after truth, both desirous of documentary proof prior to staking a firm position. Noting a lengthy hiatus in their correspondence, Bancroft asked Swain, "Has any thing come to light to change the views so forcibly and clearly expressed by you in your letter to Mr. Lossing, of December 20, 1851?" In that letter, Swain had laid bare his skepticism about the declaration. "There may have been a meeting of the Committee on the 20th," he said, "and resolutions may have been adopted, but there is no evidence satisfactory to my mind, if it be so, that the papers purporting to be Mecklenburg declarations are true copies of the original record. If they be, where were they made and by whom?"[20]

In response to Bancroft, Swain lamented their inability "to have a personal conference... in relation to the Mecklenburg Resolutions and other topics in our revolutionary history." Although "very few," his discussions with Hawks had been "full," and he wished he could cover the same ground with Bancroft. He and Hawks, Swain said, were now "more nearly together in opinion." He then quoted Hawks (not clear, but apparently) as saying, "The documentary evidence in my possession satisfies me, that there was a meeting of the citizens of Mecklenburg at Charlotte on the 19th and 20th May 1775, and that resolutions in relation to independence were discussed and adopted." Bancroft understandably interpreted this as indicating Swain's concurrence in the Hawks view. "Pray send me," he responded, "an account of the *documentary evidence* on which you build your faith that there was a meeting at Charlotte town on the 19th and 20th, and that resolves were then adopted relating to independence." The documentary evidence known to him, he said, would not fix the date so exactly. Bancroft faced a publication deadline, so his request carried some urgency.

Swain's reply is brief, tepid, and inconclusive. No account, he conceded, fixed the date with certainty. A series of doggerel verses had recently come into his possession; with that exception, there were no papers with direct reference to the subject that predated September 1800, five months after the John McKnitt Alexander house fire in which the original declaration was supposedly destroyed. In a personal conference, with the papers before them, he could present the chain of facts and inferences that formed the basis of his conclusion. They were difficult to explicate in writing, however.[21]

Lossing had solicited the Swain letter to which Bancroft had referred. Bancroft had informed Lossing that in the old files of newspapers he had examined, he had found no notices of the resolutions of May 20, 1775. In the 1831 North Carolina pamphlet on the declaration, Lossing had perceived "discrepancy in the testimony of living witnesses, and evident error in their recollection of dates." He thus doubted "the genuineness of the resolutions purported to have been adopted on the 20th of May" for three reasons: (1) contemporary newspapers, so far as was known, made no allusion to them, but did publish those of May 31, known as the Mecklenburg Resolves; (2) the general testimony collected to substantiate the claims about May 20 applied also to those about May 31; and (3) the statements that the meeting occurred on May 20 were unreliable. He wanted Swain's opinion, however, not for publication, but to aid him "in arriving at a truthful conclusion upon a subject, which, to North Carolinians, is a delicate one."

Lossing thus found it gratifying when Swain agreed with him. Swain's position was, he said, "coincident with the only logical conclusion to which our mind could arrive." Swain soon claimed possession of a "good deal" of unshared information about the declaration that he would not share, absent a visit from Lossing. This incentive did not produce the desired visit, but Lossing continued their long-distance correspondence. He hoped, he told Swain, to find a copy of the resolution in the Hugh Williamson papers. The "Davie paper," if it was not, as Swain had stated, written after the 1800 fire that consumed the original documents, could also be most important, and perhaps conclusive, "in favor of the 19th and 20th of May." While Lossing could not visit Swain, he was pleased that Hawks could. When Swain and Hawks "canvas the matter," Lossing naively forecast, "truth is certain to be evolved by such attrition of inquiry and earnest minds."[22]

There were other national-level historians with whom Swain processed this subject. When Peter Force published a work containing the May 31 (not May 20) Mecklenburg Resolves, Swain inquired about his source and whether there was a copy of those resolutions his work had omitted. Force was to forward the information to Swain through Congressman D. M. Barringer, who represented the Mecklenburg district. After a friendly reminder from Congressman Barringer that he was to respond to Swain through him—Swain, importunately, had written Barringer twice on the subject—Force responded. He revealed two sources and noted that he had found no other copy. Swain later informed Force that after much search he had succeeded in locating "a perfect copy of the 20 Resolutions of the 31 May 1775." He made further inquiry regarding Force's sources and named other publications in which the resolutions could be found. He was now engaged to collect and arrange all obtainable evidence on the Mecklenburg Declaration, and he would communicate the results of his inquiries.[23]

Henry S. Randall authored a three-volume biography of Thomas Jefferson, published in 1858. Bancroft had sent Randall Swain's letters on the Mecklenburg Declaration, noting that he could not authorize Randall's use of them. Their use was not Randall's interest, however. The charges that Jefferson had plagiarized certain passages of the National Declaration of Independence from the Mecklenburg Declaration obviously were serious. If true, Randall said to Swain, "he was further guilty of writing a most false and dishonorable letter to John Adams on the subject in 1819." As Jefferson's authorized biographer, Randall could not "pass over such questions in silence." Randall, however, wished to treat the question "in a quiet and temperate tone," with due respect to North Carolina and its witnesses on the subject. It needed "a calm, simple, good tempered explanation," he said to Swain, and "[n]o North Carolinian can do this probably as authoritatively as yourself." The genuineness of the Alexander or Davie copies of the declaration was the issue. Any explanation Swain considered appropriate would be thankfully received and published in Randall's work. A "simple and popular" explanation would be acceptable; if that was not possible, could Randall use Swain's communications to Bancroft?

Swain demurred that his letters to Bancroft were hastily written and unworthy of incorporation in Randall's publication. They did not say anything, however, that he did not believe and the truth of which he could not prove. The Alexander copy was genuine but was not the record of the Mecklenburg Committee. That, unfortunately, had been destroyed in the Alexander house fire in 1800. The copy was a remembrance, not a record. Regrettably, Swain could not "with propriety, enter at present upon the preparation of such a paper as you desire."

Ultimately Randall decided not to use even the facts in Swain's letters to Bancroft. It was possible, he said, that Swain did not regard his "opinions as among that class of facts, which you expected one to use." Further, he was sensitive to political problems such publication might present for Swain. Swain was, after all, a North Carolinian, Randall said, and "you occupied your present position."[24]

In the text of his Jefferson biography Randall indeed treated the "Meck Dec" problem in rather summary fashion. He related the 1819 *Raleigh Register* publication of the declaration; the resulting charge to Jefferson of "want of originality, or . . . direct plagiarism"; Jefferson's denial of having seen, or even heard of, the document; and the ensuing controversy. Without elaboration he sweepingly concluded, "But later discoveries—the discovery of the contemporaneously published and recognized Mecklenburg Declaration—has [sic] effectively disposed of the question." Only perhaps three lines of the two documents contained duplication, Randall noted. Yet, he conceded, "in one or two of the coincidences, the language is so unusual, that it is difficult to believe those coincidences were accidental." When referring to the search to discover the Mecklenburg Declaration's publication, Randall observed that no one took "so active a part in the investigation as the Hon. David L. Swain, ex-Governor of North Carolina."[25]

Like Randall, Harvard historian Jared Sparks downplayed the controversy's significance. "[I]t does not seem to me of much importance, historically considered," he opined to Swain, "which way the question is settled." The resolves, he said, "are quite as strong in their political character, as the *Declaration*," and they afforded an equally convincing proof of the sentiments and spirit of the people. Because the declaration had attracted so much attention, however, even receiving the sanction of the North Carolina Legislature, Sparks, like others, was curious about it. He thus wanted any particulars Swain could give him on the subject.

When a publication by William H. Foote, Virginia minister and author, stated affirmatively that there were two conventions—one on May 20, the other on May 30—and that the first produced the *declaration* and the second the *resolutions*, Sparks was appropriately skeptical. The author had not, he said, produced sufficient proof "to clear up all historical doubt" on a matter "which has become a subject of so much controversy." If the resolves purportedly passed on May 20th could be found in any contemporary newspaper, he posited, "it will settle the matter." "If not," however, "I fear there will still be doubts." Swain, Sparks hoped, would be able to "unravel this web of perplexities."[26]

At the state level the political class had a natural interest in the subject. General Joseph Graham, Governor Graham's father, claimed to have witnessed in his youth the adoption and signing of the Mecklenburg Declaration. It is thus unsurprising that Governor Graham was attracted to the issue, or that his friend Swain considered it with him. Swain once informed Graham that the Reverend James Hall, Iredell County minister and teacher, had obtained the original instructions for the delegates of Mecklenburg County. They were, Swain thought, "important collateral testimony in support of the Mecklenburg Declaration of Independence." Swain's powers of persuasion had induced Hall to leave the original manuscript in his possession. He hoped Graham would find time for full conferences with him "in relation to the general subject, and on numerous points of his history."[27]

Soon Swain enlisted Graham to compare a printed copy of these instructions with the original paper now in Swain's possession.[28] At other times Swain offered Graham "an authentic copy of the 20 Resolutions adopted by the Mecklenburg Committee on the 31 May 1775"; inquired about Graham's knowledge "of the Mecklenburg *Female* Declaration" (Swain had sent Jared Sparks "a paragraph in relation to it"); and informed him of a letter from former Alabama governor Israel Pickens "in relation to the Mecklenburg Declaration of Independence." But, Swain said, no doubt with regret, "I find no paper reflecting new light on the subject."[29]

On one occasion Swain had seen, on Governor David Reid's table, a file of papers relating to the declaration, papers Graham had obtained in Cabarrus County. A thoughtful and careful preservationist, Swain suggested that Graham had left the file there inadvertently. He requested authority to reclaim it, "either to be retained for you, or transferred to the Historical Society, as you may direct." If permitted to remain where they were, Swain feared, the papers would "in all probability be lost, or abstracted, before a great while."[30]

Finally, shortly before he became governor of North Carolina, John W. Ellis wrote to Swain, "The Mecklenburg Declaration is on my mind again.... I hope to get more certain lights upon this subject."[31] Throughout his life, Swain would have said the same; indeed, so could even modern historians, their near-consensus toward disbelief notwithstanding.

In the years immediately following Swain's death, intense debate on the subject persisted. There were declaration advocates who saw Swain's papers as a possible source of clarity. Those seeking more light on the subject, the Reverend Charles Phillips warned Eleanor Swain, would beset her with requests for access to Swain's papers.[32] As the centennial of May 20, 1775 approached, Phillips's sister, Cornelia Phillips Spencer, thought constantly of Governor Swain. Yet, she said unequivocally, he did not believe in the declaration. Her other brother, Samuel Phillips, was equally clear in his perception. "[O]n no question," he said, "was our dear old friend more decided for the last 20 years of his life than this."[33]

Charles Phillips was an adamant declaration denier.[34] As a consequence, his statements and those of his siblings could be viewed with suspicion, their close relationship with Swain notwithstanding. A contemporaneous comment that Swain did not "disguise the opinion that the paper [referring specifically to the 'Davie Copy'] is untrustworthy" is probably more reliable.[35] It also probably best describes Swain's overall view of the declaration controversy. A pilgrimage over his adult lifetime took him from steadfast advocacy, publicly at least, to serious skepticism, perhaps even disbelief. Throughout he was earnestly seeking historiographically sound proof and was willing to sacrifice personal popularity and state pride in the effort to ascertain it. As with the controversy itself, the verdict on Swain's position on it must remain somewhat inconclusive.[36]

Collecting "autograph letters" was a favorite activity for men of Swain's era, and Swain was a prime source. Two historians with whom he had processed the Mecklenburg Declaration issue, Benson Lossing and Lyman Draper, were among those entreating him. Lossing requested an autograph of Governor Richard Caswell, which Swain furnished and Lossing returned. Swain was not modest about the breadth of his collection. He possessed hundreds of Revolutionary letters, he informed Lossing, among which might well be some Lossing was lacking.

Important personages at the national and state levels were represented. From the national level there were "letters of Washington, Green [sic], Gates, Lee, . . . LaFayette . . . and others of national fame." "I have also letters from Governor J. Rutledge of S. C., P. Henry and T. Jefferson of Va. . . . and of Caswell, Nash, Burke and Martin of this state," Swain continued: "of Genl. Marion of S. C.[,] Generals Butler, Allen Jones, Gregory, Rutherford, Lillington, Davidson, Sumner, Wm. Caswell, Col. Davie, Richard Caswell, Jr., Buford . . . [,] William Lee Davidson, William Polk, and many others." Lossing had obtained some of these, he informed Swain; but he requested a tracing of the signatures of Sumner, William Polk, David Fanning ("the Tory"), General Leslie, and Major Craig. He enclosed transparent paper for that purpose. Did Swain have several others, he asked? Embarrassed to draw further upon Swain's kindness, Lossing hoped to reciprocate.[37]

Lyman Draper wanted the autograph signatures of members of the Transylvania Land Company. He thanked Swain for sending one signature and promising others. It excited him that Swain had traced certain papers that doubtless would include those of Richard Henderson. Draper desired other autograph signatures, some of which, perhaps all, would likely be found among the Henderson papers. "I am really pleased to learn," Draper told Swain, "that your State is taking hold so earnestly in the matter of hunting up your old historical documents."[38]

When the lexicographer Noah Webster died, a Yale College correspondent returned to Swain the autograph of Webster that Swain had procured the previous summer. He had sought a private conveyance to return it but assumed Swain would not want him to wait longer for one.[39]

A Boston penman claimed the third largest collection of autograph letters in the United States, "and in New England names the richest." Serious efforts notwithstanding, however, North Carolina names had eluded him. Only four of "the signers" were missing, but three of these—John Penn, William Hooper, and Joseph Hewes—were from North Carolina. There were many others, including Richard Caswell, William R. Davie, Cornelius Harnett, James Iredell, and Samuel Johnston. He thus applied to Swain for assistance or direction. The request had an altruistic dimension: the collection ultimately would belong to the Smithsonian.

To a degree, Swain could assist. He forwarded autograph letters from Davie and Johnston, a copy of a letter from Iredell, an autograph letter from Benjamin Hawkins, and an autograph message to the General Assembly from Caswell. Autographs of Hewes, Hooper, and Penn, however, were "scarce and in demand." Swain would endeavor to find them, but if he succeeded, it would be "an achievement, which will probably not be effected a second time by anyone." With one exception Swain had letters from everyone listed. He was not sure he could spare them, however, except to Governor Graham and Senator Mangum. He would be glad to receive from the writer any such letters that he could spare. "I have a passion for the antique," Swain concluded, "and no apology is required of any one who chooses to address me, especially in relation to any subject connected with the history of the country." Ultimately, Swain sent letters from Penn, Hooper, and Hewes. With these, said the recipient, he could see his way clear to completion of "an extremely interesting series in my collection." He nevertheless enclosed "a list of my deficiencies," while sending Swain a few pieces "for your antique port folio."[40]

An autograph-letter collection significantly enhanced, but still incomplete, brought a previous solicitor back to Swain to "supply my wants." He would return the letters to the extent within his power. In response Swain produced a letter from William Hooper. Thus encouraged, the writer recalled for Swain his promise to seek for him an autograph letter of John Penn. This was a small matter, the writer acknowledged, in light of "the more serious affairs that have agitated us all since our correspondence last year." (The letter was written the day before Lincoln's first inauguration.) He renewed his application for Penn's autograph nevertheless, "as well as that of Joseph Hewes." He could reciprocate by filling gaps in Swain's university's paper money collection. The writer was "greatly obliged" upon receipt from Swain of autographs of Penn and Hewes; and, he exulted, "my series of 'signers' is now becoming very complete." His reason for troubling Swain with his pleas: "All my No. Carolina friends point to you always as the source from whence my antiquarian tastes are to be gratified, and you must blame yourself if your reputation for antiquarian researches and well known kindness and generosity make you the recipient of such a missive as I now send you."[41]

Public figures from the past were not the only subjects of requests for autograph letters. Swain once complied with a request by sending a letter from "Gov. Graham[,] late Secretary of the Navy[,] subsequently candidate for the Vice Presidency on the ticket with General Scott, and at present the favorite of North Carolina for the presidency." Graham was Swain's contemporary and still thoroughly enmeshed in current events.[42] Late in his life Swain told Graham, with evident pleasure, that within the fortnight he had "examined a great many letters, constituting almost a continuous series during a century." He could, he rightly claimed, "arrange a very interesting volume of autographs, beginning with Gen'l Washington, and including Greene, Davie, Sumner, Davidson, Polk, A. [Allen, presumably] Jones, Butler, Eaton, and others immediately connected with N.C. history, Marion, Lafayette, Rochambeau, Wayne, Lincoln, Gates, Leslie, Cornwallis, Craigg, David Fanning, etc."

Three months before his death Swain bragged, but truthfully, "I have probably the most extensive and valuable collection of autograph letters south of the Potomac." He was, he said, anxious to catalogue it. The letters from eminent North Carolinians ranged through the entire century. All North Carolina governors from William Tryon in 1767 to Jonathan Worth in 1867, with two exceptions, were represented.[43]

Swain did not live to prepare the catalogue himself, but he did not exaggerate the extent of his collection. The Southern Historical Collection at Chapel Hill and the North Carolina State Archives at Raleigh contain catalogues of his autograph letters. They begin with John Adams and end with George Wythe. Other well-known names include, at the national and international levels, John Quincy Adams, George Bancroft, James Buchanan, Thomas Jefferson, the Marquis de LaFayette, James Madison, James Monroe, James K. Polk, Benjamin Rush, John Rutledge, Roger B. Taney, George Washington, and Daniel Webster; and at the state level, in addition to James Iredell and Alfred Moore, who functioned at both the national and state levels, William R. Davie and William Gaston.[44]

Shortly before the Civil War the Mount Vernon Ladies Association sought funds for the restoration, beautification, and preservation of George Washington's homeplace and grave. "Nature," it said, "has done much to embellish the scene which surrounds these sacred grounds, but architectural taste must be employed to restore and beautify them, and the graces of art be united with the beauties of nature, to make them fitting testimonials of a nation's gratitude, and an ever living tribute to the world's most illustrious hero." The purchase price had been largely attained, but a permanent fund for repair and preservation was needed.[45]

Swain was a member of the project's North Carolina Advisory Committee. He had suggested the membership, which included the sitting governor, John W. Ellis, and former governors Graham and Morehead. It was Swain's nature to take such roles seriously. Further, the appeal for his services was flattering, probably rendering it difficult to resist. "Won't you try your voice (always listened to in North Carolina with interest and respect)," wrote a member, "and say the magic words which must unseal and throw open every true American heart." State pride and patriotism, she thought, would appeal to North Carolina to make a suitable contribution.

North Carolina was not a rich state, Swain cautioned. There were few who would be able and willing to contribute lavishly, but none, he trusted, "not disposed to give something." Dorothea Dix's efforts on behalf of the mentally ill had provided a model for what could be accomplished "when there is a lady in the case." He would obey the petitioner's commands and suggest others to assist. Confident that his students would respond positively to his requests, Swain would cheerfully represent her in Chapel Hill. Governor Graham or Paul Cameron could do so in Hillsboro. The advisory council could supply suitable names in all North Carolina counties, and newspaper editors would gladly publicize the appointments.

A Swain lecture in Chapel Hill on the next anniversary of Washington's birth would, it was thought, aid the ladies of his state in collecting an offering "upon which they can look with satisfaction." Not only did Swain accept the invitation; he also secured for the occasion the services of Henry W. Miller, "not an older but a better soldier," to repeat his lecture on the men of the eighteenth century. The event went well, Swain later reported. "[Y]our champion Mr. Miller did good service in your cause," he wrote, as he forwarded a check for $360.00. The check had been deposited, Swain soon learned, and the association was greatly indebted to him, "not only for what you have done at Chapel Hill, but for all that has been done on the 22nd." Tarboro and Goldsboro had contributed, but his correspondent feared "that Chapel Hill has been more patriotic than any other part of the State."[46]

It has been said that if one wanted to know who anybody was, he went to Governor Swain; that he was perhaps more thoroughly versed in biography than any American ever, and that certainly North Carolina never produced his equal in this respect. Once introduced, he never forgot a man or his family. Students were astounded to find that he knew more of them and their families than they did themselves. He possessed a genuine love of genealogical studies.[47]

An Ohio correspondent once advised Swain that he had referred someone to him "as an appropriate source" on "the genealogy of distinguished characters in North Carolina." He hoped Swain would give the man any information he could about the family of Governor Montford Stokes.[48] Swain's "trouble ... taken" regarding an inquiry about the Forsythe family was appreciated, and the information would be transmitted without delay.[49] Weldon Edwards, prominent Warren County political figure, had reason to be still more grateful. His great uncle, Issac Edwards, had been royal governor William Tryon's secretary. Swain advised Edwards, however, that this relative "was a staunch and genuine Whig in the War of the Revolution." This enabled a greatly obliged Edwards "to wipe out the suspicion which rested upon his character."[50]

Another correspondent was beholden to Swain for showing him his relationship to Senator Thomas L. Clingman, whose acquaintance he hoped to make.[51] A Swain request for genealogical information gave renewed stimulus to a researcher who previously had "felt that I had nearly accomplished all that I proposed to myself at the outset."[52]

Swain's storehouse of historical and genealogical knowledge rendered him a sought-after and valued resource for a great variety of such endeavors. If assisting with these proved burdensome, he had only himself to blame, for the following statement to one researcher was characteristic: "I am glad you have undertaken [the project], and will take pleasure in offering all the assistance in my power."

In that instance he could offer many "letters that you will read with pleasure and advantage."⁵³

When Joseph Gales, publisher of the *Raleigh Register*, undertook replacement of the volumes of laws and legislative journals destroyed in the 1831 State Capitol fire, Swain assisted him. Swain also advised the Smithsonian Institution on its newly developed program, blessing it as "exceedingly comprehensive and in general . . . well arranged," and offering to "cooperate in any way to help achieve 'the great design of the founder.'" The author of a proposed "Military History of America" looked to Swain for copies of relevant original materials and statements from battle participants. A Swain loan of "letters or papers, manuscript or printed, relating to our Revolutionary History" was eagerly sought; they would be safely returned unless Swain was "disposed to contribute them to Historical Collection of the Dept. of State."⁵⁴

Discovery of "a number of revolutionary papers" in the State Capitol sent Governor John W. Ellis to Swain. Had Swain, Francis Hawks, or anyone examined these, Ellis inquired, and if so, what suggestions did they have? Many were letters to Swain's marital relation, Governor Caswell. Were these, Ellis asked Swain, in Caswell's Letter Book?⁵⁵

A South Carolina writer, short on Revolutionary-era papers, turned to Swain. It would greatly assist him, he said, to have copies of any letters of Rutledge, Laurens, Lowndes, Ashe, Howe, Lillington, and others. Any letters showing views toward the Stamp Act would be helpful. He would be much obliged to Swain for extracts from his manuscripts and would gladly repay Swain's costs for the copyist.⁵⁶ A Charleston correspondent assisting the British Consul there also looked to Swain. The consul had failed in attempts to obtain information on a claim of Lord Carteret to certain North Carolina lands. Persuaded that Swain possessed these elusive facts, the writer requested them.⁵⁷

Hugh Grigsby, Virginia historian, grateful for a Swain article from the *Fayetteville Observer*, hoped Swain's life would "be long spared to guard the *historic* interests of your grand old commonwealth."⁵⁸ Matters relating to the history of that "grand old commonwealth" rarely escaped Swain's involvement. A friend of Raleigh attorney Bartholomew F. Moore desired sketches of the state's deceased lawyers, beginning with Judge John Haywood. Moore implored Swain's assistance "in getting up information, legal anecdotes, important cases, etc." Swain could also, Moore hoped, incite Judge Ruffin to assist him about certain judges, "not forgetting Judge [John Louis] Taylor." But Swain himself was the most likely one to aid him in procuring the proper material.⁵⁹

The Reverend Fordyce M. Hubbard, later a university faculty member, was engaged with Harvard historian Jared Sparks on a biographical sketch of Governor Caswell. Frustrated in his efforts to find material in Caswell's home county of Lenoir, he turned to Swain. No one, Hubbard thought, was "better provided with" such materials. He wanted Swain to undertake the sketch, but if Swain would entrust his materials to him, Hubbard would do his best to give the Caswell name "a permanent place in the historical literature of the country."[60]

A proposed biography of Ephraim Brevard, draftsman, purportedly, of the purported Mecklenburg Declaration of Independence, likewise depended on Swain. The committed biographer would do what he could "but must be aided by yourself and others." "In consenting," he wrote, "I have relied greatly on your assistance." He wanted Swain's views on the subject "at length."[61]

A New York correspondent wrote as a stranger requesting aid. He was preparing a work on "the Women of the Revolution" to show the influence of women in contributing to the great cause "and in actually promoting American Independence." Swain, according to former Governor Edward Dudley, had been collecting materials on our national history for years and would probably take pleasure in assisting. He thus requested "materials for notices of any ladies who deserve a tribute—or the wives of distinguished officers." The writer profited from information Swain sent him but was disappointed that material regarding Governor Caswell's wife was missing. He pleaded for "all the information relative to her which you can furnish."[62]

The publisher of a new newspaper wished "to foster every thing that claims to be North Carolinian, if it be tolerably respectable." He would be happy if the paper could become Swain's "medium."[63] A seeker of information on "the notorious Royalist Col Fanning" begged "leave to apply to fountain head." Swain should send any particulars of his life and adventures "from tradition or otherwise." Was it true that Fanning lost his ears, the writer asked, and if so, what were the circumstances?[64]

As Swain was dispensing historical information, he was simultaneously gathering it and brokering its exchange and publication. He spent considerable time seeking from his former student, Calvin H. Wiley, the title page and flyleaf to Lawson's history of North Carolina. Wiley was also to send Swain a book and speech by his predecessor, Joseph Caldwell, on internal improvements and common schools.[65]

Swain requested spare copies of a report on the slave trade for Spier Whitaker, a former attorney general of North Carolina who had relocated to Iowa. He received, undoubtedly with keen interest, reports on Lenoir County efforts to raise funds for a monument to his wife's grandfather, Governor Caswell. He sought and received a digest of Georgia laws containing valuable materials for history. He lamented to Governor Henry T. Clark the absence of journals of the 1715 General Assembly but was uncertain whether any ever existed. He sought a manuscript from E. W. Caruthers, assisted him with his sketch of Joseph Caldwell and other writings, and offered his influence in securing publication of Caruthers's work.[66]

Several historical artifacts came into Swain's possession. A letter from Wadesboro contained a coin found by "a Negro" while plowing a field. The locale had been the site of a house the Tories had burned in the Revolutionary War. It was sent to Swain as a token of appreciation for his efforts "in rescuing from oblivion many valuable historical reminiscences of our State and her early citizens."[67] Robert Donaldson, William Gaston's son-in-law, sent Swain a "Relic of Revolutionary times," a copper button with Washington's cypher in the center, encircled by the inscription "Long live the President," and with initial letters of the thirteen states in the links. Swain and a Baltimore correspondent exchanged specimens of old North Carolina money. A Morganton correspondent sent old continental money, including an item marked as counterfeit. One from Greensboro sent "a bullet or musket ball" found when a tree at the Guilford Courthouse battleground was split for firewood. It was "no doubt shot the 15th March 81," the sender ventured.[68]

A portrait of King George III, bearing a revolutionary wartime inscription, was in Swain's possession for many years. As General Nathanael Greene had prepared to depart Salisbury during the war, he had taken the picture from a wall and written with chalk on the back, "O GEORGE! HIDE THY FACE AND MOURNE." He then had replaced it, with the face to the wall, and ridden away. The Archibald Henderson family of Salisbury owned the portrait. How it came into Swain's possession is unclear, but entrustment of such historical artifacts to him was common.[69]

A history-related bill in Congress produced lobbying efforts from Swain. The bill provided for making copies of all documents in England relating to the history of any part of the United States. Sectional tensions presented problems; Southern and Western interests, it was thought, would oppose the measure "as they call it a Yankee project to get funds out of the Treasury." Swain wrote on behalf of the bill to Asa Biggs, then in the U.S. Senate from North Carolina. Biggs's response promised a contact with the then-absent chair of the library committee and conveyed the positive outlook of a member who forecast adoption of "some measures . . . to obtain the information from England so desirable to understand or write the early history of our country and particularly of North Carolina."[70]

Sensitive both to family feelings and to historical accuracy, Swain was a valued resource for preparation of obituaries, tombstone material, and tributes to decedents. Upon the death of Judge Duncan Cameron, his children requested that Swain write Cameron's obituary. He did so from memory and in unavoidable haste on the eve of his departure for Raleigh. When questions were raised about the date of Cameron's coming to North Carolina, Swain supported his date from history but pledged "to vindicate the truth of history" if a single date or circumstance of any importance was in error.[71]

The death of Revolutionary War figure William Lenoir brought a request for a tombstone epitaph. A son, who professed no talent for writing, desired "the most concise and appropriate inscription, commemorative of the virtues of so good a parent and ... distinguished patriot of the Revolution." In view of the son's long acquaintance with Swain, and Swain's with his deceased father, the son solicited Swain's assistance. A relative of John Grady, said to have been the first man to lose his life in the defense of liberty in North Carolina during the Revolutionary War, likewise consulted Swain about a stone for his grave.[72]

Swain was the prime source for his own family's history. A cousin once sent Swain news about his eighty-seven-year-old aunt and other family information. Swain, the aunt was quoted as saying, had "taken more trouble to trace our ancestry than anyone else living, and [knew] more about them." Swain's interesting pamphlet on the Lane family had taught this cousin much. Sadly, she had to inform him of family members lost in the Civil War and vandalism from which they would never recover.[73] Another family member requested from Swain the ages of her mother's children. She had lost the records of them and was anxious to have them again.[74]

Swain's cousin, General Joseph Lane of Oregon, was the vice-presidential candidate on the John Breckinridge ticket in the 1860 presidential sweepstakes. As Lane contemplated entering the contest, his biographer called on Swain as "the person best qualified to aid me in this labor of patriotism and friendship." General Lane had spoken of Swain often, he said, "and of the care you had taken to collect the history and genealogy of his family of which he considered yourself one of its most distinguished and useful members."[75]

Swain also endeavored to preserve his own history. He once wrote Eleanor, while on a journey, "I wish you to preserve my letters as I have no other memoranda of the incidents on my tour." Such information had current utility when requests came for information about him in his public and private capacities. More important, it enables us to know much more about him and his life than we otherwise could.[76]

General Joseph Lane of Oregon, Swain's cousin, 1860 vice-presidential candidate. Courtesy of Prints and Photographs Division, Library of Congress.

Swain's contributions to the field of history were widely recognized and honored across the country in his lifetime. The following historical organizations, and perhaps others, granted him honorary or corresponding membership: the American Historical Society, the Georgia Historical Society, the Massachusetts Historical Society, the New England Historic-Genealogical Society, and the New-York Historical Society.[77]

Personal Life

CHAPTER 20

Family
"The spontaneous offerings of a grateful heart"

LEADERS, HOWEVER DEDICATED TO the public good, have private lives. Personal joys and sorrows, successes and failures, march lock step with performance of public duties. David Swain was no exception. A wife and children brought both pleasure and pain. A large extended family harried him with their problems. Personal finances occupied much of his time and energy during limited absences from public responsibilities. He had health concerns, his share and perhaps more. His mortality presented questions for personal faith. A wide affinity for others produced friends with whom to share life's blessings and burdens. The Civil War and its aftermath dominated the last decade of Swain's life. For him it was a period of unparalleled challenges, public and private. Before contemplating these, a pause to reflect on select dimensions of the private man is fitting.

Swain's courtship of Eleanor Hope White, daughter of North Carolina Secretary of State William White and granddaughter of North Carolina Governor Richard Caswell, was long and difficult. She rejected his initial overtures, conveyed after a six-month wooing period. He waited more than a year and a half before again "ventur[ing] to express this sentiment." Even then, his approach was timid. Time and distance had not altered his feelings, but it remained "with the present arbiter of them to determine in what channel they shall flow in the future." His request now was limited; he sought only "an opportunity . . . to communicate more fully and freely on this subject."[1]

Now the response was different, and the courtship resumed. Later, however, with a wedding ten days in the offing, a brief conversation between them placed Swain "in a situation at once delicate and perplexing," one with no honorable escape apart from "a further understanding on the subject." His feelings, he pledged, were "not momentary ebullitions of youthful ardour, which blaze for an instant and expire... but... the spontaneous offerings of a grateful heart."[2]

This crisis passed, and the two were married on January 12, 1826. Eleanor, however, developed no fondness for Swain's Asheville residence. To Swain's frustration and regret, she passed considerable periods in her hometown of Raleigh. At such times she failed to mention Asheville friends in her letters. She seemed to have forgotten, Swain ventured, "the leading article in the female catechism—'Whither thou goest I will go and whither thou lodgest I will lodge and thy people shall be my people and thy God my God'" (Ruth 1:16).[3]

Without Eleanor, Swain's life in the West was "the same dull, uninteresting round." He could not recall a period when "time has hung more heavily on my hands." She must not neglect to write him, he implored, and he suffered when, with regularity, she failed to heed this admonition. There was risk in his writing, for at times his words pained her. On such occasions he trusted that she knew him too well "to suspect for one moment that I would wantonly give you pain in any way."

For an early nineteenth-century man, Swain was uncommonly deferential about how Eleanor handled "her" property, the husband then being presumed to control it. She was making arrangements regarding her share of her mother's estate (her mother still lived, so a gift or a dowry presumably). Swain wished her to manage it in her own way but wanted to be advised of her course so he could be "properly prepared to arrange our business to the best advantage with the least trouble possible."[4]

On the rare occasions when Eleanor wrote, her letters often vexed him. "They are so very short," he complained. Her concerns about his female clients, he said, were unmerited and irksome. Her societal omissions were troublesome; she could easily, he thought, "attend to little civilities" such as visiting Governor Iredell's wife. Her negativity about Buncombe County, too, bothered him.[5] The greater fault, however, was that she seldom wrote at all. "I have not yet heard a syllable from Raleigh since I left you," Swain once wrote to her, "and need not say that my anxiety on the subject is very great." When she failed to answer his questions, his letters assumed an imperative tone. "You must write me immediately on this subject," he would say, "for I am at a great loss what to do."[6]

Her own slackness notwithstanding, Eleanor fretted when dissatisfied with the frequency of his communications. "I write you nearly every week," he once told her, "and still you complain that you do not hear from me." When she complained on a specified occasion, he was unrepentant. It was the result neither of neglect nor of "any of the evil causes which you appear to have anticipated," he protested.[7]

Her husband was not the sole object of Eleanor's epistolary neglect. Once when her mother had not heard from her in ten months, Eleanor's brother-in-law directed Swain to "[t]ell [her] to be more attentive to her correspondence."[8]

There is an explanation for Eleanor's remissness. During Swain's wooing of her, a friend reported that she appeared "rather melancholy," adding "perhaps hypochondriacal would be a more proper expression." All surviving evidence confirms the accuracy of this admittedly amateur diagnosis. The condition would prove enduring. Early in their marriage Swain wrote to her, "It grieves me to hear you complain of melancholy." He iteratively conveyed to her his "great anxiety" about her health and implored her to advise him regularly regarding it. In her late sixties Eleanor herself described her affliction. "I have been much relieved," she told her daughter Ella, "from a depression of mind, one of those depressions which comes sometimes in a mysterious way, and unaccounted for."[9]

Swain received occasional word of Eleanor being well. This was the exception, however. Usually, the most positive reports were only of her being "in improved health," "much better," or "about again." Swain once conveyed Eleanor's thanks to Governor Zeb Vance for "supplying an item greatly needed" that had been unavailable from any other source. "Her health is improving," he told Vance, "and affords promise of as perfect restoration as can be hoped for at her time of life." Months later, however, Swain indicated that her "health continues to improve, but she is still very feeble."[10]

Swain once consulted a Charleston physician regarding Eleanor's health. The physician diagnosed "an enlargement of the tonsils" which "a very slight operation" would remedy. He recommended two doctors, neither of whom "could fail in performing it properly." Absent that recourse, he suggested application of leeches. "He examined your case with great care," Swain wrote Eleanor, "refused peremptorily all offers of compensation, and [offered] future services." Eleanor's action on the advice, if any, has not been found. Swain later reported to the doctor, however, that she was improving "under your prescription."[11]

Battle's history of the university states, "Mrs. Swain, a granddaughter of Governor Caswell, a woman of fine intellect but retiring disposition, cared nothing for Society, and therefore the President did not dispense a large hospitality."[12] This "retiring disposition" almost certainly stemmed from Eleanor's depression and frequent ill health. For Swain, the ultimate bonhomie personality type, it had to be a difficult cross to bear. Still, it is evident that his love for her was genuine and deep. In his frequent travels he expressed it in endearing ways. "I was married six years ago to day," reads an early diary entry, "This is and that was a Thursday." Knowledge of her affection motivated him. Early in their connubial state he told her, "The reflexion that there is another interested in my welfare, that will joy in my successes and reward my exertion, with her smiles, will always be present to my imagination, and supply me with an initiative to energy, which nothing but wedded affection can afford."[13]

When Eleanor wrote him, Swain experienced "much pleasure." He conveyed his letters to her "with real affection." He disavowed homesickness but admitted that he would "catch myself reflecting now and then" and would pray that God would "restore us to each other in health and happiness."[14] Brief separation had advantages. "I relished my freedom for a time," Swain once said. After almost three weeks of it, however, he had begun "to feel a good deal disposed to return to matrimonial bondage." A more prolonged hiatus in their togetherness he would label "so long and so cruel a separation."[15]

Sometimes when away, he saved things for when he could impress them "more feelingly" upon her. At others he had "never before thought so frequently [of her] when absent." And always he expressed deep affection from "the overflowing of a heart."[16] Eleanor's affection for him, though less frequently expressed, appears equally genuine and abiding. She once told him the time he was away seemed twice its actual length. She wished him a delightful trip but would "be happy when you are fully satisfied and to home return."[17]

Three Swain children, two sons and a daughter, died in infancy. The daughter had her mother's name, Eleanor, later given to another daughter. There is no record of names for the sons. Swain proudly recorded the birth of one of them: "At 12 Eleanor was brought to bed and at 12 ½ it was announced to me that we had a son who is said to be well grown but not handsome." Sadly, a year later William Gaston sent Swain sympathy for his "heavy domestic calamity," the loss of the boy.[18]

Sadder still, a son named for the father died late in his sixth year. From his infancy son David experienced health problems. When he was not quite a year old, his father reported to William Gaston "the apparent success of the experiment upon the health of my little son." Soon thereafter Swain apologized for a late remittance on an account, attributing it to a journey "undertaken on account of the serious indisposition of my youngest child." Shortly before young David's death Swain spoke of "the glimmer of hope with respect to David's eye" but was "very anxious for further intelligence."[19]

David's death was freakish and tragic. At his sister's birthday party, David ate "quantities of plum cake & other things." He was then "taken with fits" and died the next day. A contemporary account has him repeating Methodist hymns throughout his brief illness. When asked if he was afraid to die, he begged his mother not to cry, saying, "Ma *you know* I always told you that I loved God better than any body else."[20] The inscription on David's gravestone, placed there by his mother many years later, reads, "His days were few but lovely and full of promise." They must have been full of promise indeed. Swain had him studying Latin at age five, and his memorization of the hymns he sang on his deathbed evidences remarkable mental capacity, especially for the age of six.[21]

As to his three children who survived to adulthood, Swain is said to have been "conspicuously lenient" and to have "spoilt" them. Consequently, "his children grew up to bring him infinite anxiety and sorrow."[22] Anne Caroline Swain entered his life on October 9, 1829. He was a devoted and doting father to her. When away from home he would instruct Eleanor to "kiss our little one until you are tired, if you can be wearied of that species of well doing." He urged "early attention to the culture of her head and her heart, with the [biblical] assurance that if when a child she is trained up in the way she should go, when she is old she will not depart from it." When "*the Princess Ann*" experienced misfortunes, hopefully they would "teach her the necessity of pursuing an erect, straight forward steady course of life" that would leave her "contented, prosperous & happy." Time away produced growing anxiety to see her, during which she was "ever present" in his thoughts.[23]

Anne, sometimes called "Anna" or "Annie," would remain ever present in Swain's thoughts, but often the thoughts were painful, not pleasant. Cornelia Phillips Spencer has described Anne as "[s]ometimes partially, sometimes wholly deranged, and sometimes brighter than the best of us, yet suffering the agony of knowing that she was smitten; always affectionate, generous, charitable, humble." Spencer knew Anne quite well from Anne's childhood forward. Indeed, the "affectionate, generous, charitable" aspects of Anne's personality are well reflected in her farewell letter to Spencer when the latter married and left Chapel Hill for a time.

Anne's "little message of Goodbye" sent Spencer "many an ardent wish for your happiness." In Spencer's "far distant abiding place," Anne desired for her "a flowery path-way—roses without thorns"—this despite noting, plaintively, that the longest life is short, and the happiest life full of care. The letter reflects a deeply religious nature. "May God help you now and evermore!" Anne said to her friend, continuing, "Jesus it is who glorifies the day of our prosperity with a flood tide of sun light and bespangles our night with . . . light . . . which we shall find to be suns as our faith bears us farther up and farther out into the great balm of providence."[24]

All her life Anne's health, physical and mental, was poor. There are occasional accounts of her being "much better" or "much improved," but robust good health consistently eluded her.²⁵ In her teens Anne boarded for a time at Saint Mary's School in Raleigh, where health problems disadvantaged her academically. She recognized that she was not meeting her father's expectations, calling herself "your unworthy daughter." "I am aware Pa," she told him, "that I have never treated you with the confidence you have a right to expect from me." There was a reason, however. "I cannot but think that if it were not for my health I would," she said. She was disappointing both him and herself, though, notwithstanding that she "most wished to do well."

Her "debility," she pleaded, had never been greater. Merely walking up stairs exhausted her. Even so, she was willing to do anything for her own advantage or to please Swain. When she asked the Saint Mary's rector for permission "to go home and spend a day or so," he granted it, with instructions to tell her father he thought she should tarry there the remainder of the summer.²⁶

Soon came a medical opinion that Anne had a spinal disease which, without great care on her part, would terminate in consumption. She had "a very ugly hollow cough," which Lucy Battle feared would never leave her. Her failure to write her parents from school caused them great concern. Pain in her side became a "constant companion."²⁷ A "long jaunt" to Norfolk, it once was hoped, would produce considerable improvement. If it did the change was temporary, for her complaint was soon sufficient that a friend stayed with her throughout the day and night. "I cannot think she can live many months," Lucy Battle told her husband.²⁸

Once Swain contemplated a winter in Florida for her, but her health "rendered travelling impracticable." Then, as spring approached, she "sat up the whole day and did not seem fatigued at all." By the following spring she "had given up the use of snuff—and feels and acknowledges the benefit." An engagement, however, had "broken off—her health, the cause." Accounts continued to fluctuate between her being "so ill" and a "recovery."²⁹

The situation would have been sufficiently difficult for Swain if Anne's problems had been purely physical. They were not. There were mental and behavioral dimensions as well. There is some indication that these surfaced in her childhood. When Anne was ten, Swain directed Eleanor to tell her that she "must learn to govern her temper, and avoid evil speaking and even hasty and petulant replies." She should, he said, "prize above all things 'the attainment of a meek and quiet spirit.'" Possibly, the doting father was only conveying conventional wisdom. Considering Anne's subsequent history, however, this is doubtful.³⁰

A crisis occurred in Anne's mid-twenties, one that shook Swain to his roots. A local merchant witnessed Anne steal cash from his store. The merchant experienced a degree of astonishment that rendered him mute and unable to stop her. It was a large sum, between $2,400 and $2,500. Only $635.00 had been recovered, but there was "no clue" as to the balance. Rumor had it that Swain had promised to repay if it was not found. Probably, Lucy Battle speculated, Anne "was not in her right mind and did not have an idea that there was so much." Lucy would, she told her husband, "advise her [Anne's] father to send her to a lunatic asylum—as that is the only way she can ever be made to overcome the dreadful habit that she has been in for years past." The habit, it appears, was "taking narcotics." Anne "is and has been, for a long time," said Lucy, "one of the most miserable poor creatures I ever saw." The conclusion that Anne was deranged and had committed the theft "while in a fit of derangement" had a slight palliative effect. Still, in Lucy's view, the situation "really . . . could not be much worse than it is."[31]

Rumors that Swain would take Anne to a facility in Hartford, Connecticut, proved true. Friends were sympathetic. "Through what a furnace you have passed!" wrote one, noting that "God cares for us" and that in Him "we rest our hopes and our faith." Such encouragement notwithstanding, Swain remained dejected, especially when he did not hear from Anne for long periods. The fact that his friend was "still suffering" made Judge Battle reflective. "It is a sad affliction truly," Battle noted, "but I thought he would suffer less after he had placed her where she must necessarily be better taken care of than she could be at home." Those who had seen Anne in Western North Carolina the previous summer, Battle said, had not been surprised by news of her derangement.[32]

Anne's sojourn in the North was beneficial. News came to Swain of a visitor who found Anne "out walking with the nurse." A doctor there told the visitor Anne seemed "*very much better* than she has been." It was his opinion that "her *habits* were undoubtedly the *effect* rather than the cause of her disease, and that neuralgia has had much to do with it." The phrase "*very much better*" was repeated.[33] The physician later wrote directly to Eleanor expressing surprise at Anne's "greatly improved appearance." She had emerged from the treatment "as well as ever a mother's breast could desire." "[T]he most watchful observer," he said, "could [not] have detected any thing like insanity, or Despondency." The doctor's suggestion that Swain visit Hartford was, however, one with which he could not comply "at this inclement season of the year [late December]."[34]

Anne's improvement brought pleasure to Swain's family and friends.[35] Swain's mood, however, still fluctuated. He could appear "quite as dejected as . . . ever," yet a few days later look "much brighter." Eleanor grew "cheerful," especially when she heard from Anne.[36]

Upon Anne's return she spent time with her mother's sisters in Raleigh. Her request to her father for funds for purchases was deferred on account of expenditures Swain had just made for her brother. Swain nevertheless wanted a detailed account of her plans and assured her of "the earnest desire of your father to grant any reasonable indulgence of your desires."[37] Swain had expressed to a friend his opinion that "in view of her altered condition," Chapel Hill was not a desirable place of abode for her. On that account, the friend replied, "it is to be lamented that our Asylum [later Dorothea Dix] is not yet in condition to receive inmates, particularly as she seems to be so anxious to enter it." The statement suggests that Anne was well aware of her condition.[38]

Anne had indeed improved. She was now said to be "a completely changed person" who "abhors all kinds of stimulants." Her Raleigh aunts, at least, believed she now did not want opium at all. A few months later it was said that "she really seems now to have reformed." Swain was said to be "comforted" at her appearance.[39] While better, Anne was by no means well. Swain found small tasks to keep her occupied, but even these exhausted her. Apologizing for neglecting to write, she once told a friend, "I have so much writing to do for Pa, that I have little energy left for my own private gratification of this kind." The sight of a pen made her tired and "nervous at the thought of how much I *ought* to write when so utterly incapable." Her last employment had been "to copy for the State, a portion of the laws of 1715 . . . thirty-seven years before we had a printing press." She was at that moment preparing 126 diplomas for a graduating class of eighty-two and the applicants for the master of arts degree.[40]

Charles F. Deems, former UNC professor and now publisher of a religious newspaper, had Anne at work on a book. If she would pursue the task systematically, Deems told Swain, he thought she could do it, "and the production thereof will promote her mental and physical health." Reading between the lines, this too very likely was Swain-induced therapeutic makework.[41]

A lack of appropriate self-esteem complicated Anne's physical and mental problems. Occasionally, she once said, one of her sister Ellie's visitors would "take[ ] it in his head or heart to be kind to her sister." The implication is clear: most of Ellie's visitors were not kind to, or at least were neglectful of, Anne, and Anne seldom, if ever, had such visitors of her own. She once described a particularly confident youngster, noting dolefully, "It had been better for me in early life, I cannot help thinking, had I possessed a portion of the self-esteem that characterizes her."[42] Anne Swain's history is a sad one, and it cast a constant pall over that of her doting but deeply troubled father.

Richard Caswell Swain made his initial appearance on the Swain family stage on November 28, 1837. He was named for a distinguished ancestor, his great-grandfather Richard Caswell, governor of North Carolina from 1776–1780 and 1784–1787. He fell considerably short of adding luster to the name, however. He "was in no respect," said Cornelia Phillips Spencer, "a source of comfort to his father."[43]

Because his father was known as "Old Bunc" for his native county of Buncombe, Richard came to be known as "Little Bunc," "Bunc," or "Bunky." He clearly had endearing qualities. Kemp Battle describes an amusing incident in which "Little Bunc" had mentioned something "Thad" had done, referring to his cousin Thaddeus Siler. A student asked, "What Thad? Who is Thad?" "With great indignation little Bunk burst out, 'Don't you know Thad[.] Anybody is a fool who don't know Thad!'" Moved by Richard's endearing qualities, a nephew once said to Swain, "It may be unmanly but I confess that I could not see the lines when I began to think of writing a kind word for cousin Bunk."[44]

Like his big sister Anne, as a child Richard was sickly. Death in childhood was then common, so Richard's illnesses were a serious concern for his father. "The poor man has been quite uneasy lately about Bunc," Lucy Battle once related when Richard had been "quite sick." Later, even with one of her own children ill, Lucy was "much more uneasy about little Bunc Swain," who had "been dangerously ill with Pleuresy [sic]." Swain, Lucy later reported, "looks like a new man since Bunc has recovered." Given Richard's health history, it surely pleased Swain much later when Zeb Vance could relate to him that "Richard (your son) is here and is looking very well."[45]

Perhaps because of his physical problems, Richard was an indifferent student. A UNC session report, bearing the signature of "DAVID L. SWAIN, President," shows him absent from prayers three times and from recitations twice. "His deportment is good," the report stated, "& his instructors hope that increased interest in his studies will improve his scholarship." As to the scholarship, "[h]is relative grade . . . in his class is bad in French, tolerable in Greek, respectable in the other departments."[46]

In his sophomore year Richard seriously contemplated leaving school. When the crisis passed, with Richard deciding to resume his college duties, Charles Manly had ageless advice for the troubled father. "It is exceedingly difficult for a man to determine what is best to be done in his own case," said Manly, "much more in another's." "You must not draw the curb too tight," he continued, "let him play. Let circumstances, after a while, determine the measure of license and restraint. The wildest colts and the hardest to break generally make the best . . . horses."[47] The advice apparently had some effect. Richard graduated with the UNC Class of 1858.[48]

In those days a mediocre undergraduate record did not preclude future studies at a higher level, particularly when the prospective student had influential backing. Richard chose to pursue a medical education at the Charleston College. For a time, his habits changed. Richard was "pursuing his studies with diligence," the dean reported to Swain; his deportment was "creditable to him, and such as would meet [Swain's] approbation."[49]

All too soon Richard reverted to his old ways. James Johnston Pettigrew now told the father, who had been his teacher: "I fear he has not been making a very industrious use of his time . . . Charleston is no worse than most places, but all these cities present temptations difficult to withstand."[50]

Either Richard or his father, probably his father, acted on Pettigrew's advice, and Richard was soon continuing his medical education in Philadelphia. Doctor James H. Dickson, UNC Class of 1823 and a prominent physician there, promised Swain that he would place Richard under teachers "of entire competence and high character." The young man had "many good qualities and abundant intelligence," Dickson told Swain, but seemed to be "most desultory in his habits and to labour under absolute difficulty in the effort to become regular in any thing." Dickson further promised Swain that he would exert all the influence he could on Richard but cautioned that any sway he might have "is easily evaded if he desires to evade it."[51] Philadelphia, like Charleston, was "so full of temptations and facilities for all evil" that Dickson trembled at the responsibility of advising Richard to stay there. Dickson would speak of Richard to his professors "and engage for him their careful notice." "I will do my best in every way," he pledged, "to promote his well being."[52]

Upon commencement of the Civil War, Dickson advised Richard to go home. "This whole city of brotherly hatred . . . and fury," he told Swain, "is now converted into a disorderly barrack in which no Southern man is safe for a moment from insult and violence." Dickson's power "to control, direct, or aid him in any way" was gone. Contrary to Dickson's advice Richard had chosen to live in a hotel, "subject to all disturbance and temptation." He was "only accessible on his own terms and at such times as suited him." Finally, there was no opening for him in any hospital there.[53]

Richard completed his medical training sufficiently to meet the standards of the time. On June 1, 1862, the secretary of war of the Confederacy appointed him an assistant surgeon, North Carolina 39th Infantry. He served Confederate troops in that capacity until his discharge in Shelbyville, Tennessee, on February 4, 1864.[54]

One might conclude from this that Richard was now grown and stable. But from his youth until the year of Swain's death, Richard was irresponsible in money matters. In his freshman year at UNC, Richard made unauthorized expenditures in Raleigh of $200.00 or more. Swain himself had recently borrowed $1,500 in Raleigh; he had expected to be able to repay it in a timely fashion, but now might not be. Richard's dereliction left Swain "very much perplexed as to the course I ought to pursue."[55]

As Richard prepared to render his apparently honorable service to the Confederate Army, Swain received a demand from a woman whose husband had gone to Bermuda for his health and left his notes with her for collection. She sent Swain a sum due "by your son, Dr. Swain, as I do not know his address." "I beg you will be so kind," she implored, "as to attend to the settlement of your son's [debt]." She would then remit the note to Swain. There was a list of items of clothing Richard had "bot [bought] of" her husband.[56]

After the war a creditor in Ohio looked to Swain for payment of a debt Richard had incurred. If Swain would not pay it, he should advise the creditor of Richard's whereabouts. This demand was threatening. "I believe now that he intended to swindle me out of the money when he borrowed it," the man said to Swain, "and if it is not paid soon I will publish him in Tennessee and North Carolina papers as a swindler."[57] Almost simultaneously Judge Battle warned his son Kemp about a loan Kemp had made to Richard. Had Swain replied to Kemp's letter "about the money you lent to his son," the judge asked? If not, he said, Kemp should expect nothing from the father and should get the sum from the son as soon as he could.[58]

One of Richard's debts had to be particularly embarrassing to Swain. A creditor of Richard's employed Augustus S. Merrimon, prominent legal and political figure, to collect an indebtedness of $822.60. The creditor needed to close the matter to settle accounts with the estate of a deceased partner. Swain, Merrimon's client represented, had promised to pay.

Merrimon, then practicing law in Raleigh with Swain's close friend Samuel F. Phillips, requested a response at Swain's earliest convenience. A few weeks later Merrimon wrote again, quoting at length from a letter from his client. The client now proposed to submit the matter to Judge Battle, together with Raleigh attorneys Bartholomew F. Moore and Samuel F. Phillips, as a panel of arbitrators.

Swain rebuffed the arbitration request. The client instructed Merrimon to sue "and let the courts settle the matter." Merrimon too was now uncomfortable. "I beg to say that I extremely regret such a controversy," he told Swain. To reach a resolution, he was willing to defer action until Swain could see him again on the subject and to allow Swain to accept service of process, as Swain had suggested, if they could not agree. A month later Merrimon received from Swain a check for $400.00 and $15.00 in currency. Merrimon was to send them to his client "on account of his claim for advances" to Richard. Swain apparently entered the agreement with reluctance, for it took quite a while for the initial demand to result in a resolution.[59]

As Swain struggled to settle with Merrimon's client, he received another demand on Richard's account, this one from the remote mountain town of Hayesville, North Carolina. "In August 1862 I loaned your son—Dr. Bunk Swain—fifteen dollars," claimed the creditor, "about or before the same time I bought a Government Coat for him for which I paid $7.50." Bunk, he said, thus owed him $22.50. The creditor was now "in Needy Circumstances." Surely, the creditor wrote, Swain would "not refuse to settle this Small amount for your Son." He would swear to the debt if necessary. As to his integrity and honesty, he referred Swain "to Col. David Coleman formerly of the 39th N.C. Regt.," Swain's nephew. The creditor appealed based on his need, his patriotic service, and Swain's celebrity status. By paying the debt, he said, "you will greatly oblige to help [a] Confederate soldier. And sustain your very enviable reputation." If Swain responded, the response has not been found. The demand came less than four months before Swain's demise. Thus, from Richard's early college days until shortly before Swain died, Richard's financial irresponsibility was a source of pain and frustration for his father.[60]

There was another problem, one that perhaps explains the debt issues. Richard was an alcoholic. Supporting evidence first surfaced in Richard's college days. In his freshman year there was "[g]reat excitement on Ball night." "Among others," Lucy Battle reported to her husband, "Bunc—alias R. C. Swain" was caught drunk. At a faculty meeting that soon followed, Swain was the epitome of distress. Swain himself had "found Bunc in one of the students rooms at college—*very drunk*." "The Governor's spirits would indicate that his son is doing better," Lucy stated over a year later. Earlier, however, there had been "sad accounts of [Richard's] conduct about the time he left the Hill."[61]

James J. Philips was an Edgecombe County physician and planter. In the late summer of 1861, Richard and his wife, newlyweds, spent an extended period with Philips. Philips gave Swain an account of the visit that is detailed, analytical, insightful, and for the time enlightened as to the nature of, and cure for, alcoholism. "It is unfortunately too true," Philips told Swain bluntly, "that your son is quite wayward in his habits, and the whole arises from his habit of indulging too freely in spirituous liquors." Less than five minutes with Richard was all he had needed to discover this, the doctor said. He "formed instantly a resolution to do what I could to impress him of the danger of his state."

Philips had treated many such cases. Richard, he said, was not "degraded or demoralized." His "nicer feelings," however, needed to be stimulated to action. This would be accomplished "by bringing before [him] the responsibility of the married state, the prospects of offspring, which must be provided for, the degree to which the offspring must be subjected to the honorable or dishonorable conduct of the male parent—his provident or improvident conduct." Hope that he is not degraded, Philips continued, should be kept alive in the victim. Richard had not yet reached that "last and hopeless stage," in the doctor's opinion, "but every means should be used to avert it, and the best is that which is marked with kindness of feeling, calm advice, and a hopeful prospect of success in business, a more honourable standing in society provided reformation is accomplished." The doctor had touched the subject with Richard only "lightly and indirectly." He planned soon to "give him a more serious chat on the subject and afterward never lose an opportunity to do so when necessary." It was his practice to approach these people "with kind and charitable feeling, [not] bitter condemnation."

Richard had approached Philips about commencing the practice of medicine in Tarboro. Philips could not encourage him "without his first reforming his drinking habits." A physician, more than any other professional, he had told Richard, should "never have his intellect obscured or his judgment impaired." Having "the cure of a man's life in his hands" was no small responsibility. The doctor sympathized with Swain and assured him, "I . . . will do all in my power to promote the welfare of your only son."

A grateful Swain responded that Richard would "probably be more disposed to be governed by your opinion than that of any one else." He would be "under deep obligation" to Philips, Swain said, if he would examine Richard and render an opinion on whether he should "enter into the practice of medicine any where at this time." Unless Richard could do it under Philip's auspices and in his locale, Swain thought it best for him to return to Chapel Hill where his wife could be provided for more comfortably.

Philips attempted to get Richard back for "a serious and deliberate talk." Circumstance thwarted the plan, and Richard went to Weldon in Halifax County. Doctors there had left for the army, thereby leaving opportunity for Richard. "[H]e may succeed in business," Philips opined, "if he will keep sober, give proper attention to business, and not suffer himself [to be] discouraged if he cannot accomplish as much as he desires in the beginning." In his planned conversation with

Richard C. "Bunky" Swain and Eleanor "Ellie" Swain (later Atkins).
Courtesy of Suzy Barile.

Richard, Philips promised to appeal to everything, including Richard's "honorable parentage." If Richard then failed, it would be because the habits had become ingrained "as second nature," but Philips's conscience would be clear.[62]

Shortly before his sixteenth birthday, Richard professed faith at a Methodist meeting. His faith, however, did not result in his relating appropriately to money and alcohol. From Richard's youth until his father's passing, the son's problems were also problems for the father.[63]

On October 25, 1842, Richard acquired a younger sister, Eleanor Hope Swain. The youngster had her mother's name but was usually called "Ella" or "Ellie." She was the one Swain offspring who apparently was not a serious problem for her father in childhood. As a young adult she would compensate for this omission thoroughly and notably. That story, however, awaits a later point in this narrative.

In family matters Swain focused most intensely on the one he, with Eleanor, had established. His family of origin, however, in all its extended forms, never ceased to press him. In youth he witnessed the steady decline of his father, George

Swain Sr., mentally foremost, but physically as well. "His derangement, you know," Swain once wrote Eleanor, "is of the most melancholy cast, but since you last saw him his malady has increased to such a degree that he now seems bereft of every ray of reason." After George's 1828 demise, Swain and his siblings assembled "with a view to the arrangement of father's affairs." Soon the older siblings, like their father, experienced fragile health and decline. As the youngest, Swain suffered the deaths of most of them and their spouses.[64]

A half-brother, James Lowry, once spent a night at Swain's "quiet and pleasant and happy home at Chappel Hill," where he claimed to have experienced his best night's sleep ever. "[T]he importance of [Swain's] imployment [sic]" impressed him. "I am truly glad that you are doing great good in the world," he told his half sibling. Swain, James said, could "make it profitable to your self without the laborious fatigue that I have under went in raising my little family by farming." A sad sense of inferiority crept into the communication, as James concluded with the words "your unworthy brother and friend."[65]

There was an ingrained pattern, in which James was a participant, of extended family members petitioning the more successful younger brother for assistance. James once thanked David for a helpful loan: "the three hundred dollars that you lond me Brother David has hope me along very much and now I have nearly all my debts paid but that and will now try and make that for you as soon as I can." Now seventy-three, James feared he would not see David again unless David came to Buncombe.[66]

James's greater concern, however, was for his half-brother, David's full, George Swain Jr. George had visited James, who had found him well. "[B]ut," James told David, "I am afraid brother will hurt self he has too many wild speculations in his head."[67] James was right. Once when bemoaning his financial situation, George told David he had "been looking forward all my days for something to turn up in my favor." Several years later, George still thought "I have yet some room to hope for the better." The better never came.[68]

George pleaded a difficult childhood in mitigation of his deprived condition. Their father, he said, was no farmer. As the only son of any size, the farm work fell on him "and one negro woman." He thus had limited educational opportunities. Even when he went to school, demands from the farm were such that he frequently was only at school a little and "consequently got but a very limited Education." At eighteen he was severely injured by a horse and, he said, "neither my mind nor bodily functions have ever been the same since."[69]

Swain constantly received George's complaints about his financial situation. George would find money scarcer than ever and the currency "so bad" that money was unsafe even when he got it. A note of Swain's neighbor had not been collected because the debtor had "not yet quite gotten over the Van Buren times." George himself was the subject of several suits for small debts and was struggling to hold other creditors at bay. Without success, he was working to pay off his debts "and try once more to be a free man."[70]

Being "land poor" was part of George's problem. He had acquired more land than he could sustain. As a consequence, he viewed his chances as "truly more gloomy than at any former period of my life." Because he was unable to support her, a "little Daughter" was living elsewhere. The time came when he sold his "few remaining negroes" to pay debts, so found himself with "no negroes nor children."[71]

George was a dreamer who spent his life devising moneymaking schemes. They included various farming operations, raising honey bees, mineral and mining operations, orchards, an "experiment on rice and potatoes," stock raising (sheep, principally, and a few goats), growing tobacco, a "turpentine business," and distilling whiskey. He considered cultivating Swain's Georgia land and working on the railroad.[72]

The whiskey distillery was both the most promising and the most controversial of his schemes. He started it because he saw no other way "to turn out my corn or dispose of it so as to pay debts." He anticipated having four stills in operation within a week. George's deeply religious nature rendered him defensive about it, however. If "holy writ" said anything against the making of ardent spirits or whiskey, he wanted to know where to find it. He himself neither drank to excess nor "encourage[d] drunkenness by example or precept." So long as a person was temperate, however, the product could have "good qualities" as a medicine and would do no harm. "I defy you," he said to David, "to find me a man more temperate in drinking than myself." His objective was legitimate, "to make money—and pay my debts." At one point the pressures got to George. "My friends, Relatives and yourself seem to be so much opposed to distilling of spirits," he told David, "that I have concluded to try some other method of getting along for the present." The abstinence did not last, but neither did the operation produce significant money.[73]

Instead, David was George's financial lifeline. George frequently sought, and often obtained, loans from him. Could he borrow $2,500 at 8 percent interest, repayable over four years, an early missive asks? If he had $10,000, he could, without risk, double the amount in three years, states another. Once George expected David to pay for a lot George had already bought. David's money was also needed to save George from foreclosure on a loan from another cousin, whom it appears David had never met.[74] At times George's land was used as security for his loans from David. This could prove embarrassing. It was now talked all over the county, George once told David, that his land was mortgaged to his brother.[75]

David also held land in George's area in his own name and allowed George to farm it. This too proved problematic. Their nephew once informed David that this land had "been taken just such care of as Uncle takes care of every thing," namely, very poorly. "It is a pity," a neighbor of the property said to David, that "a farm of so much value as yours should be so wretchedly husbanded."[76]

Caroline Swain, the "little daughter" for whom George had been unable to care, married well. Her groom was Crawford W. Long, a Georgia physician who would be "the first physician to use ether in surgical anesthesia." Early in their marriage David conveyed to Long his desire to aid in promoting George's comfort. The Longs soon came to echo the aforementioned concerns. "I fear your land is being injured by a bad system of cultivation," Caroline informed her uncle, "I dislike for you to lose anything by my Father's continuing on it."[77]

Late in David's life the Longs learned that land they had thought George owned in fact was David's. Their concern was palpable. David should remove George from control, Long advised, and give the management to a responsible local person who could make it yield something for George's support. For four years it had yielded nothing. For twenty years a tenant family had lived on it and had spent thousands of dollars of George's money. To give George money was useless "as he would be swindled out of it immediately."[78]

George's was a sad case. Even when up in years, he was "still per suing [*sic*] his visionary course of making money" and "just rambling About from place to p[l]ace." He visited his native city of Asheville and found that upon inquiry about people he had known there, he was directed to their tombstones. He was deeply and genuinely grateful for his younger sibling's efforts to assist him, a gratitude he expressed in endearing terms such as: "[Dear] Brother you have indeed been a brother to me"; "You have shown me more indulgence and friendship than any body else"; and "[Thanks] for having done a kind friendly and feeling brothers part toward me." Throughout his adult life Swain devoted considerable time, energy, and money to, or on behalf of, this older sibling. His only rewards appear to be George's heartfelt gratitude and the inner satisfaction that came from having done a "brother's part" for him.[79]

George was not the only extended family member with hands in David's pockets. A host of nephews, too, avidly solicited his financial assistance. Prior favors spawned new requests. "From the many favours that you have shown my Father and Brothers," wrote one nephew, "I have concluded as I would like to borrow a thousand dollars so ask you to loan it to me." The nephew thought he "could lay it out at present very profitably." Another also wanted funds for investment purposes, thinking he "could make money for both you and myself." "You have the capital," he told his uncle, "I think I have foresight and judgment."[80]

The requests were usually from the $100 to 1,000 range. The call could be for one sum immediately, more later. The plea was usually just for money, but at times there was a stated purpose: funds for a mortgage on a house, a loan sufficient for two years of college, a sum to provide for getting established as a merchant.[81] At times an apologetic demeanor accompanied the requests, but they came nevertheless. One nephew was reluctant to seek Swain's assistance because Swain had already done so much for his family. He had failed to receive needed travel money, and though reluctant to ask for an advance, did so.[82]

When nephews could not repay, they again experienced embarrassment, but it did not generate payment. One had to explain why he had not paid a debt owed to Swain for ten years. Another felt "under obligation" to Swain but promised "if I am spared I will some day pay you that together with the remainder I owe you."[83] If a nephew learned that Swain expected funds, he did not hesitate to ask for them. A Swain debtor had "sold a negro boy for something over a thousand dollars," one once informed his uncle. If that much was coming to Swain, the nephew would "be greatly obliged . . . for the use of it for a few years." "If you could loan it," he said, "I would like to borrow a thousand dollars."[84]

At times Swain chafed under these responsibilities, especially if his own financial affairs were not in the best of condition. "[I] have also lately no money," he once said. If he could not procure a sum expected from his mother-in-law, he said, "I shall be pretty much at my wits end." The money market was "in so uncertain and unsettled a condition," he opined, "that few men should venture larger operations of any kind." At the time family members owed him around $10,000, then quite a large sum. "My relatives do not expect to pay in a short period," Swain noted, "and I have no disposition to press them." As a result he had "little capital" and was unable to avail himself "of the advantages always presenting themselves to men who have money." He was not complaining, he claimed, for he regarded his assistance to family members as both a pleasure and a duty.[85] The truth is that he was complaining, and with good reason. The foregoing is but a small sample of the demands his extended family placed on him.[86]

Swain's relatives also took advantage of his influence, which was considerable. One nephew, who thought Thomas Clingman would be elected to the U. S. House of Representatives, wished to replace him as counsel in a matter. His uncle would need to make application to the governor for him, however. A bank president was to attend UNC commencement: Would Swain ask the banker about a situation he desired, the nephew later requested? Another nephew received Swain's assistance in securing admission to West Point. En route the nephew delivered a letter from Swain to the *Whig Review*. Unfortunately, however, the nephew, "very much dissatisfied" with military life, soon withdrew.[87]

One nephew used Swain's influence and money over an extended period. David Coleman attended UNC but did not graduate. According to his father he "possesse[d] an ungovernable and disobedient disposition." Swain should arrange for him to join the navy, the father suggested, if he thought it advisable. While at UNC, David had boarded with his uncle. Although willing to pay David's expenses through his senior year, Swain was unwilling to resume his status as a boarder. This must have resulted, David thought, from "some injurious report" to Swain about him, or "some ill opinion" Swain had formed of him. He acknowledged having been "indolent and inattentive," as well as financially "extravagant," while at Chapel Hill. Still, proudly but contradictorily he claimed that "no young man in university pursued a more honorable course." He would never forget what Swain had done for him at Chapel Hill, but he could not return there.[88]

David, it seems, indeed wished to join the navy. To that end his father sought Swain's influence with their congressman. Discouraging news came; it was unlikely that there would be a place for David soon. Eventually, however, the father's concern was with lack of funds with which to purchase David's navy uniform.[89] As so often happened, the accommodating uncle came to the rescue. David acknowledged receipt of $280.00 from Swain "for the purpose of completing my education and fitting me out for the Navy." He assured his uncle that, unlike other sailors, he did not spend money on women. Further, his ship had a good library; he had bought, and was reading, a copy of Blackstone.[90]

Swain remained involved with David's naval career well beyond his enlistment. When David was threatened with reassignment from the Gulf to the Naval School, a relative sought Swain's intervention to prevent it. It is significant that Swain's information regarding David's assignments came, not through routine family channels, but from a high-level official in the Department of the Navy. Several years into his naval career, David still sought his uncle's advice and assistance. He had pecuniary difficulties and a plan to satisfy his creditors over a two-year period on his seaman's pay. He hoped Swain would "give me such aid as I need—and which I know not where else to expect."[91]

Relatives wanted not only his financial assistance but also his advice about the future in general—a proposal to go to California, a possible debt to "the Society" (probably referring to the Di or the Phi), a dysfunctional family. With amusing immodesty, one requested advice about his love life. Girls who would be called "fortunes" were "very remarkably scarce," he told his uncle, but in adjacent counties there were some who could be called "tolerable." Would it be advisable, he asked, "for so good looking a young man as my self and ... Major of the United States Army too to bight at such bate or not I cannot determine." The advice of friends would be "acceptable," and he hoped Swain would "write ... shortly and give me your opinion."[92]

Those interested in the legal profession realized that their uncle was a knowledgeable resource. One had studied several subjects but never finished anything. He dreaded the consequences of a rash vocational decision so requested Swain's advice about choosing a profession. Disposed to be a farmer, he thought that would be a hardscrabble existence until there were, in his area, "manufacturers established sufficient to create a demand for raw material." These considerations had caused him to think of reading law. Swain's opinion would be highly appreciated. A few years later the nephew sought Swain's advice again, this time about which law books it was most important for him to have. He thought Swain would recommend purchasing the *North Carolina Reports*, but if so, what was the best way to get them to Macon County? He had "read nothing but Blackstone, and obtained county license through a kindness on the part of the Judges more than anything else."[93]

Swain assisted family members with legal problems. He once took the stage to Raleigh to consult George Badger "on the subject of an injunction" for one. He also consulted others and ultimately authorized submission of a settlement proposal he thought the opposing party would accept. It was, he advised the relative, the best way to dispose of "this unpleasant subject." When Asheville attorney N. W. Woodfin and a "Col. Quinn" differed on a land-title question, two nephews told Swain they would be governed by his opinion.[94]

At least occasionally Swain received gratitude from his beneficiaries. "I am under many obligations to you Uncle," wrote one nephew, "for opportunities which I hope will assist me in carrying out views that I entertain in connection with my future course in life." That could have been said by numerous members of Swain's extended family.[95]

Less evidence survives regarding Swain's assistance to Eleanor's family, but clearly, he was an accommodating and attentive in-law. He notified Eleanor's brother-in-law when their wives' mother was unable to use her arm. The serious illness of this "venerable mother in law" precluded his personally delivering, rather than mailing, a deed. When Eleanor's brother-in-law died, there was a problem regarding the deed to the land on which he had resided. The person handling the estate requested that Swain write a corrective deed. He would consult with Mrs.

Swain's sisters, "who are the persons mainly interested, as to the course proper to be pursued," Swain replied. He was uncertain that a deed had ever been made, but if the person would give him the courses and distances he would "have a deed speedily and properly executed."[96]

Evidence about Swain's involvement with his mother's family, the Lanes, is also limited. A Georgia cousin once requested of Swain "a secular history" of his family. Swain's brother George told him of a Georgia uncle, Jesse Lane, who had a marble quarry, "the best marble in the United States," the uncle believed. In his travels Swain visited a cousin, "Judge Lane," and told Eleanor he "enjoyed hospitality of a character that will place me in an awkward position if . . . they should call upon us in their way to the north." They were "much the most interesting specimens" he had seen of the Lane family.[97] Swain's most famous Lane relative, his first cousin General Joseph Lane, born in the same house in Buncombe County, migrated to Oregon and cut quite a figure. He was a U.S. senator from Oregon and the vice-presidential candidate on the John C. Breckinridge ticket in the 1860 presidential election.

Swain's friend and fellow historian John H. Wheeler, who held several federal government positions, would encounter Lane and send Swain his greetings. "Genl. Joseph Lane has just stepped in," Wheeler once wrote, "and on learning that I was writing to you, desired his especial regards." In 1860, Wheeler regarded Lane as "the most prominent man in the Union for the [Democratic] nomination at Charleston." He was the first choice with many, the second with others, and "with all, a favorite."

When he visited Wake County in July 1860, Lane was "lavishly entertained." He was "an especially honored guest because of his kinship with the descendants of Wake's Joel Lane," including Swain. On the same excursion, Lane spent several days with Swain in Chapel Hill "and learned much about our family." The men saw each other rarely and communicated only occasionally. Each viewed the other from afar, however, with considerable interest and admiration.[98]

CHAPTER 21

Other Personal Dimensions
"Busily engaged.... in arranging my business"

WITHOUT PERSONAL WEALTH, SWAIN could not have made the gifts and loans to family members. He possessed it, but this was not always the case. In his younger years he lamented to Eleanor that he had "[a]s usual . . . but little money." "[T]hat little" he would send her, notwithstanding that "[i]t actually empties my pocket." More than three years later the lament lingered. His note was due at the bank, and he had "not yet money enough to renew it." In a fortnight he would try to send funds. Another year passed, and he was still having to renew his note in the New Bern Bank.[1] A close friend, Robert B. Vance, hoped Swain's future situation would allow him "to bid a long farewell to all these scraps." In the meantime, he invited Swain to use the Vance name and credit if he could.[2]

In a few years Swain's pecuniary circumstances had improved to the point that, while in Asheville, he expected to "be detained there a long time in the arrangement of my affairs." Soon he had settled some of his business but still had much to do. The crops were promising, the country improving. This became the pattern. Swain's interests were sufficiently extensive that he found himself "busily engaged . . . in arranging my business." Three states—North Carolina, Georgia, and Tennessee—contained Swain holdings.[3]

For the time Swain's UNC salary and benefits, primarily free housing, offered a comfortable base for personal and family sustenance. By his later years in the office, the president's annual salary was in the $2,000 to 2,500 range, subject to the university's receipt of set minimums from tuition and board. Even so, in at least two instances the university trustees loaned him money. More commonly, however, Swain was the creditor and the university the debtor. At his death the university owed him a sum considerable for the time, and the debt was not settled until long afterward.[4] To produce real wealth required something more than a university president's salary and benefits. With Swain it was numerous other interests, beginning with land ownership. From early adulthood until death, he bought and sold land, making money in the process.

At age twenty-seven, Swain purchased a five-hundred-acre tract in Macon County in far southwestern North Carolina. One half he secured at a sheriff's sale; the other, by private sale. The tract was, he said, "one of the prettiest farms in this country." He flattered himself that he had both "made a fine bargain, and . . . been enabled to make a liberal provision for a destitute branch of the family of my unfortunate friend Vance [presumably Robert Vance, who had been killed in a duel]."[5] A Swain diary entry soon recorded his "accepting a proposition with regard to a lot in Asheville." Swain then purchased land in the Asheville area at a sheriff's sale.[6]

Other Western North Carolina properties now caught his attention. A nephew apprised him of land-transaction bargains there that did not exist elsewhere in the state "or even in the West." Another Western North Carolinian wrote that he understood Swain wished to invest $5,000 in land, and he offered possibilities. A few years later Swain was selling some of his western holdings. He retained ownership of a considerable amount, however. An article on Elisha Mitchell's investigations among the mountains of Yancey County contained a map of a river headwaters there and noted that "Gov. Swain . . . still owns nearly all that this map includes." Clearly Swain acquired a considerable portion of his economic assets by buying and selling Western North Carolina lands.[7] These lands constituted the greater portion of Swain's real estate interests. He also had tracts in Georgia, however, apparently acquired through interaction with his brother George and George's business. A new railroad through the area had enhanced the value of the properties, and Swain was willing to sell them. By then he was sufficiently well-heeled that time of payment was "a matter of no great moment." [8]

Through his wife's family, Swain acquired a tract of land in Tennessee. He appears to have resisted importuning to procure an investment in Texas land. Nowhere else, he was told, "afford[s] such an opportunity to make immense fortunes." The writer offered to invest there for Swain "and take one half of the profits."[9]

Swain also had farming interests. Until he contracted to sell it, he leased out or employed a manager for a farm on Beaver Dam Creek in Buncombe County.[10] The agricultural interest to which he gave the most attention was a farm in Macon County. A Swain nephew, David R. Lowry, viewed the farm as "one of the best places to raise stock in the whole mountain country." Swain, Lowry posited, had "some capital to spare and some idol *[sic]* hands [enslaved persons, presumably]." With part ownership and some hands, Lowry thought he could make money. He would "attend to all the business," he promised his uncle, "and not cost you any trouble."[11] They entered the arrangement, holding legal title as tenants in common. Swain apparently assisted Lowry with arranging the financing for his share. Lowry was to have "exclusive possession" and to cultivate and improve the farm at his discretion.[12]

Lowry's promise to preclude "any trouble" for Swain, however, proved hollow. Swain checked on the farm during summer breaks from UNC. Lowry's plans for its operation went to Swain for review. Whether Swain would send "hands," or Lowry would hire them, was a subject for negotiation. Needed fencing repairs were made. From time to time, Lowry presented Swain with "the progress and plan of our business." "[O]ur" was the operative word; they were in it together.[13]

Swain's purchase of Lowry's interest was considered. Necessity, Lowry thought, would compel him to sell. His purchase of Swain's interest was out of the question unless he could secure a wife, for the farm should not be run by a bachelor. He supposed Swain would "be ready at any time to make the trade." It appears, however, that the joint ownership and operation continued, with Swain making periodic loans to Lowry to enable him to retain his interest.[14]

Lowry was once so seriously ill that his survival was in question. Should there be "a serious determination of his disease," another nephew suggested to Swain, "the situation of yours and his business might require some particular attention by you." There was even consideration of the other nephew's taking over Lowry's interest. He was already cultivating three farms, however, and could not assume responsibility for another. Fortunately, Lowry survived, recovered, and resumed work. For Swain, though, his operating partner's illness produced anxious moments.[15]

In 1863, Swain sold $10,000 worth of stock in the Bank of North Carolina and invested the proceeds in a plantation in Pitt County. He authorized Thomas B. Dupree, a near neighbor of the property, to rent it out and manage it for him. In the first full summer of Swain's ownership, Dupree reported the land as "looking tolerable well though not in as good order" as he would have preferred. A "tolerable fair" crop had been injured by an earlier drought.[16]

In 1865, Dupree had the land rented to two men. He understood that Swain was leaving the land "entirely in my hands for rent according to my best judgment." He had received no pay for the fodder but expected it soon. He would have to charge Swain for his "considerable trouble" in attending to the corn and fodder. The crop had not been as good as that of the previous year. It would have been better, according to Dupree, but "the Freeing of Slaves had a very great affect [*sic*] on our crops for we have not been able to command them since the surrender."[17]

The end of the Civil War cost Swain not only labor for the farm but also a market for its products. He was selling the produce to the state and Confederate governments, mainly, if not entirely, for use by Confederate troops. The disruptions of the war placed him in some degree of financial straits. It appears that some of the farm produce was also needed for feeding himself and his family.[18] Notwithstanding loss of this major market, the farm operation continued after the war. Swain had some direct dealings with tenants but maintained his confidence in Dupree's honesty and judgment. He was "willing that he shall augment the improvements to be made . . . and the terms of the lease in all respects."[19]

Swain retained an investment banker in New York. He forwarded funds to the banker to invest for him. The banker held Swain's power of attorney, with authority to collect interest on the stocks and forward the sums to Swain. At times he invested the funds temporarily in U.S. Treasury notes.[20] Swain owned other stocks, among them shares in the Asheville Female Boarding House Company. In a distress sale he purchased stock in the Hillsboro Coal Mining and Transportation Company. Hillsboro lawyer-legislator Hugh Waddell was the seller. The stock, Waddell represented to Swain, was "of one of the best coal tracts on the river." It could not fail to realize handsome profits in two or three years, and he was selling it only under "a cruel necessity." Swain could not conceive, Waddell said, of "how it pains me to make such applications to my friends."[21]

To some limited degree, while at UNC Swain enhanced his wealth by continuing to practice law. A Macon County land-surveying case once went to the state supreme court. Pursuant to Swain's advice, it was returned to the county for trial on the merits. Local counsel, noting that the case would "no doubt go up again," requested that Swain "hold yourself in readiness to defend it." Swain's was not a pro bono representation. "If you will attend this matter and have a decision," the attorney told him, "I will compensate you to your satisfaction."[22]

In Swain's time husbands controlled their wives' property, and he derived some of his wealth from Eleanor and her family. An early Swain diary entry is illustrative: "I bargained away my wifes Marsh Creek land to day to Ed Chappel." He also handled legal and financial matters for the White family, however, probably without compensation. He invested funds for the "maid servant" of one of Eleanor's sisters. He appears to have drafted documents arranging affairs between and among the sisters, including the allocation and hiring out of the family enslaved persons. He engaged in extensive financial dealings with a brother-in-law, Daniel L. Barringer, in Shelbyville, Tennessee, and was a Barringer creditor. At Barringer's death he perceived it "necessary for me to go there without delay." The subsequent death of his mother-in-law brought him "additional duties" at a time when his "previous engagements were sufficiently numerous and onerous." It was probably the settlement of her estate, with its many "perplexities," in which he was so "painfully and laboriously engaged" that he was "prevented from giving much thought to any literary subject."[23]

Swain's favorable financial situation enabled him to function as a smalltime banker, with numerous debtors. Loan purposes ranged from a sheep-raising business in Macon County to the purchase of a medical practice by a Battle son. Nicholas Woodfin, an Asheville attorney employed to collect Swain's notes, once wrote him: "so many applications have been made to you for the loan of money that I presume your patience if not your funds must be exhausted." Woodfin later informed Swain that more than $1,000 of "long deferred debts" were due him "in this country." Woodfin himself owed Swain money and was grateful that Swain was willing "to increase my debt to you & to allow it to remain unpaid for a while."[24] The debts ranged in amounts from as much as $3,000 to as little as $20.00. Even a $20.00 debt, however, could be difficult to pay. One such debtor did not "in anywise resist the justice of your claim," he told Swain, but he explained at length his reasons for nonpayment and his higher aspirations for the future.[25]

Inability-to-pay laments were common, even on these small debts. One debtor could not make payment on "the small note you hold against me" but promised to "use all my efforts to meet it." His only news was "the universal cry of hard times." Another sent $100.00 on account; this, he said, was "all the money I can with convenience command." Acknowledgment of the inability to pay was embarrassing but often necessary. Even when the sum Swain required was "small in proportion to the amount of the whole debt," it at times could not be paid without inconvenience. Swain's debtors' inability to pay him was often attributed to their own debtors' inability to pay them.[26]

Requests for indulgence were made and often granted, with due thanks to Swain. At times, however, he executed on the debt or was invited simply to take the security property. There were instances of debtors selling their "Negroes" (enslaved persons) to pay his claims. One debtor wished to substitute one set of "Negroes" for another as security for his debt. The mortgaged "Negroes," said the debtor, "are very desirous that I should allow them to find a purchaser in Raleigh and as they have been remarkably faithful I am disposed to gratify them." Another Swain debtor with "Negroes" as security planned to send them "to the South." This aroused Judge Battle's concern; "the negroes," Battle said, "must not be carried off without the express consent of the sureties."[27]

Some debtors gave Swain claims priority. One rented out his entire farm to pay off his debts, noting to Swain his intent to pay "particularly your debt." Failure to collect such sums could put Swain himself in straitened circumstances. Collection could prove difficult. Late in Swain's life an effort to secure payment from all who owed him was unproductive. "[A]ll seemed to have the same tale to tell of no money," came the report, "they mostly however speak that they will pay you if times ever get right again." Money, it was said, had never been so scarce and hard to collect.[28]

Due to the nature and extent of Swain's financial matters, he made extensive use of lawyers. In Macon County, Jacob Siler was his counsel, though during his travels, Judge Battle handled some Swain matters there. Battle also worked with Asheville lawyer Nicholas Woodfin on at least one suit brought by Swain. If the plan they had agreed upon worked, Battle told Swain, "you will have made a happy escape out of an unpleasant difficulty."[29]

Swain's most extensive legal dealings were with Woodfin. They communicated mostly by mail, though on occasion Woodfin thought it would be well for Swain to come to Buncombe "and see to the settling of some of your business there." Woodfin purchased and sold land for Swain. He collected payments and handled executions for him when payments were not forthcoming.[30]

Swain amassed, for the time, a handsome estate. The 1860 U.S. Census showed him with assets valued at $76,000. The Civil War, he told Zeb Vance, reduced his estate by more than half. His credit was as good as anyone's, he rightly claimed, yet there was no friend in the North to whom he could apply, even for $500.00, with reasonable assurance of success. For four years his UNC salary had been "merely nominal," leaving him and his family dependent on the earnings and accumulations of former years. He was unable to collect on substantial sums due to him. The laments were accurate, but the effects were hardly as calamitous as their tone might suggest. Swain had been an excellent financier, and even in the face of considerable loss, he had provided quite well for himself and his family.[31]

Finances, then, were important to Swain and consumed significant portions of his time and energy. But so, too, were friendships. He was a very friendly man, the consummate bonhomie. He clearly relished relating to Eleanor his arriving at a county court and being "immediately surrounded by friends." From a later excursion he informed her, with equal zest, "I have met with numerous friends and acquaintances and been every where received with cordiality and kindness." Among them was an old schoolmate whom he had not seen in twenty-eight years. On that journey he also recognized among the passengers "the first travelling companion I ever had except my brother James." The man has been his roommate in Columbia, South Carolina in 1820.[32]

Swain's prominence made it easy for friends to keep up with him. They took pride in his accomplishments. An old schoolmate, now living at a distance, had not returned to Buncombe in fourteen years. He was well aware, nevertheless, of Swain's "success in life" and the high esteem the people of North Carolina held for him. Although they had been separated for many years, he had never doubted "that the kind feelings ... remain in full force and only require a proper occasion for their manifestation." Another former school chum had "heard so much talk about his honor Judge Swain that ... I sometimes fancy that it can't be my good friend who changed clothes with me one Sunday morning for the purpose of astonishing the good people of church."[33]

A youthful Swain developed a special friendship with prominent eastern North Carolina lawyer and political leader William Gaston. An invitation for a Swain visit to Gaston's home in New Bern brought meticulous instructions from Gaston to his family. A room was to be fitted for Swain, while Gaston would "take a bed in the office." "I entertain a very high regard for him," Gaston said, "and desire to show him every attention in my power."[34] Gaston's family became extended family to Swain. A Swain diary entry three years later notes, "W. E. Manly marries Miss H. Gaston." Another Gaston daughter, Susan, married Robert Donaldson, UNC Class of 1818, and moved with him to New York. When in New York in 1842, Swain visited the Donaldsons. They were adding a wing to their house and thus could not make him as comfortable as they otherwise would have, Susan explained apologetically to her father.

Following Gaston's sudden death in 1844, the family turned to Swain for assistance in publishing Gaston's writings and speeches, together with a biography and selected letters. Any materials within Swain's reach were desired, as well as "your *impressions* of him." Fifteen years later found Swain still sending Susan historical pamphlets that might prove useful to a Gaston biographer.

Shortly after the Civil War ended, Swain served on the Board of Visitors at West Point. When the Donaldsons learned of this, they immediately invited him to visit. "We are anxious to see some Friend from NC," Robert wrote, "who can inform us of the conditions of old friends & acquaintances there." The visit was obviously meaningful to Swain, for he related it to his former student and faculty colleague Benjamin Hedrick, whose faculty tenure at UNC had been terminated prematurely by the events leading to the war.[35]

There was another prominent legal figure, also somewhat older, with whom Swain shared a special relationship of confidence and trust. Chief Justice Thomas Ruffin, a trustee of the university during most of Swain's presidency, coveted the company of Swain and other university savants. Ruffin at least perceived the relationship as sufficiently close that he felt free to ask his younger friend to pay his debt to a Chapel Hill resident, promising "to return it on sight." Swain was the willing recipient of Ruffin's poignant, introspective reflections upon his dissatisfaction with a late-in-life return to previously abandoned judicial labors.[36]

The intimate friendships Swain maintained with Charles Manly and Zebulon

William Gaston

Vance were not only work-related, but much more. The same can be said of the Swain-Nicholas Woodfin relationship. The Asheville attorney, whom Swain had prepared for the profession, handled considerable portions of his mentor's business. Their friendship was such, however, that Woodfin would request that Swain secure a silver cane Woodfin had left near Greensboro and return it to him "when you come up." Long after Swain's death Woodfin's daughter said, "I remember to have heard Governor Swain remark in my childhood that he knew the educated men of the state; and that not one was better read than my father for whom he seemed to entertain an admiration and affection almost paternal."[37]

There were others. John H. Wheeler evidenced their strong friendship by directing Governor Graham to remember him to Swain "[w]hen you see [him]." From his Washington, D.C., post Wheeler pledged to watch for Swain's daughter, probably Ellie, and to "make her sojourn agreeable in this City." Judge Mitchell King's home in Charleston had "[a]n apartment reserved and ready" for Swain; there would be a houseful of Kings, "young and old," but Swain was so "familiarized to numbers" that this would not inconvenience him. King "rejoiced" to his friend "in the career of usefulness and honor thro which a kind Providence has conducted and sustained you."[38]

From the time William H. Battle and his family moved to Chapel Hill, if not before, Swain, Battle, and the Battle family shared a special friendship. Theirs was an easy camaraderie, involving both small talk and mutual assistance with serious matters. In the small-talk category, Swain would discuss with Lucy Battle the temperature on particularly cold days or tease a Battle daughter about her beaux. Swain could get in trouble with Lucy by failing to note the beauty of a Battle grandchild, and Battle could suffer the same fate by reading a Swain letter prior to one from her. So common were Swain's visits to the Battle household that an unaccustomed lapse between them would leave Lucy perplexed. "I cannot but wonder why he does not visit us as formerly," she would say. When confronted with the omission, Swain pleaded travel or general busyness, and he unfailingly resumed the neighborly calls.[39]

Swain was a faithful correspondent with Battle during the latter's sojourns on the judicial circuits. Battle sometimes received family news from Swain before it arrived from Lucy.[40] During Battle's frequent absences from Chapel Hill, Swain assisted Lucy and the family in many ways. He advised Lucy on where to direct mail for her husband; delivered letters and packages from the family to Judge Battle; loaned the family corn, or purchased it for them, when needed; made purchases jointly with them; inquired after, and visited, Battle children when they were ill. When the Battles's son Kemp was a UNC student, Swain sent the standard reports on his progress: scholarship always "very good"; deportment once "very good except that he talks too much in the recitation room."[41]

No one exceeded Swain in concern for Battle's state supreme court prospects. The death of Judge Joseph J. Daniel in 1848 opened a seat, for which Battle and Richmond Pearson were the leading candidates. Swain's support for Battle was such that Lucy noted to her husband, "how sincerely attached to you he is." "[H]is anxiety about the matter," she believed, was "solely on [Battle's] account." When allegations surfaced that Swain had recommended Pearson, Swain sent Battle a detailed denial. If asked, he said, he would not hesitate to give Governor Graham his opinion favoring Battle. The outcome, Swain thought, was quite unpredictable.

Battle received the temporary appointment, a surprise to Lucy because Swain had "seemed so concerned about it beforehand." Months later, when the General Assembly gave Pearson the permanent appointment, Swain felt the loss keenly. Battle would later assume the high bench, but the interim failure to do so was painful. The experience produced this affectionate comment from Lucy to her husband: "I love the Gov: sincerely, purely I believe because he loves you."[42]

Swain shared business and political advice with Battle. He once thought, for example, that Battle should sell his interest in a factory because he lived too far

Governor
William. A. Graham

from it.⁴³ On circuit Battle, in turn, performed tasks for and gave reports to Swain. A common subject was the health of Swain's relatives whom Battle encountered in his travels. When Battle's *Almanac* arrived at his home during his absence, Swain "borrowed [it] immediately as usual," Lucy reported. He had just visited for the express purpose of returning it.⁴⁴

The David L. Swain-William A. Graham friendship, and that of their families, was clearly special. Each solicited overnight visits from the other. Graham wished Swain to stay with him during a Hillsboro meeting of the stockholders of the railroad. The possibility that he inadvertently offended Swain at that meeting disturbed Graham greatly. "I would not willingly be guilty of the slightest impropriety in a matter of respect and fidelity to you," Graham assured his friend.⁴⁵

Swain, in turn, extended similar invitations to Graham and his family. One of these is particularly affecting. Anne Swain died shortly before President Andrew Johnson's attendance at the 1867 UNC commencement, rendering Eleanor "inconsolable." She thus desired to see only intimate friends. She would, though, arrange places for Graham, Mrs. Graham, and their daughter Susan, and the Swains would be very glad to have the Grahams with them.⁴⁶ When Mrs. Graham's mother died, Graham found that Swain and Judge Battle were the witnesses to her will. "I . . . must beg you both to come to my house on some day during May Court and prove it," he wrote to Swain.[47]

The Grahams solicited and received Swain's assistance in improving their Hillsboro house and garden. Swain arranged a visit to the Graham property by New York architect A. J. Davis, who was doing work for the university. Ultimately the pressure of business precluded the Davis visit. Earlier, however, Davis had purchased furniture and oil paintings for Swain and Governor Morehead, and he offered the same service to the Grahams. Swain succeeded in loaning the university gardener to the Grahams, and upon request by Mrs. Graham, granted an extension of the time allowed for his work there.[48]

Swain was intensely human. Deaths of friends, or their imminently pending deaths, thus affected him deeply. "Heard to day of the death of A. D. Murphy [sic]," he noted in an early diary entry. A night "in my own house" in Asheville brought poignant memories of a close friend, recently killed in a duel. Only two months before, Swain told Eleanor, "my friend [Robert] Vance and myself . . . with no evil anticipation as to the future lay down in that spot and in that bed from which we rose to meet no more." These mournful thoughts had deprived him of sleep "untill [sic] day light." Upon the death of former Governor John Owen, Swain, again "with a great deal of feeling," called him "the fairest man he ever knew."[49]

Sons of friends informed Swain of their fathers' deaths or terminal illnesses. James T. Morehead, for example, advised him when Morehead's father, former Governor John M. Morehead, was "only a shade from death." Morehead expressed gratitude for Swain's "token of friendship and esteem for Father a day or two since." Knowing that another former governor, Edward B. Dudley, "held [Swain] among his cherished friends," Charles Manly gave Swain a touching account of his wife's trip to Wilmington "to visit poor Dudley in his last illness." Mrs. Manly's sister had been Dudley's first wife. The death of another prominent North Carolinian, George Badger, found Swain traveling to Raleigh for the memorial. Not wishing to grieve alone, he requested that Judge Battle accompany him.[50] Nor was it just the passings of prominent friends that pained him. Lucy Battle once reported him "very sorry to hear of the fate of his old *friend* and client (Duck Shelton)."[51]

Swain's condolences were appreciated, and their recipients shared with him the depths of their grief. While Jonathan Worth was the sitting governor, he lost a daughter. In acknowledging Swain's "kind letter of condolence," Worth noted his difficulty in recovering "from the afflicting shock."[52]

The sudden death of UNC professor James Phillips brought Zeb Vance's expressions of concern. Phillips was a "venerable and most highly respected friend,"

Vance said to Swain, whose passing had greatly affected all who knew or knew of him, "but more especially his old pupil." Swain was to convey to Mrs. Phillips the "earnest sympathy" of Vance and his wife.[53]

A friend's loss of a young child evoked Swain's heartfelt empathy. Upon the death of Kemp Battle's two-year-old daughter Penelope, Swain sent a lengthy sympathy letter, reflective both of his humanity and of his unhappy personal experiences. He assured Battle and his spouse "of Mrs. Swain's and my own deepest sympathy in this melancholy bereavement." "We have both," he continued, "like your father and mother been rendered most painfully familiar with such scenes." Only two of the Swains' six children, he stated as evidence, then survived.[54] At times these melancholy occasions made work for Swain. One friend, for example, asked that Swain write an epitaph for his late wife's tombstone. Swain, he said, had "[known] her character from childhood."[55]

Faith has long been the mechanism through which mortals handle the mysteries of death and its aftermath, if any. Swain was a man of faith. He attributed this to boyhood influences, saying: "My father was a Presbyterian elder and an Arminian; my mother was a Methodist and a Calvinist, who loved and studied Scott's Commentary. Their house was the home for preachers of all sorts west of the Blue Ridge. Bishop Asbury blessed me when a child; Mr. Newton, a Presbyterian, taught me when a boy, and Humphrey Posey, a Baptist, used to pray for me when a youth. So I love all who show that they are Christians."[56] As a young man "[a] very rainy day" might see Swain "not go to preaching." More commonly, though, Sundays found him there, not infrequently at both morning and evening services.[57]

Motivation for his piety stemmed at least in part from a serious illness when he was twenty-two. A Swain diary entry notes the tenth anniversary of a morning when he awoke "under a violent fever which confined [me] to my bed 10 days and interrupted my [law] studies for three months." "Like everyone else in affliction," Swain "thought if . . . spared[,] I should pursue a more pious course of life than I have done." He did so on that day at least, hearing "three sermons . . . in the Meth[odist] E[piscopal] Ch[urch]."[58]

Friends and acquaintances would not permit him to forget or ignore the importance of faith. One of his debtors once proposed a course that should be followed in case one of them was "called home." On their first acquaintance, he said, Swain had expressed a sincere desire to be a Christian. "Such righteous desires," the debtor continued, "are always answered." He held "an unshaken hope" that Swain would "have an inheritance with the sanctified when the Heavenly Caanan shall be divided." Charles F. Deems, Methodist minister and former UNC faculty member, told Swain he had "not ceased for long years to pray for you and yours."

Even one who had wronged Swain bringing him angry tears believed he had "long since forgiven the offense." If they, as humans, could forgive, he said, God was even better at it.[59]

Family members, too, encouraged religious devotion. Foremost among them was Swain's older brother George, the largest beneficiary of Swain's Christian charity. A George Swain letter offers insight into David Swain's devotional life. "You went to prayer with us," said George, "and in doing so first repeated the Lords prayer and then thanked the lord for having taught us how to pray and you might have gone a little farther and thanked a good old pious mother for having caused you and me to put this prayer into practice and then stopped or paused perhaps for a minute or more and I thought you was done. But you then commenced a new in a humble devout and sincere manner and with the simplicity of a child went through *your devotion*." Eternal life was of utmost concern to George. He was pleased when David "express[ed] a deep concern" about his "future welfare" but still admonished that they must "above every thing else try to prepare for our latter end." An aunt had the same concern. Late in Swain's life she wished to know whether he had thought about the saving of his soul. She also inquired whether "you and your fair lady belong to a church and to what church?"[60]

Swain shared this concern for, and belief in, the hereafter. He once told Eleanor that their "connexion [was] not to terminate with our present state of existence, but to be pure and perfect in a purer world." "[W]ith respect to preparation for another world," he said, "both of us have much to accomplish." Following Elisha Mitchell's death, Swain noted that Mitchell's remains would in due time be removed from Asheville to the loftiest peak of the Black Mountain, "where they will find their appropriate resting place until the last trump shall awake the sleeping dead." He once concluded a letter to a former student by wishing him happiness, both in the present "and eternal."

Swain also believed in "the kindness of an overruling Providence." He tried "to be content with the dispensations of Providence both in prosperity and adversity." In times of affliction, however, he read the book of Job, "a more pious and patient man than I am," he admitted. Even in his historical writings, he would say "there is a God that ruleth in the affairs of men."[61]

When informing Eleanor of the death of an acquaintance caused by "dissipation," Swain observed that she would be "very agreeably surprized at the remarkable change wrought upon him, with regard to his religious views, during his dying sufferings." His inquiry about whether a Revolutionary War general had prayer "at the head of his troops" probably stemmed more from religious than purely historical interest. His biblical scholarship was such that he could recommend a commentary. He took seriously the commandment to observe the

Sabbath and keep it holy. "It is a very unusual thing," he once said, "for me to write a business communication on the Sabbath."[62]

The Reverend Charles Phillips wrote of Swain, "Time and again he has told me that his only satisfaction was in crying out "Lord be merciful to me a sinner"— "Lord I believe—help thou mine unbelief." Phillips's sister Cornelia said Swain "was not afraid of being known as a praying man." After his daughter Anne's death, it was his daily practice to pray at her grave just before dawn.[63]

It was "at the instance of the President [Swain]" that the UNC faculty adopted the practice of opening its meetings with prayer. Swain also used his biblical knowledge to admonish the students. A "crowd of idlers" once insisted that he take a text and give them a sermon. At first he demurred, but upon increased importunings he invited "their serious consideration of . . . Matthew [20:6]: 'Why stand ye here all the day idle?'" He spoke of "duty neglected, opportunities wasted, of temptations that lie in wait for the idle, of hopes disappointed and parental hearts crushed," until one by one his audience faded away. It was said that there was "no intimation that he was ever asked for another."[64]

While ecumenical in outlook and action—for example, he contributed financially to the construction of the 1835 Catholic Church in Raleigh—by affiliation Swain was a Presbyterian. Notwithstanding regular church attendance, he did not join a church until he was forty-three. At age thirty-four, in the 1835 Constitutional Convention debates, he referred to himself as "half a member" of the Presbyterian Church. Swain perhaps spoke metaphorically. He was, however, well-versed in American history. He thus could have alluded to the New England Congregationalists' 1662 "Halfway Covenant," a form of partial church membership for children and grandchildren of church members that did not require the profession of a conversion experience. In any event, his first known church membership was in the New Hope Presbyterian congregation in Orange County, which he joined in 1844. On October 26, 1845, Swain and Charles Phillips were dismissed from New Hope by certificate to join the new Presbyterian Church in Chapel Hill, in which Swain was an organizer and a ruling elder. In 1846, he and others bought from the university, for $200.00, the lot on which that church still stands. Swain assisted James Phillips with fundraising for the building and said he contributed $450.00 of the $3,589.00 with which the building was begun. According to Swain the church had "Negro" members, both enslaved and free. A marble tablet that commemorates the "long and faithful services" of Swain and three contemporaries remains on a stairway landing in Chapel Hill's University Presbyterian Church.[65]

The North Carolina Bible Society attracted Swain's participation. He was initially elected a manager and later a vice president. The death of the society's president once elevated him to that office. In 1852, he addressed the annual meeting, reading documents prepared and issued by Congress in revolutionary times that "show[ed] the feelings of dependence upon Almighty God which possessed the minds and characterized the conduct of our forefathers." "[O]ur liberties," he said, "were bottomed on the Bible, and they could not endure if the Bible should cease to be circulated and read."[66]

Later the American Bible Society elected Swain a vice president, hoping that he would accept "and lend us your counsel from time to time." He accepted and actively participated. An account of a society meeting in Cleveland, Ohio, has him assisting "in the chair."[67] The society requested a contribution from Swain to a pamphlet containing sentiments of distinguished public men "as to *the value of the Bible*." Such a volume would, it was thought, "be attended with salutary results." The society wished to "show our young country men how you regard the Scriptures." Swain's sentiments would join those of other notables such as Adams, Clay, Jackson, Jay, Marshall, Washington, and Wilberforce.

Swain's response noted the childhood influence of his pious parents. He had then been inspired by John Quincy Adams's suggestion to his son "to read the Sacred Volume through once a year (five chapters a day)." At UNC he heard recitations from students every Sabbath and directed their attention to the Holy Scriptures. "If the Scriptures are true," Swain posited, "they are a revelation and the only revelation from the most High God, upon the most important subject that can engage the attention of men." "They are therefore . . . of inconceivable interest and importance," he continued. Even if false, which he clearly did not believe, "have they no claims to the consideration of the scholar and philosopher?" he asked. The Bible, he concluded, "continues to the present time to exert a controlling influence over the minds and hearts of estimable and amiable men."[68] Swain's will left to each of his three children "a copy of the Holy Scriptures to be selected from my Library in the order of their names [Anna Caroline, Richard Caswell, and Eleanor]."[69]

As noted, a youthful illness enhanced, perhaps produced, Swain's piety. It would perhaps be inaccurate and unfair to credit his enduring faithfulness to similar causes, but the fact is that he dealt with health concerns for much of his life. A contemporary who knew him well noted that early in his career Swain observed signs of pulmonary weakness in himself following the loss of three sisters to consumption. Battle's history states that for reasons of health, he did not often attend entertainment at night.[70]

In Swain's travels as a young lawyer, he complained of "fatigue from attendance on court" and of being generally indisposed. He received the standard nineteenth-century treatment: the doctor "took a pint of blood and gave me an oz of castor oil," he reported. The following morning brought no improvement. He could not retain a first dose of salt and tartar, but a second one "operated very well." Three weeks later Swain found himself "altho somewhat emaciated and feeble, almost entirely restored."[71]

While governor, Swain deferred a visit to New Bern, blaming "[s]ymptoms of bilious disease." Two days later he reported to William Gaston that his health was better, but he was "suffering from indigestion, accompanied by a most tormenting headache." At the time he was struggling with political problems and imploring Gaston to be his mentor. It is thus reasonable to suspect a psychosomatic dimension to the ailment.[72]

There were episodic health concerns throughout his UNC time. "The Gov. from illness gave us a snap in the afternoon," a student once recorded. Faculty minutes would show "[t]he Pres.... absent on account of indisposition." He still suffered instances of "Billous [sic] fever." There was "a crick in his neck and back" and a cold with a handicapping effect on his eyes. He once told Lucy Battle he did not feel well; "indeed," she told her husband, "he has been complaining for some time."[73]

An 1847 illness stranded Swain in Raleigh. It was sufficiently serious that William A. Graham, then the sitting governor, spent almost half his time with his friend. Judge Cameron also visited at some length.[74] An undefined "indisposition" lingered through much of 1859–1860. John H. Wheeler held an early hope that Swain's health "was restored." The hope proved vain. Swain remained "quite unwell." Governor Morehead's concern for him was "greatly heightened by the position you occupy." Swain should not concern himself with the college exercises: "we had much rather have your services a long time if not so intensely rendered than for a short period," Morehead admonished.[75]

It was sound advice, for three days later Swain reported himself "free from disease" but "unable to walk from my residence to college." A few days later still he was able to leave his room but remained absent from public events. The illness confined him to bed for three weeks. It was, Swain said later, "characterized by an incessant and racking cough, which still pursues me." He received letters of condolence "from various quarters" and gifts of oranges, lemons, fruits, and flowers.[76] "Gov. Swain," a newspaper soon related, "is slowly creeping up hill again.... [I]t must have been gratifying that so many and such prominent friends expressed lively solicitude for his recovery." He also received congratulations for how well he then got through the proceedings at commencement. Friends were happy to know that his "health is convalescent."[77]

These felicitous observations were premature. His "slowly returning strength," he said, had proven unequal to his "protracted illness." His health was still such that President James Buchanan "inquired most kindly" about it, wishing to know when Swain proposed to fulfill his promise to visit Washington. By the following winter Swain still found himself "in not very robust health." He soon said, "My health has not improved and my collegiate duties require all my attention." He was not well enough, he said, to leave Chapel Hill.[78]

In spring 1860, he recorded a specific condition. "[T]he routine of the vernal season," he told Francis Hawks, "carries with it symptoms of disease that may materially interfere with my historical inquiries." It was the spring allergies in Chapel Hill, then and now an affliction to many. By late spring Swain described himself to Hawks as "in greatly improved health, and ready to ... [examine] your permanent index of the Bancroft MSS."[79]

The winter of 1862 found Swain again "quite ill," still meeting his classes, but in his bed chamber. He depicted the onset of the illness as "a chill, succeeded by a violent pain in the right ear, ending with a fever, and prostration of strength, so that I have been virtually *hors decombate* ever since." When his health improved, it was "not so rapidly as I could desire." Even when he was "entirely restored," he had "not altogether recovered my strength." His friends told him it still would be "rashness" to undertake a journey to Raleigh.[80]

Christmas 1866 brought "a severe cold." He had not left the house for two days, he told Governor Graham. Unfortunately, reports of this nature were all too common. All of Swain's life, but particularly in his later years, his health situation could be described by the trite expression "one thing after another."[81]

Loss of hearing was the most handicapping of Swain's health problems. Just when deafness descended on him is unclear. By his mid-fifties, however, it was a serious problem. As Swain and Professor Herrisse sparred over the university's disciplinary standards and practices, Swain acknowledged that his deafness at the time was so great that he "was unable to hear a word spoken either by Mr. Herrise or [the student involved]." He later admitted to Judge Asa Biggs, "My hearing is not very acute."

Charles Manly informed him of an "almost entirely deaf" woman who had "some sort of sounding apparatus fixed in her ears" and consequently "hears very well with an ordinary tone." Swain did not pursue a similar course, and consequently Charles Phillips soon observed that "his deafness increases on him." A receipt shows him paying a doctor $50.00 "For Medical Treatment of the Ear." There is also a prescribed treatment and follow-up. The treatments probably were largely useless. The problem continued to plague him, and it was a factor in his ultimate loss of position and influence.[82]

One further personal item was conspicuous. The man's handwriting was outrageously bad. This was not, at least initially, a result of old age and palsied hands. A letter to his father written when he was twenty states, "Pardon this miserable scrawl, the offspring of hurry and necessity." A decade later Swain pleaded a fractured arm and a dislocated shoulder in mitigation, hoping soon to be able to address the recipient in a more legible hand. The mending of these body parts was of little help, however; the following year he told William Gaston he would be gratified "if the slovenly character of my writing . . . do[es] not put it out of your power to comprehend my object."[83]

Almost another decade had passed when Swain ended a letter to William A. Graham by saying, "I fear that my cal[l]igraphy gives little evidence of the favorable effects of time, upon my physical constitution." He similarly feared that "a bad pen and trembling hand" would render a letter to Eleanor difficult to read. He wished the recipient of one of his letters "great success in your pursuits, and especially in your efforts to decipher this communication."[84]

Swain's compatriots in his historical endeavors—George Bancroft, Benjamin Lossing, Francis L. Hawks, and Griffith J. McRee—all had problems with his handwriting. So, too, did his colleagues in university governance. Thomas Ruffin once told him that no matter how badly written his own composition might be, "anyone who can read your manuscript can gallop through mine!" Charles Manly once thanked Swain for his "last epistle," stating, "[i]t has furnished me with occupation for 4 days."[85] Business partners suffered the same inconvenience. Swain's brother-in-law, with whom he kept some of his enslaved persons, once told him: "I cannot read the name of your friend to whom you wish to write on the subject of your negroes. I would be pleased if you would write a letter more legibly."[86] A younger contemporary once described the handwriting of one of his correspondents as "crabbed and hieroglyphical beyond anything I ever saw, unless I except that of Gov. D. L. Swain, who once wrote me several letters which I was obliged to answer at a venture, not knowing much of their contents." "It is not surprising," he continued, "to read of Mr. S's letter to the President, 'that the whole force of experts in the Attorney General's office was necessary to decypher it for the perusal of the President.'"[87]

The gripes of Swain's contemporaries were well founded. None of them, however, had the extensive cause to scold him about his handwriting that his biographer does. They, after all, suffered only episodic bouts with singular missives from him. The biographer, by contrast, has confronted an entire cache of them, covering the man's entire lifetime. The stinting, indistinct hand in which he wrote has probably added a year or two to this endeavor to tell his life story. If the man and the biographer meet beyond the pearly gates, there will be words about this.

CHAPTER 22

The "Peculiar Institution"
"Now upon the subject of your Negroes"

David Swain owned enslaved persons. He inherited them, purchased them, sold them, hired them out, took them as security for debts, and used them in his personal life and work and that of the university. From his childhood until political and legal developments brought them freedom, enslaved persons were an important aspect of his daily life.

Swain's father, George Swain, owned enslaved persons and used them in his hat-making business. He once wrote David about a runaway enslaved person named Daniel. Daniel had fallen in with some "free people of colour and white Negroes," who, George feared, might "secrete him a long time and perhaps cause me to lose him forever." George had punished him for being "impertinent" and "very neglectful in his business." He had also reduced his weekend-pass time by requiring his return on Sunday night rather than Monday morning. Fine clothes made a fool of Daniel, so George took them away; Daniel managed, however, to secure assorted finery elsewhere. In addition to George's concerns about Daniel, he complained to David that "[t]he troops of little negroes through the town are continually robbing the gardens of fruits."[1]

The degree to which his father's attitude regarding the "peculiar institution" influenced Swain's is impossible to determine. The fact that from earliest childhood he lived with evidence of it inevitably had some bearing, however. He then married into an Eastern North Carolina family with many "Negroes" and became friendly with the enslaving interests in that area with a much larger enslaved population. In 1826, the year of his marriage, he commenced acquiring enslaved persons for himself. When Eleanor's father's estate was divided years later, Swain acquired some of the enslaved persons.[2]

As with all longtime enslavers, the number of enslaved persons Swain held fluctuated over his lifetime. The 1850 Federal Census of enslaved persons for Orange

County shows him with nineteen; the 1860 Census, with thirty-two, seventeen male and fifteen female, ranging in age from ten months to fifty years. In 1858, he executed a will leaving Eleanor his residuary estate, including "fifteen slaves in the possession of Dr. J. S. Blackman of Shelbyville, Tenn. [and] twenty slaves in my own possession." A list in the Swain papers captioned "Home Slaves Confederate Tax 1864" contains thirty-five names, with dates that appear to be birth years. In 1850, 73 percent of North Carolina families had no enslaved persons; in 1860, 72 percent had none. In 1850, more than half the enslavers had fewer than ten; in 1860, 67 percent had fewer than ten. Viewed in this context, Swain was a substantial enslaver.[3]

Accordingly, when Swain as governor championed suppression of abolitionist publications,[4] it was not just his constituents' interests that he was protecting but his own as well. His views on race and human bondage were traditional for a white male member of the propertied class of his time. As a young man prosecuting the criminal dockets in northeastern North Carolina, he described the morals of a small county as depraved, "owing," he said, "to the great proportion of free negroes and mulattoes in the county who not only grow up in vice and wretchedness themselves but spread a moral pestilence around them." Contrastingly, he displayed a capacity for humane concern for the bondsmen. He lacked respect for one of his hosts, he once said, "owing principally to his speculation in negroes." And he praised a friend by saying there was not "a kinder mistress ... in a journey of 1000 miles."[5]

As a slaveowner Swain was considered "conspicuously lenient," to the point that he "spoilt" his enslaved persons. Kemp Battle recounts a counter instance when, "irritated beyond measure by his washerwoman," Swain "seized a switch to punish her." The woman responded that she could "supply back as long as you can supply whip!" The episode is neither reported nor documented elsewhere, and the present endeavor has produced no other evidence that could be construed as physical cruelty on Swain's part toward his enslaved persons, or even the threat or likelihood of it.

Battle also notes that Swain's "female slaves multiplied rapidly, although they did not enter into the matrimonial engagements usual among enslaved persons, which though not binding in law, were as much respected in fact as are now legal marriages in some of our states." A twentieth-century dissertation speculates that Swain may have discouraged family ties that might have interfered with breeding, thereby diminishing his wealth in slave property. The assertion is conjectural, incapable of proof or refutation.[6] As to his views on colonization, on at least one occasion he made a small financial contribution to the American Colonization Society.[7]

Early in Swain's marriage to Eleanor he bought enslaved persons for her mother. The purchase was "an advantageous one," he thought, "if the description given me of the negroes is a correct one." A few months later he was making such acquisitions for himself. An 1829 memorandum in his papers states, "I have sold to David L. Swain negroe woman Cherry and her child for . . . $350." The purpose was to pay certain debts. Swain then attended a sale "to purchase a chambermaid for my wife." The personalities involved make another of his acquisition transactions interesting. James C. Johnston, by his attorney James Iredell, for $900.00 paid in land, conveyed to Swain "a negro woman named Rose, aged about twenty-three years," and her two young daughters. The acknowledgement was by Joseph J. Daniel, one of the judges of the state supreme court.[8]

Many of Swain's enslaved person dealings were with his mountain relatives. A Franklin attorney wished to sell Swain "two young negroes," a Swain nephew once wrote, but felt "some delicacy" in pricing them. If Swain would take them, the lawyer could "about pay his debts and keep his land and the balance of his negroes."[9]

Swain's half-brother then wanted Swain to take his "Negroes" and release him from his debts, owed, apparently, to Swain. Would Swain, the brother asked, consider "the negroes . . . growth equal to the interest on my notes"? Shortly there would "also be an increase in the family." Humane considerations entered the brother's thoughts. While by separating them, he could sell them with little difficulty, that would, he said, "render them unhappy and be unpleasant to me." All had been raised in the family, and he was "very loath to see them go out of it."[10]

At a sale to satisfy a nephew's debt, apparently to him, Swain purchased the nephew's "15 negroes." An agent bid them in for him for just over $3,000. In reporting the transaction to Swain, Nicholas Woodfin stated, "The woman and 4 children worth $1,000 went off at the first bid $600 tho they have cried near ½ hour." "They are as likely a lot of negroes as I ever saw together," said Woodfin, who viewed the acquisitions as "a good investment." A humane consideration crept into the description: Woodfin "was pleased to see them kept together and in hand[s] that would not for gain separate mothers and children." The nephew hoped, in a few years, to pay his debts. "And the negroes," he said to Swain, "I hope you will give me a chance to redeem."[11] The transaction appears to have been arranged within the family to clear the nephew's indebtedness. Swain was doing him a favor but clearly benefiting himself in the process. It was later said within the family that Swain had purchased the "Negroes" at considerably less than their value, apparently notwithstanding the fact that the most valuable among them, "a grown boy," had died.[12]

While on the judicial circuits Judge Battle handled some of Swain's business about the enslaved. "The negro boy Jim, whom you purchased," he once told Swain from the West, "is in the possession of Mr. McDaniel." At the "owner's" death the "owner" had intended "the little negro" for his mother's "owner." He "would have made a stretch to have redeemed him," but the power was now in Swain's hands to disappoint both the boy's "owner" and his mother's.[13]

At one point in Swain's brother George's financial difficulties, apparently at Swain's suggestion George directed the sheriff to make a levy on all his "Negroes." Swain in turn directed a nephew to bid for one or two of them "as the case might present itself." George's son-in-law, Dr. Crawford W. Long, also desired to own some of them. If Swain's agent bought them low, and Swain did not wish to keep them, Long would pay for them and take possession the first of the following year.[14]

Shortly before the Civil War, Swain paid a Tennessee man $1,400 for "a negro man [age twenty-four]," warranted to be "sound, sensible[,] healthy and a slave for life."[15] Unless the enslaved man died before the Emancipation Proclamation and the Thirteenth Amendment freed all enslaved persons, he was not, in fact, as warranted, "a slave for life." Such loss of property by operation of law, however, would have left Swain with no legal remedy against the seller.

At times the enslaved were exchanged rather than purchased. If Swain had "qualative [sic] negroes, or any that might have faults," and if he was willing to dispose of them, a trader once offered, he could do so. The trader would replace them "with such as are good." Swain could "make such a selection as you will have no just cause for complaint."[16]

Using enslaved persons as a medium of exchange was also at least contemplated. A nephew once offered to sell Swain his Asheville house "and let you pay me for it in negroes." Later, to alleviate the nephew's economic distress Swain was willing to take half his land but to allow him to have the enslaved persons for five years or longer upon terms "any judges of such property may consider f[ai]r."[17]

The enslaved were also used as security for, and in payment of, debts. If Swain knew anyone willing to lend him money, a nephew once wrote, he would give "a lean [sic] on as many negroes as will be thought sufficient security for the money." He wished to purchase "two negroe boys" to employ in his wool hats business, and Swain was to inquire for him "whether such boys could be had and at what prices." To satisfy his debt to Swain, the nephew later wrote, he would sell or set apart land "and as many negroes as will be all sufficient." Another Swain correspondent would execute "any release that you consider necessary and proper . . . of my lien upon the negroes."[18]

Swain also hired out his enslaved persons. The first page of the diary he began keeping in 1832 states, "Hired Eliza (F) to Patrige (?) for $25." A note in Swain's papers contains a promise to pay him "for the use of his negro boy John." The maker of another note "for the hire of [Swain's] boy Sam" promised, in addition to payment of $350.00, "to furnish said boy with the usual clothing."[19]

Cooks were in demand. A Swain nephew once told his uncle he was trying every way possible to secure one. If Swain could spare him "a Girl that will answer my purpose for this year," he pledged, he would "try very hard to get me a white cook by next fall." Once Swain leased his enslaved person Cherry and her daughter to cook for a family. The man of the house then wished to keep them; it would be almost impossible, he said, to find a replacement for them in the area.[20]

It was not Swain's only experience of difficulty in securing the return of his rented enslaved persons. A Shelbyville, Tennessee planter once hired several of them. At the end of the contracted year, he did not wish to surrender them. He pleaded his harvest schedule, the pregnancy of one, and other reasons. Ultimately Swain dispatched his nephew to retrieve them, but almost a year past the original due date for their return.

Undeterred by this adversity, Swain continued to rent out his enslaved persons in increasing numbers. "Now upon the subject of your negroes," Nicholas Woodfin once wrote, if Swain could send them to him, he could "yet hire them to advantage for the rest of the year."[21]

Well after the Emancipation Proclamation, Swain still rented out enslaved persons. "I have hired of David L. Swain his negro woman Caroline with her child Aetina," states a late 1864 memorandum. The renter was "to make proper provision for them in sickness and health[,] to supply them with three good suits of clothing suitable to the seasons[,] . . . good pair of shoes and a blanket or bed quilt[,] and to return her at Chapel Hill on the 25 December next to the said David L. Swain." On January 1, 1865, another renter promised to pay Swain $400.00 in Confederate money one year from date "for the hire of George." Unfortunately for Swain, when that year ended Confederate money was worthless and it was illegal to possess it.[22]

Despite owning the enslaved, on occasion Swain hired some himself. He once told Eleanor he did "not know what to say about hiring negroes." "[A]t the present price of provision," he stated, "it is desirable to reduce the number." She should do what was needed, however, to "best answer your own purposes." His object was to make her burdens "as light as possible."[23] Swain also once needed "two house servants." A nephew had recommended two to him. Unless they were indispensable to the nephew's father, Swain wished "to take them before a great while." It is unclear whether the servants were his or he was to lease them. It is clear, however, that the nephew knew more about them than Swain did.²⁴

Leasing involved movement of Swain's enslaved persons, particularly those situated in Western North Carolina and Eastern Tennessee. This could prove problematic. "I have received your anunciation of a determination to remove your negroes to Macon," Swain's Tennessee brother-in-law once told him, adding, "and of course acquiesce." He was skeptical about the benefits, however. "If the products of the mountains meet with no better market than ours," he said, "you will realize little profit." A nephew in Macon County stood ready to assist. He thought they should manage the farm themselves—hired white men, he said, "do no good"—but Swain would need to "furnish your proportional part of hands."²⁵

Swain had been on an extended tour in the North. Upon his return he was disappointed to find no missive from the brother-in-law indicating "whether you could undertake to deliver my negroes in Macon," and if not, "whether you could supply a small wagon and mule for the purpose." He saw no alternative to asking his nephew to "bring the negroes"; however, he told the brother-in-law, he "would greatly prefer [his] bringing on the negroes."²⁶

The brother-in-law, in turn, could be ready to send them any time. The winter had been unfavorable for outdoor work, but he would not delay their departure on that account. The roads were impassable, however, and other causes had "conspire[d] to delay their departure." He clearly wished to retain some of the enslaved labor and may well have delayed sending it on that account.²⁷ The delays put Swain's nephew "in a very awkward situation." He needed the labor. "[I]f your hands should not come," he now told Swain, "I will hire some and do as well as I can."²⁸

Ultimately, some of the enslaved persons arrived in Macon. "Two of your Negroes from Tennessee on there way to D R Lowry staid at Jno. Silers night before last," Swain was advised. A year later, though, some still had not been delivered. Swain's brother-in-law hoped to deliver the enslaved persons to Macon "during the year."²⁹

Just when Swain initially placed his enslaved in Tennessee is unclear. Upon his purchase of the Macon County farm, he notified his brother-in-law that the arrangement might now be short-term. For approximately two-and-one-half years he had given his nephew exclusive control of the Macon County farm. During that time, he would expect his "Negroes" to remain in Tennessee; afterward, he probably would be disposed to remove them.³⁰

When their removal later came, it was, as noted, partial. The enslaved who remained in Tennessee were multiplying, so rapidly in fact that they had become a burden. They were "of no sort of service," the brother-in-law informed Swain, "as they neither feed or clothe themselves." "[T]ell me what to do with them," he implored. Nothing came of this. Many months later the report to Swain from Tennessee was, "Your negroes are all well." The multiplication had continued. Cherry had had a son, and Tom had sired a daughter. But, the brother-in-law now repeated, "Your negroes [have become] a burden to me.... Tell me what to do with them."[31]

Steadfast inaction was Swain's response. Months later still, the brother-in-law continued to plead with Swain "to have some disposition made of your large family of negroes who hang heavily on me."[32] From Swain came more inertia. "I have very long looked for a letter from you," said his relative, "but having rec[eive]d none I have come to the conclusion to wake you up—if you be not in too profound a snooze." He was now quite hard on Swain, and rightly so. "I can continue to raise negroes for you," he said, "but I must ask for a living chance; yours have swallowed me up—and the end will be, after I am too old to work, I shall have to earn my daily bread." He blamed himself—"you will not consider this any impeachment of yourself," he stated, overly deferential—but "with the support of your negroes, and debt and Interest, you must reduce me to beggary." Swain, he now said, "must either remove them or make some adequate allowance."[33]

What allowance was made, if any, is unclear. Soon, though, the brother-in-law appeared satisfied with, or resigned to, the situation. "[T]he negroes will remain until it shall be your interest or pleasure to remove them," he told Swain, noting that he saw "no great demand here *now* for such property." The longstanding imposition on his longsuffering relative was not one of Swain's finer moments.[34]

Some of Swain's enslaved persons presented behavioral problems. Swain's brother-in- law once found himself in the middle of "a war between Tony and Cherry—originating out of some shocking attempts or advances—made by him to Jane." The "strange part" was that "Tony swore to her [Cherry] that he would not rest until he had a child by Jane." Cherry, it was said, "was not slow in arraigning Tony." In fact, she swore that she would kill him. Jane was thought blameless in the matter, but she could have no peace there and would be more valuable if separated from Tony and Cherry. "[Y]our own judgment," the brother-in-law said to Swain, "will suggest the remedy."[35]

A larger problem was "*Henderson your Boy*," as Swain's nephew farm partner called one enslaved person. Henderson first appears in Swain's story in a bereavement and illness context. Since the death of his brother, Swain's nephew reported,

Henderson had been unable to work, though he himself had "not had the feavor" but only some "pains in head, back and limbs."[36]

Apparently concluding that Henderson was unsuited for farm work, Swain soon leased him to a man in Raleigh. "[Y]our boy Henderson," the lessee soon told Swain, was "one of the most insolent negroes" he had ever seen "and in every respect unfit to live as a House servant or about any person ... in Raleigh." Henderson had refused to do anything the mistress directed, saying he would "have but one Master." Henderson had said he would not live with Swain another year, "that you might do what you please with him." The man found the idea "of whipping other folks Negroes" unappealing. Swain, he thought, would "prefer taking him home and disposing of him yourself by my paying for the time he has been with me." If Henderson remained in Raleigh, Swain might lose him altogether. He would, the man predicted, "[e]ither run away or get killed for his insolence." A postscript states that Henderson had just reported that he had been severely beaten by a white man, who had charged him with impudence. "This only confirms my suspicion," Swain's lessee said, "that he will get killed if he stays in Raleigh."[37]

Two months later the lessee's patience was exhausted. He had gotten along without whipping Henderson, but "to day," he said, "I have had him put in jail." Since the lessee's last letter to Swain, Henderson's conduct had been "very outrageous." He had "taken up with a free Negro woman and ... separated from his wife." His conduct toward her had been "outrageous." The lessee had prevented him from beating her, "though he has got his sticks several times to do so." He had, however, beaten the lessee's cook severely, and for two days had made the lessee's lot "a perfect nuisance to the whole neighborhood cursing in the most profane manner and threatening to kill." Economic considerations restrained him from whipping. "I have not had him whipped yet," he said, "thinking it might hurt the sale to whip him as severely as I should have it done if whip[p]ed at all."

He could sell Henderson at "the top price for any negro," he told Swain, and he inquired whether that would not be "the best thing you can do with him." Henderson's ultimate fate is unknown, but clearly his behavior was a serious problem to the lessee. It is equally clear that economic rather than humane concerns motivated Swain's lessee's restraints in dealing with him.[38]

By contrast, there is some evidence of humane (arguably) considerations on the part of Swain and his nephew. Henderson once wished to be hired by a man in Franklin. Swain's nephew considered a conversation with the man on the subject. He had seen the man in town drunk, however, and decided against it. "[A]s

Henderson is said to be fond of liquor," he told Swain, "I know the arrangement would not suit you."

The nephew was also encouraging Swain to move "the negroes" to Chapel Hill because he "would make more to have them taken there." Henderson, he told Swain, had requested him to say "that you have treated him too well for him to murmur at going to Chapel Hill." His preference, though, was "for you to buy his wife or that he could remain in Macon." Henderson was then "at Uncle T. R. Siler's." He would learn things there that would "be useful to him in going to Chapel Hill," and, said the nephew, "he prefers being neare his wife while here."[39]

Enslaved persons' health problems were frequent concerns. Lucy Battle once reported to her husband that Eleanor Swain was sick, and Governor Swain also had "some sick negroes." Later she noted that a "servant girl" of Swain's, "in one of the outhouses," was "thought to be as dangerously ill as Bunc." At Swain's request, Lucy had sent a Battle "servant" woman to "go and sit up with her."[40]

Swain received reports on the health of his enslaved persons in Tennessee. "Your negroes have all been in health," his brother-in-law once told him, "except Leherry (?) who I feared was going into consumption." The enslaved person was now better but not yet well. "I will some day shortly send you the ages and weight of your negroes respectively," he closed. After the brother-in-law's death, the successor custodian rendered similar accounts.[41]

Injuries from accidents affected the enslaved and altered the plans of their masters. Swain had once planned to attend the annual meeting of the UNC trustees. A serious accident the previous day to a household "servant" would, however, forbid his leaving home, he informed the board secretary.[42]

Death also came to the enslaved. A nephew once notified Swain from the West that "one of the negroes ... (a grown boy) is dead." Later a "negro child ... was burned to death on a very windy and ... cold day in the negro cabin." The doctor could do nothing, and the child died about two hours after it was burned. One of Swain's Tennessee enslaved women had a baby who died. Shortly before commencement of the Civil War, Lucy Battle advised Judge Battle that "[t]he Governors man Hansnar (?) [was] buried yesterday."[43]

Swain gave a poignant account of the passing of a "servant," almost certainly an enslaved person. "Poor old Phebe," he told Eleanor, "died last Saturday night very suddenly." Although death was sudden, she "had been seriously indisposed for some time." A week previously she had visited the Swain household in Asheville "to take her leave of the family." She had refused to leave until Swain "could come down from Court." When he entered, she cried and expressed a keen desire to see him in heaven. She had promised Swain's sister Polly that she would meet her there. Phebe was "a most faithful servant," Swain said, who was now "gone to her reward."[44]

There were other longtime "servants" in Swain's experience. One named John was his traveling companion. A diary entry from Swain's time traveling the judicial circuits notes: "set out ... with John at 8am.... Road not very good." When a carriage accident dislocated Swain's shoulder, John was with him. He "rendered very prompt and efficient service," Swain stated, "and perhaps saved my life." John had been faithful ever since. "[H]is services on this occasion," Swain acknowledged, "will excuse with me a multitude of previous shortcomings."[45]

Once Swain assigned John to work in the garden. "As usual," he told Eleanor, "his progress is not very rapid." Still, "with all his defects," Swain said, "I might not perhaps find it very easy to procure a servant that would suit me so well in every respect."[46] John's "defects" continued to manifest themselves, however. A frustrated Swain soon told Eleanor that John was "so poor a body servant, so indolent and so inattentive to horses, that I do not see how I am to get along with him." At some point, master and enslaved parted company. Joseph Seawell Jones later requested from Swain "a first rate certificate of character" for John. "Your former slave—John B. Jones alias Swain," he said, "has applied to me to take him on to the North with me—to have him emancipated—by the order of his wife—who is now his owner." Such a certificate "from the gentleman who last owned him," said Jones, would aid in effecting the emancipation. Swain should send "such a letter ... as you would like to have exhibited and published in Philadelphia."[47]

In the selling of enslaved persons, at least at times Swain and his family took humane (arguably) considerations into account. A correspondent once said he had "some scruples about separating husband and wife, and to put them together I will buy Jordan or I will sell his wife if she is willing to be sold." If he bought Jordan from Swain, he wanted his tools to be considered "a part of his appurtanances." Swain once expressed a desire to remove "my negroes" from a place "before they form connexions by marriages etc. that it would be unpleasant to dissolve."[48]

Similar considerations motivated Swain's half-brother. He was striving to wind up his business, he told Swain, stating that he found it impossible to do it "and keep that family of negroes on your Farm in Macon County." If he had had "no feeling," he could already have sold them for "cash down." He wanted, though, "to act like a Christian when I am compelled to sell them." They "would be unhappy for life," he expected, if he sold them to a stranger not knowing where they were to be taken. Later, to pay a debt to Swain, the brother had to sell an enslaved woman and her children. It was noted that he disliked parting the family if he could avoid it.[49]

A Swain nephew both brokered the time Swain would allow a purchaser to pay for his enslaved and offered to sell his "Negroes" to Swain. He would bind himself "to take them back[,] paying you your money and interest as I would nead their labor in farming." He refused to sell a "very valuable negro man," however, without finding "a good kind man that will buy him and keep him near his wife who lives in the neighborhood." The nephew's father had set an example that perhaps influenced him; the father wished to sell some of his enslaved persons "but dislike[d] to see them parted and sent in every direction." Another nephew advised Swain of his intention, as old age approached, to allow his enslaved their freedom and to reestablish themselves in California, even though it would be a financial sacrifice for him.[50]

To satisfy a debt George, Swain's brother, had to sell "two of my boys." They were "grieved and fearful of being parted," and George was "truly mortified in parting with them." Earlier he had not wanted "any of Annes children to be sold out of the family if I can possibly help it." He lamented, however, that without financial assistance from his son-in-law Crawford Long, "some one of them will have to go inspite [sic] of all I can do." Long had expressed to Swain "some desire to own the negroes to be sold." If Swain's agent were to "buy them low," and Swain did not wish to keep them, Long would pay Swain for them and take possession the first of the following year.[51]

Arguably humane considerations thus factored into trading in enslaved persons by Swain and his family. Clearly, however, they were active participants in this commerce in human property; and equally clearly, economic rather than humane considerations were dominant. Swain's Tennessee brother-in-law handled some of this business for him. He once wrote, "I have not been able to sell your negroes." If an immediate sale was desirable, he said on another occasion, he had no doubt they could be sold "upon time." Jane would be confined soon (for childbirth, presumably), and Swain should be informed that the younger ones should not be sold with their mother.[52] Swain's other foremost agent in this process was Asheville attorney Nicholas Woodfin.[53]

As the Civil War roiled, Swain came to perceive his enslaved as a burden. "My slaves are an expense to me," he now told Woodfin. The "nearness of the enemy," he said, threatened to demoralize "all the negroes in the country." "They regard the northerners as fighting their battles," he continued, "and are looking with eagerness and hope to the result of this contest." Swain thought he "must either sell, hire or colonize mine," but he perceived no opportunity "to do any one of those things to advantage." If Woodfin could "suggest a place that will answer, in the West," Swain would be "greatly obliged."[54]

Not only did Swain sell enslaved persons himself; he also assisted others in the enterprise. He once advised UNC Professor John De B. Hooper of considerations in the sale of an enslaved person. He had not had time, Swain said, to make inquiries "as to the prospect of selling her." A speculator would probably give $3,000 for the family, possibly more. A neighborhood person probably would offer no more than $2,500. With these estimates before him, Hooper was to give Swain "an intimation" if he was inclined to sell. Swain would then see what could be done. The opportunity to serve Hooper in this way, Swain closed, would afford him "sincere pleasure."[55]

Swain's enslaved were not for his personal use only. They also served as laborers for the university. In the parlance of the time, they were usually referred to as "servants." Most, if not all, however, were almost certainly enslaved. The time "for hiring servants" had arrived, Elisha Mitchell once wrote Swain. Three who belonged to "Mrs. White," probably Swain's mother-in-law, were in Chapel Hill. Only Fred, however, Mitchell thought, would answer their purpose. If Mrs. White approved, there was an understanding with Fred that he was "to return and be in our employ as a cutter of wood for the west building."

"Dave and November do the work of college," Mitchell continued. In addition to Fred, Luke cut wood for the college. Swain was to inquire "for what sum negroes board in Raleigh." Apparently in anticipation of further need of labor for the university, "Messrs. Fetter Queen and Hooper ha[d] gone negro hunting to Hillsboro."[56] Mitchell later proposed construction of a ditch to convey water away from the foundation of South Building. "[T]he college hands," he said, could dig it in a week. Swain suggested that the college "servants" be given the task of cutting "old, decayed and decaying trees" from university land to supply the students with firewood.[57]

Swain maintained "negro Houses" for his enslaved, including those devoted to university labor. In 1848, the university trustees authorized payment for a contract Swain had entered for the removal of Steward's Hall "and rebuild[ing] it as an addition to [his] negro Houses at the price of $80." Swain himself paid $2.00 for "under pinning negro house."[58]

The nighttime presence of the enslaved on campus was restricted. An 1843 faculty resolution provided "that all slaves observed within the college area after dark shall be driven off, and if necessary whipped, unless a pass from some member of the Faculty is exhibited, and that the same course shall be pursued in regard to slaves coming within the college precincts to trade on the Sabbath."[59]

One Swain enslaved person used in the university's service merits special mention. Wilson Swain, later Wilson Swain Caldwell, was the son of Rosa Burgess,

 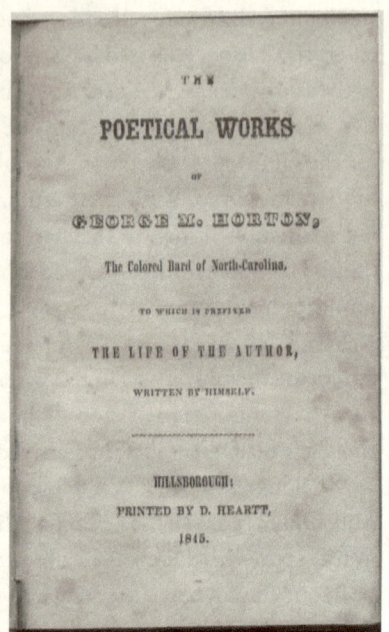

Wilson Swain Caldwell and the title page to *The Poetical Works of George Moses Horton.*

an enslaved person whom Swain had bought from Governor James Iredell, and November Caldwell, an enslaved person of Joseph Caldwell, Swain's predecessor as president of the university. Kemp Battle has observed that Governor and Mrs. Swain "were exceedingly kind and indulgent to their slaves." Consequently, Wilson "grew up quite as happy and unrestrained as any boy in the village." His first work was with Swain's son Richard "hauling with mule and cart under the orders of Mr. Paxton, the English gardener engaged in beautifying the campus." Wilson will figure later in Swain's and the university's story.[60]

Perhaps the best-known local enslaved of the time, not Swain's, but quite familiar to him, was George Moses Horton. Horton belonged to a farmer who lived about eight miles from Chapel Hill toward Pittsboro. He was a poet and, especially considering his lack of formal education, quite a good one. Horton made frequent forays into Chapel Hill where, for $.25 apiece, he wrote acrostics on the UNC boys' sweethearts. One student from the time acknowledged, "I patronized him liberally."

A limited life in captivity on a Chatham County farm was hardly the ultimate ambition of a budding literary talent. Thus, in 1844 Horton wrote the well-known Boston abolitionist William Lloyd Garrison—"a lover of the genious [sic] from every tribe and population of the human race," by Horton's description—seeking "assistance in carring [sic] my original work into publick execution." He was, Horton professed, "not alone actuated by pecuniary motives, but upon the whole, to spread the blaze [?] of african genious [sic], and thus dispel the ... gloom so prevelant in many parts of the country." His "design," Horton said, was to give Garrison "my testimony from the pen of the honorable Mr. David Swain, and president of the University of North Carolina and who is very well apprised of my condition in life," which he depicted as born a "slave," never a day of schooling, early fond of hearing people read, and early having an ear for music. He trusted that Garrison's examination "into the facts of my condition will inspire your pleasure to open to the world a volume which like a wild bird has long lain struggling in its shell impatient to transpire to the eye, a dubious world[.]" Garrison never got that chance. Horton trusted the mailing of the letter to Swain, who possessed it, unmailed, among his papers at his death.

A few years later Swain became the focus of Horton's efforts to secure increased time for his literary efforts. The long walk into Chapel Hill "to attend to my business, which chiefly lies on the Hill," he pleaded, was inconvenient. He had chosen Swain as the appropriate "Gentleman in this place to buy me." If Swain would "accede to the proposition," Horton pledged to serve him to the best of his ability. "The price," he said, "is $200 50 dollars, which i cannot but think i am worth." A touching plea concludes the letter: "Sir: i am willing to make you all the possible remuneration which i can provide i succeed in the publication of my books which i have in hand. Sir i have from this inconvenience [walking into Chapel Hill, presumably] been thrown far behind and provide you buy me i shall be under all obligation to your generosity sir you will please write a note to Master when and as you see proper[.] George M. Horton Poet[.]"

Again, Swain was unresponsive. With a later note to Swain, Horton made a final effort. Sent via a student, the note reiterated the purchase proposition and promised Swain "two-thirds on the whole of the proceeds of my book now preparing for the press." Subscriptions for the book were arriving, Horton assured Swain, and Swain would "never sustain any loss" by granting his request.

Swain rejoined in the same fashion as previously, with silence. Between the two communications, however, he apparently suggested that Horton solicit Horace Greeley's aid in promoting his literary endeavors, and perhaps his freedom. Horton's letter to Greeley, at least, implies that he is writing at Swain's behest. From the information Swain had given him, Horton said to Greeley, "i learn that you are a gentleman of philanthropic feeling." He therefore "thought it essential to apply to your beneficent hand for some assistance to remove the burden of hard servitude." Greeley would have heard of him, Horton thought, "by the fame of my work in poetry much of which i am now too closely confined to carry out and which I feel a warm interest to do." If Greeley would favor him "with the bounty of 175 dollars," Horton said, "i will endeavor to reward your generosity with my productions as soon as possible." Horton touted himself as "the only publick and recognized poet of colour in my native state or perhaps in the union born in slavery but yet craving that scope and expression whereby my literary labour of the night may be circulated throughout the whole world." Again, a poignant plea concluded the appeal: "Then o forbid that my productions should ever fall to the ground but rather soar as an eagle above the towering mountains and thus return as a triumphing spirit to the bosum of its God who gave it birth though now confined in these loathsome fetters please assist the cowering vassal to arise and live a glad denizen the remnant of his days and one of active utility, yours respect[.] George M. Horton of colour[.]"

On the back Horton penned a poem entitled "The Poet's Feeble Petition," in which he repeated his plea. This letter too Horton entrusted to Swain for dispatch. It too was found among Swain's papers at his death, never mailed, and remains among his archival materials. Swain, a Horton biographer has observed, shared the feelings of the average Southerner that to encourage "Negroes" in any endeavor outside their ordinary duties was contrary to the best interests of the South; further, he would have considered intervening between someone else's enslaved person and a noted abolitionist highly improper conduct for one of his prominent position as a servant of the state. An editor of Horton's poetry has noted, similarly, that "Swain was in all things prudential, ever cautious and discreet, seemingly fearful of offending anyone." Both are essentially correct. While Swain's omissions are offensive to a twenty-first century moral compass, in his time most of his white contemporaries would have considered them normative.

Swain did encourage Horton's literary endeavors. In the summer of 1845, Horton and his supporters circulated in Chapel Hill a subscription list for publication of a new volume of his verse. When *The Poetical Works of George M. Horton, The Colored Bard of North Carolina* was published later that year, Swain and other notables were listed among the ninety-nine subscribers. Sales were insufficient to produce the funds necessary to purchase Horton's freedom. His ultimate vindication would come only many years after his death when a dormitory on the UNC campus was named for him.[61]

There was another local enslaved person whom Swain attempted to assist. Sam Morphis, whose "owner" lived in Alamance County, was a hack driver and waiter at the university, popular with faculty, students, and townspeople. When he saved the life of a student, he particularly endeared himself to the students. Swain, 309 students, and forty-three townspeople petitioned the state legislature to emancipate Morphis. The legislature denied the petition, but the town accepted him, and he enjoyed virtual freedom. Morphis married one of William H. Battle's enslaved persons and spoke of himself as Battle's son-in-law.[62]

Civil War, Reconstruction

UNC campus view circa 1861, eve of Civil War.

CHAPTER 23

Disunion, Disruption
"The gloom thickens"

At the university's June 1859 commencement, Judge Battle presented a report from the visiting committee appointed by the trustees. The committee found the university "apparently in the highest state of prosperity." It had the largest enrollment of any college or university in the United States except Yale. The 1858–1859 student population had been 456, quite a contrast to the eighty-nine students when Swain had assumed the presidency in 1835. The trustees had contracted for "the erection of two large and commodious buildings [New East and New West] in addition to those already provided." "The site," the report stated, "is admirably located, the college grounds are beautifully adorned, and the walks are pleasant and agreeable." The university, it concluded, "has scarcely a superior and very few equals in the whole United States."[1]

Good times for the university meant good times for David Swain. The widespread and growing reputation of the college, accompanied by the related growth and prosperity of Chapel Hill, fulfilled his ambitions, both personal and institutional. His status as leading citizen of the small village was largely unquestioned and unchallenged. Cornelia Phillips Spencer reports that he "might be seen traversing the streets at early dawn to wake the town up." He was, she said, "eminently a neighborly man; always genial, kindly, often playful[,] ... his heart ... always open to sympathy with others."[2]

These halcyon days would soon fall under the heavy shadow of the impending Civil War. "The gloom thickens," Charles Manly wrote to Swain as the shadow lengthened. Powerful forces and events, beyond the control of Swain and his university, were rapidly converging to the considerable detriment of both. When these had run their course, for a few years the university's viability would hang by a thin and fragile thread. For a brief period, it would then close entirely, later to revive and recover slowly over ensuing decades. Neither the Swain presidency nor the man himself would long survive this trauma.³

The storm did not catch Swain and his contemporaries unaware. As early as 1851, William A. Graham, then secretary of the navy, advised Swain from Washington that "[t]he elements of discord have not entirely subsided either at the North or South." "Gen'l Hamilton," Graham continued, "thinks that South Carolina will not attempt secession."⁴ In 1856, Charles Manly noted to Swain a gathering in Raleigh of governors from several southern states "to hold a grand Southern Council to dissolve the Union (if Democracy [i.e., the Democratic Party] shall be beaten) I presume." The governors had departed hastily, however, upon advice that they "were concocting treason against the *Union*" and enhancing Fillmore's prospects of carrying the state in the presidential election. "With all her vacillations in Whigery and Democracy," Manly opined to Swain, "N. Car. Is a *Union State Certain*." As the sectional divide drew nearer, Manly gave Swain advice. He, Judge Matthias Manly, and Judge Battle had concluded that "due to the agitated state of the public mind in regard to national affairs," Swain should not address the General Assembly on university matters.⁵

Swain's correspondence with historian Francis L. Hawks mirrored the downward trajectory of the impending conflict. A New Yorker at the time, but southern by birth, background, and experience, Hawks found the looming breach particularly trying. "If a rupture takes place," he told Swain, "the destiny of my countrymen must be my destiny. I sink or swim with the South." The difficulty was not just personal, however. Their proposed documentary history of North Carolina was also in jeopardy. "Before we see the end of which Harper's [F]erry was the beginning," he told Swain, "the State will have need to husband her money for other purposes than that of preserving her past history."⁶ Hawks soon elaborated. The wound, he said, might be salved, even healed. It would break out again, however. No union could last long "unless there be heart in it." It would take years to restore confidence between the regions, if such could occur at all. With children and grandchildren in both regions, Hawks bemoaned, some of his foes would be from his own household.⁷

Swain's response to Hawks eloquently states his reluctance regarding southern secession. He too was "not without forebodings in relation to public affairs." "I deprecate the idea most deeply and sincerely of disunion," he said, "and cling to the hope that means will be found to avoid it." They should "look the evil boldly in the face" and "look more to our own interest." Educate the young, Swain admonished, encourage home manufactures, restrict commercial intercourse to southern cities, open direct trade with Europe.⁸

Still disheartened, Hawks continued to disengage. He disappointed Swain by not visiting him. He went mute with other friends. North Carolina Governor John W. Ellis was among the neglected and concerned. When Hawks at length responded, he pleaded the horror of war as a distraction. The attack on Fort Sumter, he told Swain, had made hostility toward the South the predominant sentiment in the North. "Political events have well nigh killed me," he moaned: "The Union (to save which I would willingly have given my life) is hopelessly broken, and the South I fear has very few friends left at the North."[9]

Closer to home, Swain's Western North Carolina friends shared Hawks's despair. "We are having troublesome times politically," James Patton wrote to Swain, "and when there is to be an end is hard to judge Now." "A Southern United Separation," Patton concluded, "is inevitable." Nicholas Woodfin had "more apprehension of the safety of the Union [than] on any former occasion." No uniting would occur, in Woodfin's opinion, except "to destroy the union."[10]

James Johnston Pettigrew, Swain's former student, now resided in South Carolina, the first state to secede. Pettigrew, who would die fighting for the Confederacy, had no desire to live "under the Independent Republic" of South Carolina. "The politicians and newspaper agitators have certainly brought things to a pretty pass," he told his old professor.[11]

As southern discomfort escalated, North Carolina participated in two last-ditch attempts to avert war. The General Assembly appointed Thomas Ruffin, D. M. Barringer, David S. Reid, John M. Morehead, and George Davis as commissioners to a peace conference held in Washington on February 4, 1861. Alabama invited the state to send delegates to Montgomery on the same date "for the purpose of forming a provisional as well as permanent government." Because North Carolina was still part of the Federal Union, the General Assembly considered itself to have "no right to send delegates for such a purpose." It nevertheless appointed Swain and two of his former students, John L. Bridgers and Matthew W. Ransom, as commissioners to "visit" the Montgomery session "for the purpose of effecting an honorable and amicable adjustment of all the difficulties that distract the country ... and ... consulting for our peace, honor, and safety."[12] William H. Battle viewed the latter appointments with skepticism. The delegation to Montgomery, he said, was "sent with restrictions, and I doubt whether they will be received." Battle devoutly hoped, nevertheless, that a compromise could be effected, for he said, "I fear nothing good can come of a Southern Confederacy."[13]

Swain's name on the list of delegates delighted a correspondent with Governor Ellis. "I could not refrain from addressing him a hasty scrawl," he told Ellis, "to express my opinion as to the course of action which I think best for North Carolina to adopt." The governor viewed Bridgers and Ransom as "warm Southern men." "Gov. Swain," he said, "has not as yet taken any decided position."[14]

The delegation departed from Raleigh on January 31, 1861, and arrived in Montgomery on February 2. Upon arrival they learned that the convention had adjourned *sine die* and the legislature was in session. In a report to Governor Ellis, which Swain authored, they informed the governor that "[a]s we were not delegates to the Southern Congress, and had no authority to participate in any consultation in relation to the contemplated formation of either a provisional or permanent government for the seceding states, we regarded our mission as restricted to the single duty of consulting for our common peace, honor and safety." The General Assembly's resolutions were read to the Southern Congress. The commissioners were invited to take seats on the floor, to attend any session, open or secret, and to communicate anything to the body they might desire. A subsequent resolution received the commissioners with pleasure and expressed hope that the body would act so as to induce North Carolina to join the new government. The commissioners, Swain reported, sampled public opinion from throughout the South, drawing on native North Carolinians now residing in other southern states. They found only a small minority favorable to "a reconstruction of our national Union." Given this finding, they did not deem it their duty to attend any of the secret sessions of the Congress. Having submitted the General Assembly's resolutions as a peace offering, Swain related, they believed they "would poorly perform the duties assigned us by entering into discussions which would serve only to enkindle strife." The commissioners forwarded to Governor Ellis a copy of the Constitution of the Provisional Government of the Confederate States of America. They notified him of the election of Jefferson Davis of Mississippi as president, and Alexander H. Stephens of Georgia as vice president, of the new confederation. They then concluded their mission.[15]

Governor Morehead's biographer attributes the choice of Morehead to lead the delegation to Washington, and Swain to head the one to Montgomery, to the facts that "[b]oth were western men and both strong Union men and not excelled in influence by any other men in the state." "They," he concluded, "best represented the commonwealth." He also cited high regard for Swain in the East and "excellent diplomatic qualities." The missions of both men, he concluded, however, were hopeless.[16] After the Civil War, Swain asserted that "[t]he failure of these overtures [was] not owing to any want of zeal or fidelity on the part of the commissioners from North Carolina, either at Washington or Montgomery."[17]

The Montgomery assignment took Swain from Chapel Hill for eighteen days. He returned to find that during his absence a public meeting had been held in the town "to deliberate upon the present state of our public affairs." Sidney Smith, who had represented Orange County in the 1846 House of Commons, had addressed the meeting on the crisis. Smith had closed his remarks by eulogizing the character and past political services of Graham and Swain and recommending them as the county's delegates to the forthcoming convention to deal with the difficulties. Graham apparently responded immediately, conveying a willingness to serve. The nominators had to await Swain's return from Montgomery, upon which he too accepted. The prospects for the two, Smith informed Graham, were "very flattering." Smith wanted the correspondence with Graham and Swain "struck off in the form of hand bills, for distribution."[18]

Not content with a perfunctory acceptance, Swain issued a philosophical discourse on the pending emergency. Although deeply grateful for the confidence of his friends and neighbors of the past quarter century, he had not sought the proposed position. "[A]t this time of trial and peril," he said, however, "no one who is deemed competent to the proper discharge of the duty should permit himself, for slight causes, to decline it." Perhaps, Swain thought, it could be ascertained before it met "what the North is disposed to concede and the South to accept."

"I most earnestly desire the preservation and perpetuation of the national Union," Swain said. He hedged, however, by adding "with proper guarantees for the maintenance of the constitutional rights of the South." He had not abandoned hope of reunion based on these principles. If that proved impossible, however, perhaps "a peaceful separation" could be obtained, "and the two great sections of the country constitute hereafter distinct, and, to a great extent, homogeneous governments." No hope should be afforded, he said, "to the enemies of free principles at home or despots abroad, that our great experiment of representative government is to prove a failure."

Concluding, Swain endorsed placing with the state's voters the call of a convention and the power to sanction or reject its proceedings. On February 28, 1861, by a very narrow margin, the voters rejected a call for a convention to consider secession. For unknown reasons, a few days earlier, apparently with his authorization, Swain's name had been withdrawn from the delegate canvass.[19]

For Swain, as for many Southern Unionists, the April 1861 firing on Fort Sumter, and Lincoln's call for troops in its wake, were watershed events. As stated by historian Bell Irvin Wiley: "Fort Sumter and Lincoln's call for volunteers took the ground from under these middle-of-the-roaders. The issue now was whether to fight with or against secessionists, and this left no choice for most southerners." A Charles Manly missive to Swain vividly depicted the sudden, dramatic shift in public opinion. "All are unanimous," said Manly: "Even those who were loudest in denouncing secession are now hottest and loudest the other way."[20]

On Saturday, April 20, 1861, before a large assembly, the Confederate States flag was raised at Chapel Hill. Swain was among the speakers. He had, it was said, "no recantations to make." "We owed Mr. Lincoln many thanks," he said, for "thus melting the hearts of our people, hitherto differing in their judgments[,] into one heart. There must now be no vacillation. Mr. Lincoln must be met at the border if he attempt[s] to cross it, and told by the musket's breath that freemen cannot be bayonetted into obedience—that eight millions of freemen cannot be dragooned into unity with eighteen or with a hundred and eighty millions of those who insist upon the bayonetting and dragooning." In the fervor of the moment, Swain badly misjudged Southern strength. The South was "invincible," he said, according to one account. Further bloodshed could be avoided "by every man in the South shouldering his musket." Lincoln would then "see our strength and know it would be useless to attempt to coerce us." "[T]he Old North State," he said, again overstating, "is fully aroused and ready."[21]

Imminent war brought Swain both information and commentary. A letter from Swain to an old Buncombe County acquaintance produced tears and reminiscences. Memories of Swain's late father surfaced, the recipient said, noting the anxiety with which George Swain must be looking down on "this once peaceful and happy country." The dark clouds of the Civil War would pit family members against one another, he foresaw, "engaged in mortal conflict, instigated by demogogues and fanatics."[22] A Swain nephew living in Texas feared that "our Union is no more." "I love my country," he told his uncle, "and feel a load on my heart when I think that our national pride is gone and the distress and wretchedness that must follow."[23]

Once war became reality, Swain remained a focal point of communications about it. A UNC graduate living in the North thought it would be "bloody and vindictive," but he was "prepared for any change that may occur." A Charleston judge with a UNC honorary degree wrote to introduce Swain to a friend who was "proceed[ing] to Richmond to attend to his duties near the government of the Confederate States—under which he now holds a very important office."[24] Swain's services in the war effort were sought. A Hillsboro group, of which William A. Graham Jr. was a member, requested his attendance at a meeting there "for the purpose of raising a volunteer company." It was hoped that Swain would address his fellow citizens on the occasion.[25]

One Swain correspondent was highly supportive of the rebel cause. "[H]ad we [r]emained under the government of that Abolitionist infidel party," he told Swain, "the abolition of slavery and the destruction of our liberties would have been the inevitable result." A misplaced optimism that the war would be brief perhaps fueled the writer's enthusiasm. He would not be surprised, he stated, "if it was settled in two or three months."[26]

Throughout the war, Charles Manly communicated with Swain faithfully. Never sanguine about the South's prospects, Manly very early saw "nothing before us but utter ruin, irretrievable bankruptcy both state and individual." Banks, he opined, could not sustain the credit of the state. Prisoners from the battle on Roanoke Island had been released, Manly reported, his own son among them. Soldiers were passing through "on their way home, on furlough to return soon." Only strict neutrality could be expected from England or France. He was striving to keep up his spirits, Manly told Swain, but it was a struggle. As the war progressed Manly saw "[o]ur disasters and defeats . . . multiplying in every direction." Loss of Roanoke Island "had a most devastating effect on the public mind." Manly questioned much of the South's strategy and accused its decision makers of being accomplices "to the murder of the men who were slain" and "guilty of high crimes."[27]

Manly's pessimism was well founded and ongoing. "We hear that the enemy is in sight of Wilmington by land and water in great force[,] while our means of defense are perfectly contemptible," he informed Swain, "Fort Macon gone, Wilmington gone." Confederate leadership left much to be desired. "The imbecility, inefficiency, obstinacy, cowardice and drunkenness of men in authority," Manly opined, "will soon destroy the Country without any aid from Yankee." North Carolina Chief Justice Richmond Pearson's liberal granting of habeas corpus petitions to discharge soldiers was not helping matters.[28]

Such communications, combined with his frequent travels, made Swain Chapel Hill's "chief medium of intercourse with the outside world." "He was the only man," wrote Cornelia Phillips Spencer, "who kept up correspondence with the men of action who were making history." Young faculty members who might otherwise have had a similar role "had all joined the Confederate army." Both the local citizens and Swain himself, Spencer thought, "a trifle overestimated his influence and importance." She may have been right, but if so, "trifle" is the operative word. Clearly Swain was extensively involved in, and knowledgeable about, the life of the state, region, and country during this turbulent time.[29]

Swain registered with Manly his complaint about the absence of mail delivery from the North. He joined Manly in noting the fall of Roanoke Island "into the hands of the enemy." Both Manly and Judge Battle, Swain noted, had sons "among the captives." Fortunately, he said, "no one of these is wounded." "The calamity is a serious one," he continued, "but we have cause to trust God that there is no loss of life or limbs."

Soon Swain reported to Manly a loss to the university: Senator Johnston of Arkansas had called home his son and a nephew. Swain had parted with the young men with much regret. "[O]ur friend Polk [Leonidas Polk, Episcopal bishop and Confederate general]," Swain observed, was "head[ing] the forlorn hope in the West."[30]

A UNC student was the beneficiary of Swain's recommendation to Governor Graham for "a lieutenancy in the regular army of this state." Swain was uncertain whether to send it to the government at Raleigh or the one at Montgomery (the Confederate government had not yet moved to Richmond). He was unfamiliar with the military bill but planned to visit Raleigh soon to confer with Graham on this and other subjects. Two days before North Carolina voted to secede, Swain suggested Samuel F. Phillips for secretary of the convention. On Monday Phillips would be in Wake Court where Graham could ascertain his wishes on the subject. Graham would be a delegate to the convention which should, Swain admonished, rewrite the parts of the state constitution that secession would render obsolete.

As the war dragged on, Graham continued to be a sounding board for Swain's concerns. Drafting young men ages seventeen and eighteen, and older men between forty-five and fifty, Swain thought a mistaken, if not fatal, policy. Implications for agriculture were profound. Every hand that could guide a plow or wield a hoe was needed to plant corn, Swain said, yet "the young and the old are summoned to spend a fortnight at Hillsboro." Lands owned by poor men subject to military service thus would remain untilled. "[W]hat is death in battle," Swain asked, compared "to the most horrible of human suffering, the lingering death by famine."

Like conscription, tax policy drew his ire. State, county, and Confederate taxes, when combined, threatened to annihilate "monied capital." "Widows, orphans, and salaried men, hitherto in comfortable circumstances," Swain said, were "in many instances greatly straitened, and in others in absolute want of the necessaries of life." Even he, Swain lamented to Graham, presumably referring to the purchase of his Pitt County farm, had been "compelled to turn agriculturalist or starve." "The necessaries of life go up," Swain continued, "while the means of purchasing are constantly diminishing."

Graham's inability to serve the unexpired Senate term of Confederate Attorney General George Davis was equally distressing to Swain. The position had then been tendered to Swain, but he "could not have left here without ruin to the

University." The university then received no state appropriations for operating expenses; the war-related decline in student enrollment significantly reduced tuition revenues without a proportionate decline in operating costs. Much evil might have been prevented, and some good perhaps effected, Swain was convinced, if one of them could have gone to Richmond at the time.[31]

To Nicholas Woodfin, relatively isolated in Western North Carolina, Swain bemoaned that "[n]o one can venture to predict what a day or an hour may bring forth." A week could make Raleigh the seat of government (Confederate, presumably), and in a fortnight North Carolina could become "the Battlefield of the Confederacy." Four important ports—Wilmington, Charleston, Savannah, and Mobile—remained in the Confederacy; these, however, Swain said, could fall into enemy hands imminently. The prospect of Edward Stanly as military governor of North Carolina concerned him. "Who shall we call on to counteract him?" Swain asked his lawyer and friend.[32]

For all of Swain's broader regional and national involvement, he had to be and was, first and foremost, focused on the university. Early 1861 found Lucy Battle "very glad that the prophecy concerning the falling off of the students here is not likely to come to pass." They continued to matriculate, Lucy stated, "tis said there will be at least 300." The 1860–1861 academic year brought an enrollment of 376 students. All southern states except Maryland and Delaware were represented in the student body. Soon, however, the Civil War severely disrupted the university's normal functioning. A precipitous decline in the student population commenced immediately, bringing long-term, devastating effects to the university.[33]

Even before North Carolina seceded, the faculty resolved that all student members of military companies who were called into service would have leaves of absence, provided they returned at commencement to receive their degrees. Seniors who were allowed to leave would be regarded as candidates for distinction at commencement.[34] Hotheads in the student body found in the war an excuse to take leave of their studies. "[F]anatics at the north," they maintained, were attempting "to wrest from the South her most cherished liberties." The students thus were "ready to forsake the peaceful duties of a college life, and take up the sword in defence of . . . sacred liberty."[35]

Viewed in context, this student militancy is not surprising. To be sure, antebellum UNC students had been subjected to counter influences. William Gaston's 1832 antislavery commencement address was among them. Later, from 1852 to 1856, all commencement speakers favored the Union. These were not the dominant voices, however. As legal historian Alfred L. Brophy has noted, "[a]fter the mid-1830s, southern universities justified themselves as places where students learned to defend southern values . . . [and] the dominant mode of thinking at [southern] colleges was support for slavery." UNC students were among those who regularly "heard about the centrality of slavery."

Moral philosophy classes were among the forums from which faculty offered, to students and the greater public, "a variety of pro-slavery arguments." In an 1848 pamphlet entitled *The Other Leaf of Nature*, Elisha Mitchell attacked Brown University President Francis Wayland and other antislavery writers. Slave owning, Wayland had posited, was sinful. It was, Mitchell countered, no more sinful than other forms of property ownership. An 1857 UNC speaker, Henry Watkins Miller, Class of 1834, gave the most radical of the university's antebellum speeches. An "ardent critic of the abolitionists," Miller viewed "oppression from the North [as] severe" and "saw the world . . . arrayed against the South." Students caught this fever, and late antebellum literary society addresses reflected their movement toward support for disunion if necessary to preserve "southern constitutional rights."[36]

When war came, underclassmen petitioned the trustees for a suspension of classes for the remainder of the session. Amid so much excitement, they argued, it was impossible to attend to their academic duties. If the war endured only two or three months, their services would not be needed; they would lose nothing, however, "since we cannot study as it is." A suspension would give them "lively strength which would enable us to prosecute our studies more vigorously next session." They hoped the trustees would "see the necessity of every arms being wielded in the coming contest and every sons participating in the defense of our homes and our firesides."[37]

The pleas were in vain. Swain was resolute in denying them. A May 1861 circular letter acknowledged "a crisis in the affairs of our country that calls for the best services we can render in the tented field if necessary, and if not there, in the sphere in which each one can make himself most useful." The faculty, Swain assured his readers, had no desire "to quench patriotic ardor, or to withhold from the public service, at the proper time, any one capable of performing the duties of a soldier." They intimated to parents and guardians, however, "the propriety of restraining the anxiety so natural to the young and inexperienced, to rush prematurely into military service."

Some students had left the university with instructions from home and the faculty's "permission and approbation." Others had gone unbeknownst to the faculty and, it feared, "in opposition to the wishes of Parents and Guardians." The latter group, it was hoped, would return in time to prepare for the annual examination. There would be no suspension of duties, and no reasonable pains spared "to render the approaching Commencement attractive." Except when dispensation had been granted for special reasons, candidates for degrees were expected to be in attendance by the beginning of commencement week.[38]

With this missive Swain commenced a war-long struggle to maintain some semblance of normality, both in the university's functioning and in the public's perception of it. He soon announced that the next collegiate year would begin on July 19, 1861. He touted the new buildings, the additions to the "Libraries and Cabinets," and the "full and efficient" corps of instructors in all departments. "[T]he means and opportunity for improvement," he boasted, were "greater than at any former period."[39]

The reality was that the university was not in its accustomed healthy state. Swain soon found himself having to trumpet the fact that it was even open and conducting business. His second circular letter, in July 1861, acknowledged the impression abroad "that the regular exercises of this Institution have been suspended." The troubled state of the country had diminished the university's numbers, Swain admitted. That temporary diminution, though, was "contributing very essentially to the public good." Former students were "in arms under the banners of every state in the Confederacy." There was probably no regiment without a UNC student or graduate. The university was now instructing in military tactics. Smaller numbers meant increased opportunities for the remaining students. In sum, Swain assured friends of the university that they "need not fear that the patronage so freely bestowed heretofore is likely to be materially diminished."[40]

This pattern would continue. In late fall 1861, Swain indicated that the university had begun its examinations for the session and would be very busy for a week. Student enrollment was indeed diminished, from more than 400 to 101. This had a positive aspect, however. Swain had "never known at any time such general attention to study and propriety of deportment as characterized our last session." With his characteristic optimism, he pronounced confidently that the next session would commence in January 1862, offering "means and opportunities of improvement" greater than ever.[41]

Difficulties notwithstanding, Swain found pleasure in some aspects of the university's situation. Its sons were making significant contributions to the war effort. In perusing the Army Register, he found "that a third of the Colonials Commandant, of the volunteer regiments now in the service of the state, are our graduates or have been students of the university." Among the new students were "promising young men from Virginia, Georgia, South Carolina, and Arkansas." The faculty was united and determined to do everything possible to sustain the institution. "I suppose," he said, "our patronage to be greater than that of any other similar seminary in the Confederacy."[42]

These relatively positive thoughts, however, could not hold at bay concerns regarding declining student enrollment. Confederate General Theophilus Holmes had a son in the sophomore class. This, plus Holmes's "high reputation," Swain thought, "entitle[d] his suggestions to the most respectful consideration." There was a pragmatic dimension to this endorsement: both men wanted to keep the students in school. Holmes told Swain he would render a great service "by diverting the enthusiasm of the students from the performance of physical service." They were not prepared, Holmes said, for positions of command. Swain should "establish a Military Attachment to the University" and put a competent officer in charge. Unless "perfectly competant [sic]," the instruction would do more harm than good. Swain's "uniform kindness" to Holmes's son invoked the general's gratitude. Only with great difficulty had he dissuaded the son from entering the army. In returning to Swain, the son had promised "to apply himself."[43]

Student fervor for the cause was not the sole problem. Even before the April 1862 Confederate conscription law, local drafts were depopulating the student body. "Three young men left us yesterday," Swain reported in January 1862, "who were drafted in the counties from which they came." The salutary feature of this, in Swain's mind, was that students subject to home-county draft could not also be subject to it in Chapel Hill. The commander of the Chapel Hill company held the same view. If his commanding general and the governor agreed, Swain thought, no reference to the trustees would be necessary.[44]

It was not that simple, however. Over the course of 1862, the student population fluctuated between 100 and 128. When the Confederacy adopted a draft law, Swain said plaintively "fear of conscription threatens great injury here." Initially the law exempted faculty at schools with twenty or more students. Swain seized on this as reflecting an intent to favor colleges and schools "as far as practicable." This agreeable interpretation hardly eased his mind, however. He asked Manly to confer with the governor on the subject immediately and to advise him of the result. "Some of our boys," he said, "are as anxious to volunteer as their parents and I are to keep them here, until they attain the muscle and grisle, requisite to efficient ... service." If he were to leave, they would be "but too ready" to follow him. Manly's visit with the governor would enable Swain, he thought, to form "a more reliable opinion" on whether the trustees should be convened.[45]

Following passage of the Conscription Act, Manly complained to Swain that no one seemed to be able to construe it or to anticipate the construction Confederate authorities would give it. Already students had departed in such numbers that the faculty resolved to allow any student so desiring to give a speech at commencement. Leaders of private institutions shared Swain's angst about effects of the draft. Braxton Craven, president of Trinity College, also hoped his students would not be conscripted. "It is all that can be done to sustain our colleges at all," he told Governor Henry T. Clark, who had succeeded Governor John W. Ellis upon Ellis's death in July 1861, "and I hope the few who will go to school will be allowed to remain." If the students were not exempted, Craven said, "we shall enevitably [sic] be broken, which I think you do not desire."[46]

As 1863 dawned, conscription remained Swain's principal concern. Why exempt faculty from conscription, Swain asked Governor Graham, if they were to be stripped of students? The January number was forty-five. It would probably rise to sixty, Swain said, but that would be "a diminution of 400 of our numbers before the war." Further, casualties continued to mount. Over the last two years deaths of graduates and students on the battlefields and from camp exposure, Swain told Graham, had exceeded all the casualties of the preceding quarter century.[47]

Such concerns notwithstanding, Swain and the faculty soldiered on to another commencement. Fewer students, but more trustees, were present for the June 1863 commencement. Among the trustees present was Swain's pupil Zeb Vance, now the state's governor. The trustees thanked university authorities for preventing a suspension of exercises. They announced their determination "to use all diligence that these efforts be so energetic hereafter." Swain occupied a morning as orator before the Literary Societies. His presentation was described as "a very interesting and useful series of Geographical and Historical parallels and contrasts between our own state and other countries on the globe."[48]

Commencement 1863 provided a transient brush with an appearance of normality. Swain's focus on the war and its effect on the student population slackened only briefly, however. He was busy preparing for future rounds with his trustees, other college and university presidents in the South, and ultimately the government of the Confederate States of America.

Autumn arrived to witness the products of that preparation. In October 1863, almost certainly at Swain's urging, the university trustees authorized him to correspond with the president of the Confederate States. He was to request a suspension of the draft for the university's students until the term ended, and for those advanced in their studies, until completion of their college course. He was also to correspond with "the Heads of other Literary Institutions of the Confederacy" to propose adoption of a general regulation exempting the two highest classes until they could attain their degrees.

Swain's letter to President Jefferson Davis detailed the effects of the war on the university. It had a small endowment, Swain wrote. Enforcement of the Conscription Act would make it difficult to sustain the institution, with revenue declining as students departed and prospective students declined to come. No appreciable addition to the army would result from the conscription of students, while their withdrawal could cause the oldest and largest of the Confederacy's public institutions to close.

Also by trustee direction, Charles Manly wrote Confederate Secretary of War James A. Seddon to the same effect. Manly also noted the draft's effects on "the able and venerable corps of Instructors," with service ranging from a quarter to nearly half a century. To disband them in the evening of life, he pleaded, would seem unjustified, and to continue their salaries without corresponding service would subject the trustees to censure.[49]

Orders of exemption for "the two senior classes" were granted. He would not grind up the seed corn, President Davis stated. Colonel Peter Mallett, the commandant of conscripts, had recommended the favorable consideration. Swain was to forward the names, ages, states, and occupations of the students eligible for exemption. Separate certificates of exemption would then be forwarded to him. Twenty-one students received such certificates.[50]

There was one cool response to Swain's plea to his fellow college heads. The University of Virginia faculty instructed its chair, Socrates Maupin, to say "that they would very cordially concur in any movement for the relief of our colleges compatible with the duty we all owe to the defense of the country in its present struggle." For many young men, mental cultivation and preparation for future usefulness could fulfill a higher duty than military service. It would not be expedient, however, they said, to exempt anyone who wished to enter college. Colleges could then become "places of refuge to the cowardly and unpatriotic," while "youth of nobler impulses would be drawn away to the army." Exemptions would be granted, the UVA faculty thought, to students who attained the draft age of eighteen during a session.[51]

With the exemptions, the university maintained its small student population. From fifty-eight in spring 1863, it rose to the sixty-five to sixty-eight range in the fall. Simultaneously, the university listed thirty-two former students as now in the 23rd North Carolina Cavalry, 41st Regiment, Confederate States Army. And sadly, Swain found himself stating, "I rarely meet my classes without informing, or hearing from them, that a recent comrade is dead, wounded or imprisoned."[52]

As former members of the community died in the war, Swain's struggle to maintain a current student body persisted. In early 1864, sixty students, a number down slightly from the fall 1863, entered the session. Swain remained "greatly concerned." His "boys," he said, were "far from manifesting any disposition to evade service." Rather, "in most instances [they were] anxious to press prematurely into the field in spite of all the influence that can be brought to bear upon them." The sophomore class, he lamented, was now reduced to six regular members.

One student missive somewhat gave the lie to Swain's assertion about the students' anxiety to leave. The student's sister was to tell their father "not to be afraid of their taking me." "Gov Swain says there is no danger of it," the student asserted, while also averring that he "would not much care if they did." He hated the idea of "skulking as it were, out of the army, when my country needs my services so much." Yet he concluded that when an exemption is offered a man, he could scarcely be blamed for taking it.[53]

Also somewhat contradictory to Swain's assertion, the Chapel Hill campus became a place of refuge for some out-of-state students who sought to avoid military service. From the capital of the Confederacy, an Arkansas senator committed to Swain's care his son and three wards. He had withdrawn them from the Virginia Military Institute in Lexington because there they would "be put in the war." Two of the wards were "sons of eminent citizens of Arks in their social position[,] wealth and respectability."[54]

Swain's inability to relax about conscription was justified. In early February 1864, an aide to Governor Vance advised him, "Colonel Mallett says there will be no change in the existing order in regards to the conscription of the students of the university." Two days later, however, Swain was directed to order students ages eighteen to forty-five, and not exempt, to report to an officer at Durham's Station. If they failed to report by the date prescribed, the officer had orders for their arrest. He hoped they would not cause him any trouble.[55]

The Confederacy now so desperately needed army men that it repealed, or was expected to, the exemption for those with hired substitutes. In early 1864, Governor Morehead conveyed to Swain his anguish about his son Eugene, who had had "a sound Englishman over conscript age as his substitute." Morehead desired his son to graduate and regretted "his having to leave college." Had Swain made any arrangements to keep his students from the operation of the conscript law, Morehead asked? Or could he "put in any plan by which [his son could] be retained in college"?[56]

On Swain's motion, in February 1864 the trustees established a committee of two to petition the chief enrolling officer of conscripts for an extension of furlough for some students. Swain and Manly constituted the committee. Soon Swain indicated, with good reason, that he still perceived that "the military bill threatens our existence." He had just learned of a notice requiring *all* white males between the ages of seventeen and fifty to report to Hillsboro. The dates specified fell during senior examination week. He thus requested an inquiry about whether such attendance could be dispensed with. The reply gave him at best minimal satisfaction. Students over age seventeen, once enrolled, would be allowed "to prosecute their studies . . . till they attain the age of eighteen years."[57]

In late October 1864, news from General Holmes rendered it certain, in Swain's view, that thirteen of fourteen seniors would immediately be conscripted "unless very earnest remonstrances of the Board can save us." The question of suspension of exercises, Swain told Governor Graham, would follow conscription.[58] The trustees again addressed the crisis. Their resolution was clearly Swain's work product, for his papers contain a draft document in his hand with identical language. The trustees resolved that the university was "as imperatively enjoined upon the General Assembly by the Constitution of the state as the maintenance of the Executive[,] legislative and judicial Departments of the government." Swain was to communicate to President Davis the sacrifices made, and services rendered, by the university's faculty, students, and graduates. These recitations and directives were preludes to a request that Davis not withdraw the exemption for the two upper classes granted pursuant to the board's resolution of October 1863.[59]

William A. Graham had advised Swain that his personal interview with Davis on the subject had not been encouraging. Davis would consider the request, but Graham was pessimistic about its prospects. Graham was right. While expressing appreciation for the importance of a college education for the country's youth, Secretary of War James A. Seddon denied the request. At that critical moment, he said, "a higher duty, that of defending the country and the colleges themselves against the ruthless Invader exacts military service from all capable of rendering it." As 1864 was ending, Graham advised Swain that there was "a rampant spirit . . . in Congress to put every body into the ranks of the Army."[60]

This spirit, and the policies it spawned, left the UNC campus almost bare of students. At commencement of the January 1865 session, Judge Battle noted that "as yet there are not very many more students than teachers." About twenty had "joined," Battle reported. If one returned as expected, there would be one senior and probably two juniors. In April when Union troops occupied Chapel Hill, only ten or twelve students—most, if not all, probably unable to fight—were still pursuing their studies. Swain notified seniors, including absent ones, that they would receive their diplomas if they delivered orations at commencement. Only four accepted his offer.[61]

Ultimately, Swain's strenuous efforts to secure draft-exempt status for his students failed. In the aftermath of Confederate defeat, diehards considered these efforts unpatriotic and detrimental to the Southern cause. Students of the time, however, revered him for it for years afterward. In the late nineteenth century, an 1861 graduate said of Swain, when describing conditions at UNC at the outbreak of the war: "He was a man filled with the milk of human kindness, dearly loved by the young men under his guidance, and every one of whom, surviving to-day, reveres his memory. The old man dearly loved his country, mourned deeply over the disruption that took place, with tears in his eyes witnessed the departure of the ninety-five members of the senior class before the commencement, and sent them their diplomas in camp." Upon the fiftieth anniversary of the outbreak of the war, an 1861 class member wrote of "the intense patriotism and the bitter sorrow of the great and good" Swain, who struggled to "keep . . . in their places" students who thought the army the "one place for them."[62]

Student departures were not the only disruption. Some faculty members, too, thought their place was in the army. William James Martin, a Virginian, had replaced the late Elisha Mitchell in the Science Department. In the fall of 1861, Martin petitioned for a twelve-month leave. He perceived a duty, he said, "to take part in our struggle for independence, if it could be done without compromising my duty to the university." John Kimberly, Benjamin Hedrick's replacement as professor of chemistry, had agreed to take Martin's classes. Swain had indicated that he thought the trustees would grant Martin leave. Thus assured, Martin had already raised a company of volunteers and been in "the service." Finding that Martin had volunteered and was now a captain in the Confederate Army, the trustees granted him a twelve-month leave.

As its expiration approached, Martin asked Swain to request an extension. He had been promoted to lieutenant colonel, and he viewed his services as even more needed than in the previous year. Many Confederate officers had been killed. He would prefer to be at his academic post, Martin told Swain, but "the country now needs the aid of every man who can bring an arm to her defence." Martin's leave was renewed "until he shall be recalled by the Board." He would be seriously wounded and spend time in a Wilmington hospital before returning to his academic post. Several of the university's tutors joined him in enlisting in the Confederate service.[63]

While younger faculty members joined students in the war effort, Swain and the other older professors remained at their posts, determined that the institution would continue to function. They, too, made sacrifices. In late fall 1861, the faculty requested Swain to advise the trustees that they had "considered the present troubled condition of the country, and its probable effect on the fortunes of this

Institution." In that light he was to make known to the trustees "their purpose to remain at their posts of duty . . . and to aid in whatever way they can the interests of the institution." Cognizant of the war's effect on the college's finances, they conveyed a willingness to accept diminished compensation if circumstances dictated.

The trustees lamented any necessity of a salary reduction and trusted that any such action would be temporary. They then promptly reduced the salaries of the president and the faculty. The reductions produced a temporary casualty. Since 1859, A. D. Hepburn had held the chair in metaphysics, rhetoric, and logic. In late 1863, through Swain, he petitioned for a leave of absence. His salary, he said, was "altogether inadequate to my support." It did not pay for his wheat and corn. With the trustees' consent, he would accept an invitation to supply the Presbyterian Church in Wilmington for a year. The trustees granted the leave.[64]

For the faculty members who stayed, the war presented a curriculum issue, whether there should be military instruction. The question was not novel. Years earlier, as the nation had moved toward war with Mexico, Manly had advised Swain that the executive committee had been authorized to establish an adjunct professorship to teach civil and military engineering. Swain consulted Albert B. Dod of Princeton, who advised that he "doubted exceedingly the expediency of putting muskets in the hands of college boys."[65] If then instituted, such instruction had long since ceased. As war clouds gathered in 1860, the issue resurfaced.

Teaching military tactics was not then within the scheme of instruction, Swain told Manly, but the trustees had discretion to enlarge the curriculum. If done, Swain perceived an issue about "whether the duty of instruction can be committed safely to anyone but a member of the faculty."[66]

In December 1860, the trustees rejected a student petition "for the organization of a Military Establishment in the College." The subject then laid largely fallow for a year until Swain wrote the board "on the importance of organizing and adopting a scheme of Military Tactics and Instruction in the College." Swain's entreaty, like that of the students, was unavailing. The board continued to perceive a need for maturation of a plan and thus held the question over for further consideration.[67]

Swain was accustomed to having his way with the board, and the issue rankled with him. In January 1862 he said to Manly, "There is no subject before us at present which occasions so much perplexity as what we shall do, in relation to organizing a military department." The trustees continued to dawdle. Manly soon informed Swain that due to the small number present and the importance of the subject, they had again postponed consideration.[68]

The faculty now weighed in, resolving that the university should provide such instruction. It appointed a committee on the subject and adopted further resolutions "concerning the propriety of a military drill, and the necessity of having one of the instructors domiciled in one of the college buildings." Frederick A. Fetter, Class of 1859 and now a Latin tutor, should be asked to reside in a college building and to give such instruction in military tactics "as might be deemed essential to the good of the university."[69]

A trustee response finally came in mid-March 1862. Fetter was to instruct in military drill and tactics, to reside at night in the Center College Building, to secure order, to supervise "the protection of the College Edifices," to call the roll at morning and evening prayers, and to perform such other duties as the faculty might prescribe. This was to augment the extant curriculum; no regular recitations were to be omitted.[70] Thus commenced some effort at military instruction on the UNC campus. Professor Martin and Tutor Fetter were the instructors at various times, and the regularity of instruction appears to have fluctuated over the course of the war depending on their availability.[71]

Late in the war the University of Alabama was said to be flourishing because of its "Military feature." This apparently aroused Swain's competitive spirit. Probably in response to Swain's concerns, the faculty resolved to recommend to the trustees a renewal of the military drill, "together with such instruction in Tactics and Engineering as can be provided with suitable books and apparatus."

In response the executive committee directed the faculty to develop a plan of practical and theoretical instruction in military tactics. Again, this was to interfere as little as possible with the extant curriculum. Faculty members were to report their opinions on the expediency of such instruction, and apparently they did. In January 1865, the executive committee referred the subject to the fall meeting of the full board. By then the war had ended, and the subject died.[72]

Even before the war, the financial aspects of university governance presented problems for Swain and the university. In early 1860, Charles Manly asked Swain, "What can be done to increase the Funds of the university?" To prepare the public mind and spur legislative action, Manly suggested a series of essays from Swain. If that failed, relief might be sought from alumni and other individuals. If the state would not sustain the institution, Manly believed there were men who would subscribe to its stock. Swain, Manly said, should think about it and make a proposal.[73]

Onset of the war exacerbated this already precarious financial condition. Tuition revenues diminished as students abandoned the classroom for military service. Day-to-day survival, to the exclusion of strategic or long-range planning, became the institution's modus operandi. Swain apparently did not respond to

Manly's plea, and more immediate concerns diverted the trustees' attention from those of the university. Manly once lamented that he had found "no favorable opportunity" for holding a conference with Judge Ruffin or Governor Graham. "Public affairs and other condition of the country," he told Swain, "have engaged all their time and you can't get them to think or talk of any thing else."[74]

The war produced one rather immediate casualty, the *University Magazine*. Due to "[t]he difficulties of the times," Swain informed Governor Graham, the editors had suspended its publication. Distressed by news of the suspension, a recent alumnus saw the need for the magazine's publication as greater than ever, "now that the glories of another Revolution are to be recorded for future generations."[75]

Swain was prescient about impending shortages of the necessities for daily subsistence. "We will wake up from this situation, before long," he told Manly, "and ask who, when and how, we are to obtain salt, pork and shoes for the coming year."[76] His forecast was sadly accurate. In the latter stages of the war the trustees appointed a committee, with Swain and Kemp Battle as members, to consider the expediency of purchasing supplies and provisions for use of the faculty, to be furnished at cost and charges. A faculty member moaned that "[a] new panic is hereabouts—The impressment of Sorghum Syrup—wheat, Beef, etc. is daily expected." He worried about the "eating houses" being unable to obtain food for the students. Swain and Kemp Battle proposed that Swain be authorized to secure delivery of articles of subsistence to boarding houses the faculty recommended as deserving of encouragement and patronage. Swain was also to secure "proper support and clothing" for faculty families "in lieu of pecuniary compensation."[77]

In September 1863, the trustees provided a fringe benefit. Faculty members could procure firewood for their families from university lands adjacent to the village. Dead and large trees were to be taken first. Thinning only was allowed, strip cutting prohibited. The bursar was to see that no permanent injury was done. The following summer the trustees extended the privilege for another twelve months and thus, though not then known, beyond the war's end. Swain and Judge Battle were to have control of the forest. Anyone who violated the governing rules and regulations forfeited his privileges. Not surprisingly, unauthorized pillaging occurred nevertheless.[78]

Difficult circumstances for his faculty brought "sore grief" to Swain. His "kindness of heart was a conspicuous trait," Kemp Battle would say of him; and while he had sufficient wealth to weather these years of hardship, he suffered with faculty whose wartime salaries did not furnish the necessities of life, and largely chose to conform to the general privation. In many respects there was no choice.

As Confederate money depreciated in value, the worth of his salary, too, diminished accordingly. The time came when bonds were issued for faculty salaries, payable on or before two years after ratification of a peace treaty between the United States and the Confederate States. With his faculty, Swain was subjected to this form of deferred payment.[79]

Wartime exigencies did not shield Swain from relatively trivial matters. Would the senior class have the traditional Commencement Ball, a ball manager inquired of him? It was doubtful, the manager acknowledged, "on account of the distress of the Confederacy." If it was to be held, financial assistance from the trustees was essential. While acknowledging the event's precarious prospects and the compelling reason for them, the manager stated that the class would consider itself slighted without it. It would be the only class for many years to graduate without "the complimentary ball."[80]

There were, however, more substantial requests. A friend of a mutual friend, now deceased, implored Swain's assistance in securing accommodations in Chapel Hill for his family, then in South Carolina, "either at a boarding house or at the Hotel." He was apologetic about imposing, but he knew of no one else to whom to turn.[81]

An 1860 graduate took seriously Swain's invitation to suggest curriculum reforms. The university's instruction in surveying, he told him, was "inadequate both in regard to the use of the compass and the plotting of instruments." Eighteen months of hard army service had injured his constitution. In his view "the wisdom and diplomacy of our statesmen has not been equal to the gallantry of our soldiers."[82]

In early 1863, Swain told Graham that the deaths of UNC graduates and students, both on the battlefields and from camp exposure, exceeded all casualties of the preceding quarter of a century. These brought responses from Swain and the faculty. When Captain George Burgywn Johnston, Class of 1859, died in the service, the faculty expressed its grief. It designated Professor John Kimberly to accompany the remains to Raleigh and to represent the faculty at the funeral. The death of "a young friend" in an unspecified engagement with Grant's forces brought a request that Swain prepare the obituary and "send it to some publication." He complied and was thanked for "a simple and just tribute to the memory of one of the purest and best of men ... couched in very acceptable language."[83]

Notes to ill or wounded former students took Swain's time. One responded, expressing his gratitude for Swain's "kind and sympathizing letter which I received while in the hospital at Richmond." It had helped keep up his spirits when wounded, he said, and was "very flattering and more especially from you of whom

I have so many pleasant recollections and so high an appreciation." Parents, too, received sympathetic missives from Swain. One father thanked him for his kind and complimentary letter regarding his son but gratefully advised that the son's wound had been very slight.[84]

Requests for Swain's aid did not cease during the war. One former student sought a certificate of his scholarship while at UNC. It may, he said, "be of great service to me in the future." He also asked for Swain's recommendation to General Clark for an appointment. It would, he said, both improve his present situation and make him more serviceable to the state "which has heretofore bestowed on me one of the richest gifts [his UNC education, presumably]."[85]

Nor did Swain discontinue his efforts to influence the placement of former students in high-level positions. The father of an 1860 graduate was deeply grateful for Swain's effort to place his son in an "advantageous position" with Governor Vance. The father doubted that the student would accept the position, but he would always be grateful to Swain for the compliment to his son and the kind way it was conveyed.[86]

CHAPTER 24

Reunion, Controversial Union
"A time ... for ... exercise of the highest power of statesmanship"

SWAIN ASSISTED MANY FORMER students during the war years, but none more so than Zebulon Baird Vance. A Vance biographer cites Vance's "lasting and stimulating acquaintance with noble David Lowry Swain" as a major influence on him. An editor of Vance's papers viewed Swain, Governor Graham, and Fayetteville newspaper editor Edward J. Hale as "the advisors on whom Vance leaned most heavily throughout his governorship."

There were antecedents to the relationship that distinguished Vance from Swain's other students. Swain had been Vance's mother's "early schoolmate and beau." Vance's uncle, Robert Vance, long since killed in a duel, had been among Swain's close friends, perhaps his closest. Vance thus arrived in Chapel Hill with enhanced stature in Swain's eyes, a status the teacher-pupil bond only deepened.[1]

In August 1862, Vance was elected governor of North Carolina. The candidate of the Conservative Party, composed mostly of former Whigs and Constitutional Unionists, he received an overwhelming 72.7 percent of the combined military and civilian vote. Charles Manly, who had voted for Vance, wanted him to "take a good start and keep it." Swain, Manly said, "doubtless [had] more influence with Vance ... than any man in the state." Manly wasted no time before urging him to use it.

The public at home and abroad, Manly told Swain, should immediately know Vance's views on public affairs. The newly elected governor's message to the General Assembly was "too far off." There should be "a *big inauguration*," with the supreme court judges, not mere justices of the peace, administering the oaths. If Swain agreed, he should write to Vance "[so] that he may prepare himself." Certainly, Swain himself should attend.[2]

Manly thus suggested, and became the courier for, one of Swain's more reflective and sentimental epistles. He now told Vance that they were "the sons of old

451

friends, natives of the same county, born under the shadow of the same mountains and nurtured under similar influences, intellectual and moral." They had been elected governor at roughly the same age. The same causes that had transferred Swain from a judicial post to an executive one had operated to withdraw Vance from the army and place him "in the chair of state." Other coincidences in their personal histories might "supply topics of conversation" when they next met.

His own election, Swain said, had been "by a respectable legislative majority over candidates greatly my senior, and of established reputation." Vance's had been "by a spontaneous expression of public sentiment[,] an almost universal uprising of the people without a parallel in our history." News of his own election had been "unwelcome intelligence," Swain said. Thankfully, however, the task had proven less difficult than Swain had expected. For the most part he had fulfilled it to the satisfaction of his friends and without bitter animosities from enemies. Vance, Swain knew, faced greater difficulties—"more is expected and more will be required at your hands"—but the greater the difficulty, the greater would be the triumph in surviving it. "I trust," he said, "you will meet it cheerfully . . . and successfully."

Manly's recommendations, transmitted through Swain, followed: a Raleigh ceremony, a judge of the superior or the supreme court to administer the oath "under as inspiring circumstances as the importance of the occasion requires," and "an opportunity to affirm your views in an inaugural address, in advance of the meeting of the General Assembly." Advice on basic governance concluded Swain's missive. "Beware of hasty committals to applicants for office," he admonished. Economy in administration was in order. Henry T. Clark, the departing governor, had two aides with high salaries. Would not "one able and trusty friend suffice?" Vance should exercise utmost care in the selection of a private secretary. "Learning, talent and integrity are indispensable," Swain said, while noting that he might "write . . . again on this head and suggest a name." (He would.)[3]

An unwell Vance replied briefly "to acknowledge your favors." He concurred in Swain's advice regarding the inaugural address and the qualifications of a private secretary. Vance would be "only too happy" to secure the services of Captain Richard H. Battle, Judge Battle's son, "if he will make the sacrifice." Swain would greatly oblige Vance by writing Battle, a choice Swain had suggested, on Vance's behalf. Battle took the position, and a Vance biographer credits him with being one of the reasons Vance was a great governor.[4]

Vance's "desire to encourage retrenchment in public and private expenditures," expressed in his inaugural address, pleased Swain. He admonished Vance on the importance of public arteries for transportation of food supplies during the war.

Despite Chapel Hill's disproportionate contributions in subscribing to its stock, the location of the railroad had not favored Chapel Hill. Swain hoped the village would not be thwarted thereby in its purpose to obtain food supplies.[5]

Vance served as a conduit for Swain's letters to Jefferson Davis on the conscription of students. Swain sought and obtained Vance's support for his efforts to defer them. "Your letter to the President has been endorsed by me and forwarded through Col. Mallett," Vance once wrote Swain.[6]

When the peace movement, led by William W. Holden and others, gained some traction in North Carolina, Vance sent a detailed, pensive, "for your eyes only" letter to his "advisor and father figure." Never, he told Swain, would he consent to this course. It would bring ruin to the state and the Confederacy and "steep the name of North Carolina in infamy and make her memory a reproach among the nations." If necessary to avoid this fate, Vance would "quietly retire to the army and find a death which will enable my children to say that their father was not consenting to their degradation." Vance acknowledged that he sounded "a little wild and bombastic, not to say foolish." "I feel Sir in many respects as a son towards you," he wrote, "and when the many acts of kindness I have received at your hands is [sic] remembered, and the parental interest you have always manifested for my welfare, the feeling is not unnatural. I therefore approach you frankly in this manner."

Vance doubted the tenacity of the people, the endurance of suffering, that "liberty and independence" would necessitate. "This requires a deep hold on the popular heart," he told his mentor, "*and our people will not pay this price* I am satisfied for their national independence!" Historians would not say, however, that the "backing down . . . was due to the weakness of their Governor." He would resist attempts "to lead them back . . . to the arms of their enemies."

No one came to Vance's mind to whom he could more appropriately go for advice than Swain. Any counsel "to throw light on my paths, or enable me to avoid the rocks before me," Vance indicated, would be gratefully received. Specifically, should he seek reelection in 1864? His own inclination was "to take the stump early and to spend all my time and strength in trying to warn and harmonize the people."[7]

Correspondence between Swain and Vance flowed steadily for the remainder of the war. Swain soon noted that if the election were "on Thursday next instead of Thursday fortnight," he "would have no doubt of a triumphant majority." If Atlanta and Petersburg fell in the meantime, Vance's prospects would suffer some, but not much.[8]

In August 1864, Vance was reelected with a substantial majority, and Swain was jubilant. "The first election flash from the army dissipated every cloud in the political sky," he told his pupil, "and killed the enemy so dead that none but a savage would have found heart to exult over the fallen foe." He had never doubted the result, Swain now claimed; indeed, he had written friends that the vote in Orange County for Vance's foe, William W. Holden, "would fall short of 200."[9]

Swain conveyed to Vance both commentary on the war's course and intelligence regarding it. At Richmond and elsewhere, Swain said, there was apprehension that the Confederate navy was preparing to attack Washington. Absent "immediate change," intelligence indicated that if attacked, Wilmington "must fall an easy prey to any considerable force." Swain grieved greatly over loss of the state-owned Confederate blockade runner *Advance*, though he supposed she had "paid for herself several times over." "[O]ur affairs in Georgia" were not "in a very promising condition," and Swain feared what Grant's forces might do there.[10]

Soon after his reelection, disheartened by Confederate prospects, Vance wished for "a long talk" with Swain. He regarded "Early's defeat in the [Shenandoah] valley" as "the turning point of this campaign" and feared that it sealed the fate of Richmond, though not immediately. It would, he told Swain, "require our utmost exertions to retain our footing in Va. until 1865 comes in." Vance viewed the Confederate Army in Georgia as "utterly demoralized." He predicted that President Davis would again display "his obstinacy in defying public sentiment and his ignorance of men in the change to a still worse commander." The Confederacy's "ruin" would then be complete. Confederate troops were deserting by the hundreds daily. More than all else, "the utter demoralization of the people" discouraged Vance. Oft-quoted lines followed. "It shows what I have always believed," Vance now told his father figure, "that the great *popular heart* is not now & never has been in this war! It was a revolution of the *politicians* not the *people*; was fought at first by the natural enthusiasm of our young men, and has been kept agoing by state and sectional pride assisted by that bitterness of feeling produced by the cruelties & brutalities of the enemy."

Vance was not "out of heart," he claimed. "Things," he said, "may come around yet." General Lee was a great man and had the "remnant of the best army on earth, bleeding, torn & overpowered though it be." As for him, just as duty had called him to resist dissolution of the Union, it now summoned him "to stand by the new union to the last gasp with truth & loyalty." He had had no hand in the war's beginning, and "should the end be bad I shall with Gods help be equally blameless." Vance longed for extended quality time with his surrogate father, however. "I hope when you come down," he concluded, "you will give yourself time to be with me a great deal."[11]

Swain now extended his commentary on the course of the war. Had Joseph Johnston remained at the head of the army (General John B. Hood had replaced him), Swain believed, the Confederates probably would have successfully defended Atlanta. That, combined with victories over Grant's armies in Virginia, Swain opined, "would probably have given such an impetus to the Peace party at the North, as would have resulted in an early armistice and subsequent peace."

Swain identified the most disloyal portions of the Confederacy: northern Georgia, northeastern South Carolina, southwestern North Carolina, southeastern Alabama, and east Tennessee. All indications, he said, pointed to their "neutrality if not hostility." The population from Nashville to Atlanta Swain viewed as "sturdy and heroic"; with "the heart to rise as one man," it might "wipe out Sherman's army in twenty days." He feared, though, that the requisite will would be "entirely wanting."

Like Vance, Swain had "unlimited confidence" in General Robert E. Lee. Even so, it would take "miracles to retrieve our failing fortunes," and Swain hoped God would provide them. "I regret that truth and conscience compel me to present so sombre a picture," Swain told his understudy, yet he could perceive nothing more Vance could do "but 'to watch and wait.'" Never wholly removed from his role as university president, Swain again beseeched the governor's aid to his institution. He needed a repetition of the succor "so promptly and effectively rendered in securing supplies for the Faculty of the University a year ago." Vance, Swain speculated, probably knew the controlling quartermaster for North Carolina and could bring personal and official influence to bear upon him, "which neither I nor anyone else can."[12]

Upon receipt of Vance's "great popular heart" letter, Swain concurred in the view "that the great popular heart never beat in union with that of the agitators who initiated the revolution." He indulged in counterfactual analysis. If Andrew Jackson rather than James Buchanan had been president in 1861, he speculated, the federal union would have been preserved. Lincoln's post-Sumter proclamation had "left the South no alternative but resistance." If the Confederate armies should "turn the battle tide in our favor," he said, reaction in the North might result in peace by the end of 1864. Unless Georgia was "redeemed promptly," however, the South would "have neither the heart nor the resources to protract the struggle for any great length of time[.]" And home-front conditions presented the prospect of starvation without some scheme for relief.[13]

Subsequent events solidified these views. Sherman's "triumphant march, his almost royal progress, from Atlanta to Savannah," Swain thought, imported verity to Vance's remark that "the great popular heart" was not in the war. Swain now spoke generally of the "submission and extermination" underway. The two Carolinas and "old Virginia" now had to maintain the war.

They could no longer assert, Swain suspected, that independence was within reach. He perceived no grounds to hope for succor from England or France. "The idea of enrolling and arming slaves and conciliating the world by the abolition of slavery," Swain further noted, "meets with little favor in this quarter." Perhaps if Clay, Calhoun, and Webster were resurrected, they could devise a remedy. In their absence, however, in North Carolina at least, "much, very much, perhaps everything depends upon the course which you shall pursue," Swain told his student.[14]

A few days later Swain noted for Vance the indication of a large minority in both the Confederate Congress and the General Assembly "anxious for peace on the best terms that can be had." Of that minority, he noted further, "no inconsiderable portion would probably prefer reconstruction to an alliance (coupled with the abolition of slavery) with England or France." In Swain's opinion the General Assembly would not pass a convention bill. If it should do so, however, he continued, he thought the people would pass it by a decided majority.[15]

Swain's macroanalysis of the war, its effects and prospects, never rendered him unavailable for lesser tasks. He remained accessible to ordinary citizens who could benefit from his assistance. And he grieved over matters of lesser import, such as the January 1865 burning of the Buncombe County Courthouse.[16]

In early 1864 George Davis of Wilmington resigned his seat in the Confederate Senate to become attorney general of the Confederacy. Vance tendered the appointment to Governor Graham, who declined for family and business reasons, and then to Swain. Vance was very desirous of Swain's acceptance. "I believe that above all men in the state," he told Swain, "your age, position, and character would enable you to modify and soften the present violent and desperate temper of Congress." It would also afford Vance great satisfaction for Swain "to receive the mark of confidence (the greatest it may ever be in my power to bestow) at *my* hands." If Swain could go to Richmond, Vance concluded, "the sooner the better."

In very broken English, a Hillsborough craftsman seconded the idea. There was "an important crisis in the history of our country," the man wrote to Swain; and "so fore as I can collect publick sentiment," he said, the desire was that Swain fill the position. "Let us use your nam agan in common with the Rest of the Citizens of the state have have every thing that is deare to fremen at stake & no good citizen can refuse under such circumstances." "As soon as I mensioned your name [at a large gathering]," he told Swain, "it mete with universal approbation & if you consent I have no idiea that there will be any opesition."

Though a good citizen, Swain did refuse. His reason, however, was compelling.

"The health of my family . . . will not admit of my leaving home immediately," he said, "and the session of Congress is too near its close, and occupied with too important subjects to admit of any delay." Swain regretted Governor Graham's declination. He presented Thomas Ruffin, John Motley Morehead, and Bedford Brown as possessing "higher claims than any others." Under all the circumstances, which he detailed and analyzed, Swain considered tender of the appointment to Bedford Brown "most judicious." While he could not himself accommodate Vance, he had no hesitation about advising him on the appointment.[17]

By the summer of 1864, Graham doubted that the war would end soon. "Unless something tending to peace shall arise out of the pending presidential election," he told Swain, "I see no prospect of the termination of the war." Swain was more optimistic; indeed, he acknowledged that he might be "too sanguine." He hoped and believed, however, "that these difficulties in which the Confederacy is involved, will close substantially with the present campaign." He saw no more cause for despondency regarding the resources of the university than regarding those of the country. They were to be sorely tried during the ensuing session, would have narrow means of subsistence, and would "endure the mortification from diminution of numbers." But, he concluded, "I have strong confidence that the new year will open with better prospects for the country and for us."[18]

Neither Swain nor Graham thought well of the late-war proposals to enlist slaves in the Confederate effort. Graham informed Swain that General Lee favored the idea of enrolling slaves, "with emancipation of themselves and families, and ultimately, of the race." "With such wild schemes and confessions of dispair [*sic*] as this," Graham said, "it [is] high time to attempt peace." When the Hampton Roads Peace Conference failed soon thereafter (February 1865), however, Graham saw "nothing in contemplation but *bella, horrida bella*."[19]

These two elder statesmen communicated frequently during this time. In the wake of the Hampton Roads impasse, Graham conveyed to Swain "the impression [in Richmond] . . . that there is no alternative but to prosecute the War." "The situation is critical," he said, "and requires a guidance beyond human ken." The military situation was "threatening." Grant had been "reinforced," and Sherman seemed "to advance almost without impediment."[20]

Swain concurred in Graham's view that the tendency at Richmond was "towards anxiety and desperation." There was good reason. "We have now no port of entry even for blockade runners," Swain told Graham (Wilmington had fallen to Union forces). Sherman had closed, or was closing, the South's railroad communication with the southwestern states. Missouri and Tennessee were organizing state governments under the United States and were following Maryland and

West Virginia in the abolition of slavery.[21] Graham soon noted that the military situation was "exceedingly critical." Sentiment was growing "in favor of new negotiations to save the wreck of our affairs, if military results continue adverse." Jefferson Davis, Graham opined to Swain, was "unequal to the crisis." He would "neither make peace, for our security, nor war with success."[22]

Swain now advocated immediate convening of the General Assembly. The governor had called his council; Swain hoped this was a prelude to a General Assembly session to determine the course of action required by passage of "the negro enlistment bill." The General Assembly also should determine whether to submit to the people the question of calling a convention. If Graham communicated his views on this to the governor, he could say that Swain concurred in them. "I regret that I cannot safely leave home and have a full conference with you on the state of public affairs," Swain lamented.[23]

Graham soon reported to Swain regarding his interview with Vance "on the subject matter referred to in your letter." The result was that the council of state would convene the following day. The war, Graham said, was now reduced to a contest between Virginia and North Carolina on one side and the United States on the other. The Confederate government was failing to "answer the present necessities of the country." The war had now touched Graham personally. "[I]n an attack by Gen'l Lee on the left of Grant's line," two of his sons had been wounded. Upon receipt of further information, he might need to go to Petersburg to attend to them.[24]

These exchanges were a prologue to probably the most significant of the discourses between these veteran statesmen. Both recognized that the war was ending, and Confederate defeat was imminent. Both wished to minimize the further spilling of blood and destruction of property. A UNC trustee had warned earlier that if the enemy invaded the state, "the Buildings and property of the university would be the special object of their attack and destructions."[25]

On April 8, 1865, with no way of knowing Lee would surrender to Grant the next day, Swain suggested to Graham a course of action, one they were uniquely equipped to pursue. North Carolina, he said, had "never passed through an ordeal more severe than that which we are about to undergo." "Unless something can be done to prevent it," he continued, "suffering, privation and death . . . is imminent to thousands, not merely men, but helpless and innocent women and children." The General Assembly was not scheduled to meet for more than a month. If the governor wished to convene it sooner, the condition of the country, especially the railroads, would likely prevent it. Absent prompt action, anarchy was likely, "from which the transit to military despotism is speedy and certain." Graham was the foremost citizen to whom the state could turn "in her present hour of peril... for the counsel and guidance demanded by the crisis." The two of them should meet in Raleigh two days later and "invit[e] a conference with the Governor on the present state of public affairs."

Swain now grew nostalgic. "I am the oldest of [Vance's] predecessors," he stated, "and at your [Graham's] entrance into public life in 1832, was called upon to discharge similar duties in a somewhat similar perilous condition of affairs." Swain was confident that Vance would listen to him kindly; as to Graham, Vance would "yield as favorable consideration to your suggestions as to the opinions of any citizen or functionary in the Confederacy." The time and circumstances called for "the exercise of the highest power of statesmanship." Perhaps they should summon Vance's other living predecessors—Governors John Motley Morehead, Charles Manly, David Settle Reid, Thomas Bragg, and Henry Toole Clarke—to join them. If Graham concurred, Swain concluded, he should "give the Governor immediate notice of our design."[26]

Graham concurred in Swain's "estimate of the dangers." He had left Richmond, where he now served in the Confederate Senate, satisfied that: Confederate independence was hopeless, there would be no peace through Davis's administration while Davis possessed "the resources of war," and the state government had a duty to move for "an adjustment of the quarrel with the United States." He had conveyed to Vance the information he possessed and his belief that Lee was "anxious for an accommodation" and Johnston could not "raise a sufficient force to encounter Sherman." It was, Graham had told Vance, "the case of a beleaguered garrison before a superior force, considering the question whether it was best to capitulate on terms, or hold out, & be put to the sword, on a false point of honor." Vance had been surprised by Graham's "statement of facts" and "incredulous... as to my conclusions." In a subsequent conversation, Vance had reluctantly agreed to convene the council of state.

Swain should now see Vance, Graham said, thinking it unnecessary that he visit the governor again. "My conversations with him," Graham said, "were very full and earnest." Graham also perceived nothing to be gained "by a convention of those who have held the office of Chief Magistrate." In the people's view, many of them were "the authors of their ruin"; they had "little respect for their judgment." Too, some of them would "swear by the administration, and wage indefinite war while other people can be found to fight it." He invited Swain to come to his house in Hillsboro the following day "and take the cars" from there to Raleigh the next morning.[27]

Soon Graham wrote again to say that the General Assembly should be convened as soon as practicable. It should pass resolutions expressing a desire to negotiate for peace, "stopping the effusion of blood, and inviting the other states of the South to unite in the movement." It should elect commissioners "to treat with" the U.S. government. In the event of Sherman's advance upon the capital, or even without it, the governor should propose a conference, "or send a commission to treat with him, for a suspension of hostilities until the further action of the State shall be ascertained in regard to the termination of the War." Graham predicated his suggestions on the belief that President Davis would not negotiate for peace except on condition of "absolute independence to the Southern Confederacy, with all the territories claimed as belonging to each State composing it."[28]

Swain accepted Graham's invitation to Hillsboro to consider matters about which Graham did not feel free to write. On Palm Sunday, April 9, they spent time together there, unaware that Lee was surrendering to Grant. They agreed that a separate peace for North Carolina constituted its best hope, and they concurred in a course of action for Swain to recommend to Vance the next day.

At Graham's urging Swain took the train from Hillsboro to Raleigh on April 10. He conveyed the discussed recommendations to Vance. If Sherman should advance on Raleigh, Vance should send a commission to him to request a suspension of hostilities until the state could determine its ultimate course. Vance was amenable to the suspension request, subject to General Joseph Johnston's concurrence. When consulted, Johnston advised Vance that if Sherman agreed to treat him with respect, he should stay in Raleigh and obtain the best terms he could.

Vance wished to confer with Graham before proceeding further. On April 11, he sent Graham the following telegram: "If you could possibly run down tonight I will be greatly obliged. This place [Raleigh] will not be held longer than tomorrow." While phrased as precatory, the message could only be regarded as peremptory. Grasping its imperative tone and purpose, Graham boarded the first train for Raleigh, departing Hillsboro at 11:00 p.m. At 3:00 a.m. on April 12, Graham arrived in Raleigh and proceeded to the executive mansion, then generally known as the "Governor's Palace." There he met Swain and Vance, the latter at his desk writing dispatches by candlelight. Colonel James G. Burr, a Vance aide, was the only other person present, Vance having sent his wife, four sons, and most of their furniture to Statesville.

Following an early breakfast, Vance, Swain, and Graham went to the State Capitol, where they composed a letter to Sherman to be sent over Vance's signature. Vance requested, "under proper safe-conduct," a personal interview at a time convenient for Sherman to confer "upon the subject of a suspension of hostilities, with a view to further communications with the authorities of the United States, touching the final termination of the existing War." William B. Harrison, the mayor of Raleigh, was authorized to surrender the city to Sherman. Vance sought Sherman's "favor to its defenseless inhabitants generally and especially to ... the charitable Institutions of the State." The Capitol with its libraries, museums, and public records, Vance "left in [Sherman's] power." He noted, however, that mutilation and destruction of these would advantage neither party. An early reply was requested. Colonel Burr reported that after signing the letter, Vance bowed his head on the desk, "completely unmanned."

Vance then appointed Swain and Graham as commissioners to meet with Sherman, deliver the letter to him, plead for the safety of Raleigh, and ascertain "upon what terms I could remain & exercise the functions of my offices." Swain and Graham had recommended that Vance seek peace with the federals. Vance was unwilling, however, to engage in unilateral peace negotiations, and was determined to do nothing that would appear to be a unilateral desertion of the Confederate cause. When a pro-Davis Raleigh editor got wind of the Swain-Graham mission and accused Vance of an intent to surrender the state, Vance denied it in characteristically colorful language. "I have no thought of such a thing," he rebuffed his accuser, "I mean to stand on Confederate soil as long as there is ground enough to pirouette on one toe, and under the Confederate flag while there is a rag enough left to flutter in the breeze."

Vance directed that Colonel Burr and another aide, Major John Devereux, accompany Swain and Graham. The state surgeon general, Dr. Edward Warren, learned of the mission and volunteered his services. The party of five commenced their journey by train around 10:00 a.m. President Davis, now in Greensboro on his flight south, had directed General Joseph Johnston to leave Confederate troops under the command of General William H. Hardee and to report to him. It thus was Hardee who gave the permit necessary for the commissioners to proceed.

The train soon reached the Confederate lines held by General Wade Hampton. The commissioners showed him Vance's letter to Sherman and General Hardee's safe-conduct permit. Hampton doubted the propriety or expediency of the mission. He nevertheless sent a message to Sherman with a note from Swain and Graham asking when and where they might confer. The train proceeded, but after a short distance a courier from General Hampton stopped it. The courier had information that Hampton had received instructions from Johnston to cancel the safe-conduct order and return the train to Raleigh. Hampton then arrived and read a dispatch he had just sent Sherman informing him that Swain and Graham were returning to Raleigh. The commissioners conveyed their disappointment, but the train reversed course, and the mission appeared to have terminated prematurely.

The train had retreated a short distance when it encountered a Union cavalry commanded by Brigadier General Smith D. Atkins. The tall, handsome Illinoisan was destined to become a member of Swain's family, but at this point they were strangers. Atkins took the party to federal cavalry chief General Judson Kilpatrick. Notwithstanding their papers and safe-conduct order from General Hardee, Kilpatrick claimed they had entered his lines while his troops were in a fight with Hampton and thus were prisoners of war. He did not intend to exercise his right to treat them as such, however. Graham stated that the party obviously had not intended to ride into a crossfire. Kilpatrick concluded the discussion by saying, "Well, as you had started to see General Sherman, see him you should." He then, to their shock and surprise, read them Sherman's order stating that he had official notice from General Grant that General Lee had surrendered his entire army to him on April 9 at the Appomatox Courthouse. There had been rumors to this effect, but this was their first official notice.

Kilpatrick now ordered Swain and Graham removed to a safe place while he communicated with Sherman. With their escort, the two men walked to the rear, the recipients of "jibes and jeers and ribald jests" from Kilpatrick's men, evoked largely because they were dressed in long-tailed coats and tall beaver hats, attire chosen for the occasion. Upon their return Kilpatrick informed them that he would send them to Sherman's headquarters when their locomotive was ready.

When the train carrying Swain and Graham arrived at Gulley's Station near Clayton, Sherman greeted them warmly and took them to his headquarters for dinner. He assured them that they were not his prisoners. When presented with Vance's proposals, Sherman was receptive and was willing to let Vance remain as governor. He replied to Vance's letter, stating, "I . . . enclose you as a safe guard for yourself and any members of the State Government that choose to remain in Raleigh." Sherman doubted that hostilities could be suspended but promised to "aid you all in my power to contribute to the end you aim to reach—the termination of the existing war." On the back of the letter, he wrote "[t]o all officers and soldiers of the U.S. Army" directing them to grant safe conduct "to the bearer of this to any point 12 miles from Raleigh and back." This was to include the governor and any member of the state or city government on his way back to the state capital.

Swain quickly made common ground with the Union commander. They had engaged in the same profession, he said. In response, Sherman noted his presidency of the Louisiana Seminary of Learning and Military Academy and Swain's presidency of the University of North Carolina. Swain observed that some of Sherman's boys had been with him for a time, and Sherman replied that many more of Swain's had been with him during the war. They had come to him before they were men, he said, and should have remained with Swain. He hoped that when they returned to Swain, they would do him (Sherman) justice by telling Swain he had treated them kindly. Swain inquired in particular of one former student, Francis Blair from Missouri, scion of a prominent political and journalistic family, who, according to a Raleigh newspaper, had wreaked considerable destruction in Fayetteville. Sherman would, he told Swain, "turn Frank over to you to answer for it in the morning."

Sherman's observation that the hour was late and they should retire ended a long conversation. The commissioners' locomotive was being repaired, he said, but would be ready early the next day. No doubt Swain and Graham suffered anxiety over this delay, but resigned to it, they settled in for the night. Graham bunked in Sherman's tent. Henry Hitchcock, a member of Sherman's staff, introduced himself to Swain as the son of a Swain playmate from his childhood; he noted that his mother often referred to Swain as "Davie Swain of Buncombe County." Swain related to Hitchcock anecdotes about his mother that made him feel like Swain was a familiar friend. After some resistance from Swain, Hitchcock turned his tent over to him for the night. A later Hitchcock account of the evening is quite revealing of Swain's personality and inclinations:

> Imagine my surprise to find in Gov. Swain an old playmate of my Mother— 'the Davie Swain' of Buncombe Co. of whom she often told me; and who when I asked him purposely—only whether he knew Col. Andrew Erwin, who lived fifty odd years ago in Buncombe, so promptly and warmly responded and find [sic] who I was spoke so warmly of my Mother and Father and of the whole family—with whom he had kept up acquaintance whenever the opportunity offered, that I quickly felt as if I had known him all my life. When they left the next morning, I went down with the General to see them off; and after a polite good-bye all round, the old gentleman—still a vigorous and interesting old man, with a remarkable memory for books, dates, and persons—called me to shake hands with 'good-bye, Major—*we are not enemies, I hope.*'

En route back to Raleigh, Swain and Graham stopped at Union General Judson Kilpatrick's headquarters five miles south of town. They presented him with Sherman's letter and safeguard, which, according to Major Devereux, he "received . . . with very great dissatisfaction." He told the commissioners they were free to continue their journey but that any resistance would be met with "hell." As they approached the capital, Swain and Graham sent Major Devereux and Dr. Warren to inform Confederate General Joseph Wheeler that the city would be surrendered. Upon their showing Wheeler a copy of Sherman's note of safeguard, Wheeler promised an immediate withdrawal of his forces.

At the capitol, to which Swain and Graham had walked from the Governor's Palace, they learned that, upon hearing that they had been captured, Vance had left Raleigh for Hillsboro. They decided that Graham, accompanied by Colonel Burr, would return to Hillsboro. Swain would await the Union advance on the capitol. Graham and Burr departed on foot, following Wheeler's cavalry. Swain, with Sherman's safeguard, assumed a position at the south entrance of the capitol. When some of Wheeler's cavalry men commenced looting stores, Swain warned the troops of Sherman's approach and that resistance might bring destruction of the city.

Graham, having temporarily abandoned his travel to Hillsboro, then rejoined Swain at the capitol. Upon Sherman's arrival, they delivered the statehouse keys to him. The general assured them that he would protect the capital and its citizens. He regretted that Vance had fled but wrote a safe-conduct for him and other government officials, which he entrusted to Swain and Graham. He also wrote a safe-conduct permitting them to return to their Chapel Hill and Hillsboro homes. Swain and Graham remained at the Governor's Palace as Sherman's guests for the evening. Swain's daughter Eleanor ("Ellie"), who would soon figure prominently in his story, had joined the party. She presented a bouquet of flowers to Sherman and his staff. Swain and Graham stayed in Raleigh overnight and left for home the next morning.

When the commissioners arrived at Graham's Hillsboro home, Vance and an aide assisted them. Graham confirmed Lee's surrender for Vance and gave him a letter from Sherman inviting his return to Raleigh. Because President Davis had requested that Vance meet him in Greensboro, Vance declined. He soon left for Greensboro and Swain for his home in Chapel Hill. Swain then led a group of villagers to greet the 10th Ohio Cavalry as it rode into Chapel Hill on the Raleigh Road. The local delegation included Wilson Swain Caldwell, former Swain enslaved person, now a freedman. Swain informed the commanding officer that Sherman had promised to spare the town and the university. His orders were the same, the officer replied. Confederate flags flying from several university buildings soon fell, however, to be replaced by the once-familiar U.S. flag. It was a peaceful surrender in which, apart from that to their pride, the university and its denizens suffered little damage.[29]

In March 1865, trustee secretary Charles Manly, anticipating arrival of federal troops, had hidden the university records for safekeeping. He was "not entirely satisfied" with the hiding place, he informed Swain, and as the war's end approached, he concluded that no place above ground was safe. He thus buried them in a thick wooden box in the woods three miles outside Raleigh. "I performed the whole operation myself," he told Swain, "digging the hole, toting off the surplus dirt... and throwing it in the branch." He then covered the spot with rubbish and leaves. "It was a terrible job," Manly said, one that left him lying on the ground exhausted. He then worried that the papers would "soon become decomposed and rot." For a time he could not recall where they were, but he soon recovered them, and they, like the university buildings, were preserved.[30]

While the university property and records thus survived intact, that cannot be said of the surrounding countryside. Despite attempted constraint by General Atkins and others, the federal troops had to have supplies. The federal occupiers thus significantly stripped the nearby properties. The pillaging activated Swain, who appealed to Sherman on behalf of the area's residents. The villagers and farmers would be without provisions or the means to sow new crops, he told him. While commending Atkins's forbearance, Swain hoped Sherman could "relax the severity of the orders under which Gen. Atkins is acting."

Sherman thanked Swain for his comments about Atkins. He promised that when the war ceased, the seizures of property would cease. Should peace negotiations fail, however, he would remain prepared to resume hostilities. The rural populations of the counties with encamped federal troops did not fare well. One correspondent told Swain that farms in Wake, Orange, and Granville counties were "completely dispoiled of everything in the shape of provisions and forage."[31]

Upon occupation of the village, the university had suspended class recitations. On April 28, the faculty ordered them resumed. On May 3, General Atkins received orders to depart for Greensboro with most of his troops. He left thirty-five men behind to guard the university.

Soon the university observed another commencement, with few students and fewer graduates. "The small number of Trustees in attendance, the small number of graduates, indeed the whole appearance of things is different from what I was accustomed to see for many years," Judge Battle told his son. It was, he said, "a sad era in the history of the university." Swain had missed this one. In response to an invitation from President Andrew Johnson to advise him on Reconstruction, he had gone to Washington to seek restoration of order and the most favorable terms possible for the state. Professor James Phillips presided over commencement in his stead.[32]

As noted, in proposing their mission to Sherman, Swain had said to Graham that it was "a time . . . calling for the exercise of the highest power of statesmanship." Like all war, the war itself was the product of a failure of statesmanship. Swain's role in bringing its North Carolina aspect to a conclusion with minimal bloodshed and destruction was arguably the most significant one in an adult lifetime characterized by acts of statesmanship. True, Sherman might have sensed the nearness of the war's end and spared Raleigh and Chapel Hill, the state's and the university's buildings and records, and the area's population. Conclusion of the war in North Carolina was more than two weeks in the future, however. Nothing in Sherman's wake suggests that he would have shown mercy until the final surrender was signed and the last rebel weapon was stacked. The probability is that Swain and Graham, as Vance's emissaries, saved the state from untold destruction with lasting effects. Swain himself considered this war-ending role "one of the most interesting and important events of his life."[33]

Historical perspective suggests that gratitude should have come to Swain in the wake of these events; not so, however. There was shock and sadness when Swain, now back in Chapel Hill, reported Lee's surrender to Grant, the terms of which had been shared with him and Graham at Union headquarters near Raleigh. Bitter-enders, unwilling to give up the cause, accused Swain and Graham of fraternizing with the enemy. Some thought they should have been hanged, not just in effigy, but literally. As federal troops marched through Chapel Hill, a Confederate general standing on Franklin Street denounced Swain and Graham as traitors who should be executed for their treason.[34]

This rancor toward Swain, and because of him toward his university, was a mere beginning, however. In the depths of his imagination Swain could not have anticipated or prepared for occurrences that soon would considerably aggravate this extant ill will. The train that had transported Swain and Graham to their negotiation with Sherman had encountered Union cavalry under the command of Brigadier General Smith D. Atkins. A Union patriot to the core, Atkins had been the first man in Stephenson County, Illinois, to volunteer in response to Lincoln's call for federal troops. He now found himself in command of the Union troops occupying Chapel Hill. The state university was the main enterprise in the small but now overpopulated village, and shortly after the arrival of his troops Atkins made a courtesy call on its president. Since Swain basically managed both the university and the town, the visit would have been considered standard protocol.[35]

Much more would evolve from this seemingly routine encounter, however. Friendly conversation revealed that the two men shared a keen interest in the Revolutionary War. Years earlier Swain had acquired an original order book from the period detailing Lord Cornwallis's movements during his 1781 expedition through North Carolina. Swain's contemporary correspondence evidences his considerable pride of ownership in the volume. He related the sequence of its orders for Governor Graham and wished to show it to him. To Griffith McRee he wrote, "It would afford me true pleasure to have an opportunity to exhibit these things to you."[36]

When Atkins visited, Swain's request for the book produced a momentous bearer, the president's attractive twenty-two-year-old daughter Eleanor ("Ellie"). Sparks flew instantly between the "delivery girl" and the waiting general. The smitten general embarked upon a new conquest, not of a military battlefield, but of a fair maiden's heart. Each evening he sent the regimental band to play in Swain's front yard. His claims that this was to honor Governor Swain lacked credence. Occupying troops and townspeople alike knew the serenades were for the object of the general's romantic inclinations. He also favored his ladylove with "a fine riding horse" and presented her father with a horse as a gift from General Sherman. The latter creature will figure prominently later in this story.[37]

The conquest was not difficult. Ellie and the general were equally enamored with each other. She shared his love letters with her father and was upset when he shared them with their close friend Cornelia Phillips Spencer. "I was never more surprised, provoked, and *distressed* in my life," Ellie told Spencer. She had shown letters intended for her eyes alone to her father, and only to him, and that "as an act of duty." Swain's perceived impropriety left Ellie irritated with him and hard on him. His "great failing," she told Spencer, was to care too much about "what 'people say.'"

Ellie left no question about her intentions. "[B]ut one voice can prevent this 'affair,'" she said, "and that is one higher than man." The world's "scoffing" mattered little. The "most noble heart and mind" had been entrusted to her keeping. When "this Yankee came among us," she told Spencer, "I had nothing to hide ... except my *self*, and this I had no fear of being stolen, but see the result!"[38]

As a dutiful father, Swain vetted the prospective groom with care. One of his sources of information and contacts was Benjamin S. Hedrick, the deposed UNC professor who was now in Washington. In early June 1865, a few weeks into the Swain-Atkins relationship, Swain served on the Board of Visitors at the U.S. Military Academy. From West Point he forwarded the following solicitation to Hedrick: "Do me the favour and advise me whether it will be in your power to obtain the desired information from Illinois." He could spare a day in Washington en route back to Chapel Hill, Swain told Hedrick, and he desired to interview "the young man in the Patent office from Illinois." Through a friend he had contacted former Governor Richard Yates, now a senator from Illinois, but had received no reply. Ultimately Swain found, apparently to his satisfaction, that Atkins was "a proper and well-connected young man."[39]

Pursuant to orders, Atkins departed Chapel Hill for Greensboro on May 3. Ellie now informed her parents that she had promised to marry him. She had attained the age of majority, she noted, and thus could make her own decisions. Again the dutiful father, Swain consented, but not without misgivings. "I have never seen any man so deeply concerned and agitated," Spencer later wrote, "as Gov. Swain at this unexpected denouement." "His whole mind and thoughts," she continued, "had been concentrated for weeks upon public affairs and the fate of the University. Suddenly his tenderest affections were touched, and in his own household, he was called upon to act in a manner requiring the most delicate and cautious management." Swain, Spencer concluded, believed similar marriages would take place all over the South, that the North and the South were coming together and were more firmly united than ever. He did not dream, she said, "of the bitterness that was to be engendered and revived."[40]

That bitterness was in evidence when the couple married at the Swain home in Chapel Hill on August 23, 1865, slightly more than four months after they met. The extent and depth of the hostile feelings were by now not news to Swain. He had volunteered to give a July 4 address, but a feeble response to his offer had discouraged him. Clearly, he had "underestimate[d] the animosity directed toward him and . . . assume[d] incorrectly that Ellie's forthcoming nuptials were of a type by then calmly accepted in the South."[41]

Hoping to attract a respectable number of guests, the Swains invited many friends. Most invitees declined, however, some more emphatically than others. There were reports of houses in which invitations were not only hastily discarded but also spit upon.[42]

As the wedding date approached, the event was "the main theme of talk" in Chapel Hill. The groom arrived a week beforehand. When nuptials day came, Governor and Mrs. Graham attended. Also present were Confederate veterans, Union army officers, UNC faculty members and their families, villagers, family members, and a few close friends. The Reverend Doctor Fordyce M. Hubbard—longtime Swain family friend, UNC faculty member, and rector of Chapel Hill's Chapel of the Cross—officiated. The town's freedmen, who considered the groom "their liberator," sent "a large and handsomely decorated cake" that was prominently displayed in the Swain home during the wedding dinner.[43] A week later the newlyweds departed for Illinois.[44] Overt hostility to the union did not lie dormant during these proceedings. Throughout the ceremony students raucously

General Smith D. Atkins and Eleanor "Ellie" Swain Atkins.

tolled the South Building bell in protest. They also hung Swain and Atkins in effigy from the building's bell tower.[45]

General and Mrs. Atkins had their well-wishers. A cousin of Eleanor's wrote Swain that she trusted that Ellie would "be happy and find many friends in the land of her adoption." Swain said laconically to Zeb Vance: "Ella was married on the 23rd ult. The Gov. and Mrs. Graham came over to the wedding and spent the next day with us." He soon told Vance that Ellie was at her new home in Freeport, Illinois, and seemed pleased "with her new relations and with the country." "No one," Ellie said, had "uttered a syllable in disparagement of the south in her presence"; she had received "universal manifestations of respect."[46]

Some journalists treated the event with jocularity. General Atkins, said one paper, had not only "accompanied the victorious armies of the Union into this department" but had also "made an important capture ... at Chapel Hill, in the person of Miss Eleanor H. Swain, daughter of Honorable David L. Swain, Ex-Governor of North Carolina, who presented the General with their prize." The Reverend Doctor Hubbard had pronounced it "a valid conquest ... in the presence of a large number of officers of the army and distinguished citizens of the state."[47]

By all accounts it was a happy time for the uniting couple. The enmity that infected the nuptials, however, was significant and persistent. Anxiety lingered in the small academic village. "I learn that Genl. Atkins and his wife are in town," wrote a resident over a year later, adding somewhat fearfully, "There has been no demonstration of any sort, and I hope everything will pass off quietly." "Most persons," said Cornelia Phillips Spencer, "think it a great pity she should come home at all in such a crisis in our affairs." And whom did they blame? "They were all full of the general talk and excitement versus Governor Swain," Spencer added. There was general agreement in the village that Swain must resign, or the university was doomed. No one would tell him so, however, and he thought he would "live it down."[48]

The abiding damage to Ellie's beleaguered father was indeed incalculable. Spencer also wrote contemporaneously: "The blight that immediately fell upon the University was directly attributable to the fact that he not only permitted his daughter to marry an invader but that he gave her a fine wedding. It was told from mouth to mouth and believed all over North Carolina that Ellie Swain went to Illinois loaded with finery and jewels stolen from the women of states farther south, and given to her by her husband."[49] Later Spencer termed the wedding "the principal agent in alienating public affection and confidence from our university for a time." After Swain's death she told Eleanor Swain, "I think that neither you nor he ever knew to what extent he was blamed for the marriage." Its effect, she quoted a professor as saying, "was very great against the Governor & the college."

It bears repeating that Swain, according to Spencer, had thought the war was over. He naively underestimated the deep feelings that lingered from the losses southern families had sustained and the resulting sense of insult and degradation. In a moment focused on a beloved family member, he was oblivious to the profound divisions and perceptions that would beset the region and the country well into the future. Little did he know, Spencer opined, that in allowing the marriage and making it a lavish, public affair, "he was condemning his ... beloved university to temporary ostracism from public favor."[50] As we shall soon see, Spencer's contemporary assessment proved depressingly and lastingly accurate.[51]

CHAPTER 25

Reconstruction
"In the days of darkness"

THE COMBINED EFFECT OF Swain's war-ending role and Ellie's impolitic marriage was a considerable diminution in his public acceptance and popularity at the local and state levels. This curtailed his extensive participation in public life little, if any, however. Instead, his involvement at the national level increased significantly.

In the immediate aftermath of the Civil War, President Andrew Johnson and Secretary of War Edwin Stanton appointed Swain to the Board of Visitors of the U.S. Military Academy at West Point. At first blush the appointment seems strange, and the rationale for it is unknown. Swain was, however, a well-recognized and well-regarded Southern elder statesman. He was now known to General Sherman and becoming so to President Johnson. At this critical juncture in American history, the federal administration may have desired to bring select Southern leaders into the national conversation. If so, Swain would have been an appealing prospect. He joined representatives from four other Southern states—Alabama, Georgia, Louisiana, and South Carolina—on the board. During the board's June 1865 attendance upon the examinations of the graduating class, one of the institution's more distinguished graduates also paid a visit. Undoubtedly recalling their recent meeting, General Sherman reportedly "shook hands cordially" with Swain.[1]

Examination of the cadets was expected to extend for twenty days. Swain foresaw the process continuing at least through mid-June, a period of detainment, he said, "longer than may be convenient for me." Inconvenience notwithstanding, his friends found gratification in the appointment: "not that such an appointment would have been, under ordinary circumstances, a matter of any remarkable note," wrote one, "but at this time, after the severe ordeal through which our country has just passed, there was special significance in it which was most grateful to me."² Swain relished both the recognition and the weightiness of the task. He could scarcely imagine a more suitable location for "a great military educational Institution." The professors impressed him favorably. The board's call upon General Winfield Scott, now venerable in age and service, brought Swain pleasure. "[V]ery feeble but more prepossessing in appearance than . . . anticipated," by Swain's description, the general had received them "very courteously" and been gratified by the visit.³

Swain had foreseen "much work." His prediction was accurate, and he took the work seriously. His post-visit report first noted the board's expansive charge: "an examination into the conditions and extent of all the means and appliances of education, which the beneficence of the government has provided." In response the committee had examined the grounds, edifices, library, and other material accumulated over more than half a century. It had made inquiries of the staff. Its members would forego detail on all aspects of the visit and "content themselves with a general reference to the satisfaction with which they contemplated the general condition in which they found them."

The board made several recommendations, among them: The services of a competent landscape gardener should be obtained. (Swain probably recalled his own service to UNC in this regard.) The cemetery should be "rendered in design and execution worthy of the institution." These improvements would cost an estimated $36,118, which Congress would need to appropriate. Extensive additions to the chemical apparatus were needed. For proper preparation, cadets should be appointed a year in advance of entrance. Upon admission they should be not less than seventeen years of age nor more than twenty-one. Acquaintance with the elements of geography and English grammar should be among the entrance requirements. Total enrollment should increase from 225 to 400, with accommodations, instructors, and other institutional accoutrements enhanced accordingly.

It was a positive feature of Swain's report that little needed to be said about hazing. Even the "intemperate use of ardent spirits" was a lesser problem than in any college or university of which the visitors had knowledge. Use of profane language, by contrast, was "unhappily very general," although "not universal." The system of discipline was "the most nearly perfect" in an institution of this kind. There should, however, be "a daily recognition of Divine Providence" under the supervision of the chaplain.⁴

Despite Swain's many roles in public life, there was a newness and a difference to this one. It was at the national level, and it involved serious military and educational policy. The inconvenience of an extended detainment in New York notwithstanding, he clearly performed the task with zest and verve.

While significant, the West Point appointment was but a small piece of Swain's postwar, national-level involvement. Shortly before the visit to the military academy, President Johnson had summoned him to Washington to consult on Reconstruction policy generally. An interesting companion accompanied Swain to the capital in response to the presidential summons: Governor Zebulon Vance, on his journey to Washington's Old Capitol Prison for a brief period of postwar incarceration.[5]

Similar presidential summonses had gone to two other North Carolinians, Bartholomew F. Moore and William Eaton Jr. John H. Wheeler, Swain's companion in historical labors, went with the three men for their late May 1865 session with the president. Johnson showed the delegation the proclamation he had prepared announcing his plan for the restoration of North Carolina to the Union. Moore objected, urging its unconstitutionality. The president, Moore thought, should allow the General Assembly to meet and call a convention to deal with the issues. Swain supported retention of the incumbent state officials and a state constitutional convention to draft a Reconstruction program.

Johnson reportedly was pleasant but unyielding in his opinion and plans. Swain later told former Chief Justice Ruffin: "He heard us patiently and unyieldingly, insisted that as the General Government was called to guarantee to each state a republican form of government that his purpose could only be effected in the existing state of things by a reconstruction of the whole fabric of government." The following day the Swain-Moore-Eaton deputation resumed their parley with the president, to find, however, that another North Carolina group with William W. Holden at its head had joined them. They had come, said Holden's *Daily Standard*, "as representatives of the radical union sentiment of the state." Their purpose: "a full and free consultation as to the best and most speedy means of reorganizing the state government." President Johnson shared with both delegations a proposed amnesty proclamation in which he had left blank the name of the provisional governor. He would, he said, appoint their nominee.

Swain, Moore, and Eaton declined the invitation and left the room. Holden also absented himself, leaving the remaining attendees to express their opinions. Swain appealed to Holden "in the most earnest tones" to decline the position if offered it, in the name of harmony. Rightly or wrongly, Holden viewed Swain's concerns about the future of the university as the impetus for the request. In his memoirs Holden recorded that he said to Swain: "Governor, I have always been a firm friend of the university, though myself not a graduate as you were not. I am not yet assured of my appointment. I may be, or I may not be, but in any event I am your friend, and the friend of Chapel Hill." Holden did not feign disinterest in the position. On the contrary, his reference to "my appointment," while the matter yet pended, connotes some perception of a possessory stake. And indeed, when the absentees rejoined the session, the office was his. The residual representatives had made their wishes known; the president, gratified by the choice, had made the appointment. Holden's duties would commence on June 5, 1865, and Swain's concerns about the appointment would prove well-founded. He soon told Governor Graham that Holden was exercising authority "not merely greater than known to his predecessors, but greater than ever were claimed for an English monarch since 1688."[6]

Swain thus did not always get his way with the Reconstruction chief executive. In the context of the time and circumstances, however, Johnson's invitation for Swain to meet with him "was no idle compliment." It was a sad condition of affairs, wrote historian John H. Wheeler, but the invitation and its aftermath showed the prominent part that Swain had in these eventful scenes.[7]

This visit left Swain with a largely favorable view of the new president. Johnson would, Swain thought, treat the conquered South as favorably as could be expected. Swain himself had been treated "with marked courtesy and hospitality" on his missions to the North. Even so, he found the experience "galling" and was glad to get back to the South. The last four years, he said, "so ruinous to us," had boosted wealth and luxury in the North. He had found himself standing up for the South and "silenc[ing] her detractors." Swain's defense of the region in the North failed to mollify his own detractors in the South. Upon his return to Chapel Hill, he offered to give an address on "the state of matters, North and South." Met with a cool reception, he dropped the idea.[8]

For the rest of his life Swain made periodic visits to, and had extensive dealings with, the capital of the now reunited nation. He returned in the early fall of 1865 and found himself well treated. He reported pleasant interviews with the president, the secretary of war, the attorney general, and the postmaster general. All were courteous and kind, he told Vance, "Mr. Seward especially." This excursion produced an even more favorable impression of President Johnson than had the previous one. Johnson, Swain opined, looked "every inch the President."[9]

In March 1866, Swain was again at the capital. He held to the view that the president was in earnest about doing the South justice and would secure the region's rights if any man could. A connection made at UNC gave Swain access to the secretary of the treasury. The man, a "mulatto" at the department, had attended President Buchanan on his 1859 visit to Chapel Hill and had stayed at Swain's home. He recognized Swain and granted him entrée.[10]

In December 1866, Jonathan Worth, who had defeated Governor Holden in the 1865 election, traveled to Washington to address General Dan Sickles's order prohibiting corporal punishment except in cases of apprenticed minors. At Worth's request Swain accompanied him, together with Justice Ruffin and Rowan County political figure Nathaniel Boyden. The president took their request for withdrawal of the order under advisement, promising to consult his cabinet and decide. When the delegation returned two days later, Johnson had concluded that Sickles's order was not warranted. He directed its suspension insofar as it conflicted with the state's laws on apprenticeship and vagrancy.[11]

John H. Wheeler forewarned Swain that the temper of Congress toward the South was not amiable. "The late election [1866] renders the future of the South more gloomy," Wheeler said. It thus was no surprise to Swain when the First Reconstruction Act passed over Johnson's veto on March 2, 1867. The relative success of the mission regarding Sickles's order prompted Governor Worth again to request assistance from Swain and Ruffin. The governor's concern now was to ascertain what, if anything, North Carolina could do "to avert total ruin." Worth regretted having to ask for further sacrifice, he told Swain, but he felt "constrained to urge your acceptance of this commission." Ruffin was ill, as was Swain's daughter Ellie. Professor James Phillips's illness also constrained Swain. Thus, neither Swain nor Ruffin made the journey. But for these restraints, however, Swain's public-service mentality would once again have had him Washington bound.[12]

Congressional takeover of Reconstruction failed to slacken Swain's cultivation of President Johnson. As noted, Johnson accepted Swain's invitation to attend the 1867 UNC commencement. He also attended Swain's dedicatory address for the monument to his father, Jacob Johnson, at Jacob's grave in Raleigh. When the address was published, together with Swain's address at the dedication of Raleigh's Tucker Hall, Swain sent the president a copy. If Johnson's children desired copies, and if Johnson would provide their addresses, Swain would be pleased to send them, he told the president.[13]

One item on which Swain addressed the national authorities was intensely personal. He owned property valued in excess of $20,000 and thus fell within the thirteenth exception to President Johnson's general amnesty proclamation. Therefore, he needed a pardon for his support of the Confederacy. He brooked little delay in seeking it. His petition is a model of ably crafted legal advocacy. It emphasizes his efforts to thwart secession, the reluctance with which he ultimately accepted it, and his declination to accept office under the Confederate government when offered.

Notwithstanding over a 50 percent diminution of his estate from effects of the war, Swain now acknowledged ownership of an estate valued at more than

$20,000, and thus his embrace within "the 13th Section" of the Amnesty Proclamation, which exempted those of that wealth level. He had taken the amnesty oath and "ha[d] availed and will avail himself of every fair opportunity to encourage harmony and secure fidelity to the Union." He thus sought "pardon for the errors of omission and commission in the performance of his public duties," promising "for the future to fulfill all the obligations of a good citizen to the best of his ability."

The petition was an appealing entreaty, minimalist in its depiction of Swain's ultimately secessionist course, yet devoid of falsehood. The relationship of trust and confidence its author had developed with the new president undoubtedly aided its course. Finally, this endorsement on the petition helped: "A pardon is respectfully recommended in this case," signed "W. W. Holden, P[rovisional] Gov[ernor]." Holden signed it on September 14, 1865 (most North Carolina pardon requests were processed through Holden, who made a recommendation in each case). Andrew Johnson granted the petition on September 28, 1865, five months and two days after the surrender of Confederate troops from Swain's state at the Bennett Place.[14]

Swain assisted others in this quest. He "succeeded in obtaining" pardons for Judge Thomas Ruffin and Paul Cameron of Orange County. In the process he bypassed Holden, who had denied Cameron's request, and went directly to Johnson, who ordered the pardons prepared for his signature.[15] George Davis—Wilmington lawyer, member of the Confederate Senate, and Confederate attorney general—thanked Swain for his assistance, and Dr. Crawford W. Long, Swain's niece's husband, sought it. Davis was newly married to a "Miss Fairfax" from Weldon in Halifax County. His parole status limited his movements between Wilmington and Weldon. It was an "unusual arrangement" that Davis obviously wished to alter.[16]

Weldon N. Edwards, prominent Warren County political figure and presiding officer of the North Carolina Secession Convention, like Swain, fell within the economic class exempted from the general amnesty proclamation. As "[a]n entire stranger to the President," he perceived a need for "backers" for his thus needed pardon application. He sought a letter from Swain to the president "speaking of me as I am," especially on whether he was an orderly and peaceable citizen. He needed assistance, he told Swain, "from those who, like you, are in better favor." Swain wrote, Edwards later said, a "more than kind letter to the President in my behalf." Edwards was grateful beyond measure "[f]or its very flattering commendations."[17]

Former North Carolina Governor Henry T. Clark considered Swain's presence in Washington "a favorable opportunity of presenting to the President my application for a pardon." He had served the Confederacy faithfully, he told Swain, but now offered the "same zeal and fidelity" to the United States. He was a supporter of President Johnson's policy, yet "subject[ed] to the criticism of those who would check my efforts and impair my influence." Clark's spirits as well as his usefulness were thereby impaired, and he would, he said, be greatly obliged if Swain could draw the president's attention to his petition.[18]

The pardon effort for another of most concern to Swain was that of Zebulon Vance. In October 1865, following one of his trips to the North, Swain advised Vance of inquiries he had made on his behalf. He had learned from these that Johnson was now inclined to conduct personal interviews with pardon applicants. Vance might ultimately find it necessary to visit Washington and see the president, Swain advised. If so authorized, however, Swain said he would be pleased "to bear the application" and to engage "in an effort on your behalf."[19] Vance's pessimism about his chances grew, however, as President Johnson's influence over Reconstruction waned. "I have pretty much given it up," he told Swain, "as the longer it is put off the further is the President from being in a position to grant it." Except for a few extraordinarily importunate applicants, a tactic Vance would feel ashamed to resort to, he foresaw no more pardons for men of prominence.[20]

Soon, though, the General Assembly passed a resolution on Vance's behalf. Notwithstanding his efforts to avoid importunity, Vance desired that Swain be "the bearer of the Resolution . . . to the Prest. on my behalf." Vance's parole had been extended to the limits of the state, a status he did not wish to jeopardize by pressing his pardon "injudiciously." His keen desire for a pardon was trumping his innate caution, however. "The presentation of these Resolutions," he thus now rationalized, "could . . . be hardly set down as importunity on my part."[21]

In response Swain indicated that he had written the governor and the public treasurer. He had requested that they ascertain whether Governor Holden had transmitted the resolutions recommending Vance's pardon and those assuring the loyalty of the state. If not, he had suggested "their immediate communication, in the most inspiring manner." Swain had received no answer. Cornelia Phillips Spencer's publication, *The Last Ninety Days of the War in North-Carolina*, would reach Raleigh about the time the General Assembly reconvened, Swain said. The work would attract attention to Vance's case "and probably offer fair opportunities to determine what is best to be done." For the moment Swain recommended "[m]asterly inactivity" on Vance's part as "the safest and wisest course." Vance took the advice seriously, so much so that he declined speaking invitations "for fear of doing harm."[22]

A lengthy period of "no direct communication" followed. When correspondence resumed, Swain assured Vance that he was not forgotten, indeed, that he was always "the object of friendly interest and solicitude." Swain was "far from supposing that all avenues for advancement in other directions are permanently closed."[23] They were not. President Johnson granted Vance a pardon on March 11, 1867. On May 2, Vance took the prescribed oath. He later reoccupied the governor's office, then spent the remainder of his life as a member of the U.S. Senate. His prospects had appeared grim for a time, but a long and distinguished political career followed.[24]

Next to Vance's the pardon of most interest to Swain was Graham's. From the outset of his efforts, Graham observed manifestation in their interviews with Swain of "coldness both of the President & Secretary [of State, presumably] in regard to me." Graham thought, he told Swain, that he "had been the subject of special communication between the former and the Prov[isional] Gov[ernor], and marked for proscription." "There has been so much prevarication by the latter [Holden] in regard to my case," Graham continued, "that no reliance is due his statements." Holden, Graham said, had told people he had recommended his application "and manifested a desire for my pardon." Information had reached him, however, suggesting "the want of truth in this." Graham was said to be "much excited" that several other leading men had been pardoned at once, while his application and those of others had been "suspended."[25]

Swain soon advised Graham of his efforts on Graham's behalf. He had called on Edmund Cooper, President Johnson's private secretary, who was "understood to have more influence at the White House than anyone else." There was nothing Cooper would not do for Graham, he had assured Swain. Swain was to write Cooper on the subject that morning. Holden, Swain advised Graham, was saying that Secretary of State Seward was "the great obstacle." Seward, according to Holden, had said Graham had been very prominent in the country but would never occupy a seat in either house of Congress. Holden had attempted to justify not asking for a pardon for Graham but had said he had never opposed it. By now, Swain thought, Judge Ruffin, too, would have advised Graham on "how matters stand in relation to your pardon."[26]

Ruffin had, for which Graham was grateful. The "personal objection" to his pardon, Graham said, "not having been 'reasoned up, cannot be reasoned down.'" It had "long since ceased to give [him] any concern," Graham told Swain, adding, "I shall make no further movement in the matter." If true, which is doubtful, Graham's lack of concern was a good thing, for he was destined for a long wait.[27]

One other matter lingered from the Civil War that had a personal dimension for Swain. The story of its closing days needed to be told. This should be done while events were recent and memories fresh. More important, the account needed to be accurate; accurate, that is, from Swain's perspective and those of his compatriots Graham and Vance. The three men were under fire for their roles and conduct in those days. Indeed, their conduct had called into question the abiding loyalty of the state to the Confederate cause. A "truthful" representation, one that would put these charges of cowardice and disloyalty to rest, thus was in order.

The governors were too busy for such an undertaking. With appropriate sensitivity to their positions of public leadership during the Confederacy, Swain and Vance also believed another writer would have freedom that circumstances would deny them. They had a candidate in Cornelia Phillips Spencer, Swain's neighbor, daughter of James Phillips and sister of Charles Phillips, UNC professors. Married briefly to an Alabama lawyer and now widowed, Spencer lived with her family in Chapel Hill. The Swain and Phillips families resided in close proximity and were on intimate terms. Given her loyalty and devotion to Swain, Spencer would have been hard pressed to refuse his request that she write the account.

Spencer was to embody in the work her personal knowledge of those final scenes. She had assistance, however. According to her brother Charles, Swain was "busy superintending the preparation of [the] account." "He furnishes the material," Charles said, while "[t]he writing, comments etc. come from my widowed sister Mrs. Spencer who with her daughter lives at my father's." Spencer made no attempt to conceal Swain's paternal role. "Whatever I may write is subject to Gov Swain's criticism," she told Graham, adding later, "no step of my present undertaking is advanced without Gov Swain's concurrence and advice." When her narrative reached book stage, the dedication page read:

To The

Hon. D. L. Swain, LL. D

At Whose Suggestion It Was Undertaken, And By Whose Invaluable Advice, Encouragement And

Assistance It Has Been Completed, This Book Is Most Respectfully Dedicated.

That Swain and Spencer were neighbors is a loss to history in relation to this work. They mostly conversed rather than wrote, thus leaving little historical record of their communications.[28]

By contrast, Vance and Spencer exchanged letters with regularity in the pro-

Cornelia Phillips Spencer, author of *The Last Ninety Days of the War in North-Carolina*.

cess. Vance, still young and ambitious, had the most at stake. Keenly aware of this, Swain also communicated with Vance often during Spencer's endeavor. Vance was, said Swain, a victim of "plottings and counter plottings." In Washington and among Northern people, it was thought that Northern prisoners of war in North Carolina had been "treated with a savage brutality." To enable Spencer to place Vance "in the true light," Swain would furnish her with a letter that apparently proved the contrary. If Spencer's initial chapters, published as articles, met a favorable reception, Swain said, they would then probably take on book form. Once the shackles of his unpardoned status were removed, Vance could again be elected to office. For now, however, he should "be quiet and bide your time," Swain instructed.[29]

Almost simultaneous Spencer-Vance exchanges depict Swain's motives and purposes in relation to Vance with clarity. As Spencer begged Vance to review her manuscript, she told him it "was written at the suggestion of Governor Swain" and had been sent to him at Swain's suggestion. "He wished a record made of North Carolina's position at the close of the war," Spencer said. It was to include "certain admirable interesting letters addressed to him by various distinguished gentlemen during that time." Swain's main object was "to have honor due and deserved justice done to *Gov. Vance*, as far as can be done in so slight an affair." Vance could determine what use Spencer made of his private correspondence; all of it that she had seen, however, did him honor. A postscript is telling as to Swain's influence: "Please return me the M.S. at your earliest convenience with an *opinion* annexed," Spencer instructed, "unless it should be *too* unfavorable, in which case I think I should prefer you to send it to Governor Swain."[30]

Vance was glad to see the manuscript, for there was a slight error he wished to correct. As to the propriety of publishing his letters, he left that to Spencer and Swain. Given their "friendly zeal" toward him, he had confidence in their selections. Vance was sensitive about some of his comments on Jefferson Davis. There had been tension between the two through much of the war, and it was cowardly to strike a fallen foe; therefore, if his remarks about Davis could be so construed, Spencer should "*draw your pen through them.*"[31]

Spencer quibbled over this. "Governor Swain wants to present a fair record of your opinions and position," she admonished, "and among other things it will be well for some people to know that you were no blind follower of President Davis." If Davis was still a prisoner (he was), however, she said, "your generous view will of course be adopted." Only Swain, Vance, and her father would see the manuscript before its publication. The benefit of Vance's "advice and criticism" was thus important.[32]

Vance's only criticism was that "some of the subjects" were "a little awkwardly brought in," did not "seem materially to follow the preceding matters." Swain, he feared, was plying her with letters and other documents so freely that weaving them in presented problems. If the title were "A Vindication of Governor Vance," not "The last ninety days of the war in N. Ca.," this would not be a problem. The latter was preferable, however, both to make the work more readable "and to vindicate me, provided the vindication don't [*sic*] stick out too plainly." Notwithstanding differences with Swain, Vance remained deferential to him. "I would hack and hew without mercy at your composition," he told Spencer, "while I would be afraid to dot an i or cross a t of his." As to content, Vance "shed tears freely over some parts of it." "To own the truth," he poignantly confessed, "wherever the sufferings and heroism of our people for the last four years are forcibly brought to my mind, my heart takes the lead of my judgment and I am almost as bad as a school girl over the last novel."[33]

Vance detailed for Spencer his efforts to save state property as the war was ending. Only after he had obtained permission from Confederate General Hardee in General Johnston's absence, he said, did he send a flag of truce with a letter to Sherman. Swain and Graham had delivered the letter, and Swain could give Spencer "full information." Vance had then left Raleigh only when Swain and Graham failed to return from their mission to Sherman; he had not been "willing to trust myself in their [Union] hands without terms so long as 8,000 North Carolina soldiers under Gen. Hoke remained under arms." Many of his friends thought he should have returned to Raleigh. He did not. Indeed, no act of his administration gave him more pleasure: "It kept the NC troops to their colors and enabled Johnston to get a treaty out of Sherman which if approved by the Govt. would have recognized the state governments and avoided all the misery, humiliation, and ruin now upon us. It enables me to say that whilst there was a soldier in the field I stood with him, and it saved me the humiliation of being afterwards thrust out of my office and treated with personal indignity. I would not have it otherwise." In a subsequent letter Vance described and defended his war-end travels, noting in particular his night at Graham's home when Swain and Graham delivered Sherman's reply to his letter.[34]

While grateful for Vance's reply, Spencer raised a delicate point. Was it advisable to "let on" about Vance's being hindered from returning to Raleigh? She was writing about "the few last desperate days of the Confederacy when the bottom fell out so unexpectedly," and was having difficulty understanding what Davis or his advisors "hoped to effect by attempting to trip you up." Many of Vance's friends, she told him, including Swain, had always regretted that he had left Raleigh. Would it be advisable to say that Confederate military authorities would not permit him to pass their lines while the negotiations were pending?

A telling statement follows, again indicative of the party in charge. "I have this statement all written," Spencer said to Vance, "and going over to the Gov. to read the M.S. to him this afternoon he demurred to mentioning the check upon you—even in this general way." Spencer preferred "to state *the whole truth*," but Swain had suggested that she ask Vance. Swain was "reluctant to make any exposé of President Davis which may irritate our friends the secessionists —who, you know all agree to idolize President D[avis] now." He was also "fearful of my saying anything that may bring you into any thing like reproach from these friends."

As for Spencer, she had questioned why Vance had left Raleigh. She now agreed with his decision. She had not known "upon what principals [*sic*] you acted, never understood your motives." Now, though, she was proud of him and wanted everyone to understand, "to vindicate you from any charge of folly—refusing to give up when all was lost—running after Davis, etc. etc."[35]

Vance could not give "a good reason for Davis's conduct in endeavoring to 'trip me up' at Greensboro." Davis seemed, Vance said, to think he could prolong the war. A "man of imperfectly constituted genius," Vance opined, Davis was unyielding in his opinions and could "*blind himself* to those things which his prejudices or hopes did not desire to see." As to whether Spencer reported the history of his attempts to return to Raleigh, Vance expressed indifference. He preferred "being thought a brave and true man to a wise one." "My heart was with that retreating army," he said, "and it cost me the bitterest tears of my life to write that letter to Sherman! Yet truth and nothing else should constitute history . . . that is, all which it is material to tell. . . . Do then as you think best."

Tensions surfaced between the subjects of Spencer's narrative. Vance now complained mildly that an unspecified letter of Graham's had done him "some injustice." This, though, was for Spencer's eyes only. If she showed it to Swain, Vance said, "I doubt not but he would approach Governor Graham and have in writing mutual letters of explanation etc. which there is not the slightest occasion for." Orange County citizens considered Graham infallible, Vance continued, and "to suggest a friendly doubt of the fact is treason with most people." Despite his respect for his elder mentors, Vance thus had differences with them. Graham could be somewhat unjust; Swain, a manipulator of history, and unnecessarily so. His advice to their mutual chronicler was simple: "I pray you to let the truth come, whoever it may hurt. You have done me so far ample justice and I thank you."[36]

Spencer acknowledged the tensions. She had asked Swain whether publication of the Graham letter would not cast some blame on Vance. It had, she admitted, given her an unfavorable impression. She had supposed that Vance's wisdom had been "under some temporary eclipse," that he was "hold[ing] onto some wild and visionary hopes for the Confederacy." Vance's account of his journey from Raleigh, and the reasons for it, however, had enabled her to "understand enough to do you justice."

Swain had assured her repeatedly, Spencer said, that Vance would not object to use of the Graham letter, even that he had read it to Vance and Vance had "endorsed it." She assured Vance that "Gov. Swain loves and admires you as if he were your own Father." She continued, "You may rely upon it that if the '90 days' fails to enhance your merit in the eyes of the people of North Carolina, the Gov. will feel that it has missed its aim." This was Spencer's purpose, too, to show that the state, "through our Executive," "*could not* have done otherwise than it did." This effort was wearing on Spencer, though. She was finding it "very hard to satisfy all parties." Her frustration is palpable from her now lament to Vance that among the most difficult things to do is "to write clearly while the actors' minds are still heated and ten thousand contradictory views of one point are continually presented."[37]

The endeavor produced tension even between Spencer and Swain, whom she idolized. She had been reluctant, she told Vance, "[t]o cram so much of the uni[versity] down the public throat." It was a very interesting subject, but "not quite so much so" as Swain thought, "nor so nearly connected with the events of the last 90 days of the war as he wishes me to 'make believe.'" Spencer, indeed, did not wish to see the book published. "[B]ut I am letting myself be overruled by others [namely, Swain]," she said. "I am going at the revision," she concluded "with very little elasticity of feeling or interest in it."[38]

When publication time arrived, Vance pleaded incapacity to make suggestions and lack of competency to criticize. His only regret was that Spencer had not recounted the entire four-year history of the war. The tensions between the subjects again surfaced. "I confess ... that in your last chapter," Vance wrote, "there are some things a little too Swain-ish, if the Gov. will pardon me." Vance soon repeated his unwillingness to attempt the critique Spencer seemed "totally desirous" that he give her work. In any rewriting, he said, "the more 'Miss Corney' has to do with it and the less anyone else—the better!"[39]

Spencer had shared with him her concern about mentioning General Atkins and the alleged depredations by him and his troops. Atkins had consistently denied these, insisting that "he left the South as poor as he entered it." Vance appreciated her "embarrassment" on the question. She should not mention Atkins at all, he opined, but should "withhold nothing of the truth of the outrages of Shermans Army." It would be an outrage, said Vance, "to suppress the truth of history under such circumstances."[40]

When Spencer's work was published, Vance congratulated her. He had read it "with sincere pleasure" and considered it "a decided success." Now, however, he was willing to correct an error for purposes of "another edition." The book stated that when Swain and Graham found Vance at Hillsboro following their mission to Sherman, they had given him his first information of Lee's surrender. In fact, he had known of it before he sent them as commissioners: "this knowledge was the cause of my sending them at all," he claimed. He had learned of this while General Johnston's Confederate troops were passing through Raleigh. His telegram to President Davis at Greensboro had brought "no positive information of a *surrender*." The response, though, had given "reason to suppose that the disaster was extreme." It was then that he had asked General Johnston's advice about sending a letter to Sherman.[41]

Vance was a special object of Spencer's efforts, prompted by Swain, at vindication. He was not alone in this regard, however. Swain and Graham were equally objects of concern. A portion of a chapter heading in Spencer's published work removes any doubt about this. It reads "Governors Graham and Swain Misunderstood." A brief portion of an introductory paragraph explicates the heading: "The mission of Governors Graham and Swain [to Sherman] was not generally understood, even by their near neighbors. That any reliable attempt to check the ruin and devastation that had hitherto accompanied that army [Union] could be made, or was even consistent with honor and our allegiance to the Confederate Government, very few believed. A distinguished Confederate general, standing on our sidewalk, as his division of infantry marched through on Friday, fourteenth, said, in reference to the commissioners, that they were a couple of traitors, and ought to be hung." Hence Spencer perceived a need to rehabilitate Swain and Graham in the public mind as well.[42]

She had Swain's approval, indeed virtual command, to do so. She now sought Graham's. In writing these "sketches . . . at Gov Swain's instance," she informed Graham, it would be necessary to allude to his "course of action, & the influence exerted by him in certain public affairs." "This, in the present delicate & critical juncture," she told Graham deferentially, "I am unwilling to do without obtaining [your] permission." If desired she would send him the manuscript upon completion; he then could "judge of the prudence & delicacy of your *annalist*." Graham's "name and fame" were "very dear to North Carolinians," and to none more so than to her. Her product was "subject to Gov Swain's criticism," and it was "at his suggestion" that she sought Graham's blessings.[43]

In reply Graham was the archetype of a nineteenth-century gentleman. He thanked Spencer for her "kind interest . . . in a just exposition of my humble course and efforts for the public weal in the late tremendous revolution." He had been somewhat reluctant about publication of facts in his letters to Swain "in the latter scenes of the War, lest it might occasion my being called as a witness in the trial of Mr. Davis [i.e., the anticipated trial of Confederate President Jefferson Davis for treason]." Now that General Lee had testified to the congressional Committee on Reconstruction, however, Graham thought this improbable. He thus was "aware of no serious objections to the reference you propose to make to the facts in question." Graham did not want to add to Davis's embarrassments "or appear to exhibit towards him harshness or indifference." But for these sentiments he might himself have brought "to public notice" some of the facts in his exchanges with Swain. Graham now followed with a "prolix narrative," his own words, of his entire public life, culminating in his role in the Civil War. His purpose was "that my motives may be understood in the scenes to which you refer."[44]

Spencer viewed Graham's approval as implicit, if not explicit. She thanked him for his "mark of confidence" and promised every effort to prove herself "neither insensible nor unworthy." She further assured him that no step would be taken "without *Gov Swain's* Concurrence & advice." Graham could consider the manuscript prior to its publication. "A matter requiring so much circumspection & delicacy in the execution," Spencer concluded, "cannot be too carefully revised."[45]

Vance's letters during this period were unavailable. In the evacuation of the capital, they had been packed with his Governor's Letter Book. The box containing them had been left in Greensboro, presumably when Vance had met a fleeing Jefferson Davis there. It had then been captured and taken to Washington, where it remained. Governor Jonathan Worth had "applied to the Pres[ident] for it through Gov. Swain" but without success. "The letters that you wish as well as others written at that time by the Governor [Vance] reflect great honor on his noble and true heart," Spencer was assured.[46]

Charles Manly had no objection to Spencer's publication of "the facts" in his letter to Swain "as to the ravages and ruin of my property by Sherman's Army." Mention of his private grief would be wrong, however, since others had suffered "still greater outrages."[47] Kemp Battle did not share Manly's reluctance. He suggested material on his role with the Chatham Railroad that Spencer could incorporate in her work. Swain had informed him of the project, and he approved. "The book," he said, "will be very valuable and interesting."[48]

Though busy with other endeavors, Swain was by no means on the sidelines of this one. He, too, solicited information for the publication. He joined Spencer in requesting an account of Union General Stoneman's late-war raid in Western North Carolina. Their correspondent had suffered severely in the raid yet pleaded insufficient information about it. Swain later reported that Spencer had obtained "full and interesting information" on it elsewhere. Swain sought information from two Battle brothers, Kemp and Richard, for an appendix relating to the university. "To what extent can each of you supply reminiscences of your respective classes?" he asked. Kemp responded with information Spencer described as "invaluable." She longed for "a dozen such [letters] from a dozen such gentlemen as you." In another example of the tensions between the principals, Spencer questioned why Battle had also sent the materials to Swain. He "overrules me," she noted, "sometimes very greatly to my advantage, and then again sometimes *not*."[49]

In 1842, Swain had brought the Reverend Charles Force Deems to the university as adjunct professor of logic and rhetoric. After several years Deems left Chapel Hill for other academic posts and the Methodist ministry before moving to New York City following the Civil War. There he founded a religious newspaper, the *Watchman*, to promote sectional reconciliation. Deems now published Spencer's work, first as a series of articles in the *Watchman*, then in a bound volume entitled *The Last Ninety Days of the War in North-Carolina*.⁵⁰ A shaky start launched the publication process. It was "a great mistake," Deems complained to Spencer, to commence the series without at least two numbers in hand. She should forward two numbers as soon as practicable, to be followed by one per week thereafter. "The articles," Deems assured Spencer, "will make an impression." Upon Spencer's request, he would send copies to her acquaintances "in any part of the world." He planned to send one to the president of the United States. She was to make corrections as she wished.⁵¹

Swain maintained a controlling hand. On one occasion Spencer forwarded to a friend the *Watchman* issue containing numbers two and three of "90 Days." She noted a letter in the account that Vance had not wished published. "[B]ut Gov. Swain and Dr. Deems voted the other way," she said, "so there you have it." Swain attempted to dictate even the method by which the volume was published. This greatly perturbed Fayetteville publisher E. J. Hale. Hale expressed "great deference" to Swain but told Spencer emphatically that he was "wrong... in advising the issue of a small edition without stereotyping [making a metal plate for repetitive use]." This would cost only two-thirds as much as an edition "with the plates." If there was a second edition, however, that expense would recur. For a known number of copies, "stereotyping would be a waste; but for an uncertain number, stereotyping is the thing."⁵²

Financing the project produced stresses between Swain and Deems. Deems was sympathetic with Swain's commitment to it. "All your views in regard to Mrs. Spencer's book are correct," he conceded. But lack of means cramped his style. The sum of $5,000 to 10,000 would allow him to "push many things that would be interesting to the South," Deems told Swain as he requested a loan of $500.00 or $1,000. Deems had real estate in North Carolina, "but that," he said, "avails me nothing among these people [i.e., in the post-Civil War North]." Swain's response was cool. "[I]t is entirely out of my power to make the advance you desire," Swain wrote, "As soon as I can realize the amount I will send you $50 in advance for your publication and this is all I can."⁵³ When installment two arrived, Deems lamented to Swain, "I have no capital to go forward with." The *Watchman* was absorbing all his resources. With $500.00, he could make a go of it; without it, he must hold up. "Can you not accomplish that?" he asked Swain as he tendered security for the loan and promised the first proceeds from sales to repay him.⁵⁴

Deems's next communication to Spencer contained a note of bitterness. He was proceeding, he said, "without $100 a head, without anything indeed." "[T]he book," he told its author, "will do more to hand Gov. Swain, Vance and Graham over handsomely to posterity than anything else that I know." Thus, he said, "they ought not to see you and me out of pocket." Deems would not enter upon the endeavor without hope for success, "[b]ut all hands now must push the sale." Arranging the book for the press had kept Deems up late the previous night. He was tired and anxious. They were immortalizing Governors Graham and Vance and Judge Ruffin, Deems concluded, and they had "not even subscribed to *The Watchman!*"[55]

Ultimately Swain loaned funds to assist with publication and secured assistance from Kemp Battle. Deems thanked him. The book was almost completed, he told Swain, and much larger than he had expected. A portion of the appendix would have to be omitted, he feared. He had no fear, however, about the book's effect on Swain's reputation. "It will do more good for your good and just reputation than anything else ever written by any of your friends," Deems assured Swain, and he was "happy to have [a] hand in doing what will make the present generation and those to come revere you." If Swain could live another ten years, his "old age" would "be covered with honor." Those who did him "injustice" now would in five years "be striving to prove that they thought just as Gov. Swain did!"[56]

To Spencer, Deems expressed anxiety about paying Swain and Battle. His goal was to secure them from any loss. To accomplish this, they needed to create a Southern market. If they could sell two thousand copies, the volume would not only pay for itself but yield a profit.[57]

To Spencer's disappointment, Swain was away when she received the book. "The surprise of the dedication is what I wanted," she said. It pleased her, though, to give "my dear old Father his copy." When Swain returned, he had much to tell her "about *Ninety Days*, many compliments," she said, "to repeat to me." Like Deems, however, she was more concerned about the financial dimensions. "I want to know that the book *sells*," she wrote in her diary.[58]

Meanwhile Swain became a distribution agent for the volume. One New York recipient, although not having had time to read it, had noticed a couple of passages "which might not have been expected considering all that has become known." A South Carolina reader viewed the work "with special interest." He had been in Columbia "when Sherman's desolating host took possession of the city and destroyed it." A Swain failure to send the volume to a friend brought a request for it. "I am anxious to possess 'the Last 90 days of the War,'" John H. Wheeler told him, "Send me a copy and the cost."[59]

President Andrew Johnson received a copy of *Ninety Days* from Swain. If placed in the hands of some of Johnson's friends in Congress, Swain ventured, "it might suggest a new line of defence for your policy of reconstruction." Johnson's veto of the Civil Rights Bill had his hearty concurrence, Swain assured the president, and no administration's policies, not even those of Andrew Jackson, had "been more universally acceptable to the great body of the people of North Carolina."[60]

In Pennsylvania, former President James Buchanan found a copy in his mail, a "favor" from Swain. Buchanan anticipated "both pleasure and profit from the perusal," especially since it had been published "under [Swain's] sanction." He had fond memories of his 1859 visit to Chapel Hill. He wished for Swain and the state, "after your severe reverses," a return to their former "peace tranquility and prosperity" in the Union.[61]

Swain was fearless in his choice of donees. Horace Greeley, Northern editor and leading abolitionist, received the book and other documents related to North Carolina history. When Spencer traveled to the North, Swain suggested, it would be a good idea for her to see Greeley. Swain also sent the book "to . . . leading Northern radicals beginning with [Thaddeus] Stevens, [Charles] Sumner, and Wendell Phillips." He told Spencer he would be glad "to have 15 or 20 copies of the Ninety Days for distribution among my friends here and elsewhere."[62]

The *Watchman* had failed financially, a blow from which Deems was finding it difficult to recover. All looked dark to him. His letters from the South were "full of painful statements of the condition of affairs." He feared matters would only "grow worse." He nevertheless persevered with his work on *Ninety Days*, once noting that he had sent Swain a dozen copies "by Express to Durham's."[63]

Perseverance never suggested roseate financial circumstances, however. Deems once acknowledged receipt of $450.00 from Swain but later "look[ed] anxiously" for the $500.00 Swain had informed him he would send, jointly, apparently, with Kemp Battle. "The book," Deems whined, "brought me no money and no fame." In accordance with Spencer's "special desire," his name did not even appear on the title page. A personal release from financial responsibility from Swain would be a great comfort to him; if Swain held him to the debt, however, he would endeavor to work it out. "Believing you and Gov. Swain to be honorable men and my personal friends," he told Battle, "I shall leave you to say what I must do." Battle was to show Deems's missive to Swain.[64]

Details are unclear, but the venture continued, with Battle now an active participant. Swain informed Battle that he had written Deems with notice that he, Battle, and Spencer had accepted "his proposition." He had "designed an early conference with [Spencer] on the best mode of carrying the contemplated scheme into execution." A "few corrections and additions," Swain thought, would "render a second edition more attractive than the first."[65]

Swain wanted a second edition to list the names and military rank of all students and alumni of the university "who fell in the late war, or who having fought through it, survived." A once-missing "Roll of Honor" had been recovered, was in Raleigh, and would aid in this. Swain sought further aid from Spencer and Battle in composing the list. He would bear the expense of the additional material. Too, he would peruse the university catalogues for information. These, with the "Rolls of Honor," would not suffice, however. They must "resort to numerous other sources of information." Swain's rationale was poignant. "Many children of the college attained distinction or fell in battle in other states where names are not to be found on the rolls of honor, or any other known record," he told Battle, "To obtain them it will be necessary that Mrs. S or we shall prepare a circular calling forth information from friends in other states."[66]

Spencer drafted the circular, and Swain sent it to Battle for his "revision correction and amendation." The final, printed version noted the planned second edition of *Ninety Days* and the desire to list UNC alumni who were in the Confederate Army, with their rank and fate if ascertainable. The tone conveyed a sense of urgency. If done at all, the work must be done immediately. It would give the book a permanent interest and value that would increase through the years. "[G]ive us such information as you possess, or can gather," the authors begged, "of such Confederate soldiers as were known to have been students at Chapel Hill." Communications could be addressed to Spencer or Swain at Chapel Hill, to Battle at Raleigh.[67]

The solicitation was productive. A second edition contained the appendix with information regarding the Civil War role of the students and graduates. Swain was pleased and thought it would have the desired effect. "Mrs. Spencers defense of your administration," he told Vance, "will have a wide circulation and produce a salutary effect wherever it goes." Swain's assessment was that Graham had performed as a Confederate senator should have, Vance had fulfilled an appropriate role for the governor, and Swain had conducted himself properly as a public-minded citizen. He sincerely believed Spencer's book established this beyond cavil. Despite her occasional grousing in the process, Spencer, too, ultimately found pleasure in her product. "You and Gov. Graham and Gov. S[wain] will be handed down to immortality . . . in a few weeks," she told Vance.[68]

A modern assessment is less charitable: Each of the male subjects attempted to influence Spencer's interpretation of their Civil War actions and, to some degree, their entire careers. The result was a careful synthesis of truth, opinion, and propaganda. While harsh, the appraisal is well-founded. The appropriate historical concern is not so much distortion as omission. Clearly no material entered the narrative without Swain's blessing, and little, if any, without Graham's and Vance's.[69]

Swain was not repaid for his loans. Deems never overcame the debtor status he incurred from the endeavor. Was it worth this? Almost certainly Swain had no regrets. To use a phrase later coined by Justice Oliver Wendell Holmes Jr., "the felt necessities of the time" justified it. That, at least, would have been the perception of the man who formulated the idea and pushed it vigorously to its conclusion.[70]

To a lesser extent than *Ninety Days*, other matters of history received Swain's attention. "In the discharge of my functions as Historical Agent of the State," he told Graham, "I must make an effort to secure the return of the Tryon Letter Book, the Council Journal and the M.S.S. purchased of the representatives of F. X. Martin [manuscripts Martin had acquired while preparing his North Carolina history, which had been displaced when Raleigh fell to Sherman]." He wished to make General Rosecrans's acquaintance so he could "appeal to him for aid in the recovery of lost materials for history."[71]

Swain assisted Graham with a memorial to prominent political figure George E. Badger. He sent Graham notes "containing some memorials of Mr. Badger." To Graham it was new material, for which he was grateful. With an assist from Eleanor, Swain confirmed the age of Badger's father at his death. Another note from Swain on Badger's career was helpful to Graham. Swain then aided in distribution of the discourse. He was glad when Graham sent him twenty copies, for he had already disposed of most of the twenty-five copies he had procured earlier.[72]

Such collaboration between the two former governors was common. When philanthropist George Peabody established a fund to support public education in the South, Peabody and the trustees invited Graham to serve as a trustee and to recommend objects for their bounty. This, Graham told Swain, "induced a shower of letters" from institutions in North Carolina, South Carolina, and Tennessee. It was natural, then, that he would seek Swain's assistance in identifying "proper subjects of patronage." "[C]ome and spend a night with me next week to discuss them," Graham urged.[73]

Numerous other matters concerned Swain during these difficult days of Reconstruction.[74] A tax, by Swain's claim ten times the average levied by the state since adoption of its 1776 constitution, vexed him. He thus sought repeal of the law "under which such authority [was] claimed."[75] Equally vexing was "a great want of tact upon the part of leading gentlemen in Raleigh in their interviews with Federal officers." Intemperate remarks and newspaper diatribes in the South had, Swain believed, done more to promote radicalism in the North "than all the speeches of Brownlow, Stephens [*sic*] and Sumner." He trusted, however, that "[t]he demoniacal notions of the extreme radicals" would "be over-ruled by 'the sober second thought.'" He could then revert to his 1860 position of "'fighting for the Union in the Union.'" A year after the war's end, he thought no state more dedicated to the Union than North Carolina.⁷⁶

Swain's customary assistance to friends in employment matters continued. He was gratified when President Johnson gave John H. Wheeler "the precise species of employment for which I wrote to assure him he was best qualified." When Wheeler performed services for the state, Swain was an intermediary with the governor and state treasurer regarding Wheeler's invoices. Other correspondents sought letters of recommendation from him.⁷⁷

Further, he was, as always, a focal point for informative commentary on the times and circumstances. Correspondents shared their wartime grief experiences with him. "Two of my brothers were killed in the Southern Army," wrote one poignantly, "[o]ne at Fort Donaldson [sic] and one at Knoxville T." Postwar economic afflictions were brought to him. "The Great Revolutionary Storm which has just passed over us," wrote one acquaintance, had rendered him lacking in employment to support his family. He waited "calmly and submissively for better days," while trusting "a Gracious Providence."⁷⁸

An 1859 UNC graduate, now in Tennessee, foresaw trouble from the freedmen. Two white men had been murdered "by them" without provocation, a mere foretaste of what would come "unless Congress will do away with the Freedmen's Bureau." The "Yankees" were urging them on, he told Swain, and the white population was comparatively "destitute of arms." Absent pursuit of a different course, one of the races would have to be exterminated, "and probably the sooner the better." The writer fervently desired "the pleasure of killing the scoundrels that are inciting the negro."⁷⁹

Closer to home, Swain's neighbor Charles Phillips saw little comfort in living "with negroes around us ... inflamed against us white folks." Would their neighbors' "affections and ... confidence" be withheld from them, yet "bestowed on any Northerner that may stroll into our state"? How could they "get our white folks esp[ecially] those of the poorer class ... to go to the polls to save themselves from the negro?" Phillips asked. "These pets of the nation," he said, "are in danger of becoming spoiled children." Phillips feared that the land scrip funds might come "with the condition that you take on board ... men of all colors in our state." Doctor Hubbard was considering an invitation from the bishop of Connecticut, Phillips said, "and so getting out of sight (& smell) of negro-dom."

Phillips was not alone in his racially based angst. "This splendid place of learning, so beautifully improved and adorned," Charles Manly told his brother Basil in Alabama, "I regard as lost forever; an old field school for n----- [with] some old field school masters of high salaries may be located there; but the glory of our beloved *Alma Mater* is gone forever." Graham conveyed similar concerns, perceiving "so great a dread of Radical revenge among our people, and so little concert of action even among conservative men."[80]

A depressed Swain relative, while allegedly not "tak[ing] our defeat near as hard as some of my acquaintances," nevertheless did not feel like writing or visiting in the wake of the South's defeat. While regretting the rupture, he had thought "we should have our slaves." Instead, they had "failed and lost our negroes[,] lost our money[,] and almost every thing we had[,] but the worst of all, lost so many of our dear friends." If "on honorable terms," he had become reconciled to reunion, and felt "no unkindness" toward the former enslaved persons for leaving. Indeed, he opined to Swain, they should be encouraged to support and improve themselves and to educate their children. Their former "owners," he later added, must "wait on a just god" from whom "our enemy may receive a portion of what we have seen and felt."[81] This "enemy" was not altogether lacking in sympathy. One former Union soldier told Swain he wished he could help restore North Carolina to its former status.[82]

Politically and personally, the problems posed by the freedmen were Swain's problems. He and Graham concurred that "with reference to Emancipation, we are at the beginning of the war." The former enslaved persons, Swain told Graham, were "utterly demoralized and almost entirely idle." Four of his had left; three had returned, "but only one is on my premises." The women and children, he thought, wanted to stay. "I cannot afford to keep them," he told Graham, "but am loath to drive them away."[83]

Graham had also experienced departures. The freedmen, he told Swain, were "not capable of determining for themselves, in a matter of such moment, and leave home in search of freedom, like knights errant in search of adventures." They should first seek a means of livelihood; only then could they reach a state of prosperity that would enable them to educate and elevate their children. Had Oliver Otis Howard, the Freedmen's Bureau commissioner, allowed him to speak without threat of arrest, Graham confided to Swain, he would have told him "that the whole policy in regard to negroes commenced in error."[84]

Swain, meanwhile, faced student unrest over the suddenly liberated bondsmen. On two occasions after the war, white UNC students made uninvited incursions into peaceful black meetings: one a gathering of delegates to a state-level black convention, the other a meeting of a black "secret society" with a speaker from Raleigh.[85]

If the qualification of freehold ownership for voting for state senators was restored, Swain favored restricted black voting for the State House of Commons. The proposed Howard Amendment (it would become the Fourteenth), however, profoundly disturbed him. It would disqualify from voting numerous white citizens, including the state's leading men, who had participated in or supported the rebellion. Swain anxiously awaited the fall 1866 election returns from Indiana, Ohio, and Pennsylvania. They would be, he feared, "a warning to prepare to swallow or submit to the Howard Amendment with what grace we may." The disfranchisement of large numbers of voters and former officeholders distressed him. If the suffrage was extended to the freedmen, they could outnumber the whites at the polls and theirs could become the dominant race. The same influences that had spawned the Civil War, he said, were now "operating most powerfully in favor of the Howard amendment, and will probably secure its adoption."[86]

The North did not realize the inevitable effect of adoption of the amendment, Swain posited. If it did, it would not propose it. Something, he hoped, would yet intervene "that may open northern eyes." The effect in North Carolina would be that "the more originally opposed to secession, and anxious for quiet submission to free government, will be ineligible, and the most violent and unreasoning will frequently be the successful candidates."

These complex times required "caution prudence forbearance and high statesmanship." Fewer than ten thousand white voters would be disfranchised, Swain thought, "and the proportion of colored voters little more than a third of the aggregate." There were practical implications for North Carolina politics: if Holden succeeded in his efforts "to command an undivided colored vote," the effect would be "to produce equal unanimity among the whites in opposition."[87]

Comparisons between the 1835 and 1868 North Carolina constitutional conventions illustrated the problem. Swain, a delegate to the 1835 convention, thought any well-informed man would regard its members as equal in ability, character, and statesmanship to any legislative body ever convened in the state. Only forty of the 120 members of that convention survived. Their considerable ability notwithstanding, none were members of the 1868 convention. Probably, indeed, none were even allowed to vote for members of that body. Between the two conventions, the number of "colored persons" admitted to the suffrage was equal to the number of whites "disfranchised by the reconstruction acts." The result was, Swain said, "[w]e have in place of all those whose age, experience, intelligence, and position in the community had secured reputation for statesmanship, an equal number of illiterate African boys." The delegates to the 1835 convention, and the state's congressional delegation at that time, bore no comparison to "the peculiarly *un*-North Carolina like character of the principal actors in as well as the proceedings of" the 1868 convention.

Perhaps, Swain said, the 1868 convention would yet "more than equal our most favorable hopes, and frame a constitution under which we may live without degradation." Instead, however, matters could "go... from bad to worse." The entire basis of representation could be changed, and the balance of power transferred "from the white majorities of the West, to the colored members in the East."[88]

From childhood days in Asheville, Swain had a friendship with Benjamin F. Perry, whom President Johnson named provisional governor of South Carolina in June 1865. A prewar Unionist, Perry now opposed federal power, particularly ratification of the Howard Amendment. Swain elaborated on his concerns about the amendment in published letters to Perry.

In 1862, Congress adopted a "test oath" for officeholding. It required an oath that the aspirant to office had never voluntarily borne arms against the United States, or given "aid, countenance, counsel, or encouragement to persons engaged in armed hostility thereto." The oath included a statement that the individual had held no office under any authority hostile to the United States. The oath-taker also pledged to support the U.S. Constitution against all enemies, foreign and domestic.

The effect of the test oath and section three of the Howard Amendment, Swain told Perry, would be "a double disfranchisement of nine tenths of the people of North Carolina." "[N]ot one tenth," he said, would be "eligible to office under the State or Federal Government." Those who "gave aid or comfort to the insurgents" could vote, but "not for the men of their choice." Their votes, instead, would be cast "for persons selected from that tenth of the community who, as a general rule, without any reference to political opinions, have no paramount claims to consideration, mental or moral." Swain claimed, legitimately, that no one exceeded him in knowledge of the prominent men of the state; and he knew of no one, in any of the state's congressional districts, who might reasonably have aspired "to a seat in the national councils" in 1860 who could honestly take the test oath. "Is it any evidence of a want of loyalty," he asked, "to decline to accept such a system of suffrage?"

It would not be difficult, Swain continued, "to divine the character of our representatives if this role shall be forced upon us." In North and South Carolina, the most able, experienced public men would be excluded. "You," he said to Perry, "have no honest and competent men who can submit to a test of loyalty, which is, in my estimation, as clearly unconstitutional as inexpedient." Perry in South Carolina and Graham in North Carolina had been denied seats in the U.S. Senate. Had they been admitted to the seats, Swain believed, "a wiser scheme of adjustment would have been adopted, and one much more favorable to the true union men of the South, than the Howard Amendment."

A later letter detailed Swain's pre-UNC political career. From his arrival at the university, he claimed, he had "carefully abstained from all connection with party politics." The purpose was to promote the university's "success and usefulness ... by preserving its entire independence of all parties, political and religious." Rarely had he been present at a political meeting, and never when he "could properly avoid it." He further claimed, more dubiously, "[i]n no instance was I ever seduced into the discussion of any mere question of party politics."

This changed, however, when secession was the topic on virtually every tongue "and the disruption of the government was imminent." He then deemed it his duty "to stand forth in defence of the Union." Now he perceived it as "no less imperative" to contribute "influence and argument" to the issue of the proposed constitutional amendment. It "threatened a radical change in the structure of government and the frame work of society." A new objection now surfaced: the oath offered the politically ambitious a severe temptation to perjure themselves. It set "a dangerous trap for mens' consciences," and offered "the most tempting bribes for the commission of perjury." Indeed, there would be "more perjuries ... in an hour than have been punished by our Courts since the Mecklenburg Convention." The amendment further would tend to "array neighborhood against neighborhood, and man against man, for years to come." Congress's power to remove the disability could not be trusted as a solution. How could two-thirds of Congress "ascertain the true character of each of the 100,000 voters of North Carolina," Swain asked, "or the million in the southern states?" It was all, he concluded, "impracticable and absurd."[89]

The favorable notice Swain's letters to Perry received in "the press abroad" pleased Graham. "[T]hey cannot fail, I think," Graham said, "to have a good effect at the North, as well as in disarming invidious and uncharitable opposition to you at home." Like Swain, Graham hoped the Southern states would reject the amendment. They were, Graham said, "in the days of darkness." "Every day," Graham now told Swain, "impresses me more and more with the helplessness and ruin that await us at the end of the process through which we are now being driven at the point of the bayonet."[90]

Swain and Graham rarely had divergent opinions on matters of public interest. These thus were "days of darkness" for Swain as well. Just how dark he could not yet know. He would soon learn when his attention turned more pointedly from broader matters of state to pressing concerns of his university.

Endings

CHAPTER 26

Decline and Fall
"No hope for the college with Gov. Swain at its head"

SWAIN'S NEAR BOUNDLESS BUSYNESS with large-scale public affairs offered no respite from the university's problems. Like a feisty bulldog, they clung to him tenaciously, constantly nipping at his well-traveled heels.

The University of North Carolina was one of the few southern institutions of higher education to remain open throughout the Civil War. Only the determination and perseverance of Swain and his faculty kept the place operative through the "unpleasantness." These did not preclude the university, like other institutions in the South, from suffering seriously in the process, however. A Swain correspondent at the University of South Carolina aptly attributed the problems to "the deplorable state of the country at present, and the late breaking up of colleges and schools everywhere in the South."[1]

Swain once described the university's late-Civil War status as its "present forlorn condition." The description remained appropriate following the war's end. The university opened the fall semester of 1865 with twenty-two students. The 1866 commencement, featuring Zebulon Vance's "Duties of Defeat" address, had only three graduating seniors in attendance.

The university was actively advertising for students.[2] Securing operating expenses became a constant struggle. Once in the post-war period, on Swain's motion, the trustees resolved to appoint a committee on "the condition of the university[,] . . . its liabilities and assets . . ." and a "plan . . . to perpetuate its existence and secure its prosperity." The trustees authorized their executive committee to inquire into the salaries of the university's officers "in connexion with the present resources." It was to issue bonds, and with the proceeds from sale of the bonds, to pay arrearages due to the faculty. The university was also seeking to compromise its debt to the Bank of North Carolina. The executive committee established a subcommittee for that purpose. Among debts left unresolved was one to Swain for $3,000.[3]

Largely successful previously, Swain's efforts to keep the university aloof from political conflict had begun to fail as the Civil War approached. Virulent and conflicting political winds caught both him and his university in the war's aftermath. Kemp Battle aptly describes it. "[T]hose who knew the President and Professors at the old University," Battle writes, "could testify that they accepted the results of the defeat of the South with as much resignation and determination thenceforward to be loyal to the Union, as those of any institution in the land. This was shown by the words and actions of President Swain, by the conciliatory address of Governor Vance in 1866, by the hearty reception accorded to President Johnson, Secretary Seward, and other northern men in 1867, and by the general attitude of authorities and students." This posture was not universally popular with the institution's constituents, however. To some, the foregoing notwithstanding, it remained "a center of aristocracy and rebellion." To others, the foregoing represented "undue sympathy with Yankees and atheists."

Too, the town of Chapel Hill was economically dependent on the university. Its people were poor, and the university's decline was the town's as well. The circumstances, financial and political, invoked prejudice against the university and its leader from all sides, and that prejudice was steadily growing. Even the diplomatic skills of a David Swain could not thwart it.[4]

Late in the Civil War, Swain defended his stewardship of the university's finances. At the end of 1837, he said, the institution's net worth had been $120,728.22; at the end of 1863, $146,135. "[L]ive or die, sink or swim," he said, "I am satisfied with the record." Just before the war, however, he had cast the crucial swing vote when the trustees subscribed to $100,000 worth of the reserved stock in the Bank of North Carolina. He so voted "with great reluctance" for one reason: Governor Manly, for whom Swain had both "great respect" and "great affection," was voting in opposition. Swain had sought Governor Graham's opinion and appears, at least, to have heard no dissent from him.[5]

Early in the post–Civil War period, their votes came back to haunt Swain and the other trustees in the majority. Swain brought news from Raleigh to Chapel Hill that the university had lost its endowment and was now wholly dependent on tuition revenues; this, too, at a time when the war had decimated the ranks of potential students and enrollment was at a historically and perilously low ebb. The state had repudiated its war debt; and the trustees' investment in the bank stock, made without prophetic vision to foresee the coming war, was now worthless. The university thus was burdened with extensive obligations and little revenue with which to meet them. It opened its fall term 1865, William H. Battle told his son Kemp, lacking "a very brilliant prospect this session." "Want of money in this State is, I think, the main cause," Battle said all too accurately. Battle himself had only two law students, with little prospect for more any time soon.[6]

Swain understood the university's condition. "[U]ntoward circumstances," he said, had "wrought evil" to an institution that had educated many of the ablest men of North Carolina and the South. The war had forced upon the legislature "a course ... which swept away the whole monied endowment of the college and left it with no resources except those furnished by the fees for tuition." These alone did not adequately support the faculty, and some members thus had "felt compelled" to resign. The number of students had to grow, contributions from the university's friends had to increase, or, Swain reluctantly conceded, the university's "doors must be closed." The latter alternative was, to him, unthinkable. It would be a heavy blow to the cause of education and "a sorry economy as well." "There must always be," he said, "[a] university in North Carolina." Indeed, there was no better purpose for the people's resources.[7]

Swain penned these thoughts in the wake of two frustrating years of attempting, without success, to secure the university's financial position. In September 1865, the executive committee authorized him "to borrow at the North" the sum of $30,000, to be used "in purchasing the bills" of several North Carolina banks. The purpose was to liquidate the university's debt to the Bank of North Carolina, and Swain was further authorized "to pledge the whole property" of the university to secure payment of the loan. His travels for this purpose proved unproductive. "I tried very hard upon many, beginning with President Johnson and Secretary Seward," Swain told Thomas Ruffin, "[b]ut I got no money, or promise of any, from any quarter." In October Swain reported to Graham that he had spent two days in Baltimore and five in New York "without being able to effect the desired loan for the university." Among others, he had called on John Jacob Astor, who had informed him of his custom to accept as security only real estate located in the state of New York, and mostly in New York City. Out-of-state loans, Astor reasoned, would require employment of attorneys versed in the laws of the borrowers' states, thus rendering them unprofitable.[8]

Usual sources of assistance had proven unhelpful. Two friends of the Astor Library, Swain had thought, were "sufficiently well acquainted with the university [and] the character of the Trustees" to place the matter before potential creditors. It did not happen. He had sought the aid of his and the university's New York friend Francis L. Hawks. This, too, was unproductive. Hawks could only inquire through a friend, he told Swain, for as a native Southerner he was "among the proscribed." Northern contempt for the South was, Hawks said, "more intense now than . . . when the parties were fighting."⁹

Only once before had the General Assembly appropriated funds for the university. In December 1791, it made a loan to it, subsequently converted to a gift. Faced with a desperate plight, the trustees now implored further legislative assistance to the university. They appointed a committee, with Swain as a member, "to prepare and present to the General Assembly . . . a Memorial . . . setting forth the state and condition of the university." Thomas Bragg, a former governor, introduced the resolution, which passed unanimously. With a sense of the importance to the state of the education of its youth, the trustees pledged to sustain the university "to the last moment that its means will enable them."

Swain prepared the "Memorial." He requested Chief Justice Ruffin's views on it, and Ruffin thought every legislator—indeed, "every man who is informed of the condition of the university, and understands, at all the value of education"—would "intuitively perceive" the needs and vote accordingly. The "Memorial," not surprisingly, with Swain as the draftsman, contained an extensive recitation of the university's history and historic value to the state. A respectable fund, it said, had been established for the university's support by the estates of private persons. This, however, the war had "swept utterly away," with the result that "the university has *not* now the means to sustain itself." Without legislative aid, the trustees pleaded, "it must speedily cease to exist." Without exaggeration, they were submitting what they believed to be "the question of its life or death."¹⁰

The General Assembly responded with an appropriation of $7,000. Although small, it was welcome, Cornelia Spencer said. In Swain's view it was a great wonder, Spencer said, that he got an inefficient legislature to do anything. The first $3,000 of the appropriation went to faculty salaries, to be prorated "in proportion to their salaries anterior to the late War." The sum of $500.00 went to a faculty committee of Swain, Manuel Fetter, and Charles Phillips, to be used in their discretion to purchase necessary articles, make necessary building repairs, and perform grounds upkeep. Use of the remainder was left unsettled for the moment.¹¹

The federal Morrill Land-Grant Colleges Act of 1862 provided funding for the establishment of many of the public colleges and universities in the United States. Swain attempted to salvage the university's finances, in part, by securing for it land scrip funds provided by that legislation. He again solicited and received assistance from deposed UNC professor Benjamin Hedrick, now ensconced in the federal bureaucracy in Washington. The repudiation of the state's war debt, Swain explained to Hedrick, had annihilated the university's endowment and a large portion of the common-school fund. It was "a matter of so much moment,"

Swain later told Hedrick, "that I know you will snatch a moment to attend to it." The president and his cabinet had determined that "nothing in the existing statutes" excluded North Carolina from the benefits under the act. The scrip thus should soon be forthcoming, and Hedrick would please advise him "on the state of things at present."[12]

Swain's "unwearied exertion [and] personal influence" in the nation's capital paid dividends. Kemp Battle, the state treasurer, reported that the General Assembly had authorized him "to receive and invest the land script [*sic*] donated to this State." He then commissioned a Swain trip to Washington to "procure the issue." "[T]he scrip was forwarded to Raleigh," Battle stated, "and is now in the Treasury." It was for the General Assembly to determine how these funds would be used, however, and this was not without controversy. Some, a Raleigh correspondent informed Swain, desired a separate college. Ultimately, however, the House, by 54 to 52, passed the bill donating the funds to the university. The dissension was in no way personal to Swain: "no one expressed any other than the highest personal regard and respect for yourself and the faculty," he was assured.[13]

With the funds now secured for the university, their disposition became the issue. Swain noted that Congress required establishment of a professorship in agriculture and one in the mechanical arts. The North Carolina legislation, which he had drafted with B. F. Moore's assistance and Judge Ruffin's approval, authorized the state treasurer to sell the scrip and invest the proceeds. Ruffin advised immediate sale at the highest price possible and investment of the proceeds "in old N.C. 6 per cents, which may now be had at 50 c. on the dollar."[14]

University trustees now authorized Kemp Battle, the state treasurer, to open negotiations for sale of the scrip. Swain and Battle commenced a weeks-long exchange with G. F. Lewis in Cleveland, Ohio, who touted his firm as the country's largest dealer in land scrip. Lewis sought from Swain the price at which he would sell all the scrip for cash. Quite assertive, Lewis insisted that it was in the university's best interest to sell for cash as soon as possible. Eventually Battle held a long interview with Lewis but found him unwilling "to buy the script [*sic*] outright except at . . . say half price." Graham advised Swain against accepting this. Swain, too, had hoped for more, with immediate benefits to the university. The outcome of the negotiations disappointed him.[15]

Ultimately the trustees agreed with Lewis to sell the land at $.50 per acre, with $10,000 to be paid at once and the remainder when Congress recognized the state (allowed it to again participate in national affairs). A small part was applied to "running expenses," with the balance invested in special tax and other state bonds. In the university's dire financial straits, even this small amount helped.

It was hardly the panacea for which Swain had hoped and which the university desperately needed, however.[16]

The Civil War had rendered the state and region infertile ground for fundraising from private sources. "The region was all but bankrupt," writes a leading historian of Reconstruction, "for the collapse of Confederate bonds and currency wiped out the savings of countless individuals and the resources and endowments of colleges, churches, and other institutions." "Times have never been so hard in Richmond since the war," a student in the UNC Class of 1868 told Swain. Professional men, the student said, did not make half what they had before the war. "There is hardly a merchant in Richmond except some Jews," he added, "who would be solvent were they obliged to meet their liabilities without due notice."[17]

After leaving UNC for financial reasons, Professor A. D. Hepburn offered to seek contributions from his friends and acquaintances. The situation, he said, should "induce every friend of the university or State in the North to aid in the work." But he had seen the fundraising efforts of too many colleges fail "in spite of agencies, and schemes of every description to raise contributions."[18]

Reduced expectations did not diminish what was expected from Swain. "I don't believe you have the least intention of seeing our College . . . closed," one North Carolina citizen wrote him, "after keeping [it] open during the entire war." Historian Benjamin Lossing hoped UNC was "in a fair way for a speedy return to its most prosperous condition." Thomas Ruffin saw no reason why the people of North Carolina, especially the legislature, should have any jealousy or prejudice against the university, its faculty, or the trustees. Other states had pride in their institutions, Ruffin said, why should that not be true in the Old North State?[19]

William H. Battle joined Swain in favoring the employment of Zebulon Vance "to canvas the State," "to embark upon a crusade in behalf of the university." Swain was inclined to offer Vance "very liberal terms." If Vance accepted, Swain hoped Graham would "post him up fully" regarding the university's history and present condition. Swain would "tell him many things, which he can tell with such great effect to the people, that cannot so well be communicated in writing." If a way could be found for him to make money for himself, as well as for the university, Vance said, "I should not mind putting in there monthly this winter."[20]

The trustees requested that Swain prepare a brief address to the state's colleges, showing the university's condition and the necessity of donations to it. In response Swain depicted all involved with the university as "incumbered with pressing and perplexing engagements." All, nevertheless, were "disposed to do the best we can under the circumstances." Even the students found these circumstances sobering. Swain had never known them to be more punctual, well behaved, and devoted to their studies. "No student," he said, "has been summoned before the Faculty, to answer for any impropriety whatsoever."[21]

The trustees also composed a circular letter to the people of the state, with this dire warning: "The University must receive assistance, or it must cease to be." To arouse pride in the institution, they noted the prewar expansion of its endowment and its enrollment. Among the alumni were "many of the most honorable names in the whole country," men who had occupied offices of church and state with distinction. Repudiation of the state's war debt had extinguished the endowment, they explained; and since the outbreak of the war, the number of students had been insufficient to pay the faculty's salaries. Faculty members thus had resigned. While reforms were contemplated, "no step," they avowed, "can be taken without aid." Unless the people came forward promptly with substantial benefactions, the university, they concluded, "must soon go down."[22]

Faculty members were indeed departing. At one point the university was a session behind in paying faculty salaries. Arrearages persisted a session later. Swain was making personal loans to faculty members. A bond sale, of not more than $7,300, was under consideration. Barely adequate when paid, at times faculty salaries were not paid at all, or at least not until well beyond their due dates. Generally lacking personal wealth, professors could not sustain themselves and their families in these severely straitened circumstances. Their flight thus was virtually inevitable.[23]

Following a year's furlough for study in Europe, Professor A. D. Hepburn returned to the university and resigned. Without a thorough reorganization, Hepburn was convinced, the university could not regain its lost standing with the public. A desire to assist with the reform effort both induced his return to the state and made him hesitant to resign. His decision to withdraw, he said, was "an indication of a state of things that demanded a prompt and energetic action on the part of the Trustees."

Some students were concerned that Hepburn's political sentiments had prompted his resignation. Any personal unpopularity was not a factor, Hepburn said. Rather, the university had for years pursued a "wrong" policy, from which it was now "reaping the fruits." The community was unanimous, Hepburn avowed, in a "determination to do nothing to sustain the university under its present system and administration." The depth of the bitterness surprised him, but it reflected a state of public opinion that rendered "all efforts to revive and elevate our university fruitless." "An alienated public feeling," Hepburn stated, "is the call for reform." Every chair "and every office" should be declared vacant. Professors should then be elected on their merits. The extensive feeling adverse to the university,

Hepburn concluded, "was indication that a new state of things was demanded." Accordingly, he had "intimated to Gov. Swain my purpose to resign." Clearly Swain himself was a major element in Hepburn's dissatisfaction.[24]

Professor W. J. Martin soon followed, resigning "reluctantly and painfully." Previously he had refused all overtures. Now, however, he said, "the ... condition of the college is so gloomy, and its prosperity in the immediate future so precarious that I do not feel justified in any further effort to weather the storm." In Judge Battle's view, there was a serious omission from Martin's statement. He should have added that for two years he had been unable to stay out of debt despite "living as plainly and self-denyingly" as he should. Martin did say it was "the saddest move" of his life, but one, he said, "to which I have conceived myself driven of necessity."[25]

Solomon Pool requested a furlough while he served as assessor of internal revenue. His time on leave would somewhat enhance the compensation of his faculty colleagues, he told the trustees, thereby reducing the university's "present pecuniary embarrassment." The trustees allowed Pool's application but considered themselves free to deny subsequent reinstatement. Charles Manly regarded the "furlough" as a "final resignation or dismissal," and the faculty appointed Professor Charles Phillips to replace Pool as its secretary.[26]

Other faculty losses ensued, with all members ultimately resigning, some of their own volition, others under pressure. F. M. Hubbard left his post as professor of Latin language and literature. His resignation was not, he said, "because I wish to abandon the university in the low estate of its fortunes ... but simply because I do not wish to be thought to be in any way or degree a hindrance to its prosperity." He was applying to be professor of Latin at Columbia College in New York City. The "gloomy prospects here," he told Graham, "enforced my offering myself among the candidates."[27]

With the benefit of a judicial salary, William H. Battle faced less financial adversity than other faculty members. He was, however, struggling to rebuild his law program. "I have few law students now on the Hill," he said in March 1867, "and I hope I shall have more after a while." A year later he commenced his school with seven students. He again hoped others would come, though he expected none with certainty. "[O]ught I to advertise?" he asked his son Kemp. Three students enrolled in the fall session 1868. Battle repeated his lament, though with slightly elevated sanguinity. "I think it probable that the number will be increased during the session," he said, "but I certainly do not calculate on a large number."[28]

Faculty woes were Swain's woes. The loss of Professor Hepburn, with that of state geologist W. C. Kerr, who also taught at the university, left him "very busy."

More important, the loss of key faculty members produced student discontent at a time when under-enrollment of students was the foremost cause of the university's financial problems. One student decried the vacancy in the chair of metaphysics, logic, and rhetoric. Soon his class would also experience the "*very serious loss*" of the professor of chemistry, mineralogy, and geology. Because of the war, the student had already lost much time; he thus was anxious to make the most rapid progress in his studies possible. His parents were very dissatisfied with his situation at UNC and wished to send him elsewhere.[29]

Admissions at Trinity and Wake Forest colleges were said to have exceeded those at UNC. The more serious competition, however, came from schools just beyond the state's northern border. The University of Virginia claimed superiority, and prospective students and their families bought into the assertion. "[T]he faculty at Chapel Hill is much inferior to the faculty here," a UVA representative once bragged to UNC Professor Charles Phillips, while graciously excepting Phillips himself.[30]

The fact that UNC had only around one hundred students, while UVA had around 450 and "the college at Lexington [Washington, later Washington and Lee]" around three hundred, deeply humiliated a Charles Manly correspondent. That many of these were from North Carolina enhanced the mortification. A nephew of Governor Morehead was at UVA "because instruction is more thorough there than here." "It would do me good," said UNC Professor Charles Phillips, "to get a student from under the shadow of the University of Va." Phillips had to concede, though, that students were being "advised to keep on to Virginia." And former UNC Professor Hepburn told Swain that students who did so wrote "glowing accounts" of it while disparaging the "system of instruction at UNC."[31]

With General Robert E. Lee now ensconced as president of Washington College, some thought UNC, too, needed a Southern hero, perhaps General Joseph Johnston, at its head. The press assailed Swain as "an old fogy, a fossil, who with his colleagues should be forced to give way to more wide awake and truly southern patriotic men." One paper professed "no unkind feeling" for Swain. The prevailing opinion, however, it stated, was "that there ought to be a change in the head of the institution." With Lee's election as president of a Virginia college, "it might have been expected that our university would decay unless some man like Gen. Joe Johns[t]on was placed at its head." With such action, the paper confidently predicted, "in one year the present buildings will not be sufficient to accommodate the large number of students."[32]

A more pointed and virulent critique came from William Bingham, founder of the Bingham School in Orange County, a feeder of students to the university.

Absence of students at UNC, Bingham said, was attributable to "a want of confidence in the administration of the college." Without changes, he posited, "it is idle to stop the tide of young men setting Virginia-ward, to the great detriment of all our educational interests." Bingham was direct and unsparing in blaming Swain for UNC's deficiencies that were driving students to Virginia. "Gov. Swain's administration," he said, "has placed a premium on idleness and vice by letting anybody enter, and letting anybody graduate." This, he concluded, "*has killed the college*, I fear beyond the hope of resurrection."[33]

Similarly adverse appraisals of Swain and his administration were now rampant. Often, they were close to home. One citizen conceded that Swain had probably managed the university's finances "better than any other man." For years, however, his influence had weighed against academic reforms suggested by faculty colleagues. Upon finding an able younger man "of a suitable turn of mind," he said, "it will be well to make the change." Samuel Phillips and Kemp Battle were considered possibilities.[34]

Parting comments of resigning faculty members were telling. In explaining the university's problems, Hepburn bluntly told Swain, there was "too much stress... upon mere political considerations." These were not the cause. Rather, the university needed a "new order" and "new men" to implement it. Adherence to the old system, Hepburn told the university's old president, would leave the university outstripped by every college with sufficient wisdom to conform to the new conditions.[35]

W. J. Martin exceeded Hepburn in candor. The university had failed to furnish essential funds for books and appliances. "A chemist without a well equipped laboratory," Martin said, "is about as well off as a farmer without farm or stock." In UNC management, Martin continued, more pointedly critical of Swain, there was too much "that is effete... to allow any one disposed to develop his department to its highest excellence a fair chance." UNC was satisfied with practices from twenty-five years earlier, "if indeed we do as well." Both "new measures" and "new men" were needed.

"The long and the short of it all," Martin said, "is that I have no hope for the college with Gov. Swain at its head." Swain's presence deprived it of public support, and Swain, Martin thought, would not resign. "Poor Gov.," Martin said: "I have the highest personal regard for him, but he is very weak, and very blind to his own interests in this matter. He has lost such a good chance at gracefully ending a long and popular career."[36]

Professor Charles Phillips and his family were Swain's neighbors and among his closest friends. Yet Phillips could hardly have been more pointed in his criticism of Swain. He had "nonplussed the Gov.," he once said, by asking him what a new professor would do for books in his department. Perhaps Swain thought, Phillips suggested, that "he might follow his own [Swain's] illustratious example by borrowing." In Phillips's view the life of the institution had "been misdirected for some years." Confidence in its scholarship was lacking, and students did not respect the faculty. "Gov. Swain complains of a want of proper State pride in North Carolina," Phillips said, "I tell him he ought to complain of a want of something proper to be proud of." Phillips, like Martin, lamented the absence of books. Scholarship and books were "not valued aright here."

These were not new complaints for Phillips. "Govr. Swain will bear me witness," he claimed, "that I have warned him of this state of matters here for twenty years." Phillips derided Swain's refusal to acknowledge the handicapping effect of his disability. "Gov. Swain thinks that his deafness renders him a better teacher than he was before," Phillips said, continuing, "I wonder what would be the effect of blindness." "Swain's really weak point," though, was the university's want of scholarship, and this was "now before the public as a cancer." Phillips wished Swain "would boldly take the ground that he will not serve here any longer at present and let another man be tried in his place."[37]

Except for William A. Graham, Swain had no closer friend than William H. Battle. Yet Battle, too, contributed to this adverse commentary. "I agree with you," Battle told his son Kemp, "that the public deserves a thorough reorganization here," one that would extend "to men as well as measures."

Unlike many critics, Battle had a kind word for his friend. There had been a time, he said, "when his equal could not be found." Now, however, Battle continued, "his best friends cannot shut their eyes to the fact that his great deafness had considerably impaired his former efficiency." The political objections to Swain, Battle thought, would "gradually die out." Time would not likely diminish the physical disability, however. "There will be great difficulty in selecting a suitable successor," Battle concluded, "but as the Governor cannot live always, it would have to be met in a few years, and it is perhaps best that it should be met now."[38]

Kemp, also a Swain friend, shared his father's concerns. "No first class man," Kemp said, would join the university faculty. The university, he prophesied, "will go down." While it had "very able teachers," the want of "new books, novel apparatus—telescopes and observatories etc etc," had "been fatal." He did not think Swain would resign, but such action clearly would have found favor with him.[39]

Ellie Swain's marriage, in Cornelia Phillips Spencer's view, was "the principal agent in alienating public affection from our university for a time." She found anecdotal support in the story of a North Carolinian who returned to the state from

Arkansas in the winter of 1865–1866. Wherever his North Carolina connection was known, the man said, "this marriage was flung at him . . . as a disgrace to the State." Swain failed to apprehend, Spencer said, that in yielding to his daughter's nuptials "he was condemning his . . . university to temporary ostracism from public favor." Spencer was right, but obviously there was more to the university's afflictions, and Swain's.[40]

To speak only of the many barbs thrown at Swain during this time would leave a distorted impression. A fair share of highly positive commentary still surrounded him. UNC alumni, in particular, were generous with praise. One alumnus, Class of 1852, could countenance no prejudice against the university's "honored President." No man, he thought, had "a deeper interest in the honor and prosperity of the State, the university and our historical records than Gov. Swain." He was saddened that "an unfounded and unreasonable prejudice should annoy his declining years, and injure the usefulness of a noble institution." Another, Class of 1860, found his gratitude constantly growing "for the many kind lessons and counsels I have received at your hands." He signed as "[y]our affectionate friend and former pupil."[41]

Current students were equally affectionate and appreciative. As Swain's presidential tenure approached its terminus, the senior class conveyed "deep regret" over the impending discontinuance of his service. His, they said, had been "a long and successful career," both as president of the institution and as their instructor. Swain's "wise and energetic direction," the students said, had led the university "from a state of stagnation . . . to one of unsurpassed prosperity." They would greatly miss his "valuable instruction" in political economy, moral science, constitutional law, and other areas. Any successor would lack Swain's "experience, erudition, and abundant information." Posterity would "recount with pleasure and pride" his deeds "for improvement of the present," which would ensure "the prosperity of the future generation."

Later, as "a mark of the high esteem" for Swain, students presented him with a dressing case, delivered, Swain said, "by the faithful college servant." He had been "a father to each and every one of us," they said, and they were confident that he would watch their "future course of life . . . with more than ordinary interest and anxiety." "Lovingly," they closed, "your friends and pupils." Deeply touched by the gift, Swain said he would always "cherish . . . most agreeable remembrances" of the students. He would preserve the case "among my choicest treasures."[42]

Former Governor Henry T. Clark knew of the claims that Swain had "outlived his usefulness" and that his deafness "was fatal to enforcing discipline," yet thought "it would be difficult to supply his place." "His deep abiding, unremitting zeal and interest in the University, Like a Father's love," Clark thought, "cannot be supplied [and] really supplies the place of many a deficiency."[43] Even as they moved toward Swain's removal, the trustees expressed deep gratitude "for his long, successful and eminent services as President of the University." They wanted him at the post until the appointment of his successor.[44]

These encomiums notwithstanding, negative perceptions of Swain and his administration of the university were pervasive and persistent. A dominant and demanding mood favored extensive reorganization and reform. For the time, Swain was an old man. In philosophy he was "old school," particularly regarding curriculum. One so circumstanced was unlikely to catch a tidal wave of change and ride it successfully.[45]

A more probable change agent thus emerged. Kemp Battle, age thirty-five and a four-year member of the UNC Board of Trustees, became the leader of the reform forces. Undeterred by his and his family's close friendship with Swain, in 1866 Battle moved the trustees for appointment of a committee to investigate the condition of the university. The committee was to report necessary or proper changes in the course of instruction; recommend increases, if any, in the number of professorships; recommend changes, if any, in the duties of the faculty; and recommend any needed improvements in the financial affairs and practical administration of the university. The courtesy was extended to Swain of inviting him to submit "plans of improvement or change" that he considered "expedient." The conclusion is inescapable, nevertheless, that his three-plus decades of administering the university were under critical review, if not, at least in some respects, direct attack. Indeed, Professor Charles Phillips—like Battle, with his family a close friend of Swain's—was explicit in this regard. He hoped Battle would "write such a Report as will mark '*a Crisis*' for Gov. Swain."[46]

Phillips led faculty participation in the reform effort. He solicited W. J. Martin and A. D. Hepburn to join him in recommending improvements. He defended his own UNC teaching career: "[n]either Gov. Swain nor [any]one else has ever criticized what I taught or how I taught it," he said. Yet he offered to resign if Battle thought it best "to make all things and men new." Long viewed as Swain's "pet," he acknowledged accusations of "applaud[ing] any doctrine of Governor Swain." But he was clearly ready, even eager, to shed that mantle. It was "high time," he said, for strong academic instruction at UNC, "so that boys need never feel that they go down hill in going up to the university."[47]

Hepburn, though now departed, took "a deep interest in the disruptions in the university." Pleased that "various methods of university education and discipline" were under discussion, he offered to, and did, "cheerfully render assistance." H. H.

Kemp Plummer Battle

Smith, professor of modern languages, offered thoughts on curricular reform in response to Battle's "request extended to the Faculty through the President." Battle himself wanted only able men at the university, "learned and enthusiastic men—those who will work continually and improve always." The "fossilizing of professors" was the greatest "calamity" a college could experience—"their learning their lessons by rote and afterwards quitting study."[48]

The reform committee report was, in some respects, kind to Swain. Before the war, it said, the university "had been a chief ornament, and a just source of pride to North Carolina." In the quarter of a century preceding 1861, its career had been one of "brilliant success." None, the report stated, had accomplished a better work in North Carolina "than they who ... conducted the university during the generation just ended." These were the Swain years; thus, these were words of appreciation for him and his leadership.

The trustee board also praised this chapter in the university's history. In memorializing the General Assembly to appoint a committee on reorganization of the university, it stated the purpose as "to restore its former prosperity and increase its usefulness." It gave content to the term "former prosperity." "[S]ince 1837," it said, "the university has been preeminently the nursing mother of humble talent and merit." The "poorest boys in North Carolina" had met the "favorites of fortune" from every state in the South and Southwest "on equal terms." Again, this was Swain's time, and these were his policies.

The times and their needs had changed, however. The reform committee perceived that astounding developments in novel branches of science "demand[ed] corresponding alterations in the curriculum at Chapel Hill." More thorough intellectual discipline and more adequate scholarship were required, as were tightened admission standards, increased attention to declamation and English composition, and enhanced philosophical and chemical apparatus. The library should have resources with which to exhibit advances in the various departments of science. The object: to fit the institution's graduates "for becoming in after life an ornament and a blessing to the country and to mankind."[49]

Swain solicited faculty response to the committee's report. None was immediately forthcoming. It was, the faculty said, unable to express an opinion at that time. Later it communicated its concurrence in the recommendations. Swain then moved for appointment of a committee to prepare an address to the people of North Carolina in vindication of the faculty. A laconic minute entry records the response: "The Faculty did not think it proper for a committee of itself to prepare such an address." Swain next appointed a faculty committee to audit the accounts of the bursar. The trustees had suspended their authority to perform that function, the faculty replied. This was new territory for a president who long had largely worked his will with his faculty.[50]

As Swain's status at the university entered free fall, so, too, did his personal life. Lifelong issues, both physical and mental, had plagued his oldest living child Anne, more often called Anna. In her thirties the physical dimension became severe and critical. When she was thirty-one, for four days and nights her death was thought to be imminent. "I have never known a greater sufferer," Swain then poignantly told Vance. More than two years later, Anne's struggle continued. Swain had made a trip to Raleigh, Charles Phillips told Kemp Battle, "full of vexing cares as to his private matters and as to the university."[51]

Under medical direction, Anne used opiates to relieve her pain. As the Civil War neared its end, these were in short supply, most being devoted to wounded and dying troops. A desperate father again wrote his pupil and friend, the governor of North Carolina, begging for assistance in securing pain-relieving drugs for his seriously ill child. It was, Swain told Vance, "a case of extreme necessity." He had solicited the state's surgeon general without result. He earnestly entreated Vance "to ascertain immediately whether morphine, opium or laudanum can be procured in Raleigh and if so to send it by express to Durham, with direction to be sent to me at this place."[52]

This affecting plea was fruitful. Swain soon thanked Vance for sending the medicine. "A delay of six hours might have produced most distressing results," he noted. Anna would always thank Vance for his "kindness exhibited in such a crisis." It was not long, however, until Swain again lamented to Vance, "Poor Anna is the greatest mental and physical sufferer I ever knew, and how I am to provide for her that which is absolutely essential to her continued existence, I do not know."[53]

At age thirty-seven Anne was dying from breast cancer, with lung, muscular, and rheumatic complications. Late winter 1867 brought end-stage. Eleanor remained alert and at her side throughout several nights, and Swain dared not leave home. "Anna's condition is no more promising than when I last wrote," he once told Graham, soon noting that she had "for some days ... been the source of much anxiety."[54]

Vance conveyed the hope, altogether vain, that it was nothing serious. In the early evening a few days later, on March 26, 1867, Anne died. "She closed a life of extraordinary mental and physical suffering," Swain said, "as quickly and quietly as an infant sucking with slumber on a mother's bosom." It was a quiet death, though, only after "dreadful suffering of *mind & body* ... endured for years," according to Lucy Battle, and thus one over which "every one that knew her ought to rejoice."[55]

The "loss of that amicable daughter" brought deep sympathy from Swain's friends. He "must feel a vacancy and a loss," wrote one, "at the departure of one who through so many years has been an object of affectionate solicitude." Swain was "bowed down," said Charles Phillips, "as if a very choice and rare child [not Phillips's view of her] had been taken from him."[56]

Anne joined her brother David and sister "Infant Ella" in graves in the family's backyard garden. Pursuant to her dying request, some of Chapel Hill's "colored people" sang a hymn at her grave, "many of them in tears as their simple melody rose in the air." Already burdened almost beyond human capacity to endure, the bereft father now had a new ritual in his daily routine. For the rest of his life, at or before dawn, he visited Anne's grave to pray.[57]

Anne's final illness and passing brought no moratorium on the university's "vexing problems." Obviously, however, they distracted Swain, diminishing his time and capacity for addressing them. Perhaps for that reason, though possibly by design, his normally astute political antennae failed him. The former and future governor, William W. Holden, was not invited to the 1867 UNC commencement. The presence there of the sitting president of the United States, Andrew Johnson, compounded the gravity of the omission. Holden was also denied a platform seat for Swain's address at the dedication of the Raleigh monument to Johnson's late father. Holden had now secured a political base in the state from which he could do Swain and the university considerable damage. These omissions thus were political miscalculations.[58]

Sadly, Swain himself became an object of pity. "I pity Gov. Swain very much," Charles Phillips told Kemp Battle, "[f]olks abuse him and ridicule him yet he can do more with them for others than any man I know of." Swain's hearing loss was a large factor. "A deaf man may *lecture*," Phillips said, "[b]ut how can he *teach* unless he require written essays?" To have a confidential communication with Swain was impossible, Phillips asserted, "unless you go into the middle of an old field." Consequently, efforts to inform Swain of external news would fail. "I could not make him hear so as to understand it," Judge Battle once reported, "though I howled nearly as loud as I could." Like Phillips, Battle was certain Swain could not hear a class recite. He had heard, however, "that the Governor thinks that he is giving more efficient instruction than he ever gave before."[59]

Rumors arose of a Swain resignation. "Be not surprised to hear of Gov. Swain's resignation—as a 'coup d'etat,'" Phillips now said to Kemp Battle. Swain was, Phillips said, "very down hearted at the prospect here and well he may be." Battle's father held a somewhat contrary view. He had posed to Swain a resignation of all trustees and faculty "so as to give . . . the opportunity to effect a complete reorganization of the institution." Swain's response, Battle said, left him "satisfied that he will not resign under any circumstances, unless requested by the trustees to do so." It was a time when Battle's wife Lucy did not think Swain looked "very bright."[60]

Judge Battle's guess proved wrong. Three days later Swain resigned, or at least offered to do so. As was his wont, he recited a brief history of his calling to and time in the university presidency. He was mildly defensive of his tenure. He quoted "a well-informed writer" who in June 1860 had noted the dramatic increase in the number of students and the doubling of the number of buildings and faculty under his leadership. "The result of the civil war," however, had "sadly disappointed this favorable augury." Swain cited, in exoneration, loss of the university's endowment and "other unfavorable effects upon our prospects" growing out of the war. At no other time in life, he told Governor Jonathan Worth, ex-officio trustee president, "were my labors more zealous[,] faithful and unintermitting in the service of the Institution." "[W]hatever betide me in the future," Swain said, "I am satisfied with the record of the past."[61]

Some of Swain's best friends, and the university's, questioned his decision. Earlier Swain had discussed the issue with Graham. Graham had been "inexorably opposed" to Swain's "offering to yield to an unreasonable and senseless clamor, having its origin in political considerations," as he had believed and still did. He was "much inclined to the same conclusion now." Judge Ruffin, with whom Graham had shared Swain's letter, was also opposed. In Swain's situation, however, Ruffin indicated that he would tender it.

Paul Cameron of Hillsboro communicated his sentiments directly to Swain. As a trustee as well as a citizen, he could not assent to the retirement. Cameron's critique was harsh. "For you to leave the college at this time," he told Swain, "will be as a father to turn his back on a sick child—In my judgment it will be to let it die." No known person would be as efficient as Swain, especially regarding the university's finances. Further, there should be some reward "for fidelity virtue and merit." Swain should "*hold on*—and let us avail ourselves of the recent resignation to call some one or two prominent Confederate officers to your side." This, Cameron was convinced, "will go a long way toward quieting the feeling against the organization of *your Faculty*."[62]

A UNC alumnus found news of Swain's resignation profoundly shocking, so much so that he wanted to go to the "fountainhead," Swain himself, for verification. It was sad that Swain's public tenure, in which he had "judiciously handled the reins" of the state and for more than thirty years guided the university "safely over the shoals," should "thus be dismantled." Swain should know, the alumnus said, "how much your services are needed and appreciated there."[63]

Press reviews were mixed. The *Raleigh Sentinel* was gentle and laudatory. It referred to Swain as "the honored head of the University." He did not need to impress "upon the public mind" the value of his labors "and long-continued usefulness." Swain had "no purpose of self-laudation" or "desire to magnify [his] services, which have been as valuable as they have been disinterested." Swain was retiring, the editor said, "with the respect and veneration of the whole State." It was hoped that he would remain at the university to teach history and to write a history of North Carolina. "He alone is capable of it."[64] Swain would "retire to the repose of private life," said the *Raleigh Register*, "with a consciousness of having labored assiduously for the advancement of education and civilization." There was "no man in the state to whom the people are more indebted on these accounts."[65]

The *Fayetteville News*, by contrast, was negative, indeed, nasty. It cited a "very forcible communication" that recommended "an entire change and remodeling of the institution." The course of study at the university, the quoted source had said, was "a ridiculous farce." Diplomas were granted to young men unqualified to enter the freshman class. The *News* concurred. For the good of the university, not only Swain, but the entire faculty, should resign. The people were learning the truth about the university, "alarmed at the disgraceful exposé," and requesting reform. While not inclined "to cast reproach upon the venerable head of the university," the paper continued, it was "as little inclined to hide and conceal the real causes of the want of prosperity and advancement in the college for the past two years." It then pointedly cast the blame on Swain. "The fact is simply this," it said:

> The President of the University is doing now what he ought to have done long since—tendering his resignation—before the harm was done and the evil became almost incurable. If with the close of the war, some one of our distinguished citizens, prominent and esteemed for his valuable services, and possessed of the capacity and energy to push forward, had been placed at the head of the institution, we would not now be regretting its painfully disadvantageous contrast to Yale, the Virginia University, and Washington College, or marking with shame the past two years—its numbers diminishing, its high prestige failing, its reputation waning and its President retiring at last, not to look with pride and pleasing meditative reflection upon the advancement of an institution which had been fostered by his influence, but to hear the complaints of his fellow citizens over the decline of what should have been their pride.[66]

The person whose opinion perhaps mattered most was confused. Jonathan Worth, governor and ex-officio trustee president, had problems interpreting Swain's letter. His first impression was that Swain had expressed a desire to resign and have the full board "meet and decide what is to be done." More careful consideration, however, brought the view that Swain had only expressed a willingness to resign if the trustees thought they could appoint a successor who was "more likely to better the prospects of the institution." Swain always would have resigned, Worth thought, upon the request of the trustees operating "under the belief that they could supply a superior likely to manage the University, under more favorable auspices." Worth was "embarrassed" as to the course he should take, for he could not construe the letter "as expressing any wish of Gov. Swain to resign." He thus would welcome advice from Graham and Ruffin, known for their "more constant and intelligent zeal as trustees." Worth had long thought Swain's deafness should prompt his resignation. If so, however, he should express clearly a wish to retire, "not merely to say what he would always have said—'I will resign if the Trustees request it.'" Momentarily putting aside his perplexity, Worth notified the trustees of the resignations of Swain and the faculty and of the problems of the university. He called a meeting of the board to deal with them. "*[E]very trustee,*" he urged, "*will feel it his duty to be present and share the responsibility of the trust he has accepted.*"[67]

The convoluted actions that followed suggest that the trustee board, too, was confused. Initially it accepted the resignations Swain and the faculty had tendered. It acknowledged Swain's long and able service with appreciation and tendered the trustees' "assurance of their undiminished confidence and high respect."[68] Two months later Charles Manly gave notice of an executive committee meeting for submission of the Report of the Committee on Reorganization, election of a new president, and the filling of all faculty vacancies. When the committee met, however, it postponed election of a president and faculty until the beginning of the next collegiate year. It requested that Swain and the faculty remain in place "until the new system" took effect. Swain, in particular, was asked to continue in office until the appointment of a successor at the next commencement.[69]

Swain pondered the possibility of Vance as his successor. Could Vance, he wondered, "be induced to stand now where I stood in 1835, with the assurance honestly entertained that the prospects are not less hopeful now, than they were then." Nothing came of this thought. In general Swain was insecure and perplexed, and justifiably so. "I can scarcely be surprised by anything that can be said, or done by any body about any thing in any quarter," he told Kemp Battle. Yet he was to hold his position for another academic year.[70]

The greater public sphere, too, had him feeling neglected and waxing nostalgic. He commended Kemp Battle for Battle's deft handling of an issue in the 1868 Constitutional Convention. He was bitter, though, because the convention delegates apparently had forgotten him. He had "been in constant readiness for examination," he told Battle, but had received "no intimation of a disposition to give audience to the oldest *ex governor* of the State[,] the oldest College President in the United States, and one moreover somewhat familiar with the history of the Conventions hitherto assembled from 1776 to the present period and more immediately connected with that of 1835 than any man living." "I stand in relation to them as I do to my immediate masters the trustees," he said, "ripe and ready for any thing." He was not a happy man, but he persevered.[71]

As his year of grace was ending, Swain learned that finally his tenure at the university, too, was over. "The Govr desires to decide now the old masters must vacate with propriety," Kemp Battle informed him. A brief further stay gave him a ray of hope, however. At the 1868 commencement, the trustees decided that an immediate implementation of a change in the course of studies was impractical. They thus reappointed the old faculty, including Swain. "[T]hey are respectfully requested to continue in the performance of duty in their respective Departments as heretofore," the trustees said. They even gave Swain some financial relief. After paying faculty salaries, the bursar was to pay the principal and interest due to him on a bond executed by the university.[72]

Swain, although finding some hope in the delay, recognized that the old order was passing and his hold on power was tenuous. He told Kemp Battle he was "anxious to be present" at the final meeting of the university trustees "under the old dynasty." As that meeting date approached, he stated his intent to be present "at the first meeting of the trustees," thus indicating a recognition of the coming new order. Other "old timers" were conveying to him concerns about that new order. One, a student in the late 1850s, worried that the libraries and other property of the literary societies might be falling into the hands of those not entitled to them.[73]

The trustee board that met in the state capitol's senate chamber in July 1868 was indeed newly constituted. Only four of seventy-eight former trustees remained, and they had been relatively inactive. Seats on the board, formerly considered to carry life tenure, vanished. Each of the state's counties now had one trustee on the board. Swain, once the holder of a "lifetime" appointment to the board, was not on the list. Solomon Pool, who would soon succeed Swain in another capacity, represented Orange, Swain's then county of residence. Judge James L. Henry represented Swain's native county of Buncombe.

Newly minted trustees were committed and enthusiastic. One said he could not refuse his appointment, then waxed eloquent. He trusted that the university, which had produced "some of the most distinguished sons of America," would now "more generally diffuse her usefulness." He could not resist a gratuitous swipe at Swain and the old regime, however, adding, "instead of being as she is accused of late years a nursery of narrow-minded, biggotted sectional ideas, she may become the nursery of patriotism, loyalty, love of country and devotion to this great Union!"[74]

Swain was not the only longtime university servant being deposed. His regular companion in the university's labors, former governor Charles Manly, had been secretary-treasurer of the trustees almost forty-seven years. In submitting his final accounting, Manly exercised "an old man's privilege" to make poignant parting comments. It was "with deep and unaffected pain" that he took leave of the "books and papers" of his office. They formed "a page in the annals of North Carolina unstained and ineffable." His tenure had marked the history of a "steady rise in reputation and influence," first under President Joseph Caldwell, then under "the still more extended and successful policy of her last Pres[ident] David L. Swain." Manly's prayer was "that her usefulness may increase more and more throughout all time." A clear conscience, and a resolution of appreciation, were Manly's rewards.[75]

Pursuant to its request, Swain, too, conveyed concluding thoughts to the newly constituted board. If faithfully executed, Swain said, the section of the just-adopted state constitution granting the board's existence laid the foundation of a great educational institution. Resident trustees in each county would extend the board's influence "to every nook and corner of the State." There would now be "the inseparable connection of the University with the Free Public School System of the state contemplated by the Constitution." Papers annexed to his address, which he almost certainly prepared, provided an accurate history of the university. The trustees were commencing their service to the institution under more favorable circumstances than had their predecessors. The means of education were now much greater "than those of our revolutionary Fathers." Almost a third of a century of connection with the university gave him the credentials "to ascertain the truth of its history" and "form accurate opinions" as to its future.

These credentials, Swain hoped, provided "a sufficient warrant for the freedom and frankness with which I deem it my duty to address you." A plea for united, nonpartisan management of the university followed: "the highest prosperity and usefulness of our educational Institution can be secured only by the earnest and united efforts of all good men of all parties and sects political and religious," he said, "and if this Union can be effected, success is as certain with it, as failure under divided counsel." Timing of resumption of the university's exercises was the trustees' decision. Swain did not hesitate, however, to praise their decision at commencement to retain the old faculty, or to criticize the more recent suspension of exercises. The latter was, he said, "a mistake in regard alike to expediency and authority." To continue it would compound the harm. In a six-month suspension of operations, the institution's property would inevitably deteriorate; the cost of its rehabilitation would then exceed that of two years of normal exercises.

The address was Swain's valedictory, and he was at his most eloquent and candid. The board decreed that he had addressed it "in a very able and satisfactory manner." It then adjourned until the following day, when it adopted a motion to have Swain's address "filed as part of the records and proceedings of the trustees."[76]

When the board convened the following day, July 24, 1868, newly elected Governor William W. Holden was in the chair. A committee appointed the previous day "to report to the meeting tomorrow some plan for the continuance of the

William Woods Holden, governor and thus UNC trustee chair when Swain's presidency terminated.

university" reported. Its first recommendation was for acceptance of the resignations of the president and faculty tendered in July 1867. Apparently to avoid possible legal complications from the fact that the resignations had been tendered to one board and were being accepted by another, the board not only accepted the resignations but also declared all the chairs in the university vacant. The executive committee was authorized to prepare and implement "a plan of thorough and efficient re-organization of the University," including the election of a president and faculty and the adoption of a system of instruction and government. At the earliest practical time, it was "to resume the exercises of the Institution." In a parting, again gratuitous slap at Swain, the board conveyed its "sense" that "only a man of established national reputation as a scholar and educator should be selected as President of the University."[77]

Swain, to that point still president of the university and thereby ex-officio a trustee, was present by invitation at these proceedings. His subsequent description of them to Graham prompted Graham later to comment that "[u]pon assuming their trust, the [new trustees], suddenly elevated to such duties, seemed exceedingly confident, aggressive, polemical." Based on Swain's description, Graham viewed the removal of Swain and the old faculty as done "in a most offensive manner."[78]

But done it was. "Leaves have their time to fall, . . . [a]nd stars to set."[79] Almost thirty-three years, which was almost half of Swain's lifetime, devoted to the university—and almost four-and-a-half decades with few days not occupied very actively and productively in some significant public position—had come to this.[80]

CHAPTER 27

Aftermath, Finale
"A want of vitality and strength to rally"

SWAIN'S LOSS OF PRESTIGE, power, and position can be attributed to no single cause. An infelicitous coalescence of forces—political, institutional, and personal—conspired against him. Arguably, but for the strident political forces, his presidency would have ended only of his own volition or upon the ultimate nonvolitional reality of death. Until the Civil War period he was generally popular personally, and his management of the university was well regarded. He adeptly maintained close contact with the political life of the state and nation without being openly partisan. His one overt political cause was the university, and it was not considered a partisan one.

Throughout his university presidency, however, he concerned and involved himself with public affairs on a larger scale. To sit quietly on the sidelines, in plain view of a crisis of the magnitude of national disunion, would have been altogether uncharacteristic of him. To the core of his being, he was a Unionist Whig. Thoughts of the death of the American experiment thus were deeply disturbing to him. Yet he was a lifelong Southerner, steeped in Southern institutions, culture, and customs, and a beneficiary of them. It thus was natural that he would commence as a secession opponent but morph into a supporter as those institutions, that culture, and those customs were threatened, especially when they were openly attacked and the "country" itself was invaded by a now "foreign" power.

Belated, relatively tepid support of a cause does not resonate well, however, with its earlier and more fervent advocates, especially when actions of the lukewarm latecomer impede the cause's success or are perceived to do so. A keen perception that both his students and the "country" would benefit from the students' completion of their education prior to assumption of arms almost certainly motivated Swain's efforts to secure their exemption from the Confederate draft. As the Confederate cause faltered, however, the more ardent Confederates came to view the exemptions negatively as a hindrance to the war effort.

A life of statesmanship perhaps held no more statesmanly ideas or actions than Swain's mission, with Graham, to Sherman. It was his idea. He advocated it, successfully, to Graham and Vance. It worked, saving North Carolina from much of the bloodshed and property destruction other Southern states experienced as the war was ending. This may well have been the supreme act of preservation in a lifetime of preservationist activity. But it was not thus viewed at the time, at least not universally so. To diehards for the Confederate cause, Swain and Graham were cavorting with the enemy, all but entering the state into a separate peace while Confederate troops still occupied the field. Rather than a preservationist hero, Swain was, to many of them, a traitor who should be hanged.

News of Ellie Swain and her "Yankee general" beau soon followed. Swain, it was thought, should not have allowed this wayward daughter to marry this evil man, or at least should not have provided the couple with a lavish wedding and nuptial party. All too recently the groom and his men had ravaged the South's land and people and pilfered their property. The groom's lifelong, vehement denial of these allegations in no way diminished them as "facts" in many Southern minds. Standing alone, the Atkins-Swain courtship and marriage would have been sufficiently impolitic to be problematic for Swain. Combined with his other perceived failures to measure up to the values and needs of the Southern cause, it was a final, arguably ultimately fatal, blow.

While rarely mentioned by contemporaries or historians, Swain's frequent interaction with the federal government during Reconstruction could hardly have helped his cause. This was, after all, the government from which his state had just attempted to secede. It was now devising, implementing, and enforcing policies regarding the freedmen that were malodorous to most of Swain's white North Carolina contemporaries. It was well known that he was, with regularity, seated at its councils.

Institutional problems at the university were long present but largely dormant. Swain's reputation and efforts had brought significant increases in enrollment, and with them, substantially enhanced revenues. He was a sound fiscal manager, the place was satisfactorily preparing leaders for the state and its communities, and for the most part a perception of well-being prevailed. The downside of Swain's fiscal conservatism was that it had left the university bereft of books, scientific equipment, and other academic apparatus. Moreover, a lack of adequate preparatory schools in the state had produced compromises in admissions standards. Poorly prepared admittees then graduated with significant lingering deficiencies.

The fiscal soundness that had long sustained public support for the university ended with the Civil War, which decimated the potential student population. When many of the limited number available for enrollment went elsewhere, perceiving an education from other institutions to be superior, UNC's academic deficiencies could no longer remain subsurface. Reform became the order of the day. An "old school" president, perceived to be an obstacle to a new order, became expendable. Faculty believed to harbor "Yankee proclivities" enhanced the ill will and the impetus for change; "the dislike of the people to the university" was not "due in a greater degree to Governor Swain than to other members of the Faculty of that day," in the opinion of a contemporary newspaper, the *Wilmington Journal*.

Swain's physical problems, primarily his loss of hearing, seriously compounded these political and institutional factors. By this time, he was quite deaf. This condition rendered personal interactions extremely difficult when he most needed his earlier considerable competence for them. There is no surviving evidence of extreme physical or mental disability otherwise. Almost without question, however, his prior capabilities in both areas had diminished, and not surprisingly given that he was in his mid-to-late sixties, in that era old age.[1]

By spring 1865, a tenure of office once highly respected and acclaimed had become unpopular and controversial. The holder of the office resisted suggestions that the old regime was ending. When the end came, he attempted a cheerful countenance, talked of having leisure time to visit his native county of Buncombe and to write the history of North Carolina about which he had spoken for so many years.

His effort to project a blithe spirit failed, however. The summer of the removal, 1868, found him melancholy, drooping, and for the first time showing his age. When Governor Holden sent African American troops to Chapel Hill to close the university for a time, it pained Swain deeply. He was unusually candid with one friend. "[S]ince I last saw you," he said, "my connection with the university has been brought to a close; it was a trial I dreaded."[2]

Shortly after the removal, Judge Battle thought Swain understood that he "no longer [had] any chance of being reelected as President of the University." Battle was wrong. Swain would yet bring a last-ditch challenge to his displacement grounded in legalistic reasoning. Before addressing Governor Holden, in Holden's capacity as president of the UNC board, Swain requested from Charles Manly a copy of a memorandum. It was one Swain had written when the trustees had removed Benjamin Hedrick from the faculty. In it, Swain had stated reasons why only the full board of trustees, at an annual meeting, could hire or remove a faculty member. He had the utmost confidence in Manly's careful filing system, and thus had no doubt that Manly could locate the document. If not, it would be a first failure at such an effort in over a thirty-year period. Manly, Swain said, had always been able "instantly" to find "any paper worthy of preservation, relating to the university."

Swain then penned a lengthy, legalistic epistle to Governor Holden. He recited the convoluted facts of his recent "in, then out, then in, then out" tenure in the office, leading to the convening of the new trustees on July 23, 1868. He noted a 1789 statutory provision granting the board power to hire a president and professors and to remove them "for misbehavior, inability or neglect of duty." The new board's acceptance of his and the faculty's July 1867 resignations, he claimed, took him "entirely by surprise." In his opinion "due consideration and deliberation" would have resulted in rejection of the resolution.

"Permit me," he then requested of the governor, "in no spirit of captiousness . . . to solicit a reconsideration of this Resolution." The argument for his continued tenure that followed was essentially the one the board had anticipated when it not only accepted Swain's and the faculty's resignations but also vacated and abolished the chairs they held. "[A]fter due consideration," Swain posited, surely no one would insist that a resignation tendered to, and accepted by, a board that had ceased to exist "can be resuscitated and accepted by a Board which came into existence a year after it was tendered and six months after it was accepted." Still less could this "supposed tender and acceptance constitute a valid foundation for declaring all the chairs in the Institution vacant and abolished, especially the Presidential chair," the president being "by the express terms of the Constitution . . . an integral portion of the executive Committee." The former was tantamount to abolition of the university; the latter, to annihilation of the executive committee.

Neither Holden nor the new-sprung board he now chaired was in the mood for legal niceties. A profound power shift had occurred. The old university president, so long in the power vanguard of both the state and its university, no longer had it. His largely academic legal treatise was simply ignored.[3]

A few days later Swain wrote to Robert W. Lassiter, who had replaced Charles Manly as secretary of the trustees, enclosing copies of university documents. Either forgetful of, or in denial regarding, his displacement, above the date he wrote "University of North Carolina." Manly was none too fond of his successor. He was "a jackass," Manly told his brother. He would, though, Manly understood, live in Chapel Hill with a dwelling house and a large salary.[4]

Contemporaries left touching accounts of Swain during this period:

President Swain continued to labor with all his former energy. Never did any officer give his whole heart and anxious care to the interests of his charge more devotedly than he. Right nobly and with high courage did he meet the loss of patronage and income, and the virulence of unfair criticism. The students were his children, their success brought him unalloyed joy, and his heart sorely felt their failures and was wounded by their deaths.
—Kemp Battle

I really do not know a more affecting and truly noble picture than that presented by Gov. Swain in his last days. All parties assailed him. His best friends shook their heads and were among the doubters. Even those who had eaten of bread provided by him, turned against him. But he struggled on, perhaps blindly but manfully. But his hopes that the storm would soon abate were in vain.
—Cornelia Spencer

"Live 10 years longer, Gov.," Charles Deems told Swain, "and you will be the most popular man in North Carolina."[5]

It was not to be. The man would not long survive the loss of the office. August was a week away, and it was not his favorite month. It was in August, he had said, when the evils that had befallen him had occurred. He thus always breathed a sigh of relief when the month was over. In August 1868 that sigh of relief never came.[6]

Among Swain's property holdings was a plantation called Babylon in Chatham County about six miles from Chapel Hill. Once the property of the late Professor Elisha Mitchell, it had served as security for a debt Mitchell had contracted to Swain. Mitchell's widow sold a portion of the tract, but the land continued to be security for the indebtedness to Swain. Swain then acquired the property through a mortgage default. In Judge Battle's estimation, the debt exceeded the value of the land.[7]

On August 11, 1868, eighteen days after his removal from the UNC presidency, Swain visited the plantation. Deposed Professor Manuel Fetter accompanied him. By one account Swain was preparing the place "for the comfort of his small family of old servants." A buggy, drawn by a horse Sherman had given Swain, provided transport. Swain had accepted the gift, he said, as a symbol of reconciliation. It was a mistake on many counts, however. Prevailing opinion held that Sherman had taken the horse from some Southern family; Swain thus was widely criticized for acquiescing in the gift. Thieves relieved Swain of the animal on three occasions, and he had to recover it. Finally, the horse itself was "spirited" and thus inclined to cause problems.[8]

Fetter held the reins on the return trip to Chapel Hill. When the horse ran out of control, Swain attempted to seize the reins. That, too, proved a mistake. A buggy wheel hit a stump, ejecting both Swain and Fetter. Both were injured, though the injuries to neither were thought to be serious. Swain's were sufficiently so, however, that he had to be carried on a stretcher from the accident scene across the UNC campus to his home. His faithful former "servant" (enslaved person) Wilson Swain, now, by his post-emancipation choice, Wilson Swain Caldwell, assisted with the homeward conveyance of his old master.[9]

The accident brought excitement and concern to the usually calm academic village, "so much running to and fro and calling and talking," said Cornelia Spencer the following day. Notwithstanding that his clothing had to be cut off of him, Swain was thought to be doing well but still could not be moved. Sober voices were deeply concerned for him. Swain, Judge Battle prophetically told his son Kemp, had "received injuries from which he will probably never recover." He was lying on his back at all times because he could not move one of his sides. He had never "look[ed] half so ghastly" in Battle's long experience with him. The doctor's view that Swain was "doing quite as well as could be expected" did not alter Battle's perspective that he was not "out of danger."[10]

A week after the accident Swain "appeared to be better," Spencer thought. Still, his doctor lamented a lack of proper nursing care, particularly that he was "not rubbed daily as he ought to be." Some inexplicably blamed Swain himself for this omission, while others viewed Eleanor as "not actively efficient." Fetter was now out walking with a cane, while Swain remained confined to his bed.[11]

The patient may have had a premonition that this August would be his last. To those nearest to him he had spoken a conviction "that his time was short." He had spent the winter and spring getting his personal affairs in order, arranging his valuable papers and correspondence. There was said to be "an increasing mellowness and ripeness of his many admirable traits of character."[12]

He was also putting his spiritual house in order. Long known as "a praying man," he interceded with the Almighty on behalf of his students and his brethren in the Christian faith. He was a Bible reader, with a preference for passages regarding the communion of saints, both with God and with one another. Charles Phillips, UNC professor and ordained Presbyterian clergyman, visited the confined man twice daily. Phillips reported conversations with Swain "on things of Faith and of communion in prayer—for him when in trouble—for our pupils here and for our country in its late and present distresses." Each day of Swain's confinement Phillips read the Bible to him and prayed with him. The last scripture Phillips read was Psalm 73. At the twenty-sixth verse, "My heart and my flesh faileth; but God is the strength of my heart and my portion forever," Swain requested a rereading. The last verse, "But it is good for me to draw near to God: I have put my trust in the Lord God, that I may declare all thy works" (Psalm 73:28), brought the same request.

"He seemed to love all who love the Lord Jesus," Phillips said of Swain, "and told many interesting anecdotes of his intercourse as a Christian with Christians of various denominations." Swain often told him, Phillips said, "that his only satisfaction was in crying out 'Lord be merciful to me a sinner' (Luke 18:13)—'Lord I believe—help thou mine unbelief (Mark 9:24).'" Phillips's father had also uttered these "soul-quieting exclamations," Swain told him. The dawn of these days often found Swain chanting familiar hymns. On his last evening he repeated the Lord's Prayer and remarked on its beauty.

As the spiritual nature strengthened, though, the physical one weakened. True, there were no broken bones. The doctor at least thought there were no internal injuries. The physical shock from the accident had been profound, however. Perhaps in part because of the equally profound psychological shock just endured, there was "a want of vitality and strength to rally" from it. At no time in these days was Swain thought to be *in extremis*. He had, indeed, spoken cheerfully of his prospects of getting well. On his last day he was, reportedly, "brighter than usual." He fed himself for the first time since the accident and was self-congratulatory on that account. Yet appetite was lacking, and the patient was feeble.[13]

On the morning of August 27, 1868, sixteen days after the carriage derailment, Swain sat up for about an hour. It was a first since the accident, according to Phillips. As he reclined in a chair, Eleanor fixed his bed. He ate his breakfast. He appeared no worse than previously. With assistance from Charles Phillips, aided by Swain's faithful old "servant" (former enslaved person) Fred Lane, he returned to his bed. Soon Swain complained of exhaustion. He requested a toddy to stimulate him. Stimulants were administered but to no avail. Swain struggled for breath. He asked to be raised up but, uneasy in that position, to be returned to a reclining posture. Windows were opened, and the patient was fanned.

Phillips now noticed that Swain's hand and breast were "cold and clammy" and that he was growing pale. Eleanor perceived that he was dying. Phillips went for the doctor, as Phillips's wife and his sister Cornelia arrived. Professor Fetter also came. Judge Battle was summoned but arrived too late. The doctor reached the bedside only to hear the patient's last gasp. "[A]ll kinds of stimulants were used to arouse him" but again to no avail.

"Death, a necessary end, [w]ill come when it will come."[14] At around 9:00 a.m., within half an hour after his return to bed, David Swain's earthly excursion ended. His last conversations were about his favorite subjects, the history of North Carolina, and the state's university, which "he loved better than his life."[15]

Epilogue
"That time can never dim or tarnish his reputation"

"ANY MAN'S DEATH COULD end the story."[1] As the song from "Porgy and Bess" states, however, "it ain't necessarily so." It is not the experience with every person, and it was not that of David Lowry Swain. There is more to say about him, his family, and his legacy.

Funerals, Burials

We noted at the outset that Swain's funeral, held two days after his death, attracted a crowd. Recent animosities apparently were forgotten, at least momentarily, in an outpouring of grief over the sudden loss of the community's, and one of the state's, most beloved and respected citizens. Standing at the head of his friend's coffin, Governor Graham said, "N[orth] C[arolina] will not soon look upon his like again."[2]

Swain's remains joined those of son David and daughter Anne in the garden of the Swain home. Cornelia Phillips Spencer's visits to the grave found it covered with wreathes and bouquets of flowers. The resting place would prove transient, however. Eleanor, embittered by her husband's treatment at the hands of Holden and the new UNC trustees, was eager to sever this last tie to the university community to which her husband had devoted half his life. "When I can command the means, sufficient for the purpose," she told Spencer, "I expect to remove the sacred relics that bind me still to this place."[3]

Eleanor soon accomplished her purposes. In December 1869, Swain's remains, and those of his beloved children David and Anne, were disinterred from the soil of Chapel Hill. Swain's trusted old "servant" (former enslaved person) Fred Lane performed the task, largely unknown to the small village, which experienced hard rain throughout the removal day. The bodies were placed overnight in the barn on the Swain premises in Chapel Hill, awaiting transport to Raleigh, where they would be reinterred in that city's Oakwood Cemetery. They remain there today with an impressive Scotch Granite monument adorning the site.[4]

Spencer hoped that with the passage of time Eleanor would change her mind and leave Swain's remains in Chapel Hill "where his life's work was done and where his best monument would be." It was she, not Eleanor, however, who experienced a mental shift. That there would be "no returning sense of gratitude or even decent remembrance and respect [for Swain]," she then told Eleanor, had become "too evident." "I am glad," Spencer thus regretfully concluded, that "you have taken him away."

When she considered how Swain had given his life to the university, however, the thoughts were "very, very bitter." "[S]urely the day will come," she predicted, "when his services will be rewarded in the outspoken love and gratitude of the whole State." She hoped to live to see that day. In the meantime, she continued to stop by the garden wall at the former Swain home "and look over at the spot where Anne and her father slept together."[5]

Estate

Swain left a will dated May 9, 1858. He bequeathed to each of his three children "a copy of the Holy Scriptures to be selected from my Library in the order of their names [oldest to youngest]." To Anne he gave "the Bureau known as hers," and to Richard the gold watch Swain had inherited from his friend Robert Vance. Eleanor ("Ellie"), at a suitable age, was to receive an article of furniture equal in value to Anne's bureau. Her mother was to make the selection. Anne's legacy lapsed with her death before Swain's.

The remainder of the estate was wife Eleanor's. As recited by Swain, it consisted principally of a riverside tract of land in Henderson County, North Carolina; a 320-acre tract in Whitfield County, Georgia; fifteen enslaved persons in the possession of Dr. J. S. Blakeman of Shelbyville, Tennessee; twenty enslaved persons in Swain's possession; twenty shares of stock in the Bank of the State of North Carolina; other stocks and life insurance; and debts owed to Swain in excess of $25,000.

Upon receipt of money due Swain from his brother-in-law William Coleman, Eleanor was to convey the enslaved persons in Swain's possession to Coleman's wife for her life, remainder to her children. By the time of Swain's death, these provisions had been rendered nugatory by the Emancipation Proclamation and Amendment XIII to the U.S. Constitution.

Even in death Swain remained a supportive brother. If George's circumstances rendered it necessary, Eleanor was, from the assets of the estate, to provide him an annual stipend of $200. This, Swain posited, "will be a competent provision to enable him to adopt the mode of life most agreeable to him."[6]

It was not an idle provision. Soon after Swain's death his nephew-in-law, Dr. Crawford W. Long, contacted Judge Battle, executor of the Swain estate. George, Long said, was "quite an old man and so enfeebled in mind as to be unfit for business." In February 1861, while returning to Chapel Hill from the Confederation Congress in Montgomery, Swain had visited the Longs. He had then told Long he had made provision for George if George outlived him. Long himself at that time "had a good property of my own" and had thought he could support George if necessary. Long's property, however, had been in "Negroes" and bank stock, "all of which is lost." He thus needed to know: Had Swain made the provision for George of which he had spoken? This might well have changed, Long acknowledged, "as [Swain] no doubt suffered something from war, in his pecuniary condition."

For eight years after Swain's death Battle provided George with the designated level of support. At length he could advise Eleanor of George's demise, which, he said, "under the circumstance cannot be the subject of regret." The annuity from her husband, Battle further advised, had now ceased. Due to the "considerable expense" he had encountered for George, Long nevertheless requested further assistance. Battle appears to have ignored the request.[7]

Battle apparently administered the estate without the involvement of William A. Graham and Eleanor Swain, whom Swain also named as personal representatives. Nicholas Woodfin, who had read law under Swain and handled much of his business in Western North Carolina, soon informed Battle regarding Swain's interests there. A "great and good man has been called away," Woodfin noted, "and . . . his place will scarcely be filled." Samuel Phillips notified Battle of a situation in which Swain was surety for a debtor. His estate, Phillips said, would be liable for the debt. Swain himself, Phillips observed accurately, "no doubt owed very little."[8]

Eleanor's ambulations after Swain's death at times posed problems for Battle. Once he had taken money collected for her to her sisters' home in Raleigh, only to find that she had "gone with General Atkins." He would await her advice about how to handle the matter. It was undoubtedly painful, for both Battle and Eleanor, when he informed her of his inability to locate the deed under which Swain had acquired his plantation Babylon, a trip to which had led to Swain's fatal accident. A later sale of the plantation to "a trifling fellow," in Battle's view, ended happily, despite the fellow's failure to comply with his contract. A bid of $2,800 at a foreclosure sale meant that Eleanor suffered no loss by his failure to comply.⁹

Richard

In Swain's absence his family did not fare well. After Anne's 1867 death Richard Caswell Swain, "Bunky," was the oldest living Swain child. Late in the Civil War he had gone to Tennessee as a surgeon in his cousin's regiment of the North Carolina troops. When the Confederate Army fell back from Shelbyville, near which he had relatives on Eleanor's side of the family, he stayed in the area, marrying there for a second time. A post-surrender visit to Chapel Hill gave him "such cold comfort that he staid [sic] but a short time."¹⁰

In 1866, Richard migrated to Shannon, Illinois, near his sister Ellie's home in Freeport. He advertised his medical practice in Freeport papers: "R. C. Swain, M.D., Physician and Surgeon, Northey House, Shannon, Illinois." "My brother is poor," Ellie wrote Eleanor when Richard opened his practice, "[b]ut for the first time in his life a Man & worthy of every assistance & encouragement his friends can give." How successful his practice was cannot now be determined. His earlier pattern of financial irresponsibility, however, persisted. On one occasion Judge Battle wrote Eleanor, regretful that Richard had not applied funds she had given him to the payment of his debts.

Quite possibly, as a result of his experience as a Civil War surgeon, Richard suffered from what today would be diagnosed as posttraumatic stress disorder. He clearly could not function altogether independently. He once told Ellie that her marriage should be considered a blessing, for he would have been lost had he not come under General Atkins's care.¹¹

On January 29, 1872, at age thirty-four, Richard attempted to board a moving train in Shannon. He slipped, fell under the train, and was killed more or less instantly. By one account he lived for about twenty minutes. For some time, he had labored under a "painful illness," not identified (perhaps the PTSD), states one account, which had diminished his strength, leaving him "too weak to recover himself when he slipped." Richard left a wife and one child, a daughter named Lula.¹²

Now at Davidson College, Charles Phillips lamented to Eleanor this tragic loss of her only remaining son. Richard had been, said Phillips, "cut off from the land of the living, in the prime of his life." The obituary, Phillips said, told "some of the reasons why Richard's friends should mourn his untimely death." John Evans, a former Swain "servant" (enslaved person), was now living with Phillips. To Ev-

Richard C. "Bunky" Swain shortly after he opened his medical practice in Illinois.

ans it was "mighty true that the poor would miss Marse Richard." The Freeport paper wrote, similarly, that his many mourners would include "the poor and unfortunate, who were always certain of his generous sympathy, and frequently of his bounty."[13]

There is a modern-day sequel to Richard's story. He was buried in the Freeport City Cemetery. A 1932 cemetery census by the Freeport Chapter of the Daughters of the American Revolution revealed that his gravestone was in poor condition. Only the name and a portion of the description remained. By the early twenty-first century, the tombstone was missing altogether. Ellie Swain Atkins's great-great granddaughter, Suzy Barile, discovered this while doing research for a book on her ancestors. She notified the U.S. Veterans Administration, and in the late spring of 2011 a new marker was placed on the grave.[14]

Ellie

North Carolinians who hoped Ellie's marriage to the "Yankee" general "had turned out badly" were disappointed. The marriage lasted, and by all appearances was a happy one. While obituaries should be read with some skepticism, Ellie's was probably accurate in saying the bereaved husband had worshipped his wife.[15]

Their first child, a son, David Swain Atkins, named for Ellie's father, died on June 3, 1868, shortly before his grandfather Swain's death. Ellie wrote her parents of her "Desolate home" and of having nothing except "to sit and wait the coming of future events." Those events came, as she bore four more children: Eleanor Hope (Dot) in 1869, named for Ellie's mother; Smith Dykins (Dyke) in 1872; Richard, who died in infancy in 1874; and Susan Anne in 1877. In her will Eleanor Swain left to Dyke the sum due to David Swain from the University of North Carolina. Dyke died on October 27, 1885, long before the debt was settled, so he never received it.[16]

In the summers Ellie returned to North Carolina with the children to spend time with her widowed mother, now living with her sisters in the White family homeplace in Raleigh. In 1881, influenza visited the White household. Ellie nursed the stricken family members and assured the general that she and the children were well. She too was then stricken, however, and on June 13, 1881, at age thirty-eight, she died. Eleanor Swain, having now lost all her children, begged General Atkins not to return the grandchildren to Illinois with him. The general yielded to her importuning, and Dot, Dyke, and Susie remained with their grandmother in North Carolina through the fall and winter of 1881.[17]

Smith Atkins survived his wife by almost thirty-two years, dying in Freeport, Illinois on March 27, 1913. A leading citizen and an active civic leader, he was the Freeport postmaster, first appointed by Lincoln and last appointed by Taft. He served in the position consistently except for the two Democratic administrations of Grover Cleveland. A piano in his house at his death was "an heirloom picked out for Governor Swain in 1833 by George Bancroft, the historian."[18]

In 1993 when UNC celebrated its bicentennial, the Swain-Atkins alliance was remembered. A musical revue written for the occasion closed with a "Ballad of Ellie Swain" that recounted the fated love affair.[19]

Eleanor

David Swain's widow Eleanor met the saddest of fates. She outlived her entire immediate family, husband and children, and two of her grandchildren. She suffered intensely from the experience. Penning pitiful musings about her lost descendants occupied some of her declining years.

Her most poignant reflections related to son David, who had died "in the 6th year of his age." "His days were few but lovely, and full of promise," she wrote on the thirty-second anniversary of his death. These words still rest on his grave marker in Raleigh's Oakwood Cemetery. "[M]y smart, my noble, my beautiful boy—since thy pure spirit returned to God who gave it," Eleanor moaned, "and where Oh! where! is the mother you loved, . . . [t]he Mother who bore you to this world of suffering?" "Suffering still on the shores of time," she lamented, "stripped of every earthly attraction." "Oh how I long to go," she cried, to join "dear David," her father, her husband, "dear dear Anne," "dear Bunky," "my little babies three." David's "presence while passing through the agency of dying," Eleanor said, "is lived over again." "Alone alone," she was, "of the family circle that gathered around that couch of death."[20]

On the thirty-fifth anniversary of David's death, October 15, 1875, from Freeport, Illinois, Eleanor again wrote agonizing reflections about him. David's "bro Bunk," his "little play-mate," was now with him in spirit, while his body was "here [Illinois] surrounded by strangers." A grandson, Richard Swain Atkins, had recently joined them, "so lately fled," Eleanor wrote, "that the perfume of his precious mouth still lingers with us, and our love for this most lovely babe lives fresh in our hearts . . . still bleeding for the loss of him!" Passage of the years had not dimmed her memory of "[t]he scene around [David's] departure." The hope of reunion lingered as her years declined.[21]

There was one further Eleanor Swain memorial "[t]o my darling little David Swain." She had been forty years old when he had left her. In another six months she would have lived twice that long. Soon her "weary feet," too, "must cross the cold river of death." Then she would meet her "darling boy." "Oh God grant it is my prayer!" she concluded, signing as "Your Mother."[22]

Almost a year later, the first anniversary of the passing of grandson Richard Swain Atkins brought Eleanor back to her writing desk. Like little David Swain, Richard had gone to heaven while a "precious babe." "When those heavenly eyes pulled upward," Eleanor wrote, "I felt all the glory of this world as having vanished in view of this *one immortal* soul." "Then," she said, "his drooping lids closed forever. Oh lovely sweetest babe."[23]

On the fifth anniversary of Richard Swain's tragic death, Eleanor again inscribed a mournful dirge. That "fatal day" had seen his "precious life . . . mashed out under the weight of two heavy Rail R Carrs [sic]." She was "waiting and hoping to find you again," she said, addressing herself to Richard, "in a reunion with your Father and all our children and dear relatives and friends who have gone before." The reunion would be "[i]n the land of life and happiness eternal beyond this vale of suffering and separation." "Oh Father above grant it" was her fervent prayer.[24]

Following her husband's displacement at the university and his sudden demise in its wake, Chapel Hill held no charm for Eleanor Swain. She soon returned to her family home in Raleigh to live with her sisters, interrupted by extended stays with Ellie and her family in Illinois.[25]

Throughout Eleanor's widowhood Cornelia Phillips Spencer was her faithful correspondent. Spring 1869 found Spencer apologetic for not having written in a long time. She had "not had the heart to," she pleaded in mitigation, because all was "so sad around Chapel Hill" and all were "in such a constant state of exasperation and gloom." She had not wanted to inflict Eleanor with this ambiance. Everything was now beautiful, though, as the oaks formed new leaves "as if unmindful of their old friends who have been cut down"—an allusion to the cutting of trees in Chapel Hill by the new UNC regime, which Spencer deplored.[26]

The first anniversary of Swain's accident made Spencer think of Eleanor, who would be "living over again the events of last summer." How fortunate she was to have known, and believed in, "[d]ear and honored" Governor Swain. "[A]ssurance of his eternal safety—his never-ending happiness" assuaged seasonal "bitter remembrances."[27]

As the second anniversary of Swain's death approached Spencer's mind again turned toward Eleanor. Every day of the season, she sympathized, "recalling the last hours of a life so precious to you," must inevitably renew her "desolation." What sighs he would heave, she speculated, but with reason, if he could now see "an Institution so degraded as this [UNC] has been." It was now her chief object in life to see the place "restored in triumph . . . to hear due honor paid to Gov. Swain's memory and justice done to his life-long services—and those of his colleagues, and to be assured that time can never dim or tarnish his reputation, but will only add to the grateful affection with which his native state remembers him."[28]

Richard's death again moved Spencer to an outpouring of sympathy for Eleanor. Spencer had thought Eleanor would soon bring Richard's remains to Raleigh, but, she supposed, "the severe weather still detains you in Illinois." She was glad Eleanor had been in Illinois with Ellie at the time. Spencer was curious, though, to know more about Richard's last days and the illness which, it seemed, was indirectly the cause of his death.

A year after Richard's demise Spencer still thought of him. Many around Chapel Hill, she said, spoke of him with affection. One woman had said there was no one like Dr. Swain. Too, many there yet loved Anne. Spencer was distributing money Eleanor had sent among some of her poor acquaintances in Chapel Hill, some of them former "servants" or enslaved persons.[29] This letter produced a rare response from Eleanor. She gratefully acknowledged Spencer's "faithful remembrance, as each annual season returns commemorative of my great bereavements." Based on Spencer's communications, Eleanor feared that "[p]oor Chapel Hill... has gone irrecoverably." There were still poignant moments for her, however. Anne had now been gone six years, but Eleanor had recently received a letter to her from a woman in an insane asylum in Connecticut.[30]

On the eighth anniversary of Swain's accident, August 11, 1876, Spencer noted the commencement of a sixteen-day anniversary period in Eleanor's mind, as she relived the days between the mishap and Swain's passing. Swain's name was yet often mentioned by his friends. The new UNC president, Kemp Battle, was saying he wished "to run this college as the Gov. did —with the same aims and success." "Yes, Gov. Swain's name is still a household word in Chapel Hill," Spencer concluded, "and I think remembered more affectionately and with truer appreciation as time rolls on." There had been many improvements to the Swain house, and Spencer wished Eleanor could see it. Spencer's brother Charles Phillips had returned to the university and was now living there. He did not like it, however, because the memories "oppressed him dreadfully."[31]

Spencer fretted over Eleanor's extended stays in Illinois. She did not like the thought that Eleanor might end her days and take the "long last sleep" there, "where North Carolina turf cannot lie over you and your own native soil enfold you." With a son and grandchildren buried in Illinois soil, a willingness to lie there would be understandable. Still, Eleanor belonged, Spencer thought, by the side of her husband. "I feel he would have wished it," she said.[32]

Upon receipt of another rare missive from Eleanor, Spencer expressed both delight and concern that Eleanor had become "indifferent to your old friends hereabouts." She again paid Eleanor's late husband a compliment. "Bro C [Charles]," Spencer said, "so often begins a chat with—'Gov. Swain used to say.'" Judge Battle was contemplating a return to Chapel Hill and the reopening of his law school. It would be sad for him, Spencer opined, because he would "miss all that formerly made Chapel Hill." "Without Gov. Swain," she said, "it can never be what it once was to the Gov.'s old friends."[33]

Like her extended visits to Illinois, Eleanor's fixed intent never to return to Chapel Hill bothered Spencer. Eleanor, Spencer was persuaded, "would not like to meet those who have gone before—on the shining shore, and tell them you have never revisited your and their old home since that awful day when I saw you getting into your carriage in the grove—with no friend to accompany you on that long and distant ride to R[aleigh]." A later letter from Eleanor was "welcome as being from you" but "did not bring a welcome announcement in telling me of your determination never to see C. H. again." "I had not thought it was so settled and *final*," Spencer told her long-absent friend.[34]

Ellie's death in June 1881 brought keen sympathy from Spencer to her "much afflicted friend." Why God had "chosen to bereave you of *all* in your old age" was a mystery to Spencer. "Now you sit a *childless* widow," she said. Spencer's "heart melt[ed]" when she thought of Ellie; she had loved both Ellie and Anne. She requested a keepsake for each of them. Spencer's brother Charles Phillips also assured Eleanor of his sympathy at a time when her "earthly supports are fewer than ever."[35]

Eleanor's "earthly supports" were diminishing in ways other than loss of her descendants. In fall 1882 her sisters, Emma and Susan White, died. In both instances, Spencer was again a sympathetic friend. She noted particularly the high esteem Governor Swain had had for Susan's "sense, integrity and *insight*." She was glad Eleanor had her grandchildren to comfort her.[36]

There was another casualty. Never a faithful correspondent, Eleanor now apparently ceased altogether to respond to Spencer's letters. Spencer did not let this deter her own missives to Eleanor, however. If Eleanor reached heaven's gates before Spencer did, she was directed to "tell *the Governor* that of all his and your old Chapel Hill neighbors *Cornelia* most faithfully remembered you both." She reported lifting a glass of wine with her brother Sam "to our old friends memory" on Swain's eighty-first birthday, January 4, 1882. They recalled "the traits of character that endeared him to those who knew him and that make his memory pleasant now."[37]

In 1882, Eleanor experienced the last August of her life. Spencer, her faithful correspondent, was again retrospective. "When August comes," she assured her now unresponsive friend, "I always think more than usual of you." "On the 27th," she said, "he left these scenes of his labors on earth for higher employments and pleasures." On "the 27th" she noted that Swain's departure had been "to-day fourteen years ago." "How vividly it all comes back as I think of it," she told the still-grieving widow.[38]

Former Swain enslaved person Wilson Swain Caldwell had been one of the bearers of his former master's stretcher through the campus on that fateful August 27. As noted, his father had been President Joseph Caldwell's enslaved person, and following emancipation he chose to bear his father's last name, with Swain as a middle name. Caldwell remained a university servant after the Civil War. He once complained that he had received "nary cent" for his work. As Swain lay dying, Professor Manuel Fetter wrote to the superintendent of public works on Caldwell's behalf. In his employment for the past eleven years Caldwell had cared for the university buildings and grounds and had waited on its students. Always, said Fetter, Caldwell had "been *faithful, honest,* and *attentive* to his duties." Fetter vouched for Caldwell's bill and hoped it would be paid.[39]

When the university reopened in 1875 following a four-year closure, Spencer advised Eleanor that Caldwell was again among the college servants. He was, Kemp Battle has said, "an exceedingly intelligent, courteous, faithful man, reliable always, and had the unbounded regard and confidence of the Faculty and students."[40] Following Wilson Caldwell's death in 1898, UNC students erected a monument in his honor. When the original Joseph Caldwell monument on the UNC campus was replaced with a marble monument on McCorkle Place, students placed the former Caldwell monument in the African American section of the old Chapel Hill Cemetery. They engraved on it an epitaph for Wilson Swain Caldwell, their "friend and servant, . . . ever respectful . . . [and] always respected." "Let him rest here till he's ready for work again," they wrote. The monument and its inscription still stand.[41] In 2014, David Caldwell, Wilson's great-grandson, conducted a credible, but ultimately unsuccessful, campaign for the office of sheriff of Orange County, North Carolina.[42]

Eleanor's later years brought news, usually sad, of other former Swain enslaved persons. "Your old servant Louisa is passing slowly away," Spencer once informed her. Eleanor sent money to the dying Louisa, a "bounty," which Spencer hastened to deliver. She soon advised Eleanor of Louisa's passing, noting "how much Anne would have felt her death." "How sad it is," Eleanor now bemoaned to Ellie, "to think of that *high* family of Blacks Wils and John are all that is left."[43]

Spencer's sister-in-law Laura Phillips posted Eleanor on the problems and desires of another former enslaved person. "[O]ld Aunt Milly Walker," Phillips said, was "laid up with Dropsy." She longed to see Eleanor once more but did not think she would "live to see her again." She would be much obliged if Mrs. Swain could spare her some money. "Miss Laura, please mam," said Milly, "write as affectionate as you can—for I think a heap of Miss [*sic*] Swain." No response from Eleanor has been found, but she at times sent Spencer money to be distributed to some of her poor acquaintances in Chapel Hill, probably mostly former servants or enslaved persons.[44]

After Swain's death Judge Battle continued to handle Eleanor's business and legal matters. When he contemplated a return to Chapel Hill from Raleigh, again to teach law, he offered to continue or resign. There is no indication that Eleanor released him from his responsibilities to her.[45]

On February 5, 1883, after a brief illness, Eleanor Swain died at her Raleigh residence. To her friends, and perhaps to herself, Cornelia Spencer speculated, her death was sudden and unexpected. Shortly before Eleanor's passing, Spencer's daughter June had visited her and had found her "well and bright." The loss was, Spencer told June, "a real pain and grief to me." The White family home at the corner of Morgan and Blount Streets in Raleigh, Eleanor's primary residence since shortly after her husband's passing, was the scene of her funeral on the day after her death.[46]

Eleanor's will largely divided her estate among her grandchildren—Ellie's Dot, Dyke, and Susan, and Richard's Lula. Lifetime support was provided for her sister Felton. Household goods were to be divided between the grandchildren and her sister Felton. Some such items went to former "servants." Books and other items "not especially named" could be "given or sold." There was to be a memorial stone to Richard, buried in Freeport, Illinois, at the Swain family plot in Raleigh's Oakwood Cemetery. Walter Clark, who had married Governor and Mrs. Graham's daughter, and Richard Battle, Judge Battle's son, were designated as "trustees" of the will.[47]

On Christmas Day 1886, fire destroyed the university-owned home the Swains had occupied in Chapel Hill. The event would have deeply grieved Eleanor, her bitter breakup with Chapel Hill following Swain's death notwithstanding.[48] In 2014, she would have been equally interested, probably fascinated, when archeological digs uncovered artifacts from the site, some no doubt left by her family. Construction on then UNC President Tom Ross's driveway uncovered remnants of this nineteenth-century home of the university's earliest presidents.[49]

History

In one respect Eleanor did not serve her husband's legacy well. The fault is not entirely hers, however. Swain himself must share in the blame. At Swain's death his labors for history received accolades equal to, perhaps even surpassing, those commemorating his contributions to education. University trustees resolved "that the University of North Carolina, and the cause of education generally, *and its historical literature especially*, have sustained in his death an irreparable loss." "[H]is labors in exploring the sources and preserving the materials of [the state's] history," they later said, "were zealous and unremitting." The Historical Society was still more effusive. It had lost "its Founder, its first and only President, and its most useful member." It "would commemorate his love for his native state, his indefatigable zeal in collecting the memorials of its history—his minute, extensive, and most accurate knowledge of men and events connected with it, and his unfailing readiness to communicate to all inquirers his ample store of information—which make his loss not only sorrowful but irreparable."[50]

For all his care and diligence in collecting these materials, however, Swain failed to provide for their disposition upon his demise. Surprisingly, given its importance to him, on this subject his will was silent. In the absence of a stipulation on his part, Eleanor ultimately left the collection with Richard Battle and Walter Clark, as executors of her estate, "to dispose of by a sale, or a gift, as they believe to be best, to ensure a fulfillment of the work to the state of North Carolina." She did this, however, only after a long period of resistance to efforts to secure and preserve the collection for public purposes, and only after some of the documents were scattered to other venues and lost to the state of North Carolina, almost certainly forever.[51]

In October 1872, Judge Battle informed Eleanor that he would send her "a paper which you may execute as your will." He had consulted Governor Graham and others "about the bequest of the Historical papers." The document he had prepared "expressed the substance of their opinions."[52] Eleanor's response reflected her uncertainty and insecurity in the matter. She was, she said, very ignorant of the course she should pursue. She knew only that "[t]o preserve the value of the work," she "must not permit the removal, or use made, of any important paper among the collection." In her will, Eleanor stated, she had bequeathed the materials to the state or the university. She now added a proviso, however: her daughter Ellie must acquiesce in the gift, or withhold it for her own pleasure, "as no better memento of her dear father could exist." This should be "put in more formal shape," Battle responded, "to make it operate as a codicil to your will."[53]

As she had requested, friends, quite "interested and competent," soon came forward. In spring 1875, the General Assembly chartered the Historical Society of North Carolina, a revival of the old society. Among its first proceedings was a directive to Governors Graham and Vance, and Mrs. Cornelia P. Spencer. They were to correspond with Eleanor for the purpose of establishing the society as the "appropriate repository" for Governor Swain's collection of North Carolina history materials. Graham requested that Spencer "write at once to Mrs. Swain" to convey the society's request. Graham had no doubt that Spencer would "be highly influential in effecting a successful result."[54]

Subsequent events proved Graham overly sanguine. Spencer immediately wrote Eleanor a beseeching letter. She recognized the magnitude of the society's request. "It seems to me the Historical Society is very coolly asking you to make them a very valuable present," she said, "[y]et . . . I suppose it has always been your intention to let the State possess this material for History." It would be "a noble surrender" on Eleanor's part, Spencer told her, but "highly appreciated." There was no more appropriate way to "link [Swain's] name permanently with that of North Carolina" or to "bestow a more solid benefit upon your fellow citizens."

A "P. S." states that Spencer originally had thought she was asking Eleanor "to bestow private property on the Society." Subsequent conversations with Judge Battle and others suggested that she was mistaken. It was their view that Swain never considered the papers he had collected "with such zeal and diligence" private property. Why Judge Battle had never told Eleanor this was a mystery to Spencer. The gentlemen who had given Spencer this information were, Spencer informed Eleanor, prepared "to *prove*" that Swain never considered the property his "except in *trust*."[55]

Eleanor's response was cryptic and cool, notwithstanding that the plea came from three of her closest friends. She must, she said, decline the request, "at present at least." The materials, she assured them, would "be carefully preserved, and disposition will be made of them in the future as will in my judgment the most nearly comply with the intentions and desires of my late husband." The chilly nature of her reply did not preclude Eleanor's "highest esteem for the members of the Committee individually and as a Committee."[56]

Eleanor was mistaken, in Graham's view, in thinking Swain had considered the historical material "which he was so curious in collecting and which was so freely yielded to him, as individual property." He knew of no recourse, however, but to report the exchange with Eleanor to the society for its further consideration.[57]

A few weeks later Spencer made a second effort. She reminded Eleanor of her previous request and the negative response. Now, she said, donors of the papers were moving to reclaim them on grounds that they were donated to the society, not to Governor Swain. "What will you do about it [?]" she asked. Spencer enclosed Graham's reply to Eleanor's former refusal. Other prominent men held his opinion: the papers were never intended to be private property, and Governor Swain "so understood it all." Eleanor should consult Judge Battle "and take his opinion." There was misunderstanding, and likely to be misrepresentations, about the matter. The Historical Society had no papers other than Governor Swain's, "and has not them if you say no."[58]

This time Eleanor's response was more elaborate but equally frigid. She found it strange that seven years after her husband's death anyone should question his right "to the historical collection which he had been so curious in obtaining." If the contributors wanted the papers back, that was fine; she had "no disposition to withhold them." "But the demand," she continued, "is for the *whole*, as property belonging to the State."

Her friends' treatment of the subject irritated her. Graham had had frequent opportunities to give her his thoughts "but took no real interest in the matter." Spencer had acknowledged that the society was "very cooly" asking her "to make them a very valuable present." If Battle considered the collection state property, he should have so reminded her when she was disposing of it otherwise in her will. She had had opportunities to dispose of some of it and felt "fully privileged" to do so. She had not, however, "knowing it was a work of so much pleasure and value to him [Swain], and there might be derived something from it, of profit to his children."

Eleanor was now feeling "very much like one groping in the dark without a leader." Ellie had grown "indignant at the proceeding" and had "no thought of letting this favorite work of her father slip from her so easily." Ellie's interest was now greater than her mother's, so Spencer should direct further correspondence to her.[59]

As late as six months before Eleanor's death, Spencer was begging her not to give away or burn "the letters and papers we were talking about." "You don't know," she said, "how I long to get my hands on them." With the Swain papers not under the Historical Society's control, she was writing letters to editors lamenting the society's lack of acquisitions.[60]

The society thus did not get the papers during Eleanor's lifetime. Her executors, given a choice between the state and the university as a repository, opted for the university. A large portion of the collection thus was preserved, and it is a valuable portion of the university's archival materials. As Kemp Battle notes, however, "There are lamentable gaps in it." Some of the papers were lost. Eleanor sold or gave away some, as did her executors. Some have disappeared. What remained for the Historical Society, and thus the university, was "only a part of the papers." Some almost certainly remain in private hands. H. G. Jones has made the most thorough study of the subject to date. He concluded that the location of all of the papers Swain collected cannot be determined. It is a virtual certainty that this will never change. Accordingly, the Swain legacy in this area, while perhaps unsurpassed by that of any other North Carolinian, is inevitably somewhat diminished.[61]

There were other losses to history, both shortly before and after Swain's death. In the year of his passing a New Bern correspondent, from whom Swain had solicited historical materials, advised him they were no longer available. His father had possessed many papers and manuscripts and had written an essay or two "bearing upon the scenes and occurrences of the 'olden times.'" These, however, had "fallen prey to the 'Trophy finders' of the U.S. Army, or been swept away by some unlettered hand, as the worthless rubbish of a rebel's house."[62]

Two months before his accident Swain had noted to Governor Holden that the Civil War had "greatly impeded but did not entirely suspend [his] researches" as the state's historical agent. When convenient for them, he would submit the result to the governor or to a committee of the General Assembly. The report was never made, and the agency terminated with his death. Among the matters he probably would have reported were: that "the outbreak of our unhappy and ill advised civil war" had frustrated his plans "to go abroad in the prosecution of [his] research"; and his plans, if the governor failed to do it, to attempt "to secure the return of Governor V[ance]'s Letter Books and other records, ... among them Gov. Tryon's Letter Book, Council Journal, etc." He never stopped thinking about historical acquisitions for the State, and only death stopped his efforts to pursue them.[63]

"And what a mine of North Carolina History is now forever lost in him!" lamented a posthumous letter to the *North Carolina Presbyterian*. He had "left many things unfinished," said a later issue, "which none but he could have done, and which we fear must now be left forever undone." Having just acquired a satisfactory understanding of some aspects of the state's history, he had at last felt himself qualified to write it. But whom had he left to do it? The question went unanswered.[64]

Former UNC Professor A. D. Hepburn, sickened by the changes that had occurred in Chapel Hill, desired a memorial volume on the university's history, with biographies of its early faculty. Such a work had been expected from Swain, Hepburn said, and presumably he had collected much of the needed material. The reminiscences that could only be gathered from old graduates, however, an ideal task for Swain, he now feared would be lost. They were.[65]

Spencer noted, after Swain's death, his loan of an "invaluable" book on the history of the university, "as collected by himself—a collection of facts—newspaper articles etc. etc." The "new owners" of the university were "exceedingly anxious to get hold of all such things," she told Eleanor, as she requested permission to recover it for forwarding to her. Its fate, however, is unknown.[66]

Despite all her efforts at recovering and preserving aspects of the Swain collection, Spencer herself contributed to the losses. In 1903, she wrote a friend that her accumulation of old letters distressed her. She had bundles of them, including some from Swain. "Yes," she said, "these would all be read in 2000, but I cannot wait." She had, instead, "burned cart-loads" of them. What a loss to history.[67]

Losses notwithstanding, long after his death Swain's materials were in use or sought after. The historian Lyman Draper once wrote Graham regarding a William R. Davie manuscript he thought to be among Swain's papers. "Mrs. Gov. Swain" had given Judge Battle permission to loan Draper the manuscript or to cause a transcript to be made for him. If Governor Swain had papers bearing on General Sumter, Graham should so inform Draper. Graham had the manuscript; he "had borrowed it from Gov. Swain in his lifetime."[68]

Judge Ruffin, too, had historical materials borrowed from Swain. He had last seen Swain at the June 1868 university commencement. "[A]s was his custom," Swain had then "discoursed a good deal upon the historical incidents and documents of the Revolution of '76." Ruffin had borrowed an imprint Swain had then mentioned. He now returned it to Judge Battle, executor of the Swain estate, "regretting most deeply that it goes back to his representative, instead of himself."[69]

The University

Swain's university, too, did not fare well in his absence. In what would have been the fall session 1868, it did not function. It reopened in January 1869 with, reportedly, a single student "from abroad." According to one account, that student soon disappeared. By another, a second student joined him, but upon grasping the situation, left after three days.

Dependent on the university, the town was so poor its citizens lacked funds with which to pay their local taxes. The university's new president soon stated the obvious to its alumni and friends. "[T]he present unfortunate condition of the University," he said, "has resulted from its financial embarrassment." Ultimately it was all too much, and the university closed for four years. A departing student wrote in chalk in one of the recitation rooms, "This old university has busted and gone to hell today."[70]

In January 1869, the university trustees had elected a new president, the Reverend Solomon Pool. Pool suffered when compared to his predecessors. "Drop him into the boots of Dr. Caldwell or of Gov. Swain," said Cornelia Spencer, and "he may peep over the tops, but he can only stumble about in it." Pool himself recognized his problem. "I was aware," he later told the university's alumni and friends, "that my predecessor had been a gentleman of rare talents and long experience, and that his place would be difficult to fill. I foresaw that every act of mine would be the subject of keen criticism, and dreaded to undertake the performance of a task so hazardous."[71]

Spencer never had a kind word for Pool. Her letters to Eleanor through the Pool years, including those in which the university was closed, were disparaging in the extreme. Pool's denomination, the Methodists, had snubbed him so severely, Spencer said, that he was about to turn Presbyterian. She recognized that she was violating the biblical proscription against judging others. "I do find it very hard to be a Christian in Chapel Hill these days," she confessed. Less charitably still, she reported seeing the president one morning "looking more sleepy and dull and solemn than usual." "He always reminds me," she continued, "of a large tom-cat."[72]

"You have no idea of the degradation," Spencer told Eleanor while the university was closed. She had walked over its buildings and grounds and had found valuable articles exposed to pillage, "doors and windows *all open*." She had picked up a letter from twenty years ago addressed to Governor Swain and introducing a new student to him. A visit to the Phi Hall revealed the tragic loss of Swain-collected historical artifacts. He had gathered and preserved Confederate relics, perhaps the only such collection in the state, one of incalculable future value. These, though, were "now all gone."[73]

Spencer was not alone in mourning loss of the old and decrying the new. A North Carolina native who had lived in Alabama for thirty-six years wrote her of "his veneration for the men who made the university what it was." He enclosed a large gold ring with an inside engraving, "In memory of the University of North Carolina *as it was* —Caldwell, Swain, Phillips, Mitchell, Hooper." Zebulon Vance wondered how Spencer managed yet to live in Chapel Hill. "Alas. alas.," he wrote, "your own pleasant village is broken up and destroyed indeed." "How I miss my dear friend Gov. Swain," he moaned.[74] A former Swain pupil appreciated a newspaper's "timely, manly and triumphant vindication of the memory and character of Gov. Swain."[75]

As to Swain's successor, even Spencer's comments were mild compared to those of former UNC faculty member Fordyce M. Hubbard. Supportive of Spencer's efforts to keep the university's condition before the public, Hubbard especially implored her to attack Pool relentlessly. "Most of all," he said "hit *him* who had the impudent self conceit to imagine himself fit to stand in the place of Gov. Swain." "I have no patience with the scamp," Hubbard continued: "He has no scholarship, no discipline, no power to control young men, no love of truth, a mean, malignant, revengeful, unscrupulous, false-hearted scoundral [*sic*]. I have no wish ever to see him again."[76]

The university's reopening in 1875 marked the end of the brief Pool era. Many tears were shed at the reopening ceremony. "The tears," Spencer informed Eleanor, "rolled down Gov. Vance's cheeks." A portrait of Swain was prominently displayed. "It looked better than I ever saw it," Spencer said, "and many said, seemed as if it would speak." The portrait "seemed to look down approvingly" as Judge Battle and Charles Phillips offered laudatory remarks about its subject. A proper order had been restored, and in a few years, Spencer could inform Eleanor that the university's prospects were "very good" as students and faculty were "coming in rapidly."77

Memorials and Remembrances

With improved prospects, the university began to consider an appropriate memorial to its late president. At the June 1883 commencement the trustees requested appointment of a committee from the alumni "to solicit contributions to a fund to provide a monument similar to that erected to Dr. Caldwell to be placed near it, to commemorate [Swain's] services." For thirty-three years, the trustees said, Swain had "directed the interests and affairs of this institution with such conspicuous and marked ability." Absence of a monument was not occasioned by lack of gratitude "or of full recognition of his services," but by "the embarrassed financial condition of the alumni" and other, more pressing demands on the Alumni Association. In a slap at the recently departed Reconstruction-era regime, one other excuse for the neglect was recited: "above all, to the transfer of the property for ten years to unknown men."78

The thought soon emerged that construction of a large hall for commencement and other public occasions would be "a better use of money" devoted to the memory of a man "so practical and averse to waste in idle show." A memorial chapel would "embalm [Swain's] memory, and keep it alive as long as the University of North Carolina remains." Contributions beyond those from alumni should be sought; Western North Carolinians in particular should delight in contributing to a memorial for one who, as a native son, "reflected so much honor on them." If they were solicited, said an Asheville paper, "there is not an individual who would deny his portion."79

It was a Pollyannaish view of the requisite fundraising. A committee of the Alumni Association sent a circular letter to the membership seeking "material aid" in the erection of a building to be called "Swain Memorial Hall." Some letters were returned noting the death of the intended recipient. Some recipients pleaded inability to pay. One alumnus found it very painful to be denied by his financial circumstances "an alumnus' and old pupil's part in commemorating in this most suitable way the worth and high esteem in which the noble old President was held by us all." Perhaps before the work was underway, he could "add my mite." Another was "little able to do any contributing to any Memorial Halls." If able, he "would do so readily and cheerfully," for his "regard, respect and reverence for Gov. Swain was very great." Still another was prevented from assisting by a desire for a home for disabled Confederate soldiers, to which he was devoting his leisure time and spare money. He too said, in effect, "maybe later."[80]

The most poignant appeal was from Cornelia Spencer to Eleanor Swain, written on the ninth anniversary of Swain's passing. She should "offer to have a fine steel engraving made from the fine portrait in your possession." The university, Spencer said, "is crippled and moving along on donations." "Can you not devote one or two hundred dollars to this object," Spencer asked, "to let the State have as elegant a reminder of *Gov. Swain* as the Graham family have given it of Gov. Graham? *Please do*." Eleanor's contribution would "be doing more to perpetuate his fame and his memory than has yet been done," Spencer claimed. She was "sure he would approve of such an appropriation." If Eleanor responded, the response has not been found.[81]

As fundraising efforts faltered and construction costs exceeded estimates, the potential honorees of the proposed edifice expanded. The trustees' secretary soon solicited names of UNC students who were killed or died "in the Confederate Service" for purposes of a tablet in their honor in Swain Hall. Ultimately the new president, Kemp Battle, conceived the idea of making the structure a more general memorial to Swain, those who had fallen in the service of the Confederate States, and "others connected with the university who by honorable living in civil or military service deserve commemoration." William L. Saunders, board secretary, proposed a compromise that was accepted: the name would be simply Memorial Hall, and a tablet honoring Swain would have the highest place and be inscribed with a summary of his distinguished career. Plaques honoring others would occupy other places surrounding it.

At the building's dedication on June 3, 1885, Governor Alfred Moore Scales "gave a most feeling and intelligent history of the services of President Swain." Later the original Memorial Hall had outlived its usefulness. In 1930 it was dismantled and a new edifice with the same name was erected in its place. The tablet honoring Swain remains in the new structure to the present. A plaque on the front exterior also recognizes his service to the university and the state.[82]

In 1913, the executive committee authorized construction of a new dining hall on the UNC campus. Completed in 1914 on the site of the first UNC president's house, it bore, and still does, the name "Swain Hall." Given its name and function,

Swain Hall on the UNC campus, completed 1914.

it was perhaps inevitable that the facility would come to be popularly known as "Swine Hall." Soon after construction of the facility, the future novelist Thomas Wolfe became one of its student patrons. He informed his brother that the food at Swain Hall "costs only $12.50 a month." With completion of Lenoir Hall in 1940, Swain Hall became an office building. It later housed the university's Department of Radio, Television, and Motion Pictures.[83]

The twenty-first century still sees university entities memorializing the Swain name. Today the Carolina Performing Arts Society serves as a support organization for the university's commitment to bring outstanding professional artists to perform and teach on the campus. When it recently established recognized levels of giving, donors of $10,000 or more annually were granted membership in the David Lowry Swain Society.[84]

For decades the university's North Carolina Collection, which Swain founded, displayed a portrait of him. The university's collection of portraits of its former presidents and chancellors contains another one of Swain. The walls of the Carolina Club in the George Watts Hill Alumni Center contain an etching of him.[85]

"He is not forgotten," Spencer told Eleanor in the first year following Swain's passing. For a long time, it was true. At the university's 1870 commencement, James F. Taylor gave an elaborate paper on Swain, Mitchell, and Phillips. In 1877, at the request of President Battle, seconded by Governor Vance, the executive committee established October 12 for perpetual observance of the laying of the cornerstone of Old East on that date in 1793. Vance paid tribute to Swain, and Swain's was among the portraits on the rostrum. At the 1886 commencement, a judge of the Supreme Court of New York, an 1864 UNC honor graduate, addressed the two societies. "His eulogy of President Swain," Battle's *History* states, "was particularly hearty and happy."[86]

In 1889, the UNC Class of 1868, the last to graduate under Swain's presidency, held a reunion. The class address recollected Swain's July 1865 boast to the students that during the four years of the Civil War, the old college bell had never ceased to toll the hours for prayers and recitations. The year 1889 was also that of the university's centennial celebration. The sixth toast was to "President David L. Swain and the Faculty and Trustees of His Administration." "As long as this University shall stand," it was then said, "President Swain will have a worthy monument, and as century after century shall move by . . . , may it be reared higher amidst the effulgent light of advancing knowledge and eternal truth."[87]

Swain was again mentioned at the 1895 commencement, and his portrait was displayed at that of 1897. The 1898 commencement included a ceremony for laying the cornerstone of Alumni Hall. Among the items included in it was a sketch of Swain.[88]

One matter between Swain, or his estate, and the university was slow to settle. At his death the university was indebted to him, both for uncompensated services and for money he had advanced to sustain it in straitened times. Even his successor Solomon Pool, not one of his greatest admirers, acknowledged in 1871 that the university's debt to Swain's estate was "entirely just and should be met." In 1874, Kemp Battle, state treasurer but soon to be president of the university, reported to the trustees on a note held by Mrs. Swain. The note was for $3,000 "for money lent to aid in building the New East and New West, and about $2,300 bonds issued to pay the Faculty." Professor Alexander McIver, Class of 1853, acknowledged the just nature of this debt and others but thought the holders would not hesitate to relinquish them if their payment would hinder the revival of the university.

In 1907, the debt remained unpaid. The amount due, with interest, had risen to $23,377.64. Beneficial title was in two surviving Swain granddaughters, with legal title in Walter Clark, now chief justice of the state supreme court, and Richard H. Battle, as executors under Eleanor Swain's will. The university was believed to have no income or property "not necessary to its use which can be applied to the settlement of the debt." In 1909, the General Assembly appropriated $3,500 "in full satisfaction and discharge of the debt."[89]

The university was not alone in memorializing the Swain name. In 1871, the General Assembly carved a new county from parts of Jackson and Macon. They named it "Swain." The act is silent as to the namesake, but without question it was named for David Lowry Swain. The recognition undoubtedly would have pleased him. Given his ardent commitment to education, however, a recent statistic regarding the county would have displeased him. In 2017 it was, and for several years had been, last among the state's one hundred counties in the amount of local money appropriated for education.[90]

In 1919, the Supreme Court of North Carolina celebrated its centennial. The principal speaker referred to "The vision of Archibald D. Murphey, the wisdom of Swain." This affirmative linkage of his name with Murphey's would have pleased Swain.[91] In 1938, the State of North Carolina placed a historical marker to Swain near his Buncombe County birthplace. The state's capital city of Raleigh has a Swain Street. The Governors Club, a late twentieth-century suburban development near Chapel Hill, also has a street named for Swain.[92]

Early in World War II, the North Carolina Shipbuilding Company at Wilmington constructed and delivered 126 Liberty Ships for war purposes. Each was named for a prominent figure in American history, especially the history of North Carolina and South Carolina. A ten thousand-ton Liberty Ship, completed in March 1943, was named the *SS David L. Swain*. It provided supplies for American forces that landed at Anzio, Italy, in January 1944.[93]

Parting Assessment

On the first anniversary of the accident that precipitated Swain's demise, Cornelia Phillips Spencer said of him, "That he erred sometimes—that his judgment was not infallible, nor he himself free from some weaknesses, it will be the duty of his biographer to point out." "[S]uch close criticism," she continued, "is one of the penalties which all men who stand on eminences must pay."[94]

The surviving historical record, and the commentary thereon, paint a largely favorable portrait of David Lowry Swain. His positive contributions, to his own time and well beyond, were manifold and superlative, even for a notable "eminence." Still, Spencer knew him as well as any contemporary did, and she was right. He was human, and his humanity embodied fallibility and flaws. Mindful throughout this endeavor of Spencer's imposition, when Swain's blemishes have surfaced, the present biographer has attempted to narrate them. As we conclude this consideration of a mostly well-lived life, a brief recapitulation of some of its less sterling aspects should satisfy Spencer's directive.

Immensely popular as a young man, even then Swain had detractors. He was at least viewed as vain and subject to flattery. William A. Blount, an Eastern member of the North Carolina House of Commons in Swain's time there, once said of him, "He is flattered with the attentions he has received and the favors that have been done him." James Graham, a congressman from Western North Carolina and brother of William A. Graham, spoke similarly. "[P]opular preferment," Graham said, "is the ruling passion of his soul." Support for a competitor for a U.S. Senate seat was all the stronger, in one view, "when David L. Swain is to be the man who is to supplant him."

Shortly after Swain's death, an offensive occurrence suggested that he was less than universally loved and respected. Cornelia Spencer sent to historian Benjamin Lossing a portrait of Swain "carefully enveloped in stiff newspaper." Upon receipt the package had been opened, presumably in the Chapel Hill Post Office, and the portrait badly torn. Lossing returned it a year later "in precisely the mutilated condition" in which he had received it. "[I]t would be a sin against the finest of human affections for such a man to have an enemy," a newspaper had said of Swain. Clearly, though, he had one, and even more.[95]

No active practitioner of the legal profession altogether escapes criticism. Little perceived negative from Swain's brief legal career survives, yet he cannot have been an exception. Foregoing commentary notes that as a young lawyer he was hypersensitive to reputational concerns; likewise, to criticism over legal fees the State had paid him.

Swain's tenure as a jurist was brief. It, too, left little in the way of critical appraisal. We have noted the objection that he was lenient to criminals, that he found appeals for mercy or tales of distress irresistible: a demurrer tempered, however, with the observation that this was hardly a damning criticism for one whose religious precepts taught that the merciful are themselves blessed and shall obtain mercy.

Modern-day appraisals would view critically aspects of Swain's legislative service that almost certainly pleased his white male, nineteenth-century constituency. He introduced a bill for a capitation tax on the migration of free persons of color into Buncombe County. He voted for a bill to prevent free persons of color from migrating into the state and to provide for "the good government of such persons already in residence." He voted for a bill to prohibit trading with enslaved persons except in a prescribed manner. He voted against a bill to emancipate certain named enslaved persons and one to regulate the emancipation of enslaved persons. He voted against a bill to place certain religious groups on an equal footing with other freemen of the state.

As North Carolina's chief executive, Swain supported the slavocracy with pronouncements that seem extreme even for his own time. The rights of the state's citizens to their enslaved persons, free from domestic aggression, he told the 1834 General Assembly, demanded protection. His last gubernatorial message to the legislature virulently attacked the fanaticism, in his view, of the abolitionists. The General Assembly had made publication of incendiary newspapers and pamphlets on abolition a felony. A first offense was punishable by fine, whipping, and the pillory; a second, by death. Dissatisfied with single-state imposition of such penalties, Swain urged the General Assembly to request that other states adopt similar measures to suppress these dangerous publications "totally and promptly." It was a matter of common safety, not subject to differences of opinion, and over which even the drastic choice of going to war might be in order.

While voiced in a public capacity, the pronouncements also upheld Swain's private interests. His status as a large enslaver, a source of stature and influence in his time, draws condemnation in ours. Swain's refusal to assist Chatham County enslaved person George Moses Horton with Northern contacts to further his literary ambitions was normative behavior in his time. One white man would rarely, if ever, have aided another white man's enslaved person in ways that might have resulted in the enslaved person's liberation. The conduct, however, offends modern sensibilities, from both humane and cultural standpoints. So, too, does Swain's apparently casual acceptance of his debtors' practice of selling their enslaved persons to pay his claims. His views on race and human bondage, traditional for a white, male member of the propertied class of his time, like his enslaver status, draw condemnation in ours.

Modern-day appraisals would also condemn Swain's strong support, as governor, for removal of the Cherokee Indians from their Western North Carolina lands. Likewise, in both his time and ours his failure to pardon Frankie Silver for the alleged murder of her apparently abusive husband has drawn criticism. During these censures, his generally liberal exercise of the pardoning power has been largely forgotten.

Abiding devotion to the preservation and perpetuation of history was a distinctive Swain hallmark. Even in this area, however, he could fall short. Friendship and self-interest could trump his usual penchant for accuracy. At best the factual foundation for naming North Carolina's highest peak for Elisha Mitchell was shaky. Swain's respect and affection for his old professor, later faculty colleague and friend, was such, however, that he knowingly and willingly (apparently) used questionable information to accomplish the designation. With the publication of Cornelia Spencer's *The Last Ninety Days*, he became a repeat offender. To vindicate his own, Zebulon Vance's, and William A. Graham's conduct in the closing days of the Civil War, he became a willing manipulator of history. Vance viewed this as unnecessary, and even Spencer, as uncritical an admirer as Swain had, saw him as unwilling "to state *the whole* truth."

For most of Swain's long tenure as president of the University of North Carolina, his administration was well regarded. With rare exceptions, the man himself was quite popular. Even then, however, student misconduct was a perpetual and serious problem. Rightly or wrongly, Swain's lax disciplinary style was blamed. Two faculty members, Henri Herrisse and John DeBerniere Hooper, resigned over these concerns. Too, even then there were occasional instances of overt student hostility toward Swain, and his pedagogical methods did not altogether escape criticism.

Antebellum UNC history strongly suggests that without the Civil War's intervention, the status quo there would have continued indefinitely. There was no compelling impetus toward major university reform. A crisis of confidence came, however, with the war-related exodus of students and the resulting loss of revenues. The crisis, in turn, evoked a critical examination, both internal and external, of the university's condition. Deficiencies, long present but long ignored, surfaced.

One critic overstated the problem. Under Governor Swain and his associates, he said, "the University was 'a nuisance,' 'a nursery for aristocrats,' 'a nest of rowdies,' 'no better than a bawdy house.'" Even Swain's friends found considerable fault, however. Kemp Battle and Charles Phillips led the academic-reform effort. Swain, Cornelia Spencer said, was "a man of the world" but "not a bookish man." "He lacked sympathy," Spencer said, "with scholarship per se, as a source of sweetness and light." Consequently, with one exception, the university remained at the Swain administration's end, as to numbers and value, "pretty much as [President Joseph Caldwell] had left it." The one exception was the acquisition of Professor Elisha Mitchell's library. Even antebellum, Professor Henri Herrisse had noted critically the failure to build the university library. For thirty years, Herrisse said, no books had been purchased, and the library was more appropriately called a "Ball room." Spencer also freely criticized Swain's "consulting too many interests and conciliating too many parties." He would, she said, hire "an inferior man" to appease concerns regarding relative representation of religious denominations on the faculty.[96]

Zeb Vance's 1877 University Day tribute to Swain drew one auditor who filed a partial dissenting opinion. Vance's highly positive assessment, the dissenter said, "does not receive the unanimous endorsement of all who knew [Swain]." By some, he continued, Swain was thought "to have been guilty of favoritism, to have lacked nerve for discipline, and to have shown too great partiality for families of wealth and influence."[97]

Kemp Battle was Swain's younger contemporary, his friend, and his eventual successor in the university presidency. His assessment, critical but also explanatory and somewhat exculpatory, is more balanced and merits quotation. "I think it cannot be denied," Battle wrote, "that according to modern standards he was lacking some essentials of a great College President." "He did not," Battle said,

> like Elliot [Charles Eliot, longtime Harvard president], direct the streams of public or private generosity to the University. [H]e bought no books, and provided no apparatus for scientific instruction. He seemed not to strive for the University's reputation in the literary and scientific world. In his carefully drawn ... resignation, ... he mentions nothing but the increase of numbers, of endowment by saving from income, and of buildings.
>
> What can be said in favor of his policy of increasing numbers and buildings? of granting diplomas without requiring proficiency in studies? Undoubtedly that he gave what the public demanded. The estimate of the success of the University was measured by numbers. Governor Swain's policy coincided with public opinion. The usual question about the success of the University was, "how many boys do you have?"

Swain's university, Battle continued, "admirably supplied the public demand of the South." It was a place for the preparation of professional men, "not ... scientific specialists, ... [or] scholars in history, literature or philosophy." While not proving great scholarship, the UNC diploma of Swain's time "yet was of great value." Above all, a Swain-era UNC diploma gave its holder "a preference for public life" and a thorough preparation for it.[98]

His nineteenth-century contemporaries would not have been critical of Swain's role in Benjamin Hedrick's removal from his UNC faculty position. We and our contemporaries would be. It was a flagrant denial of both First Amendment freedom-of-speech rights and academic freedom. In the 1850s, neither concept had implanted itself in serious fashion into the legal lore or the public consciousness. As legal historian Alfred L. Brophy has noted: "Tenure is a development of the twentieth century. Faculty members in the antebellum period were routinely fired for political reasons." On that account, and in the context of time and place, Hedrick's removal is altogether comprehensible. From a twenty-first century perspective, however, its omission from a recitation of Swain's perceived blemishes would leave a serious gap.[99]

Finally, as to his university service, he must share the blame for its unhappy ending. Early in his post-presidency period, Thomas Jefferson told his friend Benjamin Rush that "there is a fulness of time when men should go, & not occupy too long the ground to which others have a right to advance."[100] Lack of discernment as to when to "go" is a common human failure. Life is a process of giving up things, and wisdom consists of selecting the optimal times for the surrenders.

Like many others, Swain failed in this respect. He rationalized that his severely defective hearing made him a better teacher rather than a partially disabled one. True, he was in many respects a victim of circumstances beyond his control. A lifelong strength of character and competitive nature impelled him to strive to overcome them. Age, physical condition, and multiple strenuous post-war pressures provided excellent rationales for resigning with dignity, but he could not bring himself to do it.

A catalogue of Swain's faults, real or merely perceived, neither negates nor diminishes his many strengths and manifold accomplishments. Like all who attain high position, he had enemies and critics. They were dwarfed, however, by friends and admirers far more numerous. A small but representative sample of posthumous encomiums is illustrative:

> We shall not forget his ready sympathy with his neighbors, his many acts of kindness to those who were in doubt or in trouble, his unequalled sagacity as a counsellor, the affection and tolerance that marked his intercourse with men among us, his courteous manners and the thorough piety of his life.
> —Chapel Hill Village Commissioners

> He was one of the most eminent men of North Carolina, distinguished alike for his ability, erudition, and versatility of attainments.
> —*Daily Evening Telegraph*, Philadelphia

> A remarkable man. No son of the state was more jealous of her honor, more careful of her interests, more proud of her history, or so conversant with her annals. Few men in the Union were distinguished for greater and more useful versatility of attainments, more vigorous intellect, more lofty patriotism, and no man, anywhere, for more conspicuous probity of private and public character.
> —*The Episcopal Methodist*

> One of the great leaders who were chiefly responsible for the transformation of North Carolina from the unprogressive, if indeed not retrograding, state

of 1840 which lagged at the bottom in almost every list of the states, save in that of natural resources and opportunity, to the highly prosperous, genuinely progressive commonwealth of 1860.
—J. G. deRoulhac Hamilton

Perhaps no man has ever so entirely devoted his life to the advancement and vindication of North Carolina. No one ever so loved the state and people and understood them so well. To his tireless research and intelligent collection of detached facts, we owe much of what is known of the buried past. As a statesman, in the few years he devoted to political affairs, no man has surpassed him in the measure of his accomplishment.
—John W. Moore

The more I see of others who filled similar stations in life the more do I see how wise and good he was. His interest in his pupils I have never seen equaled. His contriving something better than what was then doing was unwearied and if not insisted on as often or as pertenaciously as others thought proper, it was because he exercised more foresight than others. Few men have ever had so few failures in such an active and prominent life as he led.
—Charles Phillips

No man had ever lived in North Carolina whose opportunities for ... influencing those who control her destinies have been greater than Governor Swain's were; and ... no man ever more diligently and earnestly improved those opportunities. [I]n many things he was entitled to be called great, if we mean by that term that he so used the faculties he possessed that he raised himself beyond and above the great mass of his fellows. In him there was a rounded fullness of qualities, intellectual and moral, which constitute the excellence of manhood.
—Zebulon Vance

Few men have lived in North Carolina who have made a deeper or more lasting impression on her history.
—John Hill Wheeler[101]

In his youth Swain told his father he wished neither to be a great man nor to be insignificant. "I have no disposition, if it were in my power, to become a great man," he said, "neither do I wish to move in the lowest station, and on this account I do not think I shall ever be very industrious or very idle."[102] Like beauty, greatness is in the eye of the beholder, and its assessment involves value judgments. Arguably Swain attained it; clearly, he avoided the obscurity and insignificance that results from "mov[ing] in the lowest station."

As a very young holder of public office, Swain bought into the Archibald Murphey program for lifting North Carolina out of its "Rip Van Winkle" status. Murphey was the visionary, but Swain was the pragmatist with the interpersonal skills essential to the implementation of Murphey's vision of progress for the state: economic development, largely through internal improvements, resulting in revenues sufficient to support universal public education. Throughout his life Swain was an active and vigorous promoter of both internal improvements and public education at all levels. Probably his foremost tangible achievement in internal improvements was the Buncombe Turnpike, which opened his native Western North Carolina to commerce with neighboring states. In the field of education, he not only led the state's public university for almost thirty-three years; the state also turned to him for a plan when the time for secondary public education arrived.

In a parting assessment of Swain's life and public service, his successful efforts for more equitable legislative representation for Western North Carolina merit mention. The discrimination against the western counties and their citizens was flagrant, and the West was verging on revolt. Swain led the reform forces in the 1835 Constitutional Convention. His efforts arguably kept the state together and certainly enabled its various sections to function as a unit more harmoniously. While from a twenty-first century perspective Swain gets critical reviews on issues of racial treatment and equity, it should be noted that these 1835 reforms that he championed diminished the influence of the Eastern North Carolina slaveocracy. His vote in that convention against eliminating the voting rights of persons then known as "free Negroes" also merits favorable mention, as do his frequent recommendations that his students read William Gaston's 1832 address to the Dialectic and Philanthropic Societies in which he called slavery the "worst evil that afflicts the South."[103]

Edmund Burke once said, "A disposition to preserve, and an ability to improve, taken together, would be my definition of a statesman."[104] Judged by Burke's criteria, David Swain was the consummate statesman. The foregoing commentary amply demonstrates his "ability to improve." Earlier pages of this narrative have detailed his "disposition to preserve." We have said that "[a]s governor his leadership in matters of history [was] uncommon and exemplary."

Lingering evidence of Swain's "disposition to preserve" is all around us, perhaps most notably in the North Carolina Collection of the University of North Carolina Library. Started by Swain in 1844, it is now the largest collection regarding a single state in the United States. The UNC Library's Southern Historical Collection, the North Carolina State Archives, and the state records published by William L. Saunders and Walter Clark bear multiple placements of his fingerprints.

He is rightly credited with having done perhaps more than any other antebellum citizen to stimulate interest in his state's literature and having gathered "one of the most interesting and valuable collections of manuscripts of North Carolina history in existence." His long and indefatigable labors in collecting these materials, Cornelia Spencer rightly said, are not among the least of the debts the state owes to him.[105]

Even after Swain's death, his history materials were considered important. In 1870, Zeb Vance sought a letter he had written. It had been in Governor Swain's possession, he told Cornelia Spencer, and perhaps Mrs. Swain had it. She did, Spencer secured it, and Vance granted permission to publish it. In 1873, Spencer noted how much it would "rejoice Gov. Swain's inmost heart" if he could know that inquirers from Wisconsin were requesting "stray numbers" of the *North Carolina University Magazine*, "that somebody was taking an interest in North Carolina history." Indeed, it would have. In 1907 William A. Graham Jr. admonished historian R. D. W. Connor to remember the letters to Swain in Spencer's *Last Ninety Days*.[106]

The end-of-tenure critique of Swain's UNC administration notwithstanding, the fact remains that in the antebellum period his leadership brought the university "to a place of prominence . . . attracting attention both North and South." It "became the leading college in the Southern States and approached a position of national significance." At the halfway point of Swain's presidency, William D. Moseley, one of the trustees who had selected him and who later was governor of Florida, wrote to Elisha Mitchell: "I see Gov. Swain is still at the head of the institution—much of its present reputation is owing no doubt to his great abilities and untiring energy, to say nothing of the high reputation of his associates. The last vote I ever gave as a member of the board of trustees, was *for him as President. I have seen no cause to regret that vote*, but much to approve it." As recently as following the October 12, 2012, death of longtime UNC President William C. Friday, an alumnus recognized Swain as one of the "giants" on whose shoulders Friday had stood.[107]

Although David Lowry Swain's large share of life narrowed somewhat toward its end, even then he remained, as since his youth, a vital and vibrant presence in his community, state, and nation. Arguably he was the most influential and consequential North Carolinian of the nineteenth century. Indisputably his name must appear prominently on any respectable short list from which that selection is made.

The foregoing inventory of his accomplishments should amply justify these admittedly bold claims. If perchance it falls somewhat short, one addition should fulfill that purpose.

Wendell Berry's poem, the first line of which is quoted above, continues as follows:

> There is a grave, too, in each survivor. By it, the dead one lives.
> He enters us, a broken blade, sharp, clear as a lens or mirror.[108]

"A teacher," Henry Adams said similarly, "affects eternity; he can never tell where his influence stops."[109]

Above all else, David Swain was a teacher. Over the course of a third of a century, the most talented young men in North Carolina, and many from beyond, were entrusted to his care and instruction. They acquired from him "a feel of political leadership, and interest in public leaders, in political trends in state and nation." He was "training the future statesmen, jurists and divines in our country," and "his pupils filled every possible position of honor, trust or profit."

Many prominent men credited him for their success in later life.[110] "[B]y precept and example during his long administration," an early twentieth-century commentator has observed, "he impressed himself upon the sons of North Carolina as no other man has ever done—an impression that is shown in our mature manhood of this day, and will be felt in North Carolina as long as time lasts." Swain himself had some sense of his lasting pedagogic influence. In his postbellum pardon petition he noted, with evident feeling and pride, his receipt of "gratifying assurances that [his lectures] were not without effect upon the subsequent course of life of some of his pupils."[111]

Swain thus lived on, in Wendell Berry's words, "a broken blade, sharp, clear as a lens or mirror" in hundreds of his "boys," and through them, in many others. His claim to a place of durable influence and consequence thus comes, not just from his own considerable accomplishments, but also from the achievements of the many whom he prepared for, and stimulated to, significant contributions to their communities, state, and nation.

Professor Charles Force Deems, for example, became a distinguished minister in New York. He listed Swain as one of the people who most influenced his life. Samuel F. Phillips, long the solicitor general of the United States, told Eleanor Swain some five years after Swain's passing: "Your honored and kind husband's intercourse with me lies like a long ray of sunshine upon my earlier life.... There would be little of me left if I were to subtract all I owe him."[112]

Of the many whom Swain mentored into, and in, roles of leadership, Zebulon Baird Vance likely owed him the most. Too, Vance probably, by his own contributions, gave the most back to his state and country. Of all Swain's pupils, Vance alone might begin to rival him for claim to the mantle of most influential and consequential. Vance's significant role, though, highlights the importance of Swain's. Without a David Swain, whether there would have been a Zebulon Vance, as a major public personage, is a legitimate question.

Vance himself was faithful in acknowledging, with proper gratitude, his immense debt to his benefactor and mentor. His 1877 UNC University Day tribute to Swain drew tears. "Many a handkerchief was pressed to eyes at his close," Cornelia Spencer told Eleanor Swain.[113] Vance there noted the impossibility of measuring the power "of the able and faithful teacher." All of Swain's influence, Vance said, "was exerted in behalf of good morals, good government, patriotism, and religion." No North Carolinian, he said, had possessed greater opportunities for controlling the state's destinies, and "no man ever more diligently and earnestly improved those opportunities." "[T]here are none," Vance continued, "whom as a whole we can contemplate with more interest, affection, and admiration; none whose work for North Carolina will prove to be more valuable, or more lasting, or more important to future generations."[114]

Modern critics often judge past actors, not by the moral calculus of their time, but by that of ours. In these pages they will find ample grounds to censure David Swain on such issues as slavery, race, freedom of speech, and academic freedom. Others, however, perceive wisdom in historian David M. Potter's admonition that "the supreme task of the historian, and the one of most superlative difficulty, is to see the past through the imperfect eyes of those who lived it."[115] They thus strive to evaluate figures from the past by accepting history on its own terms. They at least conscientiously attempt to understand and appreciate the world of the past as its inhabitants did, uninfluenced by how later generations might wish they had, or by moral and ethical perceptions that evolved long after the past actor's time. For those who appraise accordingly, if not for all, Vance's closing tribute to Swain remains a fitting one: "The soil of our State holds the dust of no son who loved her more or served her better."[116]

NOTES

Abbreviations

Minutes

BOTM Board of Trustees Minutes, University of North Carolina, Chapel Hill, North Carolina, SHC, UNC
ECM   Executive Committee Minutes, Board of Trustees, University of North Carolina, Chapel Hill, North Carolina, SHC, UNC
FM   Faculty Minutes, University of North Carolina, Chapel Hill, North Carolina, SHC, UNC

Papers

BFP Battle Family Papers, SHC, UNC
EC   David L. Swain Epistolary Correspondence, NCC, UNC
GLB Governors Letter Books, State of North Carolina, SANC, Raleigh, North Carolina
GP   Governors Papers, State of North Carolina, SANC, Raleigh, North Carolina
UP   University Papers, University of North Carolina, SHC, UNC, Chapel Hill, North Carolina

Persons

KPB Kemp Plummer Battle
LMB Lucy Martin Battle
WHB William Horn Battle
WAG William Alexander Graham
WPM Willie Person Mangum
CM   Charles Manly
CLS Caroline Lowry Swain
CPS Cornelia Phillips Spencer
GS   George Swain Senior

DLS	David Lowry Swain
EHS	Eleanor Hope Swain
ZBV	Zebulon Baird Vance

Publications

DNCB	William S. Powell, *Dictionary of North Carolina Biography*. Chapel Hill: University of North Carolina Press, 6 volumes, 1979–1996.
NCHR	*North Carolina Historical Review*, published by the North Carolina Office of Archives and History, Raleigh, North Carolina.

Repositories

Duke	Rare Book, Manuscript, and Special Collections Library, Perkins Library, Duke University, Durham, North Carolina.
ECU	Special Collections, Joyner Library, East Carolina University, Greenville, North Carolina.
NCC	North Carolina Collection, Wilson Library, University of North Carolina at Chapel Hill, Chapel Hill, North Carolina.
SANC	Office of Archives and History, Department of Natural and Cultural Resources, State of North Carolina, Raleigh, North Carolina.
SHC	Southern Historical Collection, Wilson Library, University of North Carolina at Chapel Hill, Chapel Hill, North Carolina.

University Entities

BOT	Board of Trustees, University of North Carolina
EC	Executive Committee, Board of Trustees, University of North Carolina
UNC	University of North Carolina

Foreword

Note: All spellings and emphasis within quotes have been retained from the original documents.

1. Frederick Law Olmsted, *The Cotton Kingdom: A Traveller's Observations on Cotton and Slavery in the American Slave States* (New York: Mason Brothers, 1861); Hinton Rowan Helper, *The Impending Crisis of the South: How to Meet It* (New York: Burdick Bros., 1857).

2. Timothy J. Williams, *Intellectual Manhood: University, Self, and Society in the*

Antebellum South (Chapel Hill: University of North Carolina Press, 2015), chapter 7. For Benjamin Hedrick, see chapter 12, infra.

3. William Gaston, "Address Delivered Before the Philanthropic and Dialectic Societies at Chapel Hill, June 20, 1832" (Raleigh, NC: Jos. Gales & Son, 1832), 14.

4. James Graham to William Alexander Graham, November 9, 1817, in J. G. deRoulhac Hamilton, ed., *The Papers of Thomas Ruffin*, 4 vols. (Raleigh, NC: Edwards & Broughton, (1918), I, 198.

5. Kemp P. Battle, *History of the University of North Carolina. Volume I: From its Beginning to the Death of President Swain, 1789–1868* (Raleigh: Edwards & Broughton Printing Company, 1907), 780.

Prologue

1. *Daily Sentinel*, September 3, 1868. The Swains' daughter Anne had died in the preceding year.

2. Crofts, *Reluctant Confederates*, xviii, 335–37, 360.

3. Lefler and Newsome, *North Carolina*, 448, states that Vance sent Graham and Swain "at their insistence." No citations back the "insistence" assertion, and the author has found no supporting documentation for it. Swain suggested to Graham that they invite "a conference with the Governor on the present state of public affairs." Graham agreed and opined that the governor might "send a Commission to treat with [Sherman]." They met with Governor Vance, who bought into the idea and appointed the two elder statesmen commissioners to negotiate with Sherman. DLS to WAG, April 8, 1865, and WAG to DLS, April 8, [9?], 1865, Hamilton et al., *Papers of Graham*, 6:292–98; Spencer, *Last Ninety Days*, 134–64.

4. Clement Dowd to KPB, August 2, 1887, UP. Solomon Pool was the first to succeed Swain in the UNC presidency. Between Pool and Battle, Charles Phillips served briefly as the university's senior administrator while chair of the faculty, but he never held the title of president. See Battle, *History*, 2:88, 91. Hence the reference to Battle as the second of Swain's successors in the university presidency.

5. Lefler, "North Carolina History–A Summary View," 38 NCHR 216, 226.

6. Churchill, *Marlborough*, 1:7.

7. U.S. Census, 1800, 1870.

8. E.g., Johnson, *Ante-Bellum North Carolina*, 20 (quoting Swain but noting that it was a commonly used figure of speech); Powell, *Four Centuries*, 245.

9. Francis L. Hawks to DLS, September 11, 1858, Swain Papers, SHC.

10. Wilson, *Chronicles of the Sesquicentennial*, 53

11. Crow, Escott, and Hatley, *History of African Americans in North Carolina*, 51

Chapter 1: Origins, Youth

1. E.g., Vance, *Life of Swain*, 2; Wheeler, *Reminiscenses*, 57.

2. L. S. Swain to DLS, March 4, 1831, EC, NCC; Reuben Swain to DLS, June (?) 6, 1838, Swain Papers, SHC.

3. Reuben Swain to DLS, supra note 2; Frederic Kidder to DLS, May 29, 1856, Swain Papers, SANC; Joseph C. Swain to DLS, September 20, 1838, EC, NCC.

4. Brewer, *Memoir of Swain*, 3; GS to DLS, June 28, July 19, 1822, EC, NCC; Thomas L. Swain to DLS, December 29, 1830, ibid.; Frederic Kidder to DLS, supra note 3.

5. Bennett, *Chronology of North Carolina*, 25–27; Brewer, supra note 4; Daniel, *Early Career*, 3–5; Daniel, *Swain*, 3–7; Wheeler, *Reminiscences*, 57; DLS to (recipient not shown), June 9, 1856, EC, NCC.

6. Battle, *History*, 1:425; Daniel, *Early Career*, 9; Daniel, *Swain*, 10; Dunbar, "Silas McDowell," 41 NCHR 425, 434; Sondley, *Buncombe County*, 1:436; Perry, *Reminiscences*, in Meats and Arnold, *Writings of Perry*, 3:307–8; Vance, *Life of Swain*, 2; Hicklin, "D. L. Swain and Joseph Lane Born in Same House in 1801," *Charlotte Observer*, May 1, 1932; DLS to Pliny Miles, November 12, 1847, Swain Papers, SHC.

7. Commission as Deputy Postmaster, EC, NCC; Appointment as Postmaster, Swain Papers, SHC; Bennett, *Chronology of North Carolina*, 25–27; Sondley, *Buncombe County*, 2:725.

8. Sondley, *Buncombe County*, 2:712–13; Jones, "Calvin Jones, M.D.," 49 NCHR 56, 57–58; J. R. Liles to DLS, September 5 (?), 1822, EC, NCC; GS to DLS September 6, 1822, ibid; DLS to Pliny Miles, November 12, 1847, Swain Papers, SHC.

9. Daniel, *Early Career*, 7–8; Daniel, *Swain*, 8; *Laws of North Carolina*, 1797, ch. 54, 1865, ch. 38, 1807, ch. 49.

10. Coon, *North Carolina Schools and Academies*, 14–15; Daniel, *Early Career*, 10; Daniel, *Swain*, 11; Sondley, *Buncombe County*, 2:644–45, 704; Newsome, "A Miscellany from the Thomas Henderson Letter Book, 1810–1811," 6 NCHR 398, 406–8 (on George Swain's April 27, 1810 letter to the *Raleigh Star*); Newsome, "Twelve North Carolina Counties in 1810–1811," 5 NCHR 413, 415n.9 (same); *Raleigh Star*, January 24, 1812.

11. Bennett, *Chronology of North Carolina*, 25–27; Brewer, *Memoir of Swain*, 3; Camp, *Swain*, 8; Daniel, *Early Career*, 4; Daniel, *Swain*, 4; Wellman, *Kingdom of Madison*, 36–37; Wheeler, *Reminiscences*, 57.

12. Swain Genealogy Materials, Pack Memorial Library, Asheville, NC; Battle, *History*, 1:425; Daniel, *Early Career*, 4; Daniel, *Swain*, 4–5; Vance, *Life of Swain*, 2. Swain came to appreciate his Lane heritage. While in Raleigh in his youth, he wrote to his father: "Tell mother that I yesterday viewed with no ordinary sensations the house in which her uncle Col. Lane formerly lived, and where she sported as a girl." DLS to GS, April, 24, 1822, EC, NCC.

13. E.g., Brewer, *Memoir of Swain*, 3; Dykeman, *French Broad*, 344.

14. Ashe, *Biographical History*, 1:448; Brewer, *Memoir of Swain*, 3; Bridges, *Masonic Governors*, 150–51; Swain Biographical Notes, Corbitt Papers, SANC; Daniel, *Early Career*, 11–12; Daniel, *Swain*, 11–13; Perry, *Reminiscences*, in Meats and Arnold, *Writings of Perry*, 3:307; Vance, *Life of Swain*, 4. Swain and Perry were said to have "had a first-rate academy teacher in Asheville, who delighted them by reading Homer aloud in class." Fox Genovese and Genovese, *Mind of the Master Class*, 255.

15. See *Biennial Report of the Superintendent of Public Instruction of North Carolina for the Scholastic Years 1898–'99 and 1899–1900*, 414.

16. DLS to GS, November 21, December 5, 1820, May 10 (?), 1822; GS to DLS, August 2, 1822, EC, NCC.

17. GS to DLS, May 10, August 16, 1822, EC, NCC.

18. Camp, *Swain*, 14 (four days); Connor, *Ante-Bellum Builders*, 66 (four months); Vance, *Life of Swain*, 4 (four months).

19. *Catalogue of the Dialectic Society*, 49; Battle, *History*, 1:821 (William Polk as trustee); Carroll, "Life and Times of David Swain," *News and Observer*, June 2, 1968.

20. Elisha Mitchell to EC, UNC BOT, December 11, 1854, UP.

21. Daniel, *Swain*, 17; GS to DLS, May (?) 3, 1822, DLS to GS, April 24, 25, May 2, July (no date given), 1822, EC, NCC. When seriously ill in Raleigh (see infra text this chapter), David doubted that he would have survived if he had been in Chapel Hill. DLS to GS, September 16 (?), 1822, ibid.

22. GS TO DLS, May 3, 10, 31, June 7, 14, July 12, 19, 26, August 16, 1822; DLS to GS, April 25, July (no date given), 1822; Joseph Gales to GS, May 11, 1822; J. R. Liles to DLS, September 5 (?), 1822, EC, NCC. On Judge Taylor's school and Swain's attendance, see Murray, *Wake: Capital County*, 1:187.

23. GS to DLS, September 21, November 9, 22, 25, December 20, 27, 1822, January 31, March 7, 21, May 2, 9, 17, 23, 1823; DLS to GS, September 21, 1822, March 1, May 24, July 1, 1823, EC, NCC.

24. DLS to GS, May 20, 1822, January 4, May 17, June 14, 1823; William Harris Avery to DLS, May 17, July 15, 1823, EC, NCC. Swain passed the exam and obtained his license to practice in the county courts of North Carolina on June 16, 1823. Camp, *Swain*, 15–16.

25. DLS to GS, April 24, May 18, 20, June 22, September 6, 21, October 4 (?), November 16 (?), 1822, May 2, 17, 24, 1823, EC, NCC; Connor, *William Gaston: A Southern Federalist*, 8 (in Swain's opinion Gaston was *facile princeps*); Daniel, *Early Career*, 30, 174–76; Swain, *Early Times*, 26. In David's letter to George of May 2, 1823, he enclosed a certificate of his service as a juror in the Federal Circuit Court, District of North Carolina.

26. DLS to GS, August 21, October 4, November 16 (?), 24, 1822, February 22, 1823 (says 1822 but is almost certainly 1823), EC, NCC.

27. GS to DLS, June 21, July 26, August 2, 9, October 11, 18, 25, November 8, 1822, EC, NCC; Daniel, *Early Career*, 45–46.

28. GS to DLS, June 21, July 19, August 29, November 8, 9, December 28, 1822, February 21, 1823; J. R. Liles to DLS, September 5 (?), 1822, EC, NCC; Camp, *Swain*, 15–16; Daniel, *Early Career*, 35.

29. DLS to Elizabeth Patton, August 25, 1822; R. B. Vance to DLS, March 26, 1823; GS to DLS, May 23, 1823; DLS to GS, July 1, 1823; W. R. Gales to DLS, September 15, 1823, EC, NCC.

30. DLS to GS, February 15, 1823, EC, NCC.

31. DLS to GS, August 2, 18, 1822, February 22, 1823, EC, NCC.

32. DLS to GS, February 1, 1822, March 22, 1823; GS to DLS, May (?) 3, November 1, 29, 1822; R. B. Vance to DLS, November 17, 1823; P. Brittain to DLS, November (?) 28, December 18, 1823, EC, NCC; Daniel, *Early Career*, 57–58. The Epistolary Correspondence contains a handwritten draft of a bill to incorporate the Fulton Turnpike Company "for the improvement of the road from Asheville by way of Warm-Springs to the Tennessee line." The bill was in the state senate on December 6, 1822. Swain was then Judge Taylor's student and not yet a legislator, which suggests that he was working actively on internal-improvements legislation even then.

33. John L. Ellis to DLS, October 30, 1823; R. B. Vance to DLS, November 17, 1823; P. Brittain to DLS, November (?) 28, 1823; W. R. Gales to DLS, March 24, 1824; T. A. Howard to DLS, July 29, 1824; W. Harris Avery to DLS, September 21 (?), 1824; DLS to "My dear Sister" (not named), December 21, 1822, EC, NCC; see Lefler and Newsome, *North Carolina*, 328 (Swain "never favored Jackson, even in 1824").

34. DLS to GS, November 1, 1822; W. R. Gales to DLS, July 19, August 9, 1823; Eccletchete to DLS, September 30, 1823, EC, NCC. Swain apparently referred to Tryon Palace in New Bern, built for royal governor William Tryon. Tryon's successor, Josiah Martin, was the second occupant. See Barefoot, Daniel J., "Tryon Palace," in Powell, *Encyclopedia of North Carolina*, 1136–39. Further research has revealed no additional information regarding "Eccletchete" or his relationship with Swain. The author also consulted the following individuals with expertise in American Indian history and law: Stacy Leeds, former justice of the Cherokee Nation Supreme Court and dean emeritus, University of Arkansas School of Law; John D. Loftin, J.D., Ph.D., of Hillsborough, NC; and J. Matthew Martin, former justice of the Cherokee Nation Supreme Court and author of *The Cherokee Nation Supreme Court: 1823–1835* (Durham, NC: Carolina Academic Press, 2020). They, too, could discover or provide no further information on "Eccletchete."

35. Murray, *Wake: Capital County*, 1:435–36.

36. DLS to GS, August 10, 18, 21, September 16 (?), 21, 27, October 4 (?), 8, 25, November 1, 9, 1822, March 8, April 12, June 14, 24, 1823; GS to DLS, September 6, 13/14,

20, October 25, November 9, 1822, January 17, February 21, 1823; GS and CLS to DLS, September 27, 1822; W. R. Gales to GS, August 31, September 7, October 11, 1822; DLS to W. R. Gales, October 8, 1822; William Gaston to DLS, April 22, 1824, EC, NCC.

37. DLS to GS, September 5, 1820; GS to DLS, April 26, June 28, July 12, 19, October 18, 1822, May 23, 1823, EC, NCC.

38. Bennett, *Chronology of North Carolina*, 25–27; Daniel, *Early Career*, 8; Daniel, *Swain*, 9; Wellman, *Kingdom of Madison*, 30; Wheeler, *Reminiscences*, 62; DLS to GS, June 28, 1822, EC, NCC.

39. GS to DLS, April 18, May (?) 3, 31, June 14, July 26, August 16, 23, 29, September 6, 1822, March 7, 1823; GS and CLS to DLS, October 5, 1822; DLS to GS, August 10, 1822, March 1, 1823; CLS to DLS, two undated letters and undated writing in script form, but clearly CLS to DLS; Althia Swain to DLS, May 18, 1822; unidentified sender (but obviously a sister, probably the youngest) to DLS, April 17, 1827, EC, NCC.

40. GS to DLS, April 26, 1822; Mary Swain to GS, February 15, 1827, EC, NCC.

41. DLS to GS, April 24, 1822; John L. Ellis to DLS, October 30, 1823, February 6, March 4, 1824; J. R. Liles to DLS, September 5, 1822; R. B. Vance to DLS, March 26, 1823, EC, NCC.

42. R. B. Vance to DLS, August 9, 1822, March 26, 1823, December 21, 1825; Will H. H. Jr. to DLS, April 21, 1824; William H. Avery to DLS, February 3, 27, 1823; W. Harris Avery to DLS, undated; John L. Ellis to DLS, February 6, 1824; DLS to GS, September 21, 1822, February 15, April 12, 1823, ibid.

43. DLS to GS, June 28, 1822, EC, NCC; Murray, *Wake: Capital County*, 1:195.

44. William H. Avery to DLS, April 4, July 18, 1823; Lucius J. Polk to DLS, August 3, 1823; W. R. Gales to DLS, August 9, 1823; Eclletchete to DLS, September 30, 1823; E. Patton to DLS, May 8, 1823; DLS to Eleanor White, December 29, 1824, EC, NCC; Daniel, *Early Career*, 29, 159–61; Murray, *Wake: Capital County*, 1:118.

45. Document in Swain's hand, undated, and DLS to Eleanor White, December 29, 1824, EC, NCC; John Haywood to DLS, March 4, 1826, ibid.; Daniel, *Early Career*, 28–29; Daniel, *Swain*, 32–33; Neal, *Abstracts of Vital Records*, 2:683; *Raleigh Register*, January 14, 1826.

46. Lucius J. Polk to DLS, December 20, 1823; DLS to GS, May 30, 1823, EC, NCC.

47. DLS to GS, April 12, May 3, 1822; E. J. Hale to DLS, February 17, 1868, *Walter Clark Papers*, SANC.

48. J. L. Taylor to DLS, (month illegible) 4, 1823; DLS to GS, March 1, 1823; GS to DLS, March 7, 14, April 26, 1823; J. L. Taylor to GS, April 29, 1823; Calvin Jones to GS, May 30 (year not shown but almost certainly 1823), EC, NCC.

Chapter 2: Law, Statecraft

1. Bennett, *Chronology of North Carolina*, 95–97; Camp, *Swain*, 20; Daniel, *Swain*, 62; Sondley, *Buncombe County*, 2:651; Vance, *Life of Swain*, 4; Certificate dated December 28, 1824, EC, NCC; *Western Carolinian*, July 4, 1823, January 18, 1825; *Raleigh Register*, December 31, 1824.

2. *Biennial Report of the Superintendent of Public Instruction of North Carolina for the Scholastic Years 1898–'99 and 1899–1900*, 414; Vance, *Life of Swain*, 4.

3. DLS to EHS, August 25, 1826, April 21, 1827, June 20, 27, July 25, October 10, 1828, EC, NCC.

4. Ibid., August 25, 1826, April 14, 21, May 6, 1827, June 27, July 25, 1828, February 19, 1830, EC, NCC.

5. Ibid., April 18, June 27, October 10, 1828, EC, NCC.

6. Ibid., September 24, 1828, EC, NCC.

7. Burton Executive Order, April 9, 1825; Iredell Executive Order, February 28, 1828; Iredell Executive Order, November 26, 1828 (William Hill, secretary of state, and James Grant were also parties to this order; Grant's capacity is unclear); Owen Executive Order, January 8, 1830, EC, NCC.

8. Ashe, *Biographical History*, 1:451; Camp, *Swain*, 23; Peele, *Lives*, 235–36.

9. Priscilla Vance, mother and beneficiary under will of Robert Vance, document releasing Swain from duties as coexecutor, October 6, 1835, Swain Papers, SHC; George D. Phillips to DLS, November 8, 1827, EC, NCC; William Siler et al., document granting Swain power to petition the court for sale or division of George Swain's real estate, March 9, 1830, Swain Papers, SHC; William Coleman, receipt to DLS as administrator of George Swain's estate, March 20, 1832, Swain Papers, SHC (typescript). The Swain Papers, SHC, contain other typescripts showing Swain as the administrator of George's estate. For a report on the duel in which Vance was killed, see *Raleigh Register and North-Carolina Gazette*, November 20, 1827.

10. Peele, *Lives*, 246; Swain, *Early Times*, 246.

11. James Graham to WAG, February 2, 1831, Hamilton et al., *Papers of Graham*, 1:199; Robert Love to Thomas H. Blount and William A. Blount, February 11, 1834, Blount Papers, SANC.

12. G. E. Badger and DLS to Governor Owen, January 16, 1830, Swain Papers, SHC; W. M. Sneed to WPM, November 18, 1830, Shanks, *Papers of Mangum*, 1:381; Thomas Ruffin to DLS, August 6, 1829, EC, NCC.

13. Joshua Roberts Memo, March 3, 1830; R. M. Saunders Memo, June 11, 1830; F. Nash Memo, June 19, 1830, Swain Papers, SHC. See also B. Shipp Memo, March 27, 1830, ibid. For a general treatment of Swain's role in the land-claim cases, and the conclusion that the testimonials disarmed the critics, see Daniel, *Early Career*, 135–45.

14. Camp, *Swain*, 18; Daniel, *Swain*, 60; W. Harris Avery to DLS, August (no day and year stated, but probably 1824), EC, NCC.

15. Powell, *Four Centuries*, 245, 253–66; Williams, Wiley J., "Rip Van Winkle State," in Powell, *Encyclopedia of North Carolina*, 974. For the Murphey program, see Hoyt, *Papers of Murphey*, 2:51–56, 63–87, 100–101, 105–51, 176–202. For further commentary on it, see Connor, *North Carolina*, 1:475–97; Lefler and Newsome, *North Carolina*, 298 (Rip Van Winkle), 312–22; Watson, "Man with the Dirty Black Beard," *Journal of the Early Republic*, 32:1, 11–12. The Graham quotes are in Graham, "Memoir of Hon. Archibald D. Murphey," *North Carolina University Magazine*, 10:1, 5–6 (August 1860), reprinted in Hoyt, *Papers of Murphey*, 1: xix–xxxiv.

16. Brewer, *Memoir of Swain*, 4; Daniel, *Swain*, 163; Connor, *Ante-Bellum Builders*, 66–67; Powell, *Four Centuries*, 253; DLS to GS, January 27, 1827, EC, NCC.

17. DLS, "Letter to Constituents of Buncombe County," from Raleigh, February 12, 1827, NCC; DLS to Captain William Siler, February 12, 1827, EC, NCC.

18. G. Baird to DLS, May 29, 1823, EC, NCC.

19. DLS to GS, December 11, 1824, EC, NCC; *N.C. House Journal*, November 30, December 8, 11, 1824.

20. Sondley, *Buncombe County*, 2:617; Hill, Michael, "Buncombe Turnpike," in Powell, *Encyclopedia of North Carolina*, 155–56.

21. Patton, *Story of Henderson County*, 96; Wellman, *Kingdom of Madison*, 41–43. For Allen's representation, see Cheney, *North Carolina Government*, 289; for the Supreme Court opinion, see *Allen v. Turnpike Co.*, 16 N.C. 119 (1827).

22. Calvin Jones to GS, February 17, 1825, EC, NCC; Hill, "Buncombe Turnpike," in Powell, *Encyclopedia of North Carolina*, 155–56; Sondley, *Buncombe County*, 2:617; Tucker, *Zeb Vance*, 41; Vance, *Life of Swain*, 5.

23. DLS to EHS, August 7, 1828, EC, NCC; Wellman, *Kingdom of Madison*, 43; *Report of the Board of Internal Improvements: 1830*, 6. The quotation from the *Raleigh Register* is in Wellman, *Kingdom of Madison*, supra. Wellman does not cite the issue, and the author has not identified it. Numerous issues of that publication are no longer extant.

24. *N.C. House Journal*, December 29, 1824, November 28, December 12, 1825; *Report*, supra note 23, 6.

25. *N.C. House Journal*, December 22, 31, 1824, January 1, 1825.

26. Ibid., January 4, 1825.

27. Ibid., November 23, December 21, 23, 26, 1825.

28. George D. Phillips to DLS, December 6, 1827, EC, NCC.

29. *Journal of the Board for Internal Improvements, 1821–1835*, November 23, 27, 1829; Daniel, *Early Career*, 81.

30. *N.C. House Journal*, January 8, December 31, 1829; Daniel, *Early Career*, 81;

Wheeler, *Reminiscences*, 57; *Raleigh Register and North-Carolina Gazette*, January 13, 1829, January 4, 1830.

31. Daniel, *Swain*, 129; *Raleigh Register and North-Carolina Gazette*, June 17, 1830 (account of Cape Fear tour).

32. DLS to Captain William Siler, February 12, 1827, EC, NCC; DLS, "Letter to Constituents," February 12, 1827, NCC.

33. *Report*, supra note 23, 7–8; Daniel, *Early Career*, 81–87.

34. *N.C. House Journal*, December 27, 1826, November 19, 1828, November 18, December 16, 31, 1829; Camp, *Swain*, 28; Coon, *Beginnings of Public Education in North Carolina*, 1:421, 445, 448; Daniel, *Swain*, 129–32.

35. *N.C. House Journal*, December 19, 22, 1825, January 3, 5, 1827, November 25, 1828, December 10, 16, 19, 1829; DLS, "Letter to Constituents," February 12, 1827, NCC; Daniel, *Swain*, 133–36, 166–68; *Raleigh Register and North-Carolina Gazette*, February 23, 1827.

36. *N.C. House Journal*, December 6, 1824, January 30, 1827, December 17, 1828; DLS, "Letter to Constituents," February 12, 1827, NCC; DLS to Captain William Siler, February 12, 1827, EC, NCC; Daniel, *Swain*, 146–47; Johnson, *Ante-Bellum North Carolina*, 584–85. "Free Negroes" and their status remained an issue in Buncombe County until Emancipation; see Franklin, *Free Negro in North Carolina*, 214–15.

37. *N.C. House Journal*, December 18, 1828, December 28, 1829.

38. Ibid., December 3, 4, 6, 21, 1824, December 26, 1825, December 18, 22, 1828, December 24, 28, 1829; Daniel, *Early Career*, 149–50; Daniel, *Swain*, 163–64. On the vesting of power at the county level, see Johnson, *Ante-Bellum North Carolina*, 76–77.

39. *N.C. House Journal*, December 2, 1829.

40. *N.C. House Journal*, December 29, 1824, December 7, 9, 14, 1825; R. B. Vance to DLS, December 17, 1825, June 1, 1827, EC, NCC; Daniel, *Early Career*, 151–52, 155–56, 159; Daniel, *Swain*, 165.

41. *N.C. House Journal*, December 31, 1824, January 1, November 28, 1825, January 2, 10, 19, 1827, November 24, December 3, 10, 22, 29, 1828, November 20, 25, 26, 1829. In his first session Swain told his father that the bill to reorganize the supreme court and have it sit at multiple sites "excites more interest than any other question now before us." DLS to GS, December 22, 1824, EC, NCC.

42. E.g., *N.C. House Journal*, December 5, 1828.

43. Ibid., December 29, 1826, January 17, 18, 1829.

44. Ibid., February 8, 1827, January 4, 1830.

45. Ibid., November 19, 1828, January 9, 1829.

46. Ibid., December 3, 31, 1828, November 18, 1829, January 6, 1830; Blackmun, *Western North Carolina*, 204; Daniel, *Early Career*, 133–34; Peele, *Lives*, 233; Tucker, *Zeb Vance*, 41; Vance, *Life of Swain*, 4.

47. *N.C. House Journal*, December 20, 22, 23, 26, 1825.

48. Ibid., January 24, 1827, December 18, 20, 1828, December 1, 1829.

49. Ibid., December 30, 1826, January 20, 1827; DLS to GS, December 10, 1825 (?), EC, NCC.

50. D. L. Barringer to DLS, October 9, 1825; William Robards to DLS, August 16, 1829; Thomas Ruffin to DLS, October 15, 1829, EC, NCC; Daniel, *Swain*, 221–25; Hoffman, *Andrew Jackson and North Carolina Politics*, 30–31. Archibald Murphey solicited Swain's support for the Senate seat. He had long entertained the wish "of spending a few years of my Old Age in public Employment," he told Swain, and hoped that in the Senate he could render some service to the nation and the state. He asked Swain to let members of the General Assembly know he was a candidate. A. D. Murphey to DLS, October 18, 1829, EC, NCC (Murphey did not secure the appointment).

51. See Daniel, *Swain*, 98–128. *The Raleigh Register and North-Carolina Gazette* published Swain's debate on the bank bill in its February 20, 27, 1829 issues; see also ibid., May 10, 1830.

52. D. L. Barringer to DLS, October 9, 1829; Thomas Ruffin to DLS, October 15, 1829; Weston R. Gales to DLS, undated, EC, NCC; Daniel, *Swain*, 118–19.

53. DLS to Captain Philo White, January 10, 1825, EC, NCC.

54. Frederick Nash to WPM, December 17, 1828, in Shanks, *Papers of Mangum*, 1:351.

55. DLS to GS, December 11, 22, 1824, December 3, 1825 (?), EC, NCC.

56. DLS to EHS, August 11, 1826, June 20, 27, July 18, August 7, 15, September 24, 1828, March 19, 1830, EC, NCC; Romulus M. Saunders to Bartlett Yancey, March 21, 1828, in Newsome, "Letters of Romulus M. Saunders to Bartlett Yancey," 8 NCHR 461.

57. See Daniel, *Early Career*, 183; Daniel, *Swain*, 215.

58. DLS to GS, January 27, 1827, EC, NCC; Cheney, *North Carolina Government*, 287, 350n.381; *Raleigh Register and North-Carolina Gazette*, February 2, 1827.

59. *N.C. House Journal*, February 1–10, 1827; DLS to GS, February 11, 1827, EC, NCC.

60. Original certificate, H. G. Burton, February 28, 1827, EC, NCC; newspaper clipping, paper and date not shown, EC, NCC. For brief commentary, see Brewer, *Memoir of Swain*, 4; Daniel, *Early Career*, 163–66; Daniel, *Swain*, 205–14; Peele, *Lives*, 234.

61. DLS to GS, February 11, 1827, EC, NCC.

62. Ibid.; DLS, "Letter to Constituents," February 12, 1827, NCC; DLS to Captain William Siler, February 12, 1827, EC, NCC.

63. DLS to EHS, March 22, April 21, May 6, 1827, EC, NCC.

64. Ibid., March 18, 22, April 14, 1827, EC, NCC.

65. Ibid., March 18, 22, 30, April 14, 1827, EC, NCC.

66. George D. Phillips to DLS, November 8, 1827; DLS to EHS, January 20, 1828, EC, NCC; *Raleigh Register and North-Carolina Gazette*, February 22, 1828.

67. See supra text accompanying note 61.

68. See Camp, *Swain*, 37, for a similar conclusion.

69. *North Carolina Reports*, 13:380; *Raleigh Register and North-Carolina Gazette*, December 16, 1830; *Western Carolinian*, December 21, 1830; Original Commission, Montford Stokes, January 12, 1831, EC, NCC; Cheney, *North Carolina Government*, 361, 370n.78; Connor, *Ante-Bellum Builders*, 56; Daniel, *Early Career*, 184–85; Daniel, *Swain*, 230; Moore, *History of North Carolina*, 2:21.

70. Arthur, *Western North Carolina*, 382–83.

71. James Graham to WAG, December 19, 1830, Hamilton et al., *Papers of Graham*, 1:196; [illegible] to DLS, January 1, 1831, EC, NCC.

72. *Western Carolinian*, January 31, 1831.

73. Seawell, Henry, "Seawell, Henry," in Powell, *DNCB*, 5:310–11.

74. DLS to EHS, May 13, September 11, 1831, March 22, April 26, 1832, EC, NCC; Daniel, *Swain*, 233.

75. John Mushat to WPM, November 13, 1832, in Shanks, *Papers of Mangum*, 1:585; Swain Diary, March 2, 4, May 5, 6, 1832, SANC.

76. Swain Diary, April 9–10, July 6, 1832, SANC.

77. DLS to EHS, April 27, May 13, 1831, EC, NCC; for items showing Swain holding court, see *Raleigh Register and North-Carolina Gazette*, May 5, 1831 (Catawba County), November 16, 1832 (Rutherford County).

78. See Swain Diary, May 14, 1832; Daniel, *Early Career*, 188.

79. DLS to EHS, March 14, April 26, 27, 1832, EC, NCC.

80. Ibid., October 23, 1831, March 22, 1832, EC, NCC; Mr. Seawell to Judge Swaine [*sic*], undated, Swain Papers, SHC; Swain Diary, March 13, 17, April 6, May 28, July 5, 1832, SANC. As to Judge Hall, see Cheney, *North Carolina Government*, 360.

81. Swain Diary, January 17, March 3, 6, 8, 10, 11, May 17, June 1, 29, August 13, 1832, SANC.

82. Ibid., March 11, May 20, 27, June 3, 9, 10, 24, July 1, 8, 15, 21, 22, 29, August 5, 12, 19, 24, 1832.

83. Ibid., April 10, 22, 23, June 2, July 3, 1832; DLS to EHS, May 13, 1831, EC, NCC.

84. Swain Diary, April 10, July 14, 18, 26, August 11, 1832, SANC.

85. Ibid., March 6, 7, 15, 19, 22, 26, 28, April 24, May 1, 7, 8, 1832.

86. Ibid., January 9, 10, 23, 30, February 13, 15, 23, May 19, 23, 24, 25, 26, 29, July 2, 10, 13, 24, August 1, 4, 14, 1832.

87. Daniels, "Nathaniel Macon," address in *Proceedings of the Thirteenth Annual Session of the State Literary and Historical Association of North Carolina*, 88–89.

88. Griffin, *Essays on North Carolina History*, 64–65; *Carolina Watchman*, November 7, 1872.

89. See supra text accompanying note 75.

90. Speight, D. A. H., "Reminiscences of Gov. D. L. Swain," in Swain Papers, Duke; Webb, W. R. Jr., "Anecdote and Reminiscence," *North Carolina University Magazine*, 14:267 (Feb. 1895).

91. Cf. Ashe, *Biographical History*, 1:451 (18 appeals, 5 reversals).

92. Peele, *Lives*, 247.

Chapter 3: Vision

1. N.C. Const. of 1776, section 15, in Cheney, *North Carolina Government*, 813; commentary, Sanders, John L., in ibid., 795.

2. Cheney, *North Carolina Government*, 161, 189n.20; Crabtree, *North Carolina Governors*, 78.

3. *Raleigh Register and North-Carolina Gazette*, December 7, 1832; *American Railroad Journal*, December 15, 1832; Brewer, *Memoir of Swain*, 4; Moore, *History of North Carolina*, 2:23; *N.C. House Journal*, *N.C. Senate Journal*, December 6, 1832.

4. Powell, *North Carolina: A Bicentennial History*, 116; Hoffman, "John Branch and the Origins of the Whig Party in North Carolina," 35 NCHR 299, 309; Hoffman, *Andrew Jackson and North Carolina Politics*, 59–60; Wallace, Carolyn A., "Swain, David Lowery [sic]," in Powell, *DNCB*, 5:483; Daniel, *Early Career*, 195–202; Daniel, *Swain*, 252.

5. John Owen to DLS, January 1, 1833, EC, NCC; Mr. and Mrs. J. A. Alexander to DLS, December 21, 1832, EC, NCC; David Thomas to the Freemen of Guilford County, *Greensboro Patriot*, February 27, 1833; *Fayetteville Observer*, December 4, 1832; Daniel, *Swain*, 251–52.

6. Editor's Table, *North Carolina University Magazine*, 9:643 (June 1860); John Branch to DLS, December 13, 1832; Charles Barring to DLS, December 24, 1832, EC, NCC.

7. James A. Graham to WAG, February 7, 1833, Graham Papers, SHC (in Hamilton et al., *Papers of Graham*, 1:252); *Tarboro Free Press*, December 11, 1832; *Western Carolinian*, January 21, 1833; Daniel, *Early Career*, 201; Daniel, *Swain*, 471; *N.C. Senate Journal*, January 7, 1833. As to Swain's carriage accident, see text accompanying notes 75, 89, chapter 2.

8. *N.C. Senate Journal*, November 26, 28, 30, December 7, 9, 1833; *N.C. House Journal*, November 26, 28, 30, December 3, 7, 9, 1833; McGehee, Montford, "A Memorial Oration," Hamilton et al., *Papers of Graham*, 1:9; Cheney, *North Carolina Govern-*

ment, 301, 361; Hugh Waddell to WAG, December 15, 1833, Hamilton et al., *Papers of Graham*, 1:273.

9. *N.C. Senate Journal*, November 20–26, December 5, 10, 1834; *N.C. House Journal*, November 20–27, December 10, 1834; *Western Carolinian*, November 29, December 13, 1834; Daniel, *Swain*, 482. The three ballots went as follows. On the first, David L. Swain, 93; William D. Moseley, 85; and "Scattering," 10. On the second, David L. Swain, 93; William D. Moseley, 89; and "Scattering," 6. On the third, David L. Swain, 97; William D. Moseley, 89; and "Scattering," 4.

10. DLS to William Gaston, September 6, 19, October 9, 1834, Gaston Papers, SHC; Lefler, *History of North Carolina*, 1:332; Hoffman, "John Branch and the Origins of the Whig Party in North Carolina," 35 NCHR 299, 309–13; Daniel, *Swain*, 443–82.

11. James Graham to WAG, December 8, 1834, Graham Papers, SHC (in Hamilton et al., *Papers of Graham*, 1:336) (two Rutherford members said to have voted against Swain); WHB to LMB, November 30, 1834, BFP, SHC; *Tarboro Free Press*, November 28, 1834; *N.C. Senate Journal, N.C. House Journal*, December 10, 1834; Walton, "Elections to the U.S. Senate in North Carolina, 1835–1861," 53 NCHR 168, 173n.12.

12. William Gaston to Susan Jane Donaldson (daughter), July 10, 1831, Gaston Papers, SHC; Gaston Speech, *Proceedings and Debates*, 336–37 (quoted in Daniel, *Swain*, 255). As to the capitol, see Lefler and Newsome, *North Carolina*, 335–36.

13. *Raleigh Register*, December 14, 1832; Niles, *Niles' Weekly Register*, December 22, 1832.

14. Connor, *North Carolina, 1584–1925*, 1:527–28; Connor, *Ante-Bellum Builders*, 58; Blackwelder, *Age of Orange*, 77–78; Wallace, "Swain, David Lowery [*sic*]," in Powell, *DNCB*, 5:483, 483–84.

15. See N.C. Gen. Stat. §4–1.

16. *N.C. House Journal*, November 19, 1833; also in Swain GLB 30, SANC, and *Raleigh Register*, November 26, 1833. For summary, see *New England Magazine*, 6:77–78 (1834); for brief commentary, see Cathey, *Agricultural Developments in North Carolina 1783–1860*, 90n.74.

17. *N.C. Senate Journal*, November 19–22, 1833; M. Ring to DLS, November 26, 1833, EC, NCC; John Lawrence Newby to DLS, December 13, 1833, EC, NCC.

18. *N.C. House Journal*, November 18, 1834; *Raleigh Register*, November 25, 1834; Daniel, *Swain*, 471–79 (additional newspaper commentary); Lefler and Newsome, *North Carolina*, 303.

19. *Raleigh Register*, November 25, 1834.

20. Ibid., December 16, 1834; for commentary, see Daniel, *Swain*, 486–97, Hoffman, *Andrew Jackson and North Carolina Politics*, 78.

21. *Raleigh Register*, January 20, 1835.

22. *Tarboro Free Press*, January 2, 1835; *Raleigh Standard*, December 12, 26, 1834, March 6, 20, 1835; Daniel, *Swain*, 494–96.

23. *Fayetteville Observer*, December 16, 1834; Daniel, *Swain*, 496.

24. Baptist, *Half Has Never Been Told*, 195–97, 199–200; Berry, *Price for Their Pound of Flesh*, 107–12; Brophy, *University, Court, and Slave*, xiv, 3–4, 19, 21–24; Fox-Genovese and Genovese, *Mind of the Master Class*, 229; Horton and Horton, *In Hope of Liberty*, 172–74, 211, 224; Kolchin, *American Slavery*, 197–99; Sinha, *Slave's Cause*, 205–7, 210–27; Wilentz, *Rise of American Democracy*, 239–40, 313–14, 330–41.

25. Terry Sanford, "Statement to Negro Leaders Meeting at the Capitol," June 25, 1963, in Mitchell, *Papers of Sanford*, 598.

26. *N.C. House Journal*, November 17, 1835, also in Swain GLB 30, SANC; *Western Carolinian*, November 28, 1835; excerpts in Coon, *Beginnings of Public Education in North Carolina*, 2:712–14. For the joint resolution on abolitionist publications, see *N.C. Senate Journal*, December 9, 1835. For a contemporary northern response to the portion on abolitionist publications, see "Defensor," *The Enemies of the Constitution Discovered Etc.*, 147–48: "We will voluntarily sacrifice our property and our lives to promote the welfare of our southern brethren; but if they make the demand which Governor Swain says they will make with perfect unanimity, the duties which we owe to our country, to posterity, and to the cause of freedom throughout the world, *forbid compliance*. We cannot, *will not submit*." See also Whedon, D.D., *Methodist Quarterly Review 1871*, 53:145: "This was simply asking the despotic suppression of free discussion in our entire country on the subject of slavery! . . . Very strange that good men and clear thinkers like Governor Swain could not realize the despotism they asserted!"

Chapter 4: Advancing the Vision

1. WPA Writers' Program, *Raleigh: Capital of North Carolina*, 26; Daniel, *Swain*, 290; Tucker, *Zeb Vance*, 41; Lefler and Newsome, *North Carolina*, 335; William Gaston to Susan Jane Donaldson, February 24, 1833, Gaston Papers, SHC; Terra L. Schramm, North Carolina State Capitol, Education and Public Programs Coordinator, cited in email, Michael Perdue (N.C. Senate Page Coordinator) to the author, April 16, 2012 (copy in author's files); Allcott, "Robert Donaldson, the First North Carolinian to Become Prominent in the Arts," 52 NCHR 333, 354.

2. Daniel, *Swain*, 145–46, 296–97; DLS to John MacRae, January 12, 1833; John MacRae to DLS, April 29, 1833; DLS to John MacRae, May 3, 1833, Swain GLB 30, SANC. See text accompanying note 47, chapter 2.

3. *Journal of the Internal Improvements Convention . . . 4th of July, 1833 . . . Address of the Committee to the Citizens of North Carolina*; Konkle, *Morehead*, 123–24.

4. "Memorial of the Convention on Internal Improvements," November 1833, in *Report of the Board of Internal Improvements*, 1833; Watson, *Jacksonian Politics and Community Conflict*, 156–58.

5. *Report of the Board of Internal Improvements*, 1833; *Farmers' Register*, January 1834.

6. Daniel, *Swain*, 342, 355.

7. John L. Sullivan to DLS, October 14, 1833, Gaston Papers, SHC; Will Gaston to DLS, October 24, 1833, EC, NCC; DLS to William Gaston, November 9, 1833, Gaston Papers, SHC.

8. James C. Johnston to DLS, September 22, October 7, 30, 1833, EC, NCC.

9. Joshua Forman to DLS, June 25, 1833, February 17, March 26, 1834, EC, NCC; Green, C. Sylvester, "Forman, Joshua," Powell, *DNCB*, 2:220–21.

10. Joseph Gales to DLS, October 30, 1833, EC, NCC; James Mauney to DLS, May 2, 1834, Swain GP vol. 3, SANC; Will Gaston to DLS, October 14, 1834, EC, NCC; Benjamin Wright to William Gaston, January 15, 1834, Gaston Papers, SHC.

11. M. Ring to DLS, December 12, 1833, and W. Nichols to DLS, December 22, 1833, EC, NCC.

12. Joseph Seawell Jones to DLS, January 2, 1833, January 22, 1834, EC, NCC.

13. James Wyche to DLS, February 15, 1833; DLS to James Wyche, February 18, 1833, August 23, 1834; James Wyche to DLS, August 29, 1834, Swain GLB 30, SANC.

14. *Western Carolinian*, December 2, 1833; Daniel, *Swain*, 357.

15. Will Gaston to DLS, August 16, 1833, EC, NCC; Cowan (no first name shown) to DLS, October 14, 1833, ibid.; Edward B. Dudley et al. to DLS, July 13, 1833, Swain GP vol. 2, SANC.

16. Charles J. Williams and Hugh McQueen to DLS, August 15, 1833; Thomas G. Polk to DLS, October 3, November 5, 1833; (illegible) to DLS, September 22, 1833, EC, NCC.

17. Daniel, *Swain*, 332; Powell, *Annals of Progress*, 39.

18. John H. Bryan to DLS, August 12, 1834, and DLS to John H. Bryan, August 23, 1834; DLS to William Gaston, September 6, 1834, Gaston Papers, SHC; Will Gaston to DLS, September 11, 1834, EC, NCC.

19. *N.C. House Journal*, November 25, 27, 30, December 5, 1833, December 13, 20, 1834, January 3, 9, December 7, 9, 1835; *N.C. Senate Journal*, November 30, December 6, 12, 1834; DLS to General Assembly, December 4, 1833, December 10, 20, 1834, December 7, 1835, Swain GLB 30, SANC.

20. DLS to President, Secretary or Treasurer of several Turnpike Companies, September 23, 1833, Swain GLB 30, SANC.

21. Wm. (?) Welch to DLS, November 15, 1834, Swain GP vol. 5, SANC; James Owen to DLS, February 22, 1834, EC, NCC.

22. DLS to John H. Bryan, August 20, 1833, Bryan Papers, SANC.

23. DLS to Joseph B. Skinner et al. (12 recipients), September 26, 1833, Swain GLB 30, SANC; W.S. Mhoon (Treasury Department) to DLS, August 28, 1833, Swain GLB 30, SANC.

24. DLS to Duncan Cameron, November 14, 1833, Cameron Papers, SHC; Daniel, *Swain*, 342. See generally Watson, "Squire Oldway and His Friends," 54 NCHR 105, 105, 110; Jeffrey, "Internal Improvements and Political Parties in Antebellum North Carolina, 1836–1860," 55 NCHR 111, 116, 119; Daniel, *Swain*, 321–70; Wallace, Carolyn A., "Swain, David Lowery [sic]," Powell, *DNCB*, 5:483, 484.

25. DLS to EHS, April 10, 11, 1834, EC, NCC.

26. Ibid., April 24, 1834.

27. Subscriptions: Proclamation of Governor, January 18, 1833, Swain GLB 30, SANC (also in *Greensborough Patriot*, January 30, 1833); James B. Skinner, N. Brewer, D. W. Stone to DLS, April 5, 1833, Swain GP vol. 1, SANC; Vasdry McBee to DLS, April 10, 1834, Swain GP vol. 3; C. L. Hinton to DLS, January 12, 1833, Swain GP vol. 1, SANC; document showing seven subscribers to Bank of North Carolina stock in Elizabeth City, SANC; *Raleigh Register and North-Carolina Gazette*, April 23, 1833, January 28, 1834. Meetings: DLS to William H. Haywood Jr., Spier Whitaker, Joseph A. Hill, December 2, 1833, Swain GLB 30, SANC; DLS to Gavin Hogg, December 2, 1833, ibid.; DLS to Hugh McQueen, Spier Whitaker, Joseph A. Hill, January 1, 1833, ibid.; DLS to William H. Haywood Jr., January 5, 1833, ibid.; William Hill and N. A. Stedman to DLS, July 29, 1835, ibid. (on Stedman, see Cheney, *North Carolina Government*, 182, 197n.83); DLS, William Hill, N.A. Stedman to William Boylan, September 5, 1835, Swain GLB 30, SANC; DLS to Weston R. Gales, August 30, 1834, ibid.; DLS to Gavin Hogg, May 23, 1834, January 5, 1835, ibid.; James Owen to DLS, April 10, 1835, ibid. Reports: Will H. Haywood Jr. and Spier Whitaker to DLS, July 1 1833, ibid.; R. M. Saunders to DLS, January 17, 1833, ibid.; DLS to General Assembly, December 11, 1833, ibid. (also *N.C. House Journal*, December 12, 1833, November 23, 1835; *N.C. Senate Journal*, December 13, 1833). Other: E. T. Troop (?) to DLS, January 30, 1833, Swain GP vol. 1, SANC; James Owen to DLS, February 22, 1834, EC, NCC; *Western Carolinian*, April 5, 1834; Daniel, *Swain*, 302–8; *Message of the Governor in Relation to the Stock Reserved to the State in the Bank of the State*.

28. *Report of the President and Directors of the Literary Fund of North Carolina*, 1833; *Report of the President and Directors of the Literary Fund of North Carolina*, 1835; *N.C. House Journal*, November 17, 1835; W. S. Mhoon, Treasury Department of North Carolina, to DLS, August 28, 1833, Swain GLB 30, SANC; see Coon, *Beginnings of*

Public Education in North Carolina, 2:712–14; Noble, *History of the Public Schools of North Carolina*, 77–78; Powell, *North Carolina: A Bicentennial History*, 108.

29. Samuel Wait, Wake Forest Institute, to William Gaston, June 30, 1834, Gaston Papers, SHC ("Another note will accompany this to Gov. Swain"; that note was not found); John L. Gay to William Gaston, October 21, 1837, Gaston Papers, SHC (reference to Swain's attending examinations "about three years ago").

30. Battle, *History*, 1:346, 824; Kornegay, "The North Carolina Institute of Education, 1831–1834," 36 NCHR 141, 143–46; BOTM, January 5, 1832. Swain had been nominated for a trustee position earlier, but his name was withdrawn. *Western Carolinian*, February 13, 1827.

31. BOTM, June 20, December 10, 1832.

32. Ibid., January 2, June 25, December 17, 1833.

33. Ibid., January 2, 1835.

34. Ibid., December 10, 1833, June 27, December 5, 1835; BOT Resolution, March 5, 1835, UP; see Battle, *History*, 1:124–25, 328, 350–51, 385–87, 401.

35. DLS to General Assembly, December 24, 1832, January 1, 1833, December 1833 (exact date not shown), December 20, 1834, November 23, December 1, 1835, Swain GLB 30, SANC; *N.C. House Journal*, December 26, 1832, January 2, December 21, 1833, December 20, 1834; *N.C. Senate Journal*, December 23, 1833.

36. George E. Badger to DLS, August 16, 1833; Battle, *History*, 1:259, 789, 834.

37. John H. Wheeler to DLS, June 17, 1834, EC, NCC.

38. John M. Dick to DLS, August 8, 1834, Swain GP vol. 4, SANC.

39. James H. Hooper to DLS, July 10, 1833, UP.

40. S. Whitaker to President UNC BOT, September 16, 1834, ibid.

41. Anonymous circular letter, May 28, 1834, UP.

42. Joseph Caldwell to DLS, April 1, 1834, EC, NCC; *Raleigh Register and North-Carolina Gazette*, June 17, 1834, May 12, 1835.

43. Perrin Busbee and James Crichton to DLS, February 21, 1835, and DLS to Perrin Busbee and James Crichton, February 24, 1835, Swain GLB 30, SANC.

44. BOTM, June 27, 1835.

45. See generally Daniel, *Swain*, 314–22.

46. DLS to Gavin Hogg, August 10, 1835, quoted in Coon, *Beginnings of Public Education in North Carolina*, 2:727.

47. Minutes of Meeting of Directors of the Literary Fund, Executive Office, January 13, 1834, Swain GP vol. 3, SANC. See Daniel, *Swain*, 312–14; York, Maurice C., "Library, State," in Powell, *Encyclopedia of North Carolina*, 672; Coon, *Beginnings of Public Education in North Carolina*, 2:688–89.

48. Francis L. Hawks to DLS, May 8, 1835, Swain Papers, SHC; DLS to William Gaston, September 16, 1835, Gaston Papers, SHC; Will Gaston to DLS, October 9,

1835, Swain GP vol. 6, SANC; James Donaldson to DLS, November 26, 1835, ibid.; Coon, *Beginnings of Public Education in North Carolina*, 2:721, 728–29. As to James Donaldson, see Allcott, J. V., "Donaldson, Robert, Jr.," in Powell, *DNCB*, 2:92; Anderson, *Carolinian on the Hudson*, 130–31.

49. Jonathan Worth to DLS, May 12, 1834, and DLS to Jonathan Worth, May 29, 1834, Swain GP vol. 4; V. M. Murphey to DLS, July 9, 30, August 25, September 15, 1834, Swain GP vols. 4, 5; DLS to Dr. Murphey, August 5, 1834, Swain GP vol. 4; V. M. Murphey to Wm. R. Hill, Swain GP vol. 5, SANC; book and valuation lists, Swain GP vol. 5, SANC; see Coon, *Beginnings of Public Education in North Carolina*, 2:688–89.

50. DLS to Joseph Seawell Jones, December 30, 1832, Swain Papers, SANC; *Raleigh Register*, November 18, 1834; Barile, *Undaunted Heart*, 142.

51. John C. Hamilton to DLS, July 28, September 23, 1834, EC, NCC; DLS to John C. Hamilton, September 6, 1834, Swain GLB 30, SANC; DLS to Will Gaston, August 21, September 6, 1834, Gaston Papers, SHC; Will Gaston to John C. Hamilton, August 1, 30, 1833, ibid.; Will Gaston to DLS, August 1, 30, 1833, EC, NCC; John C. Hamilton to DLS, September 25, 1834, Swain GLB 30, SANC; DLS to John C. Hamilton, October 10, 1834, ibid.; John C. Hamilton to William Gaston, September 27, 1834, Gaston Papers, SHC; "Correspondence in 1834 Between John C. Hamilton, Esq., of New York, and Judge Gaston and Governor Swain, in Relation to Interesting Events in the History of North Carolina," *North Carolina University Magazine*, 10:513–28 (May 1861).

52. Will Gaston to John C. Hamilton, July 17, 1834, Gaston Papers, SHC; Allen J. Davie to DLS, July 16, 1833, Swain GLB 30 and Swain GP vol. 2, SANC, and July 17, 1834, Gaston Papers, SHC; DLS to Allen J. Davie, July 25, 1833, Swain GLB 30, SANC; DLS to S. C. Clarke, July 25, 1833, ibid.

53. The reference is to John Lawson, *A New Voyage to Carolina* (London, 1709), and John Brickell, *The Natural History of North-Carolina* (Dublin, Ireland: James Carson, 1737).

54. DLS to [George Bancroft], August 26, 1835, Swain GLB 30, SANC; see Daniel, *Swain*, 301, 301n.118. Daniel states that Swain had lost the letter to which he was replying. The name of the addressee is not shown on this letter. Daniel was convinced that it was clearly to Bancroft; this author shares that view.

55. V. M. Murphey to DLS, January 30, 1833, Swain GP vol. 1, September 25, 1833, EC, NCC. Swain's initial letter to Murphey has not been found, but its content is clear from the first of the Murphey letters cited above.

56. Joseph Seawell Jones to DLS, January 17, August 24, October 26, 1833, January 22, February 12, October 23, 1834, EC, NCC. See generally Miles, "Joseph Seawell Jones of Shocco —Historian and Humbug," 34 NCHR 483; Miles, Edwin A., "Jones, Joseph Seawell," in Powell, *DNCB*, 3:322–23.

57. DLS to Dameron Pugh, March 5, 1834, and Dameron Pugh to DLS, May 8, 1834; DLS to John Guion, March 5, 1834, and John Guion to DLS, March 9, 15, 1834; Peter P. Lawrence to DLS, March 13, 1834; DLS to Gov. Iredell, March 19, 1834; DLS to James Harrison, Nathan Foscue, and John H. Hammond, March 27, 1834, Swain GLB 30, SANC.

58. Francis L. Hawks to DLS, May 18, 1835, Swain Papers, SHC; John Nash Johnston to DLS, April 24, 1834, Swain GP vol. 3, SANC; DLS to John Gatlin, March 3, 1834, Swain GLB 30, SANC.

59. James G. M. Ramsey to WAG, April 8, 1848, Hamilton et al., *Papers of Graham*, 3:219.

Chapter 5: Less Visionary Aspects

1. DLS to William Gaston, November 9, 1833, Gaston Papers, SHC.

2. Montford Stokes to DLS, December 14, 1832; Louis D. Wilson to DLS, December 26, 1832; DLS to Louis D. Wilson, December 26, 1832, Swain GP vol. 1, SANC.

3. N.C. Const. (1776), sec. 20; Daniel, *Swain*, 270, 278.

4. Swain GLB 30, SANC (Hill); *Raleigh Register and North-Carolina Gazette*, January 21, 1834 (Outlaw).

5. J. C. Norcam to DLS, January 1, 1835, Swain GP vol. 5, SANC; document dated June 5, 1834, Swain GLB 30, SANC.

6. DLS to: e.g. (appointments), Edward Stanley, December 1835 (solicitor, second judicial circuit); William I. Alexander, November 26, 1833 (solicitor, sixth judicial circuit); John F. Poindexter, December 1835 (attorney general); John R. I. Daniel, January 3, 1835 (solicitor general); John M. Dick, December 1835 (superior court judge); William Gaston, November 29, 1833 (supreme court judge); Bedford Brown, December 1, 1834 (U.S. senator), Swain GLB 30, SANC; e.g. (resignations), N.C. General Assembly, December 7, 1832 (John Hall as judge of supreme court); January 2, 1833 (J. J. Daniel as judge of superior court).

7. E.g., Sheriffs of Sixth Congressional District to DLS, August 16, 1835; DLS to William B. Shepard, September 25, 1833, and to Micajah T. Hawkins, October 3, 1835, Swain GLB 30, SANC.

8. Joshua Roberts to DLS, June 10, 1833; DLS to Joshua Roberts, June 19, 1833; Joshua Roberts to DLS, July 3, 1833; Swain document, January 1, 1835, Swain GLB 30, SANC.

9. Swain document, July 21, 1835, Swain GLB 30, SANC (Duncan Cameron and Alfred Jones replaced by John Beckwith and William McPheters); Daniel, *Swain*, 290–91.

10. William J. Alexander to DLS, February 10, 1833, Swain GP vol. 1, SANC; James Graham to DLS, May 23, 1833, EC, NCC; DLS to James Martin, June 20, 1833, Swain GLB 30, SANC; D. L. Barringer to DLS, June 24, 1833, Swain GP vol. 2, SANC.

11. W. B. Lockhart to DLS, May 7, 1834, and DLS to W. B. Lockhart, May 14, 1834, Swain GLB 30, SANC.

12. Swain document appointing original commissioners, January 14, 1834, Swain GLB 30, SANC; Swain document appointing Nash to replace Hogg, February 3, 1835, ibid.; *Message of the Governor Transmitting a Communication from the Commissioners appointed to Revise the Public Statutes*; James Iredell to DLS, March 29, 1834, EC, NCC; *N.C. Senate Journal*, December 5, 1834, November 26, 1835; *N.C. House Journal*, December 4, 6, 1834, November 25, December 9, 1835; *Raleigh Register and North-Carolina Gazette*, December 17, 1833, January 21, 1834; see Camp, *Swain*, 44, Daniel, *Swain*, 282–84, Edwards, *People and Their Peace*, 37, 272–73.

13. Will Gaston to Thomas P. Devereux, August 19, 1833, Gaston Papers, SHC; Will Gaston to DLS, August 18, 1833, EC, NCC; DLS to William Gaston, August 8, 15, 1833, Gaston Papers, SHC; T. P. Devereux to William Gaston, August 15, 1833, ibid.; William Gaston to Robert Donaldson, August 17, 1833, ibid.; William Gaston to Thomas P. Devereux, August 19, 1833, ibid.; T.P. Devereux to William Gaston, August 21, 1833, ibid.; DLS to William Gaston, August 27, 1833, ibid.; T. P. Devereux to William Gaston, August 30, 1833, ibid.; G. E. Badger, T. P. Devereux, and DLS to William Gaston, September 9, 1833, ibid.; William Gaston to Thomas P. Devereux, September 9, 1833, ibid.; William Gaston to Thomas Ruffin, September 9, 1833, ibid.; George E. Badger to William Gaston, November 14, 1833, ibid.; Thomas G. Polk to DLS, November 5, 1833, EC, NCC; certificate of Gaston's election, December 28, 1833, Swain GP vol. 3, SANC; *Raleigh Register*, December 3, 1833; Connor, *William Gaston: A Southern Federalist*, 39–40; Edwards, *People and Their Peace*, 52–53; Daniel, *Swain*, 272–78; Schauinger, "William Gaston and the Supreme Court of North Carolina," 21 NCHR 97, 101–5.

14. See note 12, chapter 3 and accompanying text.

15. Reuben Pickett to DLS, July 31, 1833, State Series vol. 2, SANC; Proclamation of August 5, 1833, Swain GLB 30, SANC; *Raleigh Register and North-Carolina Gazette*, August 13, September 10, October 8, 1833. A North Carolina statute dating to 1779 prohibited the taking of "any slave or slaves, the property of another," for sale to another or for personal use; the penalty was "death without benefit of clergy." *Laws of North Carolina*, chapter 34, 10, and note 10 (history) (1837).

16. Proclamation of July 24, 1833, Swain GLB 30, SANC; Solomon Pender, coroner of Edgecombe County, to DLS, July 14, 1833, Swain GP vol. 2, SANC; J. B. B. to DLS, July 1, 1835, and William Jones to DLS, July 4, 1835, Swain GLB 30, SANC; *Raleigh Register and North-Carolina Gazette*, August 13, October 8, 1833.

17. DLS to William V. Speight, December 18, 1833; DLS to N.C. General Assembly, December 11, 1834; James K. Trice to DLS, September 26, November 15, 1834; Statement, DLS to James K. Trice, W. R. Hill, Secretary (for DLS), to James K. Trice, October 1834, Swain GLB 30, SANC.

18. DLS to Governor of South Carolina, January 14, 1834, and to Governor of New York, May 23, 1834, Swain GLB 30, SANC. For other examples of Swain extradition requests, see DLS to Governor of Virginia, November 18, 1833; to Governor of South Carolina, April 3, 1834; to Governor of Georgia, July 18, August 30, 1834, ibid.

19. R. M. Saunders to DLS, July 3, 1834, Swain GP vol. 4, SANC; I. L. Bailey to DLS, November 13, 1833, Swain GP vol. 2, SANC; James McKinney to DLS, October 9, 1833, ibid.; DLS to James McKinney, October 23, 1833, Swain GLB 30, SANC; Charles Fisher to DLS, January 5, 1835, Swain GP vol. 5, SANC.

20. John H. Ezell to DLS, April 25, 1835, Swain GLB 30, SANC; F. Slater to DLS, January 29, 1835, and DLS to Fielding Slater, February 2, 1835, ibid.; F. Slater to DLS, February 12, 1835, Swain GP vol. 5, SANC. For other examples of extradition expenses, see Richard W. Ashton to DLS, August 3, 1834, and William R. Hill to Richard W. Ashton, August 13, 1834, Swain GP vol. 4, SANC; Frederic S. Blount to DLS, June 23, 1834, Swain GLB 30, SANC.

21. DLS to: Dr. J. W. Potts, October 23, 1833, Swain GP vol. 2, SANC; Colonel W. I. Alexander, September 4, 1834, Swain GLB 30, SANC; Joseph H. Wilson, Esq., September 26, 1834, Swain GP vol. 5, SANC. For examples of Swain's implementation of this philosophy, see Swain Document, May 23, 1833, Swain GLB 30, SANC (on recommendation of attorney general and "several respectable gentlemen," pardons offender and remits remainder of term); Swain Document, January 4, 1834, Swain GP vol. 3, SANC (partial pardon of John G. Womack on recommendation of attorney general and a number of respectable citizens); DLS to Romulus Saunders, February 7, 1834, Swain GLB 30, SANC (encloses petition for pardon and requests attorney general's views).

22. DLS to Rev. J. W. Capers et al., May 29, 1834, Swain GLB 30, SANC; undated document in Swain's hand and bearing his signature, responding to petitions for Benjamin S. Seaborn, Cumberland County, under sentence of death, Swain GP vol. 6, SANC; DLS to Henry Potter, May 1834 (exact date not shown), May 26, 1834, Swain GLB 30, SANC.

23. James Simpson to DLS, November 14, 1833, Swain GP vol. 2, SANC.

24. Joshua Lee et al. (numerous citizens of Davidson County) to DLS, October 29, 1833, Swain GP vol. 2, SANC; John M. Dick to DLS, November 15, 1833, ibid.; Swain document pardoning David Owens, January 7, 1834, Swain GLB 30, SANC.

25. Henry A. Martin to DLS, May 8, 1835, Swain GP vol. 6, SANC.

26. Steven Frontis to DLS, May 30, 1835, ibid. Re: "Negro stealing," see supra note 15.

27. Undated petition on behalf of "Negro Martin," ibid.

28. Petition on behalf of Emdemsy Laney, April 26, 1833, Swain GP vol. 1, and Swain proclamation, August 1, 1833, Swain GP vol. 2; 1834 petition for Jeremiah Carter, Swain GP vol. 5, SANC.

29. Illegible to DLS, November 23, 1833, Swain GP vol. 3, SANC.

30. Petition for Daniel Webb, "a free man of colour," July 22, 1834, Swain GP vol. 4, and Swain proclamation on Webb's behalf, July 25, 1834, Swain GLB 30, SANC.

31. John McMordy (?) to DLS, May 11, 1835, enclosing Step. Davis, M.D. to DLS, May 11, 1835, Swain GP vol. 6, SANC.

32. Swain pardon of Leslie Lee (?), December 17, 1834, Swain GLB 30, SANC.

33. Swain proclamations, William D. Sawyer, September 27, 1833, Swain GLB 30, SANC; Sampson Tarleton and Littleton Moore, May 27, 1834, ibid.; Jesse Davidson, June 2, 1834, ibid.; Benjamin Davis, August 15, 1834, ibid.; Wilborne Shoemaker, November 23, 1834, ibid.; John G. Wommack, January 4, 1834, ibid.

34. Swain proclamations, John L. Register, April 5, 1834, Swain GP vol. 3; William H. Blakely, October 6, 1834, Swain GP vol. 5 and Swain GLB 30; Samuel Davis, January 2, 1835, Swain GLB 30; Christopher Vandergriff, May 18, 1833, ibid.; William Jones and son Elias Jones, June 15, 1833, ibid.; Ricks Harrell, February 21, 1834, ibid.; J. L. Register, April 5, 1834, ibid.; William Newton, December 5, 1833, ibid.; Betsy Amos, November 30, 1833, ibid., SANC.

35. Swain proclamations, William R. Valentine, March 21, 1835, Swain GLB 30; Wilson Hodges, February 23, 1833, ibid.; Jo. Gillespie to Mr. Hodges, January 11, 1833, Swain GP vol. 1, SANC.

36. Reuben Pickett to DLS, May 14, 1833, Swain GP vol. 2, SANC.

37. Surry County citizens' petition, April 5, 1833, and Jo. Williams to DLS, April 12, 1833, Swain GP vol. 1, SANC. But see contra George N. Cloud (and thirteen others) to DLS, April 16, 1833, Swain GP vol. 1, SANC (prisoner seduced to commit crime and intoxicated at time); several citizens' petition (undated; "1833" penciled at top), Swain GP vol. 3, SANC (prisoner appears reformed; would "probably become an orderly and useful member of society").

38. DLS to Governor of Virginia, February 6, 1833, Swain GLB 30, SANC; John Scott to DLS, February 23, 1833, Swain GP vol. 1, SANC; W.D. Devereaux to DLS, March 4, 1833, Swain GP vol. 1, SANC; petition with fifteen signatures, March 4, 1833, ibid.; DLS to the Hon. Thomas Settle and John Scott, March 7, 1833, Swain GLB 30, SANC; Thomas Settle to DLS, March 9, 1833, and John Scott to DLS, March 9, 1833, ibid.; Swain order, March 27, 1833, ibid.; DLS to Sheriff or Jailor of Granville County, May 8, 1833, ibid.; James Wyche to DLS, May 25, 1833, Swain GP vol. 2, SANC; petition on behalf of Washington Taburn, March 31, 1834, Swain GP vol. 3, SANC; James M. Wiggins to DLS, April 2, 1834, Swain GLB 30 and Swain GP vol. 3, SANC; DLS

to James M. Wiggins, April 7, 1834, Swain GLB 30, SANC; DLS to (no addressee or date shown), Swain GP vol. 3, SANC; Daniel, *Swain*, 263-64.

39. Lewis Taylor to DLS, February 7, 1833, Swain GP vol. 1, SANC; F. Nash to DLS, August 28, 1833, Swain GP vol. 2, SANC; petition to General Assembly, William Paris et al., November 26, 1833, Swain GP vol. 3, SANC (other petitions here with same language); James A. Rupell to DLS, April 23, 1833, Swain GLB 30, SANC; Erwin Panhall to DLS, July 8, 1833, Swain GLB 30 and Swain GP vol. 2, SANC; James M. Wiggins to DLS, March 8, 1834, Swain GLB 30, SANC; DLS to James M. Wiggins, March 20, 1834, ibid.; James M. Wiggins to DLS, March 25, 1834, ibid.; Th. T. Hunt to DLS, March 24, 1834, ibid.; DLS to Thomas T. Hunt, Thomas B. Lillyjohn, D. T. Paschall, March 31, 1834, ibid.; Swain proclamation, April 17, 1834, ibid.; Robert Potter to DLS, August 6, 1834, ibid.; James M. Wiggins to DLS, August 8, 1834, ibid.; DLS to James M. Wiggins, August 11, 1834, ibid.; DLS to John Scott, Sol. Gen., August 11, 1834, ibid.; Daniel, *Swain*, 265-67.

40. H. Potter to DLS, May 23, 1834, Swain GP vol. 4 (also in Swain GLB 30), SANC; L. W. Capers to DLS, May 27, 1834, Swain GP vol. 4, SANC; DLS to Henry Potter, May 26, 1834, Swain GLB 30, SANC; document in Swain's handwriting, May 29, 1834, Swain GP vol. 4, SANC; H. Potter to DLS, May 30, 1834, Swain GP vol. 4 (also in Swain GLB 30), SANC.

41. T. W. Wilson to DLS, June 3, 1833, Swain GP vol. 2; William C. Bivens and Thomas Wilson to DLS, June 3, 1833, ibid.; (first name illegible) Thomas to DLS, June 3, 1833, ibid.; Samuel Hillman and Thomas W. Wilson to DLS, June 8, 1833, ibid.; Th. W. Wilson to DLS, June 12, 1833, ibid.; Swain respite order, June 18, 1833, Swain GLB 30; petition for Frankie Silver, June 29, 1833, Swain GP vol. 2; M. Burus (?) to DLS, June 30, 1833, ibid.; W.C. Bevans (Bivens?) to DLS, June 30, 1833, Swain GLB 30; DLS to W.C. Bevans (Bivens?), July 9, 1833, ibid.; two undated petitions for Frankie Silver ("1833" penciled at top of one), Swain GP vol. 3; Swain proclamation for Leslee Barrett, April 2, 1835, Swain GLB 30, SANC. The Young quote is in Young, *The Untold Story of Frankie Silver*, 68.

42. Young, *The Untold Story of Frankie Silver*, 101-2 (1994 petition). Books: Sheppard, *Cabin in the Laurel*; McCrumb, *Ballad of Frankie Silver*; Young, *The Untold Story of Frankie Silver*. Song: Bascom Lamar Lunsford, "The Ballad of Frankie Silver," see McCrumb, *Ballad of Frankie Silver*, 383. Plays: Howard Williams, "The Legend of Frankie Silver," and Susan Graham Erwin, "The Ballad of Frankie Silver," see Young, *The Untold Story of Frankie Silver*, 99. For briefer commentary, see Eubanks, *Literary Trails of the North Carolina Mountains*, 357; Phifer, *Burke: The History of a North Carolina County*, 345; Sondley, *History of Buncombe County*, 2:765-67. On Swain's use of the pardoning power generally, see Edwards, *People and Their Peace*, 59-61.

43. Joel Vannoy to DLS, January 29, 1833, Swain GLB 30, SANC; DLS to Joel

Vannoy, February 4, 1833, ibid.; DLS to Lewis Cass, February 4, 1833, ibid.; DLS to S.P. Carson, February 8, 1833, ibid.; DLS to Gen'l Thomas Love, March 2, 1833, ibid.; DLS to Joel Vannoy, February 4, 1833, Swain GP vol. 1, SANC; Lewis Cass to DLS, February 26, 1833, ibid.

44. Alex Macomb to DLS, March 4, 1833; Winfield Scott to DLS, March 22, 1833; DLS to George W. Gardner [sic], April 4, 1833, Swain GLB 30, SANC.

45. James Whitaker to DLS, March 22, 1833, Swain GLB 30, SANC; J. R. Siler to DLS, April 26, 1833, Swain GP vol. 1, SANC.

46. G.W. Gardner [sic] to DLS, April 20, 1833, Swain GLB 30, SANC; DLS to Capt. Geo. W. Gardner [sic], May 8, 1833, ibid.; G.W. Gardiner to DLS, May 6, 1833, ibid. (report from Lt. J. E. Brackett enclosed); DLS to Capt. F. G. (?) Belton, July 19, 1833, ibid.; Capt. F. G. (?) Belton to DLS, July 28, 1833, Swain GP vol. 2; Daniel, *Swain*, 267–70.

47. R. M. Saunders to DLS, May 15, 1834, Swain GP vol. 4 and GLB 30, SANC; DLS to R. M. Saunders, May 19, 1834, Swain GLB 30, SANC; DLS to Joshua Roberts, July 30, 1833, ibid.; DLS to Col. Montgomery, Agent of the Cherokee Nation, April 7, 1834, ibid.

48. Joshua Roberts to DLS, September 30, 1834, Swain GLB 30, SANC (Andrew Pickens to Joshua Roberts, September 4, 1834, enclosed); DLS to Joshua Roberts, September 30, 1834, ibid.; DLS to Andrew Pickens, September 30, 1834, ibid.; DLS to Governor of Georgia (apparently; not shown), April 6, 1835 (similar letter to Governor of Tennessee, same date), Swain GLB 30, SANC; R. A. Greene, Secretary to Georgia Governor Lumpkin, to DLS, April 17, 1835, Swain GLB 30, SANC; Andrew Pickens to DLS, April 1, 1835, ibid.; DLS to Andrew Pickens, April 6, 1835, ibid.; Cherokee Removal and Acting Indian Agent (no name shown) to DLS, May 29, 1835, ibid.; DLS to Lewis Cass, April 4, 1835, and Lewis Cass to DLS, April 17, 1835, ibid.

49. DLS to Louis D. Henry, Speaker, House of Commons, December 15, 1832, Swain GLB 30, SANC; DLS to N.C. General Assembly, December 6, 1834, ibid.; *N.C. House Journal*, December 15, 1832, December 2, 4, 10, 1833, January 7, 1834, December 4, 6, 1834; *N.C. Senate Journal*, December 3, 1833, January 10, 1834.

50. DLS to Lewis Cass, February 4, 1833, and to Samuel P. Carson, February 8, 1833, Swain GLB 30, SANC.

51. N.C. Const. (1776), sec. 18, in Cheney, *North Carolina Government*, 813; Daniel, *Swain*, 267, 510.

52. DLS to General Assembly, December 24, 1833, Swain GLB 30, SANC; *N.C. House Journal*, December 26, 1833; *N.C. Senate Journal*, December 27, 1833.

53. J. N. Bynum to DLS, April 30, 1833, Swain GP vol. 1; Lt. Rob. Gave to DLS, September 2, 1833, Swain GP vol. 2; John M. Woodard to DLS, August 7, 1834, Swain GP vol. 4, SANC. Other examples: Sandy Harris to DLS, February 9, 1833, Swain GP vol.

1; Gen. D. Newland to DLS, March 25, 1833, ibid.; David Matson, Col., to DLS, April 19, 1833, ibid.; A. E. Hanner to DLS, May 9, 1833, Swain GP vol. 2; James R. Hoyle to DLS, June 20, 1833, ibid.; Jesse Myrick to DLS, July 7, 1833, Swain GP vol. 1, SANC.

54. Wm. M. Allbritton to DLS, June 2, 1833, Swain GP vol. 2; W. R. Hill, Private Secretary to Gov. Swain, to Lt. Col. Wm. Albritton, September 14, 1833, ibid.; Wm. C. Emmett to DLS, February 12, 1833, Swain GP vol. 1; N. N. Podun to DLS, May 13, 1833, Swain GP vol. 2; D. M. Barringer to DLS, December 16, 1833, ibid.; J. N. Cook to DLS, March 28, 1834, Swain GP vol. 3, SANC.

55. Charles H. Winder to DLS, December 26, 1832; Col. Alex McRae to DLS, April 23, 1835; P. W. Fanning to DLS, April 25, 1835; DLS to Capt. P. W. Fanning, May 1, 1835; DLS to Col. Geo. Boniford, Ordinance Dept., May 1, 1835, Swain GLB 30, SANC.

56. Bev Daniel to DLS, January 12, 1835, Swain GLB 30, SANC.

57. Col. Jesse Myrick to DLS, March 7, 1834, and DLS to Jesse Myrick, March 16, 1834, Swain GP vol. 3, SANC.

58. John I. Pasteur, Maj. Genl., to DLS, April 15, 1834, Swain GP vol. 5; see also Alfred Dockery to DLS, February 4, 1835, Swain GP vol. 5; M. T. Hawkins, Maj. Gen., to DLS, April 27, 1835, Swain GP vol. 6, SANC. For similar instances see Thomas Battle to DLS, March 16, 1834, Swain GP vol. 3; Joseph Arrington Jr., Brigadier General, to DLS, March 1, 1834, and DLS to Joseph Arrington Jr., March 3, 1834, Swain GLB 30; Dan Coleman to DLS, March 20, 1834, Swain GP vol. 3; Louis D. Wilson to DLS, April 18, 1834, ibid., SANC.

59. DLS to Genl. Beverly Daniel, August 22, 1833; Bev Daniel, Adj. Gen., to DLS, August 26, 1833; Lewis [sic] McLane, Dept. of State, to DLS, November 30, 1833, DLS to Lewis [sic] McLane, December 14, 1833, Swain GLB 30, SANC.

60. Louis McLane to DLS, August 1, 1833, DLS to Louis McLane, September 24, 1833, Swain GLB 30; Louis McLane to DLS, September 1, 1833, Swain GP vol. 2, John Forsyth to DLS, September 20, 1834, Swain GLB 30; DLS to John Forsyth, September 26, 30, 1834, ibid.; DLS to Louis McLane, September 24, 1833, Swain GP vol. 2, SANC.

61. DLS to President of the U.S., January 15, 1833; Lew Cass to DLS, November 20, 1833; DLS to Levi Woodbury, September 3, 1834; DLS to President, Members of Congress, State Governors, January 19, 1834, and to Members of Congress, January 20, 1834, Swain GLB 30, SANC.

62. William Crawford to DLS, September 24, 1833, Swain GP vol. 2; Lewis [sic] M'Lane to DLS, November 30, 1833, Swain GP vol. 3; Walter Lourie to DLS, July 19, 1834, Swain GP vol. 4 and Swain GLB 30; John Forsyth to DLS, September 16, 1834, Swain GP vol. 5 and Swain GLB 30; DLS to John Forsyth, September 24, 1834, Swain GLB 30; Levi Woodbury to DLS, January 22, 1835, Swain GP vol. 5 and Swain GLB

30; J.L. Edwards to DLS, November 4, 1835, Swain GP vol. 6; Louis McLane to DLS, July 15, 1833, Swain GLB 30, SANC.

63. Edward Livingston to DLS, March 25, 1833; DLS to Louis McLane, July 19, 1833; Louis McLane to DLS, July 26, 1833, Swain GLB 30, SANC.

64. DLS to Edward Livingston, April 7, 1833, and Edward Livingston to DLS, April 13, 1833; DLS to William S. Mhoon, August 22, 1833; DLS to Judges of the Superior Courts, August 22, 1833; DLS to N.C. Members of Congress, August 23, 1833, Swain GLB 30, SANC.

65. Louis McLane to DLS, February 18, 1834; DLS to John Forsyth, March 4, 1835 (with accompanying document), Swain GLB 30, SANC.

66. R. M. Saunders to DLS, January 4, 1833, Swain GP vol. 1, and February 16, 1834, Swain GLB 30, SANC; DLS to Bedford Brown, February 16, 1834, Swain GLB 30, SANC; R. M. Saunders to DLS, May 10, 31, 1834, and DLS to R. M. Saunders, June 6, 1834, ibid.; R. M. Saunders to DLS, June 4, November 10, 1835, Swain GP vol. 6, SANC; L. L. Edwards to DLS, November 4, 1835, Swain GP vol. 6, SANC; DLS to N.C. General Assembly, December 9, 1834 (enclosing Saunders' communication), ibid.; *N.C. House Journal*, November 22, 1833, December 9, 1834; *N.C. Senate Journal*, December 9, 21, 1833.

67. DLS to Governors of the Several States and Territories, June 5, 1834, Swain GLB 30, SANC (replies: Robert Huas, Ohio, to DLS, June 18, 1834, Swain GP vol. 4, SANC; Pam G. Smith, Secretary's Office, Tennessee, to DLS, June 28, 1834, ibid.); Governor Roman of Louisiana to DLS, January 15, 1835, ibid.; William H. Richardson, Exec. Dept., Richmond, to DLS, October 9, 1833, Swain GP vol. 2, SANC.

68. E.g., John Reynolds, Illinois, to DLS, December 22, 1832, Swain GLB 30, SANC; Robert Z. Haynes, South Carolina, to DLS, January 5, 1833, ibid.; Henry W. Edwards, Connecticut, to DLS, August 10, 1833, ibid.; A.R. Nichols, Maine, to DLS, August 17, 1835, Swain GP vol. 6, SANC; James Thomas, Maryland, to DLS, June 6, 1834, Swain GLB 30, SANC; R. A. Greene, Georgia, to DLS, March 4, 1835, ibid.; William Ed Hayne, South Carolina, to DLS, July 22, 1834, Swain GP vol. 4, SANC.

69. DLS to N.C. General Assembly, December 28, 1832; John Reynolds to DLS, December 29, 1832; DLS to N.C. General Assembly, January 7, 1833; Levi Lincoln to DLS, January 23, 1833; C. P. Zennett (?) to DLS, January 31, 1833; Samuel E. Smith to DLS, February 20, 1833; Robert Lucas to DLS, February 26, 1833; A. M. Scott to DLS, March 6, 1833; Levi Lincoln to DLS, March 25, 1833; W. L. Marey to DLS, June 6, 1833; Robert Z. Haynes to DLS, January 5, 1833; Levi Lincoln to DLS, March 11, April 10, 12, 1833; Geo. Wolf to DLS, December 18, 1833; Samuel Dinsmoor to DLS, August 3, 1833; Wilson Lumpkin to DLS, January 1, 1834; J. Davis to DLS, March 3, 1834, Swain GLB 30, SANC.

70. *N.C. House Journal*, December 28, 1832, January 7, 1833; *N.C. Senate Journal*, December 24, 1833, January 5, 1835.

71. WPM to DLS, December 12, 1833, EC, NCC.

72. *The Register*, December 14, 1832.

73. John H. Wheeler to DLS, December 19, 1832, EC, NCC.

74. William Kennedy, Chair, to DLS, December 28, 1832, Swain GP vol. 1, SANC.

75. John C. Ehringhaus and Isaac Freeman to DLS, January 22, 1833, Swain GP vol. 1, SANC.

76. John Owen to DLS, January 1, 1833, EC, NCC.

77. Illegible to DLS, January 15, 1833, EC, NCC

78. M. O. King to DLS, June 21, 1833, and R. M. Saunders to DLS, June 25, 1833, Swain GP vol. 2, SANC.

79. J. W. Gwinn to DLS, September 11, 1834, and DLS to James W. Gwinn, September 23, 1834, Swain Papers, SHC.

80. WPM to DLS, December 22, 1833, Shanks, *Papers of Mangum*, 2:51–53.

81. D. L. Barringer to DLS, March 14, 1834, EC, NCC; McFarland, Daniel M., "Barringer, Daniel Laurens," in Powell, *DNCB*, 1:99.

82. James Iredell to DLS, March 29, 1834, EC, NCC.

83. *Georgia Journal*, December 2, 1834.

84. Blackwelder, *Age of Orange*, 75; Blackmun, *Western North Carolina*, 205, 236, 307, 311; Camp, *Swain*, 47; Hoffman, *Andrew Jackson and North Carolina Politics*, 116–17; Inscoe, *Mountain Masters*, 133; Kruman, *Parties and Politics in North Carolina, 1836–1865*, 5, 18–26, 55–59; Lefler and Newsome, *North Carolina*, 313, 328–29, 332, 335; Wallace, "David Lowry Swain, the First Whig Governor of North Carolina," 77–78.

85. George E. Badger to Mr. Webster, May 23, 1833, and Daniel Webster to George E. Badger, August 12, 1833, Swain GLB 30, SANC.

86. DLS to G. E. Badger, November 7, 1833; Geo. E. Badger to DLS, November 10, 1833; Daniel Webster to George E. Badger, May 24, 1834, Swain GLB 30, SANC.

87. DLS to General Assembly, December 2, 1833, ibid.

88. John D. Eccles to DLS, April 16, 1833, EC, NCC; Patrick Murphey to DLS, July 24, 1834, Swain GP vol. 4, SANC.

89. Will Gaston to DLS, August 30, 1834, EC, NCC; Benjamin R. Hines to DLS, June 26, 1833, Swain GP vol. 2, SANC.

90. Alfred S. Waugh to DLS, December 16, 1832, Swain GP vol. 1, SANC.

91. Robert Ball Hughes to Daniel W. Courts and Ben Sumner, Legislative Committee, December 29, 1832, Swain State Papers vol. 1, SANC.

92. Williams, Wiley J., "State Capitol," Powell, *Encyclopedia of North Carolina*, 1073; Draper, Howard, "Washington, Statues of," ibid., 1179–80; see generally Anderson, *Carolinian on the Hudson*, 144–49.

93. *N.C. House Journal*, November 22, 1833; *N.C. Senate Journal*, November 23, 1833, December 3, 1834; DLS to General Assembly, November 23, 1835, Swain GLB 30, SANC.

94. W. Montgomery to DLS, December 10, 1833, and DLS to W. Montgomery, December 12, 1833, Swain GLB 30, SANC.

95. DLS to General Assembly, December 27, 1834, Swain GLB 30, SANC; *N.C. House Journal*, December 27, 1834.

96. DLS to General Assembly, November 26, 1834, Swain GLB 30, SANC; *N.C. House Journal*, November 26, 28, 1834; *N.C. Senate Journal*, November 27, December 11, 1834.

97. DLS to House of Commons, December 3, 1834, Swain GLB 30, SANC.

98. *N.C. House Journal*, January 6, 8, 1835; *N.C. Senate Journal*, December 31, 1834, January 9, 1835.

99. Illegible (probably James Seawell, Magistrate of Police) to DLS, June 11, 1833, EC, NCC; *Raleigh Register and North-Carolina Gazette*, June 25, 1833.

100. *Greensborough Patriot*, July 24, 1833; Kiernan and D'Agnese, *Signing Their Lives Away* (book not paginated; see first entry under "Maryland").

101. *Raleigh Register and North-Carolina Gazette*, December 10, 1833, December 21, 1834; Daniel, *Swain*, 262.

102. Elliott, *The Raleigh Register 1799–1863*, 57; *Raleigh Register*, July 1, 1834; Daniel, *Swain*, 262; Alfred Graham to WAG, May 29, 1835, Graham Papers, SHC (in Hamilton et al., *Papers of Graham*, 1:382).

103. John Owen to DLS, January 1, 1833, EC, NCC; C. L. Hinton to WPM, December 30, 1833, in Shanks, *Papers of Mangum*, 2:62; DLS to WAG, December 30, 1833, Graham Papers, SANC (in Hamilton et al., *Papers of Graham*, 1:277); Daniel, *Swain*, 260.

104. George M. Moodecan (?) to DLS, September 1, 1833, EC, NCC; Will Gaston to DLS, January 31, 1834, ibid.; Anne E. G. Taylor (Gaston's niece) to William Gaston, November 11, 1834, Gaston Papers, SHC; *Raleigh Register and North-Carolina Gazette*, September 15, 29, 1835; Murray, *Wake: Capital County*, 1:220.

105. *Proceedings and Debates*, 337 (Gaston speech).

Chapter 6: Constitutional Reform

1. N.C. Const. (1776), Declaration of Rights, sec. 1.
2. Ibid., secs. 2, 3.
3. Hamilton, *Party Politics in North Carolina 1835–1860*, 10.
4. William Gaston to Robert Donaldson, December 9, 1831, Gaston Papers, SHC.

5. Joseph Kilpatrick to DLS, February 9, 1834, State Series vol. 4, Swain Papers, SANC; for general commentary, see Daniel, *Early Career*, 38–39; Daniel, *Swain*, 366–67; Griffin, *Essays on North Carolina History*, 112; Hamilton, *Party Politics in North Carolina 1835–1860*, 1–16; Kruman, *Parties and Politics in North Carolina 1836–1865*, 12; Lefler and Newsome, *North Carolina*, 214; Peele, *Lives*, 237; Sitterson, *Secession Movement in North Carolina*, 10.

6. John B. Craig to the Electors of Buncombe County, June 1821, EC, NCC. Craig lost the election but almost certainly not because of his position on this issue. See Cheney, *North Carolina Government*, 278.

7. DLS to GS, August 18, November 16, 24, 1822, EC, NCC.

8. *N.C. House Journal*, January 4, 1833; Daniel, *Swain*, 371–73.

9. *Western Carolinian*, November 25, 1833; see ibid., December 2, 1833, for further criticism for same reason.

10. DLS to the General Assembly, November 25, 1833, Swain GLB 30, SANC; Daniel, *Swain*, 376–78.

11. *Raleigh Register*, January 14, 21, 1834; *N.C. House Journal*, January 11, 1834; *Raleigh Star*, December 13, 1833; Daniel, *Swain*, 380–81.

12. David Outlaw to DLS, undated, EC, NCC; Daniel, *Swain*, 374. Daniel speculates, with reason, that the letter was written as Outlaw prepared to leave at the end of the legislative session, either in January 1833 or January 1834. Ibid., 374n.8.

13. *Raleigh Register*, January 14, 1834; Daniel, *Swain*, 382–83.

14. *N.C. House Journal*, November 17, 1834; DLS to General Assembly, November 17, 1834, Swain GLB 30, SANC; DLS to William Gaston, October 11, 1834, Gaston Papers SHC (enclosing of draft address); Blackwelder, *Age of Orange*, 77–78; Daniel, *Swain*, 383–86.

15. *Western Carolinian*, November 27, 1834; Daniel, *Swain*, 387.

16. Connor, *Ante-Bellum Builders*, 63; Powell, *North Carolina: A Bicentennial History*, 116–17; *A statement on the Number of Votes given . . . on the Convention Question, Etc.*, 1835, 4; county-by-county returns, Swain Papers, SANC; see *N.C. House Journal*, January 9, 1835, *N.C. Senate Journal*, November 29, December 11, 1834, January 1, 3, 6, 1835.

17. DLS to County Sheriffs, March 12, April 15, 1835; DLS Proclamation, May 1, 1835, Swain GLB 30, SANC; *Raleigh Register and North-Carolina Gazette*, February 10, March 17, April 21, May 19, 1835.

18. Daniel, *Swain*, 396–97, 397n.50; *Raleigh Register and North-Carolina Gazette*, June 2, 1835.

19. Daniel, *Swain*, 397–98; DLS to George Bancroft (probably), August 26, 1835, Swain GLB 30, SANC; *Proceedings and Debates, passim*; *Raleigh Christian Advocate*, February 16, 1887 (Swain and family living with his mother-in-law).

20. *Proceedings and Debates*, 5, 8–9; *Journal [Convention]*, 4–5.

21. *Proceedings and Debates*, 9, 32, 39, 345, 400; *Raleigh Register and North-Carolina Gazette*, June 2, 9, 1835.

22. *Proceedings and Debates*, 11–14.

23. Ibid., 17–20, 27; *Journal [Convention]*, 19–20; Daniel, *Swain*, 400.

24. *Proceedings and Debates*, 20.

25. Ibid., 27–31.

26. *Proceedings and Debates*, 40–42, 50, 201, 212; *Journal [Convention]*, 36, 39, 42; see generally Daniel, *Swain*, 411–14. Swain obviously gave a lot of thought to this issue, particularly to the high caliber of past representatives from the borough districts. His papers (SHC) contain a list of "Borough Representation, House of Commons," noting well-known and highly regarded names such as Thomas Ruffin and William A. Graham (Hillsboro); William R. Davie and Allen J. Davie (Halifax); Joseph Hewes, Hugh Williamson, and James Iredell (the younger)(Edenton); Richard D. Speight [*sic*], John Sitgreaves, and William Gaston (New Bern); William Hooper, Archibald McLean, and Edward B. Dudley (Wilmington); John Steele (Salisbury); and John Lewis [*sic*] Taylor (Fayetteville).

27. Cheney, *North Carolina Government*, 814.

28. *Proceedings and Debates*, 244.

29. Ibid., 249.

30. Ibid., 219, 242, 309–12, 331–32; *Journal [Convention]*, 50–51; for the entire debate, see *Proceedings and Debates*, 213–332; to compare the original with the amended section 32, see ibid., 416, 424; for commentary, see Daniel, *Swain*, 417–22.

31. *Proceedings and Debates*, 60, 80–81, 96, 351, 358; *Journal [Convention]*, 23, 73–74; *Federal Union*, December 18, 1835; Edwards, *People and Their Peace*, 279–80; Franklin, *Free Negro in North Carolina*, 110–16.

32. *Proceedings and Debates*, 332–40.

33. Ibid., 423; *Journal [Convention]*, 80–81; Cheney, *North Carolina Government*, 822.

34. *Proceedings and Debates*, 81, 376–77, 424.

35. Ibid., 358, 366; *Journal [Convention]*, 28, 76–77.

36. *Proceedings and Debates*, 181; *Journal [Convention]*, 35.

37. *Proceedings and Debates*, 193–94, 200–1; *Journal [Convention]*, 33.

38. *Proceedings and Debates*, 345–50, 369–73, 423–24; *Journal [Convention]*, 69.

39. *Proceedings and Debates*, 83–84.

40. Ibid., 86–87.

41. Ibid., 87–88.

42. Ibid., 88–91; Creecy, *Grandfather's Tales of North Carolina History*, 180–81.

43. *Proceedings and Debates*, 129–30; Creecy, *Grandfather's Tales of North Carolina History*, 181.

44. *Proceedings and Debates*, 130, 145 (for Gaston's remarks in their entirety, see ibid., 126–45).

45. *Proceedings and Debates*, 91, 92, 374, 400, 419–21; Cheney, *North Carolina Government*, 818–19.

46. *Proceedings and Debates*, 89. Daniel, *Swain*, 396–425, covers the convention. For other references, see Alderman, *Brief History of North* Carolina, 21–22; Arnett, *Story of North Carolina*, 269–70; Camp, *Swain*, 44; Connor, *Ante-Bellum Builders*, 74–85; Counihan, "The North Carolina Constitutional Convention of 1835: A Study in Jacksonian Democracy," 46 NCHR 335; Hadley, Horton, and Strowd, *Chatham County 1771–1971*, 87–88; Henderson, *North Carolina: The Old North State and The New*, 2:83–85; Hoffman, *Andrew Jackson and North Carolina Politics*, 83–87; Lefler and Newsome, *North Carolina*, 343–44; Patton, *Story of Henderson County*, 103–4; Wallace, "*Swain, David Lowery* [sic]," in Powell, *DNCB*, 5:484.

47. Thomas I. Faison to DLS, December 31, 1857, UP; Moore, *History of North Carolina*, 2:32; "Editor's Table," *North Carolina University Magazine*, 9:642, 643 (June 1860).

48. William Gaston to Mrs. Donaldson (daughter), July 12, 1835, and to Robert H.G. Moore (editor, *New Bern Spectator*), August 16, 1835, Gaston Papers, SHC; Camp, *Swain*, 48.

49. DLS to R.H. Madra, Messrs. Pasteur and Moore, Thomas Loring and E. L. Hale, July 14, 1835, Swain GLB 30, SANC; Swain Proclamation of September 15, 1835, ibid.; *Raleigh Register and North-Carolina Gazette*, September 29, 1835.

50. *Raleigh Register and North-Carolina Gazette*, August 11, 1835.

51. James Graham to WAG, October 26, 1835, Graham Papers, SHC (in Hamilton et al., *Papers of Graham*, 1:395); Daniel, *Swain*, 425–26, 516.

52. DLS to County Sheriffs, November 28, 1835, Swain GLB 30, SANC; Hamilton, *Party Politics in North Carolina 1835–1860*, 14; Konkle, *Morehead*, 169; Vote Totals by County, Swain GLB 30, SANC.

53. Proclamation of December 3, 1835, and DLS to General Assembly, December 4, 1835, Swain GLB 30, SANC; *N.C. Senate Journal*, December 8, 1835; *N.C. House Journal*, December 7, 1835; *Western Carolinian*, December 12, 1835.

54. E. J. Hale to DLS, October 24, 1833, EC, NCC; Will Gaston to DLS, October 14, 1834, ibid.; John Owen to DLS, September 8, 1834, ibid. Daniel states that Alexander had a personal grudge against Swain. She could not identify the source of the grudge ("For some reason") nor has the present author. Daniel, *Swain*, 467n.71. See also Hoffman, *Andrew Jackson and North Carolina Politics*, 75 (Alexander hated Swain).

55. Daniel, *Swain*, 335–36, 497–98, 521–24.

56. *People's Press*, Wilmington, N.C., November 6, 1833 (quoted in Daniel, *Swain*, 334).

57. *Raleigh Register and North-Carolina Gazette*, October 14, 1834.

58. James W. Osborne to WAG, June 3, 1835, in Hamilton et al., *Papers of Graham*, 1:383; Geo. Watterson to DLS, December 30, 1833, EC, NCC; George Stewart, L. Clemmons, T. Tillet to DLS, February 16, 1834, ibid.

59. Wheeler, *North Carolina: Her Past, Present and Future*, 10; Thomasson, *Swain County*, 102; Hamilton et al., *Papers of Graham*, 5:26n.1; Camp, *Swain*, 49.

60. Connor, *Ante-Bellum Builders*, 68–73; for the same conclusion, see Powell, *Four Centuries*, 276.

61. Daniel, *Swain*, 526–29; see also Zebulon Vance's conclusions in Peele, *Lives*, 238–39.

62. *N.C. Senate Journal*, November 23, December 10, 1835; *N.C. House Journal*, December 10, 1835; William Gaston to Susan Jane Donaldson, December 1, 1835, Gaston Papers, SHC.

63. Hoffman, *Andrew Jackson and North Carolina Politics*, 30–31; W.M. Sneed to WPM, November 18, December 3, 1830, Shanks, *Papers of Mangum*, 1:380, 392.

64. WPM to DLS, December 22, 1833, Shanks, *Papers of Mangum*, 2:51–56.

65. Spencer O'Brien to WPM, February 17, 1834, ibid., 2:87.

66. Richmond M. Pearson to DLS, October 18, 1834, EC, NCC; D. F. Caldwell to DLS, October 25, 1834, ibid.; James Graham to WAG, November 17, 1834, Graham Papers, SHC (in Hamilton et al., *Papers of Graham*, 1:330–31).

67. Will Gaston to DLS, September 30, November 11, 1834, EC, NCC.

68. Thomas G. Polk to DLS, October 17, 1834, EC, NCC.

69. Hoffman, *Andrew Jackson and North Carolina Politics*, 75 (quoting letter from "One of the People," *Raleigh Standard*, November 11, 1834); *N.C. House Journal*, November 20, 1834 (election of Bedford Brown to U.S. Senate).

70. Daniel, *Swain*, 525.

71. *N.C. House Journal*, November 17, 1835; also in Swain GLB 30, SANC.

Chapter 7: The University of North Carolina

1. Henderson, *Campus of the First State University*, 122.

2. Swain Diary, January 5, June 17–22, 1832, SANC; DLS to Charles Manly, November 15, 1856, UP; Battle, *History*, 1:365–66; *Raleigh Register*, July 2, 1833; Coon, *Beginnings of Public Education in North Carolina*, 1:519.

3. Battle, *History*, 1:356–57, 421; *Carolina Alumni Review*, July/August 2008, 24.

4. ECM, February 6, 1835; Battle, *History*, 1:413; Konkle, *Morehead*, 93n.2.

5. Battle, *History*, 1:423.

6. Creecy, *Grandfather's Tales of North Carolina History*, 178–81; Peele, *Lives*, 234–35; *News and Observer*, December 4, 1886.

7. BOTM, December 5, 1835, SHC; DLS to Editor, *The Spirit of the Age*, February 15, 1859 (also in *North Carolina Christian Advocate*, March 10, 1859); Battle, *Sketches of the History of the University of North Carolina*, 48; Battle, *History*, 1:423–24; Gobbel, *Church-State Relationships in Education*, 40–41; Powell, *First State University*, 55.

8. J. T. Jones to Genl. E. Jones (father), November 26, 1835, Patterson Papers, Duke.

9. *Raleigh Standard*, December 10, 1835; Daniel, *Swain*, 525–26; Speight, A. H., "Reminiscences of Gov. D. L. Swain," Swain Papers, Duke; Hamilton et al., *Papers of Graham*, 5:26n.1, 6:6–7n.15; *North Carolina Presbyterian*, August 4, 1869; Chamberlain, *Old Days in Chapel Hill*, 38–39.

10. *Western Carolinian*, December 27, 1835 (reprint from *Raleigh Star*, December 18, 1835); WHB to DLS, August 10, 1837, Swain Papers, SHC; Battle, *History* 1:528.

11. Spencer, *Pen and Ink Sketches*, 33; Vickers, *Chapel Hill Illustrated*, 46; *North Carolina Presbyterian*, August 4, 1869.

12. Will B. Rodman to "Dear Uncle," May 1836, Rodman Papers, ECU; Hamilton C. Jones to WPM, December 22, 1837, in Shanks, *Papers of Mangum*, 2:514.

13. Vance, *Life of Swain*, 9; Connor, *Ante-Bellum Builders*, 71.

14. Delderfield, *To Serve Them All My Days*, 124.

Chapter 8: Admitting, Parenting

1. See, e.g., FM, January 16, 1858 (faculty admitted students), May 13, 1859 (required president's certification); Spencer, *Pen and Ink Sketches*, 47.

2. Robert Strange to DLS, July 31, 1837, UP.

3. George E. Badger to DLS, July 9, 1857; M. E. Manly to DLS, July 5, 1841, August 3, 1866, Swain Papers, SANC.

4. D. L. Clinch to DLS, January 6, 1841; WPM to DLS, December 31, 1844 (enclosure, Joel Crawford to Gen. D. L. Clinch, November 17, 1844) (in Shanks, *Papers of Mangum*, 4:240–42), Swain Papers, SHC.

5. John Hill to DLS, August 25, 1845, Swain Papers, SANC.

6. Francis L. Hawks to DLS, January 12, 1856, ibid.

7. Nathan B. Whitfield to DLS, October 19, 1842, Swain Papers, SANC; Calvin Jones to DLS, February 28, 1841, ibid.; B. H. Cowan to DLS, August 23, 1838, ibid.

8. A. M. Boozer to DLS, August 13, 1866, Swain Papers, SANC (Boozer was in the UNC Class of 1864, Battle, *History*, 1:817); John B. Kelly to DLS, September 30, 1854, Swain Papers, SHC.

9. Sarah Potts to DLS, January 6, 1840, and Delphina E. Mendenhall to DLS, May 30, 1844, Swain Papers, SANC.

10. WPM to DLS, June 15, 1839, and CM to DLS, July 31, 1837, Swain Papers, SHC.
11. George W. Mordecai to DLS, April 10, 1841, ibid.
12. Robert Donaldson to DLS, June 16, 1856, Gaston Papers, SHC; see Anderson, *Carolinian on the Hudson*, 248.
13. LMB to WHB, November 8, 1850, BFP, SHC.
14. B. (Braxton) Craven to DLS, May 27, 1854, Swain Papers, SHC (typescript in Craven Papers, Duke).
15. J. W. Cameron to DLS, September 24, 1836, Swain Papers, SANC.
16. Philip Sindsby to DLS (?), June 5, 1839, August 8, 1850, Swain Papers, SANC.
17. J. W. Hardy to DLS, August 14, 1845, ibid.
18. Edward Everett to DLS, June 15, 1847, Swain Papers, SANC.
19. Basil Manly to DLS, April 16, 23, 1840, ibid.
20. J. (illegible) to DLS, January 19, 1862, Swain Papers, SHC.
21. WAG to DLS, June 10, 1864, and illegible to DLS, June 14, 1864, Swain Papers, SANC.
22. Spencer, *Pen and Ink Sketches*, 31; WHB to DLS, August 10, 1837, Swain Papers, SHC.
23. *Raleigh Register and North-Carolina Gazette*, August 28, 1840, January 8, 1841.
24. DLS to Genl. Daniel L. Barringer, May 19, 1838, July 22, 1840, Swain Papers, SHC (see also FM, Jan. 1838, re: Blair); DLS to WHB, April 7, 1848, BFP, SHC; DLS to WAG, April 11, 1851, Hamilton et al., *Papers of Graham*, 4:76; DLS to G. J. McRee, February 14, 1856, McRee Papers, SHC; DLS to John P. Steele, June 11, 1856, Swain Papers, SHC; DLS to Rev. Dr. Hawks, September 1, 1858, Swain Papers, SHC; Henderson, *Campus of the First State University*, 148.
25. Jones, *North Carolina Illustrated*, 191; Knight and Adams, *Graduate School Research and Publications*, 7; Lefler and Newsome, *North Carolina*, 383; Lefler and Wager, *Orange County, 1752–1952*, 150–51; Wilson, *Library of the First State University*, 13 (Jones, Knight–Adams, and the Lefler volumes have the figure 456; Wilson, 461); M. Fetter, Bursar, to CM, March 31, November 19, 1862, December 1, 1863 (two letters), UP; list, December 19, 1863, of thirty-two former students at UNC then in 23rd N.C. Cavalry, 41st Reg't, C.S. Army, UP.
26. John Irwin to DLS, August 3, 1839, Swain Papers, SANC.
27. CM to DLS, February 5, 1856, Swain Papers, SHC; for Manly's problems with a son, see Manly to DLS, February 14, 18, 1839, Swain Papers, SANC.
28. J. M. Morehead to DLS, July 18, 1849, Swain Papers, SHC.
29. W. M. Lowands (?) to DLS, July 30, 1837, ibid.; W. B. Reese to DLS, January 18, 1842, Swain Papers, SHC.
30. A. Rencher to DLS, February 14, 1859, UP; C. (Cave) Johnson to DLS, November 2, 1858, ibid.; illegible to DLS, April 5, 1847, Swain Papers, SANC.

31. W. J. Saunders to "My Dear Father," January 31, 1855, and R.M. Saunders to DLS, February 2, 1855, ibid.

32. DLS to EHS, June 18, 1847, ibid.

33. John H. Wheeler to DLS, June 24, 1849, ibid.

34. Macchin M'Clung to DLS, March 29, 1867, ibid.

35. Thomas Bragg to DLS, January 30, 1864, and J. Bragg to DLS, January 22, 1864, ibid.

36. Louis D. Wilson to DLS, July 11, 1840, UP.

37. D. L. Clinch to DLS, January 14, 1847, Swain Papers, SANC (typescript in Swain Papers, SHC).

38. Delphina E. Mendenhall to DLS, May 30, 1844, Swain Papers, SHC; T. B. W. I. Jones to DLS, January 6, 1842, Swain Papers, SANC; Robert H. Burton to DLS, December 3, 1838, ibid.

39. Joseph N. Bunch to DLS, December 19 (no year shown); J. W. Cameron to DLS, August 16, 1848; V. C. Barringer to DLS, June 29, 1848, ibid.; DLS to WHB, October 19, 1849, BFP, SHC.

40. George E. Badger to DLS, August 10, 1837, Swain Papers, SANC; John Warlick to DLS, April 5, 1847, Swain Papers, SHC (typescript).

41. C. (Cave) Johnson to DLS, October 20, 1857, November 2, 1858, UP.

42. J. M. Morehead to DLS, March 13, 1861, Swain Papers, SHC.

43. A. Rencher to DLS, February 10, 1860, ibid.; James Garland to DLS, April 4, 1843, Swain Papers, SANC (typescript in Swain Papers, SHC).

44. Unsigned letter to DLS, October 22, 1838, Swain Papers, SANC.

45. ECM, July 9, 1836; *Raleigh Register and North-Carolina Gazette*, September 20, 1836; Drake, *Higher Education in North Carolina Before 1860*, 84.

46. Circular letter, DLS to fathers and guardians of students, February 1855, UP.

47. FM, April 13, 1838, April 1, 1842, March 15, 1844; *North Carolina Presbyterian*, August 18, 1869.

48. R. H. Cowan to DLS, March 27, 1843, Swain Papers, SANC.

49. FM, January 17, 1846.

50. FM, 1: 3–423 (undated); Spencer, *Pen and Ink Sketches*, 41; DLS to WHB and LMB, March 28, 1862, BFP, SHC.

51. DLS to unnamed parent, March 22, 1856, EC, NCC; E. J. Hale to DLS, March 27, 1858, Swain Papers, SANC.

52. FM, August 2, 1850.

53. Calvin Jones to DLS, April 4, 1840, May 2, 1842, Swain Papers, SANC.

54. A. L. Erwin to DLS, August 22, 1841, ibid.

55. John L. Bridgers to DLS, April 24, 1843, ibid.

56. James G. Mhoon to DLS, January 13, 1843; Joseph S. Cannon to DLS, January 23, 1849; James W. Haskins to DLS, March 28, 1840, October 12, 1842.

57. Thomas I. Lenoir to DLS, March 9, 1843; R. N. Pearson to DLS, July 25, 1842, ibid.

58. D. W. Stone to DLS, November 8, 1842, ibid.

59. Neill McKay to DLS, January 14, 1836, Swain Papers, SHC; W. Hooper to DLS, October 28, 1839, Swain Papers, SANC.

60. Charles F. Deems to DLS, June 11, 1857, Swain Papers, SANC.

61. James W. Bryan to DLS, January 1, 1846, Swain Papers, SANC (typescript in Swain Papers, SHC).

62. C. H. Wiley to DLS, April 4, 1849, Swain Papers, SHC.

63. E. Mallett to KPB, February 11, 1864, BFP, SHC; Battle, *History*, 1:751, 802.

64. DLS Testimonial to William L. Scott, October 6, 1854, Scott Papers, Duke.

65. Robert R. Bridgers to DLS, October 16, 1849, Swain Papers, SHC; Battle, *History*, 1:797.

66. Leon F. Siler to DLS, July 9, 1857, Swain Papers, SANC.

67. Will E. Barnett to DLS, August 18, 1849, ibid.

68. DLS to Gen. Daniel Barringer, October 7, 1842, Swain Papers, SANC; DLS to CM, March 20, 1846, UP.

69. FM, February 18, 19, 1836, November 11, 1851, May 31, 1855; *Weekly Raleigh Register*, September 2, 1857.

70. LMB to WHB, October 18, 1845, and WHB to LMB, November 1, 1845, BFP, SHC.

71. James E. Beasley to DLS, May 4, 1867, Clark Papers, ibid. The writer was in the UNC Class of 1859. Battle, *History*, 1:811.

Chapter 9: Student Misconduct

1. Tolbert, *Two Hundred Years*, 59.

2. Document in Swain's hand, Swain Papers, SANC; Battle, *History*, 1:436.

3. FM, August 13, November 6, 1838, August 9, 1839, July 1840 (exact date not shown), July 16, 1842, May 31, 1844, June 1, 1848 (list follows of numerous students who pledge not to "Unite themselves with an Ugly Club or any similar riotous proceeding"), July 16, 1853; BOTM, December 12, 1842; J. J. Johnston et al. to DLS and WHB, July 22, 1843, UP; William Sidney Mullins Diary, July 17, 24, 1841, SHC; see Battle, *History*, 1: 452–54; Drake, *Higher Education in North Carolina Before 1860*, 212; Snider, *Light on the Hill*, 60; Vickers, *Chapel Hill Illustrated*, 46.

4. FM, November 1837 (exact date not shown); BOTM, June 6, 1838; Battle, *History*, 1:435.

5. DLS, circular letter to parents, September 30, 1840, NCC.

6. FM, June 4, 1857.

7. FM, September 22, 1856; senior class to BOT, November 22, 1839, UP (petition for dismissed student's reinstatement).

8. FM, February 12, 1847; DLS, circular letter of October 1, 1850, Historical Society of Pennsylvania (copy at SANC); LMB to WHB, October 17, 1846, BFP, SHC.

9. Battle, *History*, 1:575.

10. C. L. Hinton to DLS, August 4, 1845, Swain Papers, SANC; see also James W. Osborne to DLS, undated (as to Osborne's status, see Battle, *History*, 1:793, 894).

11. E.g., DLS, circular letter of March 31, 1858, UP; FM, November 20, 1839.

12. FM, May 27, 1846, October 2, 1856, March 22, 1858; *Memoirs of Robert Philip Howell*, SHC, 12.

13. FM, November 26, 1849, May 27, 1850.

14. Ibid., March 6, 1857, May 14, 1858; Henderson, *Campus of the First State University*, 130 (original letter DLS to Donaldson in Swain Papers, SHC).

15. FM, May 30, 31, June 2, 1856, SHC.

16. John M. Dick to DLS, February 27, 1842, UP; FM, November 5, 1852; CM to DLS, February 22, 1858, Swain Papers, SHC.

17. FM, June 2, 1859.

18. A. B. Longstreet to DLS, December 31, 1859, Swain Papers, SANC; Battle, *History*, 1:814 (showing the transfer student in 1861 graduating class).

19. FM, October 21, 1853; Battle, *History*, 1:581.

20. Spencer, *Pen and Ink Sketches*, 47.

21. FM, April 26, 1839, January 22, 1854, March 5, 1855, March 8, 1856; BOTM, March 12, 1855; see Snider, *Light on the Hill*, 62, Drake, *Higher Education in North Carolina Before 1860*, 226; Williams, *Intellectual Manhood*, 162–66.

22. FM, February 21, 1845 (reports of incidents follow), September 11, 1850.

23. Tolbert, *Two Hundred Years*, 69–70.

24. FM, April 15, 1853; BOTM, October 9, 1858; *Weekly Raleigh Register*, October 13, 1858; William J. Rivers to DLS, November 1, 1858, Swain Papers, SHC.

25. FM, April 26, 1844, October 18, 1852, September 8, 1856, November 22, 1857.

26. Ibid., August 14, 1856; Tolbert, *Two Hundred Years*, 61–62 (citing Joshua Perry to his father, May 18, 1839).

27. FM, September 12, 25, 1856, September 22, 1857, March 8, May 2, 1859.

28. Ibid., May 31, June 2, 1856.

29. Ibid., May 21, 1851, October 6, 1838.

30. Ibid., January 30, 1843, May 26, 1847, May 23, 1854, May 25, 1855, February 18, 1856; Tolbert, *Two Hundred Years*, 63.

31. FM, April 30, May 28, 1847; appendix to Mr. Herrisse's Memorial, UP; for further detail, see infra text accompanying notes 46–47.

32. Asa Biggs to DLS, September 22, 1858, DLS to Asa Biggs, September 25, 1858, Asa Biggs to DLS, September 30, November 11, 1858, Swain Papers, SANC; FM, September 12, 1858.

33. FM, April 27, June 28, November 7, 9, 1838, March 29, April 12, 1839; Battle, *History*, 1: 832–33, 836; *Concise Dictionary of American Biography*, 80.

34. FM, August 27, 1840 (with William H. Branch to DLS, August 22, 1840, and DLS to Gov. Branch, August 28, 1840); see also FM, September 1, 1840, re: rule prohibiting books in recitation rooms.

35. Edward B. Dudley to DLS, November 25, 1838, Swain Papers, SANC.

36. WAG to DLS, May 6, 1854, Hamilton et al., *Papers of Graham*, 8:534; FM, August 13, 1866.

37. James Iredell to DLS, November 12, 1845, Swain Papers, SHC; FM, August 21, September 8, November 9, 1846, May (no exact date shown), November 2, 1847, December 2, 1847, February 4, 1848.

38. FM, February 23, August 25, September 18, 1846, February 26, May 19, 28, 1847, May 5, 26, October 16, 1848, March 19, April 2, 27, 28, 1849; James Iredell to DLS, November 5, 1848, Swain Papers, SANC; Charles Phillips to DLS, March 31, 1849, Swain Papers, SHC.

39. Battle, *History*, 1:802.

40. CM to DLS, August 4, 1856; FM, September 8, 1849, August 25, 1856.

41. Ibid., April 11, 1858.

42. Spencer, *Pen and Ink Sketches*, 38–40, 49–50; *North Carolina Presbyterian*, August 18, 1869.

43. Samuel T. Iredell to DLS, undated, Swain Papers, SANC; Connor, "Governor Swain Believed in Building Character, Not in Breaking Students," *Daily Tar Heel*, September 21, 1965.

44. CM to DLS, May 2, 1860, Swain Papers, SHC. Manly was not always so forgiving. Earlier in Swain's time at the university, Manly had advocated a much harsher resolution of a case: "I am for *whipping the offender*, and at the same time not killing him," he told Swain. CM to DLS, July 31, 1837, ibid.

45. Battle, *History*, 1:533; Peele, *Lives*, 247; Snider, *Light on the Hill*, 63.

46. Henri Herrisse to BOT EC, September 27, 1856, UP; FM, August 14, 1856; ECM, October 4, 1856.

47. Herrisse Memorial to BOT EC, October 9, 1856, and appendix to same; DLS to CM, October 9, 16, 19, 24, 25, 28 (recipient of letters of 25th and 28th not identified, but almost certainly Manly); Henri Herrisse to DLS, October 10, 1856, and to Gov. Bragg, October 15, 1856; J. T Wheat to CM, October 28, 1856; statements from: James Phillips, M. Fetter, and J. T. Wheat, October 16, 1856; Prof. C. Phillips, October

20, 1856; Joseph B. Lucas, October 23, 1856; E. Mitchell, October 24, 1856, UP; FM, October 13, 1856; ECM, October 11, 1856 (copy also in Hedrick Papers, Duke). For a summary account of this incident, see Battle, *History*, 1:657–59.

48. FM, May 25, September 17, 1839, February 11, 1842, January 26, 1844.

49. Ibid., February 15, 1837, October 19, 1838, September 29, 1840, January 8, 1841, October 4, 1850.

50. Ibid., February 15, 1836, March 22, 1839, September 4, 1840, January 28, 1842, July 15, 1842.

51. *People's Press*, Salem, N.C., January 21, 1859; DLS, circular letter, December 10, 1858, UP (copy also in BFP); Victor C. Bannifer to DLS, January 1, 1859, Swain Papers, SHC; Battle, *History*, 1:690–92.

52. FM, August 31, 1840; J. M. Morehead to DLS, July 19, 1844, Swain Papers, SHC.

53. Memorial of BOT meeting, March 13, 1845, and WAG to DLS, March 14, 1845, UP; BOTM, September 11, December 26, 1850.

54. FM, February 22, March 10, 1851.

55. William Sidney Mullins Diary, October 31, 1840, SHC; Joseph C. Huske, William Alise Bell, and William F. Martin to DLS, November 9, 1840, Swain Papers, SHC. Swain's son David died on October 15, 1840 (from gravestone, Oakwood Cemetery, Raleigh, N.C.). Williams, *Intellectual Manhood*, 166, mentions the Suky Mayhs incident.

56. Tolbert, *Two Hundred Years*, 64; LMB to WHB, March 30, 1847, BFP, SHC; DLS, circular letter to parents, August 17, 1860, UP.

57. William Sidney Mullins Diary, January 19, 1841, and Thomas Miles Garrett Diary, September 29, 1849, SHC.

58. DLS to CM, December 4, 1838, UP; Battle, *History*, 1:334–36, 444–45.

59. Memoirs of Robert Philip Howell, SHC, 11; DLS to CM, August 20, 1856, UP; CM to DLS, March 11, 1857, Swain Papers, SHC; ECM, September 13, October 4, 1856; *Report of the Committee on Burning of the Belfry*, October 4, 1856, UP.

60. FM, May 27, 1840, August 30, 1850, August 3, 1855, July 18, 31, August 11, October 13, 28, November 25, 1856, January 26, February 2, March 20, July 27, 1857.

61. Henderson, *Campus of the First State University*, 121; FM, January 17, 1846; BOTM, December 26, 1845; DLS to CM, September 19, 1856, UP.

62. FM, September 12, 1840, August 29, September 10, 1860.

63. DLS to CM, October 20, 1857; FM, October 24, 1859.

64. FM, September 29, 1845.

65. CM to DLS, November 21, 1857, Swain Papers, SHC.

66. BOTM, September 9, 1860; for an example, see FM, September 19, 1845 (student "had left Chapel Hill when permission to do so had been denied him"; he was "committed to the President").

67. FM, April 9, 1838, April 7, September 21, October 30, 1840, April 20, 26, 1843, February 21, 1851, September 4, 1854, May 24, 1858, September 26, 1859, August 29, 1860, August 17, 1860; circular "By order of the Faculty," signed by DLS as president, September 30, 1840, UP.

68. DLS letter and EC circular, July 4, 1855, NCC; Battle, *History*, 1:677–78.

69. Thomas Ruffin Jr. to Wm. Gaston, September 24, October 4, 1842, Gaston Papers, SHC (the second letter shows a date of September 4; because it necessarily followed the letter of September 24, the correct date must be October 4). Gaston's letter has not been found, but its content is clear from Ruffin's response.

70. DLS to J. DB Hooper, Esq., December 31, 1850, Hooper Papers, SHC.

71. WHB to LMB, January 31, 1854 (probably 1856), BFP, SHC; DLS to unidentified (probably CM), February 2, 16, 1856, UP; FM, February 1, 1856; ECM, February 25, 1856; *North Carolina University Magazine*, 10:35–45 (August 1860); Battle, *History*, 1:667–69, 707–9. For an example of a UNC alumnus's complaint about the invitation, and Swain's response, see Robert G. Allison to DLS, February 25, 1856, and DLS to R.G. Allison, March 1, 1856, Swain Papers, SHC (Allison again complained when Hughes came to UNC in 1860; see Allison to DLS, March 20, 1860, Swain Papers, SHC) (Swain's response to Allison was published in the *Greensborough Patriot*, March 21, 1856, and the *Hillsboro Recorder*, March 26, 1856); re: EC approval of Swain's course, and his gratitude therefor, see CM to DLS, February 26, 1856, and DLS to CM, February 29, 1856, Swain Papers, SHC. For general treatment of the Hughes controversy, see Gobbel, *Church-State Relationships in Education in North Carolina Since 1776*, 52, 52nn.184–85.

72. Faculty resolution, May 4, 1866, and CM to DLS, May 9, 1866, UP; Charles Phillips to ZBV, May 10, 1866, Vance Papers, SANC; *Tri-Weekly Standard*, May 19, 1866; Battle, *History*, 1:755.

73. FM, April 6, 1841, November 5, 1861.

74. FM, June (exact date not shown), 1839.

75. FM, 1: 3–302–3 (student petition, November 4, 1839, and faculty rejection); BOTM, June 2, 1852.

76. Will A. Blount to DLS, November 10, 1840, Swain Papers, SANC.

77. A. Joyner to DLS, March 13, 1845, ibid.; see also Weston R. Gales to DLS, October 8, 1845, ibid. ("the Faculty discriminated properly in their selection of Hinton for an example").

78. J. G. Tompkins to DLS, March 7, 1854, ibid.

79. Alex Barrett, Co D 49, NC Regt, Ransom's Brigade, Petersburg, to DLS, July 22, 1863, Swain Papers, SHC.

80. J. C. Washington to DLS, March 8, 1847, Swain Papers, SANC.

81. George Junkin to DLS, October 28, 1846, ibid.

82. George B. Gordon to DLS, January 25, 1841, ibid.

83. FM, February 20, 1840, September 24, October 24, 1842, April 9, 1847, May 25, 1852, May 15, 1856, May 18, 23, 1857.

84. William Sidney Mullins Diary, November 24, 1840, September 26, 1841, SHC.

85. DLS to unidentified recipient, August 22, 1845 (typescript), Swain Papers, and to WHB, September 19, 1845, BFP, SHC.

86. DLS to WHB, October 19, 1849, and LMB to WHB, January 26, 1855, BFP, SHC; DLS to unidentified recipient, September 12, 1856, UP; FM, October 13, 1856.

87. LMB to WHB, September 27, 1845, March 25, 1848, BFP, SHC.

88. Battle, *History*, 1: Introduction (unnumbered page); for a long list of types of student misconduct in Swain's time, see Drake, *Higher Education in North Carolina Before 1860*, 194–96.

Chapter 10: Teacher

1. E.g., FM, September 8, 1837, August 27, September 8, 1838, January 26, 1841; see Camp, *Swain*, 51.

2. FM, January 20, 1836, May 22, July 18, 1840, September 28, 1850; BOTM, January 26, 1859; Battle, *History*, 1:555; Spencer, *Pen and Ink Sketches*, 57; DLS to KPB, February 13, 1868, BFP, SHC.

3. Battle, *History*, 1:408, 555.

4. William Sidney Mullins Diary, September 27, 1841, SHC.

5. Drake, *Higher Education in North Carolina Before 1860*, 110, 112, 117; Snider, *Light on the Hill*, 63.

6. Thomas Miles Garrett Diary, October 5, 1849, SHC (see Hamilton, "Diary of Thomas Miles Garrett," 38 NCHR 380); Stokes, "Nathaniel Rochester in North Carolina," 38 NCHR 467, 481; William H. Haigh College Journal, February 2, 1842, Haigh Papers, SHC.

7. Battle, *History*, 1:443, 480, 531; Wettach, *Century of Legal Education*, 20–21; Williams, *Intellectual Manhood*, 72–73; FM, 1:4-371 (report to BOT, May 1847); see also FM, 1:194 (report to BOT, May 1844), 1:4-257 (report to BOT, June 1845).

8. *Fayetteville Observer*, July 5, 1883; Drake, *Higher Education in North Carolina Before 1860*, 184–85.

9. William Sydney Mullins Diary, July 20, 23, 24, September 14, 23, 24, August 6, 1841, SHC.

10. Ibid., August 3, 17, 20, 27, 1841; see also ibid., February 7, June 15, August 6, 9, 1841.

11. Ibid., January 16, July 30, 1841.

12. *Register of the Officers and Faculty of the University of North Carolina 1795–1945*, 111; Brewer, *Memoir of Swain*, 5; Wettach, *Century of Legal Education*, 21.

13. Brewer, *Memoir of Swain*, 5; Wettach, *Century of Legal Education*, 30.

14. Wiley S. Putnam, New York, to DLS, November 2, 1842; receipt from Wiley S. Putnam, Importers & Booksellers, New York, December 18, 1843 (for books listed, including Kent's *Commentaries*); communication from same firm, April 5, 1844 (?) ("will forward the two copies of Kent as soon as ready"), Swain Papers, SANC; R. S. Mason to DLS, May 31, 1842, ibid.; William Sidney Mullins Diary, June 15, 16, 1841, SHC. For general commentary, see Farmer, "Legal Education in North Carolina, 1820–1860," 28 NCHR 271, 276 (Swain "among the many lawyers who instructed students in their offices").

15. Caldwell: Hamilton et al., *Papers of Graham*, 5:44n.25; Phifer Jr., *Burke: The History of a North Carolina County 1777–1920*, 147; Vickers, *Chapel Hill Illustrated*, 86; Ellis: Tolbert, *Papers of Ellis*, 1:xliii, 1n.1; Phillips: ibid., 6:31n.47, 7:30–31n.1; Miller, "Samuel Field Phillips: The Odyssey of a Southern Dissenter," 58 NCHR 263, 264, 276; Wettach, *Century of Legal Education*, 26; Woodfin: Hamilton et al., *Papers of Graham*, 5:235n.30; Farmer, "Legal Education in North Carolina," 28 NCHR 271, 276 n.26; Johnston, *Papers of Vance*, 1:92n.347.

16. FM, April 9, 1841 (table of studies follows); Battle, *History*, 1:462; William Sidney Mullins Diary, July 16, 19, 1841, SHC; Williams, *Intellectual Manhood*, 199.

17. Battle, *History*, 1:518–20, 713–16.

18. FM, May 28, June 1, 1848.

19. Petition to BOT, December 1848; DLS to unidentified recipient, December 17, 1848, UP.

20. BOTM, December 11, 1848.

21. Ibid., December 14, 1848, January 4, 1849.

22. S. A. Maverick to DLS, September 16, 1859; S.C. Josey to DLS, undated (note says 1856–1860, AB 1860), Swain Papers, SHC.

23. "Memorial from Diocese of NC Convention to President and Board of Trustees of UNC," May 9, 1860; C. B. Hassell to BOT, December 4, 1860, UP.

24. Alex Wilson to DLS, August 22, 1859, ibid.

25. BOTM, December 1, 1859, December 12, 18, 1860; WHB to LMB, December 13, 1860, BFP, SHC.

26. William Sidney Mullins Diary, July 19, 1841, SHC.

27. College Journal, William H. Haigh, January 19, 1842, Haigh Papers, SHC.

28. Prout, "He was 'The Worst Man in His Class,'" *Alumni Review*, 28:244–45 (June 1930).

29. Battle, *History*, 1:530; Speight, Dr. A. H., "Reminiscences of Gov. D. L. Swain," Swain Papers, Duke.

30. Battle, *History*, 1:531; Drake, *Higher Education in North Carolina Before 1860*, 108, 108n.93,113; Waddell, *Some Memories of My Life*, 25.

31. Francis Theodore Bryan to William Shepard Pettigrew, October 17, 1841, in Lemmon, *Pettigrew Papers*, 2:486; Thomas Miles Garrett Diary, August 18, September 20, 1849, SHC; William Sidney Mullins Diary, October 5, 1841, SHC.

32. Thomas Miles Garrett Diary, August 28, 1850, SHC.

33. William Sidney Mullins Diary, February 5, 1841, SHC.

34. Ibid., August 9, 1841; College Journal, William H. Haigh, January 18, 1842, Haigh Papers, SHC; Charles Phillips to WAG, October 24, 1859, Hamilton et al., *Papers of Graham*, 5:124; Wilson, *Papers of Spencer*, 437.

35. Thomas Miles Garrett Diary, August 31, 1849, SHC.

36. Battle, "David Lowry Swain," in *North Carolina Journal of Education*, 3:27, 29.

37. Thomas Miles Garrett Diary, August 31, 1849, SHC; N. F. Dancy to DLS, November 3, 1842, Swain Papers, SANC.

38. Wilson, *Papers of Spencer*, 211.

39. John W. Ellis to DLS, September 22, 1841, Swain Papers, SHC; see Tolbert, *Papers of Ellis*, 1:1–3.

40. Quoted in Drake, *Higher Education in North Carolina Before 1860*, 108–9 (citing Bryan Grimes Papers, 1844–1863, vol. I, 23).

41. J. N. Barksdale to DLS, December 17, 1840, Swain Papers, SANC.

42. Weeks, *History and Biography of North Carolina: Scrapbook*, 7: 218.

43. Cannon, *My Beloved Zebulon*, xii, xviii, 7n.5; Creecy, *Grandfather's Tales of North Carolina History*, 178; Dowd, *Life of Vance*, 17 (chapter by Kemp P. Battle); Drake, *Higher Education in North Carolina Before 1860*, 111; Edmunds, *Tar Heels Track the Century*, 43, 308; Johnston, *Papers of Vance*, 1:xxiii–xxiv, 3–4n.1; Mobley, "War Governor of the South," 16; Shirley, *Zeb Vance, Tarheel Spokesman*, 4; Wakelyn, *Biographical Dictionary of the Confederacy*, 419.

Swain's estate files contain a record of a note held by Swain on Vance and Robert Vance, from the 1850s, in the amount of $111.00. It is not clear that this was for Vance's educational purposes, but it was probably so related. Two of Vance's mother's schoolmates became governors: Swain, and Benjamin F. Perry, governor of South Carolina after the Civil War. Tucker, *Zebulon Vance*, 28–29.

44. ZBV to Harriett Espy, July 18, 1851, January 18, 1852, Vance Papers (Vance-Espy Letters), SANC; Cannon, *My Beloved Zebulon*, 7, 35, 41; Dowd, *Life of Vance*, 27–28; Johnston, *Papers of Vance*, 1:10.

45. Tucker, *Zebulon Vance*, 42–43, 278.

46. Dowd, *Life of Vance*, 19, 24–25; Alderman et al., *Compiled Under the Direct Supervision of Southern Men of Letters*, 14:6359.

47. DLS to ZBV, August 15, 1862, in Johnston, *Papers of Vance*, 1:152.

48. ZBV to Harriett Espy, June 25, 28, 1853, in Cannon, *My Beloved Zebulon*, 243–44, 250.

49. ZBV to DLS, January 2, 1864, Swain Papers, SHC (typescript; original in WAG Papers); Dowd, *Life of Vance*, 209–10; Peele, *Lives*, 245.

50. John W. Powell to DLS, February 22, 1848, Swain Papers, SANC.

51. John H. Wheeler to DLS, February 14, 1840, Swain Papers, SANC; illegible to DLS, August 31, 1838, Swain Papers, ibid.; Alexander M. Ives to DLS, March 30, 1857, Swain Papers, SHC; Clement Dowd to DLS, March 1857 (exact date not shown), ibid.; John P. Steele to DLS, June 23, 30, 1856, ibid.; Rankin and Pulliam to DLS, February 23, 1848, ibid.; McDowell (no other name given) to DLS, June 11, 1848 (typescript), ibid.; O. H. Prince to DLS, September 1, 1840, Swain Papers, SANC.

52. George E. Badger to DLS, January (?) 11, 1846; G. (?) McDowell to DLS, June 11, 1848, Swain Papers, SANC.

53. Tod R. Caldwell to DLS, March 16, 1841, Swain Papers, SHC.

54. Thomas Bragg to DLS, April 19, 1858, ibid.

55. Jonathan Worth to WAG, March 12, 1867, and DLS to WAG, March 16, 1867, Hamilton et al., *Papers of Graham*, 7:283, 295–96.

56. D. P. Gerebee (?), Wm. L. Brown, and Albert Shipp Jr. to DLS, October 3, 1838, Swain Papers, SHC.

57. Clarke M. Avery to DLS, February 4, 1839, and DLS to C.M. Avery, February 4, 1839, Swain Papers, SHC; Samuel D. Wharton to DLS, February 15, 1845, Swain Papers, SANC.

58. LMB to WHB, November 6, 1846, BFP, SHC.

59. CM to DLS, April 9 (?), 12, 1858; DLS to Paul C. Cameron, May 10, 1858; Paul C. Cameron to DLS, May 15, 1858, Swain Papers, SHC.

60. Unidentified Battle Child to WHB, undated ([Nov., 1854–Feb., 1855] penciled on), BFP, SHC.

61. LMB to WHB, April 6, 1847, July 3, 1850, BFP, SHC; Battle, *History*, 1:648.

62. Samuel H. Ridobel to DLS, December 11, 1841; M. Chamberlain to DLS, November 16, 1841; CM to DLS, May 8, 1841, Swain Papers, SANC.

63. George H. Colton to WPM, June 4, 1845, in Shanks, *Papers of Mangum*, 4:293–94; Spaulding & Storrs to DLS, March 24, 1840, Swain Papers, SANC; Charles F. Deems to DLS, November 8, 1842, Swain Papers, SHC.

Chapter 11: Faculty

1. WHB to DLS, August 18, 1855, Swain Papers, SHC.

2. Drake, *Higher Education in North Carolina Before 1860*, 109–12; Spencer, *Pen*

and Ink Sketches, 41; ECM, June 29, 1837; FM, July 18, 1850 (example, among many, of faculty meeting at Swain's house), April 30, 1854 (6:00 a.m. meeting). There are numerous recorded instances of faculty meetings not being held due to Swain's absence, e.g., FM, July 16, 1847, February 21, 1868.

3. Battle, *History*, 1:533; FM, March 3, 1836, July 20, 1860, March 7, 1867; BOTM, December 29, 1837, June 3, 1840, December 11, 1854; M. Fetter to DLS, January 2, 1857, UP; John Kimberly to DLS, January 5 (9?), 1858, ibid.; F. M. Hubbard to CM, November 29, 1858, ibid.; CM to DLS, November 13, 1861, Swain Papers, SHC.

4. BOTM, January 10, 1859; FM, November 6, 1840, May 28, 1842, August 3, 1855.

5. CM to DLS, November 11, 1842, April 11, 1855, Swain Papers, SHC; DLS to CM, July 30, 1849, UP; Hugh Waddell to WAG, July 27, 1845, ibid.

6. DLS to CM, July 1, 1837, UP.

7. Charles Dosett to DLS, June 28, 1842, Swain Papers, SANC; Delaware Kemper to DLS, November 1, 1856, UP; Andre Dulude to DLS, November 10, 1856, ibid.; B. R. Carroll to DLS, Swain Papers, SHC; Robert H. Labberten to DLS, October 27, 1859, UP; B. R. Carroll to DLS, November 5, 1859, Swain Papers, SHC; P. L. Taylor to DLS, November 14, 1859, UP; Edward Hammond to DLS, October 12, 1860, ibid.

8. J. Wood Johns to DLS, January 1, 1858, UP.

9. Lee M. McAfee to DLS, March 18, 1859, Swain Papers, SHC.

10. Joseph R. Wilson to DLS, November 12, 1859, UP. Numerous other letters supported Hepburn; see, e.g., William H. Ruffress to DLS, November 10, 1859, ibid.

11. ECM, June 24, 1847; Francis L. Hawks to DLS, October 27, December 9, 1859; DLS to Francis L. Hawks, December 4, 26, 1859; D. M. Barringer to DLS, November 4, 1859, Swain Papers, SHC.

12. John H. Wheeler to DLS, October 16, 1858, March 24, August 26, 1859, and to UNC BOT, undated, Swain Papers, SHC.

13. W. L. Ashe to DLS, April 28, 1859; Thomas Bragg to DLS, June 7, 1859; DLS to Gen. Lane, March 5, 1860; John H. Wheeler to DLS, May 7, 1859, April 19, 1861, Swain Papers, SHC.

14. George Bancroft to DLS, September 12, 1859, Swain Papers, SHC; DLS to George Bancroft, September 16, 1859, Swain Papers, SHC (copy) (original in New York Public Library).

15. (Illegible) R. Walker to DLS, September 28, 1838, Swain Papers, SANC.

16. DLS to Gen. Daniel L. Barringer, July 22, 1840, Swain Papers, SHC; DLS to WHB, January 20, 1842, BFP, SHC; see Gass, "A Felicitous Life: Lucy Martin Battle, 1805–1874," 52 NCHR 367, 380.

17. WHB to DLS, February 3, 1842, Swain Papers, SHC.

18. BOTM, December 12, 1842; WHB to DLS, January 24, 1843, Swain Papers, SANC.

19. WHB to LMB, March 18, 1843, BFP, SHC; ECM, July 3, 1844; LMB to WHB, March 6, April 26, 1845, March 2, April 6, 1847, BFP, SHC; Gass, "A Felicitous Life," 52 NCHR 367, 382–83.

20. DLS to CM, December 19, 1843, UP; DLS to WHB, September 19, 1845, BFP, SHC; WHB to DLS, October 3, 1845, Swain Papers, SHC.

21. ECM, October 3, 1845.

22. LMB to WHB, November 6, 1846, BFP, SHC; WHB to DLS, May 7, 1846, Swain Papers, SHC; DLS to WHB, May 17, 1848, BFP, SHC.

23. Sheppard, *History of Legal Education in the United States*, 1:470.

24. LMB to WHB, April 10, August 31, September 17, October 8, 1844, November 1, 1845, February 26, March 5, 12, 1846, March 20, 1860; DLS to WHB, September 19, 1845; WHB to LMB, May 27, 1848, BFP, SHC.

25. Spencer, *Pen and Ink Sketches*, 50; Vickers, *Chapel Hill Illustrated*, 57; LMB to WHB, April 12, September 27, October 18, 1845, March 18, 1848, April 9, 1949, BFP, SHC.

26. LMB to WHB, September 20, 1850, BFP, SHC; FM, September 20, 1850.

27. James Phillips to Rev. Alexander Wilson, December 12, 1843, Spencer Papers, SHC; DLS to CM, February 24, 1844, UP; LMB to WHB, October 13, 1849, BFP, SHC; DLS to WHB, October 19, 1849, BFP, SHC; Charles Phillips to DLS, January 1, 1853, UP; Charles Phillips to unidentified (probably KPB), January 26, 1853, BFP, SHC. Apparently, Davidson's courtship of Charles Phillips continued over a period of time. Ultimately Phillips went to Davidson but only after Swain's demise and the university's temporary closure.

28. ZBV to DLS, July 6, 1857, Swain Papers, SHC (also in Johnston, *Papers of Vance*, 1:30–31); Charles Phillips to KPB, July 11, 1857, BFP, SHC.

29. CM to DLS, July 11, 14, 1857, Swain Papers, SHC; DLS to CM, July 13, 14, 1857, UP; ECM, July 11, 14, 1857; see FM, July 17, 1857, for faculty tribute to Dr. Mitchell.

30. DLS to WAG, August 13, 1858, Hamilton et al., *Papers of Graham*, 5:47–49; WAG to DLS, August 17, 1858, Swain Papers, SHC; D.R. McAnally to DLS, August 19, 1858, ibid.; ZBV to DLS, August 30, 1858, ibid. (in Johnston, *Papers of Vance*, 1:38–40) (see ibid., 38–39nn.149, 150). Swain's June 16, 1858 address was published under the title "A vindication of the propriety of giving the name 'Mt. Mitchell' to the highest peak of 'Black Mountain.'" Brewer, "Hon. David L. Swain, LL.D," *New-England Historical and Genealogical Register and Antiquarian Journal*, 24:352 (October 1870). See also "A Memoir of the Rev. Elisha Mitchell, D.D.," 50, 77–88; Jeffrey, "'A Whole Torrent of Mean and Malevolent Abuse' Part I," 70 NCHR 241, 246; Jeffrey, "'A Whole Torrent of Mean and Malevolent Abuse' Part II," 70 NCHR 401, 416, 409n.22, 419–20; Sondley, *History of Buncombe County*, 2:531, 539, 542–48, 556; "Dr. Mitchell's Investigations

Among the Mountains of Yancey County," *North Carolina University Magazine*, 7:293–318 (March 1858); Editors' Table, *North Carolina University Magazine*, 10:504, 507–9 (April 1861); *Hillsborough Recorder*, June 30, 1858; *Weekly Raleigh Register*, July 14, 1858.

31. CM to DLS, July 11, 20, September 16, October 25, November 21, December 13, 1857, SHC; DLS to CM, October 20, 1857, UP; M. E. Mitchell to DLS, undated, Swain Papers, SHC; F. M. Hubbard to CM, February 3, 1858, UP; BOTM, January 4, December 1, 1858; ECM, November 20, 1857; *Weekly Raleigh Register*, September 9, 16, 1857; *Hillsborough Recorder*, November 11, 1857.

32. *Weekly Raleigh Register*, October 28, 1857.

33. C. Dickson to DLS, November 24, 1857; William Dinwiddie to DLS, November 27, 1857; S. Manfirn (?) to DLS, December 5, 1857; S. S. Holladay to DLS, December 15, 1857, UP. Martin himself wrote to Swain on November 25, 1857, ibid., enclosing testimonials on his behalf and requesting a UNC catalogue.

34. W. H. McGuffey to DLS, November 27, December 5, 1857, ibid.

35. DLS to W. H. McGuffey, December 2, 1857, ibid.

36. *Weekly North Carolina Standard*, February 3, 1858; *Fayetteville Observer*, February 1, 15, 1858; statement by Swain for *The Standard*, January 23, 1858, UP; Francis L. Hawks to DLS, November 10, 1857, Swain Papers, SHC; DLS to CM, January 23, 1858, UP; DLS to E. J. Hale and Son, February 3, 1858, Swain Papers, SHC.

37. WAG to DLS, January 23, 1858, Swain Papers, SHC; *Fayetteville Observer*, February 1, 1858; W. H. McGuffey to DLS, January 12, 1858, Swain Papers, SANC; WHB to LMB, February 3, 10, 1858, and LMB to WHB, February 12, 1858, BFP, SHC. For accounts of Martin's election, see BOTM, January 4, 5, 1858; *Weekly Raleigh Register*, January 13, 1858; Drake, *Higher Education in North Carolina Before 1860*, 110.

38. Drake, *Higher Education in North Carolina Before 1860*, 110.

39. FM, August 16, 1837; DLS to Rev. Thomas A. Morris, January 27, 1838; Thomas A. Morris to DLS, February 5, 1838; DLS to CM, February 10, 1838, UP; Battle, *History*, 1:454–55. Years later Swain detailed these occurrences in the *Raleigh Weekly Standard*, March 9, 1859.

40. Walter L. Steele to DLS, June 11, 1849, Swain Papers, SANC.

41. Levi Thorne to DLS, July 22, 1857, and DLS to Rev. Levi Thorne, July 23, 1857, Swain Papers, SHC; DLS to Rev. T. E. Skinner, August 8, 1857, Swain Papers, SANC.

42. John H. Wheeler to DLS, September 5, October 18, 1859; CM to DLS, May 15, 1859, Swain Papers, SHC.

43. CM to DLS, March 18, 1859, Swain Papers, SHC (copy in UP); DLS to CM, March 15, 1859, UP; DLS to Rev. Rufus T. Heflin, Editor of the *Christian Advocate*, March 16, 1859, UP; *Fayetteville Observer*, March 3, 1859 (publishing prior Swain statements on subject); *North Carolina Christian Advocate*, March 10, 1859; Keever, Homer M., "Deems, Charles Force," in Powell, *DNCB*, 2:49.

44. *Raleigh Sentinel*, April 13, 1871; *Biblical Recorder*, June 21, July 12, 1871; Spencer, *Pen and Ink Sketches*, 37.

45. DLS to CM, January 21, 1840, UP.

46. FM, January 25, 1856.

47. BOTM, ECM, extracts, December 1852.

48. L. S. Ives to DLS, March 3, 1846, Swain Papers, SANC.

49. CM to DLS, February 12, 1859, Swain Papers, SHC; Francis L. Hawks to DLS, January 3, 1860, ibid.; Robert Donaldson to DLS, November 10, 1843, UP; Anderson, *Carolinian on the Hudson*, 181.

50. FM, February 20, 1867.

51. UNC BOT Resolution, January 6, 1857.

52. FM, January 27, 1854; Blackmun, *Western North Carolina*, 239; DLS to CM, January 4, 1844, UP.

53. WAG to DLS, July 31, August 8, 1845, Hamilton et al., *Papers of Graham*, 3:52–54; Battle, *History*, 1:497.

54. FM, January 25, 1844; CM to S. Cheves Manly, January 24, 1844, Swain Papers, SHC; W. M. Green and Charles M. F. Deems to CM, January 27, 1844, UP; Bowman, Charles H. Jr., "Gaston, William," in Powell, *DNCB*, 2:285. Following Gaston's death his family and friends sought Swain's assistance in several ways. See, e.g., B. B. Minor to DLS, February 1, 1844, Gaston Papers, SHC; Robert Donaldson to DLS, December 6, 1845, Swain Papers, SHC.

55. FM, August 12, 1842, November 27, 1854; B. Silliman to Prof. O. P. Hubbard, August 19, 1842, July 30, 1845, Swain Papers, SHC.

56. Invitation from Josiah Quincy, Prest., P. B. K. Society, followed by J. E. Worcester to DLS, August 27, 1842, Swain Papers, SHC; William H. Haigh Diary, January 23, 1844, SHC; J. E. Worcester to DLS, October 5, 1846, April 22, 1847, January 24, 1860, Swain Papers, SHC, and November 11, 1847, Swain Papers, SANC.

57. DLS to J. D. B. Hooper, Esq., December 3, 1850, Hooper Papers, SHC.

58. Charles F. Deems to DLS, April 12, 1866, Swain Papers, SHC.

59. Cornelia Phillips to "My dear Charley" (presumably her brother Charles Phillips), September 23, 1851, Spencer Papers, SHC.

60. A. G. Alexander to DLS, February 27, 1861, Swain Papers, SANC.

61. George L.L. Davis to DLS, January 28, 1860, UP.

62. Battle, *History*, 1:451–52.

63. CM to DLS, January 18, 1858, Swain Papers, SHC; John Kimberly to DLS, November 12, 1859, Swain Papers, SANC.

64. James Phillips to DLS, October 17, 1843, ibid. (typescript in Swain Papers, SHC).

65. BOTM, December 1, 1858, January 8, 10, 1859; Solomon Pool et al. to DLS, January 17, 1859, UP.

66. BOTM, August 20, September 10, December 19, 1859; Francis L. Hawks to Rev. Professor Hubbard, August 20, 1859, UP; Charles F. Deems to DLS, January 26, 1860, UP.

67. A. M. Shipp to BOT, May 2, 1859, UP; BOTM, July 21, 1859; LMB to WHB, February 11, 1859, BFP, SHC; J. T. Wheat to DLS, June 11, 1859, UP; DLS to unidentified recipient, June 27, 1859, UP; DLS to WAG, June 27, 1859, Hamilton et al., *Papers of Graham*, 5:107; DLS to WHB, June 27, 1859, BFP, SHC.

68. FM, March 7, 1867 (entry follows these minutes); *Hillsborough Recorder*, March 20, 1867; DLS, "Dr. James Phillips," *The University Monthly*, 1:51–53 (May 1882); Battle, *History*, 1:758.

69. CM to DLS, January 20, 1840, Swain Papers, SHC; Battle, *History*, 1:464–65; ECM, April 4, 1867.

70. DLS statement, undated, to "Gentleman [sic] of the Faculty," UP.

71. J. D. B. Hooper to DLS, June 19, 1848, UP; Battle, *History*, 1:527, 545–46, 794.

72. DLS to CM, August 8, 1853, UP; William N. (?) Boyce to DLS, December 10, 1853, Swain Papers, SANC; A. M. Shipp to DLS, July 8, 1853, ibid.; Henri Herrisse to WAG, March 7, 1855, Hamilton et al., *Papers of Graham*, 4:591–92.

73. ECM, October 11, 1856 (copy also in Hedrick Papers, Duke); DLS to CM, October 10, 1856, UP.

74. Henri Herrisse to Marmaduke Robbins, July 5, 1856, UP; DLS to CM, October 16, 1856, and attached faculty resolution, ibid.; CM to DLS, October 18, 1856, Swain Papers, SHC; FM, 6:1– 58–62 (Appendix to FM dated August 13, 1856; follows FM dated October 6, 1856), March 20, 1856; Battle, *History*, 1:657–59.

75. Henri Herrisse to Gov. Bragg, October 15, 1856, UP; Henri Herrisse to Gov. Swain, October 24, 1856, ibid.; CM to DLS, October 14, 22, 25, 26, 1856, Swain Papers, SHC; FM, October 13, November 10, 1856.

76. DLS to unidentified recipient (probably CM), October 28, 1856, UP; Henri Herrisse to EC, October 31, 1856, ibid.; Henri Herrisse to Benjamin S. Hedrick, Election Day, 1856, Hedrick Papers, Duke.

Chapter 12: Hedrick Affair

1. Smith, *A Traitor and a Scoundrel*, 26; Battle, *History*, 1:624, 803; Swain Circular Letter, December 11, 1849, Hedrick Papers, SHC.

2. DLS to WAG, February 28, 1851, Hamilton et al., *Papers of Graham*, 4:48–49.

3. WAG to DLS, March 24, 1851, May 27, 1852, and DLS to WAG, April 11 1851, Hamilton et al., *Papers of Graham*, 4:59, 75, 304; WAG to Benjamin S. Hedrick, March 21, 1851, Hedrick Papers, SHC; Hamilton et al., *Papers of Graham*, 6:305n.120.

4. Smith, *A Traitor and a Scoundrel*, 32; WAG to DLS, May 27, 1852, Hamilton et al., *Papers of Graham*, 4:304.

5. DLS to B. S. Hedrick, December 8, 1852, Hedrick Papers, SHC; B. S. Hedrick to DLS, December 13, 1852, UP.

6. ECM, December 1, 1852; DLS to B. S. Hedrick, December 29, 1852, January 19, 1853, Hedrick Papers, SHC.

7. Charles Phillips to B. S. Hedrick, November 12, 1851, October 21, December 30, 1852, ibid.

8. B. S. Hedrick to DLS, January 15, 1853, UP.

9. Charles Phillips to B. S. Hedrick, January 3, 22, March 1, December 10, 1853, Hedrick Papers, SHC.

10. Charles Phillips to B. S. Hedrick (presumably), January 3, 1854; DLS to Charles Dewey (?), February 1, 1854; DLS to B. S. Hedrick (presumably), May 15, 1854; B. S. Hedrick to "My dear Wife," January 9, 1856; Charles Phillips to B. S. Hedrick, January 22, 1853, Hedrick Papers, SHC.

11. Battle, *History*, 1:654–57; Smith, *A Traitor and a Scoundrel*, 68.

12. Battle, *History*, 1:564, 654; FM, May 18, 1838; William H. Miller to David S. Reid, February 8, 1851, in Butler, *Papers of Reid*, 1:292.

13. *North Carolina Standard*, September 27, 1856.

14. Ibid., October 4, 1856.

15. B. S. Hedrick to Gov. Thomas Bragg, October 6, 1856, UP.

16. B. S. Hedrick to CM, October 14, 1856, UP (copy in Hedrick Papers, SHC).

17. *North Carolina Standard*, October 11, 1856.

18. Ibid., October 15, 1856.

19. FM, October 6, 1856; *North Carolina Standard*, October 11, 1856; *Republican Banner*, October 21, 1856.

20. DLS to CM, October 6, 1856, UP.

21. DLS to unidentified recipient (probably CM), October 7, 1856, ibid.

22. DLS to CM, October 17, 1856, ibid.

23. *North Carolina Standard*, October 11, 1856.

24. CM to DLS, October 4, 1856, Swain Papers, SHC.

25. CM to DLS, October 8, 1856, ibid.

26. ECM, October 11, 18, 1856; BOTM, January 5, 1857; CM to DLS, October 18, 1856, Swain Papers, SHC; Sitterson, *Secession Movement in North Carolina*, 121; Smith, *A Traitor and a Scoundrel*, 80.

27. *North Carolina Standard*, October 22, 1856.

28. M. S. Sherwood to "My Dear Nephew," August 20, 1856, Hedrick Papers, SHC.

29. A. D. Rankin to B. S. Hedrick, October 15, 1856, ibid.

30. Francis L. Hawks to WHB, November 6, 1856, BFP, SHC.

31. B. S. Hedrick to Dr. C. S. Henry, October 28, 1856, and to Hanson Robinson, October 24, 1856, Hedrick Papers, SHC.

32. B. S. Hedrick to Editor, *Wilmington Commercial*, January 30, 1857, ibid.; *The Wilmington Commercial*, February 5, 1857; B. S. Hedrick to T. Loving, February 10, 1857, Hedrick Papers, SHC.

33. B. S. Hedrick to Ellen Hedrick, October 22, November 15, 1856; Ellen Hedrick to B. S. Hedrick, November 15, 1856, Hedrick Papers, SHC.

34. B. S. Hedrick to Ellen Hedrick, November 22, 24, 25, 1856; Ellen Hedrick to B. S. Hedrick, November 24, 1856, ibid.

35. Ellen Hedrick to B. S. Hedrick, November 25 (two letters), 26, December 8, 18, 1856, ibid.

36. B. S. Hedrick to Ellen Hedrick, December 1, 1856, and to Henry Carey, January 21, 1857, ibid.

37. Ellen Hedrick to B. S. Hedrick, November 10, 11, 1856, ibid.

38. B. S. Hedrick to Ellen Hedrick, November 15, 17, 1856, ibid.

39. Ellen Hedrick to B. S. Hedrick, November 16, 1856, ibid.

40. John L. Hedrick to M. E. (Ellen) Hedrick, December 26, 1856; Ellen Hedrick to B. S. Hedrick, December 30, 1856, and December (exact date not shown) 1856, ibid.

41. Ellen Hedrick to B. S. Hedrick, January 5, 1857, and B. S. Hedrick to Ellen Hedrick, January 10, 1857, ibid.

42. Ellen Hedrick to B. S. Hedrick, November 16, 1856, ibid.

43. Ellen Hedrick to B. S. Hedrick, November 22, 1856, ibid.

44. B. S. Hedrick to CM, October 28, 1856, UP; CM to B. S. Hedrick, October 29, 1856, Hedrick Papers, Duke.

45. M. E. (Ellen) Hedrick to B. S. Hedrick, October 21, 1856, Hedrick Papers, SHC.

46. B. S. Hedrick to Ellen Hedrick, November 12, 14, 18, 1856, ibid.

47. DLS to Benj. S. Hedrick, November 19, 1856, Hedrick Papers, Duke.

48. B. S. Hedrick to Ellen Hedrick, November 23, 1856, Hedrick Papers, SHC.

49. Ellen Hedrick to B. S. Hedrick, December 5, 7, 14, 16, 1856; B. S. Hedrick to Ellen Hedrick, December 15, 1856, ibid.

50. Recommendation for B. S. Hedrick from DLS, E. Mitchell, F. M. Hubbard, J. T. Wheat, and Charles Phillips, February 7, 1857, ibid.; B. S. Hedrick to DLS, April 27, 1857, Swain Papers, NCAH.

51. Ellen Hedrick to Mrs. Rankin, December 29, 1856, and to B. S. Hedrick, December 13, 25, 1856, Hedrick Papers, SHC.

52. C. S. Henry to B. S. Hedrick, November 4, 1857; Henry Howe to B. S. Hedrick, January 7, 1858, ibid.

53. M. L. (?) Cocke to B. S. Hedrick, October 22, 1856; E. J. Hale to B. S. Hedrick, October 22, 1856, ibid.

54. B. S. Hedrick to CM, March 21, 1859, UP; CM to DLS, March 26, 1859, Swain Papers, SHC.

55. Samuel W. Fisher to Profs. Knowlton and Shipardson, December 10, 1856; Ch. D. Cleveland to Rev. Jno. Knox (?), May 6, 1857, Hedrick Papers, SHC.

56. Horace Greely to Horace Mann, December 2, 1856; B. S. Hedrick to Ellen Hedrick, December 7, 10, 1856, ibid.

57. B. S. Hedrick to Ellen Hedrick, December 12, 1856, ibid.

58. B. S. Hedrick to unidentified recipient, November 22, 1856 (possibly an uncompleted draft); B. S. Hedrick to Mr. Howe, January 15, 1857; B. S. Hedrick to Prof. Fetter, April 22, 1857, ibid.

59. Smith, *A Traitor and a Scoundrel*, 88–109, gives a detailed account of Hedrick's life and career post-UNC.

60. A. D. Hepburn to DLS, June 25, 1857, UP. For other commentary on the Hedrick affair, see Ballinger, Helms, and Holder, *Slavery and the Making of the University*, 27–30; Chapman, *Black Freedom*, 62–63; Cox, "Freedom During the Fremont Campaign: The Fate of One North Carolina Republican in 1856," 45 NCHR 359; Hamilton and Wagstaff, *Benjamin Sherwood Hedrick*, passim; Hamilton, *Party Politics in North Carolina 1835–1860*, 179; Snider, *Light on the Hill*, 65–66; Vickers, *Chapel Hill Illustrated*, 61–62. For a summary version of Michael Thomas Smith's *A Traitor and a Scoundrel*, see his article "'A Traitor and a Scoundrel': Benjamin S. Hedrick and the Making of a Dissenter in the Old South," 76 NCHR 316.

Chapter 13: Property

1. ECM, December 9, 1835; DLS to CM, February 10, 1838, UP.

2. FM, October 11, 1839; ECM, March 7, 1837; BOTM, December 12, 19, 1840.

3. ECM, March 26, 1846 (example of ratification of land sales Swain had made); CM to DLS, March 28, 1846, Swain Papers, SHC (Swain advised of same); BOTM, December 23, 1845, and FM, January 17, 1846 (Swain authorized to sell lot to Miss Sally Mallett "at such price as they may agree on").

4. DLS and WHB, memo, August 1, 1837, certificate, August 2, 1838, UP; ECM, January 23, February 6, 1849; CM to DLS, January 24, February 3, 1849, Swain Papers, SHC; DLS to CM, January 26, 1849, UP.

5. BOTM, December 14, 1849, June 5, December 26, 1850; WHB to CM, January 8, 1850, UP.

6. BOTM, June 4, 1851; DLS to BOT EC, October 4, December 12, 1851, UP.

7. DLS to WAG, October 27, 1847, UP; BOTM, December 16, 1851; ECM, January 13, 1852, September 7, 1860.

8. DLS to WHB, February 19, 18?? (in 1854 file), BFP, SHC; DLS to unidentified recipient, February 19, 1855, UP; DLS to CM, August 6, 1855, UP; BOTM, June 3, 1840.

9. DLS to WAG, August 26, 1836, Hamilton et al., *Papers of Graham*, 1:437.

10. Henderson, *Campus of the First State University*, 87–88, 363–64. Other sources give slightly, but not significantly, different dates: see Drake, *Higher Education in North Carolina Before 1860*, 85–86; UNC Facilities Planning Spreadsheet (copy in author's files). As to the completion of Gerrard Hall, see Ballinger, Helms, and Holder, *Slavery and the Making of the University*, 15.

11. ECM, February 23, 1838, October 1, 1839; CM to DLS, February 23, 1838, UP. While not altogether clear, the author interprets the records as indicating the university's purchase of both the Hooper and Caldwell houses. See note 1 and accompanying text.

12. E. Mitchell to Duncan Cameron, president of EC, August 28, 1839, and to CM, December 15, 1838, UP.

13. DLS to Gen. Daniel L. Barringer, March 6, 1840, Swain Papers, SHC.

14. BOTM, December 21, 1838, January 3, 1839.

15. CM to DLS, October 16, 1843, Swain Papers, SHC; J. H. Horner, E. C. Yellowley, and G. B. Wetmore to DLS, July 22, 1843, Swain Papers, SANC (typescript in Swain Papers, SHC); Battle, *History*, 1:511–13.

16. A. G. Foster et al. to DLS, November 22, 1843, and J. H. Horner et al. to DLS, November 23, 1843, UP.

17. BOTM, December 13, 23, 1844.

18. Henderson, *Campus of the First State University*, 153–54; DLS to WAG, September 1, 1847, UP; DLS to WHB, April 7, 1848, BFP, SHC ("Our cabinet-maker Day has not yet arrived with his materials from Milton, though we are constantly looking for him."); Thomas Day to DLS, November 7, December 6, 1847, UP; DLS to CM, January 26, 1849, UP; Day receipt, January 23, 1849, UP.

19. BOTM, June 3, 1846; Battle, *History*, 1:511–13.

20. CM to DLS and WHB, February 1, 1849, Swain Papers, SHC; A. J. Davis to DLS, March 4, May 31, 1850, Swain Papers, SHC; BOTM, May 31, 1854; Battle, *History*, 1:617; Henderson, *Campus of the First State University*, 138–45, 147–48; Spencer, *Pen and Ink Sketches*, 42.

21. WHB to LMB, August 16, 1855, BFP, SHC; BOTM, June 3, 1856, June 2, 1858; Hamilton et al., *Papers of Graham*, 5:31n.6; Henderson, *Campus of the First State University*, 150–53.

22. Allcott, "Robert Donaldson, the First North Carolinian to Become Prominent in the Arts," 52 NCHR 333, 362; Anderson, *Carolinian on the Hudson*, 219; Battle, *History*, 1:789; ECM, October 16, 1843; Robert Donaldson to DLS, November 10, 1843, UP.

23. DLS to Robert Donaldson, November 28, 1843, and to CM, December 19, 1843, UP.

24. Robert Donaldson to DLS, February 16, 1843, ibid.

25. Robert Donaldson to DLS, January 16, 1844 (typescript), and CM to DLS, February 22, 1844, Swain Papers, SHC.

26. A. J. Davis to DLS, April 17, 1844, March 24, 1845, UP.

27. DLS to Gov. Morehead, June 18, 1844, UP; for general commentary, see Anderson, *Carolinian on the Hudson*, 202, 218–28; Henderson, *Campus of the First State University*, 135–36; Powell, *First State University*, 63; Snider, *Light on the Hill*, 108; *Chapel Hill Newspaper*, May 5, 1985.

28. DLS to WAG, January 27, 1838 [1858], Hamilton et al., *Papers of Graham*, 5:31.

29. Documents in DLS's hand, April 1847, June 8, 1847, UP; list of measurements for East and West Buildings, Swain Papers, SANC; Swain exhibit showing disbursements approved January 3, 1838, ECM 15–66; ECM, October 10, 1847; ECM, October 1, 1843; Hart and Polley, Wilmington, to DLS, November 6, 1843, Swain Papers, SANC (typescript in Swain Papers, SHC).

30. John Berry to DLS, April 18, November 17, 1844, UP.

31. Receipt from Kendall B. Waitt, November 27, 1837; receipt from I. (?) J. Collier, undated; bill, December 10, 1850, to DLS for trustees; Henry Evans to DLS, August 31, 1854, UP.

32. Francis L. Hawks to DLS, December 31, 1856, UP.

33. LMB to WHB, March 6, 1845, BFP, SHC.

34. F. M. Hubbard to DLS, June 2, 1858, UP; Salina Wheat, May Wheat, Geo. P. Wheat to DLS, undated, UP; BOTM, December 16, 1852, December 10, 1861; ECM, April 21, 1847.

35. ECM, November 16, 1841, October 10, 1847; J. B. Tinney statement, December 7, 1847, UP; Battle, *History*, 1:431.

36. ECM, January 3, 1850; BOTM, December 16, 1852; DLS to CM, November 9, 1852, UP.

37. ECM, August 16, 1858; CM to DLS, September 16, 1857, Swain Papers, SHC.

38. BOTM, June 27, 1838; DLS to CM, October 12, 1842, UP; *North Carolina Presbyterian*, August 18, 1869.

39. Tucker, *Zeb Vance*, 43; LMB to WHB, March 16, 1847, BFP, SHC.

40. BOTM, December 16, 1844; Lefler and Wager, *Orange County, 1752–1952*, 149; Powell, *First State University*, 68.

41. Chapman, *Black Freedom*, 37; Vickers, *Chapel Hill Illustrated*, 56; receipt from Willis Duncan, June 4, 1848, UP.

42. Battle, "David Lowry Swain," *North Carolina Journal of Education*, 3:27, 29; Henderson, *Campus of the First State University*, 122–25; Spencer, *Pen and Ink*

Sketches, 42; "Heritage on the Hill," *The Village Advocate*, December 12, 1984; Bill Burk, "Walls Provide a Link to the past," *Chapel Hill News*, September 27, 2009; E. Mitchell to CM, December 27, 1849, UP.

43. Albert B. Dod to DLS, August 22, 1845, Swain Papers, SANC.

44. Alex J. Davis to DLS, August 25, 1845, UP.

45. A. J. Davis to DLS, October 29, 1846, Swain Papers, SANC (typescript in Swain Papers, SHC).

46. Alex J. Davis to DLS, February 13, 1847, Swain Papers, SANC (typescript in Swain Papers, SHC); P. G. McLaughlin to DLS, April 27, 1847, Swain Papers, SANC (typescript in Swain Papers, SHC). Davis must have had some doubts about the university's chances of hiring McLaughlin; while the courtship of McLaughlin was underway, he told Swain two men on Broadway were on the lookout for a gardener and discussed two prospects and what they would require. Alex J. Davis to DLS, March 9, 1847, UP.

47. ECM, October 1, 1843; Robert Donaldson to DLS, January 16, 1844, Swain Papers, SANC, September 30, 1845, UP, December 6, 1845, Swain Papers, SHC; see Anderson, *Carolinian on the Hudson*, 218–23.

48. James Donaldson to DLS, April 11, 1846, April 12, 1847, May 22, 1856 (probably), August 12, 1857, SANC.

49. Henderson, *Campus of the First State University*, 110, 158–61 (Loader), 110, 161, 165 (Paxton); CM, Secretary, December 1, 1858, ordinance re: "the Burser [*sic*] and the Campus," UP; BOTM, January 5, 1858. There are numerous examples of the trustee support; see, e.g., BOTM, January 5, 1848, December 15, 1851, December 1, 16, 1852, January 2, December 22, 1854, January 4, 1856, January 5, 1857.

50. E. Mitchell to CM, December 27, 1849, UP.

51. Battle, "David Lowry Swain," *North Carolina Journal of Education*, 3:27, 29; for other commentary, see Henderson, *Campus of the First State University*, 110, 129, 155–57, and Vickers, *Chapel Hill Illustrated*, 56.

52. W. H. Owen, Librarian, "Report on State of the Library," December 15, 1836, UP.

53. Ibid., December 20, 1837, UP.

54. Battle, *History*, 1:409; Henderson, *Campus of the First State University*, 146–47; Rush, *Library Resources*, 6; Snider, *Light on the Hill*, 63; Spencer, *Pen and Ink Sketches*, 40–41; Wilson, *Library of the First State University*, 12–13; York, "The Dialectic and Philanthropic Societies' Contributions to the Library of The University of North Carolina, 1886–1906," 59 NCHR 327, 333; *North Carolina Presbyterian*, August 18, 1869.

55. Wilson, *Library of the First State University*, 12–13.

56. James Phillips to DLS, July 8, 1841, August 27, 1842; DLS to M[iste]rs Wiley and Putnam, Book Sellers, New York, January 13, 1844, Swain Papers, SANC.

57. Geo. P. Putnam (Miles Putnam), London, to DLS, July 18, 1843, Swain Papers, SANC; DLS to Wiley and Putnam (apparently), January 13, 1844, Swain Papers, SHC (typescript); B. S. Hedrick to DLS, December 28, 1855, Swain Papers, SANC; ECM, December 12, 1864.

58. Drake, *Higher Education in North Carolina Before 1860*, 181–82; Harper & Brothers, New York, to DLS, March 3, 1839, Swain Papers, SANC.

59. Spaulding & Storrs, Hartford, to DLS, October 20, 1840; John P. Bigelow, Boston, to DLS, September 19, 1842; R. W. Brown, Wilmington, to DLS, December 15, 1842, Swain Papers, SANC.

60. Wm. H. Haywood Jr. to DLS, undated [1844, RDWC, penciled on letter], Swain Papers, SHC; W. Dickins to R.M. Saunders, House of Representatives, March 29, 1842, Swain Papers, SANC (refers to Swain's letter to him, which has not been found); George Badger to DLS, December 16, 1846, UP; Ja. Harlan, Dept. of Interior, to DLS, March 19, 1866, Swain Papers, SANC.

61. DLS to Benjamin S. Hedrick, October 24, 1865, December 1, 1866, April 24, 1867, Hedrick Papers, Duke.

62. FM, March 29, 1844.

63. Shanks, *Papers of Mangum*, 5:424–26.

64. M. King to DLS, April 17, 1861, Swain Papers, SANC, and April 22, July 22, September 3, 1861, Swain Papers, SHC.

65. FM, December 7, 1855.

66. Wilson, *Library of the First State University*, 14–15.

67. DLS to CM, June 24, 1846, UP.

68. DLS to Thomas Day, November 24, 1847, UP; *Historic Buildings and Landmarks of Chapel Hill, North Carolina*, 13; Barfield, "Thomas and John Day and the Journey to North Carolina," 78 NCHR 1, 23; Marshall, "The Legendary Thomas Day: Debunking the Popular Mythology of an African American Craftsman," 78 NCHR 32, 40–41.

69. DLS to WAG, September 1, October 27, 1847; DLS to Thomas Day, November 24, 1847; Thomas Day to DLS, November 17, December 6, 1847, UP.

70. James Donaldson to DLS, March 28, 1848 (typescript), Swain Papers, SHC.

71. G.W. to Western [*sic*] Gales, July 17, 1838, Swain Papers, SANC.

72. James W. Bryan to DLS, September 7, 1847, Swain Papers, SHC (as to Bryan, see Battle, *History*, 1:791, 824).

73. DLS to Gov. Ellis, February 24, 1859, Swain Papers, SHC.

74. E. Emmons to DLS, February 23, March 3, 1859, Swain Papers, SANC; DLS to John W. Ellis, February 24, 1859, and John W. Ellis to DLS, March 2, 1859, in Tolbert, *Papers of Ellis*, 1:223–26.

75. Drake, *Higher Education in North Carolina Before 1860*, 74; William S. Mullins to DLS, February 17, 1847, UP (as to Mullins, see Battle, *History*, 1:798).

76. BOTM, June 3, 1856; *N.C. Senate Journal,* January 23, 1857; DLS to unidentified recipient (probably CM), December 7, 1854, UP.

77. CM to DLS, undated (January–Feb. 1857 penciled at top), January 22, 1857, and undated (1–23(?)–1857 penciled at top), Swain Papers, SHC.

78. Battle, *History,* 1:621–22; *Tri-Weekly Commercial,* January 31, 1857; CM to DLS, January 20, February 3, 4, 1857; Thomas Bragg to DLS, January 15, 1857, Swain Papers, SHC. For an example of a brief interval when these funds were unavailable to the university, see BOTM, 6:162 (January 2, 1854?) (trustees denied request from literary societies for additional funds for buildings to accommodate increased number of students, citing, inter alia, "the diminution of their income by the late acts of the General Assembly withdrawing from the Institution the Escheats property of the State"); see also Battle, *History,* 1:623–24. For an example of Swain fighting this battle in the courts, see BOTM, December 30, 1853 (re: a North Carolina Supreme Court decision on legislative acts on the escheats question, "an argument of great force, impugning the constitutionality of the Acts and the legality of the decisions, was made by Governor Swain"). For a later example of escheats funds diverted for a common-schools purpose, see CM to DLS, February 16, 1859, Swain Papers, SHC.

79. Robert S. Burton to DLS, September 6, 1839, UP.

80. T. L. Clingman to DLS, July 4, 1846, Swain Papers, SHC.

81. B. F. Moore to DLS, October 26, 1857, Swain Papers, SANC.

82. J. W. Osborne to DLS, October 27, 1857, ibid.

83. CM to DLS, August 4, 1856, Swain Papers, SHC.

84. Battle, *History,* 1:623; ECM, February 11, 1854, June 15, October 6, 1857, January 9, 20, August 16, 1858; CM to DLS, December 13, 1858, Swain Papers, SHC.

85. CM to DLS (with ECM), August 16, 21, 1858, Swain Papers, SHC.

86. Matthias Manly to CM, January 22, 1839, UP; ECM, January 8, 1839; Battle, *History,* 1:320; Chapman, *Black Freedom,* 44–45.

87. CM to DLS, March 29, 1856, Swain Papers, SHC.

88. George B. Mathew to DLS, March 13, 1851, in Butler, *Papers of Reid,* 1:303.

Chapter 14: Special Events, Distinguished Guests

1. DLS to WAG, May 30, 1836, Hamilton et al., *Papers of Graham,* 1:429 (emphasis added); *Raleigh Register and North-Carolina Gazette,* July 19, 1836. In 1842 the societies' speaker, Judge John Y. Mason, could not attend, and Swain read his letter to the audience. Battle, *History,* 1:475.

2. *Raleigh Register and North-Carolina Gazette,* July 3, 1837.

3. Battle, *History,* 1:456; Cheney, *North Carolina Government,* 189n.20; *Raleigh Register and North-Carolina Gazette,* July 6, 1839.

4. Battle, *History*, 1:729; *Weekly Raleigh Register and North-Carolina Gazette*, June 7, 1854.

5. BOT document appointing committee, May 11, 1839, UP; WHB to DLS, February 5, 1855, Swain Papers, SHC; *Raleigh Register and North-Carolina Gazette*, May 16, 1837, April 30, 1841, May 30, 1845.

6. Will Gaston to DLS, June 24, 1839, Swain Papers, SANC; WAG to DLS, April 21, 1856, Hamilton et al., *Papers of Graham*, 4:636; Thomas Ruffin to DLS, May 31, 1858, Swain Papers, SHC; J. M. Morehead to DLS, April 2, 1846, UP.

7. DLS to Calvin H. Wiley, May 27, 1853, Wiley Papers, SANC; unsigned, undated note to WHB in Swain's hand, BFP, SHC.

8. Battle, *History*, 1:651–52, 2:616; FM, January 21, 1842, May 8, 1857, April 30, 1858.

9. Battle, *History*, 1:258, 504–5; Henderson, *Campus of the First State University*, 94–95; Nevins, *Polk: The Diary of a President*, 238; Connor, "Swain Had Knack of Landing Atop," *Chapel Hill Weekly*, March 31, 1960.

10. L. B. Hardin (Navy Department, Washington) to DLS, December 31, 1844, Swain Papers, SHC (typescript); Battle, *History*, 1:496.

11. DLS to WAG, April 7, 1847, Hamilton et al., *Papers of Graham*, 3:187, April 20, 1847, ibid, 3:188–89, April 23, 1847, ibid, 3:189.

12. DLS to WHB (undesignated but almost certainly to Battle), April 9, 1847, BFP, SHC.

13. LMB to WHB, March 16, 1847, BFP, SHC.

14. LMB to WHB, March 24, April 6, 28, 1847, BFP, SHC.

15. WAG to DLS, March 27, 1847, Swain Papers, SHC (in Hamilton et al., *Papers of Graham*, 3:185–86); ECM, April 21, 1847; CM, Sec., "Extract from the Journal of the Executive Committee of April 21, 1847," Swain Papers, SHC.

16. DLS to WHB (not stated but almost certainly), April 9, 1847, BFP, SHC.

17. DLS to "the President of the United States," April 24, 1847, Swain Papers, SHC; McPherson, "Unpublished Letters from North Carolinians to Polk," 17 NCHR 139, 145–46. As to Marshall Polk, see Battle, *History*, 1:300, 792.

18. Battle, *History*, 1:504–5; Henderson, *Campus of the First State University*, 91–96; *Raleigh Register and North-Carolina Gazette*, June 11, 1847. The Pettigrew quote appears in Drake, *Higher Education in North Carolina Before 1860*, 218, and Snider, *Light on the Hill*, 62.

19. W. W. Holden to DLS, June 4, 1847, Swain Papers, SHC; Battle, *History*, 1:509; Henderson, *Campus of the First State University*, 94–95; Nevins, *Polk: The Diary of a President*, 238–39.

20. DLS to "My dear Madam" (Mrs. Polk), February 10, 1849, in McPherson, "Unpublished Letters from North Carolinians to Polk," 17 NCHR 249, 261–64; FM, July 24, 1849; Battle, *History*, 1:615. Two recent publications discuss Polk's visit: Harriet King, "Presidents Visited Chapel Hill by Carriage, Train, Motorcade and Jet," *Chapel*

Hill News, August 17, 2008; William E. Leuchtenburg, "When the President Came Home to Chapel Hill," *Carolina Arts & Sciences*, 19 (Spring 2012).

21. LMB to WHB, February 8, 1858, BFP, SHC; James Buchanan to Benjamin Green et al., August 20, 1858, UP.

22. CM to DLS, April 29, May 5, 1859, Swain Papers, SHC; P. M. Butler et al. to BOT, April 18, 1859, UP; BOTM, April 29, 1859.

23. James Buchanan to John W. Ellis et al., May 12, 1859, in Tolbert, *Papers of Ellis*, 1:248.

24. John W. Ellis to DLS, May 24, 25, 26, 1859; DLS to Gov. Ellis, May 24, 1859; CM to DLS, May 25, 1859, Swain Papers, SHC. The Ellis-to-Swain and Swain-to-Ellis letters are in Tolbert, *Papers of Ellis*, 1:252–56.

25. James Buchanan to DLS, May 26, 1859, Swain Papers, SHC.

26. *Weekly Raleigh Register*, June 8, 1859; *Chapel Hill News*, August 17, 2008; Henderson, *Campus of the First State University*, 169.

27. *Wilmington Journal*, June 10, 1859; *Fayetteville Observer*, June 13, 1859.

28. Battle, *History*, 1:698–705; Battle, *Memories of an Old Time Tar Heel*, 245; Henderson, *Campus of the First State University*, 168–72.

29. *Wilmington Journal*, June 10, 1859.

30. Andrew Johnson to DLS, June 29, 1866, Johnson Papers, Library of Congress (published in Graf et al., *Papers of Johnson*, 10:639).

31. DLS to Andrew Johnson, May 15, 1867, Johnson Papers, Library of Congress.

32. DLS to unidentified recipient (probably WHB), May 22, 1867, BFP, SHC; DLS to Gov. Jonathan Worth, May 27, 1867, Worth Papers, SANC.

33. Jonathan Worth to WHB, May 24, 1867, ibid.; Andrew Johnson to DLS, May 22, 1867, Johnson Papers, Library of Congress.

34. Thomas Ruffin to DLS, June 4, 1867, Clark Papers, SANC; DLS to WAG, June 1, 1867, Hamilton et al., *Papers of Graham*, 7:330; WAG to DLS, June 1, 1867, Clark Papers, SANC.

35. Battle, *History*, 1:758–62; Battle, *Memories of an Old Time Tar Heel*, 212–13.

36. Edmunds, *Tar Heels Track the Century*, 25–26. Hamilton, *Reconstruction*, 621, briefly mentions Johnson's 1867 visit. Harriet King, "Presidents Visited Chapel Hill by Carriage, Train, Motorcade and Jet," *Chapel Hill News*, August 17, 2008, briefly considers the visits of Polk, Buchanan, and Johnson.

37. Examples in File 84.7, Swain Papers, SANC.

38. Thomas Bragg Jr. to DLS, May 26, 1846, Swain Papers, SANC; DLS to Wm. S. Pettigrew, June 30, 1868, and Wm. S. Pettigrew to DLS, July 8, 1868, Pettigrew Family Papers, SHC; J. H. Viser to DLS, December 9, 1847, Swain Papers, SANC; Battle, *History*, 1:472–73.

39. E.g., FM, March 9, 1857.

40. James K. Polk to Charles Manly, July 22, 1845, UP; John Y. Mason to Charles Manly, July 29, 1845, UP; FM, "Commencement Day," June 1845.

41. FM, June 3, 1853, February 3, 1854; Aaron V. Brown to DLS, June 15, 1857, Swain Papers, SHC.

42. M. (Judge Mitchell D.) King to DLS, June 11, 1859, Swain Papers, SANC; Bishop J. H. Otey to DLS, July 7, 1859, Swain Papers, SHC.

43. FM, April 11, 1856 (decision to invite Everett), February 15, 1858; Edward Everett to DLS, April 30, 1859, Swain Papers, SHC; DLS to unidentified recipient, May 9, 1859, Spencer Papers, SANC. "The Character of George Washington" was Everett's most famous speech; he delivered it 135 times. Howe, Daniel Walter, "Everett, Edward," in Garraty and Carnes, *American National Biography*, 7:629–30. A recent political biography of Everett discusses the speech and lists Chapel Hill as one of the places where Everett gave it. Mason, *Apostle of Union*, 1, 5, 34, 245–55, 317–18, 323–24.

44. *North Carolina University Magazine*, 10:56 (August 1860).

Chapter 15: Public Policy

1. Spencer, *Pen and Ink Sketches*, 68; Hamilton, "David Lowry Swain," in Malone, *Dictionary of American Biography*, 18:231; Battle, *History*, 1:531; D. L. Barringer to DLS, March 27, 1840, and DLS to Gen. Daniel Barringer, March 21, 1846; T. L. Clingman to DLS, September 2, 1847, Swain Papers, SANC.

2. DLS to Gov. R. D. Spaight, August 29, September 13, 1836; R. D. Spaight to DLS, September 13, 27, 1836; CM to DLS, September 16, 1836; W. N. Edwards to DLS, and DLS to W. N. Edwards, both December 24, 1836, Swain Papers, SHC.

3. DLS to W. H. Haywood, January 10, 1837, ibid.; J. M. Johnson to DLS, January 13, 22, 1858; DLS to James M. Johnson, January 18, 1858, ibid. Johnson had been in the UNC Class of 1849. Battle, *History*, 1:522–23, 802.

4. *North Carolina Standard*, July 24, 31, 1844; *Raleigh Register and North-Carolina Gazette*, August 2, 1844.

5. James W. Osborne to DLS, June 26, 1848, Swain Papers, SHC (see Battle, *History*, 1:793).

6. D. W. Siler to DLS, February 5, 1848, Swain Papers, SHC.

7. *Raleigh Register and North-Carolina Gazette*, July 13, 1839; Edward B. Dudley to DLS, November 16, 1839, Swain Papers, SHC.

8. J. M. Morehead to DLS, November 22, 1849, Swain Papers, SHC.

9. *Raleigh Register and North-Carolina Gazette*, June 27, 1849; DLS to Calvin H. Wiley, June 12, 1851, Wiley Papers, SANC; DLS to WAG, July 6, 1852, Hamilton et al., *Papers of Graham*, 4:343.

10. A. B. Cancury to DLS, December 13, 1836, Swain Papers, SHC.

11. C. G. Memminger to DLS, January 26, September 27, 1838, ibid.

12. D. W. (illegible, probably Stone) to DLS, March 15, 1840, and C.M. (probably Charles Manly) to DLS, April 20, 1840, ibid.

13. C. Bernard to DLS, October 17, November 25, 1848, ibid.

14. C. P. Mallett to DLS, November 13, 1839; Charles Baring (?) to DLS, November 6, 1839; Joshua Roberts to DLS, October 11, 1839, Swain Papers, SHC.

15. Edward B. Dudley to DLS, July 7, August 8, 1839, ibid.

16. DLS to WAG, September 10, 1849, Hamilton et al., *Papers of Graham*, 3:311–12.

17. *Carolina Watchman*, August 2, 1849; *Raleigh Register and North-Carolina Gazette*, July 25, August 3, 1849; *Hillsborough Recorder*, August 8, 1849; Jones, *North Carolina Illustrated*, 204, picture 7–12; Lefler, *North Carolina History Told by Contemporaries*, 207–8.

18. Konkle, *Morehead*, 300–1; Peele, *Lives*, 244.

19. DLS to CM, April 28, 1849, UP; *Carolina Watchman*, July 5, 1849.

20. *Carolina Watchman*, September 6, 13, 1849.

21. Cadwallader Jones to DLS, July 16, 1849, Swain Papers, SANC, and to WAG, July 19, 1849, Hamilton et al., *Papers of Graham*, 3:306; *Raleigh Register and North-Carolina Gazette*, September 5, 1849; *Carolina Watchman*, August 9, 1849.

22. C. L. Hinton to DLS, July 17, November 16, 22, 1849, Swain Papers, SHC; Cheney, *North Carolina Government*, 181.

23. *Weekly Raleigh Register and North-Carolina Gazette*, August 3, 1853 (citing "Ash. Mess.").

24. See text accompanying notes 32–33, chapter 2.

25. Edward B. Dudley to DLS, August 11, 1838, Swain Papers, SHC. According to a Swain nephew, such schools as existed before state-sponsored education were "not flourishing"; this was due to high prices, the scarcity of money, and "the want of patronage." Wm. Coleman to DLS, December 18, 1841, Swain Papers, SANC.

26. DLS to CM, August 31, 1838, UP; Edward B. Dudley to DLS, November 25, 1838, Swain Papers, SANC; CM to DLS, November 23, 1838, Swain Papers, SHC.

27. Konkle, *Morehead*, 187; Wilson, *Chronicles of the Sesquicentennial*, 148–50.

28. Noble, *History of the Public Schools of North Carolina*, 175–77.

29. Wm. H. Haywood Jr. to DLS, February 16, 1841, Swain Papers, SHC.

30. Wilson, *Chronicles of the Sesquicentennial*, 164; B. Craven to DLS, September 25, 1852, Swain Papers, SHC (typescript in Craven Papers, Duke).

31. DLS to Calvin H. Wiley, November 8, 1851, Wiley Papers, SANC; DLS to WAG, November 18, 1851, Hamilton et al., *Papers of Graham*, 4:215; Braverman, "Calvin H. Wiley's *North Carolina Reader*, 29 NCHR 500, 507–12; Whitescarver, "School Books, Publishers, and Southern Nationalists: Refashioning the Curriculum in North Carolina's Schools, 1850–1861," 79 NCHR 28, 37–38; Battle, *History*, 1:797.

32. *Southern Recorder*, April 28, 1857.

33. Samuel Buman to DLS, 1834 (year only stated), and William C. Woodbridge to DLS, October 23, 1836, EC, NCC; DLS to Calvin H. Wiley, January 17, 1856, Wiley Papers, SANC; receipt for $1.00 for one-year (1859) subscription to *N.C. Journal of Education*, Swain Papers, SANC.

34. John Beard to DLS, May 17, 1849, Swain Papers, SHC.

35. Henry Barnard to DLS, January 10, 1848, ibid.

36. B. Sears to DLS, February 29, 1868, Clark Papers, SANC.

37. *Hillsborough Recorder*, March 7, 1866.

38. See text accompanying note 12, chapter 5.

39. WHB to DLS, July 30, August 10, 1837, Swain Papers, SHC; Gass, "A Felicitous Life: Lucy Martin Battle, 1805–1874," 52 NCHR 365, 370n.9.

40. DLS to unidentified recipient (probably WHB), undated (Sept. 15, 1866, written on letter in pencil), BFP, SHC.

41. See text accompanying notes 43–50, chapter 5; E. B. Dudley to DLS, April 29, 1838, Swain Papers, SHC; J. N. Siler to DLS, June 12, 1838; DLS to EHS, July 10, 1838, Swain Papers, SANC.

42. DLS to Gen. Daniel L. Barringer, March 6, 1840, Swain Papers, SHC.

43. DLS to Gen. Daniel L. Barringer, July 22, 1840, ibid.

44. J.M. Morehead to DLS, January 25, 1841, ibid.

45. CM to DLS, October 15, 1850, ibid.

46. DLS to CM, August 15, 1862, Vance Papers, SANC.

47. D. W. Stone to DLS, November 8, 1842, Swain Papers, SANC; WHB to DLS, February 5, 1855; Samuel F. Phillips to DLS, December 6, 1854, January 24, 1855, Swain Papers, SHC.

48. Ashe, *Biographical History*, 1:455; Hamilton, *Party Politics in North Carolina 1835–1860*, 132; A. J. Davis to DLS, May 31, 1850; Dorothea L. Dix to DLS, February 15, 1850 (?), Swain Papers, SHC.

49. DLS to WAG, January 31, 1845, Hamilton et al., *Papers of Graham*, 3:21.

50. WAG to DLS, February 7, 1846, Swain Papers, SHC.

51. *Carolina Watchman*, December 26, 1850.

52. *Public Laws of North Carolina*, 1856–57, chapter 37; *The American Almanac... 1860*, 316; Thomas Ruffin to DLS, October 8, 1859, Swain Papers, SHC; *Daily Conservative*, March 21, 1865 (showing Swain still a commissioner).

53. See, e.g., WHB to DLS, January 16, 1853, Swain Papers, SHC.

54. DLS to KPB, April 19, 1868, UP.

55. Elisha Mitchell to WAG, August 28, 1845, Hamilton et al., *Papers of Graham*, 3:71–72; N. W. Woodfin to DLS, November 3, 1846, Swain Papers, SANC.

56. WAG to DLS, January 6, 1842, Swain Papers, SHC.

57. WAG to DLS, July 26, 1841, ibid. (in Hamilton et al., *Papers of Graham*, 2:218–

19); for another communication to Swain on the bank bill, see A. L. Erwin to DLS, August 22, 1841, Swain Papers, SANC (if the president vetoed the bank bill, it would be "a great triumph for the opposition").

58. WAG to DLS, December 5, 1841, Swain Papers, SANC (in Hamilton et al., *Papers of Graham*, 2:244–45).

59. WAG to DLS, March 24, 1851, Swain Papers, SHC.

60. John H. Wheeler to DLS, September 30, 1853, February 15, May 1, 1855, ibid.

61. DLS to Howell Cobb, Sec. of the Treasury, July 31, 1859, and to L. O. B. Branch, same date, Swain Papers, SHC.

62. J. R. Siler to DLS, June 15, 1846; N.W. Woodfin to DLS, March 14, 1847; Asa Biggs to DLS, April 9, 1847, Swain Papers, SANC.

63. D. L. Barringer to DLS, May 30, November 5, 1846; DLS to EHS, July 1, 1847, Swain Papers, SANC (typescripts in Swain Papers, SHC).

Chapter 16: Politics

1. DLS to Gen. Daniel L. Barringer, March 6, 1840, Swain Papers, SHC.

2. George E. Badger to DLS, August 10, 1837, Swain Papers, SANC; D. L. Barringer to DLS, June 7, 1838, ibid.; DLS to Gen. Daniel L. Barringer, May 5, 1840, ibid., and July 22, 1840, Swain Papers, SHC.

3. D. R. Lowry to DLS, May 4, 1840; DLS to Gen. Daniel L. Barringer, March 6, 1840, Swain Papers, SHC.

4. Edward B. Dudley to DLS, July 7, 1839, ibid.; G. M. Wellborn to DLS, August 20, 1840, UP.

5. George E. Badger to DLS, April 25, 1841, Swain Papers, SHC.

6. WAG to DLS, January 6, 1842, ibid.

7. William H. Haywood Jr. to DLS, November 23, 1841, ibid.

8. WPM to DLS, January 27, December 31, 1844, Swain Papers, SHC; see Cheney, *North Carolina Government*, 683.

9. WHB to DLS, April 14, 1848, Swain Papers, SHC.

10. D. L. Barringer to DLS, May 4, 1847 (typescript), Swain Papers, SHC; DLS to WHB, April 7, 1848, BFP, SHC; for a detailed account of the 1848 Whig nomination process, see Holt, *American Whig Party*, 259–330.

11. WAG to DLS, May 27, 1852, Hamilton et al., *Papers of Graham*, 4:305; see ibid., 1:xxi.

12. DLS to WAG, July 6, 1852, ibid., 4:341–42.

13. J. H. Coleman (nephew) to DLS, July 6, 1852; N. W. Woodfin to DLS, August 18 (typescript), September 1, 1852, Swain Papers, SHC.

14. WAG to DLS, October 13, 1852, ibid.

15. WAG to DLS, November 4, 1852, and DLS to WAG, November 5, 1852, Hamilton et al., *Papers of Graham*, 4:428, 429–30.

16. J. N. Siler to DLS, September 3, 1846, Swain Papers, SANC; DLS to WHB, December 16, 1848, BFP, SHC; see Cheney, *North Carolina Government*, 685, 687, 743n.72.

17. N. W. Woodfin to DLS, October 18, 1852, Swain Papers, SHC; DLS to WAG, November 1, 1852, Hamilton et al., *Papers of Graham*, 4:425–26; see Cheney, *North Carolina Government*, 687.

18. WHB to DLS, August 10, 1837, Swain Papers, SHC; Hamilton et al., *Papers of Graham*, 1:xxi.

19. N. T. Coleman to DLS, July 28, 1843; J. H. E. Hardy to DLS, May 2 (year not given, but has to be 1843), Swain Papers, SANC.

20. N. W. Woodfin to DLS, August 7, 1843, Swain Papers, SANC; J. H. Coleman to DLS, July 31, 1843 (typescript), Swain Papers, SHC, August 5, 1843, Swain Papers, SANC (typescript in Swain Papers, SHC).

21. D. W. Siler to DLS, February 5, 1848, and N. W. Woodfin to DLS, July 28, 1851 (typescript), Swain Papers, SHC.

22. LMB to WHB, August 9, 1858, BFP, SHC; Cheney, *North Carolina Government*, 743nn.79–81.

23. Wm. H. Haywood Jr. to DLS, October 25, 1841, Swain Papers, SHC; DLS to Genl. Daniel L. Barringer, July 26, 1842, Swain Papers, SANC.

24. DLS to WPM, April 20, 1843, Shanks, *Papers of Mangum*, 3:442, 442n.24.

25. DLS to Genl. Daniel L. Barringer, February 24, 1843; N. W. Woodfin to DLS, January 3, 1846, Swain Papers, SANC.

26. WHB to DLS, July 7, 1846, Swain Papers, SHC; WHB to LMB, September 29, 1846, BFP, SHC.

27. N. Coleman (nephew) to DLS, April 19, 1846, Swain Papers, SANC.

28. WHB to LMB, July 2, 1854, and LMB to WHB, August 16, 1854, BFP, SHC; Cheney, *North Carolina Government*, 322; Inscoe, *Mountain Masters*, 135 ("Despite the fact that they were nephews of David L. Swain, both David and Newton Coleman of Buncombe County were active Democrats.")

29. John H. Wheeler to DLS, March 17, 1844, Swain Papers, SANC (typescript in Swain Papers, SHC); Cheney, *North Carolina Government*, 361, 368n.48.

30. WHB to DLS, March 30, 1848, Swain Papers, SANC (typescript in Swain Papers, SHC).

31. DLS to WHB, April 7, 1848, BFP, SHC.

32. WHB to DLS, April 14, May 6, 1848, Swain Papers, SHC.

33. George S. Coleman (nephew) to DLS, January 19, 1849, Swain Papers, SANC;

Whichard, Willis P., "Battle, William Horn," in Garraty and Carnes, *American National Biography*, 2:344–45; Cheney, *North Carolina Government*, 361, 368n.50.

34. N. W. Woodfin to DLS, January 28, 1840, ibid.

35. DLS to WAG, November 18, 1851, Hamilton et al., *Papers of Graham*, 4:214–15; Cheney, *North Carolina Government*, 751.

36. CM to DLS, November 15, 1860, and DLS to CM, November 16, 1860, Swain Papers, SHC.

37. DLS to WHB, July 3, 1850, December 13, 1858; Thomas Ruffin to WHB, December 20, 1858, BFP, SHC; see Cheney, *North Carolina Government*, 360–61, 368n.37, 369n.53.

38. Samuel Field Phillips to WAG, June 20, 1850, Hamilton et al., *Papers of Graham*, 3:324.

39. John Gray Bynum to DLS, September 29, 1836, Swain Papers, SHC.

40. DLS to B. (Bartholomew) Fuller, October 13, 1854, Fuller Papers, SHC.

41. DLS to C. H. Wiley, November 1, 1858, Wiley Papers, SANC; Battle, *History*, 1:731.

42. J. H. Bissell to DLS, January 19, 1839, Swain Papers, SHC.

43. George S. Coleman to DLS, February 28, 1849, Swain Papers, SANC; R. C. Gatlin to DLS, July 14, 1849, Swain Papers, SHC, and July 31, 1850, Hamilton et al., *Papers of Graham*, 3:377; William Mercer Green to WAG, May 11, 1849, Hamilton et al., *Papers of Graham*, 3:285–86.

44. WAG to DLS, May 10, 1842, Swain Papers, SHC; WPM to DLS, January 12, 1848, ibid. (also in Shanks, *Papers of Mangum*, 5:91).

45. Thomas J. Lenoir to DLS, March 9, 1843, Swain Papers, SHC (typescript); D. R. Lowery (nephew) to DLS, November 29, 1840, Swain Papers, SANC; DLS to Benjamin S. Hedrick, June 6, 1866, Hedrick Papers, Duke.

46. Wm. Coleman to DLS, February 18, 1842, Swain Papers, SANC; N. W. Woodfin to DLS, February 28, 1845, ibid.; Wm. H. Haywood to DLS, March 21, 1845, Swain Papers, SHC.

47. DLS to Governor David S. Reid, January 21, 1851, Reid Papers, SANC; DLS to WPM, January 19, December 3, 1844, Shanks, *Papers of Mangum*, 4:23–24, 227.

48. DLS to David S. Reid, U.S. Senate, January 15, 1856, Reid Papers, SANC (in Butler, *Papers of Reid*, 2:136); David S. Reid to DLS, April 28, 1856, Swain Papers, SHC; DLS to David S. Reid, January 12, 1858, Reid Papers, SANC; David S. Reid to Minerva Tilley, May 13, 1858, Butler, *Papers of Reid*, 2:243.

49. T. L. Clingman to DLS, February 15, 1848, Swain Papers, SANC (typescript in Swain Papers, SHC); John H. Wheeler to DLS, October 9, 1858, Swain Papers, SHC; DLS to KPB, October 14, 1867, BFP, SHC.

50. E. B. Dudley to DLS, January 30, March 16, 1838, and John MacRae to DLS, March 18, 1839, Swain Papers, SHC; Konkle, *Morehead*, 182–83.

51. *Western Carolinian*, February 21, April 4, 1839 (for the same report, see *Georgia Telegraph*, February 19, 1839); A. M. Burton to DLS, June 20, 1839, Swain Papers, SANC; CM to DLS, January 7, 1839, Swain Papers, SHC.

52. *Western Carolinian*, April 11, 1839; DLS to EHS, December 10, 1839, Swain Papers, SANC.

53. WAG to James W. Bryan, November 21, 1840, Hamilton et al., *Papers of Graham*, 2:121–22; O. H. Prince to DLS, September 1, 1840, Swain Papers, SANC; M. Patton to DLS, November 19, 1840; N. W. Woodfin to DLS, September 25, November 9, 1840, Swain Papers, SHC; Walton, "Elections to the U.S. Senate in North Carolina, 1835–1861," 53 NCHR 168, 177.

54. Calvin Jones to DLS, February 28, 1841, Swain Papers, SANC.

55. C. L. Hinton to DLS, August 25, 1840, and DLS to Major Charles L. Hinton, August 26, 1840, Swain Papers, SHC.

56. Wm. Sidney Mullins Diary, January 25, 1841, SHC; B.M. Edney to DLS, December 18, 1841; D. L. Barringer to DLS, November 5, 1846, Swain Papers, SHC.

57. T. L. Clingman to DLS, February 15, 1848, Swain Papers, SANC (typescript in Swain Papers, SHC).

58. *Journal, N.C. House of Commons, 1848–49 Session*, 506, 522–25 (December 16, 1848); J. H. Coleman (nephew) to DLS, February 19, 1849, Swain Papers, SANC.

59. Andrew J. Polk to DLS, March 12, 1857, Swain Papers, SANC; Samuel F. Phillips to WHB, November 18, 1852, BFP, SHC.

60. J. N. Viser to DLS, December 9, 1847, Swain Papers, SHC (typescript).

61. Daniel Baker to DLS, December 10, 1856, January 22, 1857, Swain Papers, SHC.

Chapter 17: History Matters

1. See text accompanying note 34, chapter 1, note 83, chapter 2, notes 50–59, chapter 4, and the notes themselves; Swain Diary, February 9, 22, April 14, 1832, SANC.

2. DLS letter to editor, *Wilmington Chronicle*, October 27, 1843, *North Carolina Standard*, November 8, 1843.

3. Fox-Genovese and Genovese, *Mind of the Master Class*, 128.

4. Spencer, *Pen and Ink Sketches*, 3–4, 67–68; *North Carolina Presbyterian*, May 26, 1896; John L. Blake to DLS, February 13, 1857, Swain Papers, SHC.

5. KPB to WHB, July 7, 1851, BFP, SHC; Arthur, *Western North Carolina*, 382–83.

6. See text accompanying note 50, chapter 4; DLS to Joseph Seawell Jones, December 20, 1832, Swain Papers, SANC; Battle, *History*, 1:485–86.

7. *Raleigh Register and North-Carolina Gazette*, January 8, 1841; W. H. H. Jr. (William H. Haywood Jr.) to DLS, March 28, 1842, Swain Papers, SHC; L. S. Ives to DLS, May 31, 1842, Swain Papers, SHC.

8. Duncan Cameron to DLS, October 29, 1839; Will Gaston to DLS, July 28, 1841; Richard Washington to DLS, July 23, 1841, Swain Papers, SHC.

9. E.g., Brewer, *Memoir of Swain*, 5–6; Hamilton, "The Preservation of North Carolina History," 4 NCHR 3, 6.

10. *Carolina Watchman*, February 17, 1844; *Raleigh Register and North-Carolina Gazette*, June 21, 1844.

11. Circular Letter from DLS et al., September 5, 1845, copies in BFP and McRee Papers, SHC; Knight and Adams, *Graduate School Research and Publications*, 147.

12. *First Report of the Historical Society of the University of North Carolina June 4, 1845*, copy in Swain Papers, SANC.

13. *Raleigh Register and North-Carolina Gazette*, September 26, 1845 (citing a *Wilmington Chronicle* article).

14. DLS to G. J. McRee, September 20, 1844, McRee Papers, SHC (typescript in Swain Papers, SHC).

15. Thomas S. Ashe to DLS, December 2, 1845, UP.

16. A. A. Powers to DLS, December 16, 1844, and G. J. McRee to DLS, December 23, 1844, Swain Papers, SHC; H. [Helen] Caldwell to Mary Hooper, March 26, 1845, Hooper Papers, SHC.

17. Receipt dated November 1, 1848, UP; DLS to CM, February 6, 1849, Swain Papers, SANC.

18. F. M. Hubbard to DLS, September 8, 1846, Swain Papers, SHC.

19. Pliny Miles to DLS, November 8, 1847, and DLS to Pliny Miles, November 12, 1847, Swain Papers, SHC; Pliny Miles to DLS, December 14, 1847, Swain Papers, SANC; see Jones, *For History's Sake*, 137.

20. William J. Rivers to DLS, April 11, 1857, November 1, 1858, June 2, 1860; J. Johnston Pettigrew to DLS, December 21, 1857, Swain Papers, SHC.

21. F. M. Hubbard to DLS, May 19, 1846, Swain Papers, SHC; Frederic Kidder to DLS, April 16, 1856, Swain Papers, SANC.

22. F. M. Hubbard to DLS, December 16, 1845, and Drury Lacy to DLS, April 15, 1853, Swain Papers, SHC.

23. Charles Phillips, Secretary, Historical Society, to Hon. J. Q. Adams, H.R., May 12, 1846, and John Quincy Adams to Charles Phillips, May 23, 1846, Swain Papers, SANC. For the elder Adams's contributions to the first North Carolina Constitution, see Lefler and Newsome, *North Carolina*, 211, and Powell, *Four Centuries*, 186; on the discovery of the first draft of Adams's "Thoughts on Government," see Jones, *For History's Sake*, 188. Several secondary sources have informed this discussion of the Historical Society. See, e.g., Battle, *History*, 1:485–87, and Battle, "David Lowry Swain," *North Carolina Journal of Education*, 3:27, 29; Crittenden and Lacy, *Historical Records of North Carolina*, 5; Gass, "Kemp Plummer Battle and the Development of Histori-

cal Instruction at the University of North Carolina," 45 NCHR 1, 15–16; Hamilton, "The Preservation of North Carolina History," 4 NCHR 3, 6–7, and "The Southern Historical Collection" in Rush, *Library Resources*, 39; Haywood, *Builders of the Old North State*, 179; Johnson, *Ante-Bellum North Carolina*, 296, 819–20; Jones, *For History's Sake*, 239–47; Jones, H. G., "Historical Societies," in Powell, *Encyclopedia of North Carolina*, 570–73; Newsome, "Twelve North Carolina Counties in 1810–1811," 5 NCHR 413, 416n.18; Tauber, *Louis Round Wilson: Librarian and Administrator*, 57; Thornton, Mary L., "Collection of North Caroliniana," in Rush, *Library Resources*, 27; Whichard, Willis P., "North Carolina," in Jones, *Historical Consciousness in the Early Republic*, 92–101; Wilson, *University of North Carolina: Making a Modern University*, 240, 477, and "The Acquisition of the Stephen B. Weeks Collection of Caroliniana," 42 NCHR 424, 427–28. See also *Raleigh Register and North-Carolina Gazette*, June 13, 1845 (lengthy report by Charles Phillips, secretary of the society).

24. *Laws of the State of North Carolina . . . 1844–45* (Raleigh: Thomas l. Lemay, Printers, 1845), 140–41; Jared Sparks to DLS, March 5, 1845, Swain Papers, SHC; Jones, *For History's Sake*, 185.

25. 1846–47 *N.C. Session Laws*, 244–45; Saunders, *Colonial Records*, I: v–vi; Johnson, *Ante-Bellum North Carolina*, 819–20.

26. Battle, *History*, 1:246–47; Jones, *For History's Sake*, 169–70, 190.

27. Unidentified correspondent to John DeBerniere Hooper (apparently), February 8, 1849, Hooper Papers, SHC; DLS to CM, April 28, 1849, UP.

28. "M" to DLS, from Liverpool, May 2, 1849; C. Frank Powell to DLS, January 26, March 31, April 10, 1849, Swain Papers, SANC; Jones, *For History's Sake*, 191.

29. J. M. (John) Huske to DLS, October 10, 1845, Swain Papers, SANC (typescript in Swain Papers, SHC); P. C. Cameron to DLS, May 9, 1853, Swain Papers, SHC; F. Nash to DLS, May 22, 1853, Swain Papers, SHC.

30. Illegible to Unidentified, January 30, 1854, Swain Papers, SHC.

31. George Bancroft to DLS, October 27, November 18, 1854, Swain Papers, SHC.

32. Jared Sparks to DLS, May 25, June 6, October 1, November 11, November 28, 1855, Swain Papers, SHC.

33. DLS to WHB, January 18, 1856, BFP, SHC; DLS to WAG, November 25, 1854, Hamilton et al., *Papers of Graham*, 4:540–41.

34. *The Historical Magazine, Notes and Queries, Etc.*, 402 (January 1871); *Greensborough Patriot*, August 10, 1855. Swain gives a detailed account of his acquisition of the Tryon letter book in a November 20, 1855, letter to Governor Bragg published in the *North Carolina Standard* on November 28, 1855, in the *Hillsborough Recorder* on December 5, 1855, and in the *Greensborough Patriot* on December 7, 1855.

35. Walter L. Steele to DLS, September 27, 1845, May 19, 1846, Swain Papers, SANC. Steele was in the UNC Class of 1844. Battle, *History*, 1:799.

36. T. L. Skinner to DLS, January 18, 1854, Swain Papers, SANC.

37. Thomas H. Ashe (Wilmington) to DLS, August 25, 1854; Will B. Shepard (Elizabeth City) to DLS, March 19, 1849; A. A. Grady to DLS, March 1, 1855; John Gray Bynum to DLS, October 25, 1855; A. J. Davie to DLS, December 1, 1843, Swain Papers, SHC.

38. *Public Laws of the State of North Carolina, 1854–55*, 127; DLS to Governor Bragg, November 20, 1855, published in *North Carolina Standard*, November 28, 1855, *Hillsborough Recorder*, December 5, 1855, and *Greensborough Patriot*, December 7, 1855.

39. Circular letter, DLS to numerous recipients, January 12 (20?), 1857, copies in SANC (shows 20th) and in McRee Papers, SHC (shows 12th); DLS to WAG, January 15, 1858 (probably 1857), SHC (in Hamilton et al., *Papers of Graham*, 5:26) (enclosing the circular letter, ibid., 5:26–28). Wheeler's *Sketches* "sold more copies in North Carolina until well after the Second World War, and it may have been the most widely read book there after the Bible." Fox-Genovese and Genovese, *Mind of the Master Class*, 184.

40. E. A. Thompson to DLS, January 14, 1857, and Ralph Gorrell to DLS, January 16, 1857, Swain Papers, SHC.

41. E. G. Reade to DLS, February 9, 1857; Robert Paine to DLS, February 8, 1857; Asa Biggs to DLS, January 21, 1857, Swain Papers, SHC.

42. T. L. Skinner to DLS, February 11, 1857, and E. C. Hines to DLS, February 15, 1897, Swain Papers, SHC.

43. M. E. Manly to DLS, February 13, 1857, J. L. Bailey to DLS, February 19, 1857, W. Sanders to DLS, August 20, 1857, Swain Papers, SHC.

44. Will A. Jenkins to DLS, March 23, 1857; Will B. Rodman to DLS, March 20, 1857; Swain Papers, SHC.

45. W. H. Bailey to DLS, March 24, 1857, Swain Papers, SHC; L. W. Humphrey to DLS, July 28, 1857, ibid.; E. C. Gillenby to DLS, April 17, 1857, ibid.; Augustus M. Flythe to DLS, July 24, 1858, UP; G. W. I. Goldston to DLS, November 7, 1861, Swain Papers, SANC.

46. Alexander M. Ives to DLS, March 30, 1857; Clement Dowd to DLS, March 1857; A. W. Mangum to DLS, July 11, 1866; F.J. Kron to DLS, April 20, 1857; C. L. Hunter to DLS, September 15, 1857; Samuel H. Walkup to DLS, September 25, 1857, Swain Papers, SHC.

47. DLS to Jared Sparks, December 19, 1855, and Jared Sparks to DLS, January 23, 1857; DLS to unidentified recipient, March 1, 1856, Swain Papers, SHC. For letter of same import, see DLS to Hon. J. C. Dobbin (a North Carolinian then serving as secretary of the navy), November 22, 1855, Dobbin Papers, Duke.

48. J. K. Tifft (?) to DLS, July 30, 1857, Swain Papers, SANC.

49. J. F. H. Claiborne to DLS, July 18, 1859, Swain Papers, SHC.

50. DLS to James Johnston Pettigrew, December 29, 1856, Pettigrew Papers, SANC.

51. James H. Otey to DLS, July 16, 1860, Swain Papers, SANC; Samuel R. Walker to DLS, August 19, 1860, Swain Papers, SHC.

52. DLS to Conway Robinson, February 2, 1857, and W. C. Rives to DLS, April 27, 1858, Swain Papers, SHC.

53. J. F. H. Claiborne to DLS, April 30, 1860, and DLS to unidentified recipient, December 26, 1859, Swain Papers, SHC.

54. Document in Swain's hand (January 1, 1857, penciled in at top; apparently a report to the governor on Swain's efforts as state historical agent), Swain Papers, SHC; *Hillsborough Recorder*, February 4, 1857; *Greensborough Patriot*, August 10, 1855.

55. *Carolina Watchman*, December 30, 1843; Swain Papers, SHC; M. King to DLS, February 23, 1859, Swain Papers, SANC.

56. Will B. Rodman to Gen. Will A. Blount (uncle), June 1, 1836, Rodman Papers, ECU, and to DLS, December 19, 1867, Swain Papers, SHC.

57. *Old North State*, July 9, 1867.

58. William Lee Davidson to DLS, August 13, 1867, Clark Papers, SANC.

59. File 58, Swain Papers, SHC; Jones, *For History's Sake*, 182.

60. Hinton James to William H. Owen, October 20, 1838, in Connor, *Documentary History of the University of North Carolina 1776–1799*, 347–48.

61. FM, November 20, 1840; Samuel H. Biddel to DLS, February 2, 1842, UP; Francis L. Hawks to DLS, December 12, 1842, Swain Papers, SHC; Charles W. Harris to DLS, February 26, 1843, Swain Papers, SANC (typescript in Swain Papers, SHC).

62. CM to DLS, October 16, 1844, Swain Papers, SHC.

63. F. M. Hubbard to DLS, December 16, 1845, and E. E. Haywood to DLS, December 24, 1845, Swain Papers, SHC.

64. BOTM, December 16, 18, 1854; Battle, *History*, 1:638; *Weekly Raleigh Register and North-Carolina Gazette*, December 20, 1854.

65. Illegible at Charles Scribner, New York, to DLS, December 18, 1854, Swain Papers, SANC; Henry Barnard to DLS, December 26, 1855, Swain Papers, SHC.

66. BOTM, January 26, 1859; CPS to EHS, June 22, 26, 1869, Spencer Papers, SHC.

67. Battle, *History*, 1:535, 730.

68. DLS to William L. Scott, January 30, February 6, 15, 1858, Scott Papers, Duke.

69. James H. Dickens to DLS, February 14, 1856, DLS to James H. Dickens, February 20, 1856, James H. Dickens to DLS, May 11, 1856, Swain Papers, SHC; *Weekly North Carolina Standard*, May 14, 1856 (from *Wilmington Herald*).

70. *Semi-weekly Standard*, December 6, 1856; *Weekly Raleigh Register and North-Carolina Gazette*, December 10, 1856.

71. Swain, *Early Times*, 3–41. Swain's lament about histories ignoring women is mentioned in Fox-Genovese and Genovese, *Mind of the Master Class*, 195.

72. Swain, *Early Times*, part 2, 3–21; see WPA Writers' Program, *Raleigh: Capital of North Carolina*, 70, 125.

73. Battle, *History*, 1:535, 633; Blackwelder, *Age of Orange*, 165–66; Johnson, *Ante-Bellum North Carolina*, 797–98 (quoting from *Southern Weekly Post*, June 4, 1853); Spencer, *Pen and Ink Sketches*, 46; *Fayetteville Observer*, April 1, 1861; DLS statement, *North Carolina University Magazine*, 10:511 (April 1861).

74. Wilson, *Papers of Spencer*, 448.

75. See generally *North Carolina University Magazine*, vol. I, no. 1, March 1844.

76. Ibid., passim.

77. Ibid., vols. II–X (1853–1861), passim.

78. Ibid., 3:201–8 (June 1854) (publishing A. M. Hooper to The Hon. John B. Ashe, Congress, Wash. City, February 29, 1844).

79. Ibid., 1:132–36 (May 1852). As to Swain's position on Indian removal as governor, see text accompanying note 50, chapter 5.

80. Robert N. Githes to DLS, June 22, 1855, Swain Papers, SHC; G. McRee to DLS, August 21, 1855, ibid.; see also John L. Blake to DLS, March 17, 1853, Swain Papers, SANC.

81. "Correspondence in 1834 Between ... Hamilton, ... Gaston and ... Swain," *North Carolina University Magazine*, 10:513–28 (May 1861) (see text accompanying note 51, chapter 4); *Weekly Raleigh Register*, August 29, 1860.

82. James M. Bryan to DLS, March 18, 1857, and James Banks to DLS, September 1, 1856, Swain Papers, SHC.

83. *North Carolina University Magazine*, 10:370–71 (February 1861), 10:189 (October 1860).

84. DLS to WAG, September 5, 1855, Hamilton et al., *Papers of Graham*, 4:600–1; WAG to DLS, September 20, 1855, ibid., 602; DLS to WAG, October 5, 1855, ibid., 604–5, and December 13, 1855, ibid., 608–9; WAG to DLS, December 14, 1855, ibid., 609–10, January 21,1856, ibid., 626–27; DLS to WAG, January 23, 1856, ibid., 627–28; WAG to DLS, April 28, 1856, ibid., 638. See generally, re: the magazine, Cherry, Kevin, and Holden, Charles, "Literary Journals," in Powell, *Encyclopedia of North Carolina*, 683–85.

Chapter 18: More Courting Clio

1. DLS to WAG, September 28, 1836, Hamilton et al., *Papers of Graham*, 1:440; for Swain's involvement with the Murphey papers as governor, see text accompanying

notes 54–55, chapter 4; for commentary, see Jones, *For History's Sake*, 154–56, and Turner, *Dreamer Archibald DeBow Murphey 1777–1832*, viii, 216.

2. WAG to DLS, July 2, 1845, ibid., 3:48–49; DLS to WAG, May 13, 1848, ibid., 3:223–26. For Maurice Moore's "little tract" on taxation, see Price, *Not a Conquered People*, 37–48.

3. DLS to WAG, January 31, 1845, ibid., 3:21–22; WAG to DLS, February 8, 1845, ibid., 3:26–28.

4. DLS to WAG, January 31, 1845, ibid., 3:21–22; WAG to Mary W. Burke, February 6, 1845, ibid., 3:23–24; WAG to DLS, July 2, 1845, Swain Papers, SHC (in Hamilton et al., *Papers of Graham*, 3:48–49); WAG to DLS, August 26, 1845, Hamilton et al., *Papers of Graham*, 3:67–68; WAG to DLS, September 2, 1845, Swain Papers, SHC (in Hamilton et al., *Papers of Graham*, 3:72–73).

5. DLS to WAG, January 11, 1841 [1842], Hamilton et al., *Papers of Graham*, 2:249–50; WAG to DLS, August 26, 1845, ibid., 3:67; DLS to WAG, July 12, 1845, ibid., 3:49–50; DLS to WAG, October 28, 1845, ibid., 3:83.

6. DLS to WAG, June 9, 1845, ibid., 3:47.

7. James M. Spencer and Junius I. Scales to WAG, September 8, 1852, ibid., 4:396–97, and February 17, 1853, ibid., 4:490; WAG to DLS, December 20, 1852, ibid., 4:443; DLS to WAG, December 28, 1852, ibid., 4:446; WAG to DLS, January 8, 1853, ibid., 4:448.

8. WAG to DLS, January 8, 1853, ibid., 4:448; DLS to WAG, January 10, 1853, ibid., 4:449; WAG to DLS, June 1, 1866, ibid., 7:122, June 30, 1866, ibid., 7:142, September 8, 1866, ibid., 7:206–7; DLS to WAG, September 10, 1866, ibid., 7:209.

9. DLS to WAG, December 6, 1852, ibid., 4:438, June 6, 1853, ibid., 495–96, September 5, 1855, ibid., 600–601.

10. WAG to DLS, April 28, 1856, ibid., 638, February 29, 1856, ibid., 631; DLS to WAG, February 8, 1856, ibid., 629.

11. WAG to DLS, April 21, 1856, ibid., 637; DLS to WAG, February 2, 1859, ibid., 88–89; DLS to WAG, June 27, 1859, ibid., 5:106; DLS to WAG, January 20, 1862, ibid., 5:354–55.

12. DLS to WAG, December 4, 1861, ibid., 5:340–43.

13. G. McRee to DLS, May 13, 1842, Swain Papers, and DLS to McRee, May 28, 1842, McRee Papers, SHC.

14. G. McRee to DLS, August 7, 1844, Swain Papers, SHC (published in Saunders, *Colonial Records*, 19: 999), and DLS to McRee, September 20, 1844, McRee Papers, SHC.

15. Griffith McRee to DLS, December 23, 1844, Swain Papers, SANC, and DLS to G. J. McRee, December 31, 1844, McRee Papers, SHC.

16. DLS to G. J. McRee, May 8, 1846, McRee Papers, SHC; G. J. McRee to DLS, May 10, 1846, August 7, 1854, Swain Papers, SHC.

17. DLS to G. J. McRee, February 4, 1856, McRee Papers, and G. McRee to DLS, April 28, 1856, Swain Papers, SHC.

18. DLS to G. J. McRee, August 20, 1856, McRee Papers, SHC.

19. The volumes are Griffith J. McRee, *Life and Correspondence of James Iredell* (New York: D. Appleton and Co., 1857 (I), 1858 (II)).

20. G. McRee to DLS, undated ([1856?] penciled at top), Swain Papers, SHC; see generally, re: this and material that follows, Wilson, "Griffith John McRee: An Unromantic Historian of the Old South," 47 NCHR, 1.

21. DLS to G. J. McRee, August 22, 1854, McRee Papers, SHC.

22. G. McRee to DLS, August 12, September 15, 1855, Swain Papers; DLS to G. J. McRee, September 21, 1855, McRee Papers; G. McRee to DLS, October 20, 1855, Swain Papers, SHC.

23. DLS to G. J. McRee, October 23, 1855, February 1, 1856, McRee Papers; G. J. McRee to DLS, February 8, 1856, Swain Papers, SHC.

24. G. McRee to DLS, April 28, July 8, 1856, Swain Papers, SHC.

25. DLS to G. J. McRee, July 11(?), 1856, McRee Papers; G. McRee to DLS, August 27, 1856, and DLS to G. J. McRee, September 5, 1856, Swain Papers, SHC.

26. G. McRee to DLS, January (exact date not shown) 1857, Swain Papers; DLS to G. J. McRee, January 23, 1857, McRee Papers; G. McRee to DLS, March 12, 1857, Swain Papers, SHC.

27. DLS to G. J. McRee, August 18, 20, 1857, McRee Papers, SHC.

28. DLS to G. J. McRee, September 9, 1857, McRee Papers; G. McRee to DLS, September 13, 1857, Swain Papers; DLS to G. J. McRee, September 18, 1857, McRee Papers; G. McRee to DLS, December 9, 1857, Swain Papers; DLS to G. J. McRee, January 4, 1858, McRee Papers; G. McRee to DLS, January 12, 1858, Swain Papers, SHC.

29. Circular dated January 12, 1857, re: Swain's efforts as historical agent, containing handwritten note DLS to McRee, January 15, 1857, McRee Papers, SHC; G. McRee to DLS, July 25, 1855, January (exact date not shown), 1856, January (exact date not shown), 1857, Swain Papers, SHC.

30. Carraway, Gertrude S., "Hawks, Francis Lister," in Powell, *DNCB*, 3:76–77.

31. James W. Osborne to DLS, June 26, 1848, Swain Papers, SHC; Francis L. Hawks to WAG, December 18, 1852, Hamilton et al., *Papers of Graham*, 4:441; Francis L. Hawks to DLS, February 8, 1853, February 24, 1855, Swain Papers, SHC. Hawks' reference to the declaration of "May 30 [31], 1775" is to the Mecklenburg Resolves, which denied the authority of Parliament and the king but stopped short of declaring independence. The Mecklenburg Declaration allegedly went further and declared the residents of Mecklenburg County "free and independent people." See Norris, David A. "Resolves, Pre–revolutionary," in Powell, *Encyclopedia of North Carolina*, 965–66; and Faulkner, Ronnie W., "Mecklenburg Declaration of Independence," in ibid., 725–26. See generally Current, "That Other Declaration," 54 NCHR, 169.

32. Francis L. Hawks to DLS, October 25, 1856, Swain Papers, SHC.

33. Francis L. Hawks to DLS, December 15, 1856, ibid.

34. *Weekly Raleigh Register*, April 29, 1857; Francis L. Hawks to DLS, April 20, 1857, Swain Papers, SHC. DLS to WAG, January 15, 1858, Hamilton et al., *Papers of Graham*, 5:26; Hugh B. Grigsby to DLS, July 15, 1857, Swain Papers, SHC.

35. Francis L. Hawks to DLS, December 31, 1856, UP, April 8, 20, 1857, Swain Papers, SHC.

36. Francis L. Hawks to DLS, November 10, 1857, April 5, 1858, ibid.

37. Francis L. Hawks to DLS, April 5, July 30, August 16, 1858, ibid.

38. DLS to Rev. Dr. Hawks, September 1, 1858, and WAG to DLS, August 17, 1858, ibid.

39. E. J. Hale to DLS, November 12, 26, 1858, Swain Papers, SHC; Battle, *History*, 1:812–13 (E. J. Hale Jr. in UNC Class of 1860).

40. DLS to WHB, December 13, 1858, BFP; DLS to Rev. Dr. Hawks, December 24, 1858, Hawks Papers; J. M. Morehead to DLS, February 20, 1859, Swain Papers, SHC; Cheney, *North Carolina Government*, 325–26 (Morehead member of 1858–1859 House of Commons).

41. *Doc. 49, 1858–59 Session, Memorial to the Senate and House of Commons*, NCC.

42. John W. Ellis to DLS, September 15, 1859, Tolbert, *Papers of Ellis*, 1:293, January 18, 1860, ibid., 2:352–53; DLS and Francis L. Hawks to John W. Ellis, January 26, 1860, ibid., 2: 361–62; John W. Ellis to Francis L. Hawks and DLS, January 28, 1860, ibid., 2:362–63.

43. John W. Ellis to DLS, February 24, 1859, ibid., 1:224.

44. Francis L. Hawks to DLS, October 27, 1859, Swain Papers, SHC.

45. DLS to Francis L. Hawks, December 26, 1859; Francis L. Hawks to DLS, January 3, February 4, 1860, Swain Papers, SHC.

46. Francis L. Hawks to DLS, February 15, 1860; DLS to Francis L. Hawks, April 16, 1860; Francis L. Hawks to DLS, May 1, 1860, and DLS to Rev. Dr. Hawks, June 13, 1860, Swain Papers, SHC.

47. Francis L. Hawks to DLS, December 9, 1859; DLS to Rev. Dr. Hawks, September 13, 1860; E. J. Hale to DLS, October 17, 1860; DLS to Francis L. Hawks, April 16, 1861, Swain Papers, SHC.

48. Ashe, *Biographical History*, 1:454–55.

49. Hawks, *History of North Carolina*, 2:10.

50. Jones, H. G., "Wheeler, John Hill," in Powell, *DNCB*, 6:167–68, and Jones, *For History's Sake*, 171; Wheeler, *Historical Sketches of North Carolina From 1584 to 1851*, dedication and 2:53 (Swain); Lichtenstein, "For Whom Was Edgecombe County Named?", *N.C. Booklet* 18:116.

51. John H. Wheeler to DLS, July 9, 1843, Swain Papers, SANC.

52. John H. Wheeler to DLS, March 17, 1844, Swain Papers, SANC, June 20, 1845,

Swain Papers, SHC, May 12, 1844, Swain Papers, SANC; John H. Wheeler to David S. Reid, March 30, 1851, in Butler, *Papers of Reid*, 1:310.

53. DLS to C. H. Wiley, September 5, 1851, Wiley Papers, SHC; Cheney, *North Carolina Government*, 255, 257 (Henry).

54. DLS to John H. Wheeler, April 22, 1853, and John H. Wheeler to DLS, May 2, 1853, Swain Papers, SHC.

55. John H. Wheeler to DLS, September 27, October 9, 16, 1858, Swain Papers, SHC.

56. John H. Wheeler to DLS, March 3, 19, 1859, Swain Papers, SANC.

57. John H. Wheeler to DLS, April 19, September 17, December 18, 1861, Swain Papers, SHC.

58. John H. Wheeler to DLS, October 17, 1866, BFP, SHC; Wheeler, *Reminiscences*, 58.

59. DLS to WAG, November 29, 1841, Hamilton et al., *Papers of Graham*, 2:244; George Bancroft to DLS, May 2, 1845, Swain Papers, SHC.

60. George Bancroft to DLS, July 4, 1848, Swain Papers, SHC.

61. George Bancroft to DLS, October 27, 1854, June 25, 1855, ibid.

62. George Bancroft to DLS, June 25, August 30, 1855, May 21, 1857, ibid.

63. George Bancroft to DLS, March 1, 1858, and DLS to George Bancroft, March 6, 1858, ibid. (copy in Hoyt Papers, SHC); James Banks to DLS, February 2, 1856, Swain Papers, SHC.

64. George Bancroft to DLS, May 20, 1858, September 30, 1859, Swain Papers, SHC.

65. Benson J. Lossing to DLS, October 29, November 11, 27, 1851, and DLS to Benson J. Lossing, November 13, 22, 1851, ibid.

66. Benson J. Lossing to WAG, December 1, 1851, Hamilton et al., *Papers of Graham*, 4:219–20; DLS to WAG, January 6, 1852, ibid., 4:231; DLS to B. J. Lossing, December 10, 1851, Swain Papers, SHC.

67. DLS to Benson Lossing, January 6, 14, February 7, 1852, Swain Papers, SHC.

68. DLS to B. J. Lossing, May 29, 1852, and Benson J. Lossing to DLS, June 2, 1852, Swain Papers, SHC.

69. Benson J. Lossing to DLS, August 14, 1852; DLS to Benson J. Lossing, July 20, November 3, 1852, Swain Papers, SHC.

70. WAG to DLS, December 20, 1852; Benson J. Lossing to DLS, May 23, 1853, Swain Papers, SHC.

71. Benson J. Lossing to DLS, October 9, 1854, and DLS to Benson J. Lossing, October 24, 1854, Swain Papers, SHC.

72. Benson J. Lossing to DLS, November 1, 1854, Swain Papers, SHC.

73. Benson J. Lossing to DLS, June 25, July 12, August 27, 1855; Lyman C. Draper to DLS, May 23, 1855; William F. Henderson to DLS, July 17, 1855, Swain Papers, SHC.

74. Benson J. Lossing to DLS, November 19, 1855, and DLS to B. J. Lossing, November 24, 1855, ibid.; as to Ferguson, see Kujawa, Sheryl A., "Ferguson, Katy," Garrity and Carnes, *American National Biography*, 7:836–37; as to Wheatley, see Shields, John C., "Wheatley, Phyllis," ibid., 23:121–22, Sinha, *Slave's Cause*, 29–33, and Waldstreicher, "Ancients, Moderns, and Africans," passim.

75. Benson J. Lossing to WAG, March 18, 1872, Hamilton et al., *Papers of Graham*, 8:254–55; Benson J. Lossing to DLS, November 22, 1865, Swain Papers, SHC; Miles, "Benson J. Lossing and North Carolina Revolutionary History," 35 NCHR 11, 16–17.

76. Benson J. Lossing to WAG, March 18, 1872, Hamilton et al., *Papers of Graham*, 8:254–55; Lossing, *Lives of Celebrated Americans*, 430.

Chapter 19: Clio: Yet More

1. Lyman C. Draper to DLS, May 23, 1855, Swain Papers, SHC; as to Draper, see Gara, Larry, "Draper, Lyman Copeland," Garraty and Carnes, *American National Biography*, 6:881–82.

2. Lyman C. Draper to DLS, February 18, 1845, Swain Papers, SHC.

3. Lyman C. Draper to DLS, September 7, 1850, ibid.

4. Lyman C. Draper to DLS, April 16, 1868, ibid.

5. Lyman C. Draper to WAG, November 22, 1871, Hamilton et al., *Papers of Graham*, 8:228, and January 7, 1873, ibid., 8:292–93; Lyman C. Draper to William Johnston, January 7, 1873, ibid., 8:295; Lyman C. Draper to CPS, May 19, 1873, Spencer Papers, SANC.

6. Davidson, "Basis of a Mecklenburg Bibliography," 26 NCHR 28, 39.

7. The book, Scott Syfert, *The First American Declaration of Independence?: The Disputed History of the Mecklenburg Declaration of May 20, 1775*, takes the pro-Declaration position.

8. *Raleigh Register and North-Carolina Gazette*, April 30, 1819; John Adams to Thomas Jefferson, June 22, 1819, and Thomas Jefferson to John Adams, July 9, 1819, in Cappon, *Adams-Jefferson Letters*, 542–44; John Adams to John Williams, Senator of U.S. from Tennessee, April 30, 1822, Swain Papers, SANC.

9. "The Declaration of Independence By the Citizens of Mecklenburg County on the Twentieth Day of May, 1775, with Accompanying Documents...," 1831; for Swain as author of state pamphlet on the Declaration, see Hoyt, *Mecklenburg Declaration of Independence*, 15–16n.3, 136.

10. DLS to John C. Hamilton, September 6, 1834, Swain GLB 30, SANC; Lewis Williams to Joseph Seawell Jones, January 13, 1833, Swain Papers, SANC; Jones, *Defence of the Revolutionary History of North Carolina*, quoted portion at 297.

11. Current, "That Other Declaration," 54 NCHR 169, 173.

12. William J. Alexander et al. to DLS, May 1, 1839, Swain Papers, SHC; *North-Carolina Standard*, June 5, 1839.

13. Will J. Alexander et al. to DLS, April 7, 1844, and James W. Osbourne to DLS, May 28, 1844, Swain Papers, SHC; DLS, president, and other officers, to Genl. William A. Blount, May 21, 1844, Blount Papers, SANC; *Raleigh Register and North-Carolina Gazette*, June 7, 1844 (Swain sent letter of regret).

14. Samuel Henry Dickson to DLS, October 8, 1844, January 15, 1845; James Johnson to DLS, March 4, 27, 1847, Swain Papers, SHC.

15. Circular letter, DLS et al. for the Historical Society, September 5, 1845, BFP, SHC.

16. DLS, "British Invasion of North Carolina," Lecture Before the Historical Society of the University of North Carolina, April 1, 1853, in *Pamphlets &c North Carolina*, NCC, published in *North Carolina University Magazine*, 2:145 (May 1853); Edward D. Ingraham to DLS, June 8, 1853, Swain Papers, SHC.

17. John H. Wheeler to DLS, July 13, August 17, 1844, Swain Papers, SANC.

18. Francis L. Hawks to DLS, December 18, 1852, and DLS to Rev. Dr. Hawks, January 6, 1853, Swain Papers, SHC; Francis L. Hawks to WAG, December 18, 1852, Hamilton et al., *Papers of Graham*, 4:441.

19. Francis L. Hawks to DLS, April 8, 20, 1857, Swain Papers, SHC.

20. George Bancroft to DLS, March 1, 1858, Swain Papers, SHC; DLS to Benson J. Lossing, December 20, 1851, Hoyt Papers, SHC (copy; original in Davie Papers, SHC). Earlier Swain correspondents had referred to his exchanges with Bancroft on this subject: Jas. F. T. to DLS, January 29, 1849 (refers to disputed documents, seeks Bancroft's view thereon); Horace M. Polk to DLS, March 12, 1849 (a descendant of a Mecklenburg delegate; grateful to Swain for procuring, through Bancroft, a document, "which establishes beyond controversy what Mr. Jefferson with the great weight of his authority has attempted to discredit"); Hugh B. Grigsby (Virginia historian) to DLS, June 21, 1857 (seeks Swain paper on the subject, of which Bancroft had informed him), Swain Papers, SHC.

21. DLS to George Bancroft, March 6, 18, 1858; George Bancroft to DLS, March 11, 1858, Swain Papers, SHC.

22. Benson J. Lossing to DLS, December 14, 31, 1851, December 18, 1852, January 24, 1853; DLS to B. J. Lossing, January 14, 1852, Swain Papers, SHC; for commentary, see Miles, "Benson J. Lossing and North Carolina Revolutionary History," 35 NCHR 11, 16–17.

23. DLS to Peter Force, November 29, 1843, February 7, 1847; D. M. Barringer to Col. Peter Force, December 12, 1844; Peter Force to DLS, December 16, 1843, Force Papers, SHC.

24. Henry S. Randall to DLS, March 31, April 12, 1858; DLS to H. S. Randall, April 6, 1858, Swain Papers, SHC.

25. Randall, *Life of Thomas Jefferson*, 1:190, 3:570–82.

26. Jared Sparks to DLS, March 3, 1845, April 16, 1847, Swain Papers, SHC.

27. *Western Carolinian*, June 20, 1835; Sherrell, *Annals of Lincoln County, North Carolina*, III; DLS to WAG, October 28, 1845, Hamilton et al., *Papers of Graham*, 3:83–84.

28. DLS to WAG, January 6, 1846, Hamilton et al., *Papers of Graham*, 3:92 (enclosing William H. Foote to DLS, December 28, 1845, ibid., 3:93–94).

29. DLS to WAG, January 31, 1845, ibid., 3:21–22, April 7, 1847, ibid., 3:187, May 13, 1848, ibid., 3:226.

30. DLS to WAG, November 22, 1851, ibid., 4:217–18.

31. John W. Ellis to DLS, September 11, 1857, Swain Papers, SHC (published in Tolbert, *Papers of Ellis*, 1:166–68).

32. Charles Phillips to EHS, January 26, 1874, Graham Papers, SANC (in Hamilton et al., *Papers of Graham*, 8:339).

33. CPS to EHS, May 13, 1875, Spencer Papers, SANC (in Wilson, *Papers of Spencer*, 129–30).

34. See, e.g., Charles Phillips to CPS, May 14, 1875, Spencer Papers, SANC (calls the Declaration "this mystery—this myth—this grand humbug—this Declaration of May 20— 'falsely so called'").

35. James C. Welling to WAG, May 5, 1875, Graham Papers, SANC (in Hamilton et al., *Papers of Graham*, 8:430).

36. For other relevant post-Swain material, see Horace M. Polk to WAG, December 21, 1874, Hamilton et al., *Papers of Graham*, 8:400; J. McN. Alexander to editors of the *New York Evening Post*, May 18, 1875, ibid., 8:461–62; W. Henry Hoyt to Victor H. Pallsitts, January 27, 1907, Hoyt Papers, SHC. For newspaper items, see *Charlotte Democrat*, July 29, 1873; *New York Times*, May 17, 1875; *Tri-weekly Phoenix*, May 18, 1875; *Petersburg News*, May 15, 1875; *Daily Journal*, May 15, 1875; *Richmond Dispatch*, April 13, 1892. As noted, supra note 7, the latest book on the subject takes the pro-Declaration position. For a thorough treatment of the "con" position, see Hoyt, *Mecklenburg Declaration of Independence*.

37. Benson J. Lossing to DLS, October 29, December 31, 1851, Swain Papers, SHC; Benson J. Lossing to WAG, December 1, 1851, Hamilton et al., *Papers of Graham*, 4:219–20; DLS to B. J. Lossing, December 10, 1851, Swain Papers, SHC.

38. Lyman C. Draper to DLS, May 23, June 20, 1855, Swain Papers, SHC.

39. Denison Olmsted to DLS, May 29, 1843, ibid. (typescript in Swain Papers, SHC).

40. Mellon Chamberlain to DLS, July 30, August 18, September 11, 1852; DLS to M. Chamberlain, August 13, 1852, Swain Papers, SHC.

41. Joshua I. Cohen to DLS, June 3, 1860, Swain Papers, SHC, March 13, 1860, Swain Papers, SANC, June 17, 1860, March 3, 1861, November 5, 26, 1865, Swain Papers, SHC.

42. DLS to unidentified recipient, September 4, 1860 (?), Swain Papers, Duke.

43. DLS to WAG, July 12, 1866, Hamilton et al., *Papers of Graham*, 7:154; DLS to William Eaton Jr., Edwards Papers, SANC; for similar claims, see DLS to C. F. Keller, October 30, 1850, Historical Society of Pennsylvania Papers, SANC.

44. File 59, Swain Papers, SHC; *Catalogue of the Swain Collection of Autograph Letters*, Swain Papers, SANC.

45. *Greensboro Times*, February 25, 1860.

46. Con Robinson to DLS, April 13, 1857; Alice H. Dickinson to DLS, December 2, 1858, January 11, March 6, 1859; DLS to Alice H. Dickinson, February 4, 26, 1859, Swain Papers, SHC.

47. Peele, *Lives*, 246–48.

48. Edward Dromgoole to DLS, March 5, 1849, Swain Papers, SANC.

49. Francis Markey (?) to DLS, November 20, 1857, ibid.

50. W. (Weldon) N. Edwards to DLS, November 1, 1865, Swain Papers, SHC.

51. C. P. Woodriff (?) to DLS, February (?), 1857, Swain Papers, SHC.

52. G. W. (illegible) to DLS, September 27, 1860, Swain Papers, SANC.

53. DLS to Rev. A.W. Mangum, July 15, 1866, Mangum Family Papers, SHC.

54. Jones, *For History's Sake*, 89 (citing Daniel, *Swain*, 312); DLS to Joseph Henry, Secretary, and Charles C. Jewett, Asst. Sec., Smithsonian Institution, February 17, 1849, Swain Papers, SANC; Henry B. Dawson to DLS, October 24, 1860, ibid.; R.W. Gibbs to DLS, 1855 (exact date not shown), ibid.

55. John W. Ellis to DLS, February 24, 1859, Swain Papers, SHC.

56. Robert N. Githes to DLS, June 22, 1855, ibid.

57. Mitchell King to DLS, December 17, 1842 (typescript), ibid.

58. Hugh B. Grigsby to DLS, February 27, 1863, ibid.

59. B. F. Moore to DLS, February 26, 1866, ibid.

60. F. M. Hubbard to DLS, February 4, March 15, 1845, Swain Papers, SHC.

61. James W. Osborne to DLS, July 15, 1846, ibid.

62. E. F. Ellet to DLS, February 10, March 29, 1847, ibid.

63. Henry Toole to DLS, November 2, 1849, ibid.

64. Joseph Johnson to DLS, November 27, 1850 (typescript), ibid.

65. DLS to Calvin H. Wiley, August 25, November 14, 1853, January 8, 1854, January 17, 1856, November 1, 1858, Wiley Papers, SANC.

66. DLS to J. Johnston Pettigrew, April 15, 1858, Pettigrew Papers, SANC; G. Washington to DLS, July 6, 1859, Swain Papers, SHC; William W. Nolt to DLS, February 26, 1860, Swain Papers, SHC; DLS to Henry T. Clark, April 30, 1861, Clark Pa-

pers, Duke; E.W. Caruthers to DLS, April 6, 1853, Swain Papers, SHC; re: Whitaker, see Cheney, *North Carolina Government*, 182, and Mokris, Mark, "Whitaker, Spier," Powell, *DNCB*, 6:171; re: Caruthers, see Gass, W. Conrad, "Caruthers, Eli Washington," Powell, *DNCB*, 1:337–38.

67. H. W. Ledbetter to DLS, July 28, 1860, published in Editors' Table, *North Carolina University Magazine*, 10:374 (Feb. 1861).

68. Robert Donaldson to DLS, January 14, 1859, Swain Papers, SHC; Joshua I. Cohen to DLS, December 19, 1852, August 21, 1853, ibid.; I. T. Avery to DLS, April 5, 1854, ibid.; John L. Cole to DLS, January 20, 1858, Swain Papers, SANC.

69. *Carolina Watchman*, August 19, 1880.

70. Frederic Kidder to DLS, April 28, 1856, and Asa Biggs to DLS, May 20, 1856, Swain Papers, SANC. Swain's letter to Biggs of May 16, 1856 (referred to in Biggs's letter) has not been found, but its content is clear from Biggs's response.

71. DLS to WHB, January 13, 15, 1853, BFP, SHC; as to Cameron, see Sanders, Charles Richard, "Cameron, Duncan," Powell, *DNCB*, 1:311 (died January 6, 1853).

72. Thomas Lenoir to DLS, January 8, 1840, and A. A. Grady to DLS, July 26, 1855, Swain Papers, SHC; as to Lenoir, see Shrader, Richard A., "Lenoir, William," Powell, *DNCB*, 4:52–53.

73. Louise H. Kendall to DLS, November 22, 1867, Clark Papers, SANC.

74. Caroline Whitaker (niece) to DLS, August 11, 1856, Swain Papers, SANC.

75. R. O. Greenhew to DLS, October 14, 1859, Swain Papers, SHC.

76. DLS to EHS, June 25, 1847, Swain Papers, SANC; for an inquiry regarding Swain's personal and family information, see J.M. Eduly to DLS, July 15, August 10, 1858, ibid.

77. Joseph B. Pelf (?) to DLS, March 13, 1840, Swain Papers, SANC (American Historical Association); Certificate, October 14, 1839, EC, NCC (Georgia Historical Society); Certificate, November 26, 1839, file captioned "Honorary Societies," Swain Papers, SANC (Massachusetts Historical Society); Thaddeus M. Harris to DLS, November 28, 1839, Swain Papers, SHC (forwarding Massachusetts Historical Society diploma); Certificate, July 11, 1860, EC, NCC (New England Historic-Genealogical Society) (see Brewer, *Memoir of Swain*, 8); John Jay to DLS, December 8, 1847, Swain Papers, SANC, and Edward Robinson to DLS, April 5, 1854, Swain Papers, SANC (New-York Historical Society) (see also *New York Times*, April 6, 1854).

Chapter 20: Family

1. DLS to Miss Eleanor H. White, December 29, 1824, EC, NCC.
2. DLS to Miss Eleanor H. White, January 2, 1826, ibid.

3. DLS to EHS, September 8, 1826, ibid. (quoting Ruth 1:16).

4. DLS to EHS, September 22, October 2, 27, November 7, 1826, ibid.

5. DLS to EHS, May 6, 1827, January 20, July 18, 1828, ibid.

6. DLS to EHS, March 18, April 14, 1827, April 18, 1828, ibid. In the same vein, see DLS to EHS, May 2, 1828, April 26, 1832, ibid., and June 25, 1847, Swain Papers, SANC.

7. DLS to EHS, August 15, September 12, 1828, EC, NCC.

8. D. L. Barringer to DLS, October 9, 1829, ibid.

9. W. R. Gales to DLS, March 24, 1824, ibid.; DLS to EHS, March 30, 1827, March 21, June 27, 1828, ibid.; EHS to Ella S. Atkins, May 6, 1869, Spencer Papers, SHC.

10. DLS to EHS, July 1, 1847, Swain Papers, SANC ("all well"); Samuel Henry Dickson to DLS, February 20, 1845 ("in improved health"); LMB to WHB, March 31, 1852, BFP, SHC ("much better"); DLS to WHB, May 17, 1848, ibid. ("about again"); DLS to ZBV, January 14, 1864, Vance Papers, SANC; DLS to CM, July 5, 1864, UP. For other examples of Eleanor being unwell, or Swain's uneasiness about her health, see the following: DLS to EHS, January 11, 18, March 14 (?), 30, July 25, 1828, September 6, 1831, EC, NCC; N. W. Woodfin to DLS, May 24, 1852, Swain Papers, SHC (typescript); DLS to WAG, March 10, 1845, UP; D. L. Barringer to DLS, August 28, 1848, Swain Papers, SANC (typescript in Swain Papers, SHC); LMB to WHB, September 24, 1851, BFP, SHC; DLS to CM, September 2, 1859, UP. For another example of Eleanor being "better," see DLS to Gen. Daniel L. Barringer, February 24, 1843, Swain Papers, SANC (typescript in Swain Papers, SHC).

11. DLS to EHS, December 8, 10, 1839; DLS to Dr. S. H. Dickson, March 3, 1840, Swain Papers, SANC.

12. Battle, *History*, 1:534.

13. Swain Diary, January 12, 1832, SANC; DLS to EHS, March 30, 1829, EC, NCC.

14. DLS to EHS, March 5, 1830, ibid., July 10, 1838, May 9, June 18, 1847, Swain Papers, SANC.

15. DLS to CM, November 8, 1841, UP; DLS to EHS, August 27, 1828, EC, NCC.

16. DLS to EHS, March 19, 1830, EC, NCC, July 5, 1838, June 24, 1840, Swain Papers, SANC.

17. EHS to DLS, August 16, 1842, Swain Papers, SANC.

18. Swain Diary, August 10, 1832, SANC; DLS to EHS, April 16, 1832, EC, NCC; Will Gaston to DLS, August 18, 1833, ibid.; Daniel, *Swain*, 234; EHS memorial to deceased son David, October 15, 1875, Spencer Papers, SHC.

19. DLS to William Gaston, September 16, 1835, Gaston Papers, SHC; DLS to James Donaldson, November 20, 1835, in Coon, *Beginnings of Public Education in North Carolina*, 2:729; DLS to EHS, September 2, 1840, Swain Papers, SANC.

20. Mary Hooper (?) to Mrs. Francis Hooper, October 28, 1840, Hooper Papers, SHC.

21. David Swain Gravestone, Oakwood Cemetery, Raleigh, N.C.; DLS to EHS, June 11, 1840, Swain Papers, SANC; Peele, *Lives*, 240.

22. Battle, *History*, 1:534; Chamberlain, *Old Days in Chapel Hill*, 42.

23. DLS to EHS, March 19, 30, 1830, April 27, 1831, September 5, 1832, EC, NCC.

24. Russell, *Woman Who Rang the Bell*, 24 (quoted in Hamilton et al., *Papers of Graham*, 7:143–44n.5, and in Johnston, *Papers of Vance*, 1:143n.5); Annie Swain to Cornelia Phillips, June 18, 1855, Spencer Papers, SHC.

25. E.g., LMB to WHB, March 29, 1844, BFP, SHC; D. L. Barringer to DLS, May 14, 1844, Swain Papers, SHC (typescript).

26. Anne C. Swain to DLS, August 10, 1845, Swain Papers, SANC (typescript in Swain Papers, SHC).

27. LMB to WHB, September 5, October 11, 1845, February 26, 1846, BFP, SHC.

28. DLS to Genl. Barringer, March 21, 1846, Swain Papers, SHC (typescript); LMB to WHB, October 3, 1846, April 8, 1848, October 12, 24, 1849, BFP, SHC.

29. LMB to WHB, October 20, November 2, December 7, 1850, March 20, 1851, BFP, SHC; DLS to J. DB Hooper, Esq., December 3, 1850, Hooper Papers, SHC; Cornelia Phillips to "my dear Charley" (her brother Charles, presumably), March 23, 1851, Spencer Papers, SHC; James Henry Dickson to DLS, April 16, 1861, Swain Papers, SANC, and April 29, 1861, Swain Papers, SHC.

30. DLS to EHS, June 12, 1840, Swain Papers, SANC.

31. LMB to WHB, January 31, February 3, 11, 1854, BFP, SHC.

32. LMB to WHB, February 11, August 16, 1854, ibid.; Charles F. Deems to DLS, October 26, 1854, Swain Papers, SANC; WHB to LMB, August 20, 1854, BFP, SHC.

33. Caroline L. Scott to DLS, October (no date and year shown, but almost certainly 1854), Swain Papers, SANC.

34. E. S. Butler to EHS, December 16, 1854, and DLS to EHS, December 22, 1854, ibid.

35. George Swain (Jr.) to DLS, January 27, 1855, Swain Papers, SANC; Francis L. Hawks to DLS, March 13, 1855, and John H. Wheeler to DLS, May 1, 1855, Swain Papers, SHC.

36. LMB to WHB, January 31, February 3, 1855, BFP, SHC.

37. DLS to Annie Swain, October 31, 1855, Swain Papers, SANC.

38. Elliott C. Fistuc to DLS, November 1855, ibid.

39. LMB to WHB, February 1, 18, 1856, BFP, SHC; P. (?) Fetter to CPS, November 20, 1856, Spencer Papers, SHC.

40. Annie Swain to Mary Hooper, May 23, 1860, Hooper Papers, SHC.

41. C. F. Deems to DLS, November 15, 1865, Swain Papers, SANC.

42. Anne Swain to CPS, August 6, 1862, Spencer Papers, SHC.

43. Russell, *Woman Who Rang the Bell*, 24.

44. Battle, *History*, 1:575; D. W. Siler (nephew) to DLS, August 29, 1845, Swain Papers, SHC (typescript).

45. LMB to WHB, April 10, 1844, April 12, 19, 1845, February 21, 1860, BFP, SHC; ZBV to DLS, August 30, 1858, Swain Papers, SHC (see Johnston, *Papers of Vance*, 1:40).

46. DLS, form letter dated June 13, 1856, Swain Papers, SANC.

47. DLS to Annie Swain, October 31, 1855, Swain Papers, SANC; CM to DLS, November 5, 1855, Swain Papers, SHC.

48. Battle, *History*, 1:810.

49. Henry R. Frost, M. D., Dean, to DLS, December 1, 1860, Swain Papers, SANC.

50. J. Johnston Pettigrew to DLS, January 23, 1861, Swain Papers, SHC.

51. James Henry Dickson to DLS, April 16, 1861, Swain Papers, SANC; Battle, *History*, 1:289, 635, 791.

52. James Henry Dickson to DLS, April 19, 1861, Swain Papers, SANC.

53. J. Henry Dickson to DLS, April 29, 1861, Swain Papers, SANC (see also Dickson to DLS, April 16, 1861, ibid., re: Richard's living-quarters choice).

54. Barnes, *Medical and Surgical History of the War of the Rebellion Part III*, vol. II, *Surgical History*, 282; Brock, *Southern Historical Society Papers*, 22:255; Hewett, *Roster of Confederate Soldiers 1861–1865*, 15:37.

55. DLS to Annie Swain, October 31, 1855, Swain Papers, SANC.

56. Mrs. E. L. Harding to DLS, April 1862, ibid.

57. James Caldwell to DLS, June 17, 1867, Clark Papers, SANC.

58. WHB to KPB, July 20, 1867, BFP, SHC.

59. A. S. Merrimon to DLS, February 12, March 9, April 13, 28, May 30, 1868, Clark Papers, SANC; draft in sum of $822.60, July 13, 1865, Swain Papers, SANC. As to Merrimon, see Whichard, Willis P., "Merrimon, Augustus Summerfield," in Garraty and Carnes, *American National Biography*, 15:363–64.

60. Paschal C. Hughes to DLS, April 25, 1868, Clark Papers, SANC.

61. LMB to WHB, January 29, 1855, February 3, 1856, BFP, SHC.

62. James J. Philips to DLS, September 8, October 9, 1861; DLS to James J. Philips, September 28, 1861, Swain Papers, SANC. As to Philips, see Smith, Claiborne T. Jr., "Philips, James Jones," in Powell, *DNCB*, 5:89. Richard had married Sue E. Burt in Bedford County, Tennessee, on June 8, 1861. Lucas Jr. and Sheffield, *35,000 Tennessee Marriage Records*, 3:265; Marsh and Marsh, *Official Marriages of Bedford County Tennessee 1861–1880*, 1:48.

63. WHB to LMB, November 7, 1853, BFP, SHC; DLS to Annie Swain, October 31, 1855, Swain Papers, SHC.

64. GS to DLS, February 7, May 2, 1823, EC, NCC; DLS to EHS, December 28, 1827, January 4, 11, 18, 20, March 14, 21, 1828, March 5, 1830, ibid.; George Swain (Jr.) to DLS, July 21, 1841, Swain Papers, SANC; James Lowry to DLS, April 5, 1849, ibid.; L. F. Siler to DLS, October 9, 1857, ibid.

65. James Lowry to DLS, March 24, 1846, Swain Papers, SANC.

66. James Lowry to DLS, February 10, 1856, ibid.

67. Ibid.

68. George Swain (Jr.) to DLS, April 19, June 5, 1845, January 9, 1853, ibid.

69. George Swain (Jr.) to DLS, undated, ibid.

70. George Swain (Jr.) to DLS, December 20, 1840, March 29, June 9, 25, 1841, March 11, 1843, ibid.

71. George Swain (Jr.) to DLS, June 9, 1841, January 20, December 2, 1842, July 4, September 1, 1844, December 28, 1845, ibid.

72. George Swain (Jr.) to DLS, all SANC: farming operations, July 1, 13, 1846; honey bees, November 13, 1846, November 28, 1861; minerals and mining, June 26, October 8, 1853, August 6, November 20, 1854, January 27, July 17, September 8, 1855; orchards, July 17, 28, 1855; railroad, August 30, 1858; rice and potatoes, December 7, 1849, January 27, 1854; stockraising, February 20, March 21, 1857; Swain's land, July 25, 1849; tobacco, July 31, 1840, February 14, 1841, March 11, 1843, July 26, 1846; turpentine, October 9, 1855; whiskey, November 27, 1842.

73. George Swain (Jr.) to DLS, November 27, March 6, 1842, July 22, September 28, December 6, 1845, Swain Papers, SANC.

74. George Swain (Jr.) to DLS, August 13, 1838, February 19, August 6, October 15, 1839, October 23, 1841, January 14, 19, December 28, 1845, March 6, April 30, 1846; Alexander F. Luckie to DLS, October 21, 1846, ibid.

75. George Swain (Jr.) to DLS, May 5, 1842, ibid.

76. Geo. S. Coleman (nephew) to DLS, January 19, 22, 1849; (illegible first name) H. Moore to DLS, Feburary 7, 1849, ibid.; see also unsigned letter to DLS, August 26, 1860, ibid., urging David to remove George from management, saying, "he is not calculated to contend with the dis[h]onesty of mankind."

77. DLS to Doct. C. W. Long, December 21, 1844 (typescript), Swain Papers, SHC; M. C. Long (niece) to DLS, December 14, 1845, Swain Papers, SANC. As to the Longs' marriage, see Brown, *Cyclopedia of American Biographies*, 5:112; as to Long's being an anesthesia pioneer, see Lester, Malcolm, "Long, Crawford Williamson," in Garraty and Carnes, *American National Biography*, 13:865–67.

78. C. W. Long to DLS, August (?) 2, 1867, Swain Papers, SANC.

79. Unsigned letter to DLS, August 26, 1860; George Swain (Jr.) to DLS, one undated, and August 27, 1843, January 19, February 9, 1845, July 7, 1849, ibid.

80. J. H. Coleman to DLS, September 23, 1840, George S. Coleman to DLS, October 10, 1849, ibid.

81. D. R. Lowry to DLS, July 27, 1843 ($100); J. H. Coleman to DLS, August 26, 1847 ($1,000), December 1, 1845 (some now, more later) (typescript in Swain Papers, SHC); G. S. Coleman to DLS, August 22, 1849 (mortgage); N. Coleman to DLS, December 22, 1843 (college), Swain Papers, SANC; J. R. Siler to DLS, November 20, 1848, Swain Papers, SHC (merchant).

82. N. (Newton) Coleman to DLS, August 5, 1845, Swain Papers, SANC (typescript in Swain Papers, SHC).

83. David C. (Coleman, probably) to DLS, January 10, 1842; D. R. Lowry to DLS, March 27, 1843, ibid.

84. L. F. Siler to DLS, October 8, 1857, ibid.

85. DLS to Wm. T. Coleman, October 23, November 25, 26, 1839, Swain Papers, SANC.

86. For other examples, see the following: DLS to Wm. Coleman, March 30, 1840, Swain Papers, SANC, D. R. Lowry to DLS, January 27, 1842, ibid.; Wm. Coleman to DLS, February 25, 1842, ibid.; D. W. Siler to DLS, January 5, 1845, ibid. (typescript in Swain Papers, SHC); A. M. Burton to DLS, July 7, 1846, Swain Papers, SANC; J. H. Coleman to DLS, August 26, 1847, ibid.; J. H. Coleman to DLS, June 24, 1848, ibid.; D. Coleman to DLS, August 14, 1848, Swain Papers, SHC; J. H. Coleman to DLS, March 7, 1849, Swain Papers, SANC; J. W. Coleman to DLS, December 17, 1852, Swain Papers, SHC (typescript); J. H. Coleman to DLS, January 21, 1861, Swain Papers, SANC; N. F. Coleman to DLS, November 30 (no year shown), ibid.; undated DLS statement that Wm. Coleman owes him $2,070, Swain Papers, SHC.

87. J. H. Coleman to DLS, July 31, 1843, May 24, 1844, Swain Papers, SANC; DLS to WPM, August 20, 1844, Mangum Papers, Duke (in Shanks, *Papers of Mangum*, 4:177); Wm. H. Haywood Jr. to DLS, March 12, 1845, N. Coleman to DLS, June 7, July 23, 1845, Swain Papers, SHC.

88. William Coleman to DLS, November 4, 1840, and David Coleman to DLS, May 9, 1841, Swain Papers, SANC; Battle, *History*, 1:798.

89. William Coleman to DLS, January 22, February 20, May 7, 1841, January 22, 1842, Swain Papers, SANC.

90. David Coleman, May 30, 1842, receipt for funds received from DLS; David Coleman to DLS, May 30, 1842, ibid.

91. N. Coleman to DLS, April 19, 1846, Swain Papers, SHC; L. B. Hardin (Navy Dept.) to DLS, December 31, 1844, Swain Papers, SANC; D. Coleman to DLS, November 14, 1848, ibid.

92. N. T. Coleman to DLS, July 2, 1843, Swain Papers, SANC; Wm. Coleman to DLS, August 16, 1852, Swain Papers, SHC (typescript); D. W. Siler to DLS, February 5, 1848, ibid.; D. R. Lowry to DLS, September 9, 1839, Swain Papers, SANC.

93. D. W. Siler to DLS, June 30, 1842, October 29, 1849, Swain Papers, SANC; see also J. H. Coleman to DLS, February 2, 1840, ibid.; (another nephew seeking advice about whether he should pursue the legal profession).

94. DLS to William [Coleman, presumably], February 2, 28, 1840, ibid.; D. R. Lowry to DLS, January 19, 1840, Swain Papers, SHC (typescript).

95. D. W. Siler to DLS, August 29, 1845, Swain Papers, SANC.

96. DLS to Gen. Daniel L. Barringer, May 5, 1840; DLS to T. H. Trippe, December 15, 1849, ibid.; John P. Steele to DLS, May 20, 1856, and DLS to Steele, June 11, 1856, Swain Papers, SHC; on the relationship, see DLS to EHS, July 1, 1847, Swain Papers, SANC.

97. A. Luckie (cousin) to DLS, January 1, 1847; George Swain (Jr.) to DLS, September 7, 1840; DLS to EHS, July 1, 1847 (typescript in Swain Papers, SHC), Swain Papers, SANC.

98. John H. Wheeler to DLS, October 16, 1858, March 29, 1860, Swain Papers, SHC; Murray, *Wake: Capital County*, 1:396; *People's Press*, Salem, N.C., September 4, 1879.

Chapter 21: Other Personal Dimensions

1. DLS to EHS, January 20, 1828, April 27, 1831, EC, NCC; Swain Diary, May 8, 1832, SANC. For other instances of Swain indebtedness in his youth, see DLS to EHS, September 12, 1828, October 23, 1831, April 26, 1832, EC, NCC; Swain Diary, February 23, 1832, SANC; receipt, May 5, 1835, Swain payment of $505.12 "in full of all accounts against him except [one]," Woodfin Papers, SHC. He continued to borrow later, apparently for investment purposes. See J. H. Coleman to DLS, July 31, 1843, Swain Papers, SANC; DLS to WHB, April 7, 1848, January 30, 1860, BFP, SHC. Even late in life, he had debts with which to deal. See Anne Swain to CPS, December 1866 (penciled on), Spencer Papers, SHC (Anne lacking money at Christmas because "Pa has had some debts amounting to over two thousand dollars to pay in Tennessee and at the North, and so I wouldn't ask him for any just now").

2. R. B. Vance to DLS, August 30, September 20, 1826, EC, NCC.

3. DLS to EHS, July 5, 26, 1838, Swain Papers, SANC; DLS to EHS, June 11, 1840, ibid., and to CM, April 28, 1849, UP.

4. *Salary and Benefits:* BOT ordinance, November 5, 1855, UP; BOTM, January 5, 1858 (date penciled on, with question mark), January 26, 1859, February 5, 1862. *UNC*

Loans to Swain: BOTM, December 31, 1855; note, DLS to UNC BOT, December 15, 1862, Swain Papers, SANC. *Swain Loans to UNC:* DLS to KPB, October 23, 1867, UP; DLS to UNC BOT, July 23, 1868, Clark Papers, SANC; unsigned, undated paper listing "[d]ebts due by the university to the estate of the Hon. D.L. Swain," Swain Papers, SHC; *Semi-Weekly Messenger,* July 8, 1902 (quoting, in part, *Daily Journal,* Freeport, Illinois); *News and Observer,* January 5, 1941.

5. DLS to EHS, August 27, 1828, EC, NCC.

6. *Swain Diary,* May 23, 1832, SANC; J. H. Watkins to DLS, October 14, 1832, Swain Papers, SHC (typescript); illegible to DLS, October 18, 1838, Swain Papers, SANC.

7. D. R. Lowry (nephew) to DLS, November 8, 1838, June 10, 1839, November 2, 1844 (typescript), Swain Papers, SANC; Joseph Henry to DLS, October 14, 1839, ibid.; J. N. Siler to DLS, September 3, 1846, ibid.; DLS to J. Perkins, Esqr., September 24, 1848, Swain Papers, SHC (typescript); *North Carolina University Magazine,* 7:294, 301 (March 1858). Several documents in the Swain Papers, SANC, relate to his land transactions. The Swain Papers, SHC, contain copies of deeds to and from Swain, and a copy of a contract to sell his Beaver Dam Creek farm property in Buncombe County. Determining the interest Swain held in certain tracts could be problematic. See Wm. Murdock to DLS, January 3, 14, 1846, Swain Papers, SANC.

8. James Perkins to DLS, undated, and DLS to J. Perkins, Esq., September 26, 1848, Swain Papers, SANC; see also A. Luckie (cousin) to DLS, January 12, 1847, ibid.

9. Deed dated November 18, 1836, Daniel L. and Ann Barringer to DLS and wife EHS et al., Swain Papers, SHC; J. Pinckney to DLS, December 12, 1836, ibid. (typescript).

10. Lease agreement between DLS and John B. Whiteside, December 5, 1831; management agreement between DLS and William R. Baird, April 20, 1833 (typescript); contract of sale between DLS and Thomas Stradley, October 9, 1835 (typescript), Swain Papers, SHC.

11. D. R. Lowry (nephew) to DLS, November 21, 1838, Swain Papers, SANC.

12. Agreement between DLS and David R. Lowry, June 18, 1841, Swain Papers, SANC; D. R. Lowry to DLS, May 17, 1841, ibid.

13. D. R. Lowry to DLS, May 4, 1840, Swain Papers, SHC, November 29, 1840, February 15, March 29, 1841, Swain Papers, SANC.

14. D. R. Lowry to DLS, November 7, 1842, April 30, 1843 (typescript in Swain Papers, SHC), Swain Papers, SANC, and March 27, July 27, 1843, Swain Papers, SHC (typescripts); J. R. Siler to DLS, November 7, 1842, Swain Papers, SANC.

15. J. R. Siler to DLS, January 16, October 22, November 20, 1843, Swain Papers, SANC (typescript of January 16, 1843, letter in Swain Papers, SHC); D. R. Lowry to DLS, February 18, 1843, Swain Papers, SHC.

16. Deed A. M. and Sarah Lewis to DLS, August 14, 1863, Swain Papers, SHC;

Thomas B. Dupree to DLS, June 18, August 10, 1864, Swain Papers, SHC; DLS to Elias Carr, October 22, 1864, Carr Papers, ECU (typescript in Swain Papers, SHC).

17. Thomas B. Dupree to DLS, March 10, October 27, 1865, Swain Papers, SHC.

18. R. Norfleet to DLS, November 4, 1864; DLS to unidentified recipient, November 11, 1864; Capt. G. H. Brown to DLS, November 14, 1864; Mr. Newton to DLS, November 7, 1864; Thomas B. Dupree to DLS, November 22, 1864; DLS to Thomas B. Dupree (apparently), November 28, 1864; Mr. Newton to DLS, December 4, 1864; C. J. Austin to DLS, December 4, 1864; R. H. Austin to DLS, December 20, 29, 1864; DLS to Capt. G. H. Brown, January 4, 1865; DLS to unidentified recipient, January 7, 1865; R. Norfleet to DLS, November 9, 1865; G. H. Brown, Q. M. office, to DLS, January 13, 1865, Swain Papers, SHC; DLS to ZBV, August 24, 1864, Vance Papers, SANC.

19. DLS to B. F. Newton, September 13, 1866, BFP, SHC.

20. John J. Palmer, Merchants Bank, New York, to DLS, June 29, July 17, 1848, January 10, 1849, Swain Papers, SANC.

21. Receipt, J. Roberts, Treasurer, Asheville Boarding House Company, April 18, 1843; H. Waddell to DLS, February 22, 1856; Transfer Document, Hugh Waddell to DLS, stock of Hillsboro Coal Mining and Transportation Company, February 24, 1856, Swain Papers, SANC.

22. J. N. Siler to DLS, June 12, October 1, 1838, ibid.

23. Swain Diary, August 25, 1832, SANC; note, "settled all accounts between Mrs. Anna White and D. L. Swain," January 4, 1849, ibid.; Swain document, June 17, 1851, acknowledging receipt of sums to invest for "maid servant Peggy," ibid.; family document between and among White sisters, January 1, 1857, witnessed by WAG, ibid.; D. L. Barringer to DLS, June 7, 1838, May 14, 1844, September 30, 1845, ibid.; DLS to unidentified recipient, October 8, 1852, Swain Papers, SHC (typescript); DLS to unidentified recipient, March 28, 1850, Swain Papers, SANC (typescript in Swain Papers, SHC); DLS to Calvin H. Wiley, November 8, 1851, Wiley Papers, SANC.

24. J. N. Siler to DLS, March 18, 1839, Swain Papers, SANC; WHB to DLS, October 21, 1850, BFP, SHC; N. W. Woodfin to DLS, November 29, 1841, May 13, 1843, Swain Papers, SANC; August 8, 1847, Swain Papers, SHC (typescript).

25. Deed of trust (copy) to William Coleman as trustee, to secure Enoch H. Cunningham's debt to DLS in sum of $3,000, Woodfin Papers, SHC; J. W. Cameron (Cannon?) to DLS, November 22, 1847, Swain Papers, SANC. For an example of a $20.00 debt, owed for more than eight years, see R. C. Pearson to DLS, October 19, 1839, ibid.

26. J. H. E. Hardy to DLS, May 2 (no year shown); James W. Patton to DLS, November 30, 1842, January 14, 1849 (see also Patton to DLS, July 9, 1849, February 5, 1861); John Hall to DLS, January 3, 1842, Swain Papers, SANC.

27. James R. Love to DLS, November 24, 1842; Thomas Stradley to DLS, August

13, 1849; Wm. Coleman to DLS, February 20, 1843; Jacob Siler to DLS, May 1, 1843; J. R. Siler to DLS, January 6, 1848; E. Mallett to DLS, February 4, 1859, ibid.; WHB to LMB, October 22, 1849, BFP, SHC.

28. John Hall to DLS, April 30, 1843, Swain Papers, SANC; DLS to WHB, February 12, 1856, BFP, SHC; J.R. Siler to DLS, April 12, 1866, Swain Papers, SHC, March 4, 1867, Swain Papers, SANC. In addition to lending money directly, Swain sometimes served as security for loans. See "Indenture Tripartite," William Coleman, Joshua Roberts, and DLS, March 25, 1833 (copy), Woodfin Papers, SHC.

29. Jacob Siler to DLS, May 1, 1843, Swain Papers, SHC (typescript); WHB to DLS, June 29, 1846, BFP, SHC, July 7, 1846, April 14, 1848, Swain Papers, SHC, March 30, 1848, Swain Papers, SANC (typescript in Swain Papers, SHC).

30. N. W. Woodfin to DLS, February 19, September 1, 1838, Swain Papers, SANC; September 11, 1838, Swain Papers, SHC; March 8, 1841, Swain Papers, SANC; March 3, 1842, Swain Papers, SHC; March 14, 1847, Swain Papers, SANC; August 18, 1852, Swain Papers, SHC (typescript). The Swain Papers contain numerous additional communications between Swain and Woodfin relating to Swain's legal and business affairs.

31. DLS to ZBV, September 12, 1865, Vance Papers, SANC; DLS to Rev. Dr. Deems, September 4, 1866, Swain Papers, SHC; U.S. Census, Orange County, N.C., 1860, Schedule 1 (cited in Chapman, *Black Freedom*, 34); Ashe, *Biographical History*, 1:453; Peele, *Lives*, 255.

32. DLS to EHS, June 12, 1840, June 13, 18 (typescript in Swain Papers, SHC), 1847, Swain Papers, SANC.

33. J. Ervin Jr. to DLS, April 24, June 6, 1833; Cowan (first name not shown) to DLS, May 29, 1832, EC, NCC.

34. William Gaston to unidentified recipient ("Mrs. D" written on typescript; probably Gaston's daughter Susan, Mrs. Robert Donaldson), January 19, 1829, Gaston Papers, SHC.

35. Swain Diary, February 16, 1832, SANC; Anderson, *Carolinian on the Hudson*, 171, 200, 208–9, 230, 250; Susan G. Donaldson to William Gaston, April 19, 1840, Gaston Papers, SHC; Robert Donaldson to DLS, December 6, 1845, January 14, 1859, Swain Papers, SHC, and June 8, 1865, Swain Papers, SANC; DLS to B. S. Hedrick, June 16, 1865, Hedrick Papers, Duke.

36. Thomas Ruffin to DLS, March 10, 1846, July 22, 1858, March 19, 1859, Swain Papers, SHC; see Battle, *History*, 1:825.

37. N. W. Woodfin to DLS, May 13, 1843, Swain Papers, SHC (typescript); Anna W. Woodfin to J. Gilcrest McCormick, January 8, 1897, McCormick Papers, SHC.

38. John H. Wheeler to WAG, February 12, 1866, Hamilton et al., *Papers of Gra-*

ham, 7:37, and to DLS, October 17, 1866, BFP, SHC; M. (Judge Mitchell D.) King to DLS, February 23, 1859, November 20, 1860, Swain Papers, SANC.

39. LMB to WHB, September 7, 1849, October 20, 1850, March 20, 1851, January 11, February 1, 14, 1856; LMB to Patti Battle, December 22, 1865, BFP, SHC.

40. DLS to WHB, April 7, 1848, February 21, 1860; WHB to LMB, April 23, 1848, April 2, 1849, ibid.

41. LMB to WHB, one with no date, June 24, 1846, October 15, 1847, March 25, June 29, 1848, January 2, 6, 1854, January 9, 1855; DLS to WHB, January 18, 1856; WHB to LMB, June 25, 1854; WHB to KPB, January 13, 1865, March 31, 1868; Swain Circular Letters, September 27, December 6, 1847, ibid.; WHB to DLS, October 3, 1845, Swain Papers, SHC.

42. LMB to WHB, April 8, May 23, 1848; WHB to LMB, April 15, 1848; WAG to WHB, May 9, 1848; DLS to WHB, May 17, December 10, 13, 16, 1848, ibid.; see Holt, *American Whig Party*, 391–92, and Whichard, Willis P., "Battle, William Horn," in Garraty and Carnes, *American National Biography*, 2:344–45.

43. LMB to WHB, April 24, 1847, BFP, SHC.

44. WHB to LMB, May 27, 1848, September 8, 16, 1851, January 24, 1858; LMB to WHB, January 22, 1858, ibid.

45. WAG to DLS, July 10, 17, 1854, Swain Papers, SANC.

46. DLS to WAG, January 10, 1853, Hamilton et al., *Papers of Graham*, 4:449, June 1, 1867, ibid., 7:330.

47. WAG to DLS, April 1, 1858, Swain Papers, SANC.

48. WAG to DLS, November 4, 1852, Hamilton et al., *Papers of Graham*, 4:428; DLS to WAG, December 6, 1852, ibid., 4:438; S. (Susan) W. Graham to DLS, March 21, 1855, Swain Papers, SHC; Allcott, "Architectural Developments At 'Montrose' in the 1850's," 42 NCHR 85, 87–88, 91, 94.

49. Swain Diary, February 3, 1832, SANC; DLS to EHS, January 4, 1828, EC, NCC; William H. Haigh College Journal, October 24, 1841, Haigh Papers, SHC.

50. John S. Erwin to DLS, November 30, 1855, Swain Papers, SANC; J. T. (James Turner) Morehead to DLS, August 25, 1866, Swain Papers, SHC; CM to DLS, November 5, 1855, ibid.; WHB to KPB, July 15, 1866, BFP, SHC.

51. LMB to WHB, May 2, 1848, BFP, SHC.

52. Jonathan Worth to DLS, January 5, 1867, Swain Papers, SANC.

53. ZBV to DLS, March 20, 1867, Spencer Papers, SANC.

54. DLS to KPB, July 20, 1868, BFP, SHC; Gass, "Battle, Kemp Plummer," in Powell, *DNCB*, 1:114–15.

55. James M. Smith to DLS, January 26, 1854, Swain Papers, SANC.

56. Fitzgerald, Bishop Oscar Penn, "On Asbury's Trail in the Land of the Sky," quoted in *American Illustrated Methodist Magazine*, 4:289 (1900–1).

57. Swain Diary, January 8, 1832, SANC. See also Swain Diary, January 22, 28, February 19, March 11, April 15, May 27, June 3, 24, July 8, 1832, SANC; DLS to EHS, April 27, July 3 (?), October 23, 1831, EC, NCC, and December 8, 1839, Swain Papers, SANC; Thomasson, *Swain County*, 101–2.

58. Swain Diary, April 26, 1832, SANC.

59. Thomas Stradley to DLS, August 13, 1849; Charles F. Deems to DLS, January 24, 1867; E. G. McClure to DLS, October 21, 1843, Swain Papers, SANC.

60. George Swain to DLS, March 6, July 13, 1846, April 16, 1853, Swain Papers, SANC; Louise H. Kendall to DLS, November 22, 1867, Clark Papers, SANC.

61. DLS to EHS, September 5, 1832, EC, NCC, June 11, 1840, Swain Papers, SANC; DLS to W. L. Scott, October 7, 1854, Scott Papers, Duke; DLS to CM, July 13, 1857, UP; DLS, "British Invasion of North Carolina in 1776," *North Carolina University Magazine*, 2:155 (May 1853).

62. DLS to EHS, November 13, 1829, EC, NCC; DLS to Hon. Thomas Settle, October 4, 1856, Settle Papers, SHC; DLS to CM, April 27, 1862, UP; Thomas Pickens to DLS, January 31, 1857, Swain Papers, SANC; CPS to EHS, January 12, 1870, Spencer Papers, SANC.

63. Charles Phillips to unidentified recipient, August 27, 1868, Clark Papers, SANC; CPS, in *North Carolina Presbyterian*, September 23, 1868; Russell, *Woman Who Rang the Bell*, 24.

64. FM, January 13, 1849; Ashe, *Biographical History*, 1:452; Peele, *Lives*, 254–55; *Raleigh Register*, September 16, 1885.

65. Worsley, "Catholicism in Antebellum North Carolina," 60 NCHR 399, 422; Daniel, *Swain*, 419 (citing *Proceedings and Debates*, 250, 305); Craig, *Historical Sketch of New Hope Church*, 29; *First Hundred Years: The Chapel Hill Presbyterian Church, 1849–1949*, 13–15; Battle, *History*, 1:535; LMB to WHB, October 23, 1844, BFP, SHC; email, Mary Donna Pond, University Presbyterian Church, to Willis P. Whichard, September 23, 2010 (copy in author's files). See also Brewer, *Memoir of Swain*, 7; Bridges, *Masonic Governors*, 154; Lefler and Wager, *Orange County 1752–1952*, 295; Vickers, *Chapel Hill Illustrated*, 50; Wilson, *Papers of Spencer*, 547; *North Carolina Presbyterian*, September 9, 1868. A letter from Elisha Mitchell to CM, December 11, 1849, UP, states that Swain contributed $365.00 toward erection of the church building and was the second largest contributor. On "The Halfway Covenant," see Hall, *Worlds of Wonder*, 144, 153; Kidd, *Great Awakening*, 3, 185; Miller, *New England Mind*, 2:95–113.

66. *Raleigh Register and North-Carolina Gazette*, February 3, 1835, January 19, 1836, December 31, 1838; *North Carolina Standard*, December 22, 1852; Drury Lacy to DLS, February 1, 1854, Swain Papers, SHC.

67. J. W. Brigham to DLS, March 7, 1851, Swain Papers, SANC; *Cleveland Daily Leader*, October 14, 1865.

68. J. L. Brigham to DLS, October 24, 1852, Swain Papers, SANC (typescript in Swain Papers, SHC); "Testimony of Distinguished Laymen," 56–58 (Swain); original draft in Swain's hand, Swain Papers, SHC.

69. Will of David Lowry Swain, dated May 9, 1858, recorded in Will Book G, pages 541–42, Orange County, N.C.

70. Brewer, "Hon. David Lowry Swain, LL.D," 7; Battle, *History*, 1:534.

71. DLS to EHS, July 18, August 7, 1828, EC, NCC.

72. DLS to Will Gaston, October 9, 11, 1834, Gaston Papers, SHC.

73. William Sidney Mullins Diary, October 31, 1841, SHC; FM, August 26, 1843; J. R. Siler to DLS, October 22, 1843, Swain Papers, SHC (typescript); LMB to WHB, September 5, 1845, BFP, SHC; DLS to G. J. McRee, December 31, 1844, McRee Papers, SHC; E. Mitchell to CM, September 7, 1846, UP.

74. DLS to EHS, May 5, 1847, Swain Papers, SANC (typescript in Swain Papers, SHC).

75. John H. Wheeler to DLS, March 19, 1859, Swain Papers, SANC, March 24, 1859, Swain Papers, SHC; Charles Manly to DLS, April 5, 1859, J. M. Morehead to DLS, April 18, 1859, Swain Papers, SHC.

76. DLS to Thomas Ruffin, April 27, 1859, in Hamilton, *Papers of Ruffin*, 3:30–31; CM to DLS, April 29, 1859, Swain Papers, SHC; Edward Everett to DLS, April 30, 1859, ibid.; DLS to CPS, May 9, 1859, Spencer Papers, SANC.

77. *Fayetteville Observer*, May 2, 1859; M. (Judge Mitchell D.) King to DLS, June 11, 1859, Swain Papers, SANC; John H. Wheeler to DLS, May 7, 1859, Swain Papers, SHC.

78. DLS to Rev. Dr. Hawks, September 14, 1859; John H. Wheeler to DLS, November 16, 1859; DLS to Col. J. F. H. Claiborne, February 13, April 16, 30, 1860, Swain Papers, SHC; DLS to WHB, February 21, 1860, BFP, SHC.

79. DLS to Francis L. Hawks, April 16, June 13, 1860, and Hawks to DLS, May 1, 1860, Swain Papers, SHC.

80. DLS to WAG, January 20, 1862, Hamilton et al., *Papers of Graham*, 5:354; DLS to Paul Cameron, January 20, 1862, in Shanks, *Papers of Mangum*, 5:424–25; DLS to CM, January 24, 1862, UP; DLS to unidentified recipient (probably CM), January 28, 1862, UP; DLS to CM, February 14, 1862, UP.

81. DLS to WAG, December 27, 1866, Hamilton et al., *Papers of Graham*, 7:242.

82. DLS to CM, October 10, 1856, UP; DLS to Asa Biggs, September 25, 1858, Swain Papers, SANC; CM to DLS, August 25, 1859, Swain Papers, SHC; Charles Phillips to J.B. Killibrew, March 12, 1856, BFP, SHC; Document dated November 28, 1866, Swain Papers, SANC.

83. DLS to GS, May 18, 1822, EC, NCC; DLS to Joseph Seawell Jones, December 20, 1832, Swain Papers, SANC; DLS to William Gaston, November 9, 1833, Swain Papers, SHC.

84. DLS to WAG, January 11, 1841 [1842], Hamilton et al., *Papers of Graham*, 2:252; DLS to EHS, June 13 (typescript), 18, 1847; DLS to Pliny Miles, November 12, 1847; Swain Papers, SHC.

85. George Bancroft to B.J. Lossing, January 22, 1852, Swain Papers, SHC (enclosing DLS to Benjamin Lossing, December 20, 1851, ibid.) (copy also in Hoyt Papers, SHC); DLS to Rev. Dr. Hawks, January 6, 1853, Swain Papers, SHC; DLS to G. J. McRee, October 23, 1855, September 5, 1856, September 9, 1857; G. McRee to DLS, October 20, 1855, ibid.; Thomas Ruffin to DLS, December 9, 1857, ibid.; DLS to CM, February 4, 1862, and CM to DLS, August 31, 1864, ibid.

86. D. L. Barringer to DLS, April 4, 1849, Swain Papers, SANC.

87. Hamilton, *Papers of Shotwell*, 3:274.

Chapter 22: "Peculiar Institution"

1. GS to DLS, May 17, 23, August 23, 1822, EC, NCC; Inscoe, *Mountain Masters*, 65, 71, 99–101; Daniel, *Early Career*, 148–49.

2. Daniel, *Early Career*, 146–49; Daniel, *Swain*, 102n.11, 160–62.

3. Will of David L. Swain, May 9, 1858, Book G, 541–42, Orange County, N.C.; U.S. Census, 1850, 1860; List, "Home Slaves Confederate Tax 1864," Swain Papers, SANC; List, July 1, 1855, Swain Papers, SHC; Franklin, *Free Negro in North Carolina*, 9, 147.

4. See text accompanying note 24, chapter 3; Treadwell, *American Liberties and American Slavery*, 51.

5. DLS to EHS, March 30, 1827, April 27, 1831, EC, NCC; DLS to B. J. Lossing, November 24, 1855, Swain Papers, SHC. Until the nineteenth-century change, one scholar has noted, "unfree status of one type or another . . . was the lot of much of humankind," and the colonists would have seen "nothing particularly noteworthy about some people working—even under constraint—for the well-being of others." Kolchin, *American Slavery*, 4, 14. Viewed in this temporal light, Swain's attitudes and practices regarding race and human bondage were normative. His arguably humane concerns for the bondsmen, while less universal, were shared by many of his contemporaries. Ibid., 60, 88–89, 94, 112–18.

6. Battle, *History*, 1:534–35; Chapman, *Black Freedom*, 54, 60. Chapman later states that the enslaved person was Kemp Battle's and that Battle made the whipping threat. Ibid., 206, 256.

7. *American Repository*, 27:127 (Washington, April 1851) (Swain contributed $5.00; other Chapel Hillians who contributed included William H. Battle, Manuel Fetter, Elisha Mitchell, and James Phillips).

8. DLS to EHS, March 30, 1828, EC, NCC; memorandum by Anna Whithead (typescript), February 10, 1829, Swain Papers, SHC; Swain Diary, March 31, 1832, SANC; James C. Johnston document (typescript), January 17, 1839, Swain Papers, SHC.

9. D. R. Lowry (nephew) to DLS, November 29, 1840, and John Hall to DLS, April 26, 1841, Swain Papers, SANC.

10. D. R. Lowry to DLS, July 20, 1843, and James Lowry to DLS, September 23, 1843, ibid.

11. James M. Smith to DLS, August 14, 1843, ibid. (typescript in Swain Papers, SHC); N.W. Woodfin to DLS, August 21, October 21, 1843, Swain Papers, SANC; Wm. Coleman to DLS, September 1, 1843, ibid.

12. J. H. Coleman (nephew) to DLS, July 31, August 5, 1843; N. T. Coleman to DLS, August 4, 1843; N. W. Woodfin to DLS, August 7, 1843, Swain Papers, SANC; J. H. Coleman to DLS, September 4, 1845, Swain Papers, SHC (typescript).

13. WHB to DLS, March 30, 1848, Swain Papers, SANC (typescript in Swain Papers, SHC); John Hall to DLS, June 14, 1848, Swain Papers, SHC.

14. D. R. Lowry (nephew) to DLS, August 7, 1843, ibid. (typescript in Swain Papers, SHC); C. W. Long to DLS, July 17, 1843 (typescript), Swain Papers, SHC.

15. Document dated September 24, 1860, between DLS and Samuel Booth, Swain Papers, SANC.

16. John Hall to DLS, September 14, 1840, ibid.

17. J. H. Coleman to DLS, November 8, 1847, ibid., July 6, 1852, Swain Papers, SHC (typescript).

18. Wm. Coleman to DLS, October 30, 1839, Swain Papers, SANC, August 16, 1852, Swain Papers, SHC (typescript); DLS to unidentified recipient, December 4, 1844 (typescript), ibid.; see Inscoe, *Mountain Masters*, 283n.73.

19. Swain Diary, undated entry and notes, SANC.

20. D. R. Lowry to DLS, January 17, 1842, Swain Papers, SANC; Silas McDowell to DLS, January 1, 1831, Swain Papers, SHC; Inscoe, *Mountain Masters*, 77.

21. Account Book entries for July 1, 1855, July 1, 1866, Swain Papers, SHC; Inscoe, *Mountain Masters*, 78, 165–66; N. W. Woodfin to DLS, May 12, 1862, Clark Papers, SANC; Inscoe and McKinney, *Heart of Confederate Appalachia*, 212, 319n.17.

22. Memorandum dated December 31, 1864, and note dated January 1, 1865, Swain Papers, SANC.

23. DLS to EHS, December 22, 1854, ibid. For extensive treatment of the hiring of the enslaved, see Martin, *Divided Mastery*, passim; on the role of women like Eleanor Swain in the practice, see ibid., 114–117.

24. DLS to John Coleman (nephew), August 19, 1843, Swain Papers, SHC.

25. D. L. Barringer to DLS, June 11, 1842, and D. R. Lowry to DLS, August 26, 1842, Swain Papers, SANC.

26. DLS to Gen. Daniel L. Barringer, October 7, 1842, and D. R. Lowry to DLS, October 21, 1842, ibid.

27. D. L. Barringer to DLS, February 21, 1843, ibid. (typescript in Swain Papers, SHC).

28. D. R. Lowry to DLS, March 27, 1843, Swain Papers, SANC (typescript in Swain Papers, SHC).

29. Jacob Siler to DLS, May 1, 1843, Swain Papers, SHC (typescript); D. L. Barringer to DLS, May 14, 1844, Swain Papers, SANC.

30. DLS to Gen. Daniel L. Barringer, July 22, 1840, Swain Papers, SHC.

31. D. L. Barringer to DLS, September 30, 1845 (typescript), May 30, 1846 (typescript), Swain Papers, SHC, September 30, 1845, Swain Papers, SANC.

32. D. L. Barringer to DLS, November 5, 1846, Swain Papers, SHC.

33. D. L. Barringer to DLS, March 12, 1848, Swain Papers, SANC (typescript in Swain Papers, SHC).

34. D. L. Barringer to DLS, August 23, 1848, Swain Papers, SHC (typescript).

35. D.L. Barringer to DLS, October 25, 1842, Swain Papers, SANC.

36. D. R. Lowry to DLS, May 9, 1844, ibid. (typescript in Swain Papers, SHC).

37. N. White to DLS, March 2, 1846, Swain Papers, SANC.

38. N. White (not signed, but clearly from White) to DLS, May 2, 1846, ibid.

39. D. N. Siler to DLS, December 19, 1844, January 3, 1845 (typescript in Swain Papers, SHC), Swain Papers, SANC.

40. LMB to WHB, October 8, 1844 (penciled on), April 12, 1845, BFP, SHC.

41. D. L. Barringer to DLS, April 14, 1852, J. A. Blakemore to DLS, December 6, 1853, January 18, 1854, Swain Papers, SHC.

42. DLS to Charles Manly, December 19, 1843, UP.

43. J. H. Coleman to DLS, July 31, 1843, Swain Papers, SHC (typescript), and June 24, 1848, Swain Papers, SANC; D. L. Barringer to DLS, August 28, 1848, ibid.; LMB to WHB, February 21, 1859, BFP, SHC.

44. DLS to EHS, July 4, 1828, EC, NCC.

45. Swain Diary, March 1832, SANC; DLS to EHS and David Mebans (?), September 5, 1832, EC, NCC.

46. DLS to EHS, March 19, 1830, EC, NCC.

47. DLS to EHS, September 11, 1831, EC, NCC; Jo. Seawell Jones to DLS, February 4, 1839, Swain Papers, SANC.

48. E. F. Reade to DLS, November 23, 1846; DLS to Genl. Daniel L. Barringer, July 26, 1842, Swain Papers, SANC.

49. James Lowry to DLS, March 9, 1844, Swain Papers, SANC (typescript in

Swain Papers, SHC); J. R. Siler to DLS, December 21, 1844, Swain Papers, SHC (typescript) (it is possible that the references are to the same enslaved family, but the name given for the female enslaved person in the two letters is different).

50. J. H. Coleman to DLS, November 8, 1847, Swain Papers, SHC (typescript), February 19, 1849, Swain Papers, SANC, April 17, 1853, Clark Papers, SANC; William Coleman to DLS, August 18, 1852, Swain Papers, SHC; Inscoe, *Mountain Masters*, 91, 95.

51. George Swain to DLS, December 5, 1843, Swain Papers, SANC (typescript in Swain Papers, SHC), February 11, 1844, Swain Papers, SANC; C.W. Long to DLS, July 17, 1843, Swain Papers, SANC.

52. D. L. Barringer to DLS, May 14, 1844, Swain Papers, SHC (typescript), May 26, 1849, Swain Papers, SANC.

53. N. W. Woodfin to DLS, February 8, 1847, Swain Papers, SANC (typescript in Swain Papers, SHC), March 14, 1847, Swain Papers, SANC (typescript in Swain Papers, SHC), June 4, 1849, Swain Papers, SANC.

54. DLS to Nicholas Woodfin, May 11, 1862 (copy), Woodfin Papers, SHC.

55. DLS to J. DB Hooper, Esq., December 3, 1850, Hooper Papers, SHC.

56. E. Mitchell to DLS, December 28, 1840, Swain Papers, SHC.

57. Elisha Mitchell to DLS, December 3, 1844, DLS to CM, October 22, 1851, UP; see Ballinger, Helms, and Holder, *Slavery and the Making of the University*, 6.

58. BOTM, January 5, 1848; receipt, Willis Dunstan (?) to DLS, June 1, 1848, UP.

59. FM, January 7, 1843.

60. Battle, *Sketch of the Life and Character of Wilson Caldwell*, 3–4; Battle, *History*, 1:534; list captioned "Home Slaves Confederate Tax 1864," miscellaneous file, Swain Papers, SANC (listing Swain enslaved person named "Wilson," with date February 8, 1843).

61. *Memoirs of Robert Philip Howell*, 13; Georg [sic] M. Horton to "Mr. Garrison the Editor of a Boston paper," September 3, 1844; Horton to Horace Greeley, September 11, 1853; Horton to DLS, undated, SHC; Walser, *Black Poet*, 63–67, 75–80; Sherman, *Black Bard of North Carolina*, 20–23; Sinha, *Slave's Cause*, 434–36; *Poetical Works of George M. Horton, The Colored Bard of North-Carolina* (list of subscribers at end); *Herald-Sun*, Durham, N.C., March 31, 2006 (naming of dormitory). For related accounts, see Ballinger, Helms, and Holder, *Slavery and the Making of the University*, 37; Brown, *History of the Education of Negroes in North Carolina*, 13; Chapman, *Black Freedom*, 70; Jackson, "George Moses Horton, North Carolinian," 53 NCHR 140, 146. For a summary of Horton's life and work by a probable collateral relative, see Horton and Horton, *In Hope of Liberty*, x–xi (title taken from a Horton book of poetry).

62. Lefler and Wager, *Orange County-1752–1952*, 99; see also Chapman, *Black Free-*

dom, 4, 4n.4; Franklin, *Free Negro in North Carolina*, 33. For historical context on the enslaving society into which Swain was born and in which he lived most of his life, see Crow, Escott, and Hatley, *History of African Americans in North Carolina*, chapters 3 and 4; for historical context on that society in light of the enslaving institution over time, see Fox-Genovese and Genovese, *Mind of the Master Class*, 5–6, 69–71.

Chapter 23: Disunion, Disruption

1. FM, June 2, 1859; Henderson, *Campus of the First State University*, 173–74.
2. Spencer, *Pen and Ink Sketches*, 52.
3. Henderson, *Campus of the First State University*, 173–74; Charles Manly to DLS, January 19, 1860, Swain Papers, SHC.
4. WAG to DLS, March 24, 1851, Hamilton et al., *Papers of Graham*, 4:59–60.
5. Charles Manly to DLS, October 14, 1856, January 19, 1860, Swain Papers, SHC.
6. Francis L. Hawks to DLS, December 9, 1859, Swain Papers, SHC.
7. Francis L. Hawks to DLS, January 3, 1860, ibid.
8. DLS to Francis L. Hawks, January 13, 1860, ibid.
9. DLS to Rev. Dr. Hawks, September 13, 1860, April 16, 1861; Hawks to DLS, April 19,
1861; E. J. Hale to DLS, October 17, 1860, ibid.
10. James W. Patton to DLS, February 5, 1861, Swain Papers, SANC, and N. W. Woodfin to DLS, May 17, 1860, Swain Papers, SHC.
11. J. Johnston Pettigrew to DLS, January 11, 1861, Swain Papers, SHC.
12. *Journal of the Congress of the Confederate States of America, 1861–1865*, 1:23.
13. WHB to LMB, January 27, February 10, 1861, BFP, SHC.
14. Charles Baring to John W. Ellis, February 2, 1861, in Tolbert, *Papers of Ellis*, 2:582; John W. Ellis to Isham W. Garrett, January 30, 1861, ibid., 2:574.
15. *Journal of the Congress of the Confederate States of America, 1861–1865*, 1:24; *Documents, 1860–61*, #34 (NCC); DLS, Matt W. Ransom, and John L. Bridgers to John W. Ellis, February 11, 1861, in Tolbert, *Papers of Ellis*, 2:590–94; *Raleigh State Journal*, February 16, 1861.
16. Konkle, *Morehead*, 374–75.
17. *Semi-Weekly Raleigh Sentinel*, January 9, 1867 (letter DLS to the Honorable B. F. Perry of South Carolina). There are numerous brief, secondary references to Swain's role in the Montgomery delegation; see, e.g., William H.S. Burgwyn, "An Address on the Military and Civil Services of General Matt W. Ransom," before the Ladies Memorial Association and citizens, Raleigh, N.C., May 10, 1906, 3 (NCC); Hamilton, *Reconstruction*, 17; Hill, *History of North Carolina in the War Between the*

States, 1:30–31; Powell, *North Carolina: A Bicentennial History*, 130; Sitterson, *Secession Movement in North Carolina*, 209; Spencer, *First Steps in North Carolina History*, 199–200; Tolbert, *Papers of Ellis*, 1:xcvii–xcviii; Wakelyn, *Biographical Dictionary of the Confederacy*, 403; *North Carolina University Magazine*, 10:504–5 (April 1861); *Raleigh Weekly Register*, January 30, 1861.

18. *North Carolina University Magazine*, 10:504–5 (April 1861); Hamilton et al., *Papers of Graham*, 5:226–29; Sidney Smith to WAG, February 16, 19, 1861, ibid., 5:237–38.

19. *Hillsborough Recorder*, February 20, 1861; *North Carolina Standard*, February 23, 1861; Konkle, *Morehead*, 386; Hamilton et al., *Papers of Graham*, 5:238–40. Earlier, at a mass meeting in Hillsborough on December 22, 1860, Swain had taken the same "Whig Unionist" position. South Carolina had just seceded, and he referred to it "with indignation." He favored a convention but "opposed a Confederacy of the Southern States." He said he "would rather fight in the Union than out of it." *Fayetteville Observer*, December 31, 1860. He referred to this speech in his post-Civil War petition for a pardon.

20. Wiley, *Life of Johnny Reb*, 16; CM to DLS, April 22, 1861, Swain Papers, SANC; Crofts, *Reluctant Confederates*, xviii, 335–60; Inscoe, *Mountain Masters*, 250.

21. *North Carolina Standard*, April 27, 1861; Edward Hall Armstrong to Thomas G. Armstrong, April 20, 1861, Martin Papers, SHC; S. Henry Dickson to DLS, April 29, 1861, Swain Papers, SHC.

22. E. H. McClure to DLS, January 20, 1861, Swain Papers, SANC.

23. J. H. Coleman to DLS, January 21, 1861, ibid.

24. James H. Dickson to DLS, April 16, 1861, and M. King to DLS, June 3, 1861, ibid.

25. Lemuel Lynch, James C. Turrentine, George Laws, and Will A. Graham Jr. to DLS, June 10, 1861, Swain Papers, SHC.

26. John Walker to DLS, December 20, 1861, Swain Papers, SHC.

27. CM to DLS, February 17, 19, 1862, Swain Papers, SHC.

28. CM to DLS, April 30, May 17, 1862, March 3, 1864, ibid.

29. CPS diary entry March 1865, quoted in Chamberlain, *Old Days in Chapel Hill*, 80.

30. DLS to CM, February 14, 26, 1862, UP.

31. DLS to WAG, May 18, 1861, Hamilton et al., *Papers of Graham*, 5:256, May 3, 1864, ibid., 6:83–86; as to Graham as a delegate to the secession convention, see ibid., 1:xxii.

32. DLS to Nicholas W. Woodfin, May 11, 1862 (copy), Woodfin Papers, SHC.

33. LMB to WHB, January 21, 1861, BFP, SHC; *Weekly Raleigh Register*, May 29, 1861.

34. FM, March 25, April 25, 1861.

35. Manuscript in Davidson Papers, UP.

36. Brophy, *University, Court, and Slave*, xiv, xvi, 3–4, 9, 11, 19, 21–24, 126–27, 136–38,

206, 283–84.

37. H. H. Price, R. B. Peebles, and W. F. Avery, in behalf of the freshman, sophomore, and junior classes, to CM, April 27, 1861, UP.

38. Swain Circular Letter, May 1, 1861, UP; *North Carolina Standard*, May 11, 15, 1861; Battle, *History*, 1:719–21.

39. *Weekly Raleigh Register*, July 17, 19, 1861.

40. Swain Circular Letter, July 31, 1861, UP; Shanks, *Papers of Mangum*, 5:425–26; *Weekly Raleigh Register*, July 31, 1861.

41. DLS to unidentified recipient, November 22, 1861, UP; DLS to Hon. T. D. McDowell, December 14, 1861, McDowell Papers, Duke; *Weekly Raleigh Register*, December 18, 1861.

42. DLS to CM, January 24, 1862, UP.

43. Ibid.; Th. H. (Theophilus H.) Holmes to DLS, January 21, 1862, UP.

44. DLS to CM, January 29, 1862, UP.

45. M. Fetter, Bursar, to CM, Treasurer, March 31, November 19, 1862, UP; *Weekly Raleigh Register*, May 14, 1862; DLS to CM, April 27, 1862, UP.

46. CM to DLS, April 30, 1862, Swain Papers, SHC; FM, May 2, 1862; B. Craven to Gov. Henry T. Clark, February 24, 1862, Craven Papers, Duke (typescript).

47. DLS to WAG, January 26, 1863, Hamilton et al., *Papers of Graham*, 5:450.

48. *Weekly Raleigh Register*, June 17, 1863.

49. BOTM, October 8, 1863; CM to James A. Seddon, undated ("after 6 Nov. 1863" penciled at top), with copy of BOTM, UP; Battle, *History*, 1:732–33.

50. Battle, *History*, 1:733; Peter Mallett, Conscript Office, to DLS, November 6, 1863, UP; A. Landis Jr., En. Officer, 5th Dist., N.C., to DLS, November 11, 18, 1863, Swain Papers, SHC. See also Corbitt, D. L., "Historical Notes," 3 NCHR 363, 364–66 (1926); Henderson, *Campus of the First State University*, 182; Mitchell, *Legal Aspects of Conscription and Exemption in North Carolina 1861–1865*, 32–33; Powell, *First State University*, 88; Spencer, *Pen and Ink Sketches*, 53; Vickers, *Chapel Hill Illustrated*, 66.

51. S. Maupin to DLS, October 30, 1863, Swain Papers, SHC.

52. M. Fetter, Bursar, to CM, Treasurer, December 1, 1863, May 20, 1864; list dated December 19, 1863, UP; DLS to CM, November 11, 1861, UP.

53. WHB to LMB, February 6, 1864, BFP, SHC; DLS to unidentified recipient (probably ZBV), February 4, 1864, UP; Henry Armand London Jr. to Lil (sister), February 15, 1864, London Papers, SHC (quoted in Tolbert, *Two Hundred Years*, 115, and mentioned in Chapman, *Black Freedom*, 53).

54. R. N. Johnson to DLS, June 12, 1864, Swain Papers, SHC.

55. David A. Barnes, Aid de Camp to the Governor, to DLS, February 4, 1864, in Mobley, *Papers of Vance*, 3:87, and John Lockhart to DLS, February 6, 1864, Swain Papers, SHC.

56. J. M. Morehead to DLS, January 3, 1864, Swain Papers, SHC.

57. BOTM, February 17, 1864; DLS to WAG, April 16, 1864, Hamilton et al., *Papers of Graham*, 6:63; DLS to unidentified recipient (probably Peter Mallett), April 12, 1864, and E. J. Hardin, Conscript Office, to DLS, April 28, 1864, Swain Papers, SHC.

58. DLS to WAG, October 29, 1864, Hamilton et al., *Papers of Graham*, 6:191.

59. BOTM, October 31, 1864; undated document in Swain's hand, Swain Papers, SANC.

60. WAG to DLS, November 26, December 17, 1864, Hamilton et al., *Papers of Graham*, 6:195, 203; Graham Davis, Aid de Camp, to DLS, December 15, 1864, Swain Papers, SHC (with Seddon document dated November 28, 1864).

61. WHB to Richard B (Battle, presumably), January 17, 1865, BFP, SHC; Battle, *History*, 2:422–23.

62. Graham, Colonel H.C., "How North Carolina Went into the War," in *Under Both Flags: A Panorama of the Great Civil War*, 360; A. C. Holt to J. G. de Roulhac Hamilton, May 22, 1911, UP; Battle, *History*, 1:814 (Graham, author, in 1861 UNC class), 817 (Holt).

63. W. J. Martin to UNC BOT, November 11, 1861, and to DLS, July 21, 1862, UP; BOTM, December 10, 13, 1861, December 13, 1862; Battle, *History*, 1:660–61, 696, 726, 737.

64. Handwritten note stating faculty position, November 29, 1861, UP; BOTM, December 13, 1861, February 5, 1862; A. D. Hepburn to DLS, December 5, 1863, Swain Papers, SANC; Battle, *History*, 1:724–25; Hamilton, *Reconstruction*, 619.

65. CM to DLS, December 24, 1844, and Albert B. Dod to DLS, August 22, 1845, Swain Papers, SANC (typescripts in Swain Papers, SHC).

66. DLS to CM, October 8, 1860, Swain Papers, SHC.

67. BOTM, December 3, 1860, December 13, 1861.

68. DLS to CM, January 24, February 4, 14, 1862, UP; CM to DLS, February 6, 1862, Swain Papers, SHC; BOTM, February 5, 1862.

69. FM, February 14, 21, 28, March 7, 1862; Battle, *History*, 1:707, 811.

70. DLS to CM, March 13, 1862, UP; CM to DLS, March 18, 1862, Swain Papers, SHC; ECM, March 18, 1862; undated document in Swain's hand setting forth the proposal, Swain Papers, SANC.

71. Battle, *History*, 1:724–25, 736–37.

72. Charles Phillips to KPB, June 22, 1864, BFP, SHC; ECM, December 12, 1864, January 5, 1865. Charles Phillips and Kemp Battle viewed military instruction unfavorably. See Phillips to Battle, December 8, 1864, BFP, SHC.

73. CM to DLS, February 12, 1860, Swain Papers, SHC.

74. CM to DLS, March 1, 3, 1862, Swain Papers, SHC.

75. DLS to WAG, May 18, 1861, Hamilton et al., *Papers of Graham*, 5:255; William T. Nicholson to DLS, November 11, 1861, Swain Papers, SANC; Battle, *History*, 1:813.

76. DLS to CM, undated, on back of copy of Swain Circular Letter dated July 31, 1861, UP.

77. BOTM, July 2, 1864; Charles Phillips to "My dear Sir" (probably DLS), November 23, 1864, UP; DLS and KPB Resolutions on Faculty Salaries, July 4, 1864, UP.

78. ECM, September 30, 1863, July 5, 1864; Battle, *History*, 1:740.

79. Battle, "David Lowry Swain," *N.C. Journal of Education*, 3:27, 28; Spencer, *Pen and Ink Sketches*, 54; Webb, *Jule Carr*, 18; WAG to DLS, November 4, 1864, Hamilton et al., *Papers of Graham*, 6:191–92; CM to DLS, January 2, 1865, Swain Papers, SHC; BOTM, February 17, July 4, 1864; ECM, December 12, 1864; DLS and faculty members, receipt for specie bonds, January 2, 1865, UP.

80. R. D. Osborne to "Ex-Governor," March 11, 1862, UP.

81. Lloyd I. Beall to DLS, August 29, 1864, Swain Papers, SANC.

82. William J. Headen to DLS, October 28, 1864, ibid.; Battle, *History*, 1:813.

83. DLS to WAG, January 26, 1863, Hamilton et al., *Papers of Graham*, 5:449–51; FM, April 8, 1864; illegible to DLS, May 9, 1864, Swain Papers, SANC.

84. J. T. Morehead to DLS, November 6, 1863; E. J. Hale to DLS, May 28, 1863, Swain Papers, SHC.

85. S. N.(?) Patterson to DLS, April 1, 1862, ibid.

86. E. J. Hale to DLS, June 16, 1864, ibid.

Chapter 24: Reunion, Controversial Union

1. Tucker, *Zeb Vance*, 11; Johnston, *Papers of Vance*, 1:xxiii, 4n.16, 9n.45, 155n.634.

2. Mobley, "*War Governor of the South*," 29–32; Charles Manly to DLS, August 14, 1862, Swain Papers, SHC.

3. DLS to ZBV, August 15, 1862, Vance Papers, SANC (published in Johnston, *Papers of Vance*, 1:152–55); see Tucker, *Zeb Vance*, 158. On Manly as courier, see CM to DLS, August 18, 1862, Swain Papers, SANC.

4. ZBV to DLS, August 25, 1862, Vance Papers, SANC; R. H. Battle to ZBV, September 2, 1862, in Johnston, *Papers of Vance*, 1:162 (accepts offer of private-secretary position "made ... through our mutual friend Gov. Swain"); see Dowd, *Life of Vance*, 166, and Tucker, *Zeb Vance*, 158.

5. DLS to ZBV, September 15, 1862, Vance Papers, SANC, and November 25, 1862, in Johnston, *Papers of Vance*, 1:395–96, 395n.323.

6. ZBV to DLS, October 20, 1863, Vance Papers, SANC.

7. ZBV to DLS, January 2, 1864, in Johnston, *Papers of Vance*, 1:7–9; Mobley, *"War Governor of the South,"* 113–15; Yates, "Governor Vance and the Peace Movement," 17 NCHR 1, 23–25; Mobley, "Zebulon Baird Vance: A Confederate Nationalist in the North Carolina Gubernatorial Election of 1864," 77 NCHR 434, 440.

8. DLS to ZBV, January 14, 1864, Vance Papers, SANC; see also DLS to ZBV, February 11, 1864, ibid.

9. DLS to ZBV, August 24, 1864, ibid.

10. DLS to ZBV, September 18, 1864, ibid.

11. ZBV to DLS, September 22, 1864, in Johnston, *Papers of Vance*, 1:279–80; see Inscoe and McKinney, *Heart of Confederate Appalachia*, 232; Shirley, *Zeb Vance, Tarheel Spokesman*, 49–50; Bardolph, "Confederate Dilemma: North Carolina Troops and the Deserter Problem," 66 NCHR 179, 210; R. D. W. Connor, Book Review, 3 NCHR 377–79. The letter was referred to and quoted in the *New York Times* on January 16, 1885.

12. DLS to ZBV, September 26, 1864, Vance Papers, SANC (published in Johnston, *Papers of Vance*, 1:284–86 (and see 1:286n.2).

13. DLS to ZBV, September 28, 1864, Vance Papers, SANC.

14. DLS to ZBV, January 21, 1865, Vance Papers, SANC (published in Mobley, *Papers of Vance*, 3:393–95; Escott, *Many Excellent People*, 50. Swain was now writing his letters on what appear to be census forms, which suggests a shortage of regular paper.

15. DLS to ZBV, January 25, 1865, Vance Papers, SANC (published in Mobley, *Papers of Vance*, 3:396–97).

16. DLS to ZBV, February 8, 14, 1865, Vance Papers, SANC.

17. ZBV to DLS, January 11,1864, and DLS to ZBV, January 1< 2 >3, 1864, Vance Papers, SANC (published in Mobley, *Papers of Vance*, 3:43–44, 48–49); John Berry to DLS, January 13, 1864, Hamilton et al., *Papers of Graham*, 6:6; WAG to Edward J. Hale, January 29, 1864, ibid., 6:19. See Hamilton, J. G. de R, "Swain, David Lowry," Malone, *Dictionary of American Biography*, 18:230; Hamilton, *Reconstruction*, 56; Yearns Jr., "North Carolina in the Confederate Congress," 29 NCHR 359, 366.

18. WAG to DLS, August 15, 1864, Hamilton et al., *Papers of Graham*, 6:162; DLS to CM, July 6, 1864, UP.

19. DLS to ZBV, January 21, 1865, Vance Papers, SANC; WAG to DLS, January 28, February 12, 1865, Hamilton et al., *Papers of Graham*, 6:226–27, 233. See Bradley, "'This Monstrous Proposition': North Carolina and the Confederate Debate on Arming the Slaves," 80 NCHR 153, 169, 174.

20. WAG to DLS, February 5, 12, 1865, Hamilton et al., *Papers of Graham*, 6:228–29, 236.

21. DLS to WAG, February 18, 1865, ibid., 6:247–48.

22. WAG to DLS, February 22, March 12, 1865, ibid., 6:252–54, 283–84.

23. DLS to WAG, March 23, 1865, ibid., 6:285–86.
24. WAG to DLS, March 26, 1865, ibid., 6:289–90.
25. CM to DLS, January 6, 1865, Swain Papers, SHC.
26. DLS to WAG, April 8, 1865, Hamilton et al., *Papers of Graham*, 6:292–93.
27. WAG to DLS, April 8, 1865, ibid., 6:294–97.
28. WAG to DLS, April [9?], 1865, ibid., 6:297.
29. ZBV to Wm. T. Sherman, April 11, 1865, Spencer Papers, SHC (published in Hamilton et al., *Papers of Graham*, 6:299); WAG and DLS to Wm. T. Sherman, April 12, 1865, Hamilton et al., *Papers of Graham*, 6:298; W.T. Sherman to ZBV, April 12, 1865, Spencer Papers, SHC; Wade Hampton to WAG, April 14, 1865, Hamilton et al., *Papers of Graham*, 6:302. The Hitchcock quote is in Howe, *Marching with Sherman*, 296–97. See Battle, *History*, 1:528. There are numerous accounts of, or references to, the Swain–Graham mission to Sherman, e.g., the following:

Books: Ballard, *A Long Shadow*, 58, 84–85; Barrett, *Civil War in North Carolina*, 372–77; Barrett, *Sherman's March Through the Carolinas*, 203–65; Battle, *History*, 1:740–44; Battle, *Memories of an Old-Time Tar Heel*, 192; Battle, *Sketch of Wilson Caldwell*, 5; Blackwelder, *Age of Orange*, 185; Boyd, *History of North Carolina* (vol. 3, *North Carolina Since 1860*), 34–35; Bradley, *This Astounding Close*, 93–185; Chamberlain, *Old Days in Chapel Hill*, 84–85; Cheney, *North Carolina Government*, 384; Dowd, *Life of Vance*, 483–85; Hamilton, *Reconstruction*, 96–99; Johnston, *Papers of Vance*, 1:lxxii; Jones, *For History's Sake*, 96; Konkle, *Morehead*, 409, 409n.1; Lewis, *Sherman: Fighting Prophet*, 529–32; Mobley, "War Governor of the South," 194–99; Peele, *Lives*, 363–64; Raper, *William W. Holden*, 274n.48; Murray, *Wake: Capital County*, 1:505–7, 519; Robinson, *North Carolina Guide*, 234; Russell, *Woman Who Rang the Bell*, 54–55; Shirley, *Zeb Vance, Tarheel Spokesman*, 57; Spencer, *First Steps in North Carolina History*, 221–22; Spencer, *Last Ninety Days*, passim; Tucker, *Zeb Vance*, 390–404; Vickers, *Chapel Hill Illustrated*, 69–72; WPA Writers Program, *Raleigh: Capital of North Carolina*, 32–33; Hamilton et al., *Papers of Graham*, 6:xi; Zuber, *Jonathan Worth: A Biography of a Southern Unionist*, 187–88.

Articles: Roland Giduz, "President Swain's Locomotive Ride, Appeal to Sherman, Saved the University," *Alumni Review* (September 1977), 6–7; McKinney, "Zeb Vance and His Reconstruction of the Civil War in North Carolina," 75 NCHR 69, 72–81; Mobley, "Zebulon Baird Vance: A Confederate Nationalist in the North Carolina Gubernatorial Election of 1864," 77 NCHR 434, 449–52; Yates, "Governor Vance and the End of the War in North Carolina," 18 NCHR 315, 328–31.

Newspapers: *Daily Evening Bulletin*, April 27, 1865; *Lenoir Topic*, October 14, 1885; *Farmer and Mechanic*, March 28, 1905.

30. CM to DLS, March 29, April 8, 1865, Swain Papers, SHC, and CM to CPS, April 25, 1866, Spencer Papers, SHC; Jones, *For History's Sake*, 104.

31. DLS to Major General W. T. Sherman, April 19, 1865, and W. T. Sherman to DLS, April 22, 1865, Swain Papers, SHC; George W. Mordecai to DLS, May 15, 1865, Clark Papers, SANC; *Ninety-Second Illinois Volunteers*, 244–45; Barrett, *Sherman's March Through the Carolinas*, 250; Battle, *History*, 1:743–44; Bradley, *This Astounding Close*, 185–86; Vickers, *Chapel Hill Illustrated*, 75.

32. FM, April 28, 1865; WHB to KPB, June 1, 1865, BFP, SHC; Battle, *History*, 1:746; Chamberlain, *Old Days in Chapel Hill*, 87–89.

33. DLS to WAG, April 8, 1865, Hamilton et al., *Papers of Graham*, 6:292–93; Bridges, *Masonic Governors*, 153.

34. Battle, *History*, 1:742; Chamberlain, *Old Days in Chapel Hill*, 82–85; Henderson, *Campus of the First State University*, 182–87; Spencer, *Last Ninety Days*, 165–66; Webb, *Jule Carr*, 21, 25. See generally Phillips, *Diehard Rebels*, especially chapter 3 and the epilogue.

35. Beggin, *Primary Sources*, 14; Carpenter, "General Smith D. Atkins, In Memoriam," *Transactions of the Illinois State Historical Society for the Year 1913*, 83; *Ninety-Second Illinois Volunteers*, 27.

36. DLS to G. J. McRee, September 20, 1844, McRee Papers, SHC (typescript in Swain Papers, SHC); DLS to WAG, January 24, 1845, Hamilton et al., *Papers of Graham*, 3:16–17.

37. Menius, "Love and Looting in Chapel Hill, the Last Town Standing," *Chapel Hill News*, April 15, 2015; Bartholome, "She Married a Yankee," *Durham Morning Herald*, October 7, 1951; Chamberlain, *Old Days in Chapel Hill*, 94–95.

38. Ella Swain to CPS, May 12, 1865, Spencer Papers, SHC.

39. DLS to B. S. Hedrick, June 3, 16, 1865, Hedrick Papers, Duke; Russell, *Woman Who Rang the Bell*, 67; Spencer, *Pen and Ink Sketches*, 61.

40. Chamberlain, *Old Days in Chapel Hill*, 95–97; Russell, *Woman Who Rang the Bell*, 66–67.

41. Chamberlain, *Old Days in Chapel Hill*, 98; Russell, *Woman Who Rang the Bell*, 69; Vickers, *Chapel Hill Illustrated*, 76 (quote).

42. WHB to KPB, August 22, 1865, BFP, SHC; Barile, *Undaunted Heart*, 63; Chamberlain, *Old Days in Chapel Hill*, 99; Russell, *Woman Who Rang the Bell*, 69–70; Vickers, *Chapel Hill Illustrated*, 76.

43. WHB to KPB, August 22, 1865, BFP, SHC; Barile, *Undaunted Heart*, 63–65; Chapman, *Black Freedom*, 89–91; Russell, *Woman Who Rang the Bell*, 69.

44. Barile, *Undaunted Heart*, 65–66.

45. Ibid., 64; Powell, *First State University*, 89; Vickers, *Chapel Hill Illustrated*, 76; Webb, *Jule Carr*, 24–25.

46. Laura D. Hughes to DLS, August 26, 1865, Swain Papers, SANC; DLS to ZBV, September 12, October 18, November 1, 1865, Vance Papers, SANC.

47. *New Berne Times*, September 14, 1865.

48. Charles Peter Mallett to Margaret (Maggie) Mallett, September 30, 1866, Mallett Papers, SHC; CPS to Mrs. Summerell, September 30, 1866 (apparently), in Chamberlain, *Old Days in Chapel Hill*, 131–32.

49. Chamberlain, *Old Days in Chapel Hill*, 99.

50. Spencer, *Pen and Ink Sketches*, 58–61; CPS to EHS, June 26, 1869, Spencer Papers, SANC (published in Wilson, *Papers of Spencer*, 627–28).

51. The story of Ellie and the general is probably the best-known aspect of the Swain history. It is the subject of a full-length book by the couple's great-great-granddaughter: Barile, *Undaunted Heart*. For other accounts see Barringer, *Natural Bent: The Memoirs of Dr. Paul B. Barringer*, 109–10; Chamberlain, *Old Days in Chapel Hill*, 80–100; Ehle, "The Yankee Loves a Lady" (a fictionalized account based on fact); Jones, *For History's Sake*, 263; Murray, *Wake: Capital County*, 2:530n.163; Vickers, *Chapel Hill Illustrated*, 73–76; Hamilton et al., *Papers of Graham*, 7:92–93n.67, 8:339–40n.4; Wilson, *Library of the First State University*, 16n. In addition to the newspaper stories cited earlier in these notes, see Daniels, "The Love Story That Rocked the State," *Raleigh Times*, February 9, 1957. As recently as August 23, 2012, while this work was in process, *The Daily Tar Heel*, the UNC student newspaper, noted an anniversary date of the Atkins-Swain marriage. "Town and state residents didn't approve," the paper observed laconically. Russell, *Woman Who Rang the Bell*, 283–86, suggests that another Union general set up General Atkins for his initial encounter with Ellie Swain.

Chapter 25: Reconstruction

1. Edwin M. Stanton to DLS, May 27, 1865, Swain Papers, SHC; Ashe, *Biographical History*, 1:457; Bridges, *Masonic Governors*, 153; *Daily Intelligencer*, June 6, 1865; *New York Times*, June 7, August 1, 1865.

2. *New York Times*, June 7, 1865; DLS to B. S. Hedrick, June 3, 1865, Hedrick Papers, Duke; Joshua I. Cohen to DLS, July 24, 1865, Swain Papers, SHC.

3. DLS to B. S. Hedrick, June 3, 1865, Hedrick Papers, Duke.

4. "Swain's Report on West Point," undated, Swain Papers, SHC; *New York Times*, August 1, 1865.

5. Mobley, *"War Governor of the South,"* 212.

6. Folk and Shaw, *W. W. Holden: A Political Biography*, 197; Hamilton, *Reconstruction*, 106–7; Harris, *William Woods Holden*, 161–63; Holden, *Memoirs of W. W. Holden*, 45–47; Raper, *William W. Holden: North Carolina's Political Enigma*, 60–61; Wheeler, *Reminiscences*, 59–61; Padgett, "Reconstruction Letters from North

Carolina," 18 NCHR 278, 296–97n.65; *Daily Standard*, May 27, 1865; DLS to WAG, July 4, 1865, Graham Papers, SANC (cited and quoted in Carter, *When the War Was Over*, 26); DLS to Thomas Ruffin, September 15, 1865, in Hamilton, *Papers of Ruffin*, 4:28 (cited and quoted in Raper, *Holden*, 274n.6).

7. Wheeler, *Reminiscences*, 59, 61.

8. Chamberlain, *Old Days in Chapel Hill*, 113–14; Russell, *Woman Who Rang the Bell*, 71.

9. DLS to ZBV, October 18, 1865, Vance Papers, SANC; Chamberlain, *Old Days in Chapel Hill*, 117. While favorable, Swain's view of Johnson was not nearly so euphoric as that of his childhood friend, Benjamin F. Perry, who served as governor of South Carolina. Early in the Johnson administration Perry wrote Swain: "How admirably our friend Andy Johnson has behaved! How nobly he has exercised the powers of his high office for the good of the whole country! He is a wonderful man! . . . He has shown in the administration of the Presidency all the purity of Washington with the genius of Jefferson, and firmness of Jackson." B. F. Perry to DLS, June 27, 1866, Swain Papers, SHC. Modern historians view Johnson quite differently; see, e.g., Gordon-Reed, *Andrew Johnson*. Swain's ardor, too, later cooled somewhat, as he "spoke contemptuously of the poor boy who became president." Escott, *Many Excellent People*, 91, citing DLS to Thomas Ruffin, November 13, 1865, in Hamilton, *Papers of Ruffin*, 4:37–39.

10. Chamberlain, *Old Days in Chapel Hill*, 121.

11. Hamilton, *Reconstruction*, 168–69; Zuber, *Jonathan Worth*, 246–47; *The Conservative*, December 21, 1866; *Carolina Watchman*, December 24, 1866. Chapman's statement that the visit was "to no avail" is inaccurate; it was partially successful. See Chapman, *Black Freedom*, 109.

12. John H. Wheeler to DLS, October 17, 1866, BFP, SHC; Jonathan Worth to DLS, March 3, 1867, in Hamilton, *Correspondence of Jonathan Worth*, 2:908–9; DLS to Gov. Jonathan Worth, March 6, 7, 1867, Worth Papers, SANC; Zuber, *Jonathan Worth*, 252; Thomas Ruffin to DLS, March 14, 1867, Clark Papers, SANC.

13. DLS to Andrew Johnson, November 1, 1867, in McPherson, "Letters from North Carolina to Andrew Johnson," 29 NCHR 400, 403 (original in Johnson Papers, Library of Congress; microfilm copy in Davis Library, UNC-CH); Murray, *Wake: Capital County*, 1:586, 590–92.

14. The original petition is in the National Archives, Washington, D.C. A copy is in the North Carolina State Archives, Raleigh, N.C. See also Graf et al., *Papers of Johnson*, 9:56–57; Dorris, "Pardoning North Carolinians," 23 NCHR 360, 370. On Holden's role in pardons, see Harris, *William Woods Holden*, 164. For another reference to the diminution of Swain's estate as a result of the Civil War, see DLS to ZBV, September 12, 1865, Vance Papers, SANC ("my estate was lessened more than one half").

15. DLS to ZBV, October 18, 1865, Vance Papers, SANC; Carter, *When the War Was Over*, 52; see Dorris, "Pardoning North Carolinians," 370n.42. "[M]ore than six hundred prominent North Carolinians were pardoned just before the election of 1865." Franklin, *Reconstruction: After the Civil War*, 33.

16. (First name illegible) J. Might to DLS, May 1, 1866, Swain Papers, SHC (conveyed Davis's thanks to Swain); C. W. Long to DLS, May 18, 1866, ibid.

17. W. N. Edwards to DLS, July 5, November 1, 1865, Swain Papers, SHC.

18. Henry T. Clark to DLS, December 16, 1866, ibid.

19. DLS to ZBV, October 18, 1865, Vance Papers, SANC.

20. ZBV to DLS, January 8, 1866, ibid. The recipient is not identified, but the contents point unmistakably to Swain as the addressee.

21. ZBV to DLS, January 12, 1866, ibid.; *Resolution of N.C. General Assembly*, December 5, 1865, in Vance Papers, SANC.

22. DLS to ZBV, January 15, 1866, ibid.; Shirley, *Zeb Vance, Tarheel Spokesman*, 61.

23. DLS to ZBV, October 11, 20, 1866, Vance Papers, SANC.

24. *Vance Pardon*, March 11, 1867, SANC; Tucker, *Zeb Vance*, 429–30.

25. WAG to DLS, October 16, 1865, Hamilton et al., *Papers of Graham*, 6:412, 412n.275; John A. Gilmer to ZBV, October 14, 1865, Vance Papers, SANC.

26. DLS to WAG, December 27, 1866, Hamilton et al., *Papers of Graham*, 7:242.

27. WAG to DLS, January 25, 1867, ibid., 7:256. See ibid., 7:2n.2: "Graham's pardon was signed on December 4, 1865, but was not transmitted to him until May 2, 1867. By that time his rights were proscribed by the congressional reconstruction acts; his political disabilities were not removed until 1873." On Graham's difficulty in securing a pardon, see Harris, *William Woods Holden*, 183–85.

28. CPS to WAG, February 12, 22, 1866, Hamilton et al., *Papers of Graham*, 7:40, 53; Chamberlain, *Old Days in Chapel Hill*, 102–3; Lefler, *North Carolina History Told By Contemporaries*, 309; Gwin, "'Poisoned Arrows' From a Tar Heel Journalist," 7 (Swain a "father figure" with tremendous influence on Spencer), 18, 20, 28; Link, William A., "Cornelia Phillips Spencer," in Gillespie and McMillan, *North Carolina Women*, 138–39; Wright, "'The Grown-Up Daughter': The Case of North Carolina's Cornelia Phillips Spencer," 74 NCHR 260, 272–73; Charles Phillips to J. B. Killibrew, March 12, 1866, BFP, SHC; Spencer, *Last Ninety Days*, unnumbered dedication page.

29. DLS to ZBV, October 30, November 1, 20, 30, Vance Papers, SANC.

30. CPS to ZBV, October 30, 1865, ibid.

31. ZBV to CPS, November 1, 1865, ibid.

32. CPS to ZBV, November 11, 1865, ibid.

33. ZBV to CPS, November 15, 1865, Spencer Papers, SHC (also quoted in Chamberlain, *Old Days in Chapel Hill*, 104).

34. ZBV to CPS, February 17, April 7, 1866, Spencer Papers, SHC.

35. CPS to ZBV, February 12, April 25, 1866, Vance Papers, SANC.

36. ZBV to CPS, April 27, 1866, Spencer Papers, SHC.

37. CPS to ZBV, May 4, 1866, Vance Papers, SANC. Spencer probably was unaware of it, but she was making a good argument for leaving history to the historians, not to the immediate actors.

38. CPS to ZBV, August 28, 1866, Vance Papers, SANC.

39. ZBV to CPS, August 27, 31, 1866, Spencer Papers, SHC.

40. CPS to ZBV, October 11, 1866, Vance Papers, SANC, and ZBV to CPS, October 14, 1866, Spencer Papers, SHC.

41. ZBV to CPS, January 8, 1867, Spencer Papers, SHC.

42. Spencer, *Last Ninety Days*, 165–66.

43. CPS to WAG, February 12, 1866, Hamilton et al., *Papers of Graham*, 7:39–40.

44. WAG to CPS, February 20, 1866, ibid., 7:47–51, 51n.1.

45. CPS to WAG, February 22, 1866, ibid., 7:53–54.

46. A. M. McPheeters to CPS, April 11, 1866, Spencer Papers, SHC.

47. CM to CPS, April 25, 1866, ibid.

48. KPB to CPS, August 28, 1866, ibid.

49. S. F. Patterson to DLS, May 15, 1866, Swain Papers, SHC; DLS to KPB and R.H. Battle, Esqs., August 23, 1866; CPS to KPB, August 30, 1866; DLS to KPB (apparently), September 21, 1866, BFP, SHC.

50. Chamberlain, *Old Days in Chapel Hill*, 102–3; Russell, *Woman Who Rang the Bell*, 88, 90–91; Sutherland, "Charles Force Deems and the *Watchman*: An Early Attempt at Post-Civil War Sectional Reconciliation," 57 NCHR 410, passim.

51. Charles F. Deems to CPS, January 19, February 27, August 18, 1866, Spencer Papers, SHC.

52. CPS to ("Dr. Wilson" penciled on), March 7, 1866; E. J. Hale to CPS, July 19, 1866, Spencer Papers, SHC.

53. Charles F. Deems to DLS, August 30, 1866, and DLS to Rev. Dr. Deems, September 4, 1866, Swain Papers, SHC.

54. Charles F. Deems to DLS, September 4, 1866, ibid.

55. Charles F. Deems to CPS, September 14, 1866, Spencer Papers, SHC.

56. C. F. Deems to DLS, August 24, 1866, Swain Papers, SHC.

57. Charles F. Deems to CPS, August 20, 1866, Spencer Papers, SHC, and October 5, 1867, Spencer Papers, SANC.

58. Chamberlain, *Old Days in Chapel Hill*, 124–25.

59. Francis Lieber to DLS, February 15, 1867, and William J. (I.?) Rivers to DLS, January 23, 1868, Swain Papers, SHC; John H. Wheeler to DLS, October 17, 1866, BFP, SHC.

60. DLS to Andrew Johnson, March 31, 1866, Library of Congress (published in Graf et al., *Papers of Johnson*, 10:338).

61. James Buchanan to DLS, February 14, 1867, Clark Papers, SANC.

62. DLS to KPB, January 12, 1867, BFP, SHC, and DLS to CPS, April 24, 1867, Spencer Papers, SANC.

63. Charles F. Deems to DLS, January 24, 1867, Swain Papers, SHC.

64. Charles F. Deems to KPB, August 20, October 24, 1867, BFP, SHC.

65. DLS to KPB, October 10, 14, 1867, ibid.

66. CPS to KPB, June 11, 1868, and DLS to KPB, June 18, 1868, BFP, SHC.

67. DLS to KPB (not shown, but obvious), July 30, 1868; Printed Circular Letter, July 1868, BFP, SHC.

68. DLS to ZBV, January 20, May 10, 1866; CPS to ZBV, October 11, 1866, Vance Papers, SANC.

69. Gwin, "'Poisoned Arrows' From a Tar Heel Journalist," 34, 54.

70. Ibid., 25, 72. For an excellent account of the production of *Last Ninety Days*, see Inscoe, John C., "To Do Justice to North Carolina: The War's End according to Cornelia Phillips Spencer, Zebulon B. Vance, and David L. Swain," in Escott, *North Carolinians in the Era of the Civil War and Reconstruction*, 129–53. For the work itself, see Spencer, *Last Ninety Days*.

71. DLS to WAG, January 1, 1865 [1866], Hamilton et al., *Papers of Graham*, 7:1–2, 5n.13; DLS to KPB (not shown, but in context, almost certainly), September 21, 1866, BFP, SHC.

72. WAG to DLS, June 1, 30, September 8, 1866, Hamilton et al., *Papers of Graham*, 7:122, 142, 206; DLS to WAG, June 25, September 10, 1866, ibid., 140, 209.

73. WAG to DLS, March 9, 1867, ibid., 279.

74. See, e.g., DLS to ZBV, August 11, 1865, Vance Papers, SANC; DLS to WAG, March 19, 1867, Hamilton et al., *Papers of Graham*, 7:296.

75. *Raleigh Sentinel*, December 14, 1866.

76. DLS to KPB, September 21, 1866, July 30, 1867, BFP, SHC; DLS to B. S. Hedrick, June 6, 1866, Hedrick Papers, Duke.

77. DLS to KPB (probably), September 21, 1866, BFP, SHC; H. B. Hardy to DLS, January 13, 1866, Swain Papers, SANC.

78. Macchim M' Clung to DLS, March 29, 1867, Swain Papers, SANC; W. R. Hill to DLS, October 26, 1865, Swain Papers, SHC; see also E. J. Hale to DLS, February 17, 1868, Clark Papers, SANC.

79. James E. Beasley to DLS, December 21, 1865, in Corbett, D. L., "Historical Notes," 3 NCHR 366–67.

80. Charles Phillips to KPB, February 6, March 29, August 12, 1867, February 24, July 29, 1868, BFP, SHC; CM to Rev. Basil Manly, August 4, 1868 (copy), UP; WAG to DLS, November 11, 1867, Hamilton et al., *Papers of Graham*, 7:402.

81. J. R. Siler to DLS, April 12, 1866, Swain Papers, SHC, and March 4, 1867, Swain Papers, SANC.

82. George N. Kirk to DLS, June 23, 1865, Swain Papers, SHC.

83. DLS to WAG, May 6, July 7, 1865, Hamilton et al., *Papers of Graham*, 6:309, 324.

84. WAG to DLS, May 11, October 16, 1865, Hamilton et al., *Papers of Graham*, 6:311, 413–14.

85. Alexander, *North Carolina Faces the Freedmen*, 20; Foner, *Reconstruction*, 120 (citing Chamberlain, *Old Days in Chapel Hill*, 117); H. C. Thompson to Benjamin S. Hedrick, September 14, 1865, Hedrick Papers, Duke; *People's Press*, Salem, N.C., September 23, 1865.

86. Hamilton, *Reconstruction*, 151; Raper, *William W. Holden*, 71; DLS to ZBV, October 11, 1866, Vance Papers, SANC; DLS to KPB, October 20, 21, 1866, BFP, SHC.

87. DLS to ZBV, October 20, 1866, Vance Papers, SANC; DLS to WAG, March 15, 1867, Hamilton et al., *Papers of Graham*, 7:292.

88. DLS to WAG, February 1, March 10, 1868, Hamilton et al., *Papers of Graham*, 7:463–65, 518.

89. Letter One: Hamilton et al., *Papers of Graham*, 7:234–37; *New York Times*, November 26, 1866; *Hillsborough Recorder*, December 19, 1866. Letter Two: *Daily Journal*, December 11, 1866. Letter Three: *Semi-Weekly Raleigh Sentinel*, January 9, 1867. On Benjamin F. Perry, see West, Stephen A., "Perry, Benjamin Franklin," Garraty and Carnes, *American National Biography*, 17:362–63.

90. WAG to DLS, November 6, 1866, Hamilton et al., *Papers of Graham*, 7:222–23; January 25, 1867, ibid., 256; March 9, 1867, ibid., 279; June 1, 1867, Clark Papers, SANC.

Chapter 26: Decline and Fall

1. Battle, *Sketches of the History of the University of North Carolina*, 49; William T. Rivers to DLS, February 22, 1868, Swain Papers, SANC.

2. DLS to Elias Carr, October 22, 1864, Carr Papers, ECU; Chamberlain, *Old Days in Chapel Hill*, 115, 123; receipt from *Montgomery Advertiser*, November 1, 1865 ("To adv. U. of NC"), UP.

3. BOTM, December 11, 1865, December 10, 11, 22, 1866; ECM, January 12, 26, 1867; note signed by DLS, "Feby–1867," Swain Papers, SANC; Charles Manly to DLS, February 5 (?), 1867, Clark Papers, SANC.

4. Battle, *History*, 2:4; Chamberlain, *Old Days in Chapel Hill*, 124–25, 133; Russell, *Woman Who Rang the Bell*, 83; Snider, *Light on the Hill*, 66; CPS to Ellen Summerell, 1866 (penciled on), Spencer Papers, SHC.

5. DLS to KPB, July 14, 1864, BFP, SHC; DLS to WAG, August 8, September 15, 1859, Hamilton et al., *Papers of Graham*, 5:111, 118–19.

6. Henderson, *Campus of the First State University*, 207–8; Russell, *Woman Who Rang the Bell*, 73, 286–87; Spencer, *Pen and Ink Sketches*, 55; WHB to KPB, August 22, 1865, BFP, SHC; Charles Phillips to J. B. Killibrew, March 12, 1866, ibid.

7. Incomplete DLS drafts on the condition and needs of the university, dated October 10, 1867, UP.

8. ECM, September 19, 1865; Battle, *History*, 1:754–55, 2:50; DLS to Thomas Ruffin, November 13, 1865, in Hamilton, *Papers of Ruffin*, 4:37; DLS to WAG, Hamilton et al., *Papers of Graham*, 6:394–96; Barile, *Undaunted Heart*, 75, 107; Wright, "'The Grown-up Daughter': The Case of North Carolina's Cornelia Phillips Spencer," 74 NCHR 260, 273.

9. DLS to KPB, August 11, 1865, BFP, SHC; Francis L. Hawks to DLS, August 14, 1865, Swain Papers, SHC.

10. BOTM, December 22, 1866, January 21, 28, 1867; Thomas Ruffin to DLS, January 21, 1867, UP.

11. CPS to ("Dr. Wilson" penciled on), March 7, 1866, Spencer Papers, SHC; Chamberlain, *Old Days in Chapel Hill*, 126; Spencer, *Pen and Ink Sketches*, 62–63; ECM, March 5, 1866.

12. DLS to Benjamin S. Hedrick, April 26, May 17, 23, June 20, 1866, Hedrick Papers, Duke; Smith, *A Traitor and a Scoundrel*, 139.

13. Battle, *History*, 1:756–57; Chamberlain, *Old Days in Chapel Hill*, 124; Henderson, *Campus of the First State University*, 197; Spencer, *Pen and Ink Sketches*, 65; "Report of State Treasurer," *Old North State*, January 3, 1867; Joseph J. Davis to DLS, February 4, 8, 1867, Swain Papers, SHC.

14. DLS to WAG, March 16, 1867, Hamilton et al., *Papers of Graham*, 7:295–96; Thomas Ruffin to DLS, March 14, 1867, Clark Papers, SANC; DLS to CM, May 20, 1867, BFP, SHC.

15. BOTM, June 27, 1867; G.F. Lewis to DLS, March 4, May 14, June 19, December 23, 1867, UP; DLS to KPB, July 17, 1867, BFP, SHC; KPB to DLS, July 18, 1867, Clark Papers, SANC; KPB to DLS, July 18, 1867, ibid.; WHB to KPB, July 20, 1867, BFP, SHC; WAG to DLS, July 20, 1867, Clark Papers, SANC.

16. Battle, *History*, 1:757; Hamilton, *Reconstruction*, 620; Henderson, *Campus of the First State University*, 197; Hamilton et al., *Papers of Graham*, 7:293n.12.

17. Foner, *Reconstruction*, 125; W. H. S. Burgwyn to DLS, December 16, 1867, Clark Papers, SANC; John L. Nadly Jr. to DLS, March 14, 1868, ibid. The Burgwyn letter noted that he had met General Robert E. Lee and his family at a wedding in Richmond. "I . . . marked him particularly," Burgwyn said, "and would not have wished to have formed my opinion of him from what I saw of his intercourse with beautiful young girls."

18. A. D. Hepburn to KPB, October 16, 1867, UP.

19. (Illegible) to DLS, January 20, 1867, ibid.; Benson J. Lossing to DLS, November 22, 1865, Swain Papers, SHC; Thomas Ruffin to DLS, 24th (month not shown), 1867, Clark Papers, SANC.

20. WHB to KPB, October 12, 1857, UP; DLS to KPB, October 14, 1867, BFP, SHC; ZBV to KPB, October 7, 1867, UP.

21. ECM, September 18, 1867; DLS to (recipient not identified), October 10, 1867, UP.

22. Circular letter, UNC BOT to "the people of the State," 1867 (see ECM, September 18, 1867).

23. CM to DLS, June 4, 1866, UP; Charles Phillips to KPB, March 20, 1867, BFP, SHC; Salary Arrearages, Report of January 26, 1867, UP.

24. A. D. Hepburn to DLS, April 3, 1867, and A.D. Hepburn to KPB, June 25, 1867, UP; BOTM, June 27, 1867; Spencer, *Pen and Ink Sketches*, 63.

25. W. J. Martin to UNC BOT, July 13, 1867, UP; W. J. Martin to KPB, July 18, 1867, BFP, SHC; DLS to KPB, July 17, 1867, ibid.

26. Solomon Pool to UNC BOT, June 6, 1866, UP; FM, July 23, 1866.

27. F. M. Hubbard to Jonathan Worth, August 28, 1867, UP; F.M. Hubbard to WAG, February 6, 1868, Hamilton et al., *Papers of Graham*, 7:491.

28. WHB to KPB, March 2, 1867, March 4, 1868, July 28, 1868, BFP, SHC.

29. DLS to WAG, March 10, 1868, Hamilton et al., *Papers of Graham*, 7:519; F. Porter to Jonathan Worth, August 19, 1867. UP.

30. Unidentified and undated newspaper in Swain Papers, SANC; George M. Maverick to Charles Phillips, December 8, 1867, UP.

31. A. D. Hepburn to DLS, June 23, 1866, Swain Papers, SHC; C. B. Hassell to Charles Manly, June 12, 1867, UP; Charles Phillips to KPB, July 5, 1866, January 24, 1867, BFP, SHC. In a later letter to KPB, Phillips noted additionally the 300 students at the Virginia Military Institute. Charles Phillips to KPB, November 24, 1867, UP.

32. Spencer, *Pen and Ink Sketches*, 64; *Weekly Progress*, December 15, 1866.

33. Wm. Bingham to KPB, August 31, 1867, UP; see also Wm. Bingham to Rev. C. Phillips, September 20, 1866, ibid.

34. John Wilson Jr. to KPB, November 23, 1867, UP.

35. A. D. Hepburn to DLS, "[1866–1867]" penciled on, UP.

36. W. J. Martin to KPB, June 26, July 15, 1867, BFP, SHC.

37. Charles Phillips to KPB, June 23, July 5, 1866, August 6, 12, 1867, BFP, SHC. In this time frame Swain told a Lane relative that his son Richard Swain had been a surgeon in the Union army. Richard served in the Confederate army. This suggests the possibility that in addition to his severe hearing problem, Swain was experiencing some mental decline. DLS to Henry S. Lane, June 13, 1867, EC, NCC.

38. WHB to KPB, August 1, 1867, BFP, SHC.

39. KPB to Charles Phillips, August 7, 1867, BFP, SHC.

40. Spencer, *Pen and Ink Sketches*, 58–61.

41. R. L. Beall to CPS, July 19, 1866, Spencer Papers, SHC; H. [Hugh] Strong to DLS, October 27, 1866, UP (see Battle, *History*, 1:803, 813).

42. W. H. S. Burgwyn et al. to DLS, July 29, 1867; Wm. S. Pearson et al. to DLS, June 6, 1868; DLS to Wm. S. Pearson et al., June 10, 1868, UP.

43. Henry T. Clark to WAG, October 6, 1867, Hamilton et al., *Papers of Graham*, 7:378.

44. BOTM, December 18, 1867.

45. Battle, "David Lowry Swain," *North Carolina Journal of Education*, 3:27–30; Russell, *Woman Who Rang the Bell*, 108.

46. BOTM, June 7, 1866; WAG to DLS, September 18, 1866, Hamilton et al., *Papers of Graham*, 7:213; C. Phillips to KPB, November 11, 1867, UP.

47. Charles Phillips to KPB, July 20, 1866, December 16, 1867, January 17, 1868, BFP, SHC; Charles Phillips to unidentified recipient, June 26, 1867, UP; Phillips's suggestions re: reform, October 31, 1866, UP.

48. A. D. Hepburn to KPB, September 9, 1867, UP; H. H. Smith to KPB, November 21, 1867, and Smith's suggestions re: reform, November 1, 1866, ibid.; KPB to DLS, August 16, 1867, Clark Papers, SANC.

49. *Report of the Committee in Relation to the University*, January 28, 1867 (penciled on); Memorial, UNC BOT to N.C. General Assembly, January 21, 1867, UP.

50. FM, January 25, 26, 1867.

51. DLS to ZBV, August 15, 1862, Vance Papers, SANC (published in Johnston, *Papers of Vance*, 1:154); Charles Phillips to KPB, December 8, 1864, BFP, SHC.

52. DLS to ZBV, January 13, 1865, Vance Papers, SANC; Barile, *Undaunted Heart*, 84–85.

53. DLS to ZBV, January 21, 1865 (published in Mobley, *Papers of Vance*, 3:393), February 14, 1865, Vance Papers, SANC.

54. Anne Swain to CPS, December 1866 (penciled on), Spencer Papers, SHC; DLS to WAG, March 15, 16, 19, 1867, Hamilton et al., *Papers of Graham*, 7:290, 296, 297; Barile, *Undaunted Heart*, 81, 85.

55. ZBV to DLS, March 20, 1867, Spencer Papers, SANC; DLS to CPS, April 24, 1867, ibid.; LMB to KPB, March 1867 (penciled on), BFP, SHC.

56. G. McDowell to DLS, October 5, 1867, Clark Papers, SANC; Charles F. Deems to DLS, April 13, 1867, Swain Papers, SHC; Charles Phillips to KPB, March 29, 1867, BFP, SHC.

57. Barile, *Undaunted Heart*, 81–86, 99; Russell, *Woman Who Rang the Bell*, 24; Hamilton et al., *Papers of Graham*, 7:143–44n.5.

58. Chamberlain, *Old Days in Chapel Hill*, 137–38; Henderson, *Campus of the First State University*, 187–88; Vickers, *Chapel Hill Illustrated*, 77.

59. Charles Phillips to KPB, February 6, 1867; WHB to KPB, March 2, 1867, BFP, SHC.

60. Charles Phillips to KPB, May 11, 1867; LMB to WHB, July 2, 1867; WHB to KPB, July 20,1867, BFP, SHC.

61. DLS to Jonathan Worth, July 23, 1867, UP. Some papers published the letter in full: e.g., *Sentinel*, August 10, 1867; *Raleigh Register*, August 13, 1867.

62. WAG to DLS, July 27, 1867, Hamilton et al., *Papers of Graham*, 7:351–52; Paul C. Cameron to DLS, July 28, 1867, Clark Papers, SANC.

63. James E. Beasley to DLS, January 19, 1868, Clark Papers, SANC.

64. *Raleigh Sentinel*, August 10, 13, 1867.

65. Ibid., August 13, 1867.

66. *Fayetteville News*, August 20, 1867.

67. Jonathan Worth to WAG, July 27, 1867, Hamilton et al., *Papers of Graham*, 7: 353–54; Jonathan Worth to BOT members (form letter), July 30, 1867, UP; Gov. Jonathan Worth to KPB, July 30, 1867, BFP, SHC (same form letter).

68. BOTM, August 22, 1867.

69. CM to UNC BOT, November 26, 1867, UP (copy in BFP); BOTM, December 17, 1867.

70. DLS to KPB, July 30, September 5, 1867, BFP, SHC.

71. DLS to KPB, February 13, 1868, BFP, SHC.

72. KPB to DLS, May 12, 1868, Spencer Papers, SANC; BOTM, June 3, 4, 1868.

73. DLS to WAG, June 10, 1868, Hamilton et al., *Papers of Graham*, 7:558–59; DLS to KPB, June 18, July 20, 1868; B. R. Moore to KPB, July 16, 1868, BFP, SHC. As to Moore, see Battle, *History*, 1:809.

74. S. S. Ashley, Secretary, Board of Education, list of trustees; Solomon Pool to S.S. Ashley, July 16, 1868; D.A. Starbuck to S. S. Ashley, July 16, 1868, UP; Battle, *History*, 1:774–75.

75. CM to Gov. Holden and UNC BOT, July 20, 1868, UP; *North Carolina Presbyterian*, July 29, 1868.

76. S. S. Ashley, Secretary, to DLS, July 13, 16, 1868, Clark Papers, SANC (invitations to meeting); DLS to UNC BOT, July 23, 1868, ibid.; BOTM, July 23, 24, 1868.

77. *Report of Special Trustee Committee*, July 24, 1868, UP (copy in Swain Papers, SANC); BOTM, July 24, 1868; Harris, *William Woods Holden*, 264–65.

78. WAG to CPS, October 28, 1871, Spencer Papers, SANC (published in Hamilton et al., *Papers of Graham*, 8:223).

79. Hemans, Felicia Dorothea, "The Hour of Death," in Browne, *Golden Poems*, 335.

80. For secondary accounts of Swain's removal, see Battle, *History*, 1:763–67, 775–83, 2:4–6; Boyd, *History of North Carolina*, vol. III, *North Carolina Since 1860*, 354–56; Gobbel, *Church-State Relationships in Education*, 64; Hamilton, *Reconstruc-*

tion, 621–23; Henderson, *Campus of the First State University*, 187–93; Noble, *History of Public Schools*, 332–37; Snider, *Light on the Hill*, 70–72; Hamilton et al., *Papers of Graham*, 7:572n.2; Wilson, *Papers of Spencer*, 599–611; Wilson, *Impressions of Men and Movements at the University of North Carolina*, 10–15. Cornelia Phillips Spencer described the events in a series of articles, "Pen and Ink Sketches of the University of North Carolina, as it has been," published in the *North Carolina Presbyterian*, August-September 1869.

Chapter 27: Aftermath, Finale

1. I have drawn here on my general knowledge of the Swain historical materials, and the following in particular: Chamberlain, *Old Days in Chapel Hill*, 117; Schumann, *First State University: A Walking Guide*, 46; Spencer, *Pen and Ink Sketches*, 36, 53; Hamilton et al., *Papers of Graham*, 6:321n.146; Brabham, "Defining the American University," 57 NCHR 427, passim; John Wilson Jr. to KPB, September 18, 1867, and J. H. Horner to KPB, September 25, 1867, BFP, SHC. The newspaper quote is from the *Wilmington Journal*, July 9, 1869.

2. Bridges, *Masonic Governors*, 154; Camp, *Swain*, 59; Chamberlain, *Old Days in Chapel Hill*, 141–42; Russell, *Woman Who Rang the Bell*, 88; Wheeler, *Reminiscences*, 61.

3. WHB to KPB, July 28, 1868, BFP, SHC; DLS to CM, July 30, 1868, and DLS to Governor William W. Holden, President, BOT, August 4, 1868, UP; Battle, *History*, 1:777–79, 2:4–6.

4. DLS to Robert W. Lassiter, August 10, 1868; CM to Rev. Basil Manly, August 4, 1868, UP.

5. Battle, *History*, 1:751–52; Henderson, *Campus of the First State University*, 187–88 (Deems quote); Spencer, *Pen and Ink Sketches*, 36.

6. Battle, "David Lowry Swain," *N.C. Journal of Education*, 3:27, 28; Spencer, August 18, 1865 Diary entry, quoted in Chamberlain, *Old Days in Chapel Hill*, 98.

7. Barile, *Undaunted Heart*, 108; Battle, *History*, 1:779; WHB to EHS, August 19, 1872, Clark Papers, SANC; Book AM, page 207, Office of the Chatham County, N.C., Register of Deeds, Pittsboro, N.C.

8. Battle, *History*, 1:779; Henderson, *Campus of the First State University*, 86; Vickers, *Chapel Hill Illustrated*, 74; Smith, *History of Education in North Carolina*, 83.

9. Barile, *Undaunted Heart*, 108; Battle, *History*, 1:779–80; Battle, *Sketch of the Life and Character of Wilson Caldwell*, 5.

10. CPS to "Fanny," August 12, 1868, Spencer Papers; WHB to KPB, August 14, 1868, BFP, SHC.

11. CPS to "Fanny," August 19, 1868, Spencer Papers, SHC.
12. *North Carolina Presbyterian*, September 2, 1868 (probably by Charles Phillips).
13. Snider, *Light on the Hill*, 73; Battle, *History*, 2:778; Charles Phillips to unidentified recipient, August 27, 1868, Clark Papers, SANC; *North Carolina Presbyterian*, September 2, 23, 1868.
14. William Shakespeare, *The Tragedy of Julius Caesar* (New Haven: Yale University Press, 1919, Mason, ed.), act 2, scene 2, at 36.
15. Battle, *History*, 1:780; Battle, *Sketches of the History of the University of North Carolina*, 51; Jones, *For History's Sake*, 209; *Raleigh Episcopal Methodist*, September 2, 1868; *North Carolina Presbyterian*, September 23, 1868; Charles Phillips to unidentified recipient, August 27, 1868, Clark Papers, SANC; WHB to Richard Battle (son), August 27, 1868, BFP, SHC. For other brief accounts of Swain's death, see Barile, *Undaunted Heart*, 110–12; Henderson, *Campus of the First State University*, 188; Peele, *Lives*, 251; Raper, *William W. Holden*, 121–23, 300n.68; Webb, *Jule Carr*, 27; *Charleston Daily News*, August 28, 1868; *Intelligencer*, September 2, 1868; *Raleigh Sentinel*, September 3, 1868.

Epilogue

1. "Rising," in Berry, *New Collected Poems*, 277–80, at 279.
2. See Prologue and note 1 thereto; CPS to EHS, August 23, 1875, Spencer Papers, SANC.
3. CPS to EHS, March 6, 1869, in Chamberlain, *Old Days in Chapel Hill*, 155–57; EHS to CPS, March 9, 1869, Spencer Papers, SHC; Battle, *History*, 1:780; Hamilton et al., *Papers of Graham*, 7:639n.4.
4. Chamberlain, *Old Days in Chapel Hill*, 176–77, 181–82; Robinson, *North Carolina: A Guide to the Old North State*, 243; *Raleigh: Capital of North Carolina*, 138; CPS to Laura Phillips, December 18, 1869, Spencer Papers, SHC (published in Wilson, *Papers of Spencer*, 640); *Old North State*, December 24, 1869; Historic Oakwood Cemetery Pamphlet (published by the cemetery; copy in author's files).
5. CPS to EHS, December 20, 1869, December 20, 1873, Spencer Papers, SANC (the first letter is published in part in Chamberlain, *Old Days in Chapel Hill*, 177).
6. Will Book G, pages 541–42, Orange County, N.C., Registry; re: the watch Swain left to his son Richard, see Will of R. B. Vance, Vance Papers, SANC.
7. C. W. Long to WHB, December 1, 1868, BFP, SHC, and March 16, 1877, Clark Papers, SANC; WHB to EHS, May 1, November 17, 1876, January 26, March 14, 1877, Clark Papers, SHC.
8. Sam F. Phillips to WHB, September 9, 1868; N. W. Woodfin to WHB, October

2, 1868; LMB to WHB, October 12, 1868, BFP, SHC. For another example of Battle administering Swain's estate, see A. S. Merrimon to WHB, October 20, 1868, BFP, SHC.

9. WHB to EHS, June 23, November 13, 1871, January 19, October 7, 1872, Clark Papers, SANC.

10. Charles Phillips to J. B. Killibrew, March 12, 1866, BFP, SHC; Marsh and Marsh, *Official Marriages of Bedford County Tennessee 1861–1880*, 1:4, 12; Lucas Jr. and Sheffield, *35,000 Tennessee Marriage Records and Bonds*, 265.

11. *Freeport Journal*, March 1, 1871, January 17, 1872; *Journal Standard*, June 4, 2011; *Cary News*, April 13, 1994; WHB to EHS, September 29, 1871, Clark Papers, SANC; Barile, *Undaunted Heart*, 124.

12. *Freeport Journal*, January 31, 1872; *Sentinel*, February 16, 1872; CPS to Laura (Phillips, probably), February 15, 1862, Spencer Papers, SHC. The obituary states that Richard left one child. A later Eleanor musing states that he left two. EHS document, "1872" at top, Spencer Papers, SHC. According to a family source, a son born after Richard's death died at the age of sixteen months. Email, Suzy Barile to the author, October 22, 2016 (copy in author's files).

13. Charles Phillips to EHS, February 16, 1872, Spencer Papers, SHC; Barile, *Undaunted Heart*, 124–25.

14. *Journal Standard*, June 4, 2011; email, Suzy Barile to the author, May 20, 2011 (copy in author's files).

15. CPS to EHS, June 26, 1869, in Wilson, *Papers of Spencer*, 627–28; Suzy Brett, "Profile: Ella Swain Atkins," *Cary News*, April 13, 1994.

16. Brett, *Cary News*, April 13,1994; Barile, *Undaunted Heart*, 101, 153–55.

17. Brett, *Cary News*, April 13, 1994; Barile, *Undaunted Heart*, 134, 141; Massengill and Topkins, *Death Notices*, 7.

18. Carpenter, "General Smith D. Atkins. In Memoriam," in *Transactions of the Illinois State Historical Society for the Year 1913*, 82–85.

19. Tepper, *Chronicles of the Bicentennial Observance of the University of North Carolina at Chapel Hill*, 133–34.

20. EHS document, "1872" at top, Spencer Papers, SHC.

21. EHS document, October 15, 1875, ibid.

22. EHS document, October 15, 1879, ibid.

23. EHS document, September 16, 1876, ibid.

24. EHS document, January 29, 1877, ibid.

25. See, e.g., WHB to EHS, April 18, July 4, August 25, 1873, Clark Papers, SANC (Eleanor in Illinois so long that she will hardly recognize Raleigh upon her return to it). The 1870 U.S. Census shows Eleanor living in Raleigh with her White family sisters.

26. CPS to EHS, April 23, 1869, Spencer Papers, SANC.

27. CPS to EHS, August 11, 1869, ibid.

28. CPS to EHS, April 26, 1870, ibid.; (published in Wilson, *Papers of Spencer*, 647–48).

29. CPS to EHS, March 13, 1872, January 31, 1873, Spencer Papers, SHC.

30. EHS to Mrs. Spencer, March 11, 1873, ibid.

31. CPS to EHS, August 11, 1876, ibid.; Chamberlain, *Old Days in Chapel Hill*, 226, 232.

32. CPS to EHS, September 30, 1876, Spencer Papers, SANC.

33. CPS to EHS, January 31, 1877, ibid.

34. CPS to EHS, March 26, August 27, 1877, ibid. The author found no evidence that Eleanor ever returned to Chapel Hill once she left it following Swain's death.

35. CPS to EHS, June 21, August 26, 1881, ibid.; Charles Phillips to EHS, June 23, 1881, Spencer Papers, SHC.

36. CPS to EHS, October 9, November 2, 1882, Spencer Papers, SANC.

37. CPS to EHS, January 30, 1882, ibid.

38. CPS to EHS, August 7, 27, 1882, ibid.

39. Chamberlain, *Old Days in Chapel Hill*, 161; M. Fetter to C. S. Harris, Supt. Of Public Works, August 20, 1868, UP.

40. CPS to EHS, October 15, 1875, Spencer Papers, SANC; Russell, *Woman Who Rang the Bell*, 121; Battle, *History*, 2:84 (see also ibid., 1:535); Powell, *First State University*, 97.

41. Chapman, *Black Freedom*, 216–17; Powe, "Old Sandstone Monument," *Chapel Hill Weekly*, July 25, 1947; author's personal observation of the monument.

42. Al McSurely, letter to the editor, *Chapel Hill News*, April 30, 2014; author's personal observation of the campaign.

43. CPS to EHS, April 23, 1869, Spencer Papers, SHC, and May 6, 1869, Spencer Papers, SANC; EHS to Ella S. Atkins, May 6, 1869, Spencer Papers, SHC.

44. Laura Phillips to EHS, May 3, 1877, Spencer Papers, SHC; CPS to EHS, January 31, 1873, Spencer Papers, SANC.

45. WHB to Col. D. M. Carter, November 13, 1872, Carter Papers, SHC (with handbill); WHB to EHS, August 25, 1873, October 4, 1875, October 4, 1876, March 27, 1877, Clark Papers, SANC.

46. CPS to June Spencer, February 6, 1883, Spencer Papers, SHC; *News and Observer*, February 6, 1883; *New York Times*, February 8, 1883; Massengill and Topkins, *Death Notices*, 227.

47. Last Will and Testament of Eleanor H. Swain, copies in NCC and in Swain Papers, SANC.

48. Chamberlain, *Old Days in Chapel Hill*, 295; Russell, *Woman Who Rang the Bell*, 193; *University Magazine*, 6:208–9 (January 1887).

49. *Chapel Hill News*, August 24, 2014; *Herald-Sun*, August 23, 2014; *Daily Tar Heel*, August 25, 2014

50. W. W. Holden, Chairman, UNC BOT, resolution dated August 28, 1868, Clark Papers, SANC (emphasis added); ECM, August 28, 1868; BOTM, November 17, 1868; Charles Phillips, as Secretary of the Faculty and Secretary of the Historical Society, to EHS, August 31, 1868, Clark Papers, SANC; *Hillsborough Recorder*, September 9, 1868.

51. Last Will and Testament of Eleanor H. Swain, copies in NCC and in Swain Papers, SANC.

52. WHB to EHS, October 7, 1872, Clark Papers, SANC.

53. EHS to WHB, October 27, 1873, and WHB to EHS, November 3, 1873, ibid.; Battle, *History*, 2:36–37.

54. WAG to CPS, April 26, May 7, 1875, Spencer Papers, SANC; *Daily News*, May 12, 1875.

55. WAG, ZBV, and CPS to EHS, May 13, 1875, Clark Papers, SANC (published in part in Wilson, *Papers of Spencer*, 129–30). The "P.S." appears to have been written later. The following notation appears on the document: "[July–August–September ? 1875] H.G. Jones, 7-17-64."

56. EHS to Committee of the Historical Society of North Carolina, May 19, 1875, Clark Papers, SANC (published in Hamilton et al., *Papers of Graham*, 8:439).

57. WAG to CPS, June 7, 1875, Hamilton et al., *Papers of Graham*, 8:448.

58. CPS to EHS, August 11, 1876, Spencer Papers, SANC.

59. EHS to CPS, September 2, [1875], Spencer Papers, SANC.

60. CPS to EHS, August 7, 1882, Spencer Papers, SANC; letter to editor, February 12, 1879, in Wilson, *Papers of Spencer*, 139.

61. Battle, *History*, 2:106–8; Jones, *For History's Sake*, 211, 182–210, 258–69; Turner, *Dreamer Archibald DeBow Murphey 1777–1832*, viii, 216; BOTM, February 18, 1892 (with letters, KPB to CPS, February 13, 1892, and CPS to KPB, February 13, 1892); Fold 524, UP (Spencer's involvement).

62. James A. Bryan to DLS, February 2, 1868, Clark Papers, SANC.

63. DLS to Gov. Holden, June 11, 1868, Clark Papers, SANC; DLS to WAG, January 1, 1865 [1866], Hamilton et al., *Papers of Graham*, 7:1–2; DLS to unidentified recipient, December 9, 1867, Swain Papers, SHC; Jones, *For History's Sake*, 209.

64. *North Carolina Presbyterian*, September 2, 23, 1868 (writer probably either Cornelia Spencer or her brother Charles Phillips).

65. A. D. Hepburn to CPS, February 21, 1870, Spencer Papers, SHC.

66. CPS to EHS, June 22, 1869, Spencer Papers, SANC.

67. Chamberlain, *Old Days in Chapel Hill*, 312.

68. Lyman C. Draper to WAG, January 7, 1873, and to William Johnston, January 7, 1873, Hamilton et al., *Papers of Graham*, 8:292, 295.

69. Thomas Ruffin to WHB, November 2, 1868, BFP, SHC.

70. CPS to EHS, March 6, 1869, Spencer Papers, SANC; Chamberlain, *Old Days in Chapel Hill*, 225; Russell, *Woman Who Rang the Bell*, 115; *North Carolina Presbyterian*, March 17, 1869; Solomon Pool, "Address to the alumni and friends of the University of North Carolina," January 26, 1871.

71. Battle, *History*, 2:9; Chamberlain, *Old Days in Chapel Hill*, 152; Wilson, *Papers of Spencer*, 613; *North Carolina Presbyterian*, January 6, 1869; Pool, "Address," January 26, 1871.

72. CPS to EHS, October 4, 1869, January 12, 1870, Spencer Papers, SANC.

73. CPS to EHS, August 21, December 21, 1872, Spencer Papers, SANC; Spencer, "The Phi Library," in *Sentinel*, June 15, 1873, and Wilson, *Papers of Spencer*, 668–70.

74. CPS to Laura Phillips, October 19, 1869, in Chamberlain, *Old Days in Chapel Hill*, 176, and Wilson, *Papers of Spencer*, 636–37; ZBV to CPS, January 1, 1869, Spencer Papers, SANC.

75. *North Carolina Presbyterian*, July 28, 1869 (signed "N. McK").

76. F. M. Hubbard to CPS, April 9, 1869, Spencer Papers, SANC.

77. CPS to EHS, October 15, 1875, August 27, 1882, Spencer Papers, SANC.

78. *Weekly Raleigh Register*, September 16, 1885.

79. *Fayetteville Observer*, September 7, 13, 1883 (publishing *Asheville Citizen* editorial); *News and Observer*, June 28, 1883; *Raleigh Register*, September 16, 1885.

80. P. C. Cameron, R. H. Battle, and F. H. Busbee, Committee, Circular Letter dated July 2, 1883, SANC, with undated reply from R.H. Clarke on behalf of Thomas U. Macartney; illegible to CPS, August 8, 1883, Spencer Papers, SANC; unidentified sender to CPS, August 19, 1883, ibid.; John Gatling to CPS, September 27, 1883, ibid.

81. CPS to EHS, August 27, 1877, Spencer Papers, SANC.

82. Circular Letter, W. L. Saunders, Secretary of BOT, October 16, 1883, Spencer Papers, SANC; Battle, *History*, 2:315–27; Battle, *Sketches of the History of the University of North Carolina*, 28–32; Henderson, *Campus of the First State University*, 198–99; Powell, *First State University*, 105; Wilson, *University of North Carolina: Making a Modern University*, 29; Bushong, "A. G. Bauer, North Carolina's New South Architect," 60 NCHR 304, 311–12. Two recent university publications contain articles on Memorial Hall: Kenneth Joel Zogry, "The Forgettable Memorial," *Carolina Alumni Review* (January/February 2013), 37–45; John Blythe, "Mysteries of University Library History," *Windows*, vol. 22, no. 3 (University Library, Spring 2016), 16, 17.

83. Henderson, *Campus of the First State University*, 230–31, 291–92; Nowell, *Letters of Thomas Wolfe*, 3; Powell, *First State University*, 150; Wilson, *UNC: The Making of a Modern University*, 118, 123–25, 249, 361–62; Wilson, *Chronicles of the Sesquicentennial*, 143. From childhood the author has been familiar with the appellation "Swine Hall." His father, UNC Class of 1930, worked at Swain Hall as a student and often referred to this moniker.

84. Carolina Performing Arts Society fundraising publication (undated)(copy in author's files).

85. Battle, *History*, 2:821–22; MacMillan, *North Carolina Portrait Index*, 225; author's personal observations.

86. CPS to EHS, March 6, 1869, Spencer Papers, SANC; Battle, *History*, 2:36, 135, 360.

87. Battle, *History*, 2:411, 426–27.

88. Ibid., 2:518–19, 543, 552.

89. 1909 N.C. Session Laws, Ch. 743, 1127–28; Pool, "Address," January 26,1871; Document Acknowledging Debt, May 15, 1867, UP; Battle, *History*, 2:57; Alexander McIver to Bartholomew F. Moore, WHB, and WAG, September 18, 1872, Hamilton et al., *Papers of Graham*, 8:279, 279n.2; Pamphlet, "In the Matter of the Indebtedness of the Trustees of the University to the Estate of David L. Swain," NCC; *Semi-Weekly Messenger*, February 24, 1899 (N.C. Senate committee reports unfavorably bill to pay the debt); *News and Observer*, February 12, 1909; *Caucasian*, March 11, 1909.

90. Blackmun, *Western North Carolina*, 380; Mazzocchi, Jay, "Swain County," in Powell, *Encyclopedia of North Carolina*, 1098; Thomasson, *Swain County*, 5; *Asheville Citizen*, October 29, 1948; *Weekly North-Carolina Standard*, February 24, 1869 (initial proposal to name a county for Swain); *Smoky Mountain Times*, January 29, 2014; 2017 Local School Finance Study, Public School Forum of North Carolina, https://www.ncforum.org/publications.

91. Robert W. Winston, "A Century of Law in North Carolina," in *Centennial Celebration*, 10.

92. Hill, *Guide to North Carolina Highway Historical Markers*, 24; "Historical Notes," 15 NCHR 334, 337 (1938); Carroll, "The Life and Times of David Swain," *News and Observer*, June 2, 1968; author's personal observations (streets).

93. Jones, *Sonarman's War*, 108, and email from Dr. Jones to the author (copy in author's files); Vickers, *Chapel Hill Illustrated*, 144; "Historical Notes," 21 NCHR 88, 88 (1944); *Asheville Citizen-Times*, October 25, 1959; records in SS Jeremiah O'Brien National Liberty Ship Memorial, San Francisco, Ca., inspected by the author on August 13, 2013.

94. *North Carolina Presbyterian*, August 11, 1869; *Pen and Ink Sketches*, 37.

95. William Augustus Blount to John Gray Blount, November 23, 1827, in Morgan, *John Gray Blount Papers*, 4:476–77 (quoted in Daniel, *Early Career*, 170); James A. Graham to WAG, February 7, 1833, *Graham Papers*, SHC (published in Hamilton et al., *Papers of Graham*, 1:252); see text accompanying note 7, chapter 3, note 69, chapter 6; CPS to Laura (Mrs. Charles Phillips), September 8, 1869, in Chamberlain, *Old Days in Chapel Hill*, 175; Benjamin J. Lossing to CPS, September 6, 1870, Spencer Papers, SANC; Russell, *Woman Who Rang the Bell*, 130. The newspaper was a Rome, Georgia publication not otherwise identified.

96. Charles Phillips to WAG, July 20, 1872, Hamilton et al., *Papers of Graham*, 8:270–71 (quoting General Rufus Barringer); *Pen and Ink Sketches*, 37, 40–41; as to failure to build library holdings, see text accompanying notes 52–65, chapter 13, and "Appendix to Mr. Herrissee's Memorial," 1856, UP; as to denominational concerns in faculty hiring, see text accompanying notes 38–44, chapter 11.

97. Peele, *Lives*, 278–79.

98. Battle, *History*, 1:780–82.

99. See chapter 12, passim; Brophy, *University, Court, and Slave*, 75.

100. Thomas Jefferson to Benjamin Rush, August 17, 1811, Looney, *Papers of Jefferson*, 4:87–88.

101. Battle, *History*, 2:206–7; Resolution by Commissioners of the Village of Chapel Hill, September 9, 1868, Clark Papers, SANC (Commissioners); *Daily Evening Telegraph*, September 1, 1868; *Episcopal Methodist*, September 2, 1868; *Durham Morning Herald*, May 14, 1915 (Hamilton, reviewing Connor, *Ante-Bellum Builders of North Carolina*); Moore, *History of North Carolina*, 1:493 (Moore); Charles Phillips to CPS, January 3, 1870, Spencer Papers, SHC (Charles Phillips) (for a similar appraisal, see Charles Phillips to EHS, February 8, 1871, Spencer Papers, SHC); Vance, Z. B., "David L. Swain," in Peele, *Lives*, 241, 253 (Vance) (also in Tucker, *Zeb Vance*, 438); Wheeler, *Reminiscences*, 56 (Wheeler).

102. DLS to GS, June 28, 1822, EC, NCC; Daniel, *Early Career*, 20.

103. Williams, *Intellectual Manhood*, 193.

104. Burke, *Reflections on the Revolution in France*, 193–94.

105. Jones, *For History's Sake*, 235, and *North Carolina Illustrated*, 191; Saunders, *Colonial Records*, 1:viii; Snider, *Light on the Hill*, 193; Spencer, *Pen and Ink Sketches*, 67–68; Stroupe, "The North Carolina Department of Archives and History–The First Half Century," 31 NCHR 184, 189.

106. Zeb Vance to CPS, December 29, 1870, Spencer Papers, SANC; *North Carolina Presbyterian*, July 9, 1873 (also in Wilson, *Papers of Spencer*, 123); William A. Graham Jr. to R. D. W. Connor, September 20, 1907, Hamilton et al., *Papers of Graham*, 8:518.

107. Drake, *Higher Education in North Carolina Before 1860*, 115, 263; W. D. Moseley to E. Mitchell, August 15, 1853, UP; Al Dunn, letter to the editor, *Carolina Alumni Review* (May/June 2013), 15. As to Moseley, see Battle, *History*, 1:824, 834; Powell, William S., "Moseley, William Dunn," Powell, *DNCB*, 4:333.

108. "Rising," supra note 1.

109. Adams, *Education of Henry Adams*, 300.

110. Cornelia Phillips Spencer, in *North Carolina Presbyterian*, September 9, 1868; Wagstaff, *Impressions of Men and Movements at the University of North Carolina*, 32–33; Wheeler, *Reminiscences*, 57; Connor, "Governor Swain Believed in Building Character, Not in Breaking Students," *Daily Tar Heel*, September 21, 1965.

111. Creecy, *Grandfather's Tales of North Carolina History*, 178; Swain's pardon petition, National Archives, Washington, D.C.

112. Battle, *History*, 1:549; S. F. Phillips to Mrs. Swain, July 18, 1873, Spencer Papers, SHC.

113. Edmonds, *Tar Heels Track the Century*, 63; Chamberlain, *Old Days in Chapel Hill*, 242. Vance consulted Spencer when preparing the address. Russell, *Woman Who Rang the Bell*, 165.

114. Vance's address, in Peele, *Lives*, 240–42, 254–55.

115. Potter, *South and the Sectional Conflict*, 245–46.

116. Vance's address in Peele, *Lives*, 254–55.

BIBLIOGRAPHY

Primary Sources

Manuscripts

Chapel Hill, North Carolina
    North Carolina Collection, University of North Carolina
David L. Swain Epistolary Correspondence
    Southern Historical Collection, University of North Carolina
    George Badger Papers
    Battle Family Papers
    Hamilton Browne Papers
    David M. Carter Papers
    Thomas B. Davidson Papers
    William R. Davie Papers
    Peter Force Papers
    Bartholomew Fuller Papers
    William Gaston Papers
    William Alexander Graham Papers
    William H. Haigh Papers
    Francis Lister Hawks Papers
    Benjamin Sherwood Hedrick Papers
    John DeBerniere Hooper Papers
    William Henry Hoyt Papers
    Lenoir Family Papers
    Henry Armand London Jr. Papers
    Charles Beatty Mallett Papers
    Mangum Family Papers
    Julien Dwight Martin Papers
    J. Gilcrest McCormick Papers
    Griffith J. McRee Papers
    John F. Speight Papers
    Cornelia Phillips Spencer Papers
    David Lowry Swain Papers

University Papers
Nicholas Washington Woodfin Papers

Durham, North Carolina
Special Collections, Duke University
John Herritage Bryan Papers
Henry T. Clark Papers
Braxton Craven Papers
James Cochran Dobbin Papers
Peter Force Papers
Benjamin Sherwood Hedrick Papers
Benjamin R. Lacy Papers
Willie Person Mangum Papers
Thomas David Smith McDowell Papers
Samuel Finley Patterson Papers
William Lafayette Scott Papers
David Lowry Swain Papers

Greenville, North Carolina
Special Collections, Joyner Library, East Carolina University
Elias Carr Papers
William Blount Rodman Papers

Raleigh, North Carolina
North Carolina Division of Archives and History
John Gray Blount Papers
John H. Bryan Papers
Walter Clark Papers
David Leroy Corbitt Papers
Weldon N. Edwards Papers
Governors Letter Books, David L. Swain
Governors Papers, David L. Swain
Historical Society of Pennsylvania Papers
James Johnston Pettigrew Papers
David Settle Reid Papers
Cornelia Phillips Spencer Papers
David Lowry Swain Papers
Zebulon Baird Vance Papers
Calvin H. Wiley Papers
Jonathan Worth Papers

Washington, District of Columbia
  Library of Congress
  Andrew Johnson Papers
  United States National Archives
  David Lowry Swain Papers

Government Publications

A Statement on the Number of Votes . . . on the Convention Question, Etc. Raleigh, NC: J. Gales & Son, Printers to the Convention, 1835.

Barnes, Joseph K., ed. *The Medical and Surgical History of the War of the Rebellion Part III, Volume II, Surgical History.* Washington: Government Printing Office, 1883.

Biennial Report of the Superintendent of Public Instruction for the Scholastic Year 1898–'99 and 1899–1900. Raleigh, NC: Edwards and Broughton, 1900.

Catalogue of the Trustees, Faculty, and Students of the University of North Carolina 1848–49. Fayetteville, NC: Edward J. Hale, 1849.

The Declaration of Independence By the Citizens of Mecklenburg County on the Twentieth Day of May, 1775, with Accompanying Documents. . . . Raleigh, NC: Lawrence & LeMay, Printers to the State, 1831.

First report of the Historical Society of the University of North Carolina June 4, 1845. Hillsborough, NC: Dennis Heartt, 1845.

In the Matter of the Indebtedness of the Trustees of the University to the Estate of David L. Swain. Raleigh, NC: North Carolina General Assembly, 1899 (?).

Journal of the Board for Internal Improvements, 1821–1835.

Journal of the Congress of the Confederate States of America 1861–1865. Washington, DC: Government Printing Office, 1904–1905.

Journal of the House of Representatives of the General Assembly of the State of North Carolina. Sessions of 1824, 1825, 1826, 1827, 1828, 1829, 1830, 1832, 1833, 1834, 1835.

Journal of the Internal Improvements Convention . . . 4th of July, 1833 . . . Address of the Committee to the Citizens of North Carolina. Raleigh, NC: Joseph Gales & Son, 1833.

Journal of the Senate of the General Assembly of the State of North Carolina. Sessions of 1833, 1834, 1835.

Message of the Governor in Relation to the Stock Reserved to the State in the Bank of the State. Raleigh, NC: Philo White, Printer to the State, 1835.

Message of the Governor Transmitting a Communication from the Commissioners appointed to Revise the Public Statutes. Raleigh, NC: Philo White, Printer to the State, 1835.

Proceedings and Debates of the Convention of North Carolina Called to Amend the

Constitution of North Carolina, Which Assembled at Raleigh on June 4, 1835. Raleigh, NC: Joseph Gales and Son, 1836.

Register of the Officers and Faculty of the University of North Carolina 1795–1945. Chapel Hill: University of North Carolina Press, 1954.

Report of the Board of Internal Improvements: 1830. Raleigh, NC: Lawrence & Lemay, 1830.

Report of the Committee on Burning of the Belfry. October 4, 1856. University Papers, University of North Carolina.

Report of the President and Directors of the Literary Fund of North Carolina. Raleigh, NC: Philo White, Printer to the State, 1833.

Report of the President and Directors of the Literary Fund of North Carolina. Raleigh, NC: Philo White, Printer to the State, 1835.

Report Relative to the Statue of Washington. Raleigh, NC: Lawrence & Lemay, Printers to the State, 1831.

The Writer's Program of the Works Project Administration in the State of North Carolina. Raleigh, NC: Capital of North Carolina. New Bern, NC: Owen G. Dunn Co., 1942.

Magazines

American Railroad Journal
Carolina Alumni Review
Carolina Arts & Sciences
New-England Magazine
Niles' Weekly Register
North Carolina University Magazine
The Historical Magazine, Notes and Queries, Etc.
University of North Carolina Magazine

Newspapers

Asheville Citizen
Asheville Citizen-Times
Biblical Recorder (Raleigh)
Cary News
Carolina Watchman (Salisbury)
Chapel Hill News
Charleston (SC) Daily News
Charlotte Democrat
Charlotte Observer

Cleveland Daily Leader
Daily Conservative (Raleigh)
Daily Evening Bulletin (Philadelphia)
Daily Evening Telegraph (Philadelphia)
Daily Intelligencer (Wheeling, West Virginia)
Daily Journal (Wilmington)
Daily News (Raleigh)
Daily Sentinel (Raleigh)
Daily Tar Heel (Chapel Hill)
Durham Morning Herald
Farmer and Mechanic (Raleigh)
Farmers' Register (Richmond)
Fayetteville News
Fayetteville Observer
Federal Union (Milledgeville, Georgia)
Freeport (Ill.) Journal
Georgia Journal (Milledgeville, Georgia)
Georgia Telegraph (Macon)
Greensboro (Greensborough) Patriot
Greensboro Times
Herald-Sun (Durham)
Hillsboro (Hillsborough) Recorder
Journal Standard (Freeport, Illinois)
Lenoir Topic
Macon (Ga.) Telegraph
New Berne Times
New York Times
News and Observer (Raleigh)
North Carolina Christian Advocate (Raleigh)
North Carolina Presbyterian (Fayetteville)
North Carolina Standard (Raleigh)
Old North State (Salisbury)
People's Press (Salem)
People's Press (Wilmington)
Petersburg News (Virginia)
Raleigh Christian Advocate
Raleigh Episcopal Methodist
Raleigh Register
Raleigh Register and North-Carolina Gazette

Raleigh Standard
Raleigh Star
Raleigh State Journal
Raleigh Weekly Standard
Republican Banner (Salisbury)
Richmond Dispatch
Semi-Weekly Messenger (Wilmington)
Semi-Weekly Raleigh Sentinel
Semi-Weekly Standard (Raleigh)
Smoky Mountain Times (Bryson City)
Southern Recorder (Milledgeville, Georgia)
Tarboro Free Press
The Caucasian (Clinton)
The Conservative (M'connelsville, Ohio)
The Intelligencer (Anderson, South Carolina)
Tri-Weekly Commercial (Wilmington)
Tri-Weekly Phoenix (Columbia, South Carolina)
Tri-Weekly Standard (Raleigh)
Village Advocate (Chapel Hill)
Weekly North Carolina Standard (Raleigh)
Weekly Raleigh Register
Weekly Raleigh Standard
Western Carolinian (Salisbury)
Wilmington Commercial
Wilmington Journal

Published Primary Sources

Alderman, Edwin Anderson et al., eds. *Library of Southern Literature: Compiled Under the Direct Supervision of Southern Men of Letters*. Volumes 1–16. Atlanta: Martin and Hoyt, 1909–1913.

Beggin, Suzy, ed. *Primary Sources*. Stephenson County (Ill.) Historical Society, 2001.

Brock, R. A., ed. *Southern Historical Society Papers*. Volumes 1–52. Richmond: Southern Historical Society, 1876–1959.

Cannon, Elizabeth Roberts, ed. *My Beloved Zebulon: The Correspondence of Zebulon Baird Vance and Harriett Newell Espy*. Chapel Hill: University of North Carolina Press, 1971.

Catalogue of the Members of the Dialectic Society Instituted in the University of North Carolina June the Third 1795. Raleigh, NC: North Carolina Standard, 1841.

Connor, R. D. W. *A Documentary History of the University of North Carolina 1776–1799*. Chapel Hill: University of North Carolina, 1953.

Coon, Charles L. *North Carolina Schools and Academies, 1790–1840: A Documentary History*. Raleigh, NC: Edwards and Broughton, 1915.

———. *The Beginnings of Public Education in North Carolina: A Documentary History 1790–1840*. Raleigh, NC: Edwards and Broughton, 1908.

Garraty, John A., and Mark C. Carnes. *American National Biography*. Volumes 1–24. NewYork, Oxford: Oxford University Press, 1999.

Graf, Leroy P., and Paul Bergeron, Ralph W. Haskins, eds. *The Papers of Andrew Johnson*. Volumes 1–16. Knoxville: University of Tennessee Press, 1967–2000.

Hamilton, J. G. de Roulhac, ed. *The Correspondence of Jonathan Worth*. Raleigh, NC: Edwards and Broughton, 1909.

———. with Rebecca Cameron. *The Papers of Randolph Abbott Shotwell*. Raleigh, NC: North Carolina Historical Commission, 1936.

———. and Max R. Williams, *The Papers of William Alexander Graham*. Volumes 1–8. Raleigh, NC: State Departmentof Archives and History, 1957–1992.

Hewett, Janet B., ed. *The Roster of Confederate Soldiers*. Volumes 1–16. Wilmington, NC: Broadfoot, 1996.

Howe, M. A. DeWolfe, ed. *Marching with Sherman: Passages from the Letters and Campaign Diaries of Henry Hitchcock Major and Assistant Adjunct General of Volunteers November 1864–May 1865*. New Haven, CT: Yale University Press, 1927.

Hoyt, William Henry, ed. *The Papers of Archibald D. Murphey*. Raleigh, NC: E. M. Uzzell, 1914.

Johnston, Frontis W., ed. *The Papers of Zebulon Baird Vance*. Volume I. Raleigh, NC: State Department of Archives and History, 1963.

Keith, Alice Barnwell, and William H. Masterson, David T. Morgan. *The John Gray Blount Papers*. Volumes 1–4. Raleigh, NC: State Department of Archives and History, 1952–1982.

Lemmon, Sarah McCulloh. *The Pettigrew Papers*. Volumes 1–2. Raleigh, NC: Department of Cultural Resources, Division of Archives and History, 1988.

Lucas, Silas Emmett, and Ella Lee Sheffield, *35,000 Tennessee Marriage Records and Bonds 1783–1870*. Volumes 1–3. Easley, SC: Southern Historical Press, 1981.

Marsh, Helen Crawford, and Timothy J. Edwards, eds. *Official Marriages of Bedford County Tennessee 1861–1880*. Volumes 1–2. Greenville, SC: Southern Historical Press, 1996.

Mobley, Joe A. *The Papers of Zebulon Baird Vance*. Volumes II, III. Raleigh, NC: Division of Archives and History, Department of Cultural Resources, 1995 (II), 2013 (III).

Nevins, Alan, ed. *Polk: The Diary of a President 1845–1849*. London: Longmans, Green, 1992.
Price, William S., Jr., *Not a Conquered People: Two Carolinians View Parliamentary Taxation*. Raleigh, NC: Division of Archives and History, Department of Cultural Resources, 1975.
Shanks, Henry Thomas, ed. *The Papers of Willie Person Mangum*. Volumes 1–5. Raleigh, NC: State Department of Archives and History, 1950–1956.
Sheppard, Steve, ed. *The History of Legal Education in the United States: Commentaries and Primary Sources*. Volumes 1–2. Pasadena, CA: Salem, 1999.
Tolbert, Noble J., ed. *The Papers of John Willis Ellis*. Volumes 1–2. Raleigh, NC: State Department of Archives and History, 1964.
Wilson, Louis R., ed. *Selected Papers of Cornelia Phillips Spencer*. Chapel Hill: University of North Carolina Press, 1953.

Secondary Sources

"A Memoir of the Rev. Elisha Mitchell, D. D. Late Professor of Chemistry, Mineralogy & Geology in the University of North Carolina." Chapel Hill: J. M. Henderson, Printer to the University, 1858.
Adams, Henry. *The Education of Henry Adams: An Autobiography*. Boston: Massachusetts Historical Society, 1907, 1918.
Alderman, Edwin A. *A Brief History of North Carolina*. Boston: Gina & Co., Publishers, Athenaeum Press, 1898.
Alexander, Roberta Sue. *North Carolina Faces the Freedmen: Race Relations During Presidential Reconstruction, 1865–67*. Durham, NC: Duke University Press, 1985.
Allcott, John V. "Architectural Developments At 'Montrose' in the 1850's." *North Carolina Historical Review* 42 (1965): 85–95.
———. "Robert Donaldson, the First North Carolinian to Become Prominent in the Arts." *North Carolina Historical Review* 52 (1975): 333–66.
Anderson, Jean Bradley. *Carolinian on the Hudson: The Life of Robert Donaldson*. Raleigh, NC: Historic Preservation Foundation of North Carolina, 1996.
Arrett, Alex M., with Walter C. Jackson. *The Story of North Carolina*. Chapel Hill: University of North Carolina Press, 1942.
Arthur, John Preston. *Western North Carolina: A History from 1730–1913*. Johnson City, TN: Overmountain Press, 1914.
Ashe, Samuel A., ed. *Biographical History of North Carolina: From Colonial Times to the Present*. Volumes 1–8. Greensboro, NC: C. L. Van Noppen, 1905–1917.

Ballard, Michael B. *A Long Shadow: Jefferson Davis and the Final Days of the Confederacy*. Jackson: University of Mississippi Press, 1986.
Ballinger, Susan, Bari Helms, and Janis Holder. *Slavery and the Making of the University: Celebrating Our Unsung Heroes, Bond and Free*. Chapel Hill: University Library, 2005.
Baptist, Edward E. *The Half Has Never Been Told: Slavery and the Making of American Capitalism*. New York: Basic Books, 2014.
Bardolph, Richard. "Confederate Dilemma: North Carolina Troops and the Deserter Problem." *North Carolina Historical Review* 66 (1989): 61–86, 179–210.
Barfield, Rodney D. "Thomas and John Day and the Journey to North Carolina." *North Carolina Historical Review* 78 (2001): 1–31.
Barile, Suzy. *Undaunted Heart: The True Story of a Southern Belle and a Yankee General*. Hillsborough, NC: Eno Publishers, 2009.
Barrett, John Gilcrest. *Sherman's March Through the Carolinas*. Chapel Hill: University of North Carolina Press, 1956.
——— . *The Civil War in North Carolina*. Chapel Hill: University of North Carolina Press, 1963.
Barringer, Paul B. *The Natural Bent: The Memoirs of Dr. Paul B. Barringer*. Chapel Hill: University of North Carolina Press, 1949.
Bartholome, Robert H. "She Married a Yankee." *Durham Morning Herald*, October 7, 1951.
Battle, Kemp P. "David Lowry Swain." *North Carolina Journal of Education* 3 (1899): 27–30.
——— . *History of the University of North Carolina*. Volumes 1–2. Raleigh, NC: Edwards and Broughton, 1907, 1912.
——— . *Memories of an Old-Time Tar Heel*. Chapel Hill: University of North Carolina Press, 1945.
——— . *Sketches of the History of the University of North Carolina Together with a Catalogue of Officers and Students, 1789–1889*. Chapel Hill: The University, 1889.
——— . *Sketch of the Life and Character of Wilson Caldwell*. Chapel Hill: University Press, 1895.
Bennett, D. K. *Chronology of North Carolina*. New York: James M. Edney, 1858.
Berry, Diana Ramey. *The Price for Their Pound of Flesh: The Value of the Enslaved, from Womb to Grave, in the Building of a Nation*. Boston: Beacon, 2017.
Blackmun, Ora. *Western North Carolina: Its Mountains and Its People to 1880*. Boone, NC: Appalachian Consortium, 1977.
Blackwelder, Ruth. *The Age of Orange: Political and Intellectual Leadership in North Carolina 1752–1861*. Charlotte, NC: William Loftin, 1961.

Blythe, John. "Mysteries of University Library History." *Windows* 22 (Spring 2016): 16–17.

Boyd, William K. *History of North Carolina, Volume III, North Carolina Since 1860.* Chicago: Lewis Publishing, 1919.

Brabham, Robin. "Defining the American University: The University of North Carolina, 1865–1975." *North Carolina Historical Review* 57 (1980): 427–455.

Bradley, Mark L. *This Astounding Close: The Road to Bennett Place.* Chapel Hill: University of North Carolina Press, 2000.

———. "'This Monstrous Proposition': North Carolina and the Confederate Debate on Arming the Slaves." *North Carolina Historical Review* 80 (2003): 153–87.

Braverman, Howard. "Calvin H. Wiley's North Carolina Reader." *North Carolina Historical Review* 29 (1952): 500–22.

Brett, Suzy. "Profile: Ella Swain Atkins." *The Cary News*, Cary, NC, April 13, 1994.

Brewer, Fisk P. "Hon. David L. Swain, L.L.D." *New-England Historical and Genealogical Register and Antiquarian Journal.* Volume 24, Number 4 (October 1870).

———. *Memoir of Hon. David Lowry Swain, LL.D.* Boston: David Clapp & Son, 1870.

Brickell, John. *The Natural History of North Carolina.* Dublin, Ireland: James Carson, 1737.

Bridges, Earley Winfred. *The Masonic Governors of North Carolina.* Oxford, NC: Oxford Orphanage Press, 1937.

Brophy, Alfred L. *University, Court, and Slave: Pro-Slavery Thought in Southern Colleges and Courts and the Coming of Civil War.* New York: Oxford University Press, 2016.

Brown, Hugh Victor. *A History of the Education of Negroes in North Carolina.* Raleigh, NC: Irving Swain, 1961.

Brown, John Howard, ed. *The Cyclopedia of American Biographies.* Volumes 1–5. Boston: Cyclopedia Publishing, 1897–1903.

Browne, Francis F., ed. *Golden Poems by British and American Authors.* Chicago: Jansen, McClung, 1882.

Burgwyn, William H. S. "An Address on the Military and Civil Services of General Matt W. Ransom." Ladies Memorial Association and Citizens, Raleigh, NC, May 10, 1906.

Burk, Bill. "Walls Provide a Link to the Past." *Chapel Hill News*, September 27, 2009.

Burke, Edmund. *Reflections on the Revolution in France.* Edited by William B. Todd. New York: Rinehart, 1959.

Bushong, William B. "A. G. Bauer, North Carolina's New South Architect." *North Carolina Historical Review* 60 (1983): 304–32.

———. "William Percival, an English Architect in the Old North State, 1857–1860." *North Carolina Historical Review* 57 (1980): 310–39.
Butler, Lindley S., ed. *The Papers of David Settle Reid*. Volumes I–II. Raleigh, NC: Department of Cultural Resources, Division of Archives and History, 1993 (I), 1997 (II).
Camp, Cordelia. *David Lowry Swain: Governor and University President*. Asheville, NC: Stephens, 1963.
Cappon, Lester J. *The Adams-Jefferson Letters: The Complete Correspondence between Thomas Jefferson and Abigail & John Adams*. Chapel Hill: University of North Carolina Press, 1959.
Carpenter, Richard V. "General Smith D. Atkins, In Memoriam." In *Transactions of the Illinois State Historical Society for the Year 1913*. Springfield, IL: State Journal, State Printers, 1914.
Carroll, Grady L. E. "The Life and Times of David Swain." *News and Observer*, Raleigh, NC, June 2, 1968.
Carter, Dan T. *When the War Was Over: The Failure of Self-Reconstruction in the South, 1865–1867*. Baton Rouge: Louisiana State University Press, 1985.
Catalogue of the Swain Collection of Autograph Letters. Raleigh, NC: E. M. Uzzell, 1885.
Cathey, Cornelius O. *Agricultural Developments in North Carolina 1783–1860*. Chapel Hill: University of North Carolina Press, 1956.
Centennial Celebration of the Supreme Court of North Carolina 1819–1919 by the North Carolina Bar Association Held in the Supreme Court Room, Raleigh, January 4, 1919. Raleigh, NC: Mitchell Printing Company, 1919.
Chamberlain, Hope Summerell. *Old Days in Chapel Hill: Being the Life and Letters of Cornelia Phillips Spencer*. Chapel Hill: University of North Carolina Press, 1926.
Chapman, John Kenyon. "Black Freedom and the University of North Carolina, 1793–1960." PhD diss., University of North Carolina at Chapel Hill, 2006.
Cheney, John L., Jr., ed. *North Carolina Government, 1585–1979: A Narrative and Statistical History*. Raleigh, NC: NC Department of the Secretary of State, 1975.
Churchill, Winston S. *Marlborough, His Life and Times*. Volume I. London: George G. Harrap, new ed. rev., 1934.
Concise Dictionary of American Biography. New York: Charles Scribner's Sons, 1990.
Connor, Otelia. "Governor Swain Believed in Building Character, Not in Breaking Students." *Daily Tar Heel*, September 21, 1965.
———. "Swain Had Knack of Landing Atop." *The Chapel Hill Weekly*, March 31, 1960.

Connor, R. D. W. *Ante-Bellum Builders of North Carolina.* Raleigh, NC: State Normal College, 1914.
———. *Ante-Bellum Builders of North Carolina.* Greensboro, NC: The North Carolina College for Women, 1930.
———. *North Carolina: Rebuilding an Ancient Commonwealth, 1584–1925.* Volume I. Chicago and New York: American Historical Association, 1929.
———. *William Gaston: A Southern Federalist of the Old School and His Yankee Friends 1778–1844.* Worcester, MA: American Antiquarian Society, 1934.
Corbett, D. L. "Historical Notes." *North Carolina Historical Review* 3 (1926): 364–67.
"Correspondence in 1834 Between John C. Hamilton, Esq., of New York, and Judge Gaston and Governor Swain, in Relation to Interesting Events in the History of North Carolina." University of North Carolina Magazine 10 (1861): 513–28.
Counihan, Harold J. "The North Carolina Constitutional Convention of 1835: A Study in Jacksonian Democracy." North Carolina Historical Review 46 (1969): 335–64.
Cox, Monty Woodall. "Freedom During the Fremont Campaign: The Fate of One North Carolina Republican in 1856." *North Carolina Historical Review* 45 (1968): 357–83.
Crabtree, Beth G. *North Carolina Governors 1585–1974: Brief Sketches.* Raleigh, NC: Division of Archives and History, Department of Cultural Resources, 3rd printing, rev., 1974.
Craig, D. I. *A Historical Sketch of New Hope Church in Orange County, NC.* Reidsville, NC: N.p., rev. ed., 1891.
Creecy, Richard Benbury. *Grandfather's Tales of North Carolina History.* Raleigh, NC: Edwards and Broughton, 1901.
Crittenden, C. Christopher, and Dan Lacy, eds., *The Historical Records of North Carolina.* Raleigh, NC: The North Carolina Historical Commission, 1938.
Crofts, Daniel W. *Reluctant Confederates: Upper South Unionists in the Secession Crisis.* Chapel Hill: University of North Carolina Press, 1989.
Crow, Jeffrey J., Paul D. Escott, and Flora J. Hatley. *A History of African Americans in North Carolina.* Raleigh, NC: Office of Archives and History, Department of Cultural Resources, 1992. Rev. ed. 2002.
Current, Richard N. "That Other Declaration: May 20, 1775–May 20, 1975." *North Carolina Historical Review* 54 (1977): 169–91.
Daniel, Carolyn. "David Lowry Swain, 1801–1835." PhD diss., University of North Carolina, 1954.
———. "The Early Career of David Lowry Swain, 1801–1832." MA thesis, University of North Carolina, 1947.

Daniels, Josephus. "Nathaniel Macon." In Clarence Poe, compiler, *Proceedings of the Thirteenth Annual Session of the State Literary and Historical Association of North Carolina*, 80–93. Raleigh, NC: Edwards and Broughton, 1913.

Daniels, Lucy. "The Love Story That Rocked the State." *Raleigh Times*, February 9, 1957.

Davidson, Chalmers G. "Basis of a Mecklenburg Bibliography." *North Carolina Historical Review* 26 (1949): 28–40.

"Defensor." *The Enemies of the Constitution Discovered Etc.* New York: Leavitt, Lord & Co., 1835.

Delderfield, R. F. *To Serve Them All My Days.* New York: Simon and Shuster, 1972.

Dorris, Jonathan Truman. "Pardoning North Carolinians." *North Carolina Historical Review* 23 (1946): 360–401.

Dowd, Clement. *Life of Zebulon B. Vance.* Charlotte, NC: Observer Printing and Publishing House, 1897.

Drake, William Earle. *Higher Education in North Carolina Before 1860.* New York: Carlton, 1964.

Dunbar, Gary S. "Silas McDowell and the Early Botanical Exploration of Western North Carolina." *North Carolina Historical Review* 41 (1964): 425–35.

Dykeman, Wilma. *The French Broad.* New York: Holt, Rinehart and Winston, 1974.

Edmunds, Pocahontas Wight. *Tar Heels Track the Century.* Raleigh, NC: Edwards and Broughton, 1966.

Edwards, Laura F. *The People and Their Peace.* Chapel Hill: University of North Carolina Press, 2009.

Ehle, John. "The Yankee Loves a Lady." American Adventure Series II, January 1955.

Elliott, Robert N., Jr. *The Raleigh Register 1799–1863.* Chapel Hill: University of North Carolina Press, 1955.

Escott, Paul D., ed. *North Carolinians in the Era of Civil War and Reconstruction.* Chapel Hill: University of North Carolina Press, 2008.

———. *Many Excellent People: Power and Privilege in North Carolina 1850–1900.* Chapel Hill: University of North Carolina Press, 1985.

Eubanks, Georgann. *Literary Trails of the North Carolina Mountains: A Guidebook.* Chapel Hill: University of North Carolina Press, 2007.

Farmer, Fannie Memory. "Legal Education in North Carolina, 1820–1860." *North Carolina Historical Review* 28 (1951): 271–297.

First Report of the Historical Society of the University of North Carolina June 4, 1845. Hillsborough, NC: Dennis Heartt, 1845.

Flexner, James Thomas. *Doctors on Horseback: Pioneers of American Medicine.* New York: Dover Publications, 1969.

Folk, Edgar E., and Bynum Shaw. *W. W. Holden: A Political Biography*. Winston-Salem, NC: John F. Blair, 1982.

Franklin, John Hope. *The Free Negro in North Carolina*. Chapel Hill: University of North Carolina Press, 1943.

———. *Reconstruction: After the Civil War*. Chicago: University of Chicago Press, 1961, 1994.

Foner, Eric. *Reconstruction: America's Unfinished Revolution, 1863–1877*. New York: Harper & Row, 1988.

Gass, W. Conrad. "A Felicitous Life: Lucy Martin Battle, 1805–1874." *North Carolina Historical Review* 52 (1975): 367–93.

———. "Kemp Plummer Battle and the Development of Historical Instruction at the University of North Carolina." *North Carolina Historical Review* 45 (1968): 1–22.

Genovese, Elizabeth Fox-, and Eugene D. Genovese. *The Mind of the Master Class: History and Faith in the Southern Slaveholder's Worldview*. Cambridge: Cambridge University Press, 2005.

Giduz, Roland. "President Swain's Locomotive Ride, Appeal to Sherman, Saved the University." *Alumni Review* (September 1977): 6–7.

Gobbel, Luther L. *Church-State Relationships in Education in North Carolina Since 1776*. Durham, NC: Duke University Press, 1938.

Gordon-Reed, Annette. *Andrew Johnson*. New York: Henry Holt, 2011.

Graham, H. C., Colonel. "How North Carolina Went Into the War." In *Under Both Flags: A Panorama of the Great Civil War*, 358–62. Boston: J. S. Round, 1896.

Graham, William A. "Memoir of Hon. Archibald D. Murphey, Late a Judge of the Superior Court of North Carolina." *University of North Carolina Magazine* 10 (1860): 1–12.

Griffin, Clarence W. *Essays on North Carolina History*. Forest City, NC: *Forest City Courier*, 1951.

Gwin, Pamela Jane Blair. "'Poisoned Arrows' From a Tar Heel Journalist: The Public Career of Cornelia Phillips Spencer, 1865–1890." PhD diss., Duke University, 1983.

Hadley, Wade H., Doris G. Horton, and Nell C. Stroud. *Chatham County 1771–1971*. Durham, NC: Moore Publishing, 1976.

Hall, David D. *Worlds of Wonder, Days of Judgment: Popular Religious Belief in Early New England*. New York: Knopf, 1989.

Hamilton, J. G. de Roulhac. *Party Politics in North Carolina 1835–1860*. Durham, NC: Seeman Printery, 1916.

———. *Reconstruction in North Carolina*. New York: Columbia University, 1914.

———, ed. *The Papers of Thomas Ruffin*. Volumes 1–4. Raleigh, NC: Edwards & Broughton, 1918–1920.

———. "The Preservation of North Carolina History." *North Carolina Historical Review* 4 (1927): 3–21.

Hamilton, J. G. de Roulhac and Henry McGilbert Wagstaff, eds., *Benjamin Sherwood Hedrick*. Chapel Hill: University of North Carolina, 1910.

Hamilton, John Bowen, ed. "Diary of Thomas Miles Garrett at the University of North Carolina, 1849." *North Carolina Historical Review* 38 (1961): 380–410.

Harris, William C. *William Woods Holden: Firebrand of North Carolina Politics*. Baton Rouge: Louisiana State University Press, 1987.

Hawks, Francis L. *History of North Carolina*. Volumes 1–2. Fayetteville, NC: E. J. Hale & Son, 1857–1858.

Haywood, Marshall D. *Builders of the Old North State*. Raleigh, NC: Litho Industries, 1968.

Helper, Hinton Rowan. *The Impending Crisis of the South: How to Meet It*. New York: Burdick Bros., 1857.

Henderson, Archibald R. *North Carolina: The Old North State and the New*. Chicago: Lewis, 1941.

———. *The Campus of the First State University*. Chapel Hill: University of North Carolina Press, 1949.

Hicklin, D. L. "D. L. Swain and Joseph Lane Born in Same House in 1801." *Charlotte Observer*, May 1, 1932.

Hill, Daniel Harvey. *A History of North Carolina in the War Between the States, Bethel to Sharpsburg*. Volume I. Raleigh, NC: Edwards and Broughton, 1926.

Hill, Michael, ed. *Guide to North Carolina Highway Historical Markers*. Raleigh, NC: Office of Archives and History, Department of Cultural Resources, 10th ed., 2007.

Historic Buildings and Landmarks of Chapel Hill, North Carolina. Chapel Hill: Creative Printers for the Chapel Hill Historical Society, 1973.

Hoffman, William S. *Andrew Jackson and North Carolina Politics*. Chapel Hill: University of North Carolina Press, 1958.

———. "John Branch and the Origins of the Whig Party in North Carolina." *North Carolina Historical Review* 35 (1958): 299–315.

———. "The Downfall of the Democrats: The Reaction of North Carolinians to Jacksonian Land Policy." *North Carolina Historical Review* 33 (1956): 166–80.

———. "The Election of 1836 in North Carolina." *North Carolina Historical Review* 32 (1955): 31–51.

Holden, W. W. *Memoirs of W. W. Holden*. Durham, NC: Seeman Printery, 1911.

Holt, Michael F. *The Rise and Fall of the American Whig Party: Jacksonian Politics and the Onset of the Civil War*. New York: Oxford University Press, 1999.

Horton, George Moses. *The Poetical Works of George M. Horton, The Colored Bard of North Carolina*. Hillsborough, NC: D. Heart, 1845.

Horton, James Oliver and Lois E. Horton. *In Hope of Liberty: Culture, Community, and Protest Among Northern Free Blacks, 1700–1860*. New York: Oxford University Press, 1997.

Howell, Robert Phillip. Robert Phillip Howell memoirs #1959-z, Southern Historical Collection, The Wilson Library, University of North Carolina at Chapel Hill.

Hoyt, William Henry. *The Mecklenburg Declaration of Independence: A Study of Evidence Showing that the Alleged Early Declaration of Independence by Mecklenburg County, North Carolina, on May 20, 1775, Is Spurious*. New York: Putnam's Sons, 1907.

The Historical Magazine, Notes and Queries, Etc. Morrisiania, NY: Henry B. Dawson, January 1871.

Inscoe, John C. *Mountain Masters, Slavery and the Sectional Crisis in Western North Carolina*. Knoxville: University of Tennessee Press, 1996.

———. "To Do Justice to North Carolina: The War's End according to Cornelia Phillips Spencer, Zebulon B. Vance, and David L. Swain." In Paul D. Escott, ed., *North Carolinians in the Era of Civil War and Reconstruction*, 129–53. Chapel Hill: University of North Carolina Press, 2008.

———. and Gordon B. McKinney. *The Heart of Confederate Appalachia: Western North Carolina in the Civil War*. Chapel Hill: University of North Carolina Press, 2000.

Jackson, Blyden. "George Moses Horton, North Carolinian." *North Carolina Historical Review* 53 (1976): 140–47.

Jeffrey, Thomas E. "'A Whole Torrent of Mean and Malevolent Abuse': Party Politics and the Clingman-Mitchell Controversy Part I." *North Carolina Historical Review* 70 (1993): 241–65.

———. "'A Whole Torrent of Mean and Malevolent Abuse': Party Politics and the Clingman–Mitchell Controversy Part II." *North Carolina Historical Review* 70 (1993): 401–29.

———. "Internal Improvements and Political Parties in Antebellum North Carolina, 1836–1860." *North Carolina Historical Review* 55 (1978): 111–56.

Johnson, Guion G. *Ante-Bellum North Carolina: A Social History*. Chapel Hill: University of North Carolina Press, 1937.

Jones, H. G. *For History's Sake: The Preservation and Publication of North Carolina History 1663–1903*. Chapel Hill: University of North Carolina Press, 1966.

———. *North Carolina Illustrated 1524–1984*. Chapel Hill: University of North Carolina Press, 1983.

———. *The Sonarman's War: A Memoir of Submarine Chasing and Mine Sweeping in World War II*. Jefferson, NC: McFarland, 2010.

Jones, Thomas B. "Calvin Jones, M. D.: A Case Study in the Practice of Early American Medicine." *North Carolina Historical Review* 49 (1972): 56–71.

Jones, Joseph Seawell. *A Defense of the Revolutionary History of the State of North Carolina from the Aspersions of Mr. Jefferson*. Raleigh, NC: Turner and Hughes, 1834.

Kidd, Thomas S. *The Great Awakening: The Roots of Evangelical Christianity in Colonial America*. New Haven, CT: Yale University Press, 2007.

Kiernan, Denise, and Joseph D'Agnese. *Signing Their Lives Away: The Fame and Misfortune of the Men Who Signed the Declaration of Independence*. Philadelphia: Quirk Books, 2009.

King, Harriett. "Presidents Visited Chapel Hill by Carriage, Train, Motorcade and Jet." *The Chapel Hill News*, August 17, 2008.

Knight, Edward W., and Agatha B. Adams. *The Graduate School Research and Publications*. Chapel Hill: University of North Carolina Press, 1946.

Kolchin, Peter. *American Slavery 1619–1877*. New York: Hill and Wang, 1993.

Konkle, Burton Alva. *John Motley Morehead and the Development of North Carolina, 1796–1866*. Philadelphia: William J. Campbell, 1922.

Kornegay, William Gordon. "The North Carolina Institute of Education." *North Carolina Historical Review* 36 (1959): 141–52.

Kruman, Marc W. *Parties and Politics in North Carolina, 1836–1865*. Baton Rouge: Louisiana State University Press, 1983.

Lawson, John. *A New Voyage to Carolina*. London: N.p., 1709.

Lefler, Hugh T. *History of North Carolina*. New York: Lewis Historical Publishing, 1956.

———. *North Carolina History Told By Contemporaries*. Chapel Hill: University of North Carolina Press, 1948.

———. "North Carolina History–A Summary View of What Has Been Done and What Needs to be Done." *North Carolina Historical Review* 38 (1961): 216–27.

Lefler, Hugh T., and Albert Ray Newsome. *North Carolina: The History of a Southern State*. Chapel Hill: University of North Carolina Press, 1954.

———. and Albert Ray Newsome. *North Carolina: The History of a Southern State*. Chapel Hill: University of North Carolina Press, 1954.

———. and Paul Wager. *Orange County, 1752–1952*. Chapel Hill: Orange Print Shop, 1953.

Leuchtenburg, William E. "When the President Came Home to Chapel Hill." *Carolina Arts & Sciences* (Spring 2012): 19.

Lewis, Lloyd. *Sherman: Fighting Prophet*. New York: Harcourt, Brace, 1932.

Lichtenstein, Gaston. "For Whom Was Edgecombe County Named?" *The North Carolina Booklet* 18 (1918): 116–19.

Link, William A. "Cornelia Phillips Spencer." In *North Carolina Women: Their Lives and Times*, Volume I. Edited by Michelle Gillespie and Sallie McMillan, 133–51. Athens: University of Georgia Press, 2014.

Looney, J. Jefferson. *The Papers of Thomas Jefferson, Retirement Series*. Volume 4. Princeton, NJ: Princeton University Press, 2007.

Lossing, Benson J. *Lives of Celebrated Americans*. Hartford, CT: Thomas Belknap, 1869.

MacMillan, Laura, Compiler. *The North Carolina Portrait Index*. Chapel Hill: University of North Carolina Press, 1963.

Marshall, Patricia Phillips. "The Legendary Thomas Day: Debunking the Popular Mythology of an African American Craftsman." *North Carolina Historical Review* 78 (2001): 32–66.

Martin, Jonathan D. *Divided Mastery: Slave Hiring in the American South*. Cambridge, MA: Harvard University Press, 2004.

Martin, Francois-Xavier. *The History of North Carolina from the Earliest Period*. Volumes 1–2. New Orleans: A. T. Penniman, 1829.

Mason, Matthew. *Apostle of Union: A Political Biography of Edward Everett*. Chapel Hill: University of North Carolina Press, 2016.

Massengill, Stephen, and Robert M. Topkins, compilers. *Death Notices from the Raleigh Farmer and Mechanic November 8, 1877–June 24, 1885: An Indexed Abstract*. Raleigh, NC: The compilers, 1990.

McCrumb, Sharyn. *The Ballad of Frankie Silver*. New York: Signet, 1999.

McKinney, Gordon B. "Zebulon Vance and His Reconstruction of the Civil War in North Carolina." *North Carolina Historical Review* 75 (1998): 69–85.

McPherson, Elizabeth Gregory, ed. "Letters from North Carolina to Andrew Johnson." *North Carolina Historical Review* 29 (1952): 104–19, 259–68, 400–431, 569–78.

———. "Unpublished Letters from North Carolinians to Polk." *North Carolina Historical Review* 17 (1940): 37–66, 139–66, 249–66.

McRee, Griffith J. *Life and Correspondence of James Iredell*. Volumes 1–2. New York: D. Appleton, 1857–1858.

A Memoir of the Rev. Elisha Mitchell, D.D., Late Professor of Chemistry, Mineralogy & Geology in the University of North Carolina. Chapel Hill: J. M. Henderson, Printer to the University, 1858.

Memorial from Diocese of NC Convention to President and Board of Trustees of UNC, May 9, 1860.

Menius, Art. "Love and Looting in Chapel Hill, the Last Town Standing." *Chapel Hill News*, April 15, 2015.

Miles, Edwin A. "Benson J. Lossing and North Carolina Revolutionary History." *North Carolina Historical Review* 35 (1958): 11–19.

———. "Joseph Seawell Jones of Shocco–Historian and Humbug." *North Carolina Historical Review* 34 (1957): 483–506.

Miller, Perry. *The New England Mind: The Seventeenth Century*. Volumes 1–2. Boston: Beacon, 1939.

Miller, Robert D. "Samuel Field Phillips: The Odyssey of a Southern Dissenter." *North Carolina Historical Review* 58 (1981): 263–80.

Mitchell, Memory F. *Addresses and Papers of Governor Terry Sanford*. Raleigh, NC: Council of State, State of North Carolina, 1966.

———. *Legal Aspects of Conscription and Exemption in North Carolina 1861–1865*. Chapel Hill: University of North Carolina Press, 1965.

Meats, Stephen, and Edwin T. Arnold. *The Writings of Benjamin F. Perry*. Volumes 1–3. Spartanburg, SC: Reprint, 1980.

Mobley, Joe. *Ship Ashore! The U.S. Lifesavers of Coastal North Carolina*. Raleigh, NC: Division of Archives and History, 1994.

———. *"War Governor of the South": North Carolina's Zeb Vance in the Confederacy*. Gainesville: University Press of Florida, 2005.

———. "Zebulon Baird Vance: A Confederate Nationalist in the North Carolina Gubernatorial Election of 1864." *North Carolina Historical Review* 77 (2000): 434–54.

Moore, John W. *History of North Carolina from the Earliest Discoveries to the Present Time*. Raleigh, NC: Alfred Williams, 1880.

Murray, Elizabeth Reid. *Wake: Capital County of North Carolina*. Volume I, *Prehistory through Centennial*. Raleigh, NC: Capital County Publishing, 1983.

Neal, Lois Smathers, compiler. *Abstracts of Vital Records from Raleigh, NC Newspapers 1820–1829*. Spartanburg, SC: Reprint, 1980.

Newsome, A. R. "A Miscellany from the Thomas Henderson Letter Book, 1810–1811." *North Carolina Historical Review* 6 (1929): 398–410.

———, ed. "Letters of Romulus Sanders to Bartlett Yancey, 1821–1828." *North Carolina Historical Review* 8 (1931): 427–62.

———. "Twelve North Carolina Counties in 1810–1811." *North Carolina Historical Review* 5 (1928): 413–46.

Ninety-Second Illinois Volunteers. Freeport, IL: Journal Steam Publishing House and Bookbindery, 1875.

Noble, M. C. S. *A History of the Public Schools of North Carolina*. Chapel Hill: University of North Carolina Press, 1930.

North Carolina: A Guide to the Old North State. Chapel Hill: University of North Carolina Press, 1939.

Nowell, Elizabeth, ed. *The Letters of Thomas Wolfe*. New York: Charles Scribner's Sons, 1956.

Olmstead, Frederick Law. *The Cotton Kingdom: A Traveller's Observations on Cotton and Slavery in the American Slave States*. New York: Mason Brothers, 1861.

Owen, W. H. "Report on the State of the Library," 1836. University Papers, University of North Carolina.

———. "Report on the State of the Library," 1837. University Papers, University of North Carolina.

Padgett, James A., ed. "Reconstruction Letters from North Carolina." *North Carolina Historical Review* 18 (1941): 278–300, 373–97.

Patton, Sadie Smathers. *The Story of Henderson County*. Asheville, NC: Miller Printing, 1947.

Peele, William J. *Lives of Distinguished North Carolinians*. Raleigh, NC: North Carolina Publishing Society, 1898.

Pegg, Herbert Dale. *The Whig Party in North Carolina*. Chapel Hill: Colonial Press, undated.

Perry, Benjamin. *Reminiscences of Public Men*. Philadelphia: John D. Avil, 1883.

Phifer, Edward W., Jr. *Burke: The History of a North Carolina County, 1777–1920 With a Glimpse Beyond*. Morganton, NC: E. W. Phifer, Jr., 1977.

Phillips, Jason. *Diehard Rebels: The Confederate Culture of Invincibility*. Athens: University of Georgia Press, 2007.

Pool, Solomon. "Address to the Alumni and Friends of the University of North Carolina." January 26, 1871. Chapel Hill, 1871.

Potter, David M. *The South and the Sectional Conflict*. Baton Rouge: Louisiana State University Press, 1968.

Powe, Sibyl Goerch. "Old Sandstone Monument in Negro Graveyard Brings Back Memories of Days That Are Gone." *Chapel Hill Weekly*, July 25, 1947.

Powell, Lew. *On This Day in North Carolina*. Winston-Salem: John F. Blair, 1996.

Powell, William S. *Annals of Progress: The Story of Lenoir County and Kinston, North Carolina*. Raleigh, NC: State Department of Archives and History, 1963.

———, ed. *Dictionary of North Carolina Biography*. Volumes 1–6. Chapel Hill: University of North Carolina Press, 1979–1996.

———, ed. *Encyclopedia of North Carolina*. Chapel Hill: University of North Carolina Press, 2006.

Tepper, Steven J. *The Chronicles of the Bicentennial Observance of the University of North Carolina at Chapel Hill.* Chapel Hill: University of North Carolina at Chapel Hill, 1998.
Testimony of Distinguished Laymen to the Value of the Sacred Scriptures, Particularly in Their Bearing on Civic and Social Life. New York: American Bible Society, 1859.
The American Almanac and Repository of Useful Knowledge for the Year 1860. Boston: Crosby, Nicholas, 1860.
The First Hundred Years: The Chapel Hill Presbyterian Church, 1849–1949. Chapel Hill, NC: N.p., 1950.
Thomasson, Lillian Franklin. *Swain County: Early History and Educational Development.* Bryson City, NC: Author (?), 1977.
Tolbert, Lisa, ed. *Two Hundred Years of Student Life at Chapel Hill: Selected Letters and Diaries.* Chapel Hill: Center for the Study of the American South, 1993.
Treadwell, S. B. *American Liberties and American Slavery: Morally and Politically.* New York: John S. Taylor; Boston: Weeks, Jordan, 1838.
Tucker, Glenn. *Zeb Vance: Champion of Personal Freedom.* Indianapolis, IN: Bobbs-Merrill, 1965.
Turner, Herbert Snipes. *The Dreamer Archibald DeBow Murphey, 1777–1832.* Verona, PA: McClure Press, 1971.
Vance, Zebulon B. *Life and Character of Hon. David L. Swain, Late President of the University of North Carolina.* Durham, NC: W. T. Blackwell & Co.'s Steam Presses, 1878.
Vickers, James. *Chapel Hill, An Illustrated History.* Chapel Hill, NC: Barclay, 1985.
Waddell, Alfred Moore. *Some Memories of My Life.* Raleigh, NC: Edwards and Broughton, 1908.
Wagstaff, Henry McGilbert. *Impressions of Men and Movements at the University of North Carolina.* Chapel Hill: University of North Carolina Press, 1950.
Wakelyn, Jon L. *Biographical Dictionary of the Confederacy.* Westport, CT: Greenwood Press, 1976.
Wallace, Carolyn A. "David Lowry Swain, the First Whig Governor of North Carolina." In *Studies in Southern History*, 62–81. Edited by J. Carlyle Sitterson. Chapel Hill: University of North Carolina Press, 1957.
Walser, Richard. *The Black Poet (Being the Remarkable Story Partly Told by Himself) of George Moses Horton a North Carolina Slave.* New York: Philosophical Library, 1966.
Walton, Brian G. "Elections to the U.S. Senate in North Carolina, 1835–1861." *North Carolina Historical Review* 53 (1976): 168–92.
Watson, Harry L. *Jacksonian Politics and Community Conflict: The Emergence of the*

Second American Party System in Cumberland County, North Carolina. Baton Rouge: Louisiana State University Press, 1981.

———. "Squire Oldway and His Friends: Opposition to Internal Improvements in Antebellum North Carolina." *North Carolina Historical Review* 54 (1977): 105–19.

———. "The Man with the Dirty Black Beard: Race, Class, and Schools in the Antebellum South." *Journal of the Early Republic* 32 (2012): 1–26.

Webb, Mena. *Jule Carr: General without an Army*. Chapel Hill: University of North Carolina Press, 1987.

Webb, W. R., Jr. "Anecdote and Reminiscence." *University of North Carolina Magazine* 14 (1895): 267–71.

Weeks, Stephen B. *History and Biography of North Carolina: Scrapbook*. Unpublished.

Wellman, Manley Wade. *The Kingdom of Madison*. Chapel Hill: University of North Carolina Press, 1973.

Wettach, Robert H., ed. *A Century of Legal Education*. Chapel Hill: University of North Carolina Press, 1947.

Whedon, D. D., ed. *Methodist Quarterly Review 1871*. New York: Carlton & Lanahan, 1871.

Wheeler, John H. *Historical Sketches of North Carolina from 1584 to 1851*. Philadelphia: Lippincott, Grambe, 1851.

———. *North Carolina: Her Past, Present and Future*. Raleigh, NC: "Standard" Steam Book and Job Print, 1870.

———. *Reminiscences and Memoirs of North Carolina and Eminent North Carolinians*. Columbus, OH: Columbus Printing Works, 1884.

Whichard, Willis P. "North Carolina." In *Historical Consciousness in the Early Republic: The Origins of State Historical Societies, Museums, and Collections, 1791–1861*. Edited by H. G. Jones, 92–101. Chapel Hill: North Caroliniana Society and North Carolina Collection, 1995.

Whitescarver, Keith. "School Books, Publishers, and Southern Nationalists: Refashioning the Curriculum in North Carolina's Schools, 1850–1861." *North Carolina Historical Review* 79 (2002): 28–49.

Wilentz, Sean. *The Rise of American Democracy: Jefferson to Lincoln*. New York: W. W. Norton, 2005.

Wiley, Bell Irvine. *The Life of Johnny Reb*. Baton Rouge: Louisiana State University Press, 1943.

Williams, Timothy J. *Intellectual Manhood: University, Self, and Society in the Antebellum South*. Chapel Hill: University of North Carolina Press, 2015.

Williamson, Hugh. *History of North Carolina*. Volumes 1–2. Philadelphia: Thomas Dobson, 1812.

Wilson, Clyde. "Griffith John McRee: An Unromantic Historian of the Old South." *North Carolina Historical Review* 47 (1970): 1–23.

Wilson, Joseph M. *The Presbyterian Historical Almanac, and Annual Remembrance of the Church, for 1868*. Philadelphia: Joseph M. Wilson, 1868.

Wilson, Louis Round. "The Acquisition of the Stephen B. Weeks Collection of Caroliniana." *North Carolina Historical Review* 42 (1965): 424–29.

———, ed. *The Chronicles of the Sesquicentennial*. Chapel Hill: University of North Carolina Press, 1947.

———. *The Library of the First State University: A Review of Its Past and a Look at Its Future*. Chapel Hill: University of North Carolina Library, 1960.

———. *The University of North Carolina: Making a Modern University*. Chapel Hill: University of North Carolina Press, 1957.

Worsley, Stephen C. "Catholicism in Antebellum North Carolina." *North Carolina Historical Review* 60 (1983): 399–430.

Wright, Annette C. "'The Grown-Up Daughter': The Case of North Carolina's Cornelia Phillips Spencer." *North Carolina Historical Review* 74 (1997): 260–83.

Writers' Program of the Works Projects Administration in the State of North Carolina. *Raleigh: Capital of North Carolina*. New Bern, NC: Owen G. Dunn, 1942.

Yates, Richard E. "Governor Vance and the End of the War in North Carolina." *North Carolina Historical Review* 18 (1941): 315–38.

———. "Governor Vance and the Peace Movement." *North Carolina Historical Review* 17 (1940): 1–25, 89–113.

Yearns, Wilfred B., Jr. "North Carolina in the Confederate Congress." *North Carolina Historical Review* 29 (1952): 359–78.

York, Maurice C. "The Dialectic and Philanthropic Societies' Contributions to the Library of the University of North Carolina, 1886–1906." *North Carolina Historical Review* 59 (1982): 327–53.

Young, Perry Deane. *The Untold Story of Frankie Silver: Was She Unjustly Hanged?* Bloomington, IN: Universe, 2012.

Zogry, Kenneth Joel. "The Forgettable Memorial." *Carolina Alumni Review* (January/February 2013): 36–45.

Zuber, Richard L. *Jonathan Worth: A Biography of a Southern Unionist*. Chapel Hill: University of North Carolina Press, 1965.

ACKNOWLEDGMENTS

Reinhold Niebuhr has said, "Nothing we do, however virtuous, can be accomplished alone." The thought contains timeless wisdom. Inspiration, suggestions, and other forms of assistance from many people have aided and enhanced this endeavor.

Sometime before the University Library assigned this task to me, the late Dr. H. G. Jones urged me to undertake it. His earlier invitation had me prepared to accept when the library extended its request. Jones also read the draft manuscript and offered both useful comments and encouragement to persevere.

The staffs of the State Archives of North Carolina, and of the Southern Historical Collection and the North Carolina Collection of the University of North Carolina at Chapel Hill, were invariably kind and helpful. I am particularly indebted to Matt Turi of the Southern Historical Collection for initial assistance in organizing my research in the Southern's relevant collections. Bob Anthony, curator of the North Carolina Collection, supervises the Coates Leadership Series, of which this volume is a part. I am grateful to him and his committee for selecting me as the author and to him for his consistent interest and support. John Blythe also deserves a special word of thanks.

In addition to Dr. Jones, the following scholars read the manuscript, or portions of it, at my request: the late Jerry Cashion, Jeffrey Crow, George Lensing, Michael Perdue, William Price, John Sanders, and David Silkenat. Nick Graham, Michael Hill, and Cecelia Moore read the manuscript for the publisher, which shared their reports with me. I am indebted to all of them for their thoughtful comments.

Suzy Barile, Governor Swain's great-great-great granddaughter, generously shared family information and pictures. Kim Andersen helped with pictures from state archives, and Jason Tomberlin with those from the UNC Photo Archives. Anna Bryan provided the pictures from the Library of Congress.

Several typists assisted with the production. I again express my gratitude to them.

Governor Jim Hunt has described UNC President William Friday's legacy as not just what he did but what he inspired others to do. President Friday was not the inspiration for this book. He knew about it, however, and considered it important. Among his final words to me were, "You stick with this." At discouraging moments, his mandate inspired perseverance.

I should thank my subject for being the quintessential historic preservationist. Materials he produced, collected, and preserved greatly facilitated the compilation and telling of his story in the context of his time.

Finally, a customary but important credit to the people closest to me. An endeavor of this magnitude requires an author's absence from home, office, friends, and accustomed activities. I thus am grateful to my wife Leona, our daughters and grandchildren, my law partners and associates, and my friends for their tolerance and understanding. All of them enrich my life and enhance my work.

Missy (now deceased), Holmes, and Brandeis (now deceased) were splendid feline companions, and occasional distractions, when I brought Swain work home.

INDEX

abolition doctrines, 221
academic leadership: admissions, 137–49; disciplinary efforts, 172–76; electing new UNC president, 133–36; faculty, 192–216; faculty issues, 212–16; Hedrick affair, 217–31; *in loco parentis,* 141–49; politics, 284–97; property matters, 232–51; public policy, 264–83; role of teaching, 177–91; special events, 252–63; student misconduct, 150–76; work-study program, 144–45. *See also* Swain, David Lowry; University of North Carolina
Adams, John Quincy, 305
admissions, 137–49. *See also* University of North Carolina
African Americans. *See* enslaved persons; Negroes
Albemarle and Pamlico Sounds, 72
alcohol, 152–56; consuming, 18–19, 152–56
Alexander, Julius, 125, 139
Allen, James, 30
American Bible Society, 406
American National Review, 191
American Quarterly Registry, 191
Amnesty Proclamation, 476
Anderson, Walker, 75
Appeal to the Coloured Citizens of the World (Walker), 62
arms, requests for, 98

Articles of American Association, 306, 310, 340
Asbury, Frances, 19
Atkins, Smith D., 462, 466–70
Austin College, 296–97
Avery, Waightstill, 342

Badger, George, 27–28, 32, 75, 87, 106, 137, 144, 189, 237, 245, 284–87, 296, 333, 390, 402
Baird, Zeb, 15
Bancroft, George, 80, 195–96, 306, 324, 335, 338, 340, 353, 361, 409, 536
Barringer, D. L., 105, 284
Barringer, D. M., 355
Battle of Bentonville, 147
Battle, Kemp P., 5, 135, 199, 302, 400, 402, 500, 503, 506, 509, 511–13, 515, 518–19, 527–28, 539, 545, 550, 556–57
Battle, Lucy, 198–99, 204–05, 288
Battle, William H., 59, 135, 141, 145, 168, 179, 192, 196–200, politics and, 286–95, 400–01, 425, 501, 504, 506, 509
Biggs, Asa, 158, 190, 311, 365
Blair, Francis P., Jr., 141, 158-59
Blakeman, J. S., 532
Blount, Nathan, 110
Blount, William, 344
Board of Internal Improvements, 66–68
Board of Visitors, Reconstruction, 471–72

Bomford, J. W., 261
Boylan, William, 73
Bragg, Thomas, 143, 163, 190, 195, 203, 249
Branch, John, 37, 52, 122
Breckenridge, John C., 9, 195, 263
Brevard, Ephraim, 364
Bridgers, John L., 431
Bridgers, Robert R., 148
Brown, Bedford, 53–54, 101
Bryan, John H., 290
Buchanan, James, 155, 195, 257–63
Buckner, Polly, 36–37
Buncombe County (North Carolina), 8–9, 11, 14–15, 22, 25, 34, 36–37, 40, 42, 187, 202, 263, 372. See also Civil War; counties; North Carolina; Swain, David Lowry; University of North Carolina
Buncombe Turnpike, 29–31
Burke, Thomas, 325
Burns, Robert, 16
Burton, Hutchins G., 26–27, 39, 149
Burton, John, 149
Bynum, John Gray, 291

Caldwell, Helen, 190
Caldwell, Joseph, 3, 19, 68, 133, 205, 274; residence of, 234
Caldwell, Tod R., 181, 190
Caldwell, Wilson Swain, 421–22, 464, 528, 540–41
Calhoun, John C., 16, 68
Cameron, Duncan, 134, 307, 326
Cameron, Paul C., 190
Cape Fear River, 32
capitol building, constructing, 278–79
Carlyle, Thomas, 126–27
Caruthers, E. W., 365

Cass, Lewis, 95, 97
Caswell, Richard, 22, 44, 302, 325, 331, 339, 342, 358, 371
Catholic Church, 405
Cavanagh, Patrick, 242
Cedar Grove Cemetery, 211
Central Railroad, 273–74
Chapel Hill: Civil War disruptions in, 429, 432, 434–35, 440, 443–44, 449; enslaved persons in, 414, 418, 421–25; faculty at, 193, 195–99, 205, 211, 213–14; family in, 375, 378, 383, 389, 391; Hedrick affair, 217, 219, 226–27, 229–30; history matters, 302, 313, 315, 317, 333, 343, 361–62; personal dimensions in, 399–400, 405, 408; politics in, 292–93; property in, 232–34, 236, 238, 241–42, 246–48; public policy in, 273, 279–80; Reconstruction, 451, 464, 467–69, 473–74, 479, 489–90; special events in, 253, 255–56, 258–63; student misconduct, 150, 156, 158, 161, 170–71; Swain downfall in, 500, 513–14, 525–30, 531, 532, 538–42, 546, 548, 558; Swain origins in, 3–4, 10–12, 19; teaching at, 181–82, 187–91; UNC parenting, 134, 137–49. *See also* Swain, David Lowry, University of North Carolina
Charleston Library, 313
Chase, Salmon P., 230
Cherokee Bonds, 292
Cherokee Indians, 55–56, 95–98; and public policy, 278
Cherokee Removals and Acting Indian Agent, 97
Chunn, Samuel, 30
Churchill, Winston, 5

Civil War, 141, 319–20, 340, 420; Chapel Hill significance, 432–35; conscription, 436; delegation, 431–33; exchanges defining war end, 451–58; General Assembly meeting, 458–60; impending conflict, 429–33; Manly-Swain communication, 433–36; negotiating end to, 458–66; Reconstruction following, 471–96; Swain-Atkins relationship, 466–70; tax policy, 436; UNC exodus, 184; UNC faculty disruptions, 445–50; UNC student disruption, 437–45; watershed events of, 433–34

Clark, Henry T., 441, 476–77
Clay, Henry, 104–05, 145, 344
Clayton, John, 38
Clinch, D. L., 138
Clingman, Thomas L., 202, 264, 296, 347, 362
Clio. *See* history, collecting; collaborations, collecting history; Swain, David Lowry
Coleman, William, 34, 532
collaborations, collecting history: Bancroft-Swain, 340–42; Graham-Swain, 324–27; Hawks-Swain, 331–38; Lossing-Swain, 342–46; McRee-Swain, 327–31; Wheeler-Swain, 338–40
collectors books, 309
commencements, University of North Carolina, 252–63
Commentaries on American Law, 244
Confederacy, 270, 380, 431, 437–43, 449, 452–59, 482–83. *See also* Civil War; North Carolina
Connor, R. D. W., 126

Conscription Act, 440–42
Cooke, William D., 202–03
Cooper, Edmund, 478
Cornwallis, Charles, 4–5
counties: basis of representation, 111–15; forming, 34; representative proposal, 120
Craven, Braxton, 139
Crawford, Joel, 137–38
Crawford, William, 16
curriculum, enhancing, 193–94

Daniel, Carolyn, 127
Daniel, Joseph J., 14, 43, 51, 86, 91
Davidson County, creation of, 113
Davidson, William Lee, 315
Davie, Allen J., 79, 309
Davie, William R., 79, 349
Davis, A. J., 238, 242, 246
Davis, George, 431, 436, 456, 476
Davis, Jefferson, 4, 432, 442, 444, 453–54, 458, 464, 481–85
Day, Thomas, 236
debt, settling, 282
Declaration of Rights, 111. *See also* North Carolina: constitutional reform
decoying off, 89
Deems, Charles F., 208, 211, 214, 378, 486–89, 491
Delafield's Antiquities, 245
delinquency charges, 99
Devereux, Thomas P., 87
Dialectic (Di) Society, 139, 152, 160, 190, 235, 244, 261
Dick, John M., 76
Dix, Dorothea, 318, 361
Dod, Albert B., 241–42
Donaldson, James, 77–78, 243

Donaldson, Robert, 64, 107, 139, 154, 238
Donnell, John Robert, 40
Douglas, Stephen A., 169
Dowd, Clement, 5
Draper, Lyman, 347–48, 358–59
Dudley, Edward B., 70, 160, 269, 285, 295

Edney, Balis M., 288
Edwards, Weldon N., 119, 266, 362, 476
Ehringhaus, John C., 103
Ellis, John L., 21
Ellis, John W., 186, 257, 431
Emancipation Proclamation, 414
Encyclopedia of American Literature, An, 316
enrollment, 137–49
enslaved persons, 410–25. *See also* Swain, David Lowry
escheat matters, 248–51
Espy, Harriet, 187
extradition, 88–89

factions, 112–13
faculty, 192–216; Civil War disruptions, 445–50. *See also* University of North Carolina
Faison, Thomas I., 124
faith, importance of, 403–06
Fanning, David, 340
Fanning, Edmund, 326
Fayetteville Observer, 341, 363
Federal Census (1850), 410–11
Fetter, Frederick A., 447
First Reconstruction Act, 475
Fisher, Charles, 121
Foote, William H., 356–57
Force, Peter, 79–80, 355

Forman, Joshua, 69
Free Soil Party, 219–20
Fremont, John C., 220
fringe benefit, 448

Gaither, Burgess, 120
Gale, Christopher, 82
Gales, Joseph, 11, 69, 73, 109
Gales, W. R., 17
Gales, Weston, 37
Gallatin, Albert, 68
Gardiner, George W., 95–96
Garrison, William Lloyd, 62, 423
Gaston, William, 14, 43, 53–54, 64, 66, 71, 75, 84, 86–88, 118, 123–24, 128, 171, 186, 210–11, 238, 253, 302, 339, 361, 365, 374, 398, 407, 409, 437, 560; on factions, 112
General Assembly, 57–58, 62–63, 158; authorizing London documentary evidence, 310; and Cherokee Indian matters, 97–98; during Civil War, 458–60; Convention Question, 117–18; 1832 meeting, 78, 302; forming historical society, 302; Hughes matter, 107; pamphlet authorization, 306; rejecting bills, 113–14; session law reports, 102; student contracts, 145; two-thirds vote, 121
"Geographical and Physical History of North Carolina," 317–18
Geography and Atlas, 191, 202
geography, convenience of, 115–16
Gerrard, Major Charles, 75
Gorrell, Ralph, 311
"Governor Tryon's North Carolina Papers," 307–08
governorship: advancing vision, 64–83; basic governance, 119–20; Chero-

kee Indians, 95–98; constitutional reform, 111–30; counter convictions, 103–04; external controversies, 103–06; fugitive matters, 88–89; future following, 127–30; Hughes matter, 107; inheriting cases, 92–93; less visionary aspects, 84–110; new capitol building, 109; public dinner, 109; stating vision, 51–63; seeking tax information, 99–101; Senate candidate, 104, 127–129; state seal, 108–09; succession of, 127; Tennessee matter, 107; transmission of session laws, 102. *See also* Swain, David Lowry

Graham, James, 52

Graham, William A., 4, 29, 52–53, 160, 217, 254–63, 305, 310, 430, 451, 456–69

Granville County, cases in, 92–93

Graves, Ralph H., 199

Greeley, Horace, 230, 423–24

Green, Reverend William Mercer, 206, 211

Greene, Nathanael, 365

Grigsby, Hugh, 363

Gwinn, James W., 104

Hale, E. J., 125, 334

Hall, John, 42, 43

Hamilton, Alexander, 79

Hamilton, J. G. DeRoulhac, 264

Hampton, Wade, 461

Harper and Brothers, 244–45

Hawks, Francis L., 77, 138, 194–96, 209, 305, 331–38, 430–31

Haywood County, North Carolina, 37, 41, 250

Haywood, John, 66

Haywood, William H., Jr., 73, 285, 302

Hedrick, Benjamin Sherwood, 154–55; affair involving, 217–31; 244–46, 467

Henderson (servant), 416–18

Henderson, Leonard, 86

Henderson, Richard, 347

Henry, Joseph, 108

Henry, Louis D., 107

Hepburn, A. D., 194, 231, 446, 504, 511, 546

Herrisse, Henri, 157; memorial of, 162–64

Hill, S. P., 316

Hill, William R., 73, 85

Hilliard, Nancy, 161, 167, 256

Hinton, C. L., 45, 53, 73, 273, 295

Historical Agency of North Carolina, 314

Historical Society (UNC): collection assistance, 304–05; first report, 303–04; as formal structure for pursuing history, 305–06; "Governor Tryon's North Carolina Papers," 307–08; loans, 305; purposes of, 302–03; reception of, 304. *See also* history, collecting; Swain, David Lowry; University of North Carolina

history, collecting: autograph letters, 358–61; collaborations, 324–46; forming UNC Historical Society, 301–23; magazine publications, 319–23; Mecklenburg Declaration of Independence controversy, 348–58; other correspondence, 362–67; preserving Washington grave, 361–62; public lectures, 317–19; state history, 308–15; university history, 315–17. *See also* collaborations, collecting history; Swain, David Lowry

Hogg, Gavin, 59, 73, 86
Holden, William W., 172, 181, 220, 267, 453–54, 473–74, 520–21, 525–26
Holmes, Gabriel, 11, 14, 17
Holmes, Theophilus, 440
Home Slaves Confederate Tax, 411
Hooper, John DeBerniere, 215, 421
Hooper, William, signer of Declaration of Independence, 82
Hooper, William, UNC professor, 186, 232
Hopewell Treaty, 85
Horton, George Moses, 422–24
House of Commons (NC), 28, 30, 39, 51, 93, 103, 111, 118, 120, 123–24, 249, 280, 296, 334, 339, 433. *See also* North Carolina; Swain, David Lowry
Hubbard, Fordyce M., 173, 203, 364, 506
Hughes, John, 172
Hughes, Robert Ball, 107
human resources, 61

in loco parentis, policy, 141–43, 145–46, 150, 175
inability-to-pay laments, 396–97
inquiries, 98
instructional materials, 247–48
Iredell, Governor James, 40, 59, 65, 86, 105, 162, 196, 232, 253, 278, 412, 422; employing Swain, 26–27
Iredell, Judge James, 324, 329–31, 359, 361
Iredell, Samuel T., 160–62
Ives, L. S., 302

Jack, James, 348
Jackson, Andrew, 253

John (servant), 419
Johnson, Andrew, 260–62, 319, 471–74
Johnson, Jacob, 319
Johnson, R. W., 140
Johnston, James C., 68–69, 310, 412
Johnston, Samuel, 68
Jones, Calvin, 17, 24, 30
Jones, Hamilton C., 135–36
Jones, Joseph Seawell, 44–45, 78, 81–82, 350
Journals of Pennsylvania, 341–42
Joyner, Andrew, 235
judge, serving as, 41–47

Kerr, W. C., 506
Kilpatrick, Judson, 462–63
Kimberly, John, 213, 224
King, Mitchell D., 263

Lane, Joseph, 195, 263, 367, 391
Lane, Ralph, 9
Last Ninety Days of the War in North-Carolina, The, 477, 478–91, 556
Lawrence Scientific School, 218
Lee, Robert E., 172, 454–55, 507
Lefler, Hugh T., 5
legislation, 28–39. *See also* Swain, David Lowry
Lenoir, William, 366–67
libraries, improving, 243–48
Liles, J. R., 21
Lincoln, Abraham, 4, 195, 360, 433–34
Literary Fund, 56, 67–68, 74, 77, 100, 107–08, 250, 274–75
Livingston, Edward, 99–100
loans, 65–66
loco parentis, role, 141–49
Long, Crawford W., 413, 476, 533
Lossing, Benson J., 339–46

Lowry, Caroline Lane, 8–9
Lowry, James, 384
Lucas, Joseph Bibb, 292

Macomb, Alex, 95
Macon County Court, 85
Macon, Nathaniel, 45, 116
Mallett, Edward, 147
Mallett, Peter, 442
Mangum, Willie P., 35, 40, 41, 103, 127–28, 136, 137–38, 139, 246; politics and, 285–88
Manly, Charles, 142, 161–62, 190, 200, 203, 233, 291, 429; historical documents and, 306–07
Manly, John H., 184
Manly, Matthias, 137, 251
Mann, Horace, 230
Marshall, John, 14
Martin, James, 85
Martin, Leonard, 39
Martin, William J., appointing, 203–05, 506, 508
Mauney, James, 69–70
Mayhs, Suky, 166
McGuffey, William H., 203–05
McLaughlin, P. G., 242
McLean, John, 104–05
McRae, John, 36, 64–65
McRee, Griffith J., 327–31
Meck Dec, 352, 356
Mecklenburg Declaration of Independence, 82, 98, 109, 303, 306, 325, 364; controversy involving, 348–58. *See also* history, collecting
Mecklenburg Monument Association, 350–51
Mecklenburg Resolves, 355
Memminger, Christopher, 270–71

Mhoon, William, 100
Miller, Henry W., 362, 438
misconduct, students, 150–76
Mitchell, Elisha, 11, 133, 154, 156, 162–63; death of, 200–05
Moore, Alfred, 324, 361
Moore, Bartholomew F., 172, 244, 363
Mordecai, George W., 139
Morehead, John M., 29, 117, 142, 144, 152, 179, 260, 296, 402, 431–32
Morphis, Sam, 425
Morrill Land-Grant Colleges Act, 502–03
Morris, Thomas A., 205
Moseley, William D., 53, 561
Murphey, Archibald DeBow, 29, 36, 64, 78, 324, 553
Murphey, Victor M., 78, 81
Mutual Insurance Company, 240

Nash, Abner, 307
Nash, Frederick, 73, 75, 134, 307
Negro Martin, 90
Negroes, 153; negro Houses, 421; Negro stealing, 88, 90, 92; on UNC property, 241. *See also* enslaved persons
New Bern Academy, 147
Newton Academy, 8, 10, 187
Newton, George, 19
Nicholson, A. O. P., 262–63
North Carolina: Mount Vernon Restoration Advisory Committee, 361; apathy of, 56; burning of state capitol, 64; Cabarrus County, 357; constitutional reform, 111–30; county basis of representation, 111–15; revenue system of, 58–59; Executive Department, 59–60; Granville County, 43, 92–93; legislation in, 28–39; Lenoir County, 364–65; map of, 64–65;

North Carolina (*continued*)
  Negro voting in, 119; Northampton County, 85–86; revising statutory law of, 56–57; Rip Van Winkle status, 105; schools in, 8. *See also* Chapel Hill; University of North Carolina; Swain, David Lowry
North Carolina Bible Society, 405
North Carolina Constitution, 51, 86, 111, 179, 281, 494; debate on future amendments, 120–21; empowering governor, 84–85; section thirty-two of, 118
North Carolina Industrial Association, 281
North Carolina Institute of Education, 74–75
North Carolina Rail Road Company, 291
North Carolina Standard, 220–24, 227, 268
North Carolina University Magazine, 5, 263, 309, 319–23, 326, 328, 341, 344–45, 348, 448, 561

Otey, James H., 263, 314
Other Leaf of Nature, The (Mitchell), 438
Outlaw, David, 85
Owen, John, 27, 52, 65, 103–4, 109–10, 125, 253

pardons, 89–95
Patton, James, 30
Peabody, George, 277, 491
Pearson, Richmond M., 128, 186, 289–90
Peebles, Robert B., 291–92
Percival, William, 239

Perry, Benjamin F., 10, 495–96
Perry, J. B., 75
personal life. *See* Swain, David Lowry
Pettigrew, James Johnston, 150, 186, 313
Phebe (servant), 418–19
Phi Beta Kappa Society, 211
Philanthropic (Phi) Society, 152, 166–67, 173–74, 235, 244, 261
Phillips, Charles, 172, 199–200, 358; Hedrick affair, 218–19
Phillips, James, 184, 213, 214–15
Phillips, Samuel F., 181, 187, 358, 508, 533
Pictorial Field Book of the Revolution, 342–43
Pitt, William, 44
Polk, Ezekiel, 344
Polk, James Knox, 23, 254–57, 286
Polk, Thomas G., 51, 71, 98, 129; election withdrawal, 51
Pollock, George, 81
Pool, Solomon, 208–09, 506
Potter, Henry, 290
Potter, Robert, 93
prison sentences, remission of, 91–92
property, matters regarding, 232–51; Caldwell House, 234, 240–41; considering additional buildings, 237–40; erecting ball room, 236; escheat matters, 249–51; extant campus buildings, 234; faculty housing, 240; gardening, 241–43; library issues, 243–48; paymaster, 239; stone walls, 241. *See also* University of North Carolina
Protestant Episcopal Church of Mississippi, 206
public education, 33–34

public policy, 264–83. *See also* Swain, David Lowry; University of North Carolina

Rail Road Convention, 270
railroad meetings, 270–73
Raleigh Register and North-Carolina Gazette, The, 114, 202, 268, 332–33, 339, 348, 351, 356, 363, 516
Rand, N. G., 45
Randall, Alexander W., 261
Ransom, Matthew W., 431
Reade, Edwin G., 311
Reconstruction, 471–96; West Point Board of Visitors, 471–72; memorials, 490–91; *Ninety Days,* 490–91; Old Capitol Prison visit, 473–77; pardons, 475–78; property matters, 475–76; Spencer-Graham relationship, 485–86; Spencer-Vance exchanges, 478–85; Swain-Graham relationship, 491–96; *Watchman* project, 486–89. *See also* Civil War; Swain, David Lowry
religious instruction, 181–83
Revolutionary War, 55–56, 303, 309
Roanoke Navigation Company, 32
Roberts, Joshua, 85, 97
Rodman, William Blount, 135, 314–15
Ruffin, Thomas, 28, 37, 77, 86, 209–10
Ruskin, John, 188

Saint Matthews Episcopal Church, 206
Sanford, Terry, 107
Saunders, Romulus, 38, 96–97, 101–02
Saunders, William L., 316
Scales, Alfred Moore, 550
Scott, William L., 147–48

Seawell, Henry, 16, 41, 87, 109
sectionalism, 58
Seddon, James A., 442
session laws, 102
Seward, William H., 261
Sherman, William T., 4, 460–67
Shipp, A. M., 208, 214
Shipp, W. M., 195
Sickles, Daniel E., 261
Signal, 267–68
Silver, Frances, 94–95
Singleton, Thomas D., 109
Sinking Fund, 281
Sketches of North Carolina, 311
Smith, James S., 119
Smith, Roswell C., 202
Smoky Mountain Turnpike Company, 32
South Carolina: controversy in, 103–04
South Carolina Historical Society, 305
Spaight, Richard Dobbs, Jr., 73, 127, 265–67
Sparks, Jared, 307–08, 313, 356
Spencer, Cornelia Phillips, 155, 161, 186, 209, 264, 301–2, 316, 320, 429, 529, 531–32, 538–42, 543–47, 547–49, 550, 553–54, 556, 561
spirits. *See* alcohol
Spotswood, Alexander, 80
Stamp Act, 310–11
Stanton, Edwin, 471
statistics, 36
Stedman, N. A., 73
Stephens, Alexander H., 432
Stokes, Montford, 41–42, 51, 84, 92, 94, 253
Story, Joseph, 196
Strange, Robert, 137

students: academic policy and, 173; alcohol policy and, 152–56; campus confinement of, 169–70; Civil War disruptions, 437–45; expressing contempt, 156–58; fights among, 167; financial irresponsibility of, 171; firearms possessed by, 167–68; fires started by, 168–69; illicit sexual activity, 156; leniency toward, 162–64; mischievous misbehavior, 172–73; misconduct, 150–76; off-campus misbehavior of, 169–70; riots, 165–67; rumors, 165–66; sons of governors, 159–62. *See also* University of North Carolina

Swain, Anne, 375–78, 513–14, 531–32, 538

Swain, Caroline, 387

Swain County (North Carolina), 553

Swain, David Lowry, 3–6; academic leadership of, 131–97; annual messages of, 55; attraction to women, 21–23; *beau ideal* and, 122; becoming new UNC president, 133–36; belief in Providence, 404; broader vision, 313; and Buncombe Turnpike, 29–31; carte blanche authority, 201; championing internal improvements plan, 68–74; Cherokee Indians and, 95–98; during Civil War, 427–70; and common school materials, 277; condolences of, 402–03; constitutional reform, 111–30; contempt of, 15; death of, 529–30; decline and fall of, 499–522; Eastern interests, 34; education of, 10; elections won by, 51–54; employing friends of, 194–200; endings, 499–530; enhancing wealth, 395–96; enslaved persons of, 410–25; estate of, 532–34; extradition matters of, 88–89; faculty issues and, 211–16; faculty stability preceding Mitchell death, 200–05; family of, 371–91; farming interests, 393–95; focus on internal improvements, 58; forming new western counties, 34; fugitive matters, 88–89; funeral/burial of, 531–32; Gaston-Swain relationship, 398; governorship, 49–130; Graham-Swain friendship, 401; health concerns, 406–08; health of, 17–19; Hedrick affair, 217–31; as historian, 299–367; history following, 542–47; humor of, 183–84; importance of finances to, 397; infant children of, 374–84; inheriting cases, 92–93; internal House matters, 35–36; internal improvements conventions, 65–66; as judge, 41–47; land-transaction bargains, 392–93; law/statecraft tutelage, 25–47; legal career of, 25–28; legislative career, 28–39; library of, 80–81; Mecklenburg Declaration of Independence controversy, 348–58; melancholic attitude of, 525; morbid sensibility, 121; national-level role, 471–96; negotiating Civil War end, 451–70; nephews, 387–91; New York investment banker of, 395; non-regional matter votes, 32; opinion on constitutional questions, 190; pardoning issues, 89–95; parting assessment of, 553–63; paternal ancestors, 7–8; personal dimensions of, 392–409; personal life free fall, 513–14; personal life of, 369–425;

physical appearance, 46; physical problems, 525; politics and, 284–97; as "Professor of Things in General," 188–90; property holdings, 527; public policy and, 264–83; publishing North Carolina map, 64–65; Raleigh time of, 12–15, 23–24; reception of, 184–85; during Reconstruction, 471–96; relationship with father, 18–20; religious attendance of, 19–20; religious devotion, 403–04; remembrances, 549–53; Ruffin-Swain relationship, 398–99; as solicitor, 39–41; spiritual house, 528–29; and state issues, 16; as "storehouse of facts and anecdotes," 301–02; subject matter taught by, 179–83; Swain-A.J. Davis relationship, 238–47; taxation authority, 36; as teacher, 177–91; teaching style, 185–88; "treating" bills, 35; UNC faculty and, 192–216; UNC following passing of, 547–49; UNC presence as student, 10–11; UNC resignation, 515–22; on universal public education, 33–34; university devotion, 11–12; university presidency reflection, 523–25; Vance-Swain relationship, 187–88; votes regarding persons of color, 34–35; witnessing courts, 14; Woodfin-Swain relationship, 399; youth of, 10–24. *See also* academic leadership; governorship; history, collecting; students; University of North Carolina

Swain, Eleanor Hope ("Ellie") (David's daughter), 384, 464, 467–70, 524, 535–36

Swain, Eleanor Hope White (David's wife), 25–26, 30–31, 38–39, 40–42, 261, 316, 371–75, 377, 395, 404, 410–12, 418–19, 528–29, 531–34, 536–47

Swain, George, 7–9; alcohol hypercriticism, 18–20; religious concerns, 19–20; university devotion witnessed by, 11–15; Buncombe Turnpike, 30–31

Swain, George, Jr., 384–87, 533

Swain, Richard Caswell, 161, 378–84, 534–35, 537–38

Taborn, Washington, 92–93
Taney, Roger B., 212
Tarboro Male Academy, 148
taxes, seeking information on, 99–101
Taylor, John Louis, 11, 14, 17, 23–24, 129
teacher, position, 177–91
10th Ohio Cavalry, 464
Thompson, E. A., 311
transfer students, 139–41. *See also* students; University of North Carolina
Transylvania Land Company, 359
"treating," 35
Treaty of Ghent, 16
Treaty of Tellico, 97
Trinity College, 139, 507
trustees, 193
tutors, 192
23rd North Carolina Cavalry, 442
Tyler, John, 106

Ugly Club, 150–52
U.S. Census, 397
U.S. Congress, acquiring papers from, 245–46
U.S. Constitution, 101–2, 187, 495
U.S. Military Academy, 471

United States, House elections in, 287–88
University of Alabama, 447
University of North Carolina: academic curriculum, 209–10; agricultural instruction, 209–10; athletics, 210; avoiding political conflict, 500; Ball room erection, 236; Board of Trustees, 511; candidate selection, 137–49; chief function of, 178–79; church duties, 205–09; Civil War disruptions, 437–50; Civil War exodus, 184; Civil War occupation, 465; Columbia-*versus*-Chapel Hill debate, 10–11; considering additional buildings, 237–40; death of friends of, 210–11; Department of Modern Languages, 193; disciplinary efforts, 172–76; electing new president of, 133–36; extant campus buildings, 234; faculty issues, 212–16; faculty of, 192–216; faculty stability preceding Mitchell death, 200–205; faculty/students departing, 504–07; finance issues, 143–45; First Amendment and, 220; fiscal policy formation, 11; free from censure, 159–60; Hedrick affair, 217–31; Historical Society, 302–06; intra-faculty harmony in, 211–12; Law School commencing, 198; legal education at, 196–98; libraries of, 243–48; *loco parentis* role, 137–49; misconduct issues, 150–76; perceptions of Swain, 507–11; politics and, 284–97; post-Civil War funds, 501–03; property matters, 231–51; public policy, 264–83; reform efforts, 511–13; religious instruction at, 181–83; selling land, 503–04; South Building destruction, 168–69; special events at, 252–63; student deaths, 148–49; subject matter taught at, 179–81; Swain Memorial Hall, 549–51; Swain teaching style, 185–91; teaching at, 177–91. *See also* Civil War; Swain, David Lowry

Van Buren, Martin, 184–85
Vance Literary Society of Asheville, 36
Vance, Robert B., 15, 27, 451
Vance, Zebulon B., xv, 136, 147, 155, 172, 187–88, 200, 279; Civil War, 451–64, 556–57, 561–65
Vio, Romano, 107
Virginia Military Institute, 140

Wadsworth, Edward, 205
Wait, Samuel, 74
Waitt, Kendall, 235
Wake Forest College, 164, 507
Walker, David, 62
Walker, Felix, 15
Walker, James, 307
Warren, Edward, 311–12
Washington, George, grave of, 361–62
Washington College, 507
Watchman, 486–89
Waxhaw settlement, 313
Webster, Daniel, 27, 106
Webster, Noah, 359
Weeks, Stephen B., 186–87
Welch, Thomas, Sr., 37
Wellborn, James, 122
West, improving. *See* North Carolina: constitutional reform
Western Carolinian, The, 294–95
Wheat, John Thomas, 156, 164, 212, 214
Wheeler, John H., 103, 195–96, 207,

282, 311, 342–43, 352, 391, 400, 407, 473–75, 488, 492
Whig Party, 53, 60, 105, 128, 145, 228, 255, 264, 267–69, 282, 284, 292–93, 295–96
White, Eleanor Hope, 22
White, William, 22, 319
Wiley, Bell Irvin, 433
Wiley, Calvin H., 147, 275–77, 364
Williamson, Hugh, 305
Wilmington Commercial, 225
Wilmington Committee, 340
Wilmington Literary Association, 317

Wilson, Alexander, 183
Wilson, Joseph R., 194
Wilson, Louis Round, 244
Winston, Patrick H., 41
Woodfin, Nicholas W., 181, 286–87, 288–90, 293, 295, 412, 431
Worth, Jonathan, 78, 474–75, 515–18
Wright, James, 341
Wyche, James, 70

Yancey, Bartlett, 44
Young, Perry Deane, 94

WILLIS P. WHICHARD of Chapel Hill is a lawyer who, like his subject David Swain, has spent most of his career in public office and the academy. He is the only person in North Carolina history who has served in both the North Carolina House of Representatives and the North Carolina Senate and on both the North Carolina Court of Appeals and the North Carolina Supreme Court. Dean and Professor of Law at Campbell University from 1999-2006, he holds the A.B. and J.D. degrees from the University of North Carolina and the LL.M and S.J.D. degrees from the University of Virginia.

www.ingramcontent.com/pod-product-compliance
Lightning Source LLC
Chambersburg PA
CBHW021821220426
43663CB00005B/95